Machine Tool Operation

PART I

MACHINE TOOL OPERATION

PART I CONTAINS THE FOLLOWING DIVISIONS:

Safety   *The Drill Press*
Measuring Tools   *The Lathe*
Bench Work   *Forge Work*

PART II CONTAINS THE FOLLOWING DIVISIONS:

The Shaper   *Hydraulics*
The Planer   *Metal Band Saws*
The Milling Machine   *Metallurgy*
The Grinding Machine   *Cutting Fluids*

MACHINE TOOL OPERATION

PART I

Safety • Measuring Tools • Bench Work
The Drill Press • The Lathe • Forge Work

Henry D. Burghardt
Aaron Axelrod
and James Anderson

FIFTH EDITION

McGRAW-HILL BOOK COMPANY

New York St. Louis San Francisco Dallas Toronto London Sydney

ABOUT THE AUTHORS

HENRY D. BURGHARDT was Head of Machine Shop at Wm. L. Dickinson High School, Jersey City, New Jersey, for many years. He prepared the first three editions of this book.

AARON AXELROD has been an apprentice machinist, an inspector, a draftsman, and a shop-mathematics-and-science teacher at the Bayonne Vocational and Technical High School, New Jersey. As a teacher, he taught mathematics and science as they applied to each and every job his students did in the machine shop.

Dr. Axelrod received his doctorate from New York University in Vocational Education. His thesis was on Machine-shop Science. Although retired, he still takes an active interest in new machines and methods of manufacture.

He is the author of *Machine Shop Mathematics.*

JAMES ANDERSON began the learning of his trade at fourteen years of age when he became an indentured apprentice to a long-established chemical-engineering firm in Silvertown, London, England. Upon the completion of his apprenticeship, he spent two years as an erector in charge of machinery installation and operation.

He worked in American machine shops for fifteen years before becoming a teacher of machine-shop practice. He received his teacher training in the University of the State of New York and has taught in public schools since 1942. He is now teaching at Queens Vocational High School in New York City, and is also director of Machine Shop Training at the Kollsman Instrument Corporation, makers of precision aircraft instruments.

ISBN 07-008961-2

1516-VBVB-75432

Machine Tool Operation, Part I
Copyright © 1959 by McGraw-Hill, Inc. All Rights Reserved.

Preface

Metal working in some form has been done by man for thousands of years. The products produced were the results of skill—hand and brain. Although simple tools were used during most of those years, the products served man well in his humble beginning. The earliest writings referred to a lathe. Such machines greatly increased man's productivity and enabled him to live better. Nevertheless, they were very crude when compared with modern machine tools now used for the machining of metals.

The purpose of this text is to help the beginner of machine-shop practice obtain the simple fundamentals of machine-tool operation. Along with these fundamentals, principles of science and mathematics as applied to machine-shop practice are given and explained. Several actual jobs on the various machines are explained in detail for the easy understanding of the apprentice. For the machinist there are sections for his use on modern machine practices.

This text is planned to permit all possible flexibility in its use. Certain chapters comprise a study of operations; other chapters may be used for reference and studied in connection with these operations. The particular job on which the operation is to be made and the proper time to refer to the construction or use of the machine or tool must be decided according to conditions that exist at a given time in a given shop.

The apprentice who uses this text will learn the principles and elementary operations of machine-shop work. It is in no sense a treatise, nor is it a production manual. It is primarily designed to be used in connection with class lectures and demonstrations in the school shop. It may be used to supplement the information that an apprentice or student in the commercial shop may acquire by observation, practice, or other means.

The aim has been to adapt this text for use in vocational, industrial-technical, trade, and technical schools, and in apprenticeship courses where training in machine-shop practice is given. To this end, the necessary elementary information concerning machine-tool operation has been very carefully selected and set forth as simply and clearly as possible.

The chief function of the shop is to teach the intelligent and safe operation of machines. It must be conceded that a knowledge of the construction of the machine tools and of the principles underlying their operation makes the essential difference between a machine operator and a machinist. Therefore, the mechanisms of typical machine tools have been described, more or less, in detail. Enough information has been given to identify the major parts and their functions.

Many of the questions that are incorporated in various chapters have been revised and reworded so that the student may be able to determine the correct answers by studying the text material. New questions have been added when possible.

Chapter 2, Safety in the Machine Shop, has been revised to show right and wrong procedures in various machine-shop operations. Many new pictures have been added. It is an accepted fact that a safe worker is usually a good worker. Safety has become a very important item in cost calculations of manufacturing firms.

Chapter 11, Cutting Tools and Cutting Speeds, has been revised to include the new recommendations for cutting angles and a non-technical explanation of what actually takes place at the cutting edge of lathe tools. It is sincerely hoped that this section will materially aid all apprentices and machinists to understand clearly that phase of the trade. This chapter is well illustrated with pictures and drawings showing actual chip formations and just how the metal is peeled off the job.

Surface finishes and their measurement are of increasing importance in close-tolerance machining operations. Some industries require tolerances in the nature of a few millionths of an inch. The new machinist should realize that such tolerances are obtainable, and that modern science has provided him with the machines and measuring device that make work to such small dimensions possible. For this reason, new material on the techniques of surface measurement has been added on pages 573–576.

To the manufacturers who have cooperated in the preparation of this text, our many thanks. As teachers in vocational and technical high schools, the authors desire, at this time, to acknowledge the help that many manufacturers give to both teachers and students by their generous sending of catalogues, pamphlets, and instruction books to schools for their use.

In conclusion, the authors wish to express their appreciation to the many machine-shop teachers of vocational and technical high schools who have made so many excellent suggestions in the preparation of material. Without their help, this text would have been just another book.

To our wives, Emma J. Anderson and Edith R. Axelrod, who gave up many evenings to assist in the typing and proof reading of this text, our most sincere thanks.

AARON AXELROD
JAMES ANDERSON

Contents

BENCH WORK

4. HAMMERS, SCREW DRIVERS, WRENCHES, HACKSAWS   *105*

5. CHIPPING, FILING, SCRAPING   *121*

6. LAYING OUT   *147*

THE DRILL PRESS

7. DRILL-PRESS CONSTRUCTION   *161*

8. DRILLS AND DRILLING   *173*

9. OTHER DRILL-PRESS TOOLS AND OPERATIONS   *211*

THE LATHE

10. LATHE CONSTRUCTION AND MANIPULATION

11. CUTTING TOOLS AND CUTTING SPEEDS

12. CENTERING   *317*

13. FACING   *329*

14. TURNING IN A LATHE   *336*

15. CHUCKING WORK

16. TAPERS AND ANGLES

CONTENTS

APPENDIX

LIST OF TABLES

To the Student

This is written for the young man in the shop who hopes to be a machinist. It is written for the ambitious young man (and most young men are ambitious) who expects to be, some day, a first-class machinist, a foreman, a superintendent. It is written for the alert young man, the one who combines with his ambition a determination to work, to study, to think—a determination to make enthusiasm in his work overcome laziness, to make preparedness bring the opportunity. This shop you are in is one of a hundred, or of a thousand, or of ten thousand, where certain boys are being trained. Some boys are lazy and shiftless; they will be drudges all their lives. Others are the future foremen, superintendents, managers, owners. Are you "on the job"? Who is happier, the wide-awake fellow with his feeling of satisfaction in accomplishment, or the lazy fellow with his feeling of envy? Both have to work! What is work? Webster says, "Work is a physical or intellectual effort directed to some end." Either one, physical effort or intellectual effort, taken alone is drudgery. Properly combined they produce enthusiasm. Football is work, it is sport too; but beef alone or brains alone never made a football player. Machine-shop practice is work. Often and especially at the beginning, it may be hard work and dirty work, but combined with the proper amount of "intellectual effort" it is increasingly interesting as one progresses.

What is meant by this training—this doing and this thinking—in machine-shop work? Where does it begin and where does it end? It means a development of the hands, ears, eyes, and mind in the power to do, to listen, to observe, to remember, and to reason.

Machine-shop practice consists of certain mechanical principles that are a part of all machine-shop work everywhere—the principles of cutting tools, cutting speeds and feeds, actions of gears, screws, cams, etc.—applied in the construction of certain machines and tools and in the various machine operations: that is, in the methods of holding and doing the work. There are only a few principles, comparatively, but there is no end of methods. Machine-shop training begins with the elementary principles, the easiest mathematical problems, and the simplest methods of applying these principles and problems on some kind of machine. It advances step by step, to other principles and to the application of all these principles in the doing of work, by various methods, on the other machines.

This text has been prepared with the single purpose of helping the boys in machine shops to gain quickly a working knowledge of the principles of machine work and their application in shop practice. After all, no text, no teacher, no foreman, or no friend can help the boy who is not willing to help himself.

AARON AXELROD

JAMES ANDERSON

Introduction

CHAPTER 1

The Machinist's Trade

This has been called the *atomic age*, the *technological revolution*, and the *electronic age*. But call it what you may, this era is maintained by *machines* of all kinds, types, and sizes. Machinery is everywhere. Practically all necessities of life are made by machines. The atom bomb and all electronic equipment used in war as well as in peace are made either in part or entirely by machine tools.

In thousands of factories, foodstuffs are refined and prepared, fabrics are woven, and wood and metal are fitted to make the furnishings of civilization. Everywhere factories are building labor-saving devices for the education, recreation, and prosperity of the people. But without the machinist, there could be no engines or dynamos to furnish the power; there could be no machines because the machinist is the producer of them all. As a matter of fact, there would be no factories.

Lincoln had no telephone in the White House, and no electric light. Think of the development of the telephone and the machines that have made it possible. Think of the development of the electric light and of the huge engines and generators in the electric power stations. Think of the growth of the automobile industry, of the improvements in the product year by year, and the improvements in the methods of manufacture. Consider the motor alone—the absolute reliability of the materials used, the necessary perfection of fit of its component parts, the marvelous methods of manufacture to make these parts by the thousands. These examples could be multiplied indefinitely—sewing machines, cameras, radios, motion-picture machines, typewriters, cash registers are a few that are universally known. Everybody knows too that all these things are made by machinery. Who invents the machines? Who develops

the machines? Who builds the machines for making all these things?
The loafer? No. The worker and thinker? Yes.

A few years ago there were two kinds of steel, machine steel and
tool steel. Today there are dozens of special steels—steels for gears,
for shafts, for screws, for springs, for tools, even a kind of steel for
the particular gear or axle or tool. The new methods of heat-treatment of steel have added strength, toughness, and temper far
beyond the dreams of the past generation.

Since 1927 there has been developed, to an amazing degree, the
use of the so-called *carbide cutting tools*. Work that no one thought
possible to machine, outside of grinding, is now drilled, reamed,
turned, milled, and planed with cemented-carbide-tipped tools,
and cutting speeds so fast as to seem incredible are recommended.
These tools have also made possible greater feeds and deeper cuts,
thereby reducing the operational time. This, in turn, means greater
production and lower costs.

To take care of the increased power and speed needed, in all
kinds of machine tools, such developments as scientifically designed
main castings; ball bearings and roller bearings; heat-treated,
ground, and lapped gears; centralized oiling under pressure; individual motor drive for machines and even for machine units;
multiple-disk clutches and powerful brakes are demanded in
modern production plants. And keeping pace with other improvements are safety appliances, guards, and the electronic devices used
for the control of some moving parts of machine tools.

These typical industrial developments, together with thousands
of others, have been made possible by the cooperation of trained
men—machinists, designers, electricians, chemists, and metal-
lurgists working in harmony with progressive businessmen.

Progress means the development of improvements and the machine is the instrument of progress.

The machinist's trade is a great trade—great in its vital necessity,
great in its ever-increasing interest, and great in the opportunity
it offers for advancement. John Fritz, who founded the Bethlehem
Steel Company, was a machinist in his youth; George Westinghouse
started his lifework in a machine shop. Dr. John A. Brashear, who
was one of the greatest telescopic-instrument makers and one of the
greatest scientists America has produced, was once a machinist.

Henry Ford's knowledge of machine-shop work has served to make happy tens of millions of people.

In the light of the advance in this marvelous machine era, the machinist's trade would seem to be very difficult, but the fact is, it comprises today, as it did 50 years ago, the mastery of only a few fundamentals. To be sure there are a thousand different kinds of machines to be built and assembled, but the machine-shop principles remain the same.

The operator of a special machine for doing a certain class of work, in a machine shop or in a factory, is not classified in the machinist's trade as a machinist but is known as a *Machine Operator*. This means that he is skilled in the operation of only one machine, usually a production type machine. The machine operator must be adept in using all of the attachments of that special machine.

The young man who gets ahead is not satisfied with knowing how to operate merely one machine. He will want to know how to operate all of the machine tools in the shop. It is the wide-awake, thinking young fellow who becomes the expert journeyman mechanic, then the foreman, and finally, the plant superintendent. It is not all fun; it means work, it means study, it means sacrifice of money at the start, but it is interesting, vitally stimulating, and not deadening. Walking a treadmill is only existing; going ahead is living.

In the large industrial centers, more than half the workers are employed in the metal trades; that is, more mechanics and machine hands are employed in these trades than are at work in all the other trades taken together. It is safe to say that 90 per cent of the foremen in the great manufacturing plants have been promoted from the ranks of machinists, and that 90 per cent of the superintendents of these factories have previously been foremen.

It is admitted by all manufacturers that the proportion of expert machinists is growing constantly smaller; why then, should it be difficult for the young man in the shop to foresee the opportunities that may be his, *if he is prepared?*

During the last few years factory conditions have greatly changed; scientific management, quality control practices, improved production methods, etc., have made the machine hand more than ever before a mere part of the machine, while the standing of the real machinist is on an increasingly higher level. The same operations—

turning, boring, drilling, etc.—are performed, but are performed more easily, more quickly, and with greater accuracy. The cutting tools have more than doubled the efficiency of those of a few years ago. The machines have been built stronger, more rigid, more adaptable, more accurate. While these improvements have lessened the *manual* labor incident to machine work, the truly marvelous strides made in the manufacturing of thousands of parts exactly alike have advanced the making of the special machines, tools, and gages— that is, real machine-shop work—to a much higher plane as regards the *mental* effort necessary to do this work.

For the engineering student, a knowledge of machine-shop practice is absolutely necessary. If the engineer is to be able to design and aid in the manufacture of machine tools, he must know just what these tools are able to do. If he is to become a production engineer—one who decides which machine tools will do certain machine operations—he must have a thorough knowledge of machine-shop practice.

A SHORT MACHINE-SHOP CATECHISM

What Is a Machine Shop? A machine shop is a place in which metal parts are cut to the size required and put together to form mechanical units or machines, the machines so made to be used directly or indirectly in the production of the necessities and luxuries of civilization. Machine-shop work is the basis of all mechanical production. Figure 1-1 shows a section of a large machine shop.

What May Constitute the Equipment of a Machine Shop? Machine-shop equipment consists, in part, of certain standard machine tools, the kind, the size, and the number of machines depending, of course, upon the product of the shop. Machine-shop equipment includes the tools used at the bench and on the floor as well as the measuring and adjusting tools, the work-holding and tool-holding accessories, and the small tools used in the machines.

What Are the Standard Machine Tools? The lathe, the drill press, the shaper, the planer, the milling machine, the grinding machine, and the boring mill are usually considered standard machine tools. The turret lathe, the slotter, the gear-cutting machine, and many others are usually referred to as manufacturing machines or special machines. The propriety of the term *special machine* lies in the fact that these are modifications of standard machine tools and have been developed to meet specialized production problems.

It is difficult, and perhaps unnecessary, to draw the line between standard and special. A few years ago the milling machine, and still more recently the grinding machine, were considered special machines. Now they are regarded as very essential machines in the well-equipped shop. One who is able to operate intelligently the

Fig. 1-1. A section of a large machine shop. (*The Monarch Machine Tool Company*)

machines recognized as standard will be able, with a minimum amount of study and experience, to understand and operate any special machine.

It must be understood that all kinds of machine tools are made in a great variety of types and sizes. Fortunately for the machinist, certain basic principles of construction and operation which obtain in one size of machine, obtain in all machines of that class, and further, many of these same principles are found in other kinds of machines. The student or apprentice does not have to begin all over again to learn to operate each size and kind of machine. If he has mastered certain principles regarding one size or type of any kind.

of standard machine tool he has certain knowledge that will help considerably in understanding the construction and operation of other machines. The underlying principles of the proper cutting speeds and feeds, the grinding of the cutting tools, of adjustments and measurements, apply to all of them.

The Lathe. The lathe (Fig. 1-2) is a metal-turning machine tool

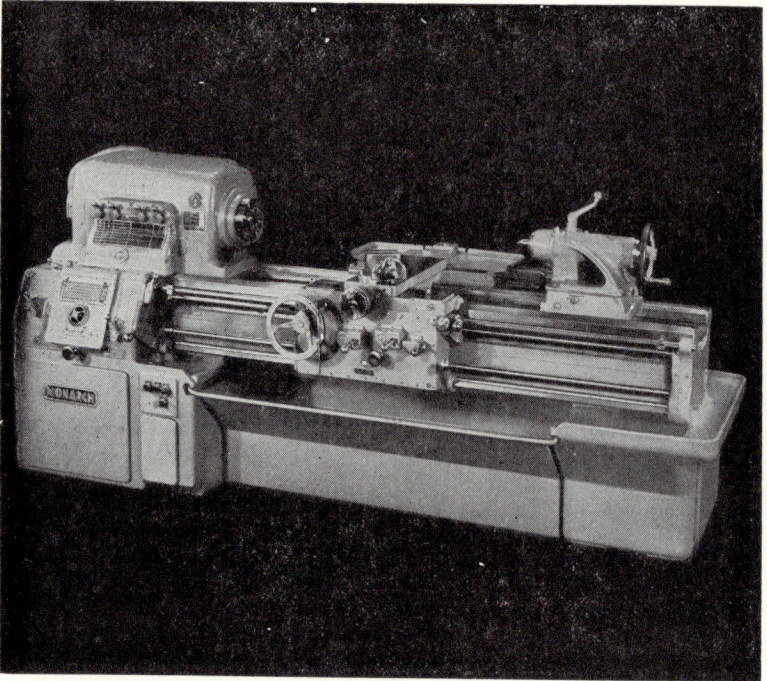

Fig. 1-2. An engine lathe. (*The Monarch Machine Tool Company*)

in which the work, while revolving on a horizontal axis, is acted upon by a cutting tool which is made to move slowly (feed) in a direction more or less parallel to the axis of the work (longitudinal feed), or in a direction at right angles to the axis of the work (cross feed). Either feed may be operated by hand or by power (automatically) as desired. When the feeding is in a direction parallel to the axis of the work, cylindrical or *straight turning* is accomplished. When the cut is in a direction at a slight angle to the axis of the work a *taper* is the result; more of an angle results in *turning to an angle*. The cut at right angles to the axis of the work (the cross-feed operation) is known as *facing* or *squaring*. Cutting inside of a hole is termed *boring*.

The Drilling Machine. The drilling machine, or drill press, is a

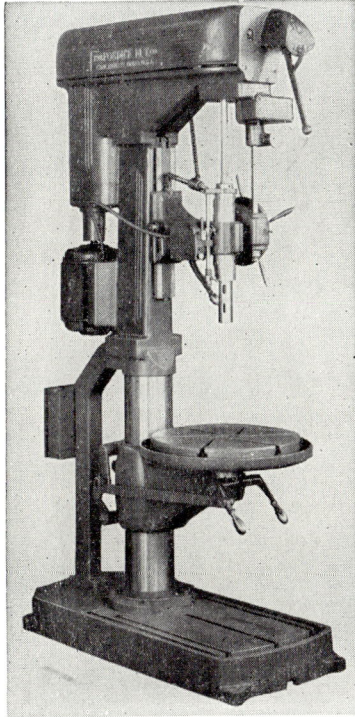

Fig. 1-3. A single spindle heavy duty drill press. (*The Fosdick Machine Tool Company*)

machine tool used mainly for producing holes in metal. In this machine the work is securely held while a revolving cutting tool is fed into it. The cutting tool most commonly used is called a *drill;* it has, in effect, an action similar to a wood *bit.* In Fig. 1-3 a single spindle heavy duty drill press is illustrated.

The Shaper. The shaper (Fig. 1-4) is ordinarily used for finishing flat or partly curved surfaces of metal pieces few in number and not usually over a foot or two long. In the shaper, the cutting tool has a reciprocating (forward and return) motion, and cuts on the forward stroke only. The work is usually held in a vise bolted to the work table and the regular feed is accomplished by causing the work table to move automatically at right angles to the direction of the

Fig. 1-4. A shaper. (*The Cincinnati Shaper Company*)

cutting tool. The construction of the tool head permits of down feed at right angles to the regular feed, or at any other angle if desired. The cutting tools used in the shaper are similar to the turning tools used in the lathe.

The Planer. The planer (Fig. 1-5) is a machine tool used in the production of flat surfaces on pieces too large or too heavy or perhaps too awkward to hold in a shaper. In this machine the table, or *platen*, on which the work is securely fastened, has a reciprocating (forward and return) motion. The tool head may be automatically fed horizontally in either direction along the heavily supported crossrail over the work, and automatic down feed is also provided. Cutting tools used in planer work are the same as those used in the shaper.

Fig. 1-5. A double-head planer. (*The G. A. Gray Company*)

The Milling Machine. The milling machine (Fig. 1-6) is a machine tool in which metal is removed by means of a revolving cutter with many *teeth*, each tooth having a cutting edge which removes its share of the stock. The work is supported by various methods on the work table, and may be fed to the cutter longitudinally, transversely, or vertically. A great variety of work may be done on a milling machine, and next to the lathe it is perhaps the most adaptable and interesting machine in the shop.

The Grinding Machine. The grinding machine (Fig. 1-7) is a machine tool in which an abrasive wheel is used as a cutting tool to obtain a very high degree of accuracy and a smooth finish on metal parts, including soft and hardened steel. A large variety of types and a number of sizes of surface-grinding machines and external and internal cylindrical-grinding machines are manufactured for ordinary and special grinding operations. The advance in the use of

Fig. 1-6. A horizontal milling machine. (*The Cincinnati Milling Machine Company*)

the grinding machine is one of the outstanding factors in present-day rapid, accurate production of metal parts.

The Boring Mill. There are two distinct types of boring-mill design, the vertical (Fig. 1-8) and the horizontal (Fig. 1-9), both of which are modifications of the lathe. Boring is the operation of enlarging a hole, usually by means of a single cutting tool, and the boring mill is designed primarily for the purpose of finishing holes that are impracticable to finish in a lathe or other machine because of the size or shape of the work.

In a vertical boring mill, the work table revolves on a vertical axis and the cutting tool (which may be a drill or a boring tool or a turning tool) is arranged above the table and may be fed laterally (toward or away from the center of the table) and up or down in any position. Because of these feeding arrangements, turning and

Fig. 1-7. A surface grinder. (*The Cincinnati Grinder Company*)

facing may be accomplished as easily as boring. In the smaller sizes the various tools are arranged in a turret head.

In a horizontal boring mill, the cutting tool revolves on a horizontal axis. The spindle which carries the cutting tool may be fed longitudinally through the spindle head and in the more recent designs the spindle head may be fed vertically. The work table may be fed longitudinally and transversely. The horizontal boring mill, while designed primarily for boring holes, may also be used for finishing horizontal and vertical flat surfaces by means of a suitable milling cutter fastened to the spindle.

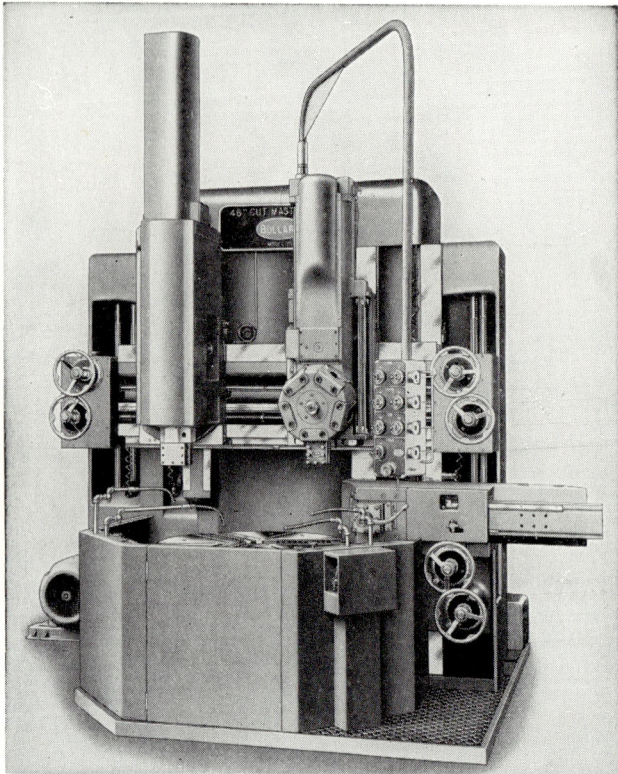

Fig. 1-8. A vertical boring mill sometimes called a *Bullard*. (*The Bullard Company*)

NOTE: Because of the size of the boring mills, vertical and horizontal, and the nature of their product, it is not customary for beginners in shop practice to operate these machines. The setup of the work, the shaping and setting of the tools, the measuring, gaging, etc., in a vertical boring mill greatly resemble chuck work in a lathe. In the horizontal boring mill these operations are similar to many found in lathe and milling-machine work. That is, the mechanical intelligence necessary to operate a boring mill can be acquired by application of like principles on smaller machines and on work less costly. Therefore, a further discussion of boring mills is nowhere included in this text.

Fig. 1-9. A horizontal boring mill. (*The Bullard Company*)

What Is Meant by Bench Work and Floor Work? *Bench work* in a machine shop consists of laying out, assembling, and the final fitting of parts. When the same operations are performed on heavy work, the term *floor work* applies.

Are There Many Specified Divisions in the Machinist's Trade? There are probably more opportunities for specializing in machine-shop work than in all the other trades taken together. Consider the range in sizes of machines and consequently the work to be done; also the opportunity of specializing on certain types of machines, such as planer, milling machine, or grinding machine. One might prefer model work, experimental work, or toolmaking. Toolmaking itself is divided into several branches such as diemaking, jig making, and gage making. In any event, the machinist of whatever class, or the toolmaker of whatever specialty, must have a certain *machine-shop sense* and a knowledge of principles and methods. These can be acquired only by experience and study.

How Are the Employees of a Commercial Manufacturing Shop Classified? The machine shop is but one of the essential units in the typical production plant. In the machine shop, the special tools and machines are developed and built, and repairs made. Elsewhere in the factory are rooms filled with special machines or "manufacturing" machines run by machine operators. These operators become very skillful in operating one machine and are able to produce accurate and acceptable work.

It has not seemed necessary or advisable for manufacturing purposes to train more than a small proportion of the employees to be anything but operators, or assemblers, or machine hands. The result is that few, indeed, are what may correctly be called *machinists.*

The employees of commercial manufacturing shops may be classified according to grades of attainment discussed in the following paragraphs.

Machine Operator. A machine operator is one who operates a manufacturing machine doing just one class of work. He is able to do many things on this machine such as starting and stopping the machine, making minor adjustments of the work and cutting tool, and removing the workpiece when the operation has been completed.

Assembler. The assembler takes the parts already made and inspected and puts them together. In general, this work calls for some skill and some common sense. In the final fitting and adjustment of the job, mechanical ability is required as well as good trade judgment.

Machine Hand. A specialized machine hand is one who has very little general machine-shop knowledge but who has operated a special machine long enough to be skillful in a variety of work on this machine, or on a machine of this class. He is able to do his own setup work and make the necessary adjustments.

Machinist's Helper. A machinist's helper knows the names and uses of the various small tools (cutting tools, measuring tools and gages, holding tools, etc.) used in machine-shop work. In addition he may be able to do elementary bench work or machine work.

A Specialized Machinist. A specialized machinist is one who has had some general machine-shop experience and has made a specialty of some one machine or some one class of work, such as lathe work

Fig. 1-10. A vertical milling machine called a *Bridgeport*. (*Bridgeport Machines, Incorporated*)

and planer work. He has a broader background of experience and more versatility than the machine hand.

Bench and Floor Hands. Bench hands and floor hands possess information and skill regarding a number of so-called *hand operations* (as differentiated from machine operations) such as filing, scraping, assembling, and adjusting. A skilled bench hand or floor hand, in general machine-shop work, has the ability also to read blueprints readily and to do layout work. In addition, a first-class bench hand or floor hand has had, usually, considerable experience in machine operation.

The Machinist. The general machinist has had enough experience, has acquired enough information, has developed enough judg-

Fig. 1-11. A jig borer used for very accurate work in drilling, reaming, and boring holes. (*The Moore Machine Tool Company*)

ment, and possesses "head" enough to be able to set up intelligently and operate any standard machine tool and perform any bench or floor operation. In addition, he is able to harden and temper machine-shop cutting tools.

The Toolmaker. The expert toolmaker qualifies substantially as the general machinist. Toolmaking is usually a lighter or smaller class of work and, generally speaking, involves more delicate workmanship, more accurate measurement than does general machine work. It also involves more mathematical calculations on the part of the workman and a more extended use of the various machine-tool attachments.

Apprentice Machinist. The grades of apprentice vary naturally from beginner apprentice to advanced apprentice. The beginner may have no previous machine-shop experience, while the advanced apprentice should have a thorough training in the fundamental knowledge of a machinist. The typical apprentice agreement is based upon an understanding that the apprentice shall be given a few months' experience on bench and floor work and on each of the standard machine tools, and, in addition, shall be given an opportunity to learn the essential principles of the operation of each. The degree of attainment of an apprentice at a given time depends of course upon the individual, other things being equal. The ambitious apprentice is keenly desirous of learning the trade. Where the employer fully meets his obligation, the apprentice is offered every advantage to learn the operations, methods, calculations, and principles involved in machine-shop practice, to the end that his development may be rapid and sure.

What Is the Knowledge One Must Have to Be an Expert Machinist? He must have an understanding of certain fixed principles which obtain in all machine-shop practice, for example:

The action of metal-cutting tools.

Elementary metallurgy.

Cutting speeds.

Feeds and feeding devices.

Strength of materials—stresses and strains—rigidity and spring.

Gear trains.

Measurements.

Adjustments, etc.

He must have a sufficient knowledge of arithmetic to read measurements from the various instruments, and to make the necessary calculations for cutting speeds, gear velocities, angles, threads, etc.

He should have a sufficient knowledge of the principles of mechanical drawing to be able at least to read blueprints of machine details.

He should have a reasonable working acquaintance with the construction and operation of the typical standard machine tools. To be an expert machinist does not imply a highly specialized knowledge of all or perhaps of any one of the machine tools, but it is an established fact that the high-class specialist on a particular kind of machine or class of work is also to a considerable extent familiar with general machine-shop practice.

He should be well acquainted with the characteristics of the metals used in machine construction, particularly cast iron, bronze, aluminum, and the various kinds of steels. And he must be familiar with the heat-treatments of carbon steel and high-speed steel.

He must be resourceful in methods. The most efficient way of doing a certain job often depends on the accuracy required, the number of pieces to be made, the available machines, and the available tools.

He must have a considerable knowledge of the sequence of operations; the knowledge of how to go at the job to assure accuracy of result in the shortest time. It is said that there are over 100 operations on the receiver of the Springfield rifle, which, when finished, weighs about a pound. Think of the satisfaction of being able to arrange the sequence of operations and to design the special tools and fixtures for such a job. It requires the knowledge of a machinist. Every job of five operations or of ten operations thoughtfully worked out is a problem solved and every problem solved is a help in solving the next.

What Chance Has a Machinist for Promotion? The chief advantage of the machinist's trade is in the opportunities it offers for promotion. Every machine-shop foreman, naturally, must have been promoted from the ranks. Further, practically every superintendent and every master mechanic of any industry manufacturing metal goods of any description is a machinist. These men may have gone through the drawing room, but they were machinists before they were draftsmen.

Thousands of successful manufacturers were once machinists. They had ideas suggested by their machine-shop experience. They put these ideas into practice and developed them. To mention only a few: Joseph R. Brown and Lucien Sharpe, founders of the Brown & Sharpe Manufacturing Company of Providence, Rhode Island; Francis A. Pratt and Amos Whitney, founders of the Pratt & Whitney Company of Hartford, Connecticut; Worcester R. Warner and Ambrose Swasey, founders of Warner & Swasey of Cleveland, Ohio, were all apprentice boys, and then machinists, before they were counted among the foremost manufacturers of the world.

Fig. 1-12. A universal heavy-duty turret lathe. (*The Warner Swasey Company*)

What Are the Essential Characteristics of a Machinist? Carefulness, orderliness, accuracy, speed, judgment, and confidence are six essential characteristics that a skilled machinist must have.

Care of Self. A machine is a good servant but a cruel teacher. It is a dreadful thing to lose a finger in order to learn that revolving gears are dangerous things to handle. It is better to be overcautious until habits are formed, which, without conscious reasoning on the part of the operator, make a dangerous move around a machine practically impossible. A well-trained machinist is careful through habit.

Care of Machine. A mechanic is always careful not only of the appearance but also of the good condition of his machine.

Orderliness. The truth of the need of "a place for everything and everything in its place" is nowhere better exemplified than in a shop where a number of people at various times use the same machines and tools. And orderliness makes one's own work easier and speedier. Orderliness and neatness about the machine and bench are the marks of a good workman. They are habits worth forming.

Accuracy. It is very often necessary for a machinist to work within $\frac{1}{1000}$ in. This is easy enough with the machine tools and measuring tools found in modern shop equipment. It means, however, that the machine must be perfectly adjusted and otherwise in first-class condition, that the cutting tool must be properly sharpened and set, and that the measuring tool is dependable for accuracy.

Speed. An expert mechanic studies the methods and means of doing a job; makes sure that the machine, cutting tools, and measuring tools are in good condition; and then with care, and without undue haste, operates the machine to obtain the maximum production. Carefulness, orderliness, thoughtfulness, and close attention to the little things make for speed.

Judgment. A man is successful in any business in about the same proportion as he acquires judgment. This is as true of a machinist, foreman, or superintendent, as it is of any other business or professional man.

Judgment is the ability to decide correctly after comparing ideas, methods, or facts. The mechanic must cultivate ideas, study methods, and learn facts regarding his trade. He must know when to rough, when to finish, where accuracy is necessary, and when and where it is not essential. He must be resourceful in ideas and methods in order to adapt himself to various shop conditions. Judgment is intelligence, and every job, well thought out and well done, sharpens the intellect and paves the way toward success.

Confidence. The man who through study, thought, and careful application has confidence in his own ability to accomplish results has in this confidence a factor which makes for success.

Safe Work Habits. An apprentice must at once learn to work safely so that the men working near him will not be injured. Poor work habits and unsafe practices often lead to disappointment to the young man entering the trade. So, from the very start, *learn to work safely and acquire good work habits.*

How Are These Characteristics Acquired? A skilled artisan is one who has the power to think and execute with knowledge and ability. To think is to employ the mental capacity of distinguishing ideas and methods. To execute with expert ability means to employ the senses with confidence and accuracy.

The man who aspires to leadership in any trade or profession must *study* and must *work*. Theory and practice walk hand in hand toward skill, knowledge, and efficiency, and a man's value to himself and to his employer is always in proportion to his efficiency.

Skill in machine work may be acquired by studying how and why certain operations are done and in connection with this study, a considerable experience in performing these or similar operations is essential.

A lifetime of merely doing is not sufficient to acquire knowledge, except in a very limited degree. One must take advantage of what others have done and are doing. A fund of information is available in the special articles in the trade papers, and in the advertisements in these magazines; in the manufacturer's catalogues and instruction bulletins; and in reference books of which dozens have been prepared regarding each of the standard machine tools. Whole volumes have been written also about machine parts such as gears and cams; and about machine-shop mechanics and machine-shop mathematics; about steel and the heat-treatment of steel for various purposes. It is unnecessary to own all these books but it surely is advisable to know where certain kinds of information can be found when wanted. It is almost as necessary for a machinist to appreciate the value of a reliable handbook as it is for him to know how to use a micrometer. To keep up to date it is well worth while to read regularly at least one of the magazines relating to the work of the machinist. The progressive machinist is a student.

Efficiency can be approached only through the application of the best methods. The selection of the best method requires sound reasoning. The power of sound reasoning is founded in the knowledge of principles. One must know *why* before he can reasonably know *how*.

This sounds serious; it is serious, but certainly not discouraging. Study is easy and work is fun when one is interested. Master the first principles and get interested, develop that interest into the right kind of enthusiasm, and your knowledge and your power, your good influence and your income, will grow and grow fast.

QUESTIONS ON THE MACHINIST'S TRADE

1. In what ways are machine tools important to man's progress?
2. Why is the machinist considered important to the welfare of all peoples?
3. Of what importance has been the development of new metals and materials to the world?
4. How did the knowledge of the machinist's trade help such men as Henry Ford, Walter Chrysler, and many others become so successful?
5. What is a machine shop?
6. Describe how an engine lathe operates.
7. Describe how a milling machine operates.
8. Describe how a shaper operates.
9. Compare the engine lathe with the milling machine as to method of operation and state the differences.
10. Compare the engine lathe with the shaper as to method of operation and state the differences.
11. Compare the milling machine with the shaper and state the differences as to operation.
12. Name three standard machine tools found in most shops.
13. Name three production machine tools usually found in production shops.
14. What is meant by *bench work?*
15. What is meant when one is called *a machine operator?*
16. What is a machinist?
17. What is meant when one is called *a toolmaker?*
18. What is meant when one is called *an apprentice?*
19. State the differences between an apprentice and a machine operator.
20. State the differences between an apprentice and a machinist.

Safety

CHAPTER 2

Safety in the Machine Shop

Working safely is the first essential an apprentice should learn even before he is taught how to operate any of the machine tools. The young man can easily learn to work safely, and it is just as easy to learn the *safe* way of doing things as it is to learn the *unsafe* way. The safe way is the efficient and correct way.

Safety is an attitude; that is, it is a frame of mind. If the mechanic's attitude toward safety is a good one, he will accept the idea that safe working habits are the ones to learn and practice for the rest of his working life. A young apprentice must make up his mind that working with other people in the shop is his business; to keep himself as well as those working with him free from accidents is also part of his attitude towards safety. Many injuries have resulted from a lack of appreciation of the fact that there are other people in the shop who are working and probably thinking of safety.

A good and safe mechanic is one who is "safety conscious," always practicing safe and accepted procedures. So, from the very beginning of his apprenticeship, the young man *must always* remember that safety is not only his concern but everybody's concern. A safe place in which to work and live is just as important and perhaps more important than merely learning a trade. A trade hasn't been learned well until safe working habits are formed and practiced, day in and day out.

Safe working habits cannot be bought or manufactured; they must be *learned* through *practice*. The young apprentice *must* practice safe working procedures at *all times*, not for a day or month or year, but *always* and for *all time*, if he is to become a *safe* worker. Rules and regulations, mechanical guards and devices placed around machinery, posters and lectures are very important, but

23

they will never replace *intelligent precautions* taken by the mechanic in doing his work.

If a student develops a sense of responsibility to himself, to his fellow workers, and to society—a spirit of cooperation and interest in doing his work safely—that student will have gone a long way toward becoming a safe worker.

Industry is always trying to reduce the number of accidents in the shops; thereby saving life and limb, let alone millions of dollars in production time and in insurance premiums.

So, *learn to work safely at all times.*

What Are Accidents? When this question is asked, the answer is likely to be cuts, bruises, etc., because most of us, when thinking about accidents, have the idea that an accident has occurred only when a serious injury has resulted. Obviously, accidents and injuries are not the same. An *accident* is a mishap. It does not have to result in an injury to anyone or damage to anything. It is well to bear this in mind.

The definition of an accident varies with its application. For example, in industry, reportable accidents are usually based on a lost-time factor; that is, has the person who had the accident lost any time from his job? The school-shop accident definition is more exacting, not determined by lost time but by bodily injury. In accordance with this concept of an accident, the following definition of a school-shop accident is used:

> *Every mishap that causes injury to the body or a member of the body should be considered as an accidental injury.*

Present Conditions. The boy comes to the school shop and usually is anxious to do things. He wants to start at once and frequently would like to finish the job in one period. In fact, he would like to work in the shop for a longer period of time, but the bell rings and classes change according to the school schedule. How does this affect safety practices? He is in a hurry. The time is too short to do all the things he wants to do. Does he fasten his material securely before he starts the machine? Or does he frequently attempt to hold with his hand the material on which he is working? Are these all so true because he is in a hurry? The answer is yes. Such procedures always end up in some form of an accident.

The old saying that "haste makes waste" is true under these conditions.

Such procedures and practices must be stopped. The teacher must allow plenty of time in which to do the job. The student must be taught safe practices and he must also stress that time, under school conditions, is not a too important factor.

Machine Tools and Their Hazards. The hazardous nature of industrial machine tools, including the mechanical power-transmission apparatus driving them, has long been recognized. Early efforts in industrial safety dealt almost exclusively with the guarding of machines, and a great deal of progress has been made in making machines less dangerous. But machines are still an important source of injuries. For example, of the 283,634 injuries reported to the Industrial Commission of Ohio during one year, 57,064, or 20 per cent, were reported as caused by machinery. Not all these injuries, of course, were due to machine tools, although these tools do cause a considerable number of injuries and particularly in those industries which use metalworking machines extensively.

Injuries due to machine tools stem primarily from two sources, the point-of-operation and the mechanical power-transmission apparatus involved in driving the machines. Injuries to machine-tool operators may occur from other causes, such as handling materials, falls, or difficulties chargeable to the job but not to the machine.

The modern trend to use individual motor drives has eliminated much of the hazard originally associated with mechanical power-transmission apparatus although a small number of plants still use the overhead drive. Individual motor drives, however, have created some new hazards, such as those from electricity in the case of a break in the insulation on the electrical controls.

All machine tools have several points in common—they use driving power of one sort or another; their tools have sharp cutting edges; they have dangerous moving parts; and they throw off flying chips. These general characteristics, plus those peculiar to each class of machine, are the source of accidents.

Let us now examine some of the machine tools of the average machine shop and note their hazards.

Milling. Milling consists of machining a piece of metal by bringing it into contact with a rotating cutter with many cutting edges. This process includes the hobbing of gears. Machine tools that perform a milling operation include horizontal milling machines, universal milling machines, vertical milling machines, planer-type milling machines, gear hobbing, profilers, and routers. Circular saws, although usually classed as cut-off machines, also do a milling job.

Fig. 2-1. The well-dressed operator—sleeves rolled up and wearing goggles—standing safely on the "going-away" side of the cutter.

The chief hazard of machine tools that perform a milling function is accidental contact with the revolving cutter. Such accidental contact may occur in removing chips, particularly if a rag instead of a brush is used. Loose clothing creates a serious hazard around a rotating cutter; the loose sleeve, necktie, or apron becomes wound around the cutter and draws the operator into contact with the cutting edges. Flying chips also create an eye hazard.

Figure 2-1 shows how a safe machine operator should be dressed when operating a machine. He has his sleeves rolled up, wears goggles, and is standing on the "going-away" side of the cutter. Figure 2-2 is another example of good and safe dress for an operator.

Accidents are also caused by unsafe operating practices, such as tightening the arbor nut by using the power of the machine, or attempting to adjust the work or tool while the machine is in motion. In most milling-function machines not only the cutter but also the

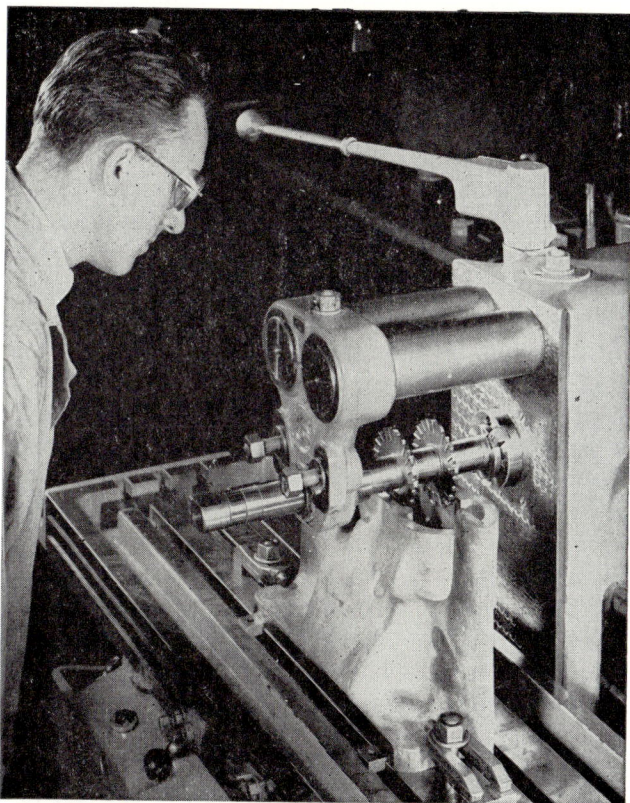

Fig. 2-2. An operator wearing goggles when milling.

material worked on is in motion. This tends to make these machines dangerous.

Safe operation depends on the knowledge and skill of the operator, plus the constant application of the rules of safe practices.

Planing and Shaping. Planing consists of machining a surface by moving the work backward and forward under a stationary cutting tool. This classification also includes shaping, the process in which the tool moves in a straight line over a stationary piece of work. Machine tools that perform a planing operation include planers, shapers, slotters, broaches, and keyseaters.

The two chief machines that make up the planing function group are planers and shapers. Operators of planers are injured by being struck by the moving table or by being caught between the table and the frame or bed of the machine. Since most planers are large machines, a fall from the table, or the top of the bed between the uprights, may be a serious matter. Unsafe practices, such as changing stop dogs while the machine is in motion or riding the table during the operation, frequently lead to severe injuries. Planers usually operate on large pieces, and considerable hazard is met in handling the material into or out of the machine.

Operating a shaper offers real danger from flying chips. It is important that the work be securely clamped to the table so that it is not displaced by the tool, and that no adjustments be attempted while the machine is in motion. Operators are also injured by being caught between the ram and some fixed object if the proper clearance at the end of the ram stroke is not maintained. There is always, of course, the chance of being caught by the tool at the point where cutting takes place. Such accidents often are due to clearing away chips with the hand or with rags.

Figure 2-3 illustrates a safe worker on the shaper. He has his sleeves rolled up, wears safety glasses, and is watching his job. He has his mind on his job. There are no tools lying on the machine or near it. His machine is clean and no chips are seen. This is the way to work on any machine tool.

Turning. Turning consists of shaping a rotating piece by means of a cutting tool, thus generating a cylindrical surface. Machine tools that perform a turning operation include engine lathes, turret lathes, hollow-spindle lathes, automatic lathes, and automatic screw machines.

Accidents from lathes occur from a number of causes: from being drawn into the lathe if loose clothing catches on the revolving work; from contact with the chuck or lathe dog; from attempting to remove chips with the hands; or from being struck by flying chips, particularly when cutting cast iron, brass, or any other nonferrous

Fig. 2-3. A shaper operator working fully equipped for safety.

Fig. 2-4. A lathe operator dressed for safe working.

metal. When a crane is used to lift the work into a lathe, considerable danger may result from the handling of the heavy material.

On many turret lathes and automatic machines, the stock extends beyond the machine and, unless properly guarded, may get caught in the clothing and cause injury to the operator or others who pass close to the machine. Many lathes, especially the screw

Fig. 2-5. Another safe worker on a lathe.

machines and the automatics, use a coolant or cutting oil which, if allowed to splash on the floor, creates a slipping hazard.

Figures 2-4 and 2-5 show safe practices when working on an engine lathe. Notice the sleeves. They are rolled up *above* the elbow. The operator is wearing safety glasses, apron, and is carefully watching his job. His mind is on the job. All of these are good safety practices. *Practice them yourself.*

Boring. Boring consists of cutting a round hole by means of a rotating cutting tool, or the work may revolve and the tool remain fixed as in the lathe. A vertical boring mill, which is also considered as performing a boring function, has a rotating table to which the work is clamped—the work rotates and the tool is stationary. Reaming, drilling, and honing are also considered boring operations. Machine tools that perform a boring operation include vertical and horizontal boring mills, jig borers, drill presses, multiple-spindle

Fig. 2-6. A radial-drill-press operator dressed for safe working. (*The Fosdick Machine Tool Company*)

drills, radial drills, gang drills, centering machines, lathes, and honers.

Hazards from such machines stem from a number of sources. If the work is not securely clamped or the proper clearances are not maintained, the operator may be injured when trying to adjust the machine without bothering to stop it.

In the case of drills, injuries occur through contact with the revolving drill or by being struck with the material being drilled. Such accidents may occur if the operator attempts to drill while holding the work in his hand (instead of clamping it to the table of the press) or if he wears loose clothing when operating a drill press. Operators of such machines are also urged to wear caps, especially those who prefer to wear their hair long. An operator's hair getting caught in the drill was a very common occurrence during the war years, especially among the women working in machine shops. Clearing away chips with the hands while the drill was in motion has also led to many serious injuries. Flying chips also create a serious eye hazard.

Figure 2-6 shows how a drill-press operator should be dressed for safe work on a drill press.

Grinding. Grinding consists of shaping a piece by bringing it into contact with a rotating abrasive wheel (the cutting tool). The process may be internal grinding (as in grinding a hole), external cylindrical grinding (as on the outside of a revolving piece), or surface grinding (as on a flat piece). The process also includes such methods of finishing as polishing, buffing, and lapping. Abrasive wheels are also used to do cutting-off or parting operations. Machine tools that perform a grinding operation include grinders, abrasive wheels, abrasive cloths, abrasive belts, abrasive disks, abrasive points, buffing wheels, polishing machines, and lapping machines.

Fig. 2-7. Grinding a tool bit on a pedestal grinder safely.

The chief accident hazards from this class of machines include eye injuries from flying particles, injuries from contact with the revolving wheels, disks, or belts, and injuries due to bursting of abrasive wheels. At times, abrasive wheels seem to "explode" when they are poorly manufactured, improperly installed, run at incorrect speeds, or used incorrectly. All wheels should be checked before using.

Fig. 2-8. Working safely on a surface grinder. (*The Brown & Sharpe Manufacturing Company*)

Inhalation of the dust made in grinding or polishing processes constitutes a serious health hazard unless the grinding is done "wet" or the dust removed by mechanical means.

Goggles *must always* be worn when grinding. Figure 2-7 illustrates an excellent work habit, safe and sure for protecting the operator's eyes. Note that he uses not only the goggles for his eyes but also the safety-glass guard usually mounted on floor grinders. *Cultivate* and *practice* this procedure.

Study Fig. 2-8 carefully. What safe practices are shown? You will notice that the operator working on the surface grinder is wearing goggles and has his sleeves rolled up. These are very good work habits and should be followed at all times.

Housekeeping. A shop may be compared to your own home. Many accidents have happened in the home because of things just lying around. This also applies to the shop. Imagine a shop where tools, scrap parts, castings, etc., are lying around in the aisles and

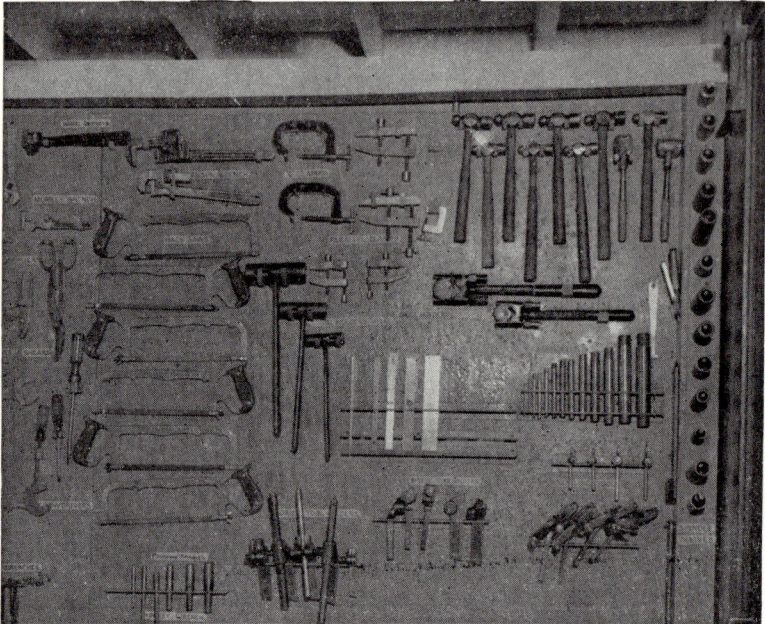

Fig. 2-9. A well-kept and safe tool crib.

piled loosely on tables or racks. Housekeeping is the term used in industry to mean the safe storage of tools, parts, and all the rest of the items used in manufacturing.

A sign of a safe shop is a clean and orderly shop; a place where everything is put away or stored so that people walking through it will not trip or fall, thereby causing a possible injury.

The slogan "*A PLACE FOR EVERY TOOL AND EVERY TOOL IN IT'S PLACE*" should be adopted by all shops whether they be machine shops or otherwise. In this way, and only in this way, may the shop be considered a safe place in which to work. Figure 2-9 illustrates a good housekeeping job for the small tools in the shop. The same procedure can be followed for all tools.

Precautions and Safe Practices for the Machine Shop. The following precautions and safe practices have been recommended by the National Safety Council and should be studied and learned by every apprentice.

GENERAL SAFETY PRECAUTIONS

1. Be sure that all machines have effective and properly working guards that are always in place when machines are operating.
2. Replace guards immediately after any repairs.
3. Do not attempt to oil, clean, adjust or repair *any* machine while it is running. Stop the machine and lock the power switch in the "Off" position.
4. Do not operate any machine unless authorized to do so by the teacher, or under his supervision.
5. Even after the power is off, do not leave the machine until it has stopped running. Some one else may not notice that it is still in motion and be injured.
6. Do not try to stop the machine with your hands or body.
7. Always see that work and cutting tools on any machine are clamped securely before starting.
8. Keep the floor clear of metal chips or curls and waste pieces. Put them in the container provided for such things. Scraps are tripping hazards, and chips or curls may cut through a shoe and injure the foot.
9. Do not operate machinery when the instructor is not in the shop.
10. All setscrews should be of flush or recessed type. If they are not, move with caution when near them. Projecting setscrews are very dangerous because they may catch on sleeves or clothing.
11. Get help for handling long or heavy pieces of material. Follow safe lifting practices—lift with your leg muscles, not your back. If you do not know how to lift safely, ask your teacher to show you.
12. When working with another student, only one should operate machine or switches.

13. Do not lean against the machines.
14. Do not run in the shop; there should be no "fooling around" in the shop at any time. Don't be a "wise guy."
15. Concentrate on the work and do not talk unnecessarily while operating the machine.
16. Don't talk to others when they are operating a machine.
17. Get first aid immediately for ANY injury.
18. Be sure you have sufficient light to see clearly. Check with the teacher if you do not have enough.

CLOTHING AND SAFETY EQUIPMENT

1. *Always* wear safety glasses, goggles, or face shields designed for the type of work when operating any machine.
2. Wear clothing suited for the job. Wear shoes with thick soles— safety shoes if heavy work is being done.
3. Do not wear rings, watches, bracelets, or other jewelry that could get caught in moving machinery.
4. Do not wear neckties or loose or torn clothing of any kind.
5. *Wear* shirts or jumpers with sleeves cut off or rolled above the elbows.
6. Always remove gloves before turning on or operating any machine. If material is rough or sharp and gloves must be worn, place or handle material with machine turned off.

HOUSEKEEPING

1. Keep floors free of oil, grease, or any other liquid. Clean up spilled liquids immediately; they are slipping hazards.
2. Aisles should be clear at all times to avoid tripping or other accidents.
3. Store materials in such a way that they cannot become tripping hazards.
4. Do not leave tools or work on the table of a machine even if the machine is not running. Tools or work may fall off and cause toe or foot injury.
5. Put tools away when not in use.
6. Place all scrap in scrap boxes.

EQUIPMENT

Shapers

1. Be sure ram, tool head, tool, work, table-support clamping screws, and vise are properly secured in place, or position, and that the tool head and tool clear the work before starting the shaper. Place a metal shield or heavy, close-mesh wire screen over the tool to catch the chips.
2. After setting the stroke length and position, check to see that adjusting nuts are tight.
3. Remove all wrenches from machine after completing setup.
4. If magnetic chuck is used, be sure current is "On" before starting machine.
5. Stand parallel to direction of stroke of machine when it is running and never reach across the table between strokes of the ram.
6. Never remove chips while ram is in motion.

Planers

1. After work is fastened, check to see that it clears crossrails; see that stop pegs are in proper places and safety dogs are secured in position.
2. See that feed rod and its attachment are properly located and in proper working order.
3. Have planer idle when adjusting length of bed stroke and speed of machine to suit work.
4. Do not reach over a moving job and never ride the bed or platen.
5. Do not leave any tools of any kind between the ways.
6. When loosening toolholders, hold tool with one hand or place a wooden support under it.

Milling Machines

1. Make sure that the cutter and arbor are secure and that cutter and arbor support clear the work.
2. Use only cutters that are correctly ground and in good condition.
3. To avoid striking hands on cutter while setting up, move table with work as far away from cutter as possible.

4. When using cutters in a vertical milling machine, do not take an excessively heavy cut or feed. Such a feed or cut could break the cutter and injure operator.

5. Do not try either to tighten or to take off arbor nut by applying power to machine. Make sure motor is "Off."

6. Check speeds and feeds, and feed work against direction in which cutter is rotating.

7. Keep hands away from work when machining.

8. Never reach over a revolving cutter, especially the side of cutter which cuts into the work.

9. Use a brush not the hands to remove chips.

Drill Press

1. Use drills properly sharpened to cut to the right size and see that the drill is running true.

2. Small drills should revolve at high speeds, large drills at low speeds. Reduce speed about 50 per cent when drilling cast iron.

3. Chuck wrenches must be removed from drill chucks before starting the machine.

4. *Never* attempt to hold work under the drill by hand. *Always* clamp work to table.

5. Run drill only at proper speed; forcing or feeding too fast may result in broken or splintered drills and serious injuries.

6. Change belt for speed regulation only when power is "Off" and machine has come to a dead stop.

7. If work should slip from clamp, never attempt to stop it with the hands. Stop the machine and make adjustments.

8. If drill stops in work, shut off the motor and start drill by hand.

9. File or scrape all burrs from drilled holes.

10. Do not reach around or in back of a revolving drill.

11. Keep your head back and well away from *ANY* moving part of the drill press.

Lathes

1. Before turning on the power, check to see that the tailstock, tool holder, and job are properly clamped.

2. Use *hand power only* when putting on or removing chuck or faceplate. *Do not use* the power that operates the lathe.

3. When assembling or removing the chuck, place board on ways to prevent damage to machine and possibly to operator in case the chuck falls. Have firm grip on chuck as it nears the end of the thread.

4. Do not leave chuck wrench or any other tool in the chuck. If machine is turned on, wrench may fly out and injure the operator or any other person.

5. Do not use wrench on revolving work or parts.

6. Never try to measure work or feel the edge, or adjust a cutting tool when lathe is running.

7. Do not take heavy cuts on long slender work. Doing so may cause the job to fly out of the machine.

8. When filing, be sure tang of file is protected by a strong wooden handle. Stand to one side so that, if the file is forced upward, it will go past the body rather than against it.

9. As a general rule, do not shift or change gears while lathe is running.

10. Stand erect. This keeps head away from flying chips.

Metal Saws

1. When turning on power, stand to one side of saw frame, then adjust speed to suit work.

2. When saw is operating, do not bend over it.

3. Mount work *only* when saw is stopped.

4. Support protruding end of long work so material cut off will not fall and possibly injure any one. Be sure that the protruding end is well guarded against any one coming in contact with it.

5. When using the sliding stock guide, do not allow fingers to project beyond the end so that they could come in contact with the saw teeth.

6. Be sure that the blades for both circular and band saws are in good condition before using. An indication that the blade is cracked is a sharp, regular clicking sound as the work is fed. Change the blade *at once* if this condition arises.

7. *Always* inspect blade before using.

8. If blade does break in work, shut off the power and do not attempt to disengage blade from work until the machine has come to a complete stop.

Grinders: PEDESTAL TYPE

1. Stand to one side out of line of wheel when starting it up, especially if wheel is new.
2. The face of the wheel must be flat and free from grooves.
3. Work should be fed slowly and gradually. Using too much pressure, or striking wheel suddenly, may cause it to break.
4. Make sure that the tool rest is *only* ⅛ in. from the face of the wheel. *Check this distance.* Too much clearance may cause job to jam the wheel and break it.
5. Do not set tool rest while machine is in motion.
6. Use face of wheel only, unless it is designed for grinding on the side; otherwise, side pressure may break the wheel. Whenever possible, use entire face of wheel to avoid grooving.
7. Never use a grinding wheel that is loose on the shaft or if its rate of speed is not safe for the number of r.p.m. of the spindle. Check with the teacher for this information.
8. Stop wheel if it chatters or vibrates excessively. This may be a danger signal that the wheel is not properly balanced or not attached securely to spindle.
9. All wheels should be tested for soundness. The teacher usually does that.
10. Hold job against wheel firmly so that it will not slip out of the hand and cause hands and fingers to come in contact with the wheel.
11. Use clamp or other suitable holding devices for grinding short pieces.
12. *Always use face shield or goggles* even if grinder is provided with protective glass shields.

SURFACE TYPE

1. Be sure magnetic chuck is thoroughly clean.
2. Test holding power of chuck before starting the machine.
3. Stand to one side of wheel before starting up.
4. Check to see that wheel properly clears work.

Hand Tools: SCREW DRIVERS

1. Select screw drivers to fit the screw head being used.
2. Keep screw-driver handles smooth.

3. Do not use a hammer on a screw-driver handle.
4. Avoid holding work in the hand when using a screw driver on it, as it may slip and cause stab wounds.
5. Never grind a screw driver to a chisel edge.

WRENCHES

1. Discard wrenches that are spread.
2. Select open-end wrenches to fit the job.
3. Where possible, avoid using an *adjustable* or *monkey* wrench.
4. If a wrench has become burred, grind off the rough spots to avoid cutting the hands.
5. It is generally safer to *pull* a wrench toward yourself than to *push* it away from you.
6. Be sure that your knuckles will clear obstructions when the wrench turns.

HAMMERS

1. Hammers that are chipped should be discarded.
2. *Never* use a hammer that has a loose or split handle.

CHISELS

1. In using a chisel and hammer, keep the chisel head free from burring by grinding it if necessary.
2. Where chips may fly, use a chip screen.
3. Hold the chisel and hammer firmly and keep the chisel head and the face of the hammer clean and free from grease.

SCRAPERS

1. Keep scrapers in a place away from the rest of the tools.
2. Keep guard from handles on all scrapers. Guard against scraping towards the body.
3. Avoid holding work in one hand and the scraper in the other; stab wounds are likely to result.
4. Scrapers that must be carried in a tool box should be guarded with a wooden or leather sheath for their own protection as well as yours.

FILES

1. Always use a file with a handle.
2. When filing in the lathe, learn to file left handed.

3. Keep the file and your hand clear of the chuck jaws or dog.
4. Do not use a file as a pry bar.
5. If filing in a lathe, do not use a pad of cloth or waste under the thumb on the end of the file.
6. Keep a firm grip on the file at all times.
7. Do not blow filings so that they can go into anyone's eyes.

HACKSAW

1. Use the correct blade for the job.
2. See that the blade is correctly secured in the frame.
3. When the saw breaks through the work, ease up on the pressure so that the hand will not strike the work or vise.
4. Be sure that the work is held securely in the vise.
5. Do not force cut.

TAPS AND DIES

1. Be sure work is firmly mounted in vise.
2. Secure the proper size of tap wrench.
3. Avoid cutting the hands on a broken tap end.
4. If a broken tap is removed by using a punch and hammer, *wear goggles.*
5. If a long thread is cut with a hand die, keep the arms and hands clear of the sharp threads coming through the die.

QUESTIONS ON SAFETY

1. There are usually five areas of hazards connected with the operation of any machine tool. These are listed below and you are to name the precautions necessary for these hazards:
   A. Machine—moving and loose parts.
   B. Tools—inserting and removing the tool and handling the wrench.
   C. Materials—holding, handling, cooling, lifting, removing from machine, and removing chips.
   D. Floor around the machine—chips, coolant, and oil.
   E. Operator—hands, eyes, and feet.
2. What should an apprentice learn to do at once? Why?
3. Name five accepted practices when operating a drill press.
4. Many accidents have occurred when handling materials. Name at least three safe methods in handling materials.

5. Lifting is also a hazard. Explain how one should lift with safety. Give a concrete example.

6. If a casting is too heavy for one person to lift, what should he do? Why?

7. Why are you cautioned against wearing rings, wristwatches, etc., when working on a machine tool?

8. What are the dangers involved in the wearing of loose clothing and ties?

9. What is meant by housekeeping when applied to the machine shop?

10. Name at least five good practices of housekeeping.

11. In the school shop, one is usually told to report any accident no matter how slight. Why?

12. Name three safe practices when using a hammer, a chisel, a screw driver.

13. Why should handles on hammers be checked before using?

14. Why are the heads of chisels always checked before using?

15. Why should deep cuts and fast cutting speeds be avoided whenever possible?

16. What should be done to a grinding wheel before it is mounted in the machine? Why is it done?

17. In chipping, why should a guard be placed around the piece being chipped?

18. What should always be worn when grinding? Why?

19. Name three safe practices when operating a lathe, a milling machine, a shaper, a grinder.

20. Revolving drills are very dangerous. Name three things that a drill-press operator should always look out for.

21. Name at least three safe practices shown in Fig. 2-10.

Fig. 2-10. Operating a drill press.

Right and Wrong Work Habits

RIGHT

Fig. 2-11. Goggles worn, hammer held at the end of the handle to get the full leverage and longest stroke, and chisel held lightly but securely.

WRONG

Fig. 2-12. No goggles, choking the hammer, clutching the chisel.

RIGHT

Fig. 2-13. File properly held, body well balanced, sleeves rolled high, and apron and goggles worn. He *is* interested in his job.

WRONG

Fig. 2-14. Body much too stiff for complete control of file and not balanced.

RIGHT

Fig. 2-15. When filing left handed, no hand is in danger.

WRONG

Fig. 2-16. When filing right handed, the left hand is in danger.

RIGHT

Fig. 2-17. Breaking up the stringy chips with a piece of wood, *not with the hands.*

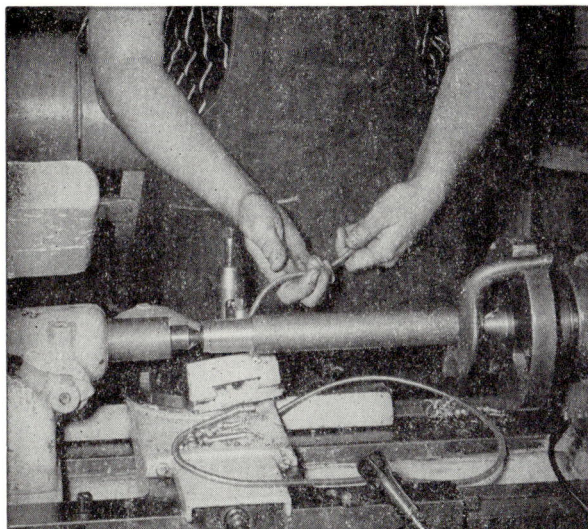

WRONG

Fig 2-18. Long chips may cut operator's hands. They may wind around the revolving job and gather all the chips into one mass of dangerously revolving cuttings.

RIGHT

Fig. 2-19. No necktie worn.

WRONG

Fig. 2-20. Wearing a long necktie.

RIGHT

Fig. 2-21. Head away from the spindle and hair combed back tightly.

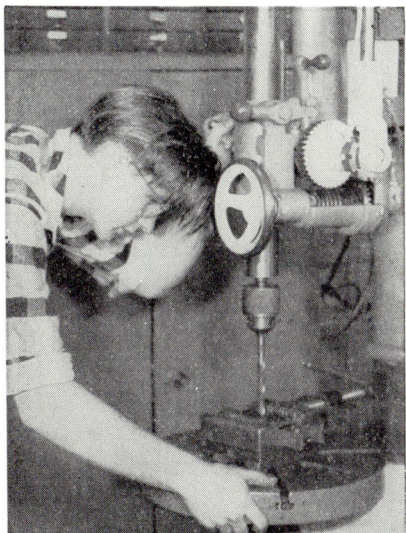

WRONG

Fig. 2-22. This fellow's hair and head are in danger.

RIGHT

Fig. 2-23. Brush the chips away on the "away" side of the cutter.

WRONG

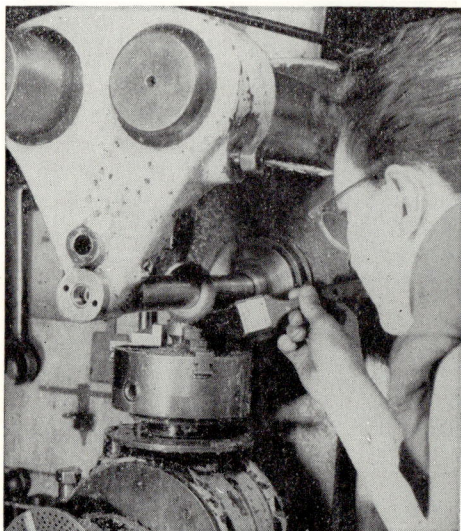

Fig. 2-24. Brushing the chips away on the wrong side of the cutter. The brush will be taken in by the cutter.

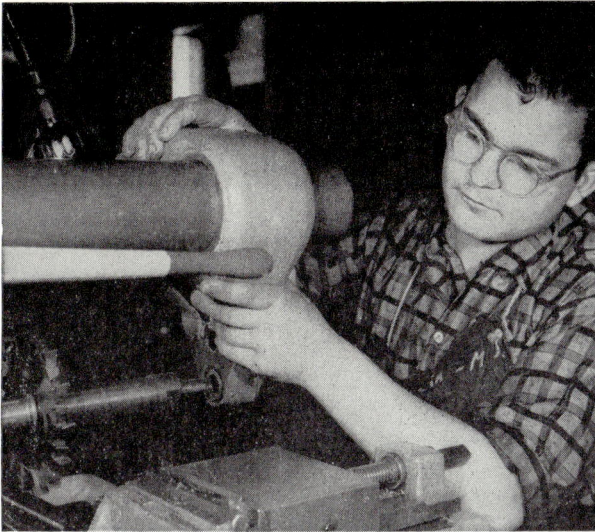

RIGHT

Fig. 2-25. His eyes are on the job and his fingers are clear of the bearing hole.

WRONG

Fig. 2-26. He is *not* watching as the overarm bracket is being pushed onto the end of the milling-machine arbor. Result: badly bruised or sometimes broken finger.

RIGHT

Fig. 2-27. Arbor is properly supported. Operator is standing well balanced. Wrench on nut is correct.

WRONG

Fig. 2-28. Tightening arbor nut when arbor is *not* supported by overarm bracket. Operator standing incorrectly; if wrench slips, a bad fall may result. Wrench has not been placed properly on nut; it should be reversed.

RIGHT

Fig. 2-29. Standing to one side of the shaper and wearing goggles and apron.

WRONG

Fig. 2-30. Standing in front of the shaper with chips flying. Ram may hit him on the head.

RIGHT

Fig. 2-31. Guard in place protecting operator. Operator stands upright closely watching the job at a safe distance.

WRONG

Fig. 2-32. Wheel guards are *not* in place. Operator in danger of getting chips in his eyes and face and/or a broken wheel in his face.

RIGHT

Fig. 2-33. Standing to one side of the furnace with hand on the gas-control valve.

WRONG

Fig. 2-34. Standing in front of a furnace when lighting it. Face and hair may be singed.

RIGHT

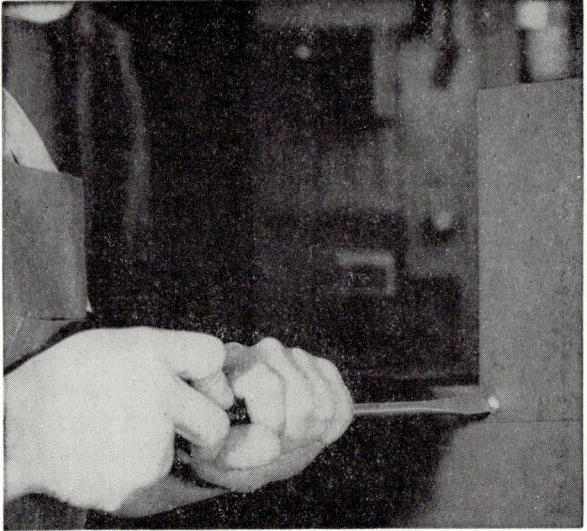

Fig. 2-35. Screw driver held level; tip square in slot of screw.

WRONG

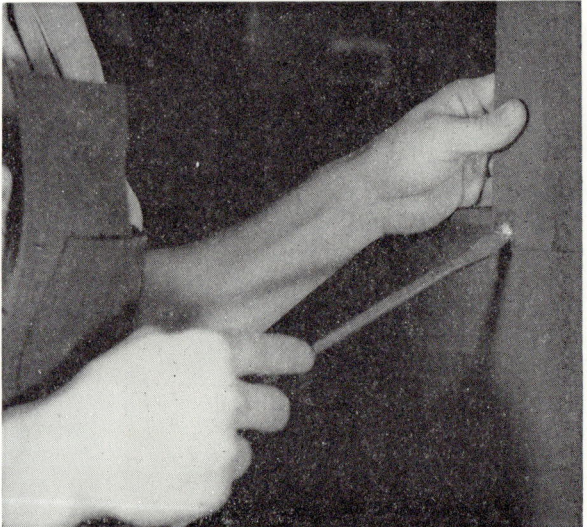

Fig. 2-36. Screw driver held at an angle; tip placed improperly in screw slot. If the screw driver slips out of the slot, a punctured hand may result.

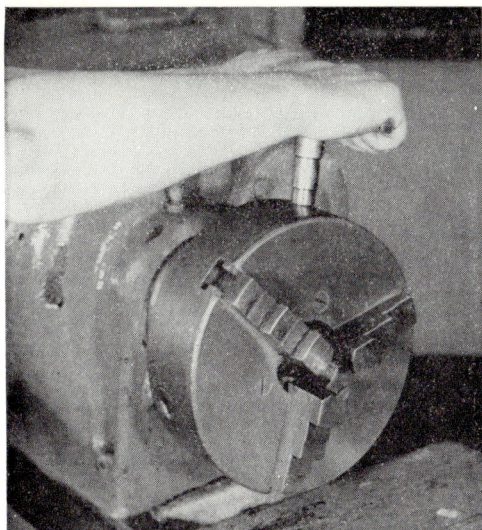

RIGHT

Fig. 2-37. Turning off the chuck safely. The board protects ways of the lathe in case the chuck drops accidentally.

WRONG

Fig. 2-38. If this chuck drops, the hand may be crushed and the lathe dented.

QUESTIONS ON MACHINE-SHOP SAFETY

1. An improperly shaped screw driver can be a hazard to safety. Explain how a screw driver should be ground and to what shape. Use sketches for your answers.
2. What should a safe worker look for *before* using a hammer.
3. How should you scrape metals, against or away from your body? Why?
4. Always use a file with a handle. Why?
5. State your reasons why filing should be done left-handed and not right-handed when working on a lathe.
6. It has been said that safety is an attitude. Explain this statement.
7. Is it necessary to learn safety or is it better to pick it up by experience? Explain.
8. How can you practice safety every day in the home, street, and shop?
9. Why does industry spend so much time and money to reduce accidents?
10. State your definition of an accident.
11. Tightening an arbor nut on a milling machine by using machine power is dangerous. What can result?
12. It is unsafe to lean against a milling machine when it is in operation. Why?
13. Shaping and planing machines do similar types of work. More accidents are caused by the planer table than the shaper table. Why?
14. How can the accidents caused by the planer table be avoided?
15. State the safe way of removing chips from a machine.
16. Lathe operators consider long sleeves a hazard to their safety. Why?
17. How should the safe worker in a machine shop be dressed? Give a complete outfit from head to toe.
18. State the slogan that should be adopted by all machine shops that consider good and safe housekeeping.
19. It is a rule not to attempt to operate a machine until given permission by the instructor. Why?
20. Setscrews projecting from a moving part are dangerous. In what way are they dangerous?

Measuring Tools

CHAPTER 3

Measuring Tools of the Machine Shop

Accuracy. The student in machine work should begin at once to understand accuracy in its relative terms. He should appreciate from the start the value of the various measuring tools in obtaining the degree of accuracy the given operation demands. For example, if the caliper measurement is easy, quick, and accurate enough, then the use of a micrometer would be poor practice. On the other hand, if it is easier, quicker, and better to use a micrometer to get the measurement, it would be wrong to use the caliper. There is no more reason why a boy should not use a micrometer the first week in the shop than there is to suppose he must chip castings for 6 months before he can run a lathe.

Care of Measuring Tools. It goes without saying that precision measuring tools should be handled with the greatest of care. Good tools are made of hardened steel and will stand a lifetime of use without breakage, but the *accuracy* of even the finest tool can be quickly impaired by careless or abusive treatment. In working with measuring tools, be careful to avoid accidental scratches or nicks that will obscure graduations or distort surfaces. Rust is the enemy of all finely finished surfaces. Tools should be wiped clean of finger prints after using and kept in separate boxes or cases. A light dressing of oil applied with a soft, lint-free cloth will protect tools in storage.

Linear Measurements. Linear measurements on flat surfaces are perhaps the most common measurements made in general practice in the machine shop. The tool used varies with the size of the dimension, the nature of the work, and the degree of accuracy required. It may range from a steel tape, rule, divider, or trammel to a micrometer or vernier caliper. The measurement may be made direct as with a steel rule or slide caliper (in which the dimension is read directly from a graduated scale or standard, using dividers, calipers, or a surface gage to transfer the measurement). Many related tools such as straightedges, steel squares, and protractors are used in conjunction with linear measuring tools to determine flatness, straightness, squareness, and angularity.

Round Work Measurements. For round work, measurements are usually made by contact, using tools with contact points or surfaces such as spring calipers, micrometers, and vernier calipers. Contact measurements are made in two ways: (1) by pre-setting the tool to the required dimension, using a steel rule, micrometer, or other tool as a gage, and then comparing the set dimension with the actual size of the work; and (2) the reverse of this method, viz., first setting the contact points to the surfaces of the work and then using a steel rule, vernier caliper, or micrometer caliper to read the size. The first method is generally preferred where repeated tests must be made, such as in machining a piece to a given size, or when checking the same dimension on a number of identical parts. The second method is preferred for determining the actual size of the piece or an accurate measure of variation from a required standard.

Rules. Among the most useful tools in the shop are the steel rules. Although these are actually rules or rulers, most machinists call them scales. They are made in a variety of kinds such as *spring tempered*, *flexible*, *narrow*, and *hooked*, and in lengths from 1 to 48 in., the most popular being the spring-tempered 6-in. rule (Fig. 3-1). Most steel rules are graduated, that is, marked by fine

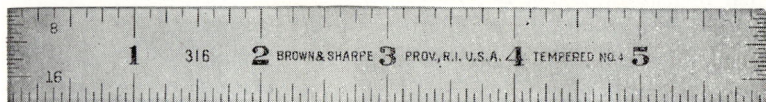

Fig. 3-1. A 6-in. rule. (*The Brown & Sharpe Manufacturing Company*)

lines upon each edge of both sides, and often at the ends, in different subdivisions of an inch. The different graduations are classified by number. For example, the No. 7 graduation, which is perhaps the most used, has 64ths, 32nds, 16ths, and 100ths on the four edges. The No. 4 graduation, which many shopmen prefer, has 64ths, 32ds, 16ths, and 8ths. The flexible rule (Fig. 3-2), is very popular with machinists and toolmakers and is graduated on only three edges, in 64ths, 32ds, and 8ths.

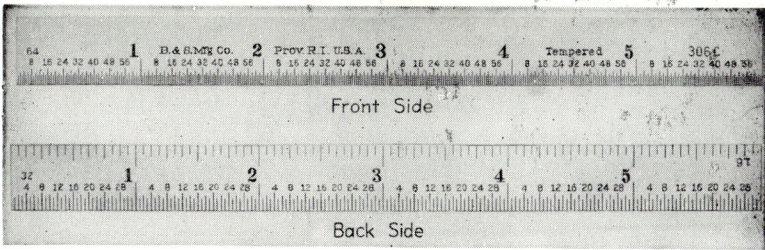

Fig. 3-2. A 6-in. flexible rule. (*The Brown & Sharpe Manufacturing Company*)

It will be observed (see Figs. 3-1 and 3-2) that the graduation lines are of different lengths, the 64ths being the shortest and the lines marking the 32ds and the 16ths, and so on, are successively longer, the inch mark being the longest. This has been so designed to make reading the rule easier and quicker.

Figure 3-3 shows a mechanic using a 6-in. steel rule. For longer measurements, longer rules are used, such as the 36- and 48-in. rules.

Another useful measuring tool is the *hooked* rule (Fig. 3-4). This rule makes possible accurate measurements against shallow shoulders. They are also very convenient in taking measurements

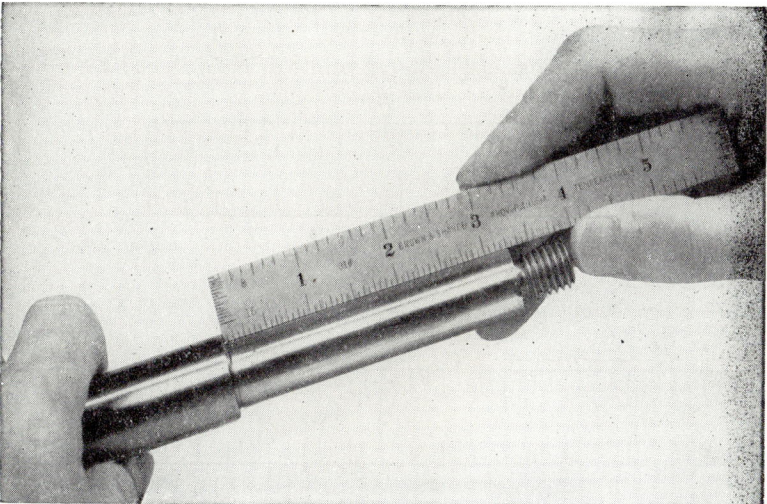

Fig. 3-3. A 6-in. steel rule being used. (*The Brown & Sharpe Manufacturing Company*)

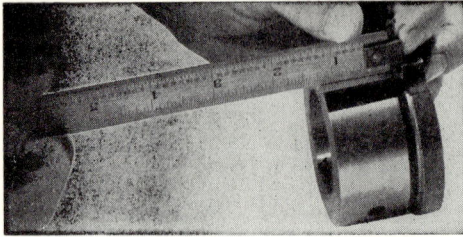

Fig. 3-4. A 6-in. hooked rule being used.

of flanges or circular pieces or through hubs of pulleys; also for setting calipers and dividers and taking measurements from points where the user cannot see if the rule is even with the measuring edge.

PROBLEMS

NOTE: Figures 3-6, 3-8, and 3-9 do not show the entire length of the rule. When reading, include in your answer that part of the rule not shown.

1. What are the readings in Fig. 3-5 at points *A*, *B*, *C*, *D*, *E*, and *F*?

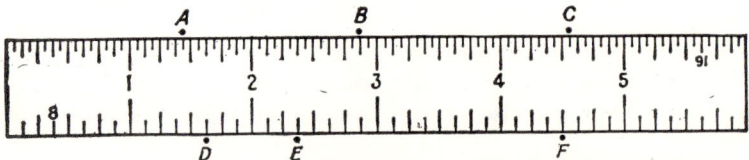

Fig. 3-5.

2. What are the readings in Fig. 3-6 at points *A*, *B*, *C*, *D*, and *E*?

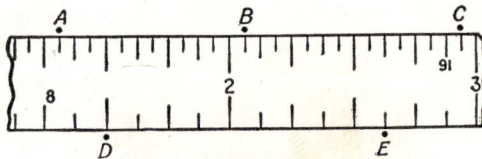

Fig. 3-6.

3. What are the readings in Fig. 3-7 at points *A*, *B*, *C*, *D*, *E*, *F*, and *G*?

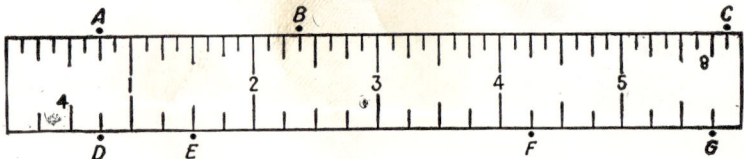

Fig. 3-7.

4. What are the readings in Fig. 3-8 at points *A*, *B*, *C*, *D*, *E*, and *F*?

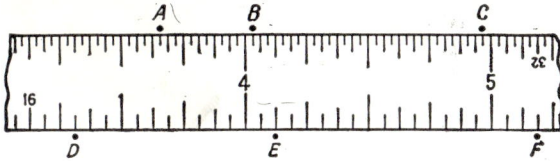

Fig. 3-8.

5. What are the readings in Fig. 3-9 at points *A*, *B*, *C*, *D*, and *E*?

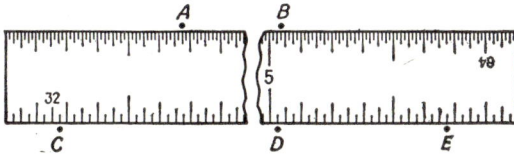

Fig. 3-9.

Calipers. A caliper is a tool used in measuring diameters. It is always used with a steel scale and, at times, with a micrometer. The caliper itself cannot be read directly as a steel scale and therefore, when a measurement is taken with a caliper, the opening is measured on the steel scale or micrometer.

Calipers are made in several styles such as the *spring-joint caliper*, *firm-joint caliper*, *transfer caliper*, for both inside and outside diameters.

Figure 3-10 illustrates an outside spring-joint caliper being used and Fig. 3-11 shows an inside spring-joint caliper being used. The spring at the top tends to keep the legs set taut against the pressure of the adjusting nut.

Figure 3-12 shows an outside firm-joint caliper. A caliper of this kind is usually preferred only in the larger sizes. Figure 3-13 shows the inside caliper.

Figure 3-14 shows a transfer caliper. The special feature of the transfer caliper is that it may be used inside of chambered cavities, over flanges, etc., removed and reset without losing the size calipered. This is done by loosening the lock nut *a* which binds one leg to the auxiliary leaf and moving this leg (while the joint *b* is tight) to clear the obstruction, then moving it back against the stop on the leaf where it will show the exact size measured.

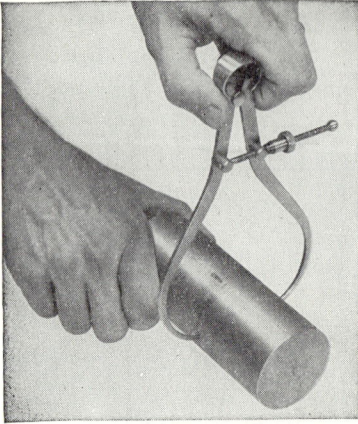

Fig. 3-10. A left-handed worker using an outside spring-joint caliper. (*The L. S. Starrett Company*)

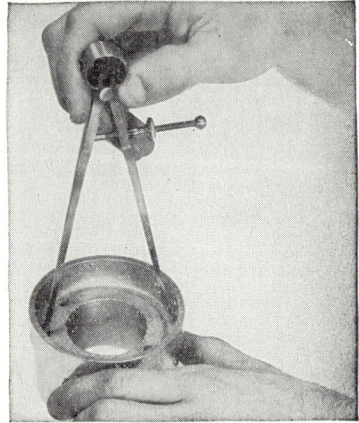

Fig. 3-11. An inside spring-joint caliper being used. (*The L. S. Starrett Company*)

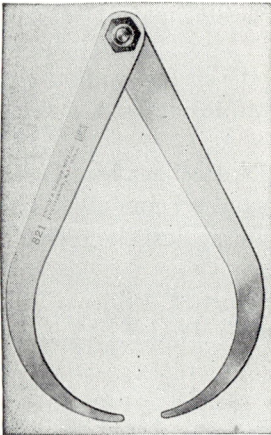

Fig. 3-12.   **Fig. 3-13.**   **Fig. 3-14.**

Fig. 3-12. An outside firm-joint caliper. (*The Brown & Sharpe Manufacturing Company*)

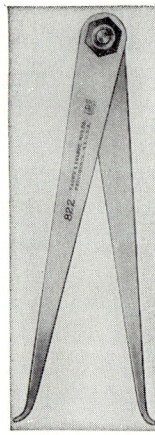

Fig. 3-13. An inside firm-joint caliper. (*The Brown & Sharpe Manufacturing Company*)

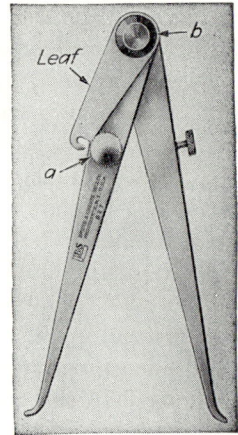

Fig. 3-14. A transfer caliper. (*The Brown & Sharpe Manufacturing Company*)

The caliper may be used as a measuring tool or as a gage. The machinist generally uses it as a *measuring tool;* he takes a cut for a short distance, measures it with the caliper, reads the measurement on the scale to see how much more of a chip he has to take, and proceeds accordingly. When the caliper is used as a gage, it is set to the size required and then used.

Measuring with a Caliper (Fig. 3-15). Accurate use of calipers requires considerable practice and the development of a sense of

Fig. 3-15. A toolmaker's outside caliper being used. (*The Brown & Sharpe Manufacturing Company*)

touch. To get a delicate sense of touch of the caliper on the work, it should be held lightly and not with a "grab grip." If the caliper will just barely hang from the work without falling off, the pressure is about right. It is possible to force calipers over or into work by using too much pressure, and thus introduce an error in reading. It is not too difficult to demonstrate the "feel" of 0.001 in. with a caliper. A lathe mandrel[1] tapers about 0.001 in. in 2 in. of its length.

---

[1] *Mandrel:* Sometimes erroneously called *arbor,* a machine-shop tool with accurate centers which may be forced into the hole in the piece to be machined (such as a pulley or gear), thus providing centers on which turning or other machine work may be done.

Get a mandrel from the toolroom or crib and carefully set the caliper as if to measure this mandrel 3 in. from one end, then without changing the setting, caliper the mandrel 5 in. from the same end and note the difference in the feel.

When measuring with outside calipers, the axis of the calipers should be held perpendicular to the axis of the work. With inside calipers, the axes of work and calipers should coincide. It is particularly important with inside calipers that the tips of both feet bear on the work, not one foot and the side of the opposite leg. *Never caliper the work while it is moving or revolving;* it is not accurate and the caliper may get caught and be broken.

Setting and Reading an Outside Caliper. To set an outside caliper hold the rule in the left hand with the end against the little finger as shown (*a*, Fig. 3-16) and in such a position that the light falls

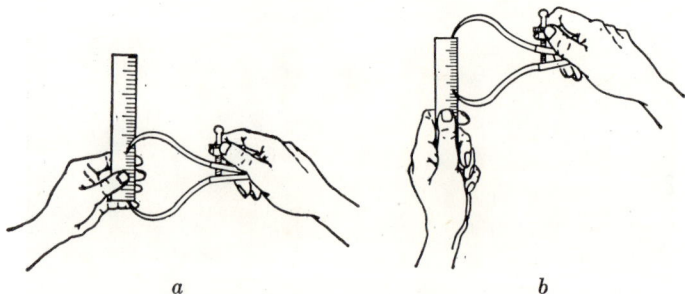

a   *b*

Fig. 3-16. (*a*) correct; (*b*) incorrect.

directly on the scale. Hold the caliper in the right hand, in such a position that it may be adjusted by the adjusting nut between the thumb and finger. Place the end of one leg of the caliper against the end of the scale and against the finger so that it will not slip around, and then adjust the other leg to the desired graduation on the rule. Hold the caliper true and looking squarely at the end to be set to the line, adjust the caliper until that end seems to split the line. In this way a caliper may easily be set to within 0.002 or 0.003 in. of the exact size required. A firm-joint caliper is held in about the same way but must be adjusted by rapping lightly against some solid object.

To read an outside caliper it is held substantially as above except that as it is not to be adjusted, the adjusting screw should not be touched.

Calipers are not *efficient* for accurate measurements, but they are efficient for measuring stock, roughing cuts, lengths, and any dimensions that need not be extremely accurate. The caliper may be used if necessary for very close measurements, but it is easier and quicker and surer to use a micrometer or a gage.

In rapid-production work it is usually advisable to use gages for determining the correct sizes. For cylindrical work the snap gage is used and where a slight variation over or under nominal size is allowable a *limit gage* is used.

Figure 3-17 illustrates but one style of limit snap gages. It will be understood that for rough turning, the difference between

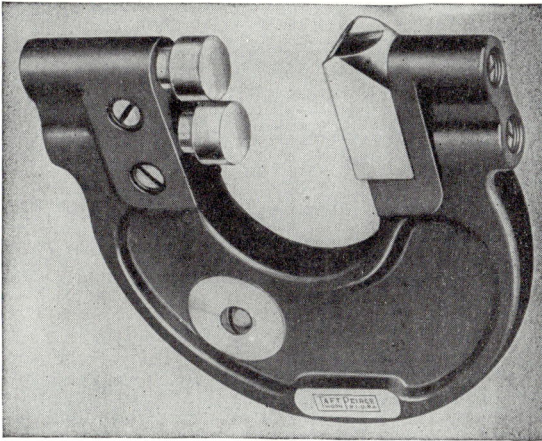

Fig. 3-17. A snap gage. (*The Taft-Pierce Manufacturing Company*)

the "go" dimension and the "no go" dimension is much greater than could be allowed in the finishing operation, and further, in different classes of work the limits allowed for finishing vary greatly. The advantage of the gage shown lies in the fact that it is adjustable. For further information concerning snap and other types of gages, see Chapter 8, "Drills and Drilling."

The Micrometer Caliper. Micrometer calipers are made in a variety of sizes ranging from ½ in. to about 48 in. However, the one

Fig. 3-18. An outside micrometer being used on stock held in a chuck. (*South Bend Lathe Works*)

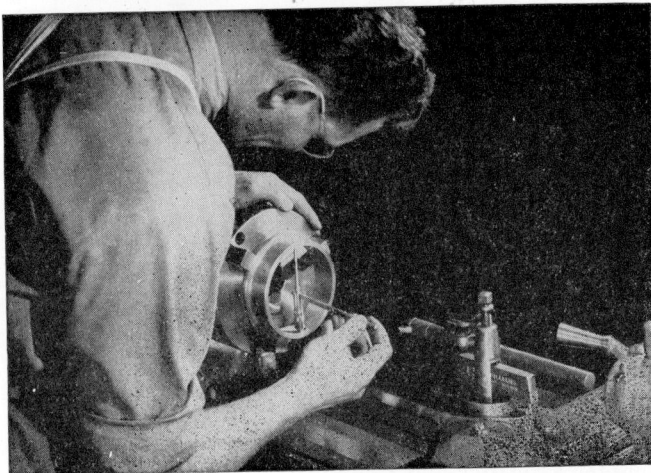

Fig. 3-19. An inside micrometer being used on a job held in a chuck. A boring setup is shown. (*The South Bend Lathe Works*)

most commonly used is the 1 in. size for measurements from 0.001 to 1.000 in. They are made also in a variety of styles such as *outside* micrometers, *inside* micrometers, *thread* micrometers, and *depth* micrometers. Figure 3-18 shows an outside micrometer in use (this one being larger than the 1 in.); Fig. 3-19 shows an inside micrometer in use; Fig. 3-20 shows a depth micrometer; Fig. 3-21 shows a thread micrometer, and Fig. 3-22 shows a very large size micrometer in use.

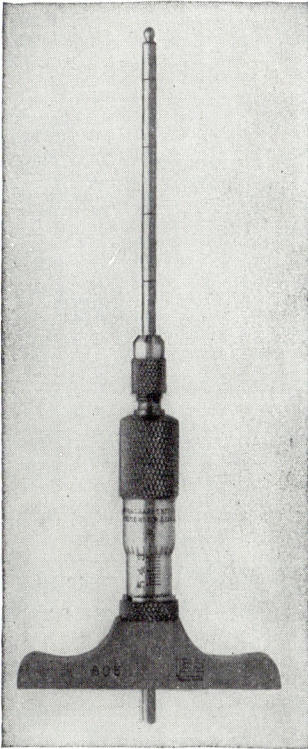

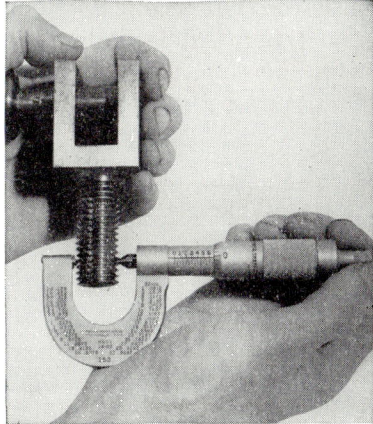

Fig. 3-21. A thread micrometer being used. (*The Brown & Sharpe Manufacturing Company*)

Fig. 3-20. A depth micrometer. (*Brown & Sharpe Manufacturing Company*)

Fig. 3-22. A worker using a large micrometer for an outside dimension. (*The Brown & Sharpe Manufacturing Company*)

Some of the reasons why the micrometer caliper is so important are:

1. It is small, portable, and strong enough to withstand normal use.

2. It retains its accuracy well and can readily be adjusted in case it wears.

3. It is easy to handle, easy to read, and can be used with only one hand.

The word *mike* is often used in reference to the micrometer. It is the machinist's abbreviation for the tool. *Miking* is another term used in the shop. It simply means using the mike to get a reading.

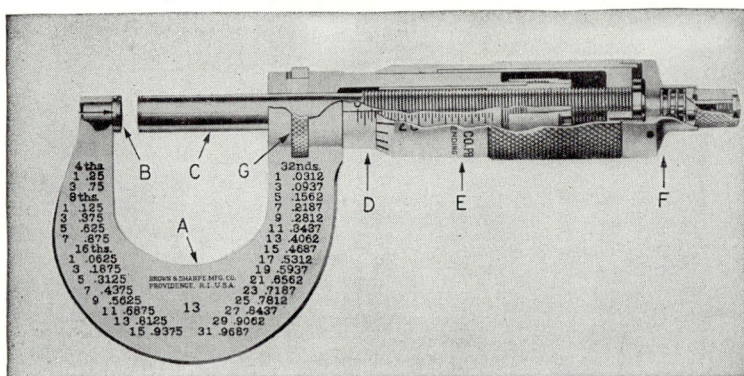

Fig. 3-23. A sectional view of a micrometer. *A*, frame; *B*, anvil; *C*, spindle; *D*, barrel; *E*, thimble; *F*, ratchet stop; *G*, clamp ring. (*The Brown & Sharpe Manufacturing Company*)

Principle of the Micrometer. Figure 3-23 shows a cross-sectional view of the micrometer. The basis of the tool is an accurate screw, which can be revolved in a fixed nut to vary the opening between the two measuring faces, one at the end of the screw spindle *C* and the other on the anvil *B*. The graduations on the barrel *D* and thimble *E* indicate precisely the position of the screw and the amount of opening between the measuring faces. The thimble rotates with the screw spindle and travels along the barrel. The graduations on the barrel conform to the pitch of the measuring screw, one line for each revolution. The graduations on the beveled edge of the thimble accurately subdivide each revolution of the screw so that readings may be taken in units, usually of 0.001 in. or 0.01 mm.

How to Read a Micrometer Caliper. The instructions that follow on how to read a micrometer caliper apply to a micrometer that reads thousandths of an inch only. How to read a micrometer graduated in ten-thousandths of an inch will be explained after the explanation of the vernier caliper.

In Fig. 3-24, the spindle C is attached to the thimble E, on the inside. The part of the spindle that is concealed within the sleeve and thimble is threaded to fit a nut in the frame A. Since the frame is stationary, the thimble E is revolved by the thumb and finger, and the spindle C, which is attached to the thimble, revolves with it and moves through the nut in the frame, approaching or receding from the anvil B. The article to be measured is placed between the anvil

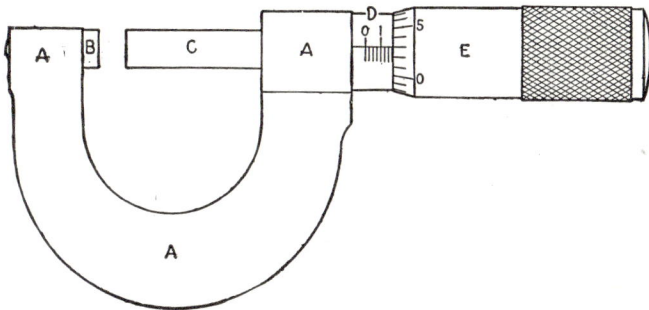

Fig. 3-24. Major parts of a micrometer. A, frame; B, anvil; C, spindle; D, sleeve or barrel; E, thimble. (*The L. S. Starrett Company*)

and spindle. The measurement of the opening between the anvil and spindle is shown by the lines and figures on the sleeve D and thimble E.

The pitch of the screw threads on the concealed part of the spindle is 40 per inch. The pitch of any screw thread is determined by the number of threads per inch of length of the bolt on which these threads are cut. On the spindle of the micrometer, 40 threads are cut per inch of length, thereby giving a pitch of 40 to an inch. One complete revolution of the spindle, therefore, moves it longitudinally $\frac{1}{40}$ or twenty-five thousandths of an inch. The sleeve D is marked with 40 lines to the inch, corresponding to the number of threads on the spindle. When the caliper is closed, the beveled edge of the thimble coincides with the line marked O on the sleeve, and the O

line on the thimble agrees with the horizontal line on the sleeve. Open the caliper by revolving the thimble one revolution, or until the O line on the thimble again coincides with the horizontal line on the sleeve; the distance between the anvil B and the spindle C is then $\frac{1}{40}$ or 0.025 in., and the beveled edge of the thimble will coincide with the *second* vertical line on the sleeve. Each vertical line on the sleeve indicates a distance of 0.025 in. Every fourth line is made longer than the others and is numbered from 0 to 10. Each numbered line indicates a distance of 0.100 in.

To read a caliper, therefore, *multiply the number of vertical divisions visible on the sleeve by 25 and add the number of divisions on the bevel of the thimble from 0 to the line that coincides with the horizontal line of the sleeve.*

EXAMPLE: Read the measurement as shown in Fig. 3-24.

SOLUTION: There are 7 divisions visible on the sleeve. Multiply that number by 25 and add the number of divisions shown on the thimble, 3. The micrometer is open to

$$7 \times 25 = 175 + 3 = 0.178 \text{ in.}$$

or

$$(0.100) + (3 \times 0.025) + (0.003) = 0.178 \text{ in.}$$

The second reading is obtained from the facts that the number 1 is visible and therefore equal to 0.100 in., that three more smaller lines are visible and each line is equal to 0.025 in., and that the number 3 on the thimble coincides with the horizontal line on the sleeve.

PROBLEMS

1. What is the reading in Fig. 3-25? Fig. 3-26? Fig. 3-27?

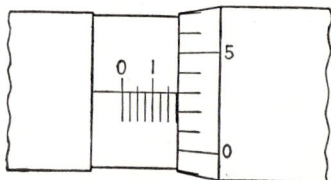

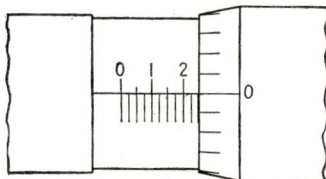

Fig. 3-25.   **Fig. 3-26.**

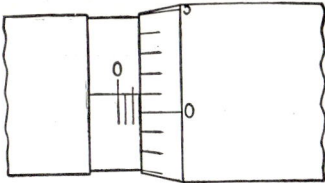

Fig. 3-27.

2. What is the reading in Fig. 3-28? Fig. 3-29? Fig. 3-30?

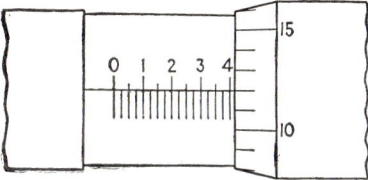

Fig. 3-28.

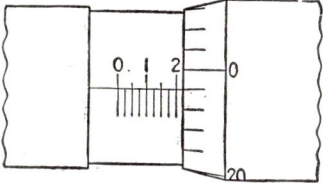

Fig. 3-29.

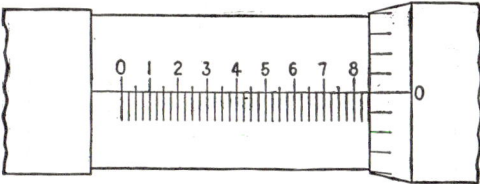

Fig. 3-30.

3. What is the reading in Fig. 3-31? Fig. 3-32? Fig. 3-33?

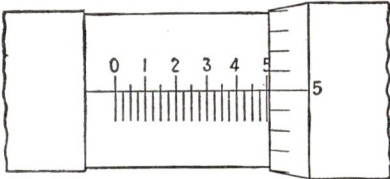

Fig. 3-31.

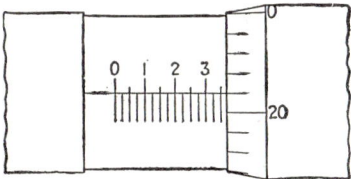

Fig. 3-32.

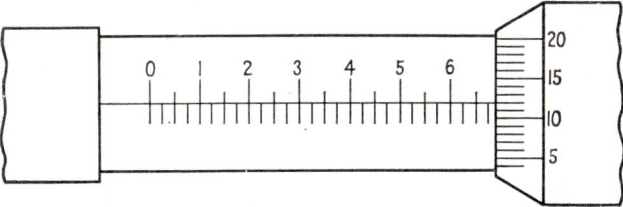

Fig. 3-33.

4. What is the reading in Fig. 3-34? Fig. 3-35? Fig. 3-36?

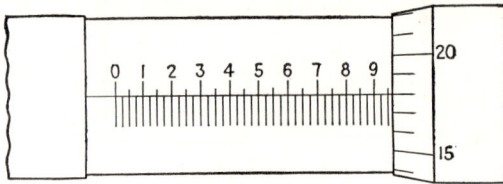

Fig. 3-34.

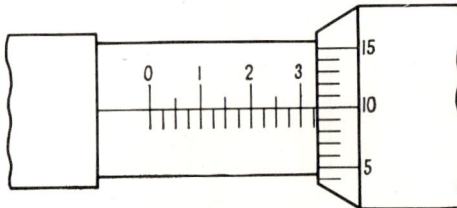

Fig. 3-35.

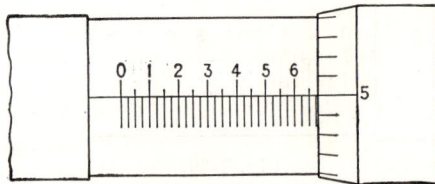

Fig. 3-36.

Holding a Micrometer. Figure 3-37 indicates clearly the proper way to hold the micrometer in order to accurately measure a piece held in the hand. Note carefully the position of the fingers; the micrometer is held by the little finger or the third finger, whichever is less awkward, against the palm of the hand, which allows the spindle to be operated in either direction with the thumb and index finger. The correct way to hold a micrometer when measuring work not held in the hand, is shown in Fig. 3-38.

When making a measurement be sure the micrometer is held square across the diameter. Turn the spindle down to the work, but not down too hard. It is easy to spring a micrometer 0.001 or 0.002 in. and this not only gives a false measurement but also injures the micrometer.

It seems easy for some people occasionally to read a micrometer

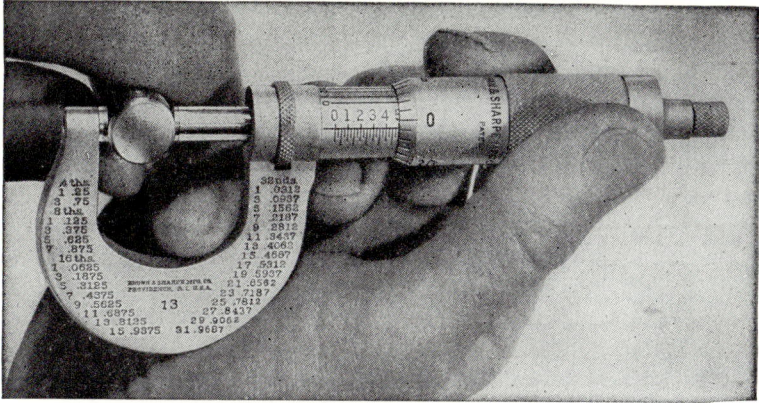

Fig. 3-37. How to hold the micrometer correctly when piece is held in the hand. Note positions of the fingers. (*The Brown & Sharpe Manufacturing Company*)

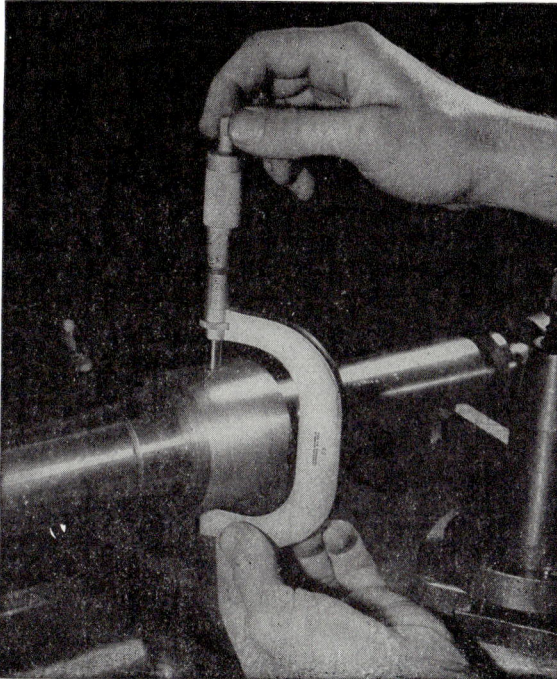

Fig. 3-38. How to hold the micrometer correctly when piece is not held in the hand. (*The Brown & Sharpe Manufacturing Company*)

0.025 over or under; such a mistake is inexcusable. It is even more careless to add 25 and 5 and call it 35, or 75 and 5 and read it 85. Be careful when using a micrometer to hold it properly, to adjust it carefully, and to read it accurately.

QUESTIONS ON MEASURING

1. How do you read a scale, using the significant graduations?

2. How do you hold a caliper to read the measurement on a scale?

3. What is the method of adjusting a firm-joint caliper?

4. What do you understand by sensitive touch?

5. What is the difference between the "go" and the "no go" dimensions of a limit gage?

6. What part of an inch does one revolution of the thimble of a micrometer move the spindle? Why?

7. Into how many divisions is the barrel graduated? How are these divisions numbered?

8. Into how many divisions is the beveled edge of the thimble graduated? How numbered? Why?

9. Describe the proper way to hold a micrometer (*a*) holding the work in the hand, (*b*) when the work is in the machine.

The Vernier Caliper. The *vernier caliper* is a measuring tool much used in machine shops, especially in tool and diemaking departments where fine and exact work is done. Figure 3-39 shows

Fig. 3-39. An outside vernier caliper is use. (*The Brown & Sharpe Manufacturing Company*)

an outside diameter being taken, and Fig. 3-40 shows an inside diameter being taken, both taken with a vernier caliper.

The beam or bar of the vernier caliper is graduated in fortieths of an inch, that is, the smallest graduation is $\frac{1}{40}$ in. long. Since $\frac{1}{40}$ in. equals 0.025 in., four graduations will be exactly $\frac{1}{10}$, or 0.100 in., long. Each fourth division line is numbered, and each number represents the distance in tenths of an inch which that division line is from the nearest inch line on the left.

Fig. 3-40. An inside vernier caliper in use. (*The Brown & Sharpe Manufacturing Company*)

Figures 3-41 and 3-42 represent two different readings. The vernier has 25 divisions, which are numbered from 0 to 25. Every fifth division is numbered. The length of the 25 divisions on the vernier is equal to the length of 24 divisions on the beam of the caliper. The graduations on the beam are in fortieths of an inch, or 0.025 in. Therefore, 24 times 0.025 equals 0.600 in. Thus, one division on the vernier equals $\frac{1}{25}$ of 0.600, or 0.024 in. The difference, therefore, between one division on the beam and one division on the vernier is equal to 0.025 minus 0.024, or 0.001 in.

When the reading is exact, with respect to the number of fortieths of an inch, the zero on the vernier coincides with a graduation on the scale—either inch, tenth, or fortieth, as the case may be. This leaves a space between the lines on the scale and 1, 2, 3, 4, etc., on the vernier of 0.001 in., 0.002 in., 0.003 in., 0.004 in., etc., respectively, the difference increasing 0.001 in. at each vernier division in numerical order until, at the twenty-fifth graduation, the lines again coincide.

Thus when the first, second, or third, etc., line on the vernier coincides with any line on the scale, the zero on the vernier has moved 1, 2, 3, etc., thousandths of an inch past the previous fortieth graduation to bring these lines together.

To read: Note the inches, tenths, and fortieths of an inch that the zero of the vernier has moved from the zero of the scale. To this reading add the number of thousandths indicated by the line on the vernier that coincides with any line on the scale.

EXAMPLE: Read the dimensions shown on Figs. 3-41 and 3-42.

Fig. 3-41. A vernier scale. (*The Brown & Sharpe Manufacturing Company*)

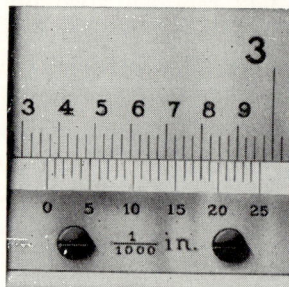

Fig. 3-42. A vernier scale. (*The Brown & Sharpe Manufacturing Company*)

SOLUTION: Figure 3-41 shows the zero graduation on the vernier coinciding with the fortieth graduation on the scale (the second fortieth beyond an even tenth graduation). This indicates that the reading is exact with respect to fortieths of an inch. The reading therefore is 2.000 + 0.300 + 0.050, or 2.350 in.

Figure 3-42, however, shows the eighteenth vernier line coinciding with a line on the scale. This indicates that 0.018 in. should be added to the scale reading. The reading, then, is 2.000 + 0.300 + 0.050 + 0.018, or 2.368 in.

Figure 3-43 shows a magnifying glass being used to read a vernier caliper. This is a common practice among machinists, since it is

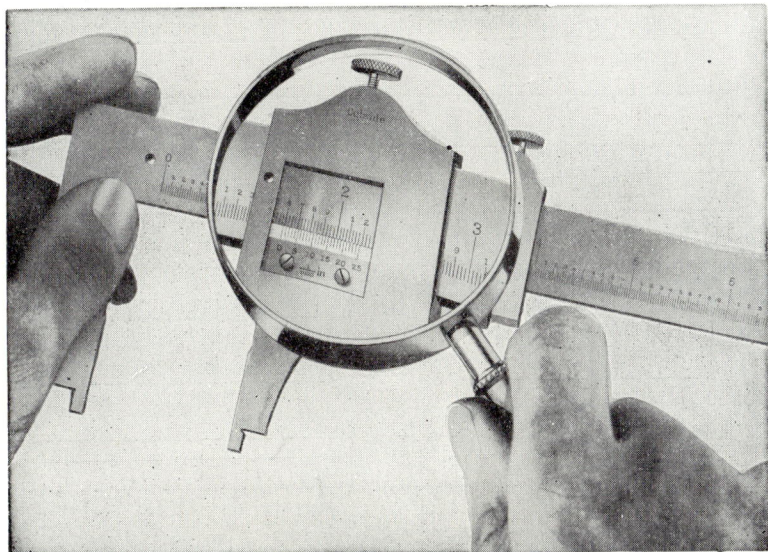

Fig. 3-43. Magnifying glass being used to read a vernier caliper. (*The Brown & Sharpe Manufacturing Company*)

hard to read without one. A magnifying glass should be used with almost all vernier reading because it assures a good view will be had of the reading.

PROBLEMS

The problems in reading a vernier caliper are shown in Fig. 3-44. The drawing in each case represents a part of the vernier caliper. The upper scale in each case represents some part of the graduations on the beam or bar of the scale. The lower part is a representation of the vernier scale. What are the readings in the problems of Fig. 3-44?

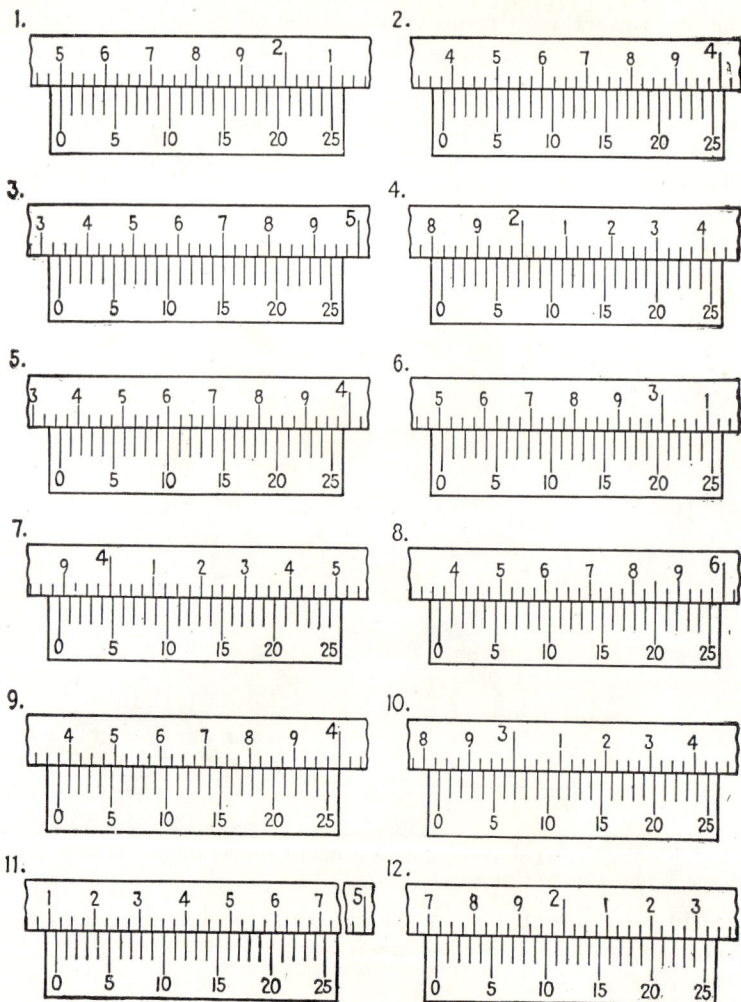

Fig. 3-44.

How to Read Micrometers Graduated in Ten-thousandths.

A micrometer graduated to read in ten-thousandths of an inch has all the graduations found on an ordinary micrometer. Such a micrometer is shown in Fig. 3-45. In addition, there are 10 longitudinal spaces laid out on the sleeve. This set of spaces is the vernier.

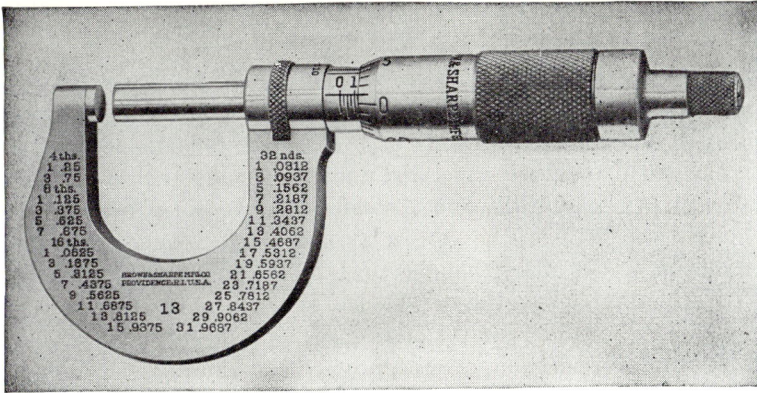

Fig. 3-45. A ten-thousandth micrometer. Note the lines at the top of the barrel. These are the lines where each one equals one ten-thousandth of an inch. (*The Brown & Sharpe Manufacturing Company*)

scale by means of which a reading as fine as 0.0001 in. can be made. Figure 3-46 is an enlarged view of the barrel showing the vernier scale.

Fig. 3-46. A close-up of the vernier scale on a ten-thousandth micrometer. (*The Brown & Sharpe Manufacturing Company*)

The vernier scale is used in reading a micrometer whenever the longitudinal line on the spindle does *not* coincide, that is, is not in alignment with a line on the thimble.

The vernier scale, consisting of 10 spaces running parallel to the longitudinal lines on the sleeve, covers exactly nine of the spaces on the beveled edge of the thimble. These lines are numbered from 0 to 0 (meaning from 0 to 10).

Since the 10 spaces or divisions of the vernier equal the over-all space of nine divisions of the thimble, then one division on the vernier equals $\frac{1}{10}$ of $\frac{9}{1000}$, or 9/10,000 in. (0.0009 in.). Graduations on the thimble equal $\frac{1}{1000}$, or 10/10,000 in. The difference between one division on the thimble and one division on the barrel is therefore (10/10,000) − (9/10,000), or 1/10,000 in. (0.0001 in.).

The *zero* lines of the vernier and thimble coincide when the reading is exact in thousandths and the differences between lines on the thimble and lines on the vernier at 1, 2, 3, etc., equals 0.0001 in., 0.0002 in., 0.0003 in., etc. Thus as the 1, 2, 3, etc., vernier lines coincide with any thimble line, the thimble has moved past the exact setting 1, 2, 3, etc., ten-thousandths of an inch.

To read a vernier micrometer, proceed as follows:

1. Obtain in thousandths of an inch as seen on the barrel and thimble. In other words, get the reading as on an ordinary micrometer.

2. Add to this reading the ten-thousandths indicated by the coinciding line of the vernier and thimble.

EXAMPLE: What is the reading in Fig. 3-47a and in Fig. 3-47b?

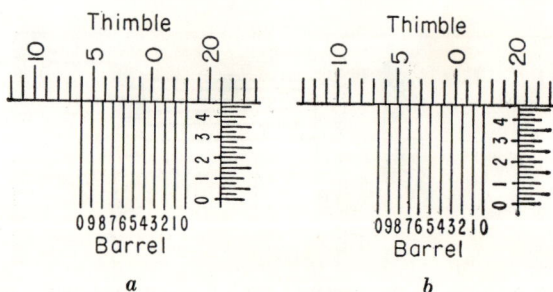

Fig. 3-47.

SOLUTION: In Fig. 3-47a, there are no ten-thousandths to add because the zero line of the vernier coincides with lines on the thimble. The reading will be in thousandths of an inch.

Reading = 0.469 in.

In Fig. 3-47b, the 7th graduation on the vernier coincides with a line on the thimble indicating 0.0007 in. should be added to the thousandths reading.

Reading = 0.4697 in.

PROBLEMS

Figure 3-48 represents the graduations and the vernier scale on the sleeve together with the graduations on the thimble as if they had been laid out on a flat surface. What are the readings in the following parts of Fig. 3-48?

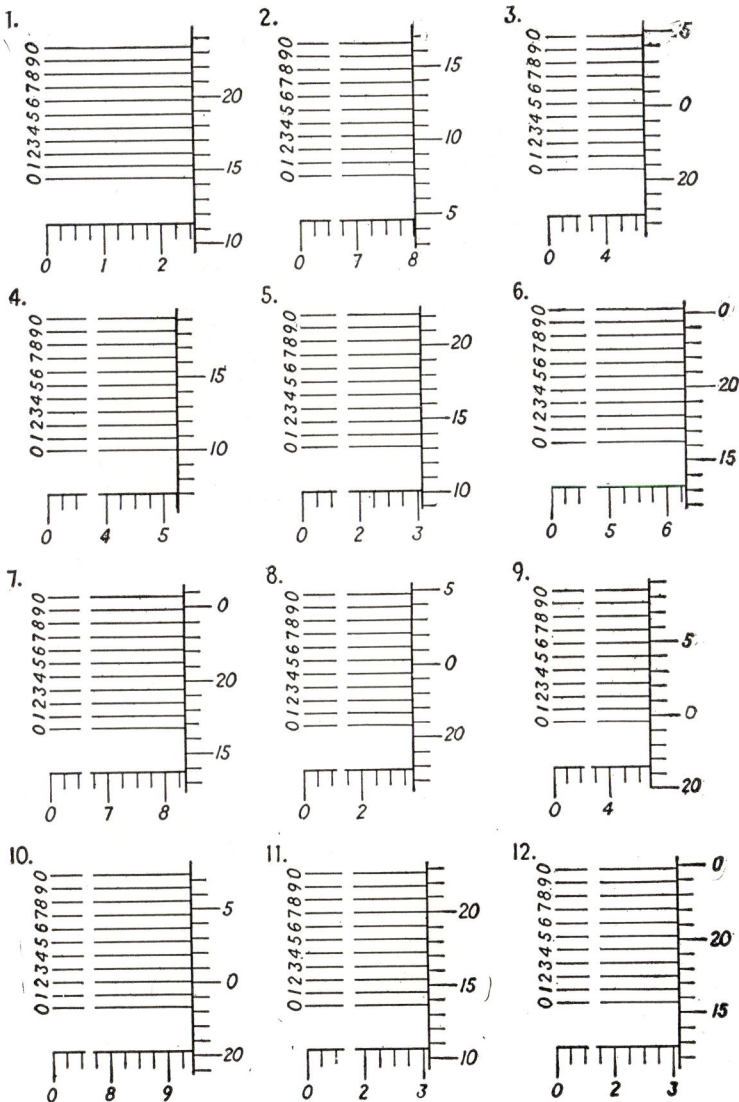

Fig. 3-48.

How to Read a Universal Bevel Protractor with a Vernier.
A *bevel protractor* is a measuring tool used to measure angles. With
the help of a vernier, it will measure angles accurately. Figure 3-49
represents a case of angle measurement using the protractor.

Fig. 3-49. Using a bevel protractor to measure a bevel on piece. (*The Brown &
Sharpe Manufacturing Company*)

Figures 3-50 and 3-51 show part of a vernier protractor. The upper
scale is the one showing *degrees*, each tenth degree being numbered.

Fig. 3-50. Close-up of a vernier scale on a protractor. (*The Brown & Sharpe
Manufacturing Company*)

Fig. 3-51. Close-up of a vernier scale on a protractor. (*The Brown & Sharpe Manufacturing Company*)

The lower scale is the vernier, each line being equal to $\frac{1}{12}$ degree, or 5 minutes. Each space on the vernier is 5 minutes shorter than two spaces on the scale.

When the zero on the vernier exactly coincides with any graduation on the scale, the reading is in exact degrees, as in Fig. 3-50 wherein the reading is 17°0′. When the graduation marked 0 on the vernier does not exactly coincide with any graduation on the scale, the graduation on the vernier that does coincide with any graduation on the scale indicates the number of twelfths of a degree to be added to the whole degree reading.

To read: Read off directly from the scale the number of whole degrees between 0 on the scale and 0 on the vernier. Then count, in the same direction, the number of divisions from the 0 on the vernier to the first line on the vernier that coincides with any line on the scale. As each division on the vernier represents 5 minutes, the number of these divisions multiplied by 5 will be the number of minutes to be added to the whole number of degrees.

EXAMPLE: Read the angle as shown in Fig. 3-51.

SOLUTION: Figure 3-51 shows the zero on the vernier between 12 and 13 on the scale. Counting to the right from zero on the scale, the zero on the vernier has traveled 12 whole degrees. In the same direction, the 10th line of the vernier, representing 50 minutes, is in line with a line on the scale. Therefore, we have 50 minutes to add to the whole number of degrees. The reading is then 12°50′.

Since the divisions, both on the scale and vernier, are numbered both to the right and left from a basis of zero, any size angle can be

measured, and the readings on the scale and on the vernier are taken
either to the right or left according to the direction in which the zero
on the vernier is moved.

PROBLEMS

What is the reading on the bevel protractor shown in Figs. 3-52
to 3-57?

Fig. 3-52.

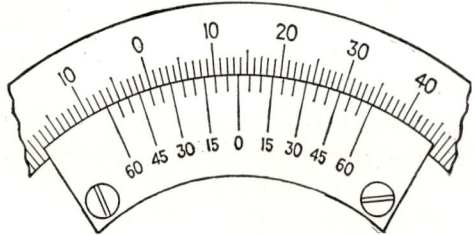

Fig. 3-53.

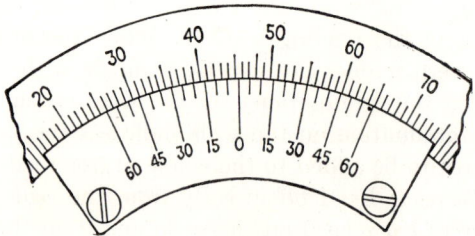

Fig. 3-54.

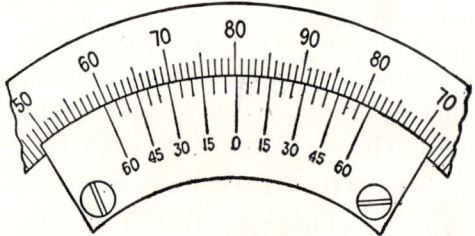

Fig. 3-55.

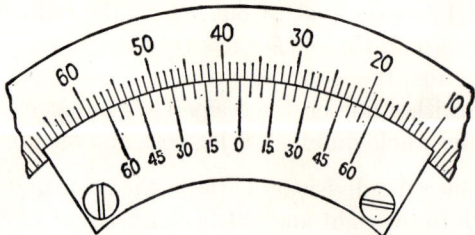

Fig. 3-56.

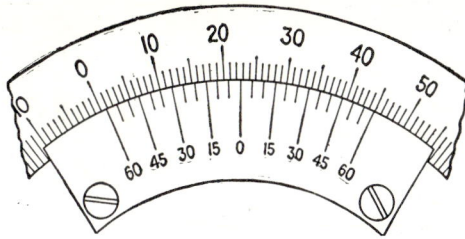

Fig. 3-57.

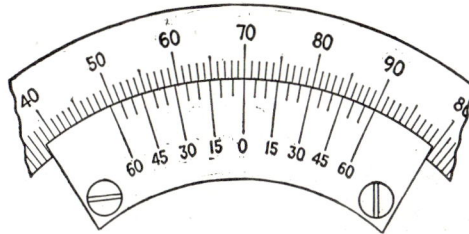

QUESTIONS ON MEASURING TOOLS

1. What measuring tool is best for measuring length?
2. What measuring tool is best for measuring diameters?
3. What measuring tool is best for measuring a diameter to ten-thousandths of an inch?
4. What measuring tool is best to measure angles?
5. What measuring tool measures an angle to its nearest 5 minutes?
6. For measuring a finished diameter, what tool would you use?
7. What kind of steel is used to make measuring tools?
8. Why must the anvil and spindle of a micrometer be exceptionally hard?
9. What is done to a measuring tool when it is "off"?
10. To what part of an inch does a vernier caliper measure?

Gage Blocks. Figure 3-58 shows a set of gage blocks usually used in machine shops where extreme accuracy is desired. They are rectangular blocks of tool steel very carefully hardened and finished. Their surfaces are so fine and parallel that when rubbed together in the proper manner they will stick together. This rubbing is known as *wringing*.

Each block is very accurate to within a few millionths of an inch. They are very often referred to as *precision* or *gage blocks*. At times, the names given to these blocks are those of the manufacturer. For example the Webber Gage Company manufactures such blocks, and

Fig. 3-58. An 81-gage block set. (*The Brown & Sharpe Manufacturing Company*)

their blocks are called *Webber blocks*. Another manufacturer of these blocks is the Johansson Company, and their blocks are called *Jo blocks*.

Sets of these blocks may be purchased in almost any combination of sizes. The common set as used in machine shops is the 81-block set. This size set enables the apprentice to produce almost any measurement in four decimal places. The table below shows the sizes of the blocks in such a set.

Series 1: One Ten-thousandth Inch—9 blocks

0.1001	0.1002	0.1003	0.1004	0.1005	0.1006	0.1007
		0.1008	0.1009			

Series 2: One-thousandth Inch—49 blocks

0.101	0.102	0.103	0.104	0.105	0.106	0.107	0.108	0.109	0.110
0.111	0.112	0.113	0.114	0.115	0.116	0.117	0.118	0.119	0.120
0.121	0.122	0.123	0.124	0.125	0.126	0.127	0.128	0.129	0.130
0.131	0.132	0.133	0.134	0.135	0.136	0.137	0.138	0.139	0.140
0.141	0.142	0.143	0.144	0.145	0.146	0.147	0.148	0.149	

Series 3: Fifty Thousandths Inch—19 blocks

0.050	0.100	0.150	0.200	0.250	0.300	0.350	0.400	0.450	0.500
0.550	0.600	0.650	0.700	0.750	0.800	0.850	0.900	0.950	

Series 4: Inch Series—4 blocks

1.000	2.000	3.000	4.000

Whenever accuracy is desired to four decimal places in any length or height dimension, these blocks are used. For example, if a machinist has a dimension of 2.467 in. that he has to use in setting up a job and that dimension has to be very accurate, he makes a combination of various size blocks whose total will equal 2.467 in. Later in this section, instruction will be given in making various combinations of blocks for desired dimensions.

Precision blocks have uses other than that of setting up dimensions. Measuring tools such as micrometers and vernier calipers are checked for accuracy with these blocks. It is good practice on the part of machinists to have their measuring instruments checked occasionally for accuracy. Figure 3-59 shows a micrometer being checked by precision blocks.

There are sets available that contain more and less than 81 blocks shown in Fig. 3-58. Extra blocks are added to the larger sets to make sets containing as high as 118 pieces. Smaller sets may contain as few as 10 or 12. It can be readily seen that the small sets cannot give the wide variety of dimensions needed by most machinists, whereas larger sets have blocks that can be combined to give almost any dimension needed.

However, for dimensions of four-decimal places, the 81-block set is satisfactory.

How to Obtain Various Dimensions Using Gage Blocks. To build up any dimension with gage blocks, the first consideration is to use **as** *few blocks* as possible. The second point to be remembered is always to work from *right to left* of the decimal point when making the combination. In other words, eliminate the last figure in the dimension sought first.

The method of combining blocks is best illustrated by examples. *For all examples, an 81-block set is used.*

EXAMPLE 1: Set up the 1.3427 in. dimension.

SOLUTION:

Step 1.	Write the dimension on paper	1.3427	*Check*
Step 2.	Eliminate the last figure to the right of the decimal point by selecting a block with a 7 in the fourth place. In this case, use the 0.1007 block. This amount must be subtracted from 1.3427 to obtain the amount still to be accounted for. The size of the block is written in the last column on the right for addition to prove our problem	0.1007	0.1007
	Result	1.2420	
Step 3.	Eliminate the last figure to the right other than zero	0.112	0.112
	Result	1.1300	
Step 4.	Eliminate the last figure again	0.130	0.130
	Result	1.000	
Step 5.	Eliminate the 1.000	1.000	1.000
	Result	0.000	1.3427

If the last column on the right is then added, it should add up to the dimension for proof.

EXAMPLE 2:   Set up blocks for 3.4817 in. dimension.

SOLUTION: Dimension sought............. 3.4817 *Check*

Step 1.	Eliminate the 7 with	0.1007	0.1007
	Result	3.3810	
Step 2.	Eliminate the 1 with	0.131	0.131
	Result	3.250	
Step 3.	Eliminate the 0.250 with	0.250	0.250
	Result	3.000	
Step 4.	Eliminate the 3.000 with	3.000	3.000
	Result	0.0000	3.4817

PROBLEMS

NOTE: Use the blocks in an 81-block set for these problems. These are listed on page 89.

1. Set up blocks for the following dimensions: (*a*) 2.0976, (*b*) 1.678, (*c*) 2.0055, (*d*) 5.864, (*e*) 7.9753, (*f*) 10.060, (*g*) 9.3578, (*h*) 0.5378, (*i*) 4.0067, (*j*) 3.0643, (*k*) 1.0372, (*l*) 6.6009.

2. Make *two* sets of blocks for *each* of the dimensions shown below. *Do not* use the blocks that were selected in making the first set. (*a*) 3.7659, (*b*) 7.9645, (*c*) 4.0765, (*d*) 1.0045, (*e*) 0.6058, (*f*) 3.9047.

Checking Micrometers Using Blocks. The good machinist always checks his measuring tools. This is usually done about once a week. The checking should be done in the toolroom—not by the machinist.

The gage block is the quickest and best method to use in checking a micrometer. Pick any size block and mike it. The reading on the barrel of the micrometer should read the exact size of the gage block used in checking. If not, adjust the micrometer to the reading. Then you are sure that your measuring tool is ready to go to work.

Figure 3-59 shows a micrometer being checked, using a 0.500-in. gage block. The micrometer reading is exactly 0.500. Therefore, this micrometer is ready to be used.

The Sine Bar. Measurement of angles, bevels, and tapers down to 30 minutes, or $\frac{1}{2}$ degree, can be done with a bevel protractor.

When accuracy to 5 minutes, or $\frac{1}{12}$ degree, is required, the vernier type of bevel protractor may be used. But a protractor, even under a glass, is difficult to set to 5 minutes and today's measurements have to be in millionths of an inch. This means that a *sine bar* must be used.

The sine bar may come in half a dozen styles, shapes, or lengths, but its purpose and principle are always the same. The purpose is to reduce all angles to terms of a right triangle, the simplest form of

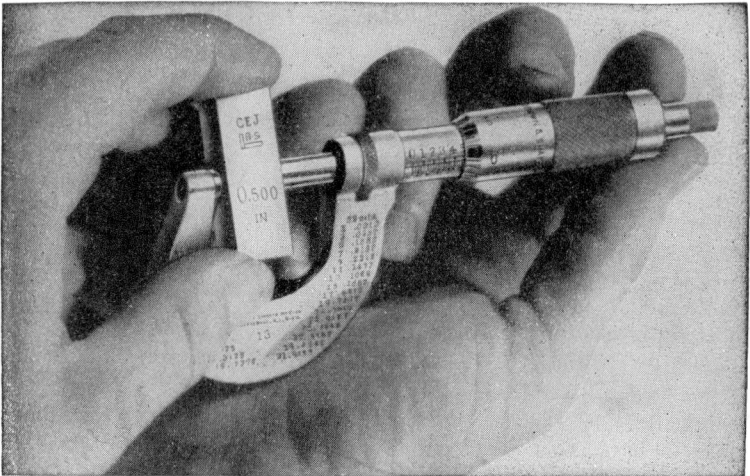

Fig. 3-59. A micrometer being checked using a gage block. (*The Brown & Sharpe Manufacturing Company*)

trigonometrical solution. Although, in your work, you may be called upon now and then to solve obtuse and acute triangles that cannot be reduced to "square" terms, you will find most of your work will lend itself to solution by the sine bar method. You may never require more than the simpler trigonometric formulas explained in the use of the sine bar.

The sine bar consists of a bar of stabilized, highly finished chrome steel, resting on two cylindrical rollers, the centers of which are 5 in. apart. Some sine bars are 10 in. between centers. The surface or face of the bar is parallel to the bottom of the rolls. The face is flat within 50 millionths of an inch between the 5-in. centers.

Figure 3-60 shows a sine bar resting on a surface plate with one end mounted on gage blocks.

Fig. 3-60. A sine bar set to a definite height. (*The DoAll Company*)

Theory of the Sine Bar. In trigonometry, the sine of an angle is defined as the ratio of the side opposite the angle whose sine is to be found *over* the hypotenuse of the right triangle. Referring to Fig. 3-61, the sine of angle *A* is side *a* over side *c*, the hypotenuse; the sine of angle *B* is *b/c*. Angle *C* is the right angle which makes triangle *ABC* a right triangle.

Now, the sine bar is *always* the hypotenuse in any solution involving its use. So, then, it is side *c*. The length of the hypotenuse, or side *c*, is always known since it can be only 5 in. if a 5-in. sine bar is used, or 10 in. if a 10-in. sine bar is used. The usual problem is to find the angle between the hypotenuse and the side *b*, or angle *A*. Since we know side *a*, or can find it by building up gage blocks to equal it, the angle is easily found. In the Appendix sine tables are already worked out for you in connection with the

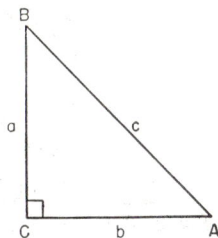

Fig. 3-61. A right-angle triangle.

5-in. sine bar. These tables are in terms of side *a*. If you have the height, or side *a*, and not the angle, all you have to do is to read down the table until you find a height corresponding to the one you have, and read across directly to the angle. The exact angle can be found since the tables are broken down to minutes.

If you have the angle and want to know the proper height of side *a*, that also is given by direct reading in the table by reversing the above process.

For example, you had a height, or side *a*, equal to 3.68497 in. and wanted to know the angle *A*. From the table you learn it lies some-

Fig. 3-62. Checking an angle plate with sine bar, gage blocks, and a comparator. (*The DoAll Company*)

where between 47°28′ and 47°29′. Choose the nearest angle; in this case, the angle is 47°29′.

Now, suppose you had an angle of 35°41′ on the blueprint and you wanted to stack up gage blocks to form side *a* for a test. From the tables, 35°41′ calls for a height of 2.916525. That is the height to which you will have to stack the gage blocks for the angle. How to check the angle will be explained in the next section.

How to Use the Sine Bar. There are many applications of the sine bar to setups and inspection problems. Some of them are shown in Figs. 3-62 to 3-64. The sine bar can readily be clamped to an angle plate after its position has been determined, with the gage blocks and the whole setup then moved under the comparator for further

Fig. 3-63. Checking an angle of a gage with sine bar–comparator setup. (*The DoAll Company*)

measurement comparisons and for determining flatness of angle pieces (see Figs. 3-62 to 3-64). One of its common applications is that of checking bevel gears, as shown in Fig. 3-65. Remember in all such applications, use either the surface plate or the master flat as a base from which to work.

To check an angle block, set it on the sine bar and build up the perpendicular (or side *a* of the right triangle) to the required height.

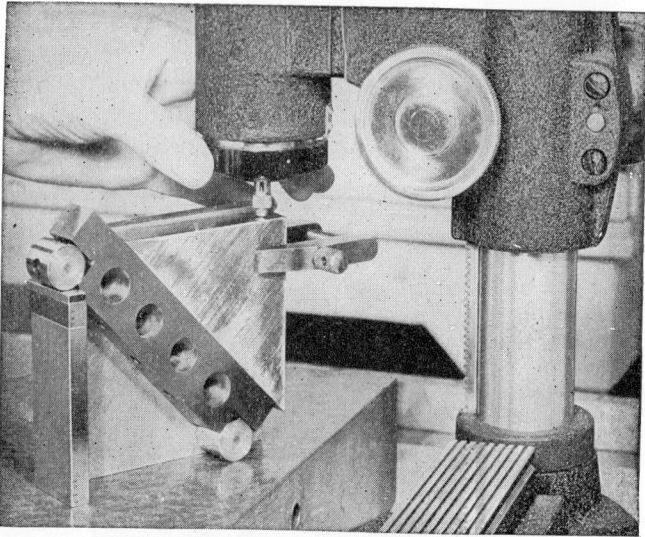

Fig. 3-64. Checking an angle plate with sine bar and comparator. (*The DoAll Company*)

Fig. 3-65. Checking a bevel gear with sine bar, master flat, and a dial indicator. (*The DoAll Company*)

Then clamp the block to the face plate and move it under the comparator or a height gage with an indicator attached. If the top surface of the angle block is flat under the comparator or indicator,

Fig. 3-66. Measuring accuracy of an angle gage with sine bar, gage blocks, and dial indicator. (*The DoAll Company*)

within the limits prescribed or the tolerances allowed, your problem is solved. If it is not flat, you can read the variance directly from the comparator or indicator, or build up or remove gage blocks to determine the amount the angle is out.

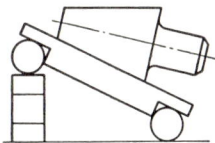

Fig. 3-67. Use of a sine bar in checking the taper of a plug gage. (*The DoAll Company*)

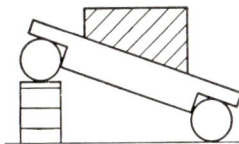

Fig. 3-68. Using a sine bar to check the taper of a taper key. (*The DoAll Company*)

Figure 3-66 shows a setup for measuring accuracy of an angle gage with sine bar, gage blocks, and dial indicator. Figure 3-67 shows a setup for checking a taper plug gage and Fig. 3-68 shows a setup for checking a taper key.

The applications pictured in the foregoing will provide a "skeleton" method from which to work. One of these setups should provide a basis from which to start.

Dial Indicators. Another measuring instrument used quite frequently in machine-shop practice is the *dial indicator*, sometimes called a *test indicator*. The illustrations that follow in this section show many different types.

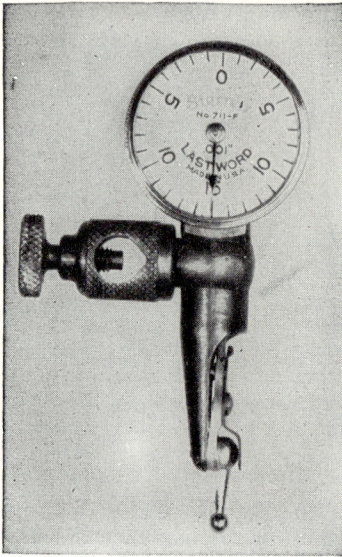

Fig. 3-69. The Last Word dial indicator, a very important checking and measuring instrument for the machine shop. (*The L. S. Starrett Company*)

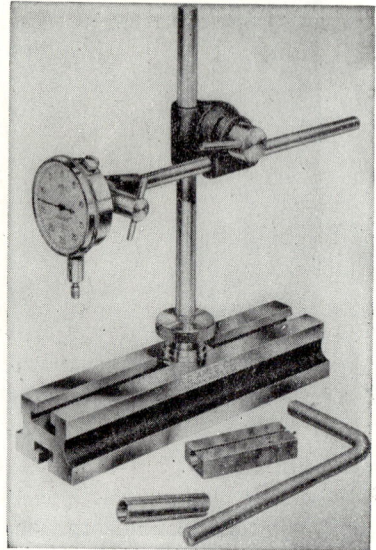

Fig. 3-70. An indicator mounted on a stand. (*B. C. Ames Company*)

Test or dial indicators are used to true and align machine tools, fixtures, and work; to test and inspect size and trueness of finished work; and to compare measurements, either heights or depths or many other measurements.

Most indicators have a range of 30-thousandths of an inch, usually arranged so that 15-thousandths are on either side of the zero mark. See Figs. 3-69 and 3-70. These particular indicators are graduated in thousandths of an inch, which is plainly marked on the face of the instrument. There are some indicators which are graduated in ten-thousandths of an inch. For most work requring an accuracy of the nearest 0.001 in., the graduations of an 0.001-in. indicator is used.

Figure 3-69 illustrates an outstanding indicator used in machine work. It is called the "Last Word" and is very flexible. It can be

Fig. 3-71. The Last Word indicator in use. (*The L. S. Starrett Company*)

turned and revolved, and has many uses. However, others of different makes can also be used.

Figures 3-71 to 3-75 illustrate some of the uses of the dial indicator. Figure 3-71 shows the Last Word being used to check the location of a cylindrical piece; it is being lined up with the center of the drill chuck. Figure 3-72 shows a dial indicator mounted on a surface gage, checking the bottom of a hole. Figure 3-73 shows an

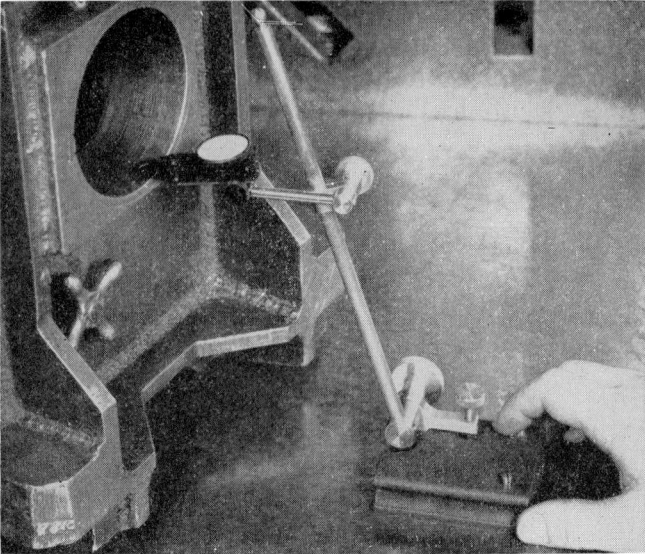

Fig. 3-72. A Brown & Sharpe indicator being used. (*The Brown & Sharpe Manufacturing Company*)

Fig. 3-73. Dial indicator being used to check the location of toolmakers' buttons. (*The Brown & Sharpe Manufacturing Company*)

indicator mounted on a stand, checking the location of toolmakers' buttons. Figure 3-74 shows an indicator mounted on a snap gage. Figure 3-75 shows an indicator checking the height of the piece. Note the Jo blocks near the indicator. As a rule, these blocks are used in first determining a specific height and then the indicator is set for that height. A more detailed explanation follows.

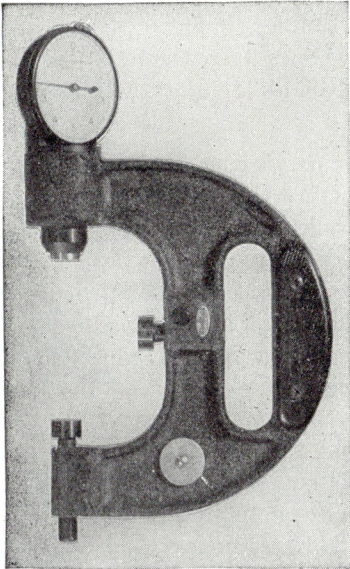

Fig. 3-74. An indicator mounted on a snap gage. (*The Sheffield Corporation*)

Fig. 3-75. Piece being checked for height. (*The L. S. Starrett Company*)

How to Use the Indicator. Refer to Fig. 3-75. Let us suppose that the height of the piece shown in the illustration is 4.387 ± 0.001 in. Here are the steps to be followed so that this height may be checked:

1. Secure a dial indicator graduated in thousandths of an inch.
2. Attach to the stand as shown. (A height gage or surface gage may be used.)

3. Secure the proper Jo blocks to make the height of 4.387 in.
4. Put combination of blocks under stem of indicator and with a little pressure adjust the reading so that the pointer of the dial is at zero.
5. Remove the blocks and place piece to be tested under the stem of the indicator.
6. If the dial pointer reaches the zero mark, then the piece is correct for the dimension.
7. Since the tolerance is ±0.001 in., then the next piece may measure so that the pointer will come to a stop *one* line *after* or *before* the zero on the dial. If it does, the piece is still acceptable.
8. If however, the pointer passes the first graduation after or before the zero line, the piece is not acceptable.
9. If the pointer stops let us say three lines *before* the zero, then the piece is 0.002 in. too short; if three lines are *after* the zero, then the piece is 0.002 in. too long.

The same piece may be tested for parallelism (that is, to check

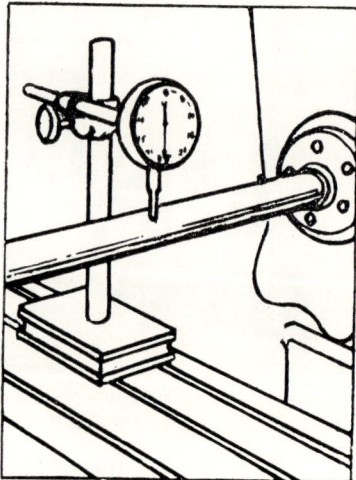

Fig. 3-76. Testing an arbor with a dial indicator.

whether the top of the piece is parallel with the bottom of the piece) by moving the piece so that the top contacts the stem of the indicator. When that is done and the pointer does *not move* from the original position, then the faces are parallel. If the pointer *does move*, then the faces are *not* parallel and the amount of variance may be noted by finding the high and low readings on the indicator.

If the tolerance on the piece just checked was ±0.0003 in., then an indicator graduated in ten-thousandths of an inch would be used. Each line would equal 0.0001 in.

Another common use of the indicator is shown in Fig. 3-76. Here it is used to check the straightness of an arbor. For other uses, especially on chucks, see Chapter 15.

QUESTIONS ON MEASURING TOOLS

1. When would you use the following measuring tools in measuring? Rule, micrometer, vernier caliper, gage block, protractor, sine bar.

2. When would you use the hooked rule? Make a sketch showing actual use of the hooked rule.

3. How accurate is any measuring tool?

4. Of what use are snap gages? Would they be used in a toolroom? In a die shop? In a lathe department? Give reasons for your answers.

5. What is meant by "go" and "no go" when applied to gages?

6. What measuring tool would you use for the following:

    a. Measuring length to the nearest $\frac{1}{64}$ in.

    b. Measuring length to the nearest 0.001 in.

    c. Measuring a diameter to the nearest $\frac{1}{64}$ in.

    d. Measuring an inside diameter to the nearest 0.001 in.

    e. Measuring the depth of a hole to the nearest $\frac{1}{32}$ in.

    f. Measuring the width of a keyway to the nearest $\frac{1}{64}$ in.

7. Can you find any angle using a sine bar? Give reasons.

8. How accurate is the bevel protractor?

9. What is the purpose of a sine bar?

10. How accurate is the sine bar?

11. Should you use the sine bar with a bench as the base?

12. Show by sketch and then explain just how you would check a taper plug gage having an included angle of 5°19′.

13. Give three uses for the dial indicator.

14. Tell how you would use the indicator to check the alignment of the centers of the lathe.

15. Describe how an arbor is checked.

16. Name three other uses of the dial indicator not mentioned in the text.

Bench Work

CHAPTER 4

Hammers, Screw Drivers, Wrenches, Hacksaws

The Use of Hand Tools. There are many operations in machine-shop work which involve the use of tools that are controlled by hand. The term *bench work* is used in reference to the operations incident to the processes of laying out, fitting, assembling, etc., when the work is placed on the bench or in a bench vise. The term *floor work* applies to the larger work which is erected on the floor of the shop. The same tools—hammers, wrenches, cutting tools, measuring tools, etc.—are used for either.

An expert machinist is skillful in the use of the hand tools of the craft. Being skillful is the opposite of being awkward or clumsy; it is the opposite of being ignorant or stupid; it is the opposite of being careless or indifferent. You would not use a tack hammer to drive a spike; why should you use a fine file for roughing stock? You would not use a sledge hammer to drive a tack, why should you use a 12-in. monkey wrench on a $\frac{1}{4}$-in. bolt? You do not mistake a chisel for a screw driver, why should you use a screw driver with the end shaped like a dull chisel?

Skill means the knowledge of the proper tool to use and how to use it in the right way; it means more than this—it means a positive unwillingness to use a tool that is not right. The real machinist is proud of his kit of tools, proud of the work he can accomplish with them. Manual skill must be acquired through practice. Information regarding the proper use of hand tools can, however, be obtained by reading and by observation.

Bench work involves the use of hammers, screw drivers, wrenches, hacksaws, chisels, files, scrapers, taps, threading dies, small drills (by means of hand drills or breast drills), hand reamers, taper reamers, and taper-pin reamers. In addition, most of the machine-shop measuring tools and gages are used in bench work. Many of these tools and gages will be described elsewhere in this book. Also the use of taps, dies, and hand-operated reamers, while perhaps belonging particularly to bench or floor work, will be described.

Care of Hand Tools. There are a few rules that should be followed in the care of hand tools. Care will make your tools last longer and keep them always in good working condition. Remember, an accepted sign of a good machinist is the excellent condition of his tools.

1. Put those tools not in actual use in a safe place while you are working. Tools may break if allowed to drop on the floor.

2. Put tools away when you are through with them. If you leave them lying around, you can easily trip over them, spraining, or perhaps breaking, your ankle.

3. To save time and avoid waste, assign each tool to a place in your toolbox and see to it that each tool is kept in its place. Before putting away your tools in the box, make sure that they are clean.

4. Do not leave sharp tools protruding from work benches. They will tear, rip, or puncture any moving object that comes in contact with them, *including yourself.* For the same reason, do not carry sharp tools in your back pocket.

5. *Always* use the right tool for a job. Use the tool designed for the job.

Follow the Rules. Tools are indispensable servants, performing many tasks beyond the power of your own hands.

Hammers. The hammer is a very simple striking tool. It is just a weighted head and a handle which directs its course. Your toolbox is not complete unless it contains at least two or three types of hammers.

Machinists' hammers are made of steel, hardened and tempered. They are made in different sizes (weights) from 6 oz. to $2\frac{1}{2}$ lb.; those weighing over $1\frac{1}{4}$ lb. are not much used. The top of the hammer head is called the *peen* and the bottom is called the *face.* The illustration, Fig. 4-1a, shows a hammer with a *ball* peen which is the common form of machinist's hammer, although the *straight* peen (*b*), and the *cross* peen (*c*), are used for swaging and riveting. The eye of the hammer head is somewhat smaller in the middle than at the ends. If the end of the handle is fitted to fill one end of the eye and wedged with soft steel wedges to fill the other end, it will be tight and secure in the hammer head. A *hammer with a loose head is dangerous.* The handle is set about square with the head and should be of such a shape and length as to give the proper grip and balance when in use.

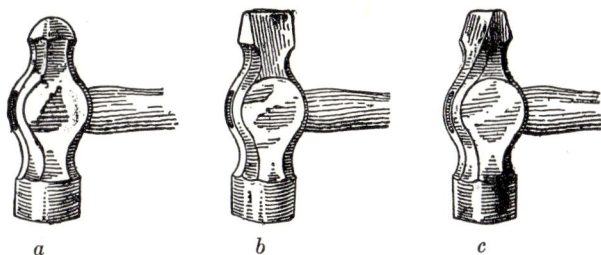

Fig. 4-1. Hammers: (*a*) ball peen; (*b*) straight peen; (*c*) cross peen.

If one is using a sledge, it is more effective to take it easy when lifting the sledge and put the snap in the blow. The same is true in all hammering; a solid snappy blow is more effective and less tiresome. Such a blow cannot be delivered if the handle is grasped too near the head or is grasped too tightly.

Soft Hammers: Soft-face hammers have pounding surfaces made of wood, brass, lead, rawhide, hard rubber, or plastic. Metal workers use them to form soft metals such as copper and aluminum. They are handy in machine shops for driving close-fitting parts together or for knocking them apart. The face may be damaged easily, so *don't use a soft-face hammer for rough work.* It is not made for striking punch heads, bolts, or nails. One of the most practical plastic hammers is shown in Fig. 4-2*a*. It has replaceable tips or faces.

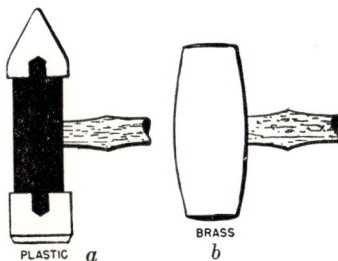

Fig. 4-2. Soft-face hammers.

Screw Drivers. Screw drivers have one main purpose—to loosen and tighten screws. However, they have been used as a substitute for everything from an ice pick to a bottle opener.

There are three main parts to a screw driver. The part that you grip is called the *handle*, the steel portion extending from the handle is the *shank*, and the end which fits into the slot of the screw is called the *blade*. See Fig. 4-3. The slim steel shank is designed to withstand considerable twisting force in proportion to its size but it will bend or crack in two if used as a pry or pinch bar.

The tip of the blade is hardened to keep it from wearing, and the harder it is, the easier it will break if much of a bending strain is applied. If the shank of the screw driver is once bent, it usually is difficult to get it perfectly

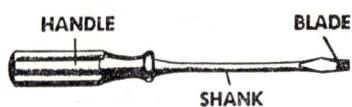

HANDLE **BLADE**

SHANK

Fig. 4-3. Parts of a screw driver.

straight again. And if the shank is not straight, it is hard to keep the blade centered in the slot of the screw.

Don't hammer on the end of a screw driver. It is not to be used in place of a cold chisel, a punch, or a drift. Hammering can break the shank, mushroom the end of the handle, or snap off the blade.

The most common types of screw drivers are the *standard, off-set,* and *ratchet* shown in Fig. 4-4

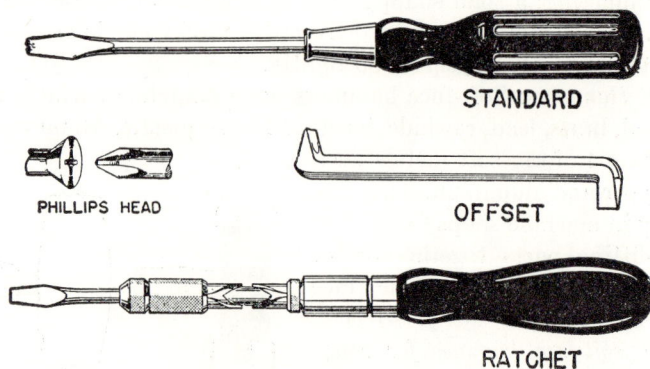

STANDARD

PHILLIPS HEAD

OFFSET

RATCHET

Fig. 4-4. Types of screw drivers.

The standard screw driver is used for most ordinary work and comes in a variety of sizes. Too much emphasis cannot be placed on selecting the correct size of screw driver so that the thickness of the blade makes a good fit in the screw slot. This not only prevents the screw slot from becoming burred and the blade tip from being damaged, but also reduces the force required to keep the screw driver in the slot.

A double-end offset screw driver is used for driving screws that cannot be reached with a straight screw driver. It has one blade forged in line with the shank of the handle and the other blade at right angles to the shank. With such an arrangement when the swinging space for the screw driver is limited, you can change ends after each swing and thus work the screw in or out of the threaded hole. Use this screw driver when there is insufficient space to work a standard screw driver.

The Phillips-type screw driver is made with a specially shaped blade that fits Phillips cross-slot screws. The heads of these screws have two slots that cross in the center. This checks the tendency of some screw drivers to slide out of the slot onto the finished surface of the work. The Phillips screw driver will not slip and burr the end of the screw if the proper size is used.

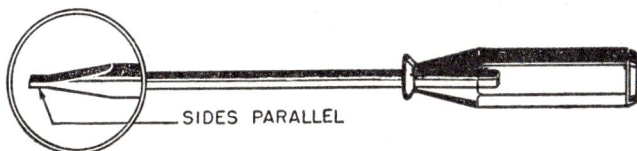

SIDES PARALLEL

Fig. 4-5. Correctly ground tip of a screw driver.

The ratchet-type screw driver is used when fast motion is wanted. It operates on a worm-type spindle and by raising the handle and pushing down on it, the blade is turned quickly.

Grinding the Blade. The tip of the screw-driver blade should be ground so that the sides of the blade are practically parallel, and the blade sides should gradually taper out to the shank body. If you should ever damage the end of the blade, make it usable again by grinding it against an emery wheel. First, grind the tip straight and at right angles to the shank. After the tip is ground, square-dress off from each face, a little at a time. Keep the faces parallel for a short distance or have them taper in a slight amount. Never grind the faces so that they taper to a sharp edge. See Fig. 4-5 for a correctly ground tip.

SAFETY RULES FOR USE OF SCREW DRIVERS

1. Never use a screw driver to check an electric circuit where the amperage is high. The electric current may be strong enough to arc and melt the screw driver blade.

2. Never hold the work in your hand while tightening or loosening a screw. If the blade slips, it can cause a bad cut. Use a vise or a solid surface that will bear the pressure of the driver.

3. Don't hold work in your hand while using a screw driver—if the point slips, it can cause a bad cut. Hold the work in a vise, with a clamp, or on a solid surface.

4. Never get any part of your body in front of the screw-driver bit tip. And that is a good safety rule for *any* sharp or pointed tool.

QUESTIONS ON THE USE OF SCREW DRIVERS

1. What happens if considerable force is exerted and the screw driver jumps out of the slot?

2. Is the slot in a screw made with parallel sides or is it V shaped?

3. If the screw-driver blade is ground to look like a dull cold chisel will it work well?

4. How is a burr thrown up on the side of the screw slot? Does filing it off fix the slot? Is it fair to leave it on? What should be done?

5. Give three reasons why a screw-driver blade should have parallel sides.

6. Of what kind of steel is a screw driver made? Why?

7. How is the tang end shaped to hold fast in the handle? What other methods of holding may be used?

8. Why are the larger sizes of screw drivers often made with square shanks (or bodies)?

Wrenches. Fundamentally, the wrench is an instrument for exerting a twisting strain, as in turning bolts and nuts. The majority of nuts and bolts have six-sided heads called *hex* heads, hex being the abbreviation of hexagon, taken from the Greek word meaning *six-cornered.* The wrench is designed to grip opposite sides of these heads when you are removing or replacing parts.

Wrenches are made in many different forms. Any form of wrench consists of a handle or handles with jaws, lugs, or an opening or socket to fit the object to be turned. They are named (1) from their shape, such as S wrench and angle wrench, (2) from the object on which they are used, such as the tap wrench and pipe wrench; and (3) from their construction, such as the spanner wrench and ratchet wrench. Several of the wrenches commonly used in machine work are illustrated in Fig. 4-6.

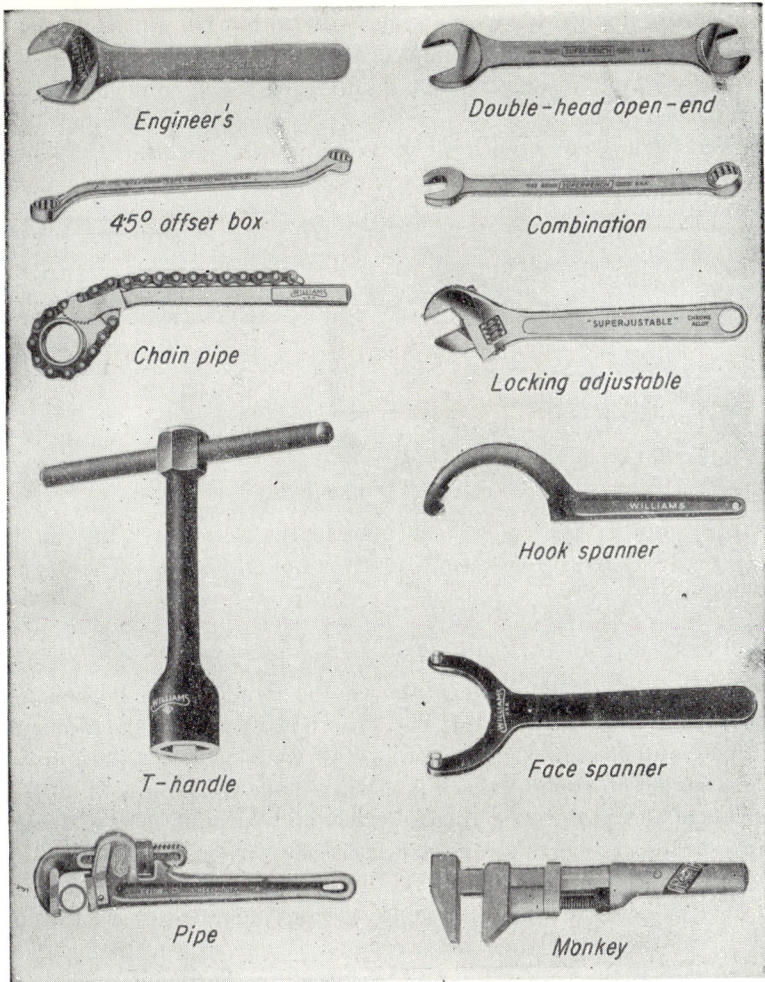

Fig. 4-6. Several types of wrenches. (*J. H. Williams Company, Ridge Tool Company, The Billings & Spencer Company*)

Another type of wrench used by machinists especially in assembling parts is the *torque* wrench, Fig. 4-7. Torque is the amount of turning or twisting force applied on the nut. A torque wrench tells you just how much of that turning or twisting force you are applying. On some makes of torque wrenches, a pointer indicates the amount of applied force on a scale or indicator. On others, you can set the dial for the exact amount of torque you want to apply. Then, when you pull on the wrench, a light flashes the instant you hit the prescribed amount.

Another type of wrench much used in machine work is the *socket* wrench on which sockets of different sizes are attached to the handle for various sizes of nuts.

Fig. 4-7. Torque wrench. (*J. H. Williams Company*)

Fig. 4-8. An Allen wrench.

Still another type of wrench used in the *Allen* wrench. This is especially designed for Allen-head screws only. Figure 4-8 shows an Allen wrench.

A Few Suggestions Regarding the Use of Wrenches

1. The wrench should fit, otherwise the corners of the bolt or nut to be turned will be rounded. The wrench is a lever and the mechanical advantage is, of course, in proportion to the length of the handle. The handle of a solid wrench is usually made to give about all the leverage the part to be turned will stand without injury. In an adjustable wrench this cannot be the case. When a large monkey wrench is used on a small bolt, or when a large tap wrench is used on a small tap or reamer, considerable care and judgment must be used. With the extra leverage the workman is not so sensitive to the resistance of the bolt or tap and may turn too hard and break it.

2. Do not use a wrench with an opening too large. When using a monkey wrench adjust the sliding jaw until it is tight on the nut.

3. When using a monkey wrench, have the jaws point in the direction the force is to be applied. There are two reasons for this; the wrench is less apt to be sprung, and it is less liable to slip off the nut or bolt.

4. A quick jerk when tightening, or a blow with the ball of the

hand when loosening a bolt or nut, is more effective than a sustained pull or push, because momentum is a factor.

5. It is distinctly *not* good practice to use a wrench for a hammer or to use a hammer on a wrench. It *is* good practice to oil the thread of a bolt or nut and occasionally to oil the screw of a monkey wrench.

6. Oftentimes bolt heads or nuts are so placed in a machine that a movement of the wrench through 90 deg. (for a square nut) or through 60 deg. (for a hexagonal nut) is impossible owing to obstructions. This difficulty is overcome by using for the square nut a 22½-deg. angle wrench and for a hexagonal nut a 15-deg. angle wrench. By turning the wrench over each time it is applied the nut may be turned completely around when the swing of the handle is limited to substantially half that required for a straight wrench. This is illustrated in Fig. 4-9.

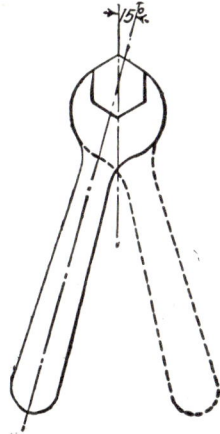

7. The ratchet wrench (Fig. 4-10) is especially useful when only a short swing of the handle is permissible; in fact the multiple ratchet wrench may be used with a swing of only 10 deg. An added advantage of the ratchet wrench lies in the fact that it is not necessary to remove it until the bolt or nut is tight.

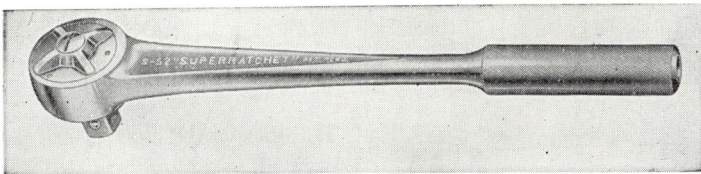

Fig. 4-9.

Fig. 4-10. Ratchet for socket wrenches. (*J. H. Williams Company*)

Action of Check Nut. The principle underlying the proper action of a check nut should be understood. The function of the check nut is to make more certain that the holding nut will not loosen, that it will stay where it is put. The check nut and the holding nut should be arranged so they bear on opposite sides of the screw thread and thus produce the effect of an extremely tight nut. It is not enough to screw the one nut down against the other. In order to make the two nuts bear on opposite sides of the thread it is necessary to use a wrench on each nut and to turn the first nut back a little as the second is turned down. If the first nut is a fairly close fit on the screw only a small fraction of a turn is necessary. It will be understood from the foregoing that the check nut is the first to be put on, and the second is the holding nut since it bears against the side of the thread that takes the reaction of the part being held. Therefore, if two nuts of unequal thickness are used the thicker one should be put on last in order to obtain the value of its greater strength.

QUESTIONS ON THE USE OF WRENCHES

1. What is the purpose of the 15-deg. offset wrench? Of the 22½-deg. offset wrench?
2. Explain the use of each of the following wrenches: single-end wrench, double-end wrench, closed-end wrench, spanner wrench, socket wrench, ratchet wrench, pipe wrench, monkey wrench, chuck key, hollow setscrew key, tap wrench.
3. What is the value of a socket wrench?
4. What is a lever? Is a wrench a lever?
5. Why are wrench handles made so short?
6. If too much force is applied to a wrench, what is liable to happen?
7. What causes the corners of bolts and nuts to become rounded? What does it indicate on the part of the workman?
8. Is a push or a blow more effective in loosening a bolt or a nut? Why?
9. Explain the principle of the action of a check nut.
10. Explain the action of a setscrew.
11. Why is a check nut sometimes used in conjunction with a setscrew?

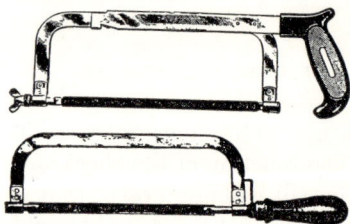

Fig. 4-11. Hacksaws. Top, adjustable; bottom, solid.

Hacksaws. Hacksaws are used to saw metal. There are two parts to a hacksaw—the frame and the blade. Common hand hacksaws have either adjustable or solid frames. See Fig. 4-11 for examples of both; top frame is adjustable, bottom solid.

However, most hacksaws are

now made with an adjustable frame. Hacksaw blades (Fig. 4-12) of various types are inserted in these adjustable frames for different kinds of work. Adjustable frames can be changed to hold blades from 8 to 16 in. long. Solid frames, although more rigid, will take only the length blade for which they are made. This length is the distance between the two pins which hold the blade in place.

The better frames are made with a pistol-grip handle. Recently, several manufacturers have put out frames with the handle in an inverted position. The idea is that the force applied on the forward stroke of the saw (the cutting stroke) is delivered in direct line with the blade.

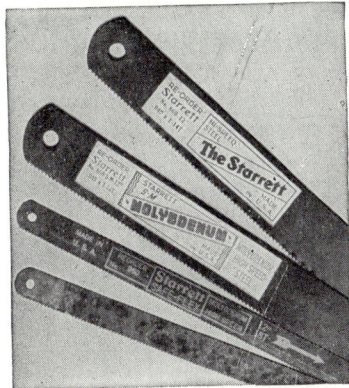

Fig. 4-12. Types of hacksaw blades. (*The L. S. Starrett Company*)

Hacksaw blades are made of high-grade tool steel, hardened and tempered. There are two types, the all-hard and the flexible. All-hard blades are hardened throughout, whereas only the teeth of the flexible blades are hardened. Hacksaw blades are about $\frac{1}{2}$ in. wide, have 14 to 32 teeth per inch, and are from 8 to 16 in. long. The blades have a hole at each end which hooks to a pin in the frame. All hacksaw frames which hold the blades either parallel or at right angles to them are provided with a wing nut or screw to permit tightening or removing the blade.

While it seems, and really is, simple and easy to use a hacksaw, this is all the more reason why one should be unwilling to exhibit his ignorance by doing this job poorly, either by hand or in the power saw. Learn how a hacksaw blade should be selected and how it should be adjusted in the frame. Be able to judge when it is cutting properly and when it should be discarded. Form the habits of arranging the work close to the vise to avoid spring, and of using judgment when tightening it in the vise.

It is easier to cut down than it is to cut sideways or up, and the usual manner of holding the frame (and the blade) is illustrated in Fig. 4-13. Sometimes, however, it is practicable to hold the frame flat, as, for example, when a long strip is to be cut from a sheet of metal. In such a case, the clips which hold the blade may be given a quarter-turn thus setting the blade at right angles to its normal position in the frame. With the blade so arranged a strip of any desired length may be cut, provided it is no wider than the distance from the blade to the back of the frame.

Proper Number of Teeth. If only a few teeth are broken the saw is ruined. One of the chief causes of breakage of saw blades is due to

Fig. 4-13. Hacksawing.

teeth unsuited to the work. Most shops buy hacksaws without specifying the number of teeth per inch or the work on which the saws are to be used, and the dealer furnishes a saw with a medium number of teeth (18 or 20 teeth per inch). This saw is all right for solid pieces of steel and cast iron, but is not right for cutting soft materials or tubing. Low-carbon (machine) steel bars as small as 1 in. in diameter may be cut efficiently in a power saw with a heavy blade of 14 teeth per inch; if, however, it is attempted to cut pipe or thin stock or small bars with such a saw the teeth will catch and break. The following saws are recommended by manufacturers for the purposes noted:

Power blades for cutting solids in soft steel—14 teeth per inch.
Hand blades for cutting solids in soft steel—18 teeth per inch.
For general use in hand frames—18 teeth per inch.
High-carbon steel (tool steel) and cast iron—24 teeth per inch.
Tubing, brass, copper, drill rod—24 teeth per inch.
Thin sheet metal and thin tubing—32 teeth per inch.

Using the Hacksaw

1. *Before you start a hacksaw cut, check again to see that you have the proper blade, and that its teeth point away from the handle.*
2. Check and adjust the blade tension, and the hacksaw is ready to go to work.
3. Secure the stock in a vise, or with clamps.
4. Saw along a scribed line and stay just *outside* that line.
5. If the saw does not start readily, file a V-shaped nick at the starting point.
6. Hold the saw at an angle that will keep at least two teeth cutting all the time, otherwise the blade will jump and individual teeth will be broken.
7. Start the cut with a light, steady, *forward* stroke.
8. At the end of the stroke, relieve the pressure and draw the blade *straight back*. Don't use any pressure on the return stroke.
9. After the first few strokes, make each stroke as long as the hacksaw frame will allow.
10. After the cut is started, use long steady strokes and do not speed. Use about 40 or 50 strokes per minute.
11. As you near the end of the cut, slow down so that you can control the saw when the stock is sawed through.
12. When finished, clean the chips from the blade, loosen the tension on the blade, and return the hacksaw to its proper place.

Hints on Hacksawing

1. Hold the work fairly close to the vise to avoid spring and chatter.

2. The smaller pieces will break off easily when the saw cut is two-thirds through.

3. Hold the work securely, otherwise it may loosen under the pressure of the cut and the blade will be broken.

4. Do not, however, pinch a frail piece too hard. Judgment must be used.

5. The tendency is to cut too fast with a hacksaw. Fifty or sixty strokes per minute is right for average work. The forward stroke is the cutting stroke, pressure should be relieved on the return stroke.

6. The amount of pressure necessary depends on the kind of material, the width of the cut, and the condition of the blade. If, for example, a fairly thick piece of machine steel is to be cut, considerable pressure will be necessary to make the teeth "bite"; if the same pressure is applied on a narrow piece, or on soft material such as copper, the teeth biting too deeply will catch and probably break. The same reasoning applies when starting a cut on a corner, or on a small rod, or any thin section. Another case of using judgment.

7. Be careful as the finish of the cut is approached or the teeth will dig in the thin section and break.

8. If a saw blade breaks when the cut is only partly finished, start the new blade in another place on the bar. This is especially important when using a power saw. The "set" of the teeth of an old blade is slightly worn and the cut is narrower than the new blade, consequently the new blade will bind if it is attempted to continue this cut.

9. Keep the saw cut straight; when the cut runs, the blade is cramped and will probably break. If it starts to run, give the bar about a quarter turn and begin a new cut; the first cut will help to keep the second one straight.

10. Never use oil as a hacksaw lubricant. A lubricant is unnecessary when hand sawing. In high-speed power sawing where the friction of the blade on the work will tend to heat the blade enough to spoil the temper, water is used to keep it cool. In such a machine, provision is made for the coolant to flow on the saw.

11. It is good practice, for the beginner at any rate, to make a small nick with the edge of a file to start the saw cut.

12. Fairly thin sheet metal may be neatly sawed if clamped between two pieces of board. Saw the boards and metal together; this will serve to steady the blade and keep it from digging so easily. If the teeth are too coarse, a blade somewhat worn is better for sawing thin metal than a new saw.

Power Sawing. Figure 4-14 shows a power saw. The general information above applies to power sawing as well as to hand sawing. In addition the following suggestions are offered:

1. Cut the pieces at least $\frac{1}{16}$ in. longer than length given on the drawing for bars up to 2 in. in diameter; allow more for larger pieces.

2. Lower the saw carefully to start the cut.

Fig. 4-14. A power hacksaw. (*Racine Tool & Machine Company*)

3. Set a stop for the length if several pieces are to be cut.

4. Production is much greater and more of the saw is used if two bars are cut at the same time.

5. When sawing comparatively thin pieces do not hold them with the edge up, because the pressure of the saw against the thin section will very likely cause the teeth to dig and break.

6. If it seems advisable to saw a pipe or tube with the regular blade, saw a piece of bar stock or a piece of wood at the same time.

7. A blade quite dull will not cut straight down. Put in a new one.

QUESTIONS ON HACKSAWS

1. When using a hacksaw, which stroke is the cutting stroke? Which way should the saw be placed in the frame? Does the saw cut on the return stroke? Give reason.

2. What is a fair cutting speed for a hand hacksaw?

3. When are blades with 18 teeth to the inch used? With 24 teeth to the inch? With 32 teeth to the inch?

4. What is the effect if one or two teeth are broken out of a hacksaw blade? Why?

5. How tightly should a hacksaw blade be strung in a frame? Why?

6. Why will a hacksaw break if the frame is tipped sideways? If it is not pushed straight? If pushed too hard?

7. When cutting off a piece of flat stock say $\frac{1}{4}$ by 1 in., how should it be held in the vise? Why?

8. Why is a hacksaw blade harder than a wood-saw blade?

9. What makes the hacksaw blade more brittle than a wood-saw?

10. State three common faults in the use of hacksaws, any one of which may result in breaking the blade.

11. What safety precautions should be taken when hand hacksawing?

12. What safety precautions should be taken when using the power hacksaw?

CHAPTER 5

Chipping, Filing, Scraping

There is a considerable satisfaction in being able to hold a cold chisel and strike it with a hammer in such a manner as to produce a surface that indicates real workmanship. Almost anyone thinks he knows how to use a hammer, and yet, excepting the screw driver, there is probably no tool in the shop that is more ignorantly or carelessly used.

The shaper, the planer, or the milling machine may usually be regarded as more efficient than the hammer and chisel for the removal of metal, but there are many times when the hammer and chisel are invaluable. There never has been a real machine shop without a cold chisel or a real machinist who did not know how to grind and use one.

CHIPPING

Cold Chisels. Cold chisels are the tools to use for cutting or chipping metals. They are made of good grade tool steel with a hardened cutting edge and a beveled head at the opposite end. They will cut any metal that is softer than they are, or any metal that can be cut with a file. The width of the cutting edge of a cold chisel denotes its size. Chisels are used with a hammer or, if much metal is to be removed, with a pneumatic gun.

Usually the bar stock from which the chisel is forged is octagonal (eight-sided), but may be hexagonal (six-sided), round, square, or rectangular. They are classified according to the shape of their points. The commonest shapes are flat, cape, round nose, and diamond point.

When chiseling, always use the type of cold chisel that has been designed for the particular job you want to do. For instance, if you are going to chip or cut thin sheet metal, remove stock from flat surfaces, cut rivets, or split nuts, use a *flat cold chisel* (Fig. 5-1).

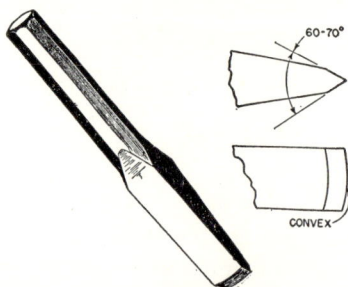

Fig. 5-1. Flat cold chisel and point angle.

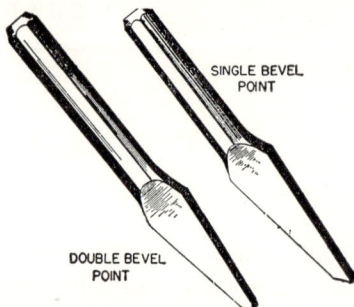

Fig. 5-2. Cape chisels.

If the work involves cutting such things as keyways, narrow grooves, square corners, or slots, use a *cape chisel* (Fig. 5-2). This tool is narrow in width and can also be used to chip flat surfaces that are too wide for a flat chisel.

Round or semicircular grooves should be cut with a *round-nose chisel*, Fig. 5-3. This tool is also the one to use for chipping inside

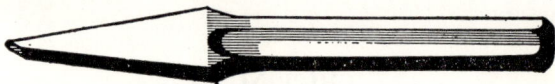

Fig. 5-3. Round-nose chisel.

corners which have a fillet (curved junction), and for drawing back drills which have "run out."

The diamond-point chisel (Fig. 5-4) is made square at the point, then ground on an angle across diagonal corners, which makes the

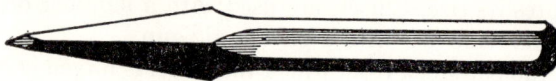

Fig. 5-4. Diamond-point chisel.

cutting face diamond shaped. Use it for cutting V grooves and square corners.

As a rule, the cold chisel is used for cutting wire or small round stock, or for cutting sheet metal or plates. Look at Fig. 5-5. It illustrates the correct way to hold the hammer and chisel and the best position for the work.

Ordinarily, you should hold a chisel in your left hand with the finger muscles relaxed. Your grip on the chisel should be steady but loose. It is best to watch the edge, *not the head*, of the chisel while working. Strike sharp, quick blows, taking care that the hammer does not slip off the end of the chisel and injure your hand.

Hold the cutting edge of the chisel at the point where the cut is desired. After each blow of the hammer, set the chisel to the correct position for the next cut. The depth of the cut depends on the angle at which the chisel is held in relation to the work. The sharper the angle, the deeper the cut will be. Do not try to take too

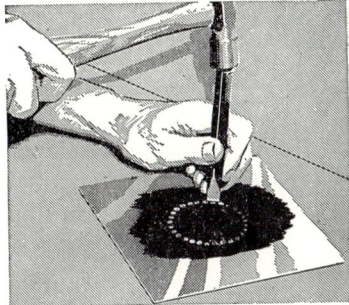

Fig. 5-5. Good chiseling technique.

deep a cut. For rough cuts, $\frac{1}{16}$ in. depth is enough, but half that much or less is plenty for finishing cuts.

Avoid cutting plate or thick sheet metal with a cold chisel whenever possible, since the metal will invariably stretch. However, when this must be done, the best procedure is as follows:

1. Draw a straight line on the work with a scriber where the cut is to be made.
2. Grip the work firmly in a vise with the scribed line even with, or just about the top of, the vise jaws.
3. The waste metal should extend above the jaws.
4. Start at the edge of the piece and cut along the scribed line with a sharp chisel.
5. Use the jaws of the vise as a base for securing shearing action.
6. Hold the chisel firmly against the piece and strike it hard.
7. *Be sure to keep the cutting edge of the chisel flat against the vise jaws.*

When chipping steel, lubricate the chisel point with light machine oil. This will make the chisel easier to drive and cause it to cut faster than it would if dry. When chipping cast iron, chip from the edges of the work toward the center to avoid breaking off corners.

SAFETY RULES FOR CHIPPING

1. Never use a chisel with a "mushroom head."
2. Always grind the end back of the head so that the mushroom disappears.
3. When using a chisel for chipping, always wear goggles.
4. If there are other men close by when chipping, see that they wear goggles or are protected from flying chips.
5. Use a hammer that is heavy enough for the job. Make sure the hammer handle is tight.
6. Keep the hammer and the head of the chisel clean and free from grease or oil to prevent the hammer from slipping.
7. If the work is held in a vise, *always* chip toward the solid jaw of the vise. *Never* chip toward the movable jaw.
8. Where possible, avoid chipping parallel with the jaws.
9. *Remember that the time to take these precautions is before you start the job. After somebody is injured, it is too late.*

Grinding a Cold Chisel. Much better control of the chisel is obtained if it is held as shown in Fig. 5-6 with the left hand resting on

Fig. 5-6. Proper way to hold a cold chisel when grinding.

the tool rest. Do not hold the chisel too hard against the wheel or the temper will be lost. A flatter and better facet will result if the chisel is held slightly canted and moved slowly back and forth across the face of the wheel, especially if the wheel is at all worn. As the tendency is to tip the chisel and thus grind more off one end of the facet, the beginner should frequently examine the facet in order to correct this fault. Efficient chipping cannot be accomplished with a chisel on which the facet curves from the cutting edge back; grind it straight. Most beginners will grind the chisel with too sharp a cutting angle; remember that 70 deg. is nearer a right angle than it is half a right angle.

To avoid unnecessary waste of the chisel, practice grinding should be done on an inexpensive piece, say, flat stock of cold-rolled steel $\frac{1}{8}$ by $\frac{3}{4}$ in., until the skill of grinding equal and parallel facets is acquired.

The Operation of Chipping. The first direction is to avoid gripping the chisel or hammer too tightly. The boy on the New England farm acquired the art of holding a plow after his hands became so tired he could no longer grip the plow handles, and the same principle applies to chipping. Grasp the hammer handle well back toward the end; don't "choke the hammer." Swing the hammer with an easy forearm movement vertically over the shoulder, but hit the chisel with a solid snappy blow. Depending upon conditions, and often upon choice, the chisel may be held with the hand over or under as desired. The surface of the facet bearing on the work is the guide and should be kept parallel to the surface desired. If the chisel is held too high it will "dig"; if held too low the cut will "run away from the line." With close attention to the line and to the chisel edge (*never look at the head of the chisel when chipping*) one will very soon automatically raise or lower the chisel as needed, and the knack of chipping is acquired.

Hints on Chipping

1. Always wear goggles, especially if another person is chipping near by.

2. Do not permit too large a "mushroom" to form on the head of the chisel; grind it off occasionally.

3. Do not try to chip with a dull chisel. When necessary to sharpen, grind off only a trifle.

4. When holding work in a vise put a packing block of wood or metal under it to keep it from slipping down in the vise.

5. Do not hammer the vise handle.

6. Use a light hammer for a small chisel and a heavier hammer (about 1 lb.) for ordinary chipping with a $\frac{3}{4}$-in. chisel.

7. Look at the guiding lines on the surface to be chipped, never at the head of the chisel, or a sore thumb will result.

8. Always chip toward the solid vise jaw, if possible.

9. When chipping cast metal it is best to begin at the ends and chip toward the middle because the force of the blow against the corner is liable to break the corner off below the finish line. And also as a second cut approaches the first cut, it is good practice to ease up on the force of the blow in order not to break out a chunk of metal.

10. Don't pet the work—chip it! Count 1001—1002—1003 and so on for time and rhythm.

11. Instead of keeping the edge of the chisel constantly against the chip, most mechanics prefer occasionally to draw it back $\frac{1}{8}$ in. or so, say, every two or three blows. This eases the hand, gives better control and a better cut. Of course the chisel edge is again in place before the next blow falls.

12. Do not take too deep a cut, $\frac{1}{16}$ or $\frac{3}{32}$ in. is enough. The chisel is less liable to break, the cutting edge will stand up longer, and more metal will be removed in a given time. Leave at least $\frac{1}{32}$ in. for the finishing cut to give the chisel a chance to "bite." When finishing, be sure the cutting edge is sharp, ease up on the force of the blows but keep them snappy.

13. If the surface to be chipped is fairly wide, use a cape chisel first to cut shallow grooves, and then the flat chisel to remove the stock between the grooves.

14. To cut off a heavy rivet head or similar projection, cut a slot through the middle with a cape chisel and remove the rest with a flat chisel.

15. To cut a hole in a thin sheet use a cape chisel and cut fairly close to the line.

16. To cut off a strip (1) use the vise jaw and the chisel for a shearing cut (Fig. 5-7), or (2) nick both sides along the top of the vise jaw and then break off the strip.

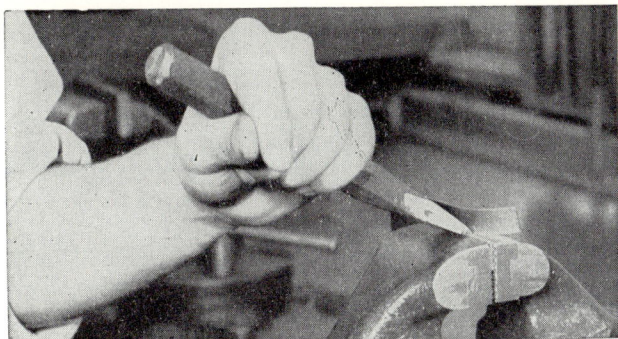

Fig. 5-7. Shearing with a cold chisel.

QUESTIONS ON CHIPPING

1. Examine the cutting edge of a properly ground cold chisel. Is the cutting edge straight? Are the facets ground flat?

2. Test the hardness of the chisel near the cutting edge with a file. Test it ¾ in. or so back from the cutting edge. Which part is harder? Is it as hard as the file?

3. How far back is a cold chisel hardened?

4. What is the proper temper color for a cold chisel? How does the temper of a cold chisel differ from the temper of a lathe tool?

5. If the cutting edge of a chisel is heated until it is red hot, or even blue, has the temper been destroyed?

6 Why will not grinding off the color restore the temper?

7. After a chisel has been sharpened several times, is it still as hard as ever on the cutting edge? Give reason.

8. How is the chisel held against the grinding wheel? Why not rest the chisel on the tool rest?

9. When the face of the grinding wheel is grooved, how may the facets of the chisel be ground flat?

10. Why is a wet grinder better for grinding tools than a dry grinder?

11. What is the best cutting angle for a cold chisel? Why not 90 deg.? Why not 50 deg.?

12. When grinding a cold chisel, or any other cutting tool, what precaution must be taken regarding the temper?

13. There is always a tendency for the beginner to grind one end of the facet wider than the other end. How do you account for this? How do you correct it?

14. If no grinder is available, how may a cold chisel be sharpened?

15. How dull should a cold chisel become before it is proper to sharpen it?

16. What is a flat chisel? What is a cape chisel? What is a gouge chisel?

17. About what weight of hammer should be used for chipping?

18. Where and how should the hammer handle be grasped? Why?

19. What is the proper position at the vise for chipping? Should the workman raise the hammer over his shoulder or toward his side?

20. How should a chisel be grasped? How tightly?

21. Should the workman look at the cutting edge or the head of the chisel when chipping? Why?

22. At about what angle with the surface being chipped should the chisel be held? Why not a greater angle? Why not a less angle?

23. How do you prevent marring the work when holding it tightly in the vise?

24. How may the piece being chipped be kept from working down in the vise?

25. What kind of a chisel is used for chipping a keyway?

26. Why is it best, if possible, to drill a hole at the end of the keyway to be chipped?

27. Is it proper to lubricate a cold chisel when chipping steel?

28. Why is it advisable to anneal a forged tool before hardening and tempering it?

FILING

The Use of Files. To know the kind of file to use, what to say when asking for the particular file, how to take care of files, and how to use them skillfully should prove a source of satisfaction to almost any boy or man. Filing is one of the accomplishments, like sharpening and using a drill, using taps and dies, soldering, and hardening and tempering, that are necessary in a machine shop and often valuable in many other places.

When fitting machine parts together there are occasions when a slight reduction in size is required, and the use of a machine tool is impracticable. In such cases the file is most useful. Further, in many classes of work such as diemaking, experimental work, and model work, surfaces must be finished and parts fashioned by filing. Therefore, it is important that a machinist shall be able to use a file skillfully.

Nothing looks much worse in the estimation of a mechanic than a poor job of filing. The art of filing, especially at the bench, is an acquired "knack." The beginner should learn all he can by reading, by observation, and by asking questions; then he may practice intelligently, and in no other line of machine-shop work is it more true that practice makes for skill.

Machine-shop Files. A file (Fig. 5-8) is a piece of high-carbon crucible steel having teeth cut upon its body by parallel rows of

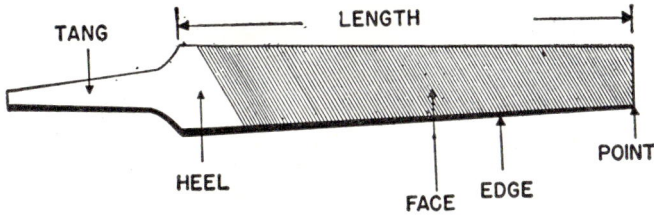

Fig. 5-8. File terminology.

chisel cuts. These cuts are made more or less diagonally across the face depending on the material on which the file is to be used and whether for roughing or finishing. When a file has a single series of cuts across its face, it is known as *single cut.* The *double-cut* file has two courses of cuts crossing each other (see Fig. 5-9). The terms

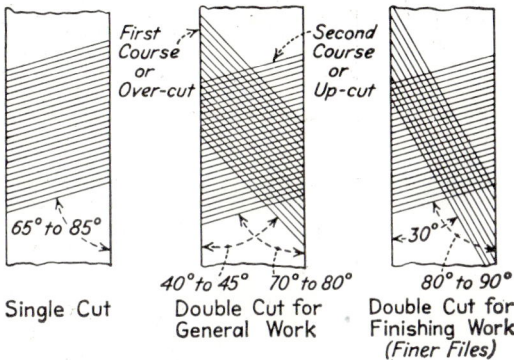

Fig. 5-9.

rough, coarse, bastard, second cut, smooth, and *dead smooth* refer to the distance apart of the parallel cuts on the larger files (10 in. or over, see Fig. 5-11), and on smaller files the Nos. 00, 0, 1, 2, 3, 4, 5, 6, 7, 8, refer to the same thing, No. 00 being the coarsest. These

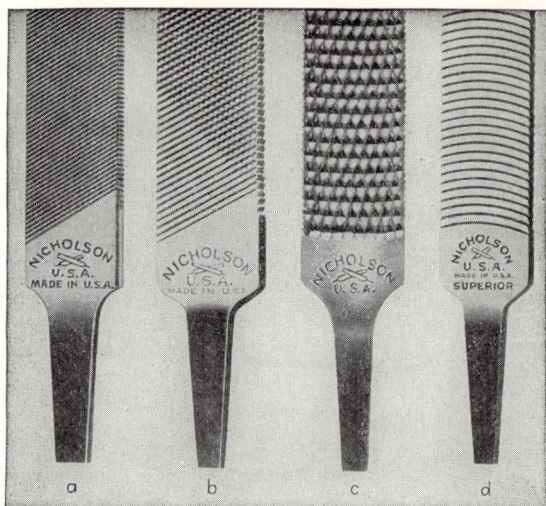

Fig. 5-10. Types of files. (*a*) Single cut, (*b*) double cut, (*c*) rasp cut, (*d*) curved tooth. (*Nicholson File Company*)

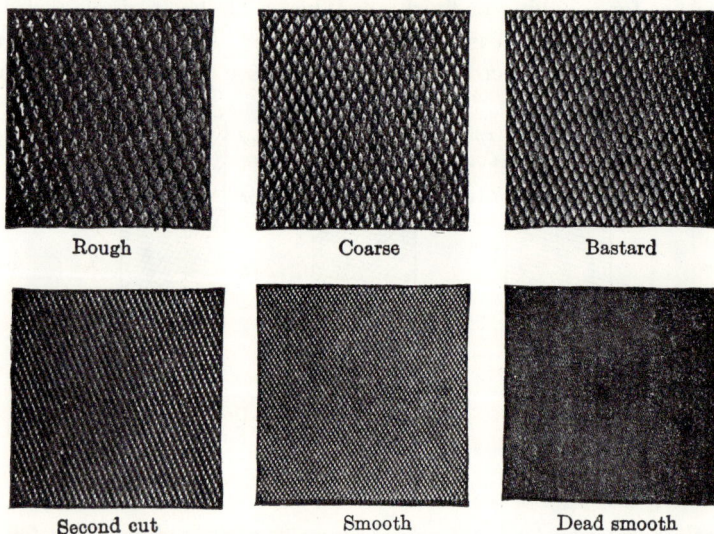

Rough Coarse Bastard

Second cut Smooth Dead smooth

Fig. 5-11. In the larger files, the relative coarseness of the given cut is known by name. In the smaller files, the cuts are distinguished by numbers. Do not get the term *second cut* confused with the term *double cut* as illustrated in Fig. 5-9.

terms are relative and depend on the length of the file; a 16-in. "second-cut" file is much coarser than a 10-in. "second-cut," and a No. 00 8-in. file is coarser than a No. 00 4-in. file. The length of a file is always measured exclusive of the tang.

In general it may be stated that a 10- or 12-in. bastard file is used for rough filing at the bench, the second cut for bringing the work fairly close to a finish, and as fine a file as desired for the finish. The *rough* and *coarse* files and the *dead-smooth* files are not much used in machine-shop work, and of the smaller files the Nos. 00 and 2 are used much more than the finer cuts.

Files may be obtained in almost any desired shape or length and are commonly known either by their cross section as *square, round, three square* (triangular), *half round*, etc.; by their general shape as *flat, hand, pillar*, etc.; or by their particular use as *mill file, warding file*, etc. Files are used in all of the metalworking trades; the shapes most commonly used in machine work are illustrated in Fig. 5-12 and a brief description of each follows.

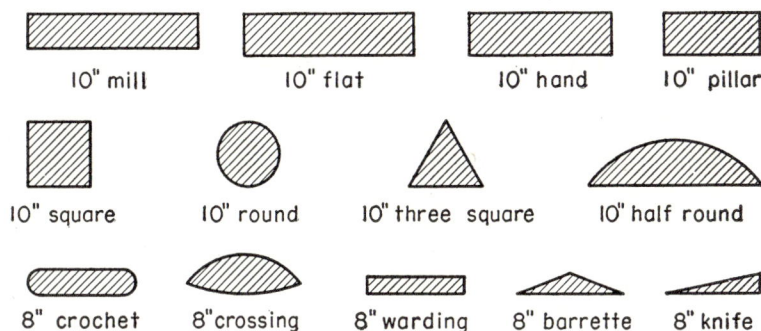

10" mill 10" flat 10" hand 10" pillar

10" square 10" round 10" three square 10" half round

8" crochet 8" crossing 8" warding 8" barrette 8" knife

Fig. 5-12. Cross sections of several files.

Mill File. Nearly all the files used in machine shops are double cut, the most notable exception being the mill file. The mill file is single cut, of substantially the shape of the flat file and most commonly 10 or 12 in. in length. It may be obtained with flat or rounded edges or one flat and one round as desired. Bastard or second cut are mostly used. The chisel teeth (single cut) give a smoother finish than the pointed teeth (double cut), but do not remove the metal so fast. It is usually regarded as better than the double-cut file for lathe work. It is much used for drawfiling, and in the bastard cut is fairly efficient for filing brass or bronze. The mill file derives its name by reason of its extensive use in woodworking mills for sharpening saws and planer knives. In machine-shop work it is often called *float* file or *lathe* file, but *mill* file is the correct name.

Flat File. The flat file is rectangular in shape and tapers slightly narrower and thinner toward the point and toward the heel. It is the most commonly used file in the shop for general work. It is usually 12 in. long and bastard cut, but may be obtained in lengths from 6 to 16 in. in any cut.

Hand File. The hand file is parallel in width with faces slightly convex. The hand second-cut file is an excellent file for removing feed marks and for bringing flat surfaces fairly close to the finish. The hand smooth is the favorite finishing file for flat surfaces and is often used for finishing surfaces of round work revolving in a lathe.

Pillar File. The pillar file is similar to the hand file except that it is narrower. An 8-in. pillar file is light and "handy." It is adaptable for a great variety of filing operations and is one of the most popular files in the shop. Used usually in No. 00, 2, or 4 cut.

Square File. The square file is used for filing the smaller square or rectangular holes, for finishing the bottoms of narrow slots, etc.

Round File. The round file is used for enlarging round holes and for finishing round corners. It is generally tapered and the small sizes are often termed "rattail" files.

Three-square Files. The three-square files are double cut on all three sides and the edges are very sharp. These files are especially valuable for finishing surfaces that meet at less than a right angle, and for backing off special taps, counterbores, etc., that frequently must be homemade.

Half-round File. The half-round file is one of the most useful files in general machine-shop work. It may be obtained in any length and cut.

Crochet File. The crochet file has both edges rounded. It is useful when filing against a filleted shoulder or a rounded corner of a hole.

Crossing File. The cross file, sometimes called the *shadbelly*, is often used in place of the half round. Each side of the file has a different curve which feature frequently is of great convenience.

Warding File. The warding file is a very thin file. It is essentially a locksmith's file for making the ward notches in keys. It is however very useful in the machine shop for filing slots and notches, and for finishing the sides of narrow grooves.

Barrette File. The barrette file has a flat triangular shape with teeth on the wide face only (safe back). It is a most useful file for finishing the sharp corners of many sorts of slots and grooves.

Knife File. The knife file is used instead of the barrette file in similar work where the thinner cross section and the safe back of the latter are not necessary.

The files mentioned above are only a few of the shapes manufactured. By referring to a catalogue of files it will be observed that there is manufactured a size, shape, and cut of file for practically every purpose and any material. When a machinist or toolmaker asks for a file he gives the *length*, the *name*, and the *cut;* for example, "10-in. hand second cut" or "8-in. pillar No. 2."

The Safe Edge. The mill file and the flat file have single-cut teeth on both edges; the hand file usually has teeth on one edge only, the other edge being termed the *safe* edge; the pillar file has two safe edges. If a safe edge is desired on any file it is easy to grind off the teeth. As a matter of fact a sharper corner may be obtained with a file so ground.

Convexity of Files. Most files are made with the faces slightly convex lengthwise or "bellied." There are good reasons for this. If when filing a broad surface all the teeth were in contact, it would require too much pressure downward to make the file "bite," as well as forward pressure to make it cut; this would mean practically double work and also make it more difficult to control the file. If the face of the file were straight, to produce a flat surface every part of the stroke would have to be perfectly straight. This is impossible. If a file were cut with flat faces and warped ever so little in hardening (and this is impossible to avoid) then one side would be concave and useless for flat work.

Taper of Files. The convexity of a file should not be confused with the taper of a file. A flat file has faces which are convex, and it also tapers slightly in width. Certain files (for example, the square, round, and triangular files) are more adaptable for a variety of work if they taper from near the middle to a very small cross section at the point, and are generally so made. There are occasions, however, when it is preferable to use a file of uniform cross section; such files are termed *blunt*.

File Handles. One important thing concerning files is too often disregarded; the file should be provided with a suitable handle properly fitted. The size of the handle depends on the size of the file, and the nature of the job. On the larger files the handle should be of a size that may be easily grasped; if too large or too small it will tire the hand in heavy filing. On the smaller files the handle should be of a size that will give balance to the file. When using a 4- or 5-in. file a piece of leather belting cut to a convenient shape makes an excellent handle. A wooden handle is fitted as follows: Drill a hole in the handle, of a size equal to the average thickness of the tang, and to a depth about equal to the length of the tang. Heat the tang of an old file to a dull red and force it about two-thirds its length into the hole and quickly withdraw it. Plunge the handle in water to stop the burning and then drive it on the new file, being careful not to split it. Practically the whole of the tang should be fitted to the handle.

Care of Files: Pinning. There is always a tendency, especially when filing narrow surfaces or corners, to have the file "pin," that is, small particles of the material being filed get wedged in front of the teeth of the file and scratch the work. Keep the file clean either with a file card (Fig. 5-13a), or by pushing the dirt from between

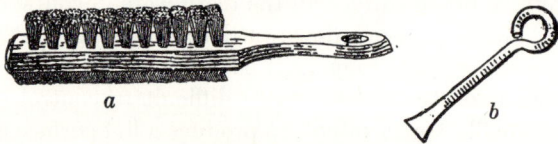

Fig. 5-13. File cleaners.

the teeth with a piece of soft steel, brass, or copper flatted thin on the end (Fig. 5-13b).

Pinning is caused often by bearing too hard on the file, especially on the finer cut files. The worst kind of pinning is caused by hard usage of a new file. The new file should be used with great care until the small burrs on the ends of the teeth are worn away. Files are expensive cutting tools and it is a sure sign of ignorance or carelessness to throw them in a drawer or on the bench. Be orderly and careful; it pays.

Cross Filing. Pushing the file endways, under more or less pressure against the work, is called *cross filing*, or merely filing. No pressure is applied to the file on the return stroke; it should not be removed from the work but may rub lightly.

Fig. 5-14. The proper way to hold the file for heavy filing.

Holding the File. Most filing is done by holding the file in both hands. The file should be held in one hand only in especially delicate work where the suitable file is too small to be held in both hands. The proper way to hold the file for heavy filing is shown in Fig. 5-14. Grasp the file handle in the right hand, with the palm of the hand against the end of the handle and the *thumb on top.* Cover the other end of the file with the base of the thumb of the left hand and curl the fingers under.

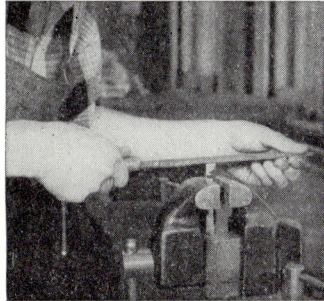

Fig. 5-15. The proper way to hold the file for lighter finishing cuts.

For the lighter finishing cuts the position of the right hand remains the same, but the left hand may be changed to the position shown in Fig. 5-15. This gives better control of the file.

The beginner will usually grasp the file too firmly. He will generally acquire about the proper grip after his hands get tired and cramped.

Position of the Body When Filing. Skillful filing is a *knack* and to acquire this knack it is essential that conditions must be right. It is easier to do a thing well by the right method than it is by the wrong method, but having once learned by the wrong method it is difficult to acquire the right. The height of the work to be filed in the vise should not be above the level of the workman's elbow as he stands erect; therefore the shorter boys should be provided with platforms to stand on. Filing at the bench, especially the heavier filing, calls for a certain harmonious action of the arms, body, and legs. Stand with the left foot pointing toward the bench, the hollow of the right foot 8 to 12 in. from the left heel, and bend the body slightly forward at the hips. Hold the file as shown in Fig. 5-14 with the right arm bent to about 90 deg. and the left arm somewhat nearer straight. Lean forward slowly for about two-thirds of the stroke, bending the knees slightly, and at the same time, push with the arms. During the last third of the stroke keep pushing with the arms, but bring the body back slightly to nearly the original posi-

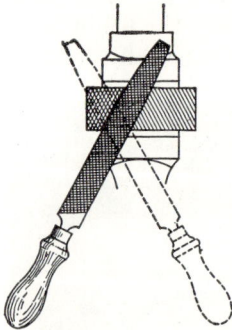

Fig. 5-16.

tion. Then bring back the file lightly on the work to position for another stroke. Keep the file level or the work will be rounded instead of flat. The great fault is too much speed. Bear on hard but take slow strokes.

Operation of Filing. If the work is cast iron the scale should be removed, possibly by chipping, before an attempt is made to file the surface. A few strokes on cast-iron scale will ruin a file. When rough filing it will be found that "crossing the stroke" (Fig. 5-16) at short intervals will rest the arms. It also serves to show the beginner where he tends to file the hardest, thus helping him to keep the surface straight, and practice in keeping the surface flat and straight is practice in learning to file. The work should be tested occasionally with a scale or with the blade of a square (Fig. 5-17a). Test it crosswise, lengthwise, and diagonally. A common fault is to rock the file. Either an over-arm or an under-arm rocking action will produce a convex surface; push the file as straight as possible.

If the surface being filed is to finish square with another surface, care must be taken to *keep it fairly square when roughing* because if one corner is filed $\frac{1}{16}$ in. low, it means either that the work is

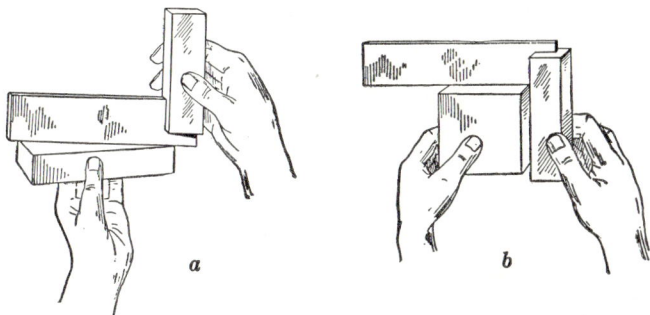

Fig. 5-17. (*a*) Testing for flat; (*b*) testing for square.

spoiled or that the sixteenth thickness must be filed off the whole surface. Test it frequently with a steel square as shown in Fig. 5-17*b*. When finishing the surface the defects will show more plainly if the work and the square are held between the light and the eye. Remember that a machinist's steel square is a tool that will not stand rough handling. If it is the least bit "out," it is worthless.

Another advantage of the convexity of the file will by this time have become apparent. The skillful workman can control the file to make the few teeth that touch the work at one time cut just about where he desires. If the middle, or one corner, or one edge is a little high, he files off the high spot and this is the art of filing a true surface.

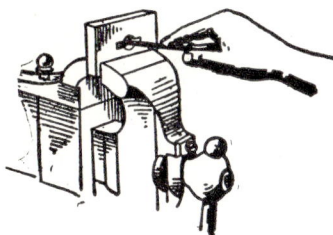

Fig. 5-18.

Filing is a skill, to acquire which one needs to pay careful attention and to have patience; "all of a sudden" you have it and filing is easy. If one has attained a reasonable amount of proficiency in two-hand filing—the sense of file balance and control—he will find no particular trouble in learning to file with one hand. A stool of a height that will bring the workman's shoulder to about the level of the work should be provided. The file may be grasped in several ways; the position of the hand as illustrated in Fig. 5-18 is suggested as one giving ease in operation and good control.

Drawfiling. When it is desired to "line" or grain a piece of work (either flat or round) lengthwise it may be done by drawfiling. Hold the file as shown in Fig. 5-19. Keep it flat, and bear on, as hard as necessary, both directions of the stroke, being careful not to scratch the work with a dirty or dull file. Removing the handle in certain cases may give better balance of the file. The single-cut file is usually regarded as best for drawfiling. After the piece is filed it may be polished by moving an emery stick, or a piece of emery cloth under the file, back and forth in the same manner as drawfiling.

Fig. 5-19. Drawfiling.

Filing Soft Metals. Filing brass, solder, lead, etc., with the ordinary double-cut file is very unsatisfactory because the teeth quickly become clogged with chips which are difficult to remove. The *brass file* (Disston) has been designed to overcome this difficulty and also to produce a better finish with a coarser file. It is made with deep teeth and open bottoms; the up-cut is on a longer angle than usual and the over-cut is almost straight across. If such a file is not avail-

Fig. 5-20. Curved-cut file.

able a single-cut file is usually more satisfactory than a regular double-cut file.

The *curved-cut file*, Fig. 5-20, has proved very efficient for filing soft metals. The shape of the grooves between the teeth reduces to a considerable extent the clogging of the teeth when filing aluminum, brass, copper, etc. The curved-cut file with its chisel edges gives an excellent finish when filing round work in a lathe.

Further, it has very free cutting action which makes it desirable when considerable stock, iron or steel as well as the softer metals, is to be removed. It is especially economical for the reason that unlike other files it may be advantageously recut or sharpened.

Needle-handle Files. The very smallest files are made in the form of "needle-handle files" (Fig. 5-21). They are much used in fine die work and are also very useful in delicate finishing touches

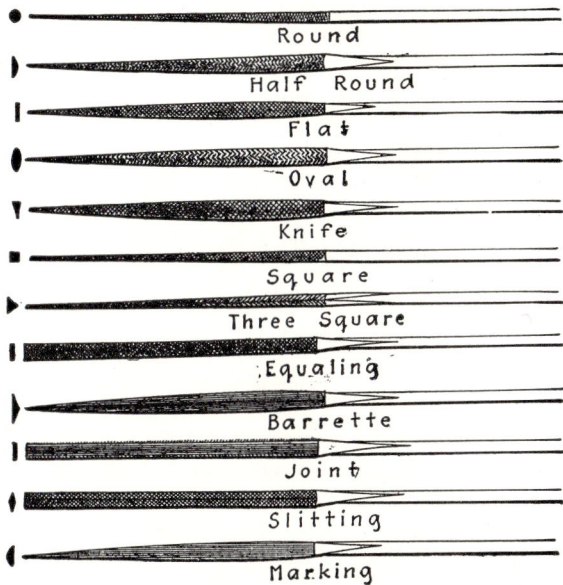

Fig. 5-21. Needle-handle files.

in a variety of filing jobs. They are made in 4- to 6-in. lengths, only a third to a half of which is file shaped and cut, the remainder forming a slender handle.

DONT'S IN FILING

Don't use a file without a handle.
Don't use a loosely fitting handle.
Don't use a worn-out file.
Don't use a dirty file.
Don't use a new file on narrow edges.

Don't use a good file on cast-iron scale.

Don't use a fine file for filing soft metal.

Don't use a bastard file for finishing.

Don't use a smooth file for roughing.

Don't let the file hit the vise jaws.

Don't allow files to scrape together.

Don't put your fingers on the cast-iron surface being filed.

Don't push the file too fast.

Don't file too much before testing the work.

QUESTIONS ON FILES AND FILING

1. What is one reason for having the file slightly convex, or bellied?
2. If the file were not bellied, and warped in hardening, would its usefulness be impaired? Explain.
3. If the file were not bellied, would it be easier to take hold or harder? Why?
4. What is the effect when filing if the right hand tends to go down and the left hand rises slightly?
5. What is the effect when filing if the right hand tends to rise and the left to go down?
6. Is it easy to file the edges and produce a convex surface? Give reason.
7. It may be stated that in order to produce a flat surface with a 10- or a 12-in. file, a harmonic movement of the arms, body, and legs is necessary. What does this mean?
8. What do you mean by a knack? Is filing a flat surface a knack? How is a knack acquired?
9. What is meant by crossing the cut in filing?
10. Should the file be lifted from the work on the return stroke? What is the reason?
11. What are the differences between a flat file and a hand file?
12. What is the difference between a bastard file and a second-cut file?
13. In what way does the mill file differ from the other files?
14. What do you understand by bastard? Second cut? Smooth?
15. How is the length of a file measured?
16. What is the difference between a double-cut file and a single-cut file?
17. What is the difference between a double-cut file and a second-cut file?
18. Which is the easier metal to cut with a file, cast iron or wrought iron?
19. How should the scale on castings be removed before filing the surfaces?
20. What is the reason a file should not be used to remove the scale from cast iron?

21. When should the coarser files be used? When should the finer files be used?
22. On narrow work, should an old file or a new file be used? Why?
23. What can be done to keep cast-iron filings from clogging the file?
24. How is the handle properly fitted on the tang of a file?
25. What is meant by a safe edge on a file? When is it advisable to use a file with a safe edge? If necessary could you grind a safe edge on a file?
26. What commonly used file has two safe edges?
27. Is a half-round file half round?
28. On what kind of surfaces is a half-round file used? What is the purpose of having teeth cut on the flat side?
29. How is the cut of a file designated in the smaller sizes?
30. What is a file card? How may a piece of brass or copper rod be made into a most efficient file cleaner?
31. What causes pinning? How may the pin be removed?
32. In your judgment, why should a single-cut file be best for filing in a lathe?
33. What is a needle-handle file?

SCRAPING

Scraping in machine work is the operation of *pushing* off, rather than *peeling* off, a small chip with a very sharp tool having no rake. For example, hand reaming is really a *scraping* action. Ordinarily, however, the term is confined to the finishing of flat and curved surfaces with hand scrapers as explained here.

Reasons for Scraping. (1) It is practically impossible to produce a true flat surface in a machine or with a file. (2) Most of the flat bearing surfaces are iron surfaces, and the condition of an iron surface as it comes from a planer or shaper or milling machine is not suitable for a first-class bearing surface; first, because it is not exactly flat and true, and second, because even the sharpest cutting tool does not produce the *close grained* and *smooth* surface that is necessary for such a bearing. (3) There are many curved bearing surfaces, for example in the bearing boxes and caps for shafts, spindles, etc. These surfaces, whether of cast iron, babbitt, or bronze, must be scraped to obtain the alignment and fit necessary in high-grade work.

Tools Used for Scraping a Flat Surface. To produce an accurate flat bearing surface the "high spots," although they are only two or three thousandths of an inch high, must be located and scraped off. The tools used for locating the high spots and for otherwise gaging the shape and accuracy are special gage plates, such as for the ways of a lathe or a dovetail slide; surface plates (Fig. 5-22*a*),

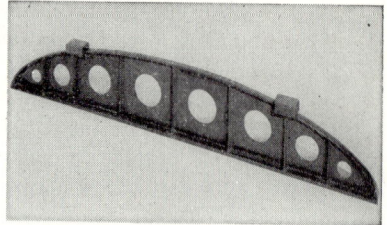

Fig. 5-22*a*. Surface plate. (*Taft-Pierce Manufacturing Company*)

Fig. 5-22*b*. Cast-iron straightedge. (*Brown & Sharpe Manufacturing Company*)

which are made in a variety of shapes and sizes; and iron straightedges (Fig. 5-22*b*), which are practically long narrow surface plates. These plates are scientifically designed to retain their shape. They are very expensive and should be handled and used with the greatest care.

The tools used to remove the high spots are called *scrapers*. Figure 5-23 shows the commonly used forms of scrapers for flat work either of which may be made of a size convenient for the job at hand. The flat scraper (Fig. 5-23*a*) for general machine-shop use is usually about the size of a 10- or 12-in. hand file. It is drawn down on the end to about $\frac{1}{16}$ in. thick, hardened, and the "snap" taken out, that is, heated just enough so that a drop of water will bubble on it. In other words, a scraper should be as hard as it is possible to make it. Scrapers are often made from old files, but they are not so good as those made of special scraper steel. The hook scraper (Fig. 5-23*b*) is used for *flowering* or *frosting*, which are the terms used

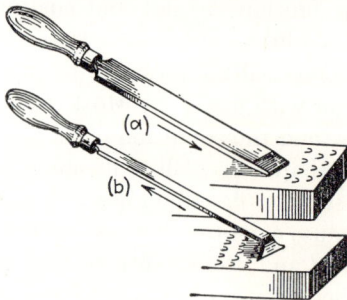

Fig. 5-23. Scrapers for flat work: (*a*) flat scraper, (*b*) hook scraper.

for the more or less regular scroll or patchwork design which is sometimes used to finish a scraped surface. They are also used for scraping surfaces where it is inconvenient to use a flat scraper, as for instance in the angle of a dovetail bearing surface.

Sharpening the Flat Scraper. The taper sides of the cutting edge are ground flat and smooth, and the end is ground square edgewise but slightly convex lengthwise. The object of the slight curve of the cutting edge is to enable the user to cant it ever so little to one side or the other to scrape exactly the spot desired without danger of scratching under the surface of the work with the corner of the scraper. After grinding, the scraper is oilstoned, the flat sides first and then the end. When stoning the end, hold as shown in Fig. 5-24 and move the scraper for a distance of about 3 in. back and forth on the oilstone. Tip the handle ever so little forward and bear down on the push stroke, easing up on the return. When one cutting edge is sharp, turn the scraper half around and oilstone the other edge. Do not hold the edge square to the direction of the stroke but at

Fig. 5-24.

about 45 deg., as shown in the figure. This will tend to give a better edge if the oilstone is uneven, and also give the slight convexity desired.

The Scraping Operation. To mark the high spots a thin application of venetian red or prussian blue paint is rubbed on the surface plate, and the work rubbed on the plate or the plate on the work, whichever is the more convenient. The high spots on the work will then show plainly, being marked with the paint. Only a few spots will show the first time and these will be more or less isolated. These are scraped off and the operation of marking repeated. As the scraping continues, the number of the spots will increase, and strange as it may seem, the greater the number of spots evenly distributed the more perfect the scraped surface.

Figure 5-25 shows the correct position for holding the scraper. With the flat scraper the forward stroke is the cutting stroke and

the usual stroke is seldom over ½ in. in length. The effect should
be clean cut and smooth—no scratches. Keep the scraper *sharp;*
when one edge becomes dull turn it over and use the other edge.
Oilstone it when necessary and grind it a little every three or four
times it is oilstoned. Not more than two or three thousandths
should be scraped; if the work is more uneven it probably should
be machined again although it may perhaps be more economical

Fig. 5-25. Correct position for holding the scraper.

to file it. As the spots increase in
number and decrease in size, considerable judgment must be used
as to just where and how much to
scrape. Turpentine may be used
instead of the paint when close to
the finish to show the high spots
which will appear bright. The
turpentine acts also as a lubricant
between the work and the plate,
which is often an advantage, and further it serves to make the
scraper cut better.

Hints on Scraping

1. Do not allow any oil, not even your fingers which are naturally
oily, to touch the surface being scraped.

2. Until the surface is substantially true it is necessary, to accomplish anything, to scrape hard. As the spots begin to show
evenly over the surface, ease up on the chip.

3. Dipping the scraper occasionally in turpentine (or water) will
help it to cut easier and better.

4. When roughing, especially, try to keep the cuts about square
in shape and cross them in succeeding courses. This will help to
make the marking more easily distinguishable.

5. The best way to apply the paint is with a rag swab or by hand.
Apply it more generously when roughing than when finishing.

6. Be extremely careful that no grit or dirt gets on the surface
plate and that none remains on the work when being tested. Keep
the paint box covered.

7. Use the whole plate—not one spot.

8. Keep the scraper *sharp* or it will scratch. Scratches spoil a scraped surface.

Scraping Curved Surfaces. Round bearings and other curved surfaces have often to be scraped to fit running or sliding parts. The scrapers used are shown in Fig. 5-26. The half-round bent scraper in Fig. 5–26a is mostly used. It has two cutting edges and the cutting stroke may be either toward or away from the user as desired. The proper way to hold this scraper is shown in Fig. 5-27. For the larger curves the scraper shown in Fig. 5-26b, is preferred by many; it is ground to conform to the curve of the work and

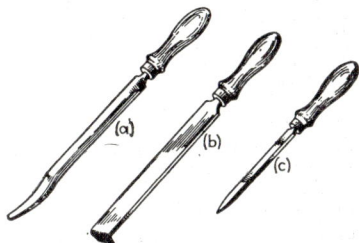

Fig. 5-26. Scrapers for curved surfaces: (a) half-round bent scraper, (b) scraper ground to conform to the curve of the work, (c) three-cornered scraper.

sharpened to cut on the pull stroke. Scraping a curved surface to fit a shaft or a gage is not particularly different in principle or operation from scraping a plane surface.

The three-cornered scraper (Fig. 5-26c) is used to break (remove the sharp edge), or round as desired, the corners of holes or other

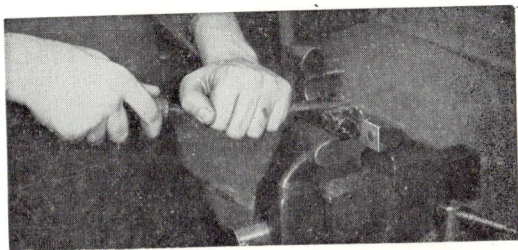

Fig. 5-27. Scraping a bearing with a half-round scraper.

curved edges. It is usually made from an old file by grinding off the teeth. The three corners of the body back of the cutting edges should be well rounded in order not to cut the hands of the user.

QUESTIONS ON SCRAPING

1. Is there a difference between the cutting angle of a flat scraper and a scraper for curved work?

2. Is the end of a flat scraper straight? What shape is it lengthwise? Crosswise?

3. What is the difference between a scraper for a round bearing and a three-cornered scraper? Could a three-cornered scraper be used for scraping a round bearing?

4. Why is a scraper for round bearings curved slightly?

5. When is a three-cornered scraper used? How is it usually made in the shop?

6. Of what kind of steel is a scraper made? Why?

7. How is a scraper hardened? How is it tempered?

8. What care must be taken when grinding a scraper?

9. Why is a scraper oilstoned after grinding?

10. How is a scraper for a round bearing oilstoned?

11. How is a flat scraper held when being oilstoned?

12. What are the advantages of a scraped surface?

13. What is a surface plate? Why must great care be taken of a surface plate?

14. How is a flat bearing surface tested?

15. How is a round bearing surface tested?

16. Why is a thin coating of red lead or prussian blue applied to a surface plate? Which is better? Why?

17. How do you determine when a surface is sufficiently scraped?

CHAPTER 6

Laying Out

Laying out is the shop term used to include the marking or scribing of center points, circles, arcs, or straight lines upon metal surfaces, either curved or flat, for the guidance of the worker. It is
much used in drill-press work and in shaper and planer work. The
layout, to be worth while, must be right for the job at hand; therefore, the dimensions on the blueprint must be carefully followed and
the layout lines made sharp and clear. The degree of accuracy necessary depends on the job; a great amount of layout work is done
on rough castings and it is not to be expected that the dimensions
will be in thousandths of an inch. On the other hand, it often requires more calculation and judgment—head work—to lay out a
casting so that it will machine to size (especially if it is scant here
or there) than it does to lay out *accurately* two or three holes on a
finished surface.

Tools Used for Laying-out Work

Bench Plate or Surface Plate (Fig. 6-1). The cast-iron plate of convenient size, ribbed to give strength and staying qualities, machined on top and bottom, and usually on sides and ends is called

Fig. 6-1. Bench plate. (*The Taft-Peirce Manufacturing Company*)

the *bench* or *surface* plate. It is used when laying out work as a base upon which to rest the work, gages, and other tools. (A bench plate may be differentiated from a surface plate in that the surface plate is scraped or lapped flat. It is an expensive piece of apparatus, especially in the larger sizes.) Surface plates are also made of granite and ceramic materials. Usually laying-out plates used for floor work are often 4 to 5 ft. wide and 8 to 10 ft. long.

Hammer (Fig. 4-1). The hammer usually used in machine work is the ball-peen.

Center Punch (Fig. 6-2). These punches are hardened and both ends are tempered. Center punches are about 4 in. long and have

Fig. 6-2. Center punch being used. (*The Brown & Sharpe Manufacturing Company*)

nicely knurled finger grips. Points are ground carefully at an angle which will give maximum strength and penetration and at the same time provide a punch mark in which drills and other pointed tools will start easily. Some center punches are automatic in that the striking mechanism is enclosed in the handle which is of such size and form as to be held conveniently in the hand. A downward pressure releases the striking mechanism and makes the impression.

Prick Punch. This punch is similar to the center punch except that the point is much sharper, the angle being about 30 deg. while the center punch is ground about 90 deg.

Scriber (Fig. 6-3). This is a slender piece of tool steel 8 or 10 in. long, sharp pointed at both ends, one end bent to approximately a

Fig. 6-3. Scriber. (*The Brown & Sharpe Manufacturing Company*)

right angle, points hardened and tempered, and is used for marking or scribing on metal.

Divider (Fig. 6-4). This is a tool with hardened-steel points used for scribing circles or laying off distances. It is adjustable and is classified according to size by the maximum opening between the points such as 3 in., 4 in., etc., divider. Divider points must be slender and sharp.

To set the divider, place one point in a convenient graduation line on a scale (for example, the 1-in. line) and adjust the other point until it exactly splits the graduation line the correct distance away. Since the graduation lines are V shaped, a divider may often be set more nearly exact by feeling than by seeing. Adjust it until no "give" can be felt on either side of the V. Check with a magnifying glass if desirable. When the divider is fully opened, the exact adjustment is difficult because of the wide angle; consequently, a larger divider will be required, or possibly it would be better to use trammel points (Fig. 6-17).

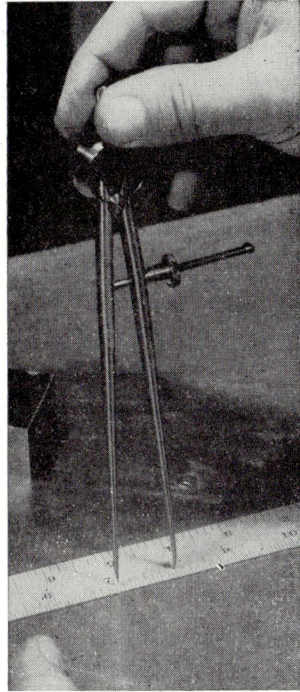

Fig. 6-4. A divider being used. (*The Lufkin Rule Company*)

The Vernier Caliper (See Fig. 3-39). This tool may be used for accurate settings of dividers and trammels. Near the zero mark on the beam is a tiny indentation in the center of a small circle, and on the sliding jaw is another small cone-shaped mark. Set the vernier to the dimension required and then adjust the points of the dividers

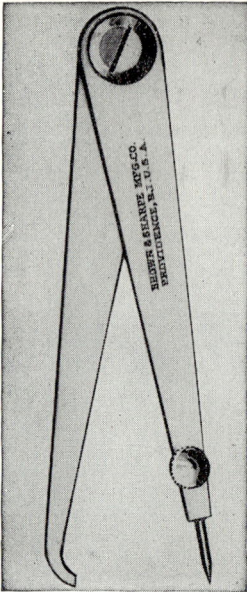

Fig. 6-5. Hermaphrodite caliper. (*The Brown & Sharpe Manufacturing Company*)

or trammels, by "feel" or with the aid of an eyeglass, exactly in the two marks.

Hermaphrodite Caliper (Fig. 6-5). This caliper is usually used to locate approximate centers of work. It is also called a *morphy* caliper.

Scale. See Fig. 3-1, page 60.

Bevel Protractor (Fig. 6-6). Use this tool for laying out angles.

Parallels (Fig. 6-7). These are used to rest work on, usually for finished surfaces. At times, *box parallels* (Fig. 6-8) are used instead of the regular parallels. They are usually used for larger work. All sides are finished and parallel.

Square (Fig. 6-9). The beam and the blade edge of this tool are hardened. The length of the blade is from the inner edge of the beam to the end of the blade. It is used to test squareness and right angles.

Angle Plates (Fig. 6-10). These are used to clamp work on to it.

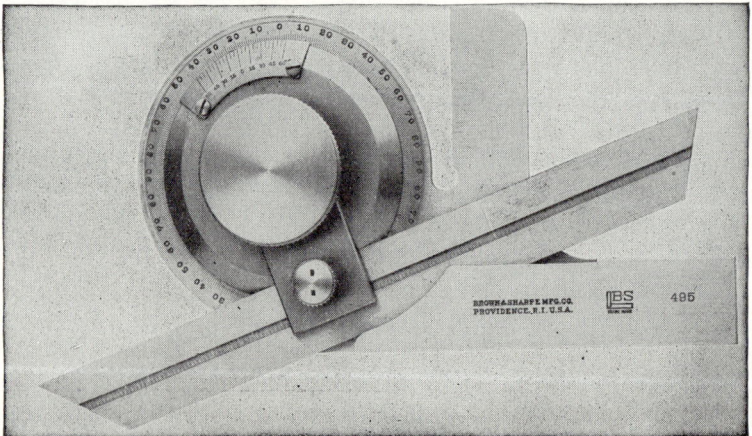

Fig. 6-6. Bevel protractor. (*The Brown & Sharpe Manufacturing Company*)

Fig. 6-7. Various sizes of parallels. (*The Brown & Sharpe Manufacturing Company*)

Fig. 6-8. Box parallels. (*The Taft-Peirce Manufacturing Company*)

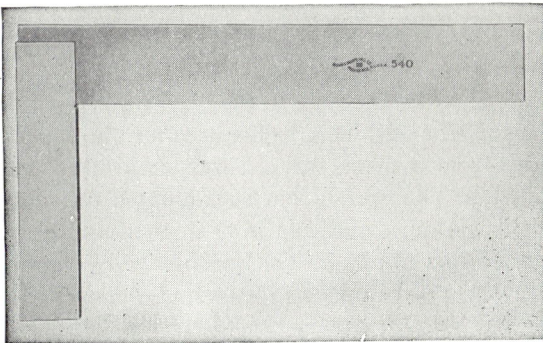

Fig. 6-9. Square. (*The Brown & Sharpe Manufacturing Company*)

Fig. 6-10. Angle plates. (*The Taft-Peirce Manufacturing Company*)

Parallel Clamp (Fig. 6-11). This is used to clamp work.

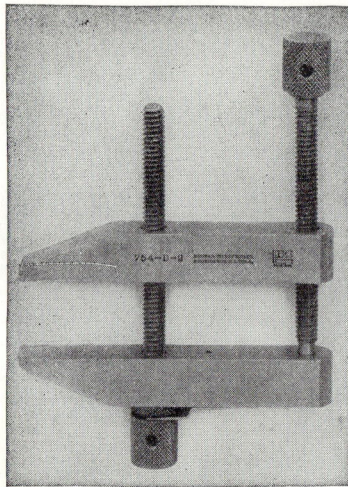

Fig. 6-11. Parallel clamp. (*The Brown & Sharpe Manufacturing Company*)

Height Gage (Fig. 6-12). This tool is used for obtaining the height of projections from a plane surface and for locating and scribing dimensional lines. The upright bar is graduated to read, by means of a vernier[1] scale on a movable jaw, to thousandths of an inch. The fixed jaw forms the base. The sharp edge of the extension of the movable jaw may be used to scribe lines on surfaces that have

[1] See page 76 for the reading of the vernier.

the scale removed. Figure 6-13 shows the scribing of lines using the height gage. In this case, the offset scriber is used.

The Surface Gage (Fig. 6-14). Surface gages are designed so that a wide range of adjustments can be made readily. The spindle can

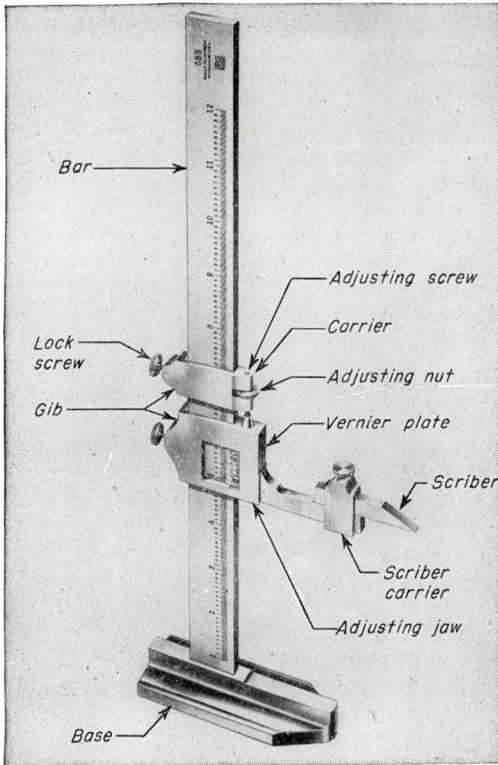

Fig. 6-12. Height gage. (*The Brown & Sharpe Manufacturing Company*)

be adjusted quickly in a swivel bolt and set at any angle above or below the base and locked in an approximate position by the large knurled adjusting screw. The fine adjustment is then made by the small knurled screw on top of the base. The base is of a form most convenient to handle and a V groove in the bottom adapts it for cylindrical work. Two gage pins in the rear end of the base can be pushed down and used against the edge of a surface plate or against the side of a T slot. The scriber may be used below the base as a depth gage, and for small work, it may be inserted and adjusted in the swivel bolt in place of the spindle.

Figure 6-15 shows a surface gage being set for a specific height and Fig. 6-16 shows a line being scribed on many pieces, all having

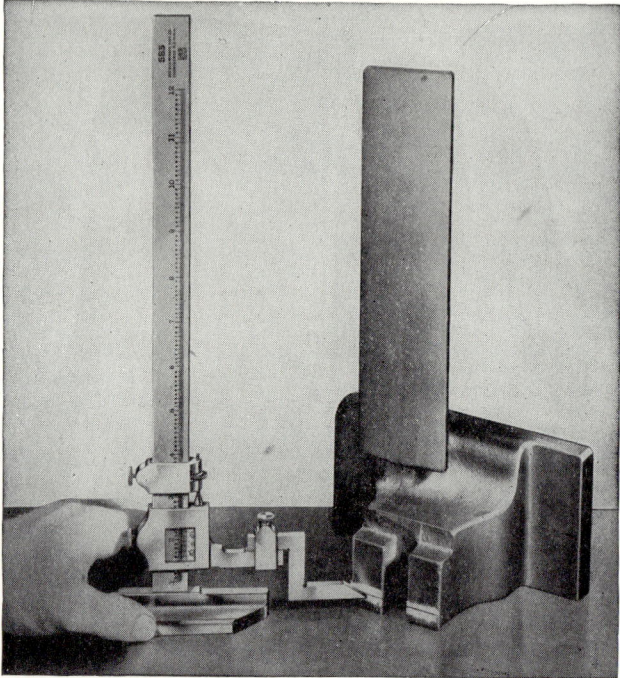

Fig. 6-13. Lines being scribed with height gage. (*The Brown & Sharpe Manufacturing Company*)

the same height line marked. These pieces will later be planed to that scribed line.

Trammel Points (Fig. 6-17). This tool is practically a beam compass or divider used for drawing arcs or circles having a large radius. An advantage lies in the fact that the point holders are perpendicular to the surface being scribed. It will be noticed that caliper legs, a pencil point, or a pen point may be substituted for the divider points. A ball is also provided to enable an arc or circle to be scribed, using a hole as a center.

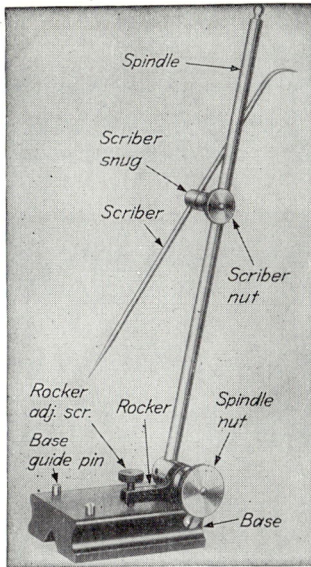

Fig. 6-14. Parts of the surface gage. (*The Brown & Sharpe Manufacturing Company*)

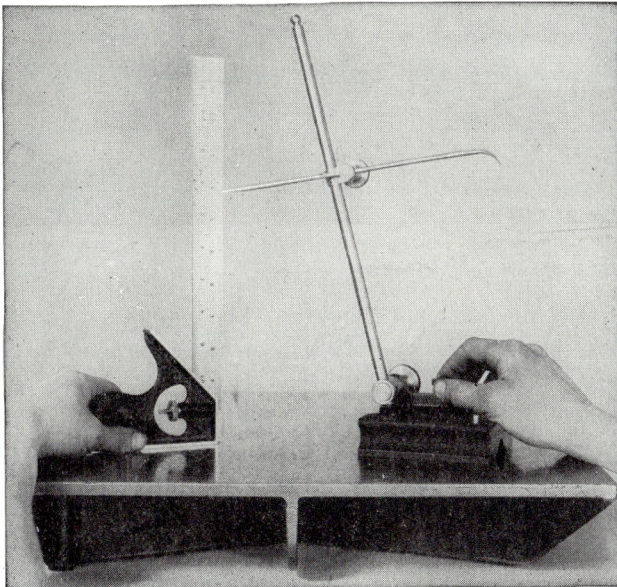

Fig. 6-15. Surface gage being set for a specific height. (*The Brown & Sharpe Manufacturing Company*)

Notice some applications of the various points used on the trammel shown in Fig. 6-17.

Scribing the Lines. The process of laying out work calls for intelligent reasoning on the part of the workman. It is impossible to give more than a few rules or directions since each job is practically a problem in itself. Laying out is line work. The surface to be ma-

Fig. 6-16. Many pieces being scribed using the surface gage. (*The Brown & Sharpe Manufacturing Company*)

chined is indicated by a line either straight or curved, and the centers of holes are located by the intersections of lines. A double line, or a blurred line, is worse than useless; have the point of the scribing tool *sharp* and *draw one line*. Chalk well rubbed into the surface of a casting will help to make the lines more distinct. White lead mixed with turpentine is quicker and better for the larger work. To make the lines more distinct on a finished surface apply blue vitriol solution, sometimes called "copper solution," with a piece of waste. To make blue vitriol solution, dissolve a small handful

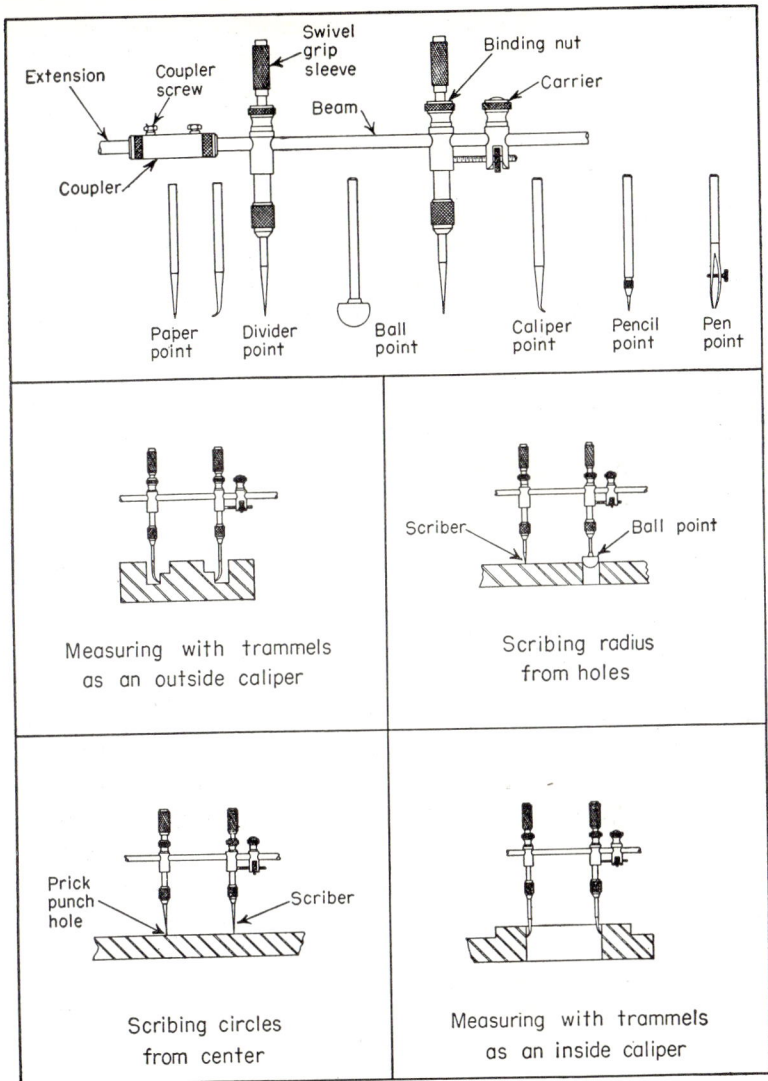

Fig. 6-17. Trammel points and some uses. (*The L. S. Starret Company*)

of copper sulphate (blue vitriol crystals) in a half pint of water and add a few drops of nitric acid.[2] A cream jar or a pickle bottle with a good-sized neck makes a good container. The diemaker frequently heats the steel for the die or punch until it is blue. In this oxidized surface the finest line is clearly visible.

The Operation of Laying Out. It is usually advisable to work from a given surface or "seat." If several lines are to be scribed, a *base line*, to which the other lines may be referred, should be drawn. The base line may be valuable later to relevel or square up by if it is necessary to move the piece during the layout. If a bench plate is used as a seat for the work and the tools, the surface gage may be adjusted to a scale held vertically. By carefully adjusting the point of the surface-gage scriber to the dimensions given on the drawing, parallel lines of the required distances apart may be easily scribed on the work. If greater accuracy is required a height gage may be used.

The intersections on these lines may then be laid off by scale measurement from a finished surface, from previously located square or angle plate, or by means of a divider from a given point. Angular lines may be laid off by using a bevel protractor.

If it is not convenient to seat the work directly on the bench plate, it may be supported on parallels placed on the plate or it may be clamped to an angle plate and the lines scribed as suggested above.

In drill press work the centers of the holes are located by the intersections of lines. A light indentation is made at the point of intersection with a prick punch and, using this mark as a center, a circle the size of the hole required is scribed with a divider. After the circles are scribed, make a deeper indentation with the center punch to make it easier to start the drill central.

In layout work if the intersection of lines comes in an opening, as for example in a cored hole or between projections of a casting, it is customary to bridge across the opening with soft wood. A small piece of sheet copper or tin with corners bent down to drive into the wood is used as a surface upon which to scribe the lines and make the slight indentation for the divider point.

Oftentimes in cored work, the core may move a little in the mold which will cause the hole to be out of center. Such a casting may

---

[2] Dykem blue may also be used.

often be saved by compensating on some other surface for the error. In such a case a preliminary layout may be advisable to determine if this surface will clean.

If there is a likelihood of the lines on the rough surface of a casting becoming obliterated, it is good practice to make a series of light center punch marks $\frac{1}{4}$ in. or so apart along the line. This is not done on finished surfaces.

It will be well for the beginner to check his layout to be sure it is right.

Oftentimes it is necessary to lay off a number of equally spaced holes in a given circumference. The following table of chords (distances between centers of holes) for a circle having a diameter of 1 in. may be used by multiplying the constant for the required number of spaces by the diameter of the given circle.

Number of divisions in circle	3	4	5	6	7	8	9	10	11	12
Length of chord. Diameter of circle 1 in......	0.866	0.707	0.588	0.500	0.434	0.383	0.343	0.309	0.282	0.259

QUESTIONS ON LAYING OUT

1. What is chalk used for in layout work? When is whiting used?
2. What solution is used on surfaces which have been machined, to make the lines show more distinctly? How is it made?
3. What is the difference between a prick punch and a center punch?
4. What do you mean by a light indentation with a prick punch? For what purpose is a light indentation used?
5. Why is a divider set by feel more accurate than when set by sight?
6. What tool is used for a heavy indentation? Why? When is a heavy indentation made? Give reasons.
7. Why is a series of prick punch marks sometimes made to show the location of the circle? When are they used in other line work?
8. On finished work is this necessary? Is it advisable? Give reasons.
9. How are lines parallel to each other or parallel to a base usually scribed?
10. How are lines at an angle to a given line or base usually scribed?

11. How are intersections accurately laid off from a finished surface? From an established point?

12. What do you mean by checking the layout? When is it advisable?

13. Explain the use of the following tools used in layout work: scale, scriber, hermaphrodite caliper, divider, surface gage, prick punch, center punch.

14. Explain the use of the following tools used in layout work: bench plate, angle plate, parallels, parallel clamps, C clamps, square, bevel protractor, height gage.

15. What is the distance across the flats of the largest square that can be filed on the end of a cylinder 1 in. in diameter? 2 in. in diameter?

16. To what dimension should a divider be set to space equally ten holes in a 5-in. circle? Five holes in a 10-in. circle?

The Drill Press

CHAPTER 7

Drill-press Construction

In every machine shop many sizes and sorts of holes must be made in metal parts. Some of these holes must be very smooth and straight, of an exact size and accurately placed. Others are not so particular as to size or location. In any case, to be produced *efficiently*, all holes must be made with the proper tools for the purpose, and in machines properly set up and operated. A knowledge of drilling machines and the tools used is one of the most important factors in machine-shop practice. A machinist must have this knowledge.

Study the mechanical features of speed changes, feed changes, adjustments of spindle and worktable. Get acquainted as soon as possible with the names and uses and the particular characteristics of the cutting tools and their holding devices. Learn to tell by the "feel," by the sound, by the chip, whether or not a drill or other cutting tool is working as it should. Have the setup look as if a mechanic did the job—neat and trim, with the clamps or stop correctly placed. Almost anybody can drill a hole, but the machinist's job is to know the why of the construction of the machine, the characteristics of the tools used, the successive steps of the operations involved, and how to lay out the work, set up the job, and finish the holes to specifications.

Although other cutting tools are often used, the twist drill is most important. Whether the drill is large or small, carbon or high-speed steel, held in a chuck or otherwise, used with a jig or not, the principles of its operation are the same. And whatever size or design of drilling machine is used, with any method of speed and feed changes, the fact remains that sharpening the drill, holding the work, setting the speed and feed, and drilling the hole, call for machine-shop training—study and practice. It is not an involved training, but it does call for understanding and judgment.

The Drilling Machine. The common mechanical feature of all drilling machines consists of a spindle (which carries the drill or

Fig. 7-1. A gang drill press in the drill press department of a machine shop. (*International Harvester Company*)

other cutting tool) revolving in a fixed relative position in a sleeve which does not revolve but which may slide in its bearing in a direction parallel to its axis. When the sleeve carrying the spindle with the cutting tool is caused to move in the advance direction (usually downward), the cutting tool approaches or is fed into the work, and when moved in the opposite direction, the cutting tool is withdrawn from the work. That is, the spindle holds the drill, and the nonrevolving sleeve *carries* the revolving spindle and drill. Feeding pressure is applied to the sleeve by hand or power and causes the revolving drill to cut its way into the work a few thousandths of an inch each revolution. In most drilling machines the spindle is vertical and the work is supported on a horizontal table.

Like all other machine tools, drilling machines are of many kinds, with a wide range of sizes. The mechanical principles of speed and feed changes differ in no particular respect from those found, for example, in lathe construction. The machine may be driven by a belt or by motor direct. The various speeds and feeds may be obtained through cone pulleys or gears. All except the smaller sizes (sensitive drills) have power feeds.

Several manufacturers now feature drilling machines having hydraulic feeds. This is an especially important development in machines used in manufacturing large quantities of duplicate parts.

Fig. 7-2. A standard floor-model superservice drill press with a cutting lubricant system. (*The Cincinnati Bickford Tool Company*)

The Standard Drill Press: Floor Type. This machine (Fig. 7-2), sometimes called upright drill press or simply drill press, has six or more spindle speeds and three or more automatic feeds. Most drill presses have circular columns, although some have square box-section construction. The head, which carries the sleeve, spindle, and feed gears, is in many models bolted to the frame and, to accommodate different heights of work, the worktable is vertically adjustable or may be swung entirely out of the way and the work seated on the base. On other types, especially those having gear feed instead of belt feed, the head also has considerable vertical adjustment on a finished flat surface on the front of the column. This gives a wider range for heights of work. The head is balanced by a counter-weight within the column.

The standard drill press may have either a rectangular or a round worktable. In the machines with the round column the worktable is supported on an arm which is girdled on the finished lower section of the column. There are three ways in which this worktable may be adjusted for position: (1) The supporting arm (and table) may be raised or lowered; this provides for different heights of work. (2) The supporting arm may be swung to substantially 90 deg. either side of center, and (3) the table itself, being pivoted at its center, may be swiveled[1] through 360 deg. The adjustments (2) and (3) in combination provide for locating, directly under the cutting tool, any given spot on the work when the work is clamped or is for some other reason impracticable to move about on the table.

A *compound table*, rectangular in shape, having both longitudinal and lateral movements as desired, is shown in Fig. 7-3. Some of these tables are merely adjustable; others are made for extreme accuracy. Note in Fig. 7-3 the two dials for reading the location, or the movement, of each slide; one dial reads thousandths and the other in ten-thousandths of an inch.

Upright drill presses are classified as to size by the diameter of the largest piece that can be centrally drilled, that is, by approximately the diameter of the table, as 15 in., 21 in., up to 42 in.

Care of the Table. The accuracy of the machine is determined to a large extent by the condition of the table of the drill press. Consequently, the utmost care of the table must be taken. Here are several precautions to be taken whenever the table is used:

1. The table of drill presses having movable tables must be properly locked to the column after the table is raised or lowered.

2. The drill press table should be kept free from chips. No chips

---

[1] *Swivel:* In machine tools, a construction which permits a part to turn or swing on a column or pivot through more or less of an arc with (usually) provision for clamping in the desired position.

can be allowed between the table and the work, or the table and the work holding device. Chips between locating surfaces mar the table, and work or work-holding device. Chips should not be removed with the bare hands; a brush or leather scraper should be used.

3. Only work, work-holding devices, and measuring tools should be placed on the table. Other tools may just as well be placed on a bench and any unnecessary marring of the table be prevented.

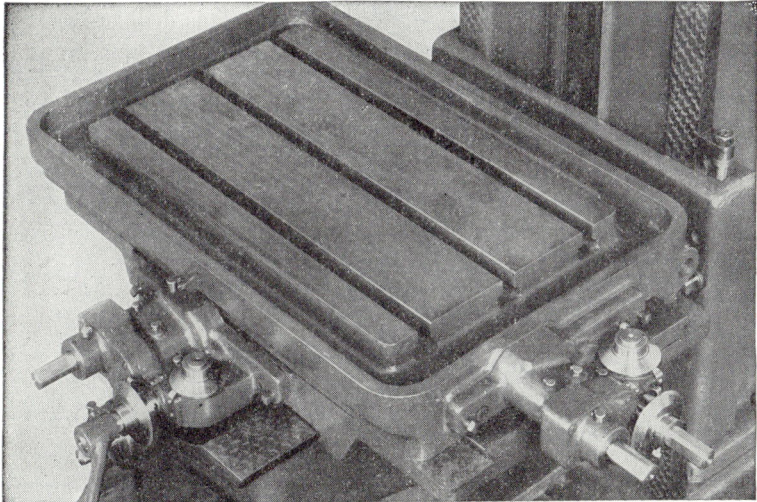

Fig. 7-3. A compound table having multiple dial arrangement and quick traverse. The adjusting dials move with the table and are visible at all positions of the table. (*The Cincinnati Bickford Tool Company*)

When anything is placed on the table, it must be gently placed there.

4. Care must be taken to prevent a drill or similar cutting tool from being driven out against the table when being drifted from its socket. A board placed under the tool is a reasonable precaution.

5. Work and work-holding devices should be securely fastened to the drill table and properly blocked on the sensitive drill press to prevent damage to the table, as well as injury to the operator and damage to the cutting tool, holding device, and work.

6. Rough-surfaced work must not be strapped directly to the table. Cardboard should be used between the table and work.

7. Care must be taken on all drill presses not to tighten T bolts unduly when strapping work or work-holding devices to the table.

8. To prevent drilling into the table when drilling through-holes, the work should not be placed directly on the table. It should be supported by parallel bars, placed in a V block, clamped in a vise, or put in a jig or fixture. Before drilling the piece, set a stop so that the drill can go just through the piece into the table or the holding device.

The Standard Drill Press: Bench Type. This drill press, Fig. 7-4, is found in many school shops as well as in many small manu-

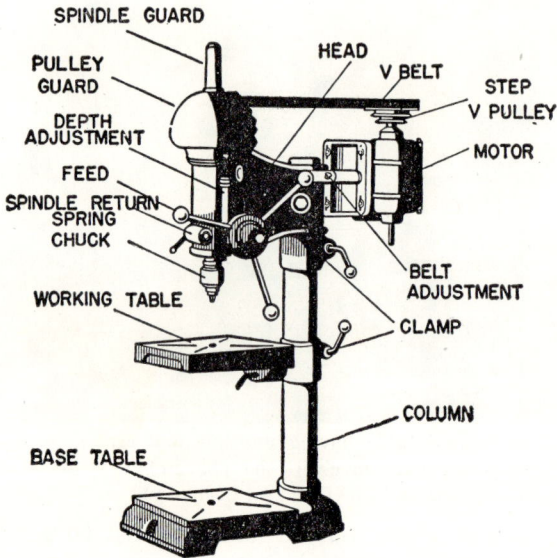

Fig. 7-4. Parts of a standard bench drill press.

facturing plants. They are usually used for small drilling jobs. However, they do have all the important parts of the larger model, usually called the *standard drill press*.

These machines have a separate motor which drives the drill spindle and chuck by means of a V belt. Four grooves are usually found on the *cone step pulley* of the motor and four on the *spindle pulley*. The drill press shown here has four speeds, and the belt is shown as adjusted for the highest possible speed. Notice that it is on the *largest-diameter* groove of the *motor* pulley. This high speed—3,000 to 3,600 r.p.m.—is suitable for small drills but is about 10 times too fast for a ½-in. drill. When in doubt as to the speed needed for a job, use the *slowest* speed. That means changing the belt to the *smallest-diameter* groove of the *motor* pulley.

The feed pressure is easily controlled on the drill press by means of a feed wheel with long handles. A *depth* stop is provided to stop the progress of the drill at a predetermined depth. That is very important when blind holes are being drilled (holes that do not go all the way through).

The working table may be raised or lowered by simply loosening the clamp holding it to the column. This is to accommodate small and large pieces of work.

Bench drill presses usually have a capacity for drills up to ½ in. Any drill larger than that is usually put in the spindle of a floortype standard drill press.

The Sensitive Drill Press. This machine (Fig. 7-5) is used for drilling small holes with hand (sensitive) feed. They are made in various sizes and may have from one to eight spindles (see Fig. 7-7 for similar gang drill).

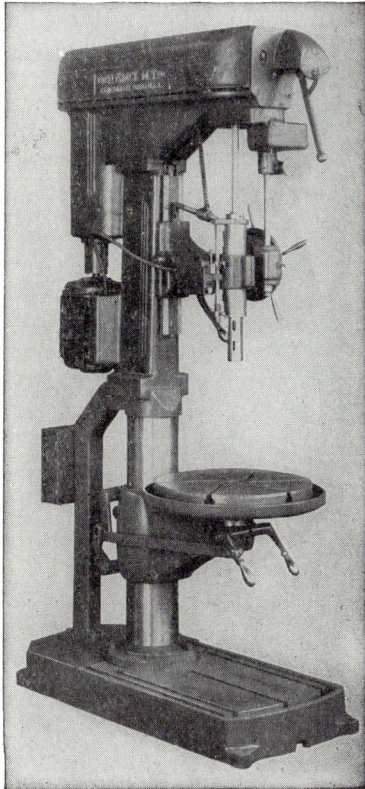

Fig. 7-5. A sensitive drill press. (*The Cincinnati Bickford Tool Company*)

Some of the smaller sizes are set on the bench and are called bench drills. The head and worktable have vertical adjustments; no other adjustment of the table is needed.

The Radial Drill. This machine (Fig. 7-6) is especially useful when drilling several holes in the larger and heavier pieces. It has taken the place, to a considerable extent, of the larger upright drills because it has a much wider range, is more convenient to handle, and greater production is possible. The spindle head is mounted on a radial arm which is girdled on the column. The head is adjustable along the arm, and the arm may be swung in a horizontal plane to any desired position within limits. These features permit of quickly

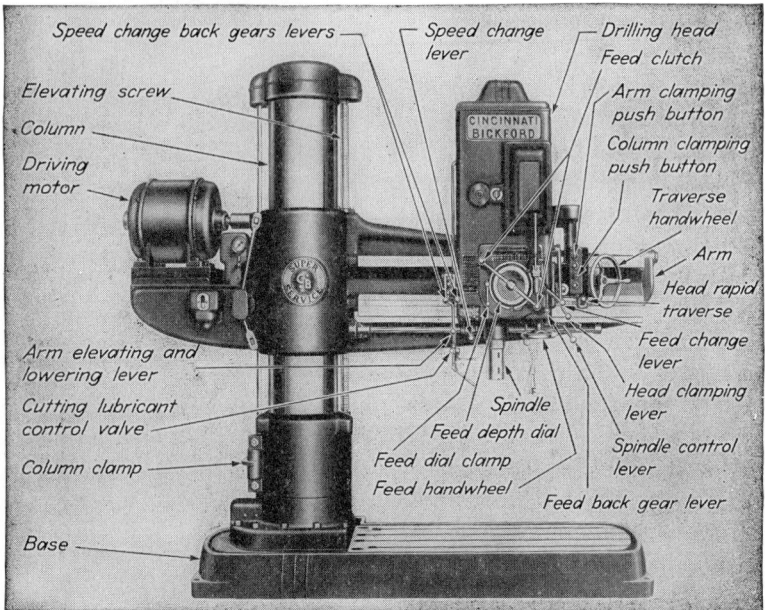

Fig. 7-6. A superservice radial drill press with the important parts identified. (*The Cincinnati Bickford Tool Company*)

locating the cutting tool over any point within a considerable area. Further, the arm may be raised or lowered to accommodate a wide range in heights of work. Various kinds and sizes of tables, plain and adjustable, are made which, when in use, are bolted to the base. Radial drills are classified as to size by the length of the arm. Figure 7-6 shows the important parts of the radial drill press.

The Gang Drill. This is a collection in one machine (Fig. 7-7) of the essential speed and feed units of from two to eight single drill presses mounted on one base and provided usually with one vertically adjustable worktable extending under all the spindles. The speed and feed units, also the vertical adjustments of the heads, are individual and independent. One or more of the spindles may be provided with the reversing gears or "tapping attachment."

Fig. 7-7. A four-spindle gang drill press. (*The Cincinnati Bickford Tool Company*)

This type of machine is a manufacturing machine and is primarily intended for work held in a jig which may be easily slid from spindle to spindle for successive operations. A very wide range of sizes and kinds of gang drills are manufactured, from the smallest sensitive drills to the heavy-duty power-feed machines. Gang drills designed and fitted especially for the production of a given part are not uncommon.

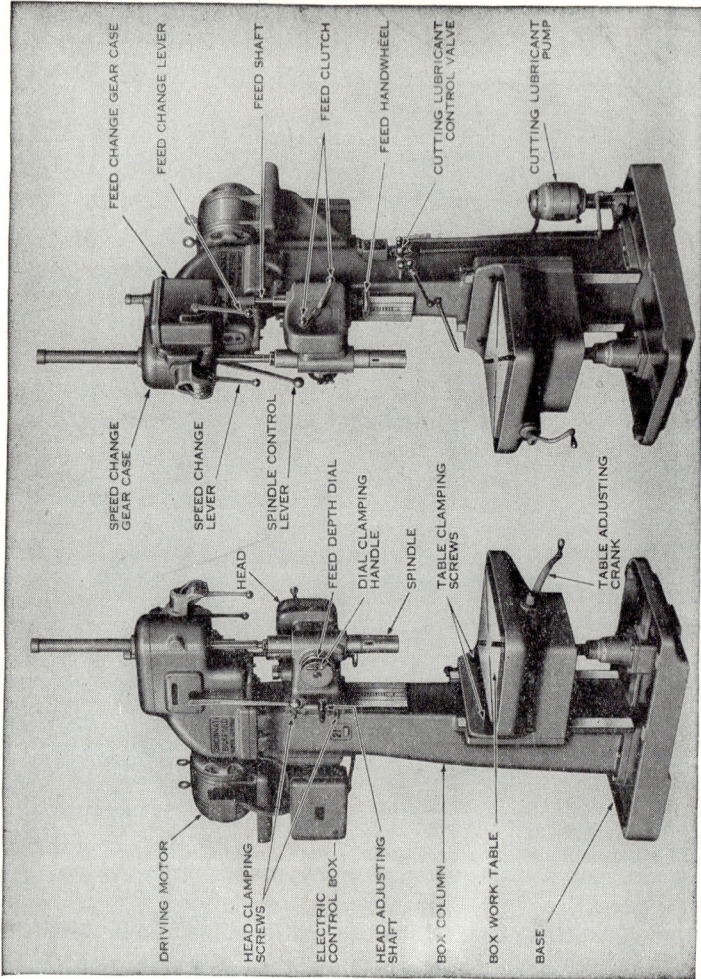

Fig. 7-8. A standard floor-model drill press with the important parts identified. (*The Cincinnati Bickford Tool Company*)

FEED CHANGE GEAR CASE

FEED CHANGE LEVER

FEED SHAFT

FEED CLUTCH

FEED HANDWHEEL

CUTTING LUBRICANT CONTROL VALVE

CUTTING LUBRICANT PUMP

SPEED CHANGE GEAR CASE

SPEED CHANGE LEVER

SPINDLE CONTROL LEVER

FEED DEPTH DIAL

DIAL CLAMPING HANDLE

SPINDLE

TABLE CLAMPING SCREWS

TABLE ADJUSTING CRANK

HEAD

DRIVING MOTOR

HEAD CLAMPING SCREWS

ELECTRIC CONTROL BOX

HEAD ADJUSTING SHAFT

BOX COLUMN

BOX WORK TABLE

BASE

DEFINITIONS: PARTS OF THE DRILL PRESS

In Fig. 7-8, a standard drill press is illustrated, and the parts are named. Brief descriptions of the mechanisms are given. These part names and descriptions apply practically to any drill press and similar constructions are found in all drilling machines. Do not be satisfied merely to operate the machine—real satisfaction comes in knowing the construction and capabilities of the machine.

Driving Motor. Drives all of the mechanism of the machine. It does not drive the cutting lubricant pump.

Head Clamping Screws. Clamps head to the column.

Head Adjusting Shaft. Moves the head up and down to the desired position.

Box Column. Column on which the head rides.

Box Work Table. Table of machine on which work is clamped or on which the vise and other holding devices are placed or clamped.

Base. Provides a steady foundation for the column and table. Also serves as a reservoir for the cutting lubricant when used.

Speed-change Gearcase. Houses the gears that control the speed of the spindle.

Speed-change Lever. Controls the speed-change gears. Sets these gears for the desired spindle speed.

Spindle-control Lever. Operates the start, stop, forward, and reverse of the machine.

Feed Depth Dial. Dial indicator used to determine the depth of the hole when feeding the drill into it.

Dial Clamping Handle. Lever used to change dial setting positions.

Spindle. Part holding the drill chuck or socket.

Feed-change Gearcase. Houses the feed mechanism.

Feed-change Lever. Controls the setting of the feed.

Feed Clutch. Permits the operator to engage or disengage the feed without removing his hand from the lever that controls the advance and return of the spindle.

Feed Handwheel. Wheel used to control hand feed.

Cutting-lubricant Control Valve. Regulates the flow of the lubricant when the cutting lubricant pump is operating.

Electric Control Box. Box containing the electrical controls for the machine.

Table Adjusting Crank. Crank used to adjust the height of the table.

Feed Shaft. Shaft used to control the feed.

Cutting Lubricant Pump. Pump that feeds the cutting lubricant to the drill and work.

QUESTIONS ON DRILL-PRESS CONSTRUCTION

1. Clean the taper hole in the drill-press spindle. Why is it especially dangerous to clean a taper hole in a revolving spindle? How do you clean this hole? Why must it be clean and dry?

2. How is the table raised or lowered? How is it swung to the right or left on the column? How is it turned on its own axis?

3. Why, in some drilling machines, is provision made for raising or lowering the spindle head on the front of the column?

4. What is the maximum amount of the adjustment of the spindle head?

5. In operation, the drill-press spindle revolves in the spindle sleeve. Does the sleeve revolve?

6. How does the sleeve move in its bearing? What does it carry with it?

7. How is the spindle supported at its upper end? How is it made to revolve? Why is a long keyway, or spline, cut in the spindle?

8. How is the drill press started and stopped?

9. When are the back gears used? Why?

10. How are the back gears engaged?

11. Is it safe to engage the back gears when the machine is running? Give reason.

12. What is the use of the rack fastened to the spindle sleeve? What engages it?

13. What kind of a hole is in the end of the spindle? Why?

14. What is a sensitive drill press? Why is it so named?

15. What type of drilling machine is usually called simply *drill press*? Why?

16. What is a radial drill?

17. What is the advantage of a radial drill?

18. What is the value of a multiple-spindle drill?

19. What mechanical feature is common in all drilling machines?

20. How are drilling machines classified as to size?

21. What is the difference between an eight-spindle sensitive drill and a multiple drill?

CHAPTER 8

Drills and Drilling

Drilling-machine Operations. There are several operations involving holes that are usually done on the drill press (Fig. 8-1).

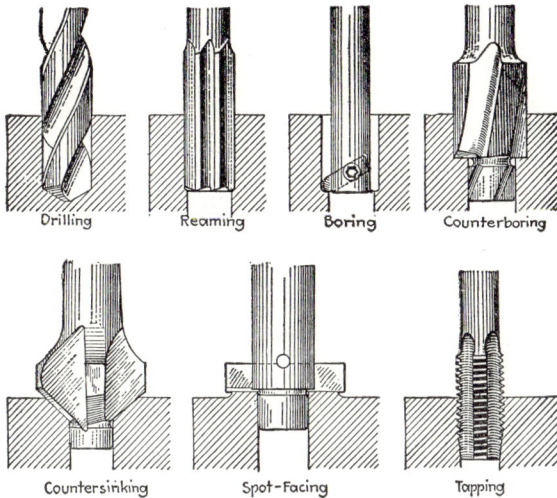

Drilling   Reaming   Boring   Counterboring

Countersinking   Spot-Facing   Tapping

Fig. 8-1. Drilling-machine operations.

Drilling is the operation of producing a circular hole by removing solid metal. The cutting tool used is called a *drill*.

Reaming is an operation of sizing and finishing a hole by means of a cutting tool having several cutting edges. This tool is called a *reamer.* Reaming serves to make the hole smoother, straighter, and more accurate.

Boring is the operation of enlarging a hole by means of an adjustable cutting tool with only one cutting edge.

Counterboring is the operation of enlarging the end of a hole cylindrically, as for a recess for a fillister-head screw.

Countersinking is the operation of making a cone-shaped enlargement of the end of a hole, as for a recess for a flathead screw.

Spot-facing is the operation of smoothing and squaring the surface around a hole, as for the seat for a nut or the head of a cap screw.

Tapping is the operation of forming internal threads by means of a tool called a *tap*. To withdraw the tap by power in a drill press requires either a reversible motor or a reversing attachment or *tapping attachment*. To withdraw a tap by hand, loosen the chuck or other holding device and remove.

In this chapter, information may be found concerning drills, methods of holding work, and the operations incident to drilling. If the student gathers an understanding of drills and drilling, he may apply the knowledge to other drill-press operations, brief discussions of which are in the next chapter.

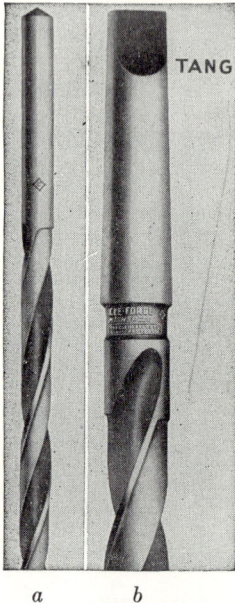

a   b

Fig. 8-2. (*a*) Straight and (*b*) taper shank drills. (*The Cleveland Twist Drill Company*)

Tool-holding Devices. The revolving spindle of the drill press carries the cutting tool. Some tools may be held directly in the spindle hole of the machine, others must be held in a taper socket, or drill chuck, or other device, the shank of which fits the tapered hole in the spindle.

The cutting tools used for any of the drill-press operations (except tapping) may be made either with straight shanks or taper shanks (Morse standard). It is usually considered best to have the smaller sizes of drills (drills under $\frac{1}{2}$ in.) provided with straight shanks because they can be conveniently and firmly held in a chuck (Fig. 8-6), and the extra cost of the taper shank on these sizes is unnecessary. In the larger sizes, the difference in cost between straight and taper shanks is not so great, and it is nearly

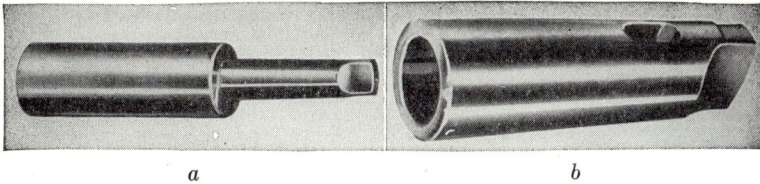

a   *b*

Fig. 8-3. (*a*) Drill-press socket and (*b*) sleeve. Cutting tools with taper shanks that are too small to fit the taper hole in the spindle of the machine are held in a small taper hole in a socket, the shank of which fits the spindle hole. If the socket makes too long an extension, a sleeve may be used. Sockets and sleeves are made in all necessary sizes, No. 1 to No. 2; No. 1 to No. 3; No. 3 to No. 4, etc., the first number denoting the size of the taper hole and the second number, the size of the taper shank. If a suitable socket or sleeve is not at hand, a combination of socket and sleeve or of two sockets or two sleeves may be used.

always more convenient to hold them by means of the taper shank. Figure 8-2 shows drills with a straight and taper shank.

Sockets and Sleeves. The drilling-machine spindle is provided with a Morse standard taper hole of a size in proportion to the size of the machine. Several sizes of drills, for example, have shanks which will fit the spindle,[1] others are too small and, to step the sizes, sockets or sleeves (Fig. 8-3) are used.

A tapered key or *drift* is used, as shown in Fig. 8-4, to remove the taper shank from the taper hole. Do not use anything but a drift for this purpose and use the rounded edge against the rounded edge of the hole.

The taper shanks of drills, reamers, counterbores, etc., and

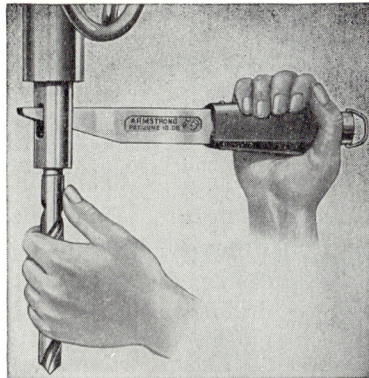

Fig. 8-4. Drift or taper key in use. (*The Armstrong Bros. Tool Company*)

also of the sockets and sleeves, have the end flattened to form a *tang* which fits in a suitable slot at the end of the taper hole in which

---

[1] The range of sizes of drills provided with a given size of shank is usually as follows: Sizes up to $9/16$-in. diam., No. 1 Morse taper; sizes $37/64$ to $29/32$ in., No. 2 Morse taper; sizes $59/64$ to $1\frac{1}{4}$ in., No. 3 Morse taper; sizes $117/64$ to 2 in., No. 4 Morse taper; sizes $21/64$ to 3 in., No. 5 Morse taper; sizes $31/16$ to 4 in., No. 6 Morse taper.

the shank is held (Fig. 8-4). The purpose of the tang is to help drive the drill, since the hold of the taper alone is not sufficient. It must be understood, however, that the tang alone is not sufficient to drive the drill or other cutting tool, and consequently, the taper shank and hole must be properly fitted, clean, and dry, and the shank must be firmly driven home or the taper will not do its share, and the result will be a twisted-off tang.

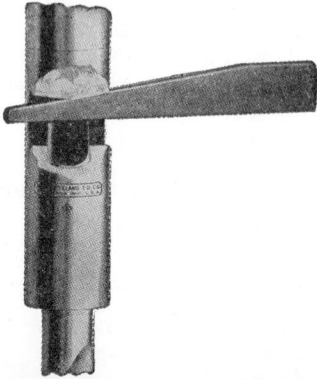

Fig. 8-5. Using the drift with Cleveland sockets and Cleveland drills. (*The Cleveland Twist Drill Company*)

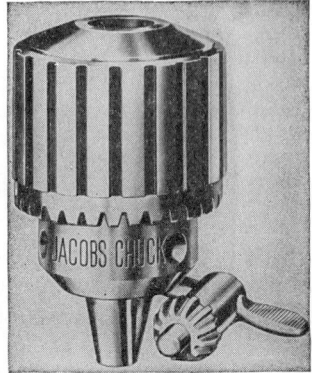

Fig. 8-6. A Jacobs drill chuck. (*The Jacobs Manufacturing Company*)

To mount a taper shank drill into the spindle, thrust the taper shank of the drill (or of the drill chuck, if a chuck is used) into the socket and the socket into the spindle. To secure the drill and drill socket, put a block of wood on the table and with the feed handle, bring the drill down sharply against the block to drive the drill and socket tight. If a drill chuck is used, secure it in the same manner and then grip the drill in the chuck. Figure 8-5 shows how to use a drift with Cleveland sockets and drills. Cleveland sockets, drifts, and drills are designed to prevent the battering or upsetting of the corners of the drill tangs by providing a bevel in the upper surface of the drift slot. This gives the wedge-shaped drift flat bearing surfaces above and below without lessening its driving power.

Drill Chucks (Fig. 8-6). A chuck is a gripping device with two or more adjustable jaws set radially. A drill chuck is made especially for holding *straight-shank* drills or other cutting tools in the spindle of the machine and is itself provided with a *taper shank* which fits the taper hole in the spindle. They are made in various sizes, and a series of three or four chucks will hold drills from the smallest size up to 1 in. in diameter. Figure 8-7 shows a drill chuck in a drill press.

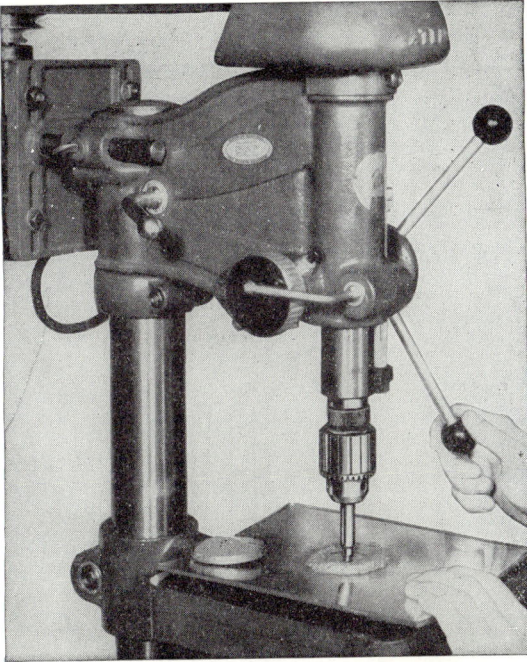

Fig. 8-7. A drill chuck in use. (*The Jacobs Manufacturing Company*)

Another type of chuck constantly used in production work is the *Magic chuck* (Fig. 8-8). This chuck makes possible the accurate locating of an unlimited number of successive tools in a drill press. Tools may be taken out while the spindle is revolving and other tools put in. Figure 8-9 shows how this is done. This chuck also saves time in changing tools whenever such changes are necessary. For example, if a hole is to be drilled and then tapped, the drill is put in first, the hole is drilled, and then the drill is taken out and replaced by the tap. It should be mentioned that the drill and tap must be mounted in special sockets or collets when used with this chuck. It is a simple operation using very little time. In production, time is

Fig. 8-8. A Magic chuck. (*The Collis Company*)

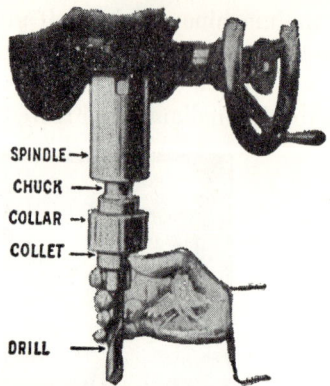

Fig. 8-9. Raise collar with thumb; collet and drill drops into hand. Only one hand required to change tools. (*The Collis Company*)

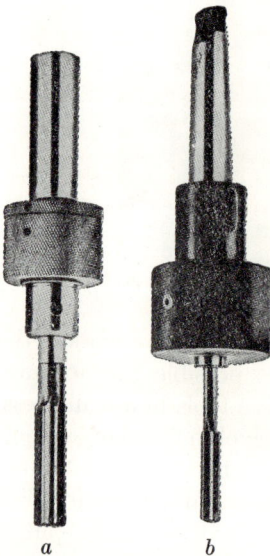

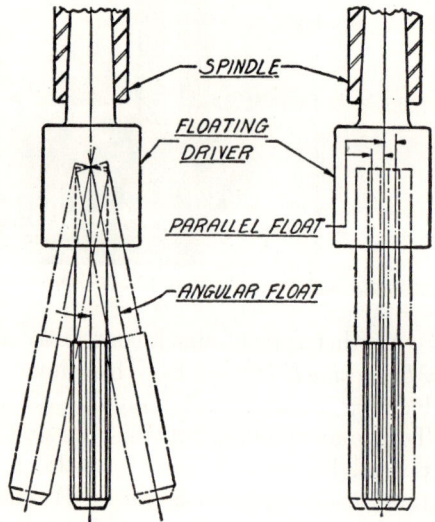

Fig. 8-10. Floating holders. (*a*) Straight shank and (*b*) taper shank. (*The United Aircraft Corporation*)

Fig. 8-11. Motions floating holder must permit. (*The United Aircraft Corporation*) very important since the cost of the article being manufactured is directly related to the time taken to make that article.

Another holding device used in machine shops is the *floating holder*. Figure 8-10 shows one with a straight shank and one with a taper shank. These holders are used to compensate for out-of-alignment of drill spindles or work, holders for reamers, counterbores, taps, etc., and permits self-aligning of the tool. Such holders are less necessary when jigs are used because the work is likely to be properly aligned and worn tools can be forced into alignment by jig bushings. Figure 8-11 shows the motions that floating holders must permit.

QUESTIONS ON DRILLING-MACHINE ACCESSORIES

1. What is a drill chuck? What kind of a shank has it? Why is the shank provided with a tang?
2. If the taper shank of the drill is too small for the hole in the spindle of the machine, how is the drill held?
3. What is a drift key used for? How is it used? What is the objection to using a drift upside down?
4. Give reason for wiping shank of drill or chuck clean and dry before being thrust into spindle.
5. Is the hold of the taper alone sufficient to keep the drill from turning in the socket? What two things hold the drill from turning?
6. What faults in the setting of the drill might result in the tang being twisted off?
7. Why are the smaller sizes of drills made with straight shanks?
8. Define drilling, reaming, boring, and spot-facing.
9. What is the difference between counterboring and countersinking?
10. If the taper shank of the chuck is too small for the spindle hole, what do you use? How is the chuck made secure in the spindle?
11. When would you use a Magic chuck? Why?
12. When would you use a floating holder? Why?

Twist Drills. The drills most commonly used in the machine shop are twist drills. The twist drill is probably the most used and most efficient tool in the shop. Figure 8-12 shows such a drill with the main parts identified.

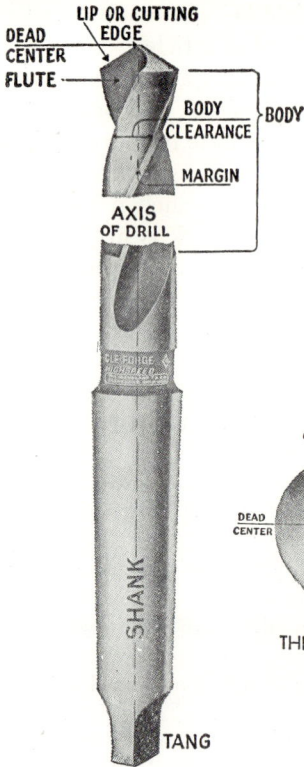

Fig. 8-12. Parts of a twist drill. (*The Cleveland Twist Drill Company*)

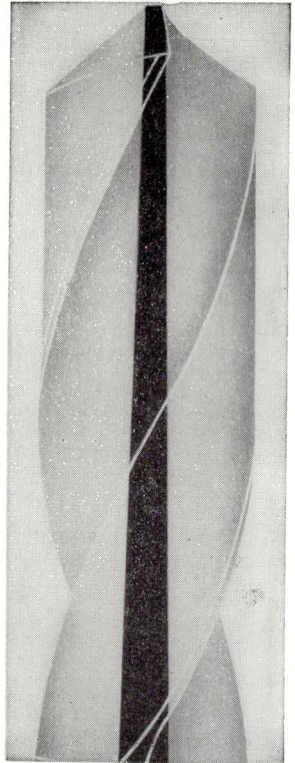

Fig. 8-13. The web of a drill. (*The Cleveland Twist Drill Company*)

DEFINITIONS: DRILL PARTS AND FUNCTIONS

Point. The point is the conical part of the drill. On the point, the cutting lips are ground.

Body. The body is the part of the drill that is fluted and relieved.

Shank. The shank is the part that fits into the holding device.

Flute. The flute is the groove of the drill. It carries out the chips and admits the coolant.

Tang. The tang is the flattened end of the taper shank. It helps drive the drill and provides means for driving the drill from the socket without injuring the shank.

Dead Center. Dead center is the point at which the two lips, properly ground, meet.

Lips. The lips of a drill are its cutting edges.

Margin. The margin is the narrow surface along the groove that determines the size of the drill and keeps the drill aligned.

Web. The web is the narrow section between the flutes. It is the "backbone" on the drill (Fig. 8-13).

Twist drills are made in *number* sizes; No. 1 (0.228 in. diameter) to No. 80 (0.0135 in. diameter). They are also made in *letter* sizes; A (0.234 in. diameter) to Z (0.413 in. diameter). See Table 18, page 542, for all sizes of number and letter drills. They are also made in sizes ranging from $\frac{1}{64}$ in., in sixty-fourths of an inch to 4 in. or larger, and in metric sizes as well. The smaller sizes of drills are not usually marked and the size is found by the use of a *drill gage* (Fig. 8-14).

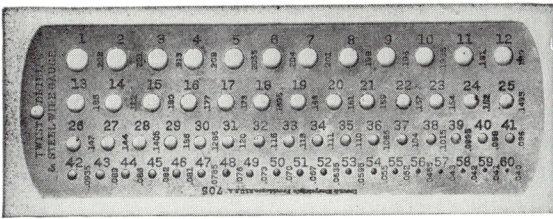

Fig. 8-14. A twist drill and steel wire gage. (*The Brown & Sharpe Manufacturing Company*)

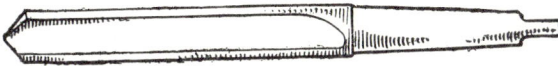

Fig. 8-15. Taper-shank straight-fluted drill.

The Straight-fluted Drill. For drilling brass, copper, and other soft metals, a drill with rake (a twist drill) has a tendency to "dig," or "grab." A straight-fluted Farmer drill (Fig. 8-15) is the best to use for soft metals, but a twist drill may be used if the fronts of the lips are ground as shown in Fig. 8-16. It is also advisable to use a drill without rake when drilling very thin stock because of the tendency of the drill to "hook" into the work when it is breaking through.

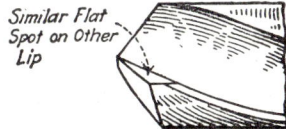

Similar Flat Spot on Other Lip

Fig. 8-16. Twist drill ground for use on brass.

A drill ground in this manner is very effective for drilling unannealed steel and hard spots in cast iron when turpentine is used as a lubricant.

The Flat Drill. Occasionally when it is required to drill a hole of a size for which a twist drill is not at hand, it is convenient to know that a flat drill (Fig. 8-17) will do good work. It may be made easily

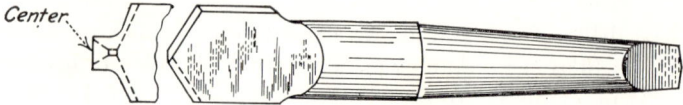

Fig. 8-17. Homemade flat drill.

and quickly. A piece of round carbon steel or drill rod of a suitable diameter is forged flat on one end so that it will be wider than the body, centered, the shank turned straight or tapered as desired, and the narrow sides of the flat portion turned to the size required. If the drill is of a sufficient size to warrant the extra operation, the cutting edges can be turned to the included angle of 118 deg., leaving a teat which may then be filed off. If greater accuracy is required, the shank and body may be left large enough to grind on centers after hardening and tempering. In this case the teat will, of course, be left on until these surfaces are finished and will be ground off when the drill is sharpened.

The three-fluted drill (Fig. 8-18), so called because it resembles a twist drill, would perhaps more properly have been named a *three-*

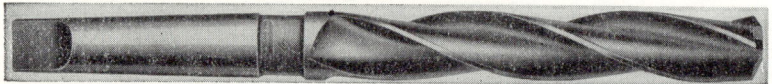

Fig. 8-18. Three-fluted drill. (*The Cleveland Twist Drill Company*)

tooth spiral reamer, since its function is enlarging cored, punched, or drilled holes. It will not drill the initial hole, but being very sturdy and having wide cutting edges, it is an efficient tool when a hole must be considerably enlarged.

Oil-tube Drills. When manufacturing quantities of steel parts in which it is required to have holes ½ in. or more in diameter drilled fairly deep, it has often proved economical to use drills with oil tubes (or holes) running lengthwise spirally through the body to carry the oil directly to the cutting lips. Such a drill with the necessary oil-feeding socket is illustrated in Fig. 8-19. The oil is carried from the reservoir (any suitable can or pail set fairly high to give sufficient pressure and provided with a stopcock will do) through a pipe to the tube on the side of the collar. The collar may be held from turning with the socket by using a piece of ¼ in. gas pipe long enough to reach the column of the machine or other suitable stop.

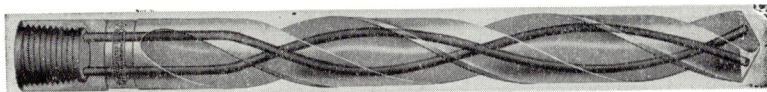

Fig. 8-19a. Oil-tube drill. (*The Cleveland Twist Drill Company*)

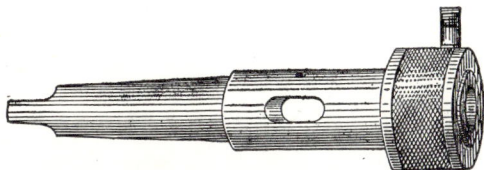

Fig. 8-19b. Oil-feeding socket.

The collar and also the body of the socket are provided with channels through which the oil is forced into the holes in the shank of the drill, which register with the channels, and thence through the tubes in the drill to the cutting edges.

SHARPENING A DRILL

Drill-grinding Machine (Fig. 8-20). In shops where any considerable amount of drilling is done, it is economical to have a drill-grinding machine. This machine may be quickly adjusted to support a drill of any length or diameter in a wide range of sizes and is so designed that it is a very simple matter to grind the drill properly, that is, with the lips of equal length, at the correct angle with the axis, and with the correct clearance. However, there are many times when it is advisable and even necessary to grind a drill by hand, and every *real* machinist knows how to do it correctly and quickly.

Principles of Sharpening a Drill. Drills are made of carbon steel and high-speed steel. Some special drills are carbide-tipped. These are used for special jobs when the two other types of drills are unsatisfactory.

Although high-speed drills have gained place in production work, it is still possible to obtain the smaller sizes ($\frac{1}{4}$-in. and under) made of carbon steel. Industry stopped using carbon drills because they were too soft and did not hold up under production methods. How-

Fig. 8-20. A drill grinder. (*The Hisey-Wolf Machine Company*)

ever, school machine shops still use the carbon drill because of its cheapness in comparison with the high-speed drill.

When sharpening or using a carbon-steel drill, extra care must be taken not to let it get hot enough to lose the temper. If the cutting edge shows blue, it indicates the temper has been lost in that part, and the drill must be shortened that much in order to grind the soft part away. This means not only extra work but also waste of the drill. Have plenty of water ready and use care. If necessary to grind a high-speed drill dry, never dip it in water to cool it, because this is likely to crack the lips.

Drills, like other cutting tools, have a cutting angle, a cutting edge, and various *clearance angles*. These angles are explained and described in the paragraphs that follow.

Lip Clearance. In order to cut properly, the drill must have a certain lip clearance. *Lip clearance* is the "relief" that is given to the cutting edges in order to allow them to enter the metal without interference. Figure 8-21 shows a properly ground drill with the

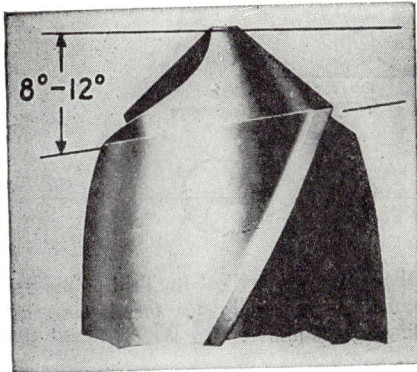

Fig. 8-21. Properly ground drill showing correct angle for lip clearance. (*The Cleveland Twist Drill Company*)

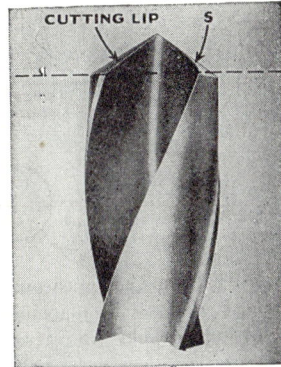

Fig. 8-22. A drill point without any clearance. Note that both the cutting lip and the heel *S* are in the same plane. (*The Cleveland Twist Drill Company*)

proper lip clearance. The heel has been ground below the lip, giving the lip an opportunity to feed in. General purpose drills are given a lip clearance of 8 to 12 deg. Figure 8-22 shows lips without clearance. Such a surface can only rub on the stock with which it comes into contact. The heel, which is on the same plane as the lip, prevents the lip from cutting the work.

Angle of Clearance at Center of Drill. The angle of clearance at the center of the drill should be greater than the angle at the circumference of the drill. The reason for this is clear. When 0.002 in. of stock is removed as the drill turns one-quarter of a revolution, it is distributed around a much larger sector on the circumference

of the drill than at the center. The angle of clearance at the center
must be proportional to the angle at the outside. The clearance on
a drill is about 12 deg. at the cutting edge. If correctly sharpened,
the edge of the angle across the web of the drill (the *dead center* of
the drill) will be about 45 deg. with the line of the cutting edges
(Fig. 8-23a). The appearance of the dead center is therefore an
index to the clearance; when it is like Fig. 8-23b, the lips have too

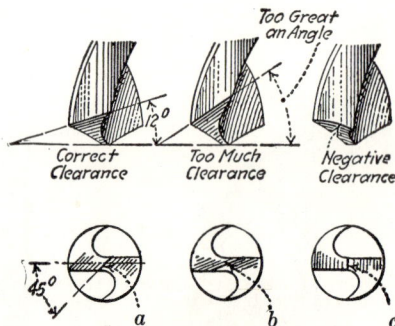

Fig. 8-23. From the appearance of the "dead centers" of the drill points—the
lines *a*, *b*, and *c*—the machinist would know if the lip clearance is correct or
not, as indicated in the corresponding figures above.

much clearance, and when it is like Fig. 8-23c, the lips have no clearance. Lip clearance is very important as it takes considerable pressure to feed the drill into the work under the best possible conditions, owing to the nature of the point, and if the lips are not
properly backed off, the drill will break under feeding pressure
simply because it cannot cut.

A drill must not be given too much clearance because excess clearance leaves insufficient thickness of lip to carry off the generated
heat. It also leaves insufficient stock behind the cutting edge usually required for its support, thereby weakening the cutting edge.

A drill must have sufficient clearance. A drill lacking enough clearance will not be able to cut properly but will be forced into the
work until it breaks. It causes the drill to "wander," making oversized holes.

The following table shows the amount of clearance in degrees for
various metals:

Metals	Degrees
Soft and medium steels	12 to 15
Hard steels	7 to 12
Aluminum	12 to 15
Brass	12

Angle and Length of Lip. In grinding a drill, it is important that the angle of the point be correct, that the angles and lengths of the

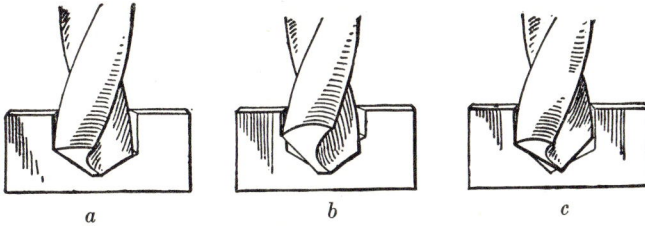

Fig. 8-24. (a) Lips of different lengths; drill will cut oversize. (b) Lips with different angles with axis of drill; drill will wobble and cut oversize. (c) Lips with different inclinations; one lip does practically all the work, which tends to crowd the drill toward the opposite side and wear off the land.

lips be equal. Drills having unequal angles or unequal lengths of lips, or both, will result in oversize holes.

Great care must be taken to get the lips exactly the same length and both at the same angle with the axis of the drill. Figure 8-24 illustrates just what happens if the lengths of the lips are not exactly the same or the angles are not the same.

Theoretically, if the edges of the drill are ground at an angle of 59 deg. with the axis, the best results will be obtained in most materials. Therefore, the drill should be held at about 59 deg. with the face of the grinding wheel (Fig. 8-25). For testing the angles and the relative lengths of the cutting edges, there are several types of gages, four types being made by The Morse Twist Drill and Machine Company. Any protractor will check the angles if these special gages are not handy.

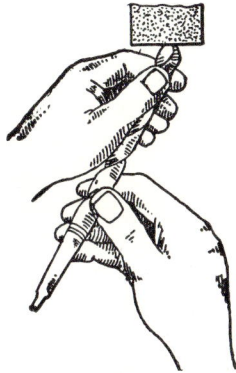

Fig. 8-25. About 59 deg. is the correct angle at which to hold drill against the face of the grinding wheel.

In order not to waste an expensive drill, practice grinding the end of a flat piece of stock, say ⅛ by 1 in., to the shape of the cutting edges of a flat drill (Fig. 8-17).

Figure 8-26 shows a lip angle for drills used in general work.

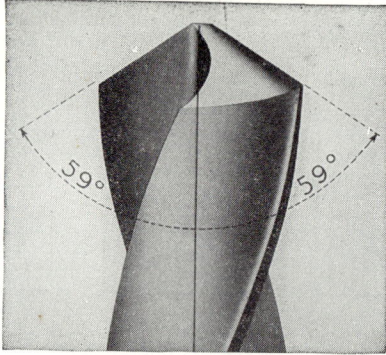

Fig. 8-26. Lip angles for drills used in general work. (*The Cleveland Twist Drill Company*)

Rake. Rake is an angle that forms the cutting wedge. It increases the keenness of a tool. As commonly considered, the angle of rake is not the angle the flute makes with the work. This would be true if there were no point angle, but when the drill is pointed, the actual rake is less than the angle the flute makes with the work. The smaller the angle of the point, the less the rake angle. This is illustrated by Fig. 8-27.

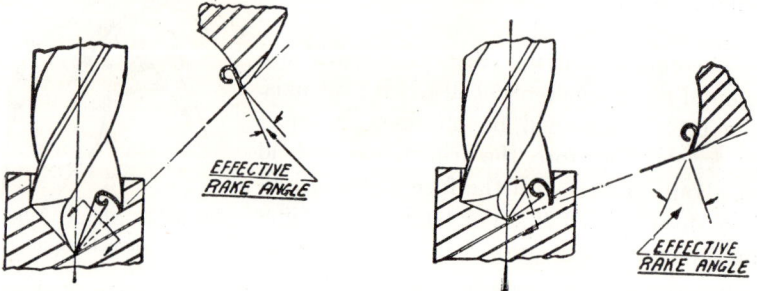

Fig. 8-27.

Rake angle is determined pretty much by the manufacturer. However, in two cases, it is changed by grinding the drill: very hard steel requires that the rake be reduced in order to increase the support behind the cutting edge; brass and bronze require no rake.

The Operation of Sharpening a Drill

1. Hold the drill with hands placed about as shown in Fig. 8-25. (Hands may be reversed if this is found to be easier operation.)
2. Have the axis of the drill (or practice piece) about 60 deg. with the face of the grinding wheel. This will give the desired angle between the cutting edges.
3. Hold the edge to be sharpened parallel to the top of the tool rest, that is, in a horizontal position.
4. Hold the right hand (and the shank of the drill) a little lower than the left hand and press the drill against the grinding wheel. Holding the shank a little lower serves to give the clearance.
5. Grind the other lip in the same manner.
6. If the right hand is too far down, too much clearance will be ground, and the end will look like Fig. 8-23*b*; if not down far enough, no clearance or *negative* clearance may result, like Fig. 8-23*c*.
7. Do not grind too much off one lip before grinding the other; keep them pretty much alike, and when finished, they should be of the same length and the same angle with the axis of the drill.
8. When both lips are ground correctly, then grind the heel—the remainder of the end of the drill—just enough to make a finished job.
9. Do not *twist* the drill when grinding it; pivot it a little (rock it) in the left hand, enough to give the clearance, and later to grind off the heel.
10. Grind in a direction *from* the edge *to* the heel, never from the heel to the edge.

Drill Points for Different Materials. The point angles of twist drills vary for different materials from 60 to 150 deg. with about 118 deg. for average work (see Fig. 8-28). The Morse Twist Drill and Machine Company, after many experiments with different angles of points in various grades of materials, recommend the following (refer to Fig. 8-28):

150 deg. for hard materials, flatted as in *b*, and with not over 10-deg. clearance.
125 deg. for heat-treated steel and drop forgings.
118 deg. for average class of work (shown in *a*).
100 deg. for copper.
 90 deg. for soft cast iron.
 60 deg. as in *c*, for wood, hard rubber, bakelite, and fiber.

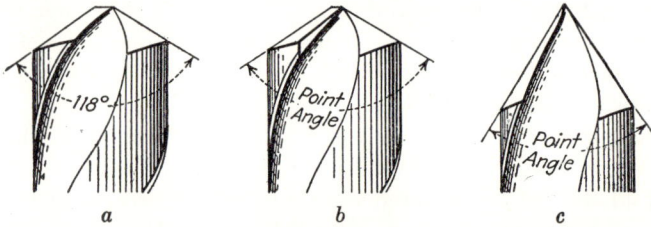

Fig. 8-28.

Thinning the Point of a Drill. To strengthen a drill the web is made thicker toward the shank. This is not noticeable on drills under ¾ in. in diameter; but on larger sizes, as the drill is shortened, it becomes necessary to grind the point somewhat thinner as shown in Fig. 8-29. Use a narrow grinding wheel and be careful to preserve the center by grinding an equal amount from each side, and also not to weaken the web unnecessarily by thinning too far back.

Fig. 8-29. Thinning the point of a drill.

Speeds and Feeds of Twist Drills. Owing to the variations of the hardness and toughness of the materials used in machine-shop practice, no hard and fast rule can be given for the speeds and feeds of twist drills.

The correct speeds and feeds must be determined by the judgment of the operator, and the following hints will help the beginner to obtain this necessary knowledge.

1. When the cutting edge breaks off, the feed is too heavy or the drill has been given too much clearance.

2. When the drill splits, there is too much feed or the drill has not been given enough clearance. *There seems to be a tendency for the beginner to give insufficient lip clearance toward the center of the drill. The whole length of the lip must be backed off or the drill will surely break under the feeding pressure.*

3. The rapid dulling of the drill especially at the outer ends of the lips (the corners) is evidence of too much speed and too much clearance.

4. When a drill squeaks, it is usually an indication of a crooked hole or dullness caused by the margin of the drill becoming worn. Never allow a drill to squeak.

The following tables of speeds and feeds are given here as having proved practical for average conditions:

Average Cutting Speeds with Drills of High-speed Steel*

Stainless steel and Monel metal	50 ft. per min.
Annealed high-carbon (tool) steel	60 ft. per min.
Low-carbon (machine) steel	80 ft. per min.
Very soft steel and soft gray iron	100 ft. per min.
Brass and copper	200 ft. per min.
Aluminum	300 ft. per min.

* Average cutting speeds with carbon steel are about half the above.

Average Feeds for Drills

Same feeds *per revolution* for high-speed as for carbon-steel drills.
Sensitive (hand) feed for number-size drills.
0.005 in. per revolution for $\frac{1}{4}$ to 0.015 in. for $1\frac{1}{2}$ in. and up.

Calculation for R.P.M. of a Drill. To know how to get the number of revolutions per minute (r.p.m.) of the spindle to give the proper cutting speed (CS) for a given diameter of drill is very important. The method and formula are given here.

METHOD: To obtain the number of revolutions of the drill-press spindle necessary to give the proper cutting speed for the drill, proceed as follows: (1) know whether the drill is carbon steel or high-speed steel; (2) determine what cutting speed is suitable for that kind of drill and the material it is to cut (from experience or from a table); (3) divide four times the cutting speed by the diameter of the drill; (4) set the drill for the nearest available speed.

FORMULA:

$$r.p.m. = \frac{4CS}{D}$$

EXAMPLE: To find the r.p.m. of a carbon-steel drill $\frac{5}{8}$ in. in diameter to cut soft machine steel.

SOLUTION:

1. Carbon-steel drill to be used.
2. To cut machine steel with a carbon-steel drill, the recommended speed is one-half that of a high-speed drill, or 40 ft. per min. (f.p.m.).
3. $r.p.m. = \dfrac{4 \times 40}{\frac{5}{8}} = 256$ f.p.m.
4. Nearest spindle speed is, say, 235.

The Use of Cutting Fluids and Coolants. It is a well-known fact that the use of some kind of cutting fluid and coolant when cutting metal, with the exception of cast iron, makes for greater production, better finish, and longer tool life. In ordinary lathe turning, and in shaper and planer work, cutting fluid is not used because the advantages to be obtained from using enough fluid do not compensate for the untidiness. However, in mass production procedures, cutting fluids are used. In drill-press work, however, it is necessary to use a lubricant in order not to tear the surface of the holes, drilled, reamed, or tapped, and also not to ruin the cutting tool.

In drilling or otherwise machining cast iron, a cutting fluid is not necessary because the chips break easily, and the graphite in the casting acts to reduce the friction. The mixture of chips and fluid often clogs the drill and other cutters and it is always very dirty. Because cast iron contains some sand, this mixture of sand and fluid often acts like an abrasive which produces poor surfaces and shortens tool life.

Lard oil is the original fluid used and is still highly prized, but it is expensive. Sulfur added to lard oil has an advantage in drilling hard or tough materials. Oil manufacturers make a sulfurized mineral-lard cutting oil which is recommended for the more difficult drilling.

For machining stainless steel, a cutting compound made of two parts of sulfurized cutting oil and one part of carbon tetrachloride is recommended. *CAUTION:* Carbon tetrachloride is poisonous and its use is forbidden as a coolant in some states.

For ordinary drilling, there are a number of soluble oils on the market which, when mixed with from 10 to 20 parts water, make very satisfactory lubricants and coolants.

Cutting Lubricants Used in Drilling, Reaming, and Tapping

Metal	Lubricant
High-carbon steel	Lard oil or a reliable soluble oil
Low-carbon steel and wrought iron	Lard oil or soluble oil
Unannealed steel and hard spots in cast iron	Turpentine
Malleable iron	Soda water or soluble oil
Aluminum and copper	Kerosene or kerosene and lard oil mixed
Brass and bronze	Dry or a flood of soluble oil
Cast iron	Dry

QUESTIONS ON DRILLS AND DRILL GRINDING

1. How is the drill held when grinding by hand? Is it placed on the hand rest, or held in the hand? Why?

2. How is the drill grasped with the right hand?

3. What angle does the center line of the drill, as properly held, make with the face of the grinding wheel? Why not 45 deg.? Why not 30 deg.?

4. Why is the drill held with the cutting edge up and in a horizontal position?

5. How is the drill moved against the wheel to "back off" the cutting edge? Why not give it a twisting motion?

6. What do you mean by fulcruming the drill in the left hand?

7. Why must care be taken to have plenty of water available when grinding a drill?

8. How much clearance has the cutting edge of the drill?

9. What part of the twist drill is the lip? The point? The land?

10. What is the effect of too much lip clearance? Of not enough lip clearance?

11. How can you tell by looking at the point of a drill whether or not the drill has been given sufficient lip clearance?

12. Has the drill any other clearance?

13. What is *rake* on any cutting tool?
14. What governs the amount of rake on a twist drill?
15. Why can no set rule be given for the speeds and feeds of drills?
16. What does the squeak of a drill indicate?
17. What do you mean by the land of the drill being worn away? What causes this? How do you repair the drill?
18. How many revolutions per minute should a ¾-in. drill be run to give a cutting speed of 35 ft. per min.?
19. State two advantages of the spiral flute.
20. On what kinds of work is a straight-fluted drill used?
21. State two advantages of using a cutting compound when drilling steel.
22. When is turpentine used as a cutting lubricant?
23. What is the advantage of an oil-tube drill? When is it used?
24 State how you would make a flat drill 1½ in. in diameter.
25. What is the purpose of thinning the point of a drill?
26. What care should be taken when thinning the point?

WORK-HOLDING DEVICES

Work is held on the drill press by means of clamps, vises, and jigs. Production work is rarely clamped onto the table. Equipment necessary for clamping down work is simple and inexpensive, consisting merely of clamps of various sorts, bolts, and sometimes parallels. But locating work to be clamped is very slow, accurate only when painstakingly performed, and even then not altogether sure. Furthermore, the method provides no means for holding the cutting tool in alignment as does the drill jig. The method is reserved for the repair shop and the tool room where jigs would be too expensive and whose mechanics are highly skilled.

Occasionally, production work is held in a vise. However, even a vise does not accurately locate work and in addition does not provide means for holding cutting tools in alignment. Vises are also largely used for holding work in the repair shop and toolroom.

Jigs (Fig. 8-30). This figure shows work held in a drill jig while the work is being drilled. Jigs are the production means of holding work for drilling. Quantity production allows the building of expensive fixtures for holding work. Jigs hold work securely. They are quickly loaded and unloaded. They provide means for guiding tools into work at proper relative positions and for holding holes to size.

Fig. 8-30. Work being drilled in a jig. (*Moore Drop Forge Company*)

Jigs have hardened steel bushings, through which the drill is guided so that the holes are accurately located in the work. Figure 8-31 shows various types of jig bushings.

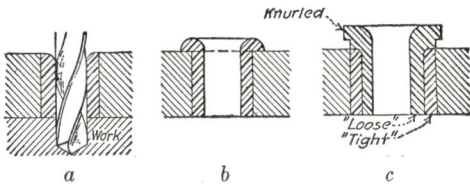

Fig. 8-31. Types of jig bushings. (*a*) Headless type bushing, (*b*) head type bushing, (*c*) slip-type bushing.

Where two or more different sizes of holes are to be drilled, it is customary to use a multiple-spindle drill (or to set up a gang drill or even several machines with the drills or other cutting tools in proper sequence in the respective spindles) and pass the jig from one spindle to the next.

In the larger toolmaking departments the holes for the jig bushings are bored to the ten-thousandth of an inch in *jig borers*. A jig borer is a precision-built drilling and boring machine resembling a drill press. It is provided with a compound table of extreme accuracy, and other facilities for adjusting and machining the work within limits of less than the ten-thousandth of an inch.

In the absence of a jig borer, jigs may be bored in a lathe, or in a milling machine, or in a drill press provided with a precision compound table (Fig. 7-3).

Jigs vary in cost from a few dollars to several hundreds of dollars, depending on the number and location of the holes, the accuracy required, and the size of the jig. The jig is used in manufacturing numbers of duplicate pieces. It is one of the most important of the rapid-production tools in that it saves the time of laying out and also the extra expense of drilling to a layout.

For run-of-shop jobs, toolmaking, and model work, jigs are not available. The work must first be laid out and then either held against a stop or clamped in some manner and drilled.

Generally speaking, it calls for more intelligence and skill to set up the job in a vise or on the table, and drill the holes to layout, than is involved in the use of a jig; consequently it is more interesting. It is important that every machinist shall be able to lay out and set up the work and drill the holes accurately without the use of a jig. An example of laying out, a description of clamping accessories, and a few hints on clamping the work follow.

The Use of Clamps and Stops. All drill-press work, except the heavy pieces, should be either clamped to the table, or located

Fig. 8-32. One type of drill vise. (*Desmond-Stephan Manufacturing Company*)

against a stop. A flat clamp or similar piece makes a suitable stop (Fig. 8-43). When a vise (Fig. 8-32) is used to hold the work, the vise should be clamped to the table or located against a stop. A jig also should be located against a stop. *Never should the work be held by hand against the force of a revolving drill or other cutting tool.*

As a matter of fact, a stop is sufficient for most jobs, and in many cases is better than a clamp. It allows the work to move a little and "find its own center," and there is less likelihood of inaccurate alignment with the drill point. This is especially true when the spot has been gouged with the chisel (Fig. 8-42).

If the work is fairly high, and a stop is used, have the stop high enough to counteract the tendency of the work to tip. If the work tips, the hole will be incorrect. In many jobs it is best to spot the hole the full diameter of the drill when against the stop, and then clamp the work before drilling the remainder of the hole.

The success of any job that must be clamped to the table of any machine such as the shaper, drill press, boring mill, or milling machine, the faceplate of a lathe, or the platen of a planer, depends almost entirely on the manner in which it is clamped.

Bolts. The worktable is provided with enough T slots to enable the operator to locate, conveniently, the necessary bolts for the stops and clamps.

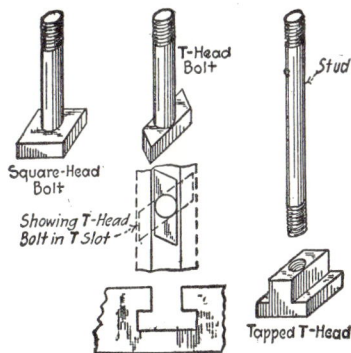

Fig. 8-33. Bolts.

The square-head bolt (Fig. 8-33) is satisfactory for ordinary clamping purposes, but to place it in position it must be pushed along the T slot from one end. The T-head bolt is placed by simply dropping the head lengthwise in the slot and turning it to the right, and is especially convenient when clamping inside of castings which would otherwise have to be lifted over the bolt. Many prefer the tapped T head, the stud of which may be removed and the head pushed along the slot under the work to the desired position. Studs of various lengths may be used as needed, requiring only a comparatively small number of heads.

Clamps (Fig. 8-34). The *plain slot* clamp, or *strap*, is provided with a bolt hole somewhat nearer the front end, or work end. The front end is usually beveled (Fig. 8-34*a*).

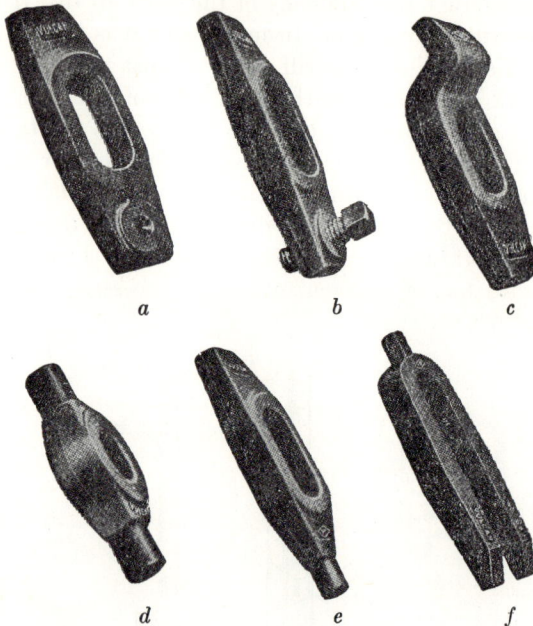

a   *b*   *c*

d   *e*   *f*

Fig. 8-34. Clamps. (*The United Aircraft Corporation*)

The *adjustable step* clamp has an adjusting screw which permits the leveling of the strap from the work to the step block (Fig. 8-34*b*).

The *goose neck* clamp permits clamping of work of large thicknesses without the use of long clamping bolts. It reduces the height of the step block required (Fig. 8-34*c*).

The *finger, double end*, clamp is used mostly in production work, each finger being inserted in a hole to clamp the work (Fig. 8-34*d*).

The *finger, single end*, clamp is made to use in a hole in the job using the ordinary block in clamping (Fig. 8-34*e*).

The U clamp may be removed from the bolt without removing the nut. It is very convenient for purposes of adjustment (Fig. 8-34*f*).

Clamping Blocks. The block under the outer end of the clamp may consist of a piece of handy scrap metal of the required dimensions, or if of considerable height, suitable pieces of hard wood may be used. Have the wood of sufficient cross section to give the needed stiffness, and arrange it under the clamp so that the pressure will be exerted *lengthwise of the grain*, so that it will not crush. Figure 8-35 shows a step block which is very useful. Both bases are finished and either may be used.

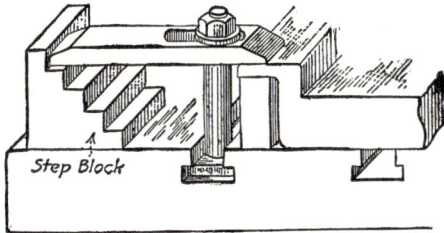

Fig. 8-35. Using step block.

Shims. A shim is a piece placed between the table and the work or for that matter between any two pieces or parts for purposes of adjustment or to give support. A shim may be rectangular or tapered slightly, and may be of metal, wood, or paper. Usually, however, a shim is considered as a thin piece of metal, while the heavier pieces are called *packing blocks.*

Hints on Clamping

1. A clamp should be properly placed and the clamping block must be the correct height or the work will become loosened, with probable damage to both work and machine.

2. The clamping bolt should be placed as close to the work as conditions will permit. By the principle of levers, the pressures on the work and on the clamping block are inversely proportional to their distances from the bolt. This is illustrated in Fig. 8-36.

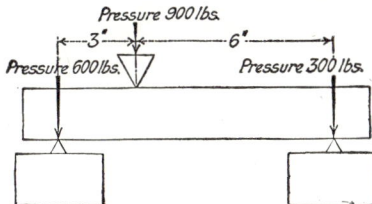

Fig. 8-36. The principle of levers. A mechanical principle that should be applied when clamping work.

3. The clamp should have a firm seat on both the work and the clamping block. The block should be at least high enough to bring the clamp parallel to the surface on which the work rests. It may be a trifle higher to ensure against an edge contact.

4. The clamp must not be placed over a part that will spring under pressure until a shim or packing block is placed under that part (Fig. 8-35).

5. Many pieces are spoiled owing to carelessness in cleaning the parts against which the work is seated or is clamped. When a piece is to be clamped in a vise, or against an angle iron or similar tool, care must be taken to clean away all chips and dirt.

6. Never use a nut without a washer.

7. The selection of the wrench, the way it is held and *controlled,* and the judgment as to force used are indications of a mechanic's skill. (Don't "bark" your knuckles because of an uncontrolled wrench!)

8. Oil the threads of the bolt or nut when dry.

9. Avoid using bolts that are much too long, and never use a bolt with only three or four threads catching in the nut.

10. Return clamps, bolts, and all other clamping accessories to the place where they belong. This is only fair to all concerned.

11. *A Very Important Precaution.* When setting up for drilling holes through the work, make sure that the work is so arranged as to permit the drill to go through without drilling into the vise or the table or the parallels.

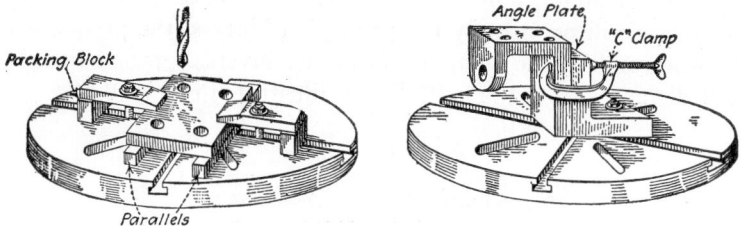

Fig. 8-37. Holding work on drill-press table.

Examples of Drilling Setups. Figure 8-37 shows methods of clamping work for drilling that are self-explanatory. Figure 8-38 illustrates a cylindrical piece held in V blocks and also the method of arranging the center-punch mark exactly over the axis of the cylinder, or *central*.

Laying Out for Drilling.[1] The process of laying out work for drilling consists of indicating by means of intersecting lines the

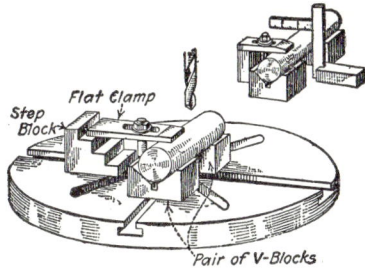

Fig. 8-38. If cylindrical piece is not too large, it may be clamped in a vise; if this is inconvenient, it may be clamped as shown. In either case, when setting up, have the work clamped lightly with the center-punch mark as nearly over the axis of the cylinder as may be judged by eye. Then, holding a square on the table and against the cylinder, roll the work until the measurement between the blade of the square and the center-punch marks equals one-half the diameter of the work. Finally, tighten securely.

positions of the *centers* of the holes to be drilled. At the point of intersection, a slight prick-punch mark is made, and using this as a center, a circle indicating the size of the hole is scribed with a divider. If the surface on which the layout is to be made has been machined, a coating of blue vitriol solution (copper sulfate) or dykem blue (a quick-drying solution used like copper sulfate) may be applied and allowed a moment to dry. The lines scribed on this surface will show very distinctly. Chalk, rubbed well into the unfinished surface of a casting, will serve the same purpose. A simple example is given here to illustrate two methods of laying out.

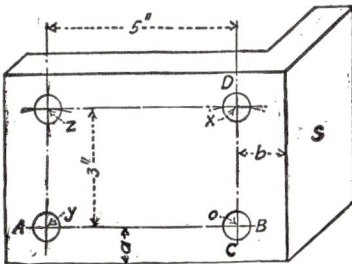

Fig. 8-39.

Example of Laying Out. Lay out and drill four ⅝-in. holes, symmetrically located, in the face of an angle plate as per the dimensions given in the sketch, Fig. 8-39.

[1] See also Chapter 6, page 158.

1. Measure the width of the plate, subtract 3 in., and divide by 2 to obtain the distance a.

2. Place the angle plate on a suitable parallel on a surface plate and with the surface gage scriber set the distance a above the parallel, scribe the line AB.

3. Measure the height of the angle plate, subtract 5 in., and divide by 2 to obtain the distance b.

4. Adjusting the surface gage to the distance b above the parallel and placing the angle plate on surface S, square-up line AB if necessary and scribe line CD.

5. The point of intersection of the lines AB and CD is the center o of one hole. Make a slight indentation at this point with a prick punch.

6. Set a divider to 3 in. and, on o as a center, scribe an arc intersecting the line CD at x. Make a slight prick-punch mark at x. This is the center of the second hole.

7. Set the divider to 5 in. and, with o as a center, scribe an arc intersecting the line AB at y, and, with x as a center and the same divider setting, scribe a fairly long arc at z. Make a prick-punch mark at the intersection of the arc at y and the line AB. This is the center of the third hole.

8. Carefully set the divider to 3 in. once more and, with y as a center, scribe another arc at z intersecting the arc already scribed. Make a prick-punch mark at the intersection of these two arcs. This is the center of the fourth hole.

9. Set the divider to $5\!/\!16$ in. and, with o, x, y, and z as centers, scribe the $5\!/\!8$-in. diam. circles to indicate the positions of the four holes.

Another method of finding the centers of the four holes is as follows: After line AB is drawn, set the scriber of the surface gage 3 in. higher and draw line through zx; after line CD is drawn set the scriber 5 in. higher and draw line through yz. Which method is more practicable depends upon the location of the holes and the size of the work and the available tools. The given example serves merely to illustrate the methods.

Whoever drills these holes will make larger indentations at the centers with a center punch. By the time the job reaches him, the circles may have become more or less obliterated and the rescribing should be done from a *prick-punch mark* rather than from a *center-punch mark*.

When the surface on which the layout is to be made is *unfinished* (for example, cast iron without the scale removed), a series of a half-dozen or more small center-punch marks ("witness" marks, used where accuracy is essential, but jigs are impractical) around the circle will serve to make the layout plainer (Fig. 8-40a). Take care to locate the marks exactly on the line, or they are worse than useless.

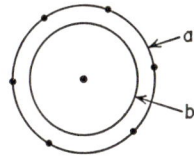

Fig. 8-40.

It is a good plan for the beginner when laying out holes he is to drill to scribe also from each center a circle somewhat smaller than the finished size of the hole, to help in gaging the central position of the spot made before the drill cuts its full diameter (Fig. 8-40b).

Use of Toolmakers' Buttons in Drilling. Figure 8-41 shows a set of toolmakers' buttons usually used in accurately locating holes to be drilled. These buttons are steel bushings which are tightened in exact positions on the work after the holes have been laid out. They are hardened and ground to a given diameter in even tenths of an inch, such as 0.300, 0.400, and 0.500 in. The ends, which

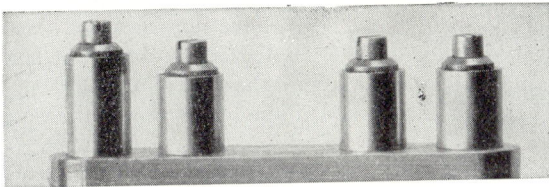

Fig. 8-41. Toolmakers' buttons. (*The Brown & Sharpe Manufacturing Company*)

rest firmly on the surface of the work, are ground square, permitting the button to seat firmly and squarely over the center of the proposed hole. These buttons are nearly always used with a vernier height gage, although in many cases micrometers and gage blocks may be used.

In using these buttons, the work to which they are clamped should be true, for if not, the buttons will slant parallel with the base and cause error in measurements. Once the work has been ground or planed true, any hole or series of holes to be drilled or bored should be laid out with scriber, scale, and dividers, which can be done within approximately 0.010 in. Prick-punch lines intersecting at points to be drilled or bored, drill and tap to sufficient depth, so that the 5"—40 pitch screw shall enable the button to be clamped tight. File the burr caused by tapping and screw the buttons to work just hard enough so that they may be tapped to position while locating.

The work should now be placed on a surface plate for final adjustment of buttons with the height gage. When in position for accurate boring, tighten clamping screws so that they will not move while being trued up and bored. Next, clamp to table and tap the work to bring buttons to run true with their axis by using a test indicator. See that the work is held fast to the table, being careful that the buttons have not moved while clamping in position; then remove the buttons, drill and bore.

QUESTIONS ON HOLDING WORK

1. What is the first care when setting up a drilling job?
2. Why is a stop usually sufficient for holding a vise? Why is it better for most work than a clamp?
3. Why is it necessary to use either a stop or a clamp?
4. Do the same principles apply to pieces not held in a vise?
5. If the work is fairly high, how are the stops arranged? Why two stops?
6. On what shape of work is the V block a convenient holding device? What angle with each other are the sides of a V block?
7. How is the V block secured to the table? How is the work held in the V block?
8. When is an angle iron a convenient tool for holding work? How is it fastened to the work table?
9. How is the work fastened to the angle iron?
10. What is a C clamp?
11. What care must be taken when applying a clamp?
12. Certain pieces are often supported by parallels and then clamped. What are parallels? Why are parallels used?
13. What is the advantage of a T-head bolt?
14. When clamping a piece of work why should the bolt be placed near the work?
15. Why is a packing block used under the clamp? How high should it be? Why?

16. What is a U clamp? What advantages has it?

17. What is a pin clamp (finger clamp) used for?

18. What do you mean by shimming a piece of work? What is the difference between blocking and shimming?

19. Why must the work be solid under the clamp? If the part where the clamp is applied overhangs, what must be done before clamping?

20. What are the objections to springing the work when drilling? How may it be avoided?

21. Make a sketch of a piece properly clamped, showing the work, the bolt, the clamp, and the packing block.

22 What is the use of a washer? Should a nut ever be used without a washer? Give reasons.

23. How far should a nut be screwed on a bolt? Give reasons.

24. What are the advantages of a jig?

25. In your opinion when is it profitable to make a jig?

26. For what reasons, do you think, is it more expensive to drill to a layout than to use a jig?

Hints on Drilling

1. Always examine a drill for size and sharpness before using it.

2. It often happens, through ignorance or carelessness, that a drill is used after it becomes dull, which causes the land to wear away for a distance back from the cutting edge. The diameter of the end of the drill is reduced, thus making the drill bind and squeak. It will be necessary to grind off the damaged end and then sharpen the drill.

3. Examine the job or the blueprint or both to determine the tools, bolts, clamps, etc., to use. Get these things together without making extra trips to the toolroom or elsewhere.

4. Have the shank of the drill and socket, or of the chuck, clean, dry, and tight in the spindle.

5. Be sure the setup is arranged so the drill will clear as it goes through the work, and not cut into the parallels, table, or vise.

6. Sometimes the condition of the drill, dull or with uneven lips, or the lips not ground to the proper angle with the axis, will cause the drill to wobble. Also, an uneven surface where the drill starts may cause the drill to run away from the center and to wobble. Forcing the feed, before the drill gets a chance to start evenly, will cause these troubles. To have the drill properly sharpened, and all

other conditions right, and then to start the drill carefully will save time in the end.

7. A drill will "follow" a hole already made, and many times it is a good plan to drill a hole, say $\frac{1}{8}$ in. in diameter and about $\frac{1}{4}$ in. deep, to keep the larger drill from running.

8. When the drill "breaks through" at the end of the cut, it has a tendency to "dig in," especially when drilling thin pieces, and also when drilling through a cylinder at right angles to the axis, or into another hole at right angles. Such pieces should be clamped down, and, especially when hand feed is used, care must be taken or a broken drill will result. The tendency to dig is greatly increased by lost motion in the thrust bearing between the spindle and sleeve.

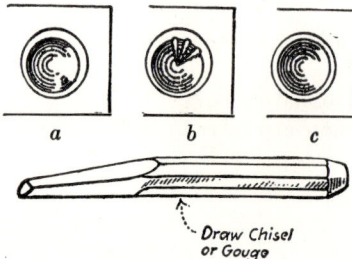

Fig. 8-42. Use of gouge to draw the spot to center.

9. When drilling small pieces, and thin pieces especially, it is often more convenient to place them on a suitable piece of board. Set the depth gage to allow the drill to go through the piece but not through the board. Such pieces may be stopped from turning by a nail driven in the board or they may be held by a clamp.

10. A squeak indicates undue friction. The cause should be looked for immediately and the fault corrected. Occasionally when drilling cast iron, it is advisable to rub a little oil or grease on the *lands* of the drill.

11. When a machine is overworked, it will "groan." A dull cutting tool, a chip under the cutting edge, a lack of lip clearance, and overfeeding are frequent causes. Throw out the feed at once and proceed to find and correct the fault.

12. Read carefully on pages 190–191 the causes of spoiled work and broken drills due to faulty grinding.

Drilling the Hole. Be sure that the drill is the right size, sharp, and securely held. If the work is not clamped, a stop must be provided. Be sure to clamp table securely before drilling.

Align the point of the drill carefully with the center-punch mark, start the machine and make a spot half or two thirds the diameter of the drill. Back the drill away from the work and note if the spot is central with the scribed circle. If not central, (Fig. 8-42*a*), chip one or more shallow grooves *b* on the heavy side. A drill will go toward the least resistance and chipping away stock on the heavy side will tend to make the drill cut toward that side. This operation may have to be repeated. Watch carefully and be sure the spot is central before it is the full diameter of the drill (Fig. 8-42*c*).

When a drill is properly ground, and operated at the correct speed and feed, the chips should appear as illustrated in Fig. 8-43.

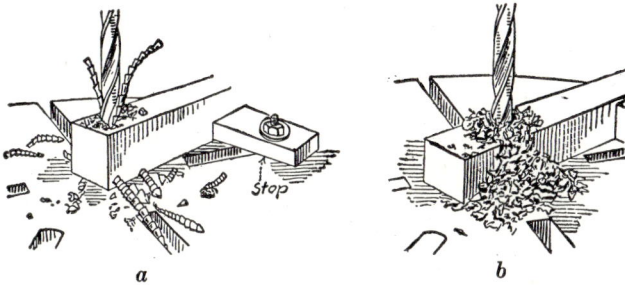

Fig. 8-43. Shows appearance (*a*) of steel chips and (*b*) of cast iron chips when properly sharpened drill is used. Shows also, the use of a stop to keep the work from swinging around as the drill revolves.

As the hole becomes deeper the chips break up more or less while being forced out. When the depth of the hole is several times the diameter of the drill, the removal of the chips becomes more difficult and it is often advisable to slightly increase the feed and decrease the speed as this gives a greater freedom of chip movement. Sometimes it is necessary to remove the drill from the hole to clean the chips (and if drilling steel to apply the cutting compound). A round file that has been magnetized is very useful for removing chips from the hole.

If, when drilling steel, the drill is removed from the hole, *great care must be taken when the drill is re-entered that a chip is not lodged between the point of the drill and the bottom of the hole.* When this happens the drill will ride on the chip, and if the feed is thrown in, the machine will be subjected to an enormous overstrain, and, if continued, either the machine or the drill will be broken. Always start the feed by hand, make sure the drill is cutting, then throw in the power feed.

When all conditions are right a fairly deep hole may be drilled straight. If, however, a hard spot or a blowhole is encountered, or if the work is not properly seated or held, or if the drill is improperly ground or dull, the hole is likely to "run." One can usually tell when a drill or other cutting tool is not acting properly by the "feel," by the sound, or by the appearance of the chip.

Drilling Large Holes. The larger the drill, the greater the thickness of the web between the flutes, and consequently the wider the point or dead center. The dead center of the drill has a very ineffective scraping action rather than a keen cutting action, and to feed efficiently a drill, say $1\frac{1}{2}$ in. in diameter, in a 20-in. drill press will unduly strain the machine. In such a case it will save time and trouble to thin the point of the drill as described on page 190.

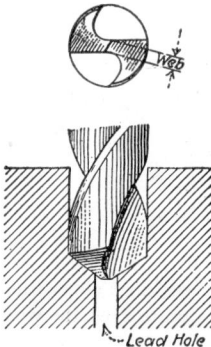

Fig. 8-44. Following a lead hole or pilot hole.

Some machinists prefer to drill a lead hole (Fig. 8-44) of a diameter equal to about the thickness of the web of the larger drill. It is very necessary to drill this hole accurately to layout because the larger drill will surely follow the small hole. Do not drill a lead hole much larger than necessary or the following drill may chatter and drill out of round or at least spoil the "mouth" (top) of the hole. In any event do not crowd the drill, that is, feed it too fast, when starting.

Do not brush the chips carelessly about and do not permit the cutting compound to flood the table and floor. When through using the bolts, clamps, or other tools, clean them and put them where they belong. An expert workman is neat and orderly.

QUESTIONS ON DRILLING

1. Secure a drill from the tool crib. Examine it. Is the drill properly sharpened? Have the cutting edges been given sufficient clearance?

2. If the hole is to be drilled through the piece, what precaution must be taken?

3. If the hole does not go through the piece, how may the depth be gaged on the spindle?

4. Is the depth of a drilled hole measured from the point or from the corner?
5. When, in general, is it necessary to use a clamp to hold the work? When is it better to use a stop? Why is it nearly always best to use one or the other? When may it be unnecessary?
6. How is a straight-shank drill held?
7. How is a taper-shank drill held? Why should the taper be clean and free from oil? How is the drill removed?
8. What is the difference between a prick-punch mark and a center-punch mark? When is each used?
9. When is chalk or whiting used in a layout? When is blue vitriol solution used in the layout?
10. Why are prick-punch marks sometimes made in the circles showing size and position of holes?
11. If two or more holes are to be drilled in a piece securely clamped to the table, how may they be located in turn under the drill without loosening the clamps?
12. State two things that will cause a drill to wobble.
13. If the center-punch mark in the layout is practically true, why will not the drill always start true and cut true?
14. If the spot shows out of center with the layout, a gouge chisel should be used. On which side of the spot is it used? How many chisel cuts should be made? How deep?
15. If a piece is clamped to the table before it is located exactly under the drill, is it necessary to adjust the table before drilling the hole if a draw chisel is used? Give reason?
16. How may chips be removed from a hole?
17. Is a lubricant used when drilling cast iron?
18. Does a squeak indicate proper or improper conditions? Why?
19. If a fairly deep hole is being drilled in cast iron, how may oil be used?
20. It is sometimes necessary to remove the drill from a partly finished hole. If a steel chip lies under the point of the drill when it is run back into the hole, what is the result? What is the remedy?
21. When does a machine groan?
22. Why is it best always to feed by hand until you are sure the drill is cutting?
23. If no chip is under the drill and the machine groans, what is indicated?
24. What is indicated when the extreme outer corners of the cutting edges of the drill wear away rapidly? What will happen if this fault is not immediately corrected?
25. Either one of two faults may cause the lips to chip. What are these two faults?

26. A very common fault in grinding causes a drill to split up the web; what is it?

27. How is the proper cutting speed of a drill determined?

28. How many revolutions per minute are necessary to cut 30 ft. per min. with a $\frac{7}{8}$-in. drill? To cut 40 ft.?

29. How many revolutions per minute are necessary to cut 40 ft. per min. with a drill $1\frac{1}{4}$ in. in diameter?

30. How many revolutions per minute are necessary to cut 35 ft. per min. with a $\frac{1}{4}$-in. drill?

31. What lubricant is used when drilling soft steel or wrought iron? When drilling unannnealed steel? When drilling aluminum?

32. How is a twist drill ground for drilling brass? Why?

32. What is meant by thinning the point of a drill? When is it advisable?

34. When is it advisable to use a pilot drill?

CHAPTER 9

Other Drill-press Tools and Operations

It is practically impossible to drill a hole to the exact size of the drill. Therefore, to obtain a hole of standard size, round and smooth, it is practical to drill or bore to $\frac{1}{64}$ in. undersize and then machine ream. If greater accuracy is required, it may be bored or machine-reamed to within 0.005 to 0.015 in. undersize, depending upon the size of the hole.

REAMERS

Reamers are made of either carbon-tool steel, high-speed steel or are carbide tipped; in hundreds of sizes; for general or specific purposes; in various types and kinds, straight, and in all standard and many special tapers. They are made with straight or taper shanks for machine use, and with squared shanks for hand reaming, and many sizes are available in either expansion or adjustable types.

Spiral teeth in a reamer cut more freely, and tend to prevent chatter and catching if there is a longitudinal slot or keyway in the hole.

The work is held for reaming in the same way as for drilling. In fact, it is the usual practice to follow the drill with the reamer under the same conditions that the drilling was done. However, there are times when a slower speed will give better results to the finished hole.

Reamer Terms. Most reamers are made up of three parts, *angle of chamfer*, *body*, and *shank* (Fig. 9-1).

The *angle of chamfer* is the part of the reamer that does the cutting, and is ground on every flute uniformly. It is so ground on each flute that there is clearance behind the chamfered cutting edges. This applies specifically to rose-type reamers. On fluted reamers, most of the cutting is done by the blades.

The *body* is made up of several flutes and lands, that is, the land being the part between each flute. On top of each land is a margin which runs from the angle of chamfer to the back end of the flute. There is relief or clearance in back of the margin known as the *body clearance angle*. The cutting face of most reamer lands form an angle with a line drawn from a point on the front marginal edge

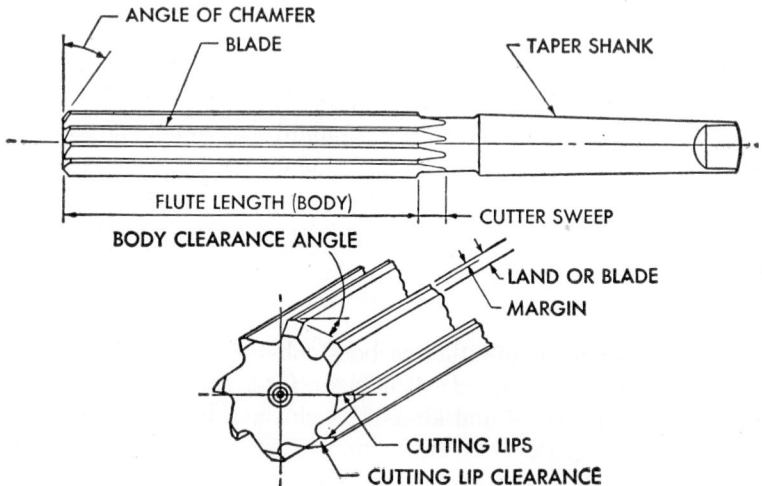

Fig. 9-1. Reamer terms. (*Whitman & Barnes*)

through the center. This angle is called the *rake angle*. If there is no angle, the cutting face of the land is said to be *radial*.

The *shank* (straight or tapered) is the driving end of the reamer and fits into the chuck or holder of the machine in which it is to be used.

Handling Reamers. A reamer has two edges on each blade that must be kept sharp in order that it may be a smooth-machining, free-cutting, and a long-lived tool. These are the end, or chamfered, cutting edge and the marginal, or blade edge. To keep these parts of the tools sharp and unbroken, keep reamers in separate containers and well protected. Reamers should not be thrown onto or rolled across hard metal surfaces such as steel bench tops.

Stock Removal Allowance. The life of reamers on many jobs is shortened because of insufficient amount of stock for the reamer to remove. The reason may be that the drill is to near the reamer size, or that the drill is cutting too much oversize.

Many jobs are so set that only 0.015 to 0.020 in. is left for the reamer to remove. If this is true, the reamer must start to cut under very abnormal conditions, as illustrated in Fig. 9-2. Owing to a lack of bushings, certain operating conditions, or improperly pointed drills, some holes may be drilled that are tapered or bell-mouthed. The tendency of the reamer is to wedge in the hole rather than to cut it. The result is severe reamer wear and breakage.

In ferrous metals an even greater amount of reaming stock should be provided. For the smaller diameters, this should be approximately $\frac{1}{64}$ in., but on sizes larger than $\frac{1}{2}$ in., the recommended amount of stock to leave is $\frac{1}{32}$ in.

Alignment of Reamers. To facilitate reamer and bushing life and to produce straight and well-machined holes, the spindle, reamer,

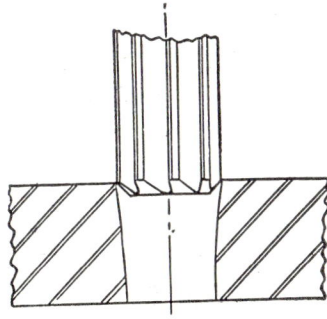

Fig. 9-2. A bell-mouthed hole. (*Whitman & Barnes*)

bushing (if one is used), and hole to be reamed should be in proper center-line alignment.

If there should be any misalignment between spindle and bushing, the result will be a worn bushing, which will result in a bell-mouthed hole plus a worn reamer. It is for this reason that many slip-type bushings are made of hardened steel.

Types of Reamers. Reamers are made in several types among which are the chucking or machine reamers, shell reamers, hand reamers, adjustable reamers, expansion reamers, and taper reamers. Each will be described briefly.

Chucking or Machine Reamers (Fig. 9-3). There are two types of machine reamers, rose reamers and fluted reamers. In the *rose reamer*, the teeth are beveled on the end, backed off, and cut only on the end. The lands are nearly as wide as the grooves and are not relieved (backed off). The flutes or grooves are provided for conveying oil to the cut and chips away from the cut. The rose reamer tapers slightly smaller toward the shank (about 0.001 in. per inch of length) to prevent binding; it does not cut a particularly smooth hole but is very useful to bring the hole to within a few thousandths of size, when it may be finished with the hand reamer. Rose reamers, therefore, are usually made 0.003 to 0.005 in. under nominal size.

The *fluted reamer* has more teeth for a given diameter than the rose reamer. The lands are narrower, and are backed off the whole length. The front ends of the teeth are beveled or rounded and then relieved. It is a valuable finishing reamer when extreme accuracy is not required.

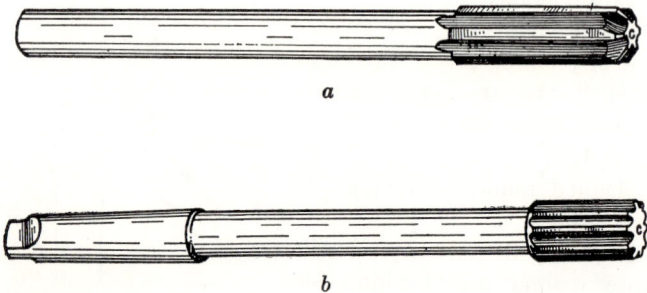

a

b

Fig. 9-3. Machine reamers: (*a*) straight-shank rose reamer and (*b*) taper-shank fluted reamer.

Both the rose reamer and the fluted reamer are made with either straight or taper shanks. It is not usually advisable on account of the extra cost to buy taper-shank reamers under $7/16$ in. diameter; and it is not usually good practice to buy straight-shank reamers of over 1 in. in diameter because of the difficulty in holding them.

Shell Reamers. For reasons of economy, many manufacturers prefer the shell reamers and arbors illustrated in Fig. 9-4. These reamers are made in either rose-reamer style or fluted-reamer style and the arbors with either straight or taper shanks. They differ in no particular respect from the ordinary solid reamer except that one arbor may be fitted to a number of reamers, and when a reamer is worn out it may be thrown away without discarding the arbor.

Hand Reamers (Fig. 9-5). Where a particularly accurate hole is required it is first drilled, bored, or machine-reamed to about 0.005 in. undersize and then hand-reamed.

STRAIGHT FLUTED
SHELL RFAMER
a

SPIRAL FLUTED
SHELL REAMER
b

ARBOR FOR SHELL REAMERS
c

ARBOR FOR SHELL REAMERS
d

Fig. 9-4. (*a*) Straight-fluted shell reamer, (*b*) Spiral-fluted shell reamer, (*c*) arbor for shell reamers, taper shank, (*d*) arbor for shell reamer, straight shank. (*National Twist Drill & Tool Company*)

A hand reamer is essentially a finishing tool, a scraping tool, and is ground straight for nearly the whole length of the teeth. It is slightly tapered, smaller toward the end, for a distance about equal to its diameter, to permit of its entering the hole to be reamed. The teeth are relieved a very little for clearance. The shank end is machined square to receive the wrench. *The hand reamer should never be operated by mechanical power.* Care should be exercised to start

HAND REAMER-STRAIGHT FLUTES
a

HAND REAMER-SPIRAL FLUTES
b

Fig. 9-5. Hand reamers: (*a*) straight flute and (*b*) spiral flute. (*National Twist Drill & Tool Company*)

it true and keep it straight. It is often advisable to start the hand reamer when aligned and steadied by the dead center of the lathe or a center placed in the drill-press spindle, as the case may be. *Do not leave over 0.005 in. for a hand reamer.*

Adjustable Reamers (Fig. 9-6). Probably the most efficient kind

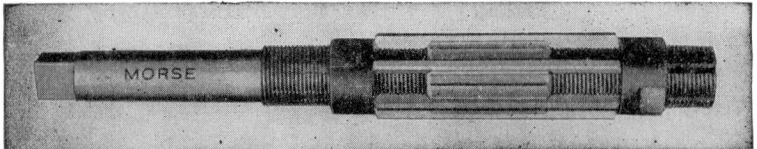

Fig. 9-6. Adjustable inserted-tooth reamer. (*Morse Twist Drill & Machine Company*)

of reamer for any purpose is the adjustable-blade reamer. The best types of these reamers can be adjusted to sizes within a considerable range over or under nominal size, often a valuable feature. While they cost more than the solid type of reamer, the fact that they may be easily sharpened and quickly adjusted to an exact size, and their corresponding long life, make them a particularly efficient tool. These reamers are made in all standard sizes, either hand or machine, with the body and shank in one piece or as shell reamers.

Fig. 9-7. Expansion hand reamer, spiral flute. (*The Cleveland Twist Drill Company*)

The Expansion Reamer. The body of the expansion reamer (Fig. 9-7) is bored slightly taper and slitted to permit a slight expansion (about 0.005 in. in a 1-in. hand reamer and proportional amounts in other sizes $\frac{1}{4}$ in. and over). A tapered plug, threaded through the end (guide) and squared for a wrench, is the expander. This reamer is not meant for an oversize reamer, or for an adjustable reamer; it is meant to give longer life to a reamer for finishing standard-size holes.

Taper Reamers. Taper reamers, both for roughing and finishing (Fig. 9-8), are made for all of the standard sizes of tapers. The end of the shank of the hand reamer is cut square to receive the wrench, and the reamer should always be turned by hand. As the chips do not fall out readily a taper reamer should be removed often and cleaned.

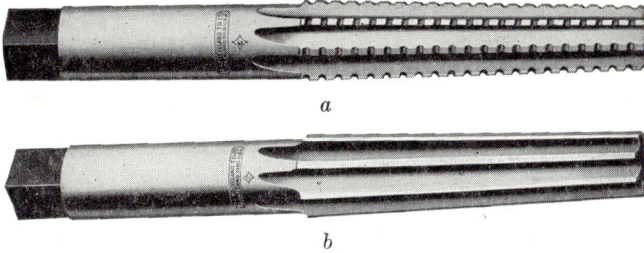

a

b

Fig. 9-8. Hand reamers for tapered holes: (*a*) roughing and (*b*) finishing. (*The Cleveland Twist Drill Company*)

By reason of the shearing cut such as is given to a reamer by the spiral flutes, there is less strain upon the reamer, less clogging with chips, and a smoother and more accurate hole results. This is especially true with steep-spiral taper reamers for use in machines (Fig. 9-9). Rough with the coarser tooth and finish with the finer tooth reamer. Feed slowly.

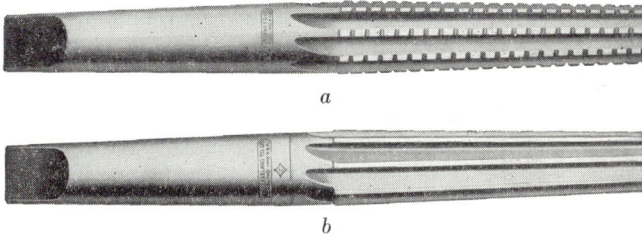

a

b

Fig. 9-9. Machine reamers for tapered holes: (*a*) roughing and (*b*) finishing. (*The Cleveland Twist Drill Company*)

Taper reamers are common in modern industry in the tapering of holes for the many sized and commonly used taper pins and the production of taper sleeves and sockets. Such reamers are made in pairs, roughing and finishing.

High-speed Reamers. Cutting tools made of high-speed steel will cut at least twice as fast and often four or five times as fast as similar tools made of carbon steel. It follows that where it is practicable to obtain the increased speed, it is profitable to use high-speed cutting tools. For example, in production work where considerable machine reaming is to be done, it is economical to use high-speed reamers. An adjustable machine reamer with high-speed steel blades has the advantage of the tough steel body.

Carbide-tipped Reamers. Because of the ever increasing demand for a reamer that would stand up under heavy loads, a reamer with hard inserts made up of a carbide was designed. Figure 9-10 shows such a reamer.

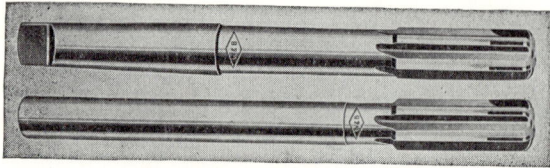

Fig. 9-10. Carbide-tipped reamers, straight and taper shank. (*Whitman & Barnes*)

The ability of the carbide to retain a sharp edge under high temperature, plus its excellent abrasion-resistant qualities, makes it particularly advantageous for use in reamers. Carbide-tipped reamers have proven economical in all of the common metals including steel, as well as in plastics. Their ability to hold size longer makes their use profitable in long production runs. Carbide reamers will outlast high-speed reamers many times in castings where sand or hard scale is encountered.

No specific rule can be given for speeds and feeds except to start with the same speeds and feeds as were used with high-speed reamers. The finish required, the condition of the machine, and tool life are usually the determining factors in speed.

The amount of stock to be removed must be sufficient to allow the reamer to cut at all times. A good rule is to leave about 3 per cent of the finished diameter for reaming. A good rule to start with for the feed is at least 0.002 in. per tooth per revolution of the reamer.

Emergency Reamers. A drill may be used as a reamer to give a satisfactory result if the corners are slightly rounded with an oilstone. A hole must be undersized before using this reaming drill. Run at fairly high speed and feed slowly.

A small-size reamer that will work well and can be easily sharpened may be quickly made from a piece of drill rod of the size desired. Cut off to length, square the end, and round the corner somewhat. Then reduce the diameter a thousandth or two except for an eighth of an inch or so from this end, either by filing or with emery cloth. Now bevel the end 45 deg. or more, leaving about half of it; back off the single cutting edge a very little and harden and temper. Grind and oilstone the flat beveled surface, oilstone the rounded cutting edge a trifle, and the reamer is ready to use. Feed slowly as there is only one cutting edge.

To Avoid Chattering of Reamers. Chattering is a more or less rapid vibration of the work or the tool which produces a wavelike unevenness in the surface being finished. It may be caused by improperly adjusted bearings, too much spring of the tool or work, too wide a cut, or too much clearance on the tool.

To lessen the tendency of chattering, reamers are *increment cut*, that is, the teeth are unequally spaced. With such teeth chatter marks cannot occur at the same rate for succeeding teeth—cannot *synchronize*—and, therefore, the tendency is for the reamer to cut smooth. Also, in hand reamers, the faces of the teeth are radial or slightly ahead of radial to give a scraping cut, and the lands are relieved only a small amount.

To further lessen the tendency to chatter, the teeth of reamers may be cut on a spiral. In the case of a spiral-cut reamer, the spiral should be left-hand, that is, the twist should be opposite that of a twist drill, otherwise the tendency is for the reamer to pull into the hole, and this would tend to increase rather than to diminish the trouble.

By reason of the shearing cut such as is given to a reamer by the spiral flutes, there is less strain upon the reamer, less clogging with chips, and a smoother and more accurate hole results. This is especially true with steep-spiral taper reamers.

Hints on Reaming

1. A burr on the tooth of a hand reamer will spoil the hole. When any reamer is obtained from the toolroom, feel along the cutting edge or the land of each tooth, and if any burr is noticed, oilstone it off.

2. Always use lard oil or other suitable cutting compound when reaming steel or wrought metal.

3. It should be emphasized that *never under any circumstances* should a reamer be turned backward.

4. Oil is not used as a cutting lubricant when reaming cast iron. It is very often advisable, however, to put oil on the lands of a rose reamer to reduce the friction in the hole and prevent scoring.

5. Do not attempt to start a reamer on an uneven surface. The reamer as it starts tends to go toward the point of least resistance and if not started true will not ream a straight round hole.

6. To avoid tearing at the beginning, bring the reamer to the edge of the hole before starting it, and feed carefully.

The Operation of Reaming. It depends upon the degree of accuracy and finish desired whether or not a hole should be reamed at all and also whether it should be merely machine-reamed or finished with a hand reamer. For example, bolt holes or cap-screw holes, whether body size or tap-drill size are not reamed, while holes for dowel pins, pivot pins, hinge pins, etc., must be reamed. Further, a hole in which a mandrel is to be used for other machine operations (for instance, the hole in a pulley or in a gear blank) must be reamed. When the hole is fairly long in proportion to the diameter and an extra smooth surface is not required, a fluted machine reamer will give the desired result. When a high degree of accuracy and finish is desired, a hole had best be hand-reamed. It is first machine-reamed with a fluted reamer or rose reamer 0.002 to 0.005 in. undersize which leaves the correct scraping chip for the hand reamer.

A hole that is to be reamed is drilled with a *reamer drill* which is usually 0.005 in. *undersize* (less than the finished diameter of the hole).

It is customary immediately to follow the drill with the reamer, especially if the work is clamped, to ensure alignment. The speed for reaming is usually somewhat less than for drilling to avoid any tendency to overheat and ruin the cutting edge. The feed should not be crowded or the reamer may tear the surface of the hole. Be sure the reamer runs true and take care in starting the cut, otherwise a chatter may develop which will spoil the mouth of the hole. If the reamer chatters, stop the machine and then start very slowly, pulling the belt by hand if convenient.

If the hole is to be hand-reamed, it may be well to put a center in the drill-press spindle to align and steady the reamer until it is well started. As the reamer is turned with a tap wrench (Fig. 9-20) and cuts its way into the hole, follow it up with the center but do not crowd it; feed by hand. Assistance will probably be necessary.

Duplicating a Drilled and Reamed Part. When, as frequently happens, it is desired to duplicate a flat piece having two or more holes already drilled and reamed, a quick accurate method is as follows: Obtain a drill, the size of the reamed hole, to be used as a *spotting* drill, a machine reamer of the desired size, also a reamer drill $\frac{1}{64}$ or $\frac{1}{32}$ in. smaller. Clamp or otherwise arrange the two pieces with the one to be drilled and reamed in position under the piece already reamed, with the first hole aligned under the spotting drill in the machine spindle. Spot this hole, then remove the spotting drill and put in the reamer drill (undersize drill), and drill the hole. Then ream with the machine reamer. After reaming and before proceeding to the next hole, insert any suitable pin or plug through the two pieces to keep them in exact relationship while the next hole is being spotted, drilled, and reamed. If three or more holes are to be made, it will be wise to use a second plug as this will prevent any shifting of either piece while the other holes are being made.

QUESTIONS ON REAMERS AND REAMING

1. It is assumed that the hole has been drilled. Select a reamer of the proper size. When is a machine reamer used as a finishing reamer?
2. If it is not to be used for finishing the hole, how much undersize is it made? Why?
3. How is a taper-shank reamer held in the spindle?
4. If the shank is too small to fit the spindle hole, what do you do?
5. Why is it necessary to wipe the taper clean and dry?
6. How is a straight-shank reamer held?
7. What are the advantages of the taper-shank reamer? Of the straight-shank reamer?
8. Is it necessary to clamp or "stop" the work when using a machine reamer? Give reasons.
9. What part of the machine rose reamer does the cutting? Fluted reamer? Where is the tooth clearance? What other clearance has a machine reamer?

10. What is the use of the flutes in a machine reamer?

11. How much metal is usually left for a machine reamer to remove? Why not $\frac{1}{16}$ or $\frac{1}{8}$ in.?

12. What is the cutting speed of a machine reamer as compared with a twist drill? How do the feeds compare?

13. When is a lubricant used in reaming?

14. What are the advantages of facing around the hole before machine reaming?

15. How should a reamer be started? If it chatters what is indicated?

16. If a machine reamer squeaks when used in cast iron, what does it indicate? How may it be avoided?

17. If several holes are to be drilled or reamed through two pieces clamped together what precaution should be taken?

18. What is a machine reamer? Fluted reamer? Rose reamer?

19. What is an adjustable reamer? What are its advantages?

20. What is a shell reamer? What are its advantages?

21. How may a drill be used for a reamer if no reamer of the size is available?

22. What is a hand reamer? Why is part of the body ground slightly tapered?

23. Should a hand reamer be operated by mechanical power? How may it be used in the drill press?

24. When using a hand reamer in a drill press or lathe, why is it wise to follow it up with the center? How is this done? What precaution should be observed?

25. State at least three precautions that should be observed when using a reamer.

26. Why does a reamer tend to follow the hole already made?

27. If the work is *clamped*, and the drilled hole is not exactly in line with the machine spindle, what will be the result when the hole is reamed?

28. Explain the process of duplicating a flat piece with two or more holes.

29. What is meant by a carbide-tipped reamer?

30. What advantages has the carbide-tipped reamer over the high-speed reamer?

31. Why does such a reamer keep its sharp edge longer than any other type of reamer?

The Counterbore. This tool is used to face around a hole, in order that a nut or bolt may set square with the hole; or to enlarge a hole to a given depth, as for the fillister head of a machine screw and a cap screw.

The standard solid counterbore (Fig. 9-11) consists of the *guide* (sometimes called thè teat or the pilot) which is the size of the original hole; the *cutter head* which is the size of the enlarged hole, and on the end of which the cutting teeth are formed; the *necked*

Fig. 9-11. Solid counterbore with tapered shank. (*The Cleveland Twist Drill Company*)

portion which in the counterbore may be long to permit of enlarging a hole to a considerable depth if desired; and the *shank* which may be straight or tapered. Grooves are cut either straight or spiral in the head to form the upper faces of the cutting teeth. These grooves usually extend the whole length of the head to provide for the escape of chips, and to provide also a way for lubricating the cut. The teeth are backed off about 10 or 12 deg. to give clearance to the cutting edges. The cutter head is slightly tapered, smaller toward the shank, so that it will not bind.

Counterbores are made solid in the smaller sizes, (Fig. 9-11) and usually with removable cutters or blades in the larger sizes (Figs. 9-12 and 9-13). In any case, the cutting edges are at right angles

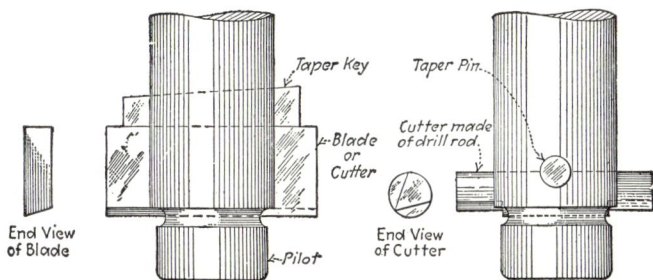

Fig. 9-12. Two types of homemade counterbores with removable blades or cutters.

to the axis of the counterbore in order to cut a *flat* surface. However, many counterbores of any size may be procured with removable pilots. The advantage of having a removable pilot lies in the fact that the size of the pilot to be used depends upon the size of the hole to be counterbored and the size of the counterbore. Even small counterbores are now supplied with removable pilots.

A counterbore should have at least two cutting edges. They should be carefully and evenly ground in order to balance the cut. Sometimes one tooth of a counterbore with a wide cut is ground to cut only in the middle and a little deeper than the other tooth. This is to break the chip and narrow the width of cut. It should, however, be so ground as to allow each tooth to do its share.

The counterbore is not designed for extremely accurate work; therefore the body is usually made a trifle (0.003 to 0.005 in.) over the nominal size, and the guide is made one- or two-thousandths

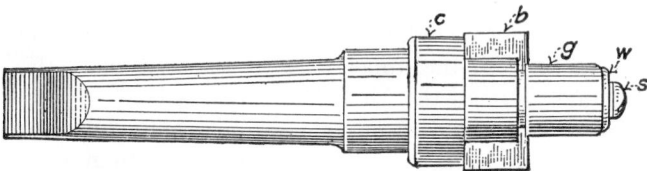

Fig. 9-13. Combination counterbore. The large part c of the cutter head is a hardened-steel collar forced into place after the slot for the blade b is cut. It projects somewhat over the slot and is ground true on the face. The blade is centered by a turned projection which fits the collar and is held square against the ground face of the collar by the guide bushing g, the washer w, and the screw s. The bushing is slotted to fit over the blade and is hardened and ground. Various sizes of blades and bushings are quickly interchangeable. (*Cleveland Twist Drill Company*)

under the size of the hole to be enlarged so that it will not bind. Oil the guide before using so that it will not rough up.

A cold chisel is much cheaper to make and much easier to sharpen than a counterbore, and it is often desirable to chip off the scale around the hole before spot-facing or counterboring cast iron.

To avoid any danger of overheating and drawing the temper of a counterbore, run it at a somewhat slower speed than for drilling a hole of corresponding size, and apply the cutting lubricant freely.

The countersink may be differentiated from the counterbore in that it is used to enlarge the end of a hole to a cone shape, as for a flathead machine screw or a wood screw. The terms *center reaming* and *countersinking* are both applied to the operation of making the center holes in work to be machined "on centers." The combination drill and countersink is the best tool to use for this operation. An

important fact should be kept in mind—the included angle of a
center hole is 60 deg. and the included angle of the countersunk hole
for the head of a wood screw or a standard flat machine screw is
82 deg.; do not get the 82-deg. countersink and the 60-deg. center
reamer mixed.

Three different kinds of countersinks for screw-heads are illustrated in Fig. 9-14. Countersinks are run at fairly
slow speed to avoid chattering. Hand feed is commonly used, and plenty of cutting lubricant should be
applied.

Boring in a Drill Press. It is sometimes practicable to use a drill-press for boring a hole, for example,
when a drill or reamer of a suitable size may not be
available. Further, when a perfectly straight hole is
desired and a high degree of accuracy as to location
is necessary, it is frequently drilled $\frac{1}{16}$ in. or more
undersize, then *bored*, and finally reamed. If it is under-

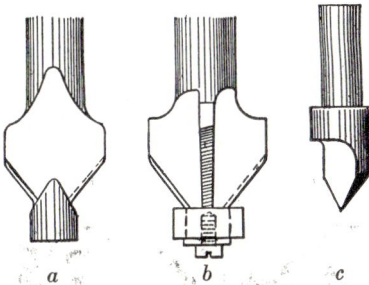

Fig. 9-14. Types of countersinks for flathead screws. The
included angle is 82 deg. as in a center reamer. (*a*) Two-lip with
guide, (*b*) four-lip with guide bushing and provided with screw
and washer for holding various sizes of bushings to fit holes of
different diameters, (*c*) the cheapest and best form of countersink for small screws.

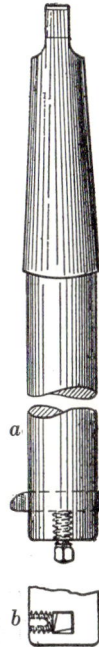

Fig. 9-15.
Boring tool
for drill
press.

stood that a reamer will tend to follow the hole already made but
that a boring tool tends to go straight (cutting more from one side
of the hole than from the other side if necessary), the value of boring
a hole to insure accuracy of shape and of location will be apparent.

Drill-press boring tools are made in many varieties and sizes.
Figure 9-15 illustrates a common type: The cutting tool is held in

position by a setscrew in the end of the bar as at (*a*), or by a hollow setscrew in the side of the bar as at (*b*). When the boring tool is for any reason long and slender and inclined to spring, it is necessary to take light cuts.

QUESTIONS ON BORING, COUNTERBORING, ETC.

1. What is the difference between boring and counterboring a hole?
2. What is the difference between counterboring and countersinking?
3. What is the difference between a machine-screw countersink and a countersink (center reamer) for a lathe center?
4. Some shops provide three different sizes of counterbores for each of the most used sizes of fillister-head screws, namely, the body-size to head-size counterbore; the tap-drill size to head-size counterbore; and the tap-drill size to body-size counterbore. What is meant by these terms? What is the purpose of each of these counterbores?
5. Why do you put oil on the teat of a counterbore? Is this true when counterboring cast iron?

TAPS AND TAPPING

Tapping is an operation that is very frequently done in machine work. Tapping may be defined as the process of cutting internal threads by means of a cutting tool called a *tap* (Fig. 9-16). Produc-

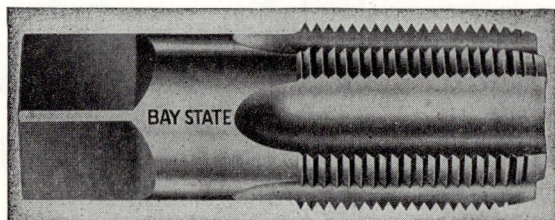

Fig. 9-16. A tap. (*Bay State Tap & Die Company*)

ing threads of the best possible quality is the objective of every tapping operation. Tapping, however, is one of the most difficult of machining operations because of the problems of chip removal and lubrication at the cutting edges and the fact that speed and feed cannot be varied independently because the relationship between them is fixed by the lead of the tap. However, in the production of tapped holes, the type of tap used, the use of the proper lubricating fluids, and the skill of the operator are the most important factors to be considered.

Taps should cut freely and maintain uniformly accurate tapped holes. Taps should never be forced into a hole at any time. Taps, like all cutting tools, should be handled with the greatest of care.

Figure 9-17 shows spindles holding taps of different sizes ready to be used in tapping the many holes of a casting. This practice of

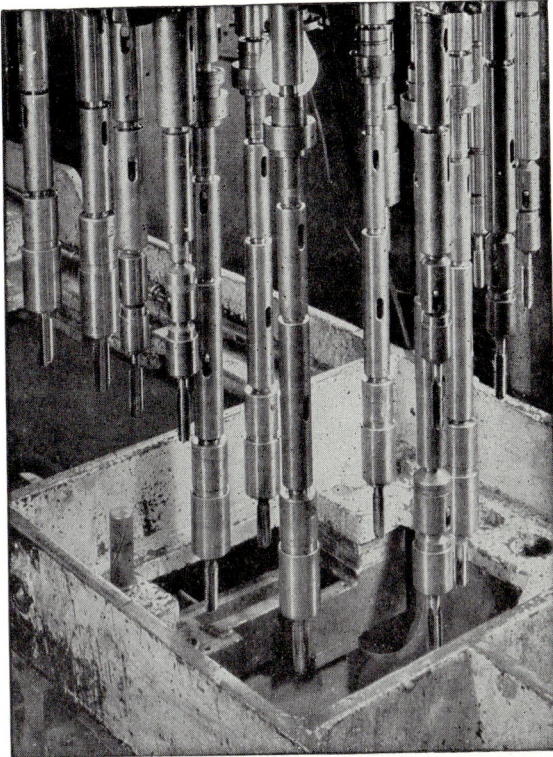

Fig. 9-17. A gang-tap set up. (*Charles H. Besly & Company*)

having separate spindles for different size taps is accepted practice in production work. It saves a great deal of time when taps do not have to be removed in order to tap a different size hole.

DEFINITIONS: TAP TERMS

Figure 9-18 shows a line drawing of a tap with its parts labelled. So that the student will readily understand and correctly interpret the various technical terms used in dealing with taps, definitions are included of those terms most commonly used.

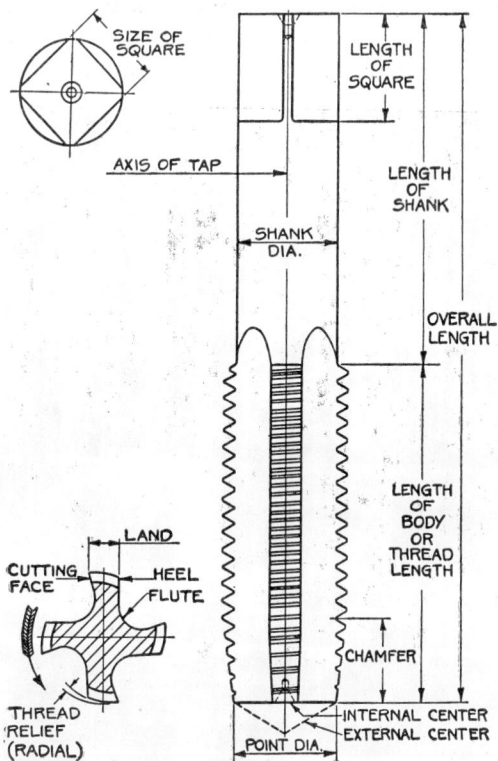

Fig. 9-18. Graphic illustration of tap terms. (*Greenfield Tap & Die Company*)

Axis of Tap. The longitudinal central line through the tap.

Chamfer. The tapered outside diameter at the front end of the threaded section.

Cutting Face. The front part of the threaded section of the land.

External (Male) Center. Sometimes termed *male* center and is the cone-shaped end of the tap. It is incorporated for manufacturing purposes and usually at the threaded end of small taps only.

Flute. The groove providing for the cutting faces of the threads or teeth, chip passage, and lubrication.

Heel. The back part of the threaded section of the land.

Internal (Female) Center. Sometimes termed *female* center and is a small drilled and countersunk hole at the end of the tap, necessary for manufacturing purposes.

Land. The threaded web between the flutes.

Point Diameter. The outside diameter at the front end of the chamfered portion.

Square. The squared end of the tap shank.

Thread Relief. The section of tap thread that is backed off to give the cutting edge.

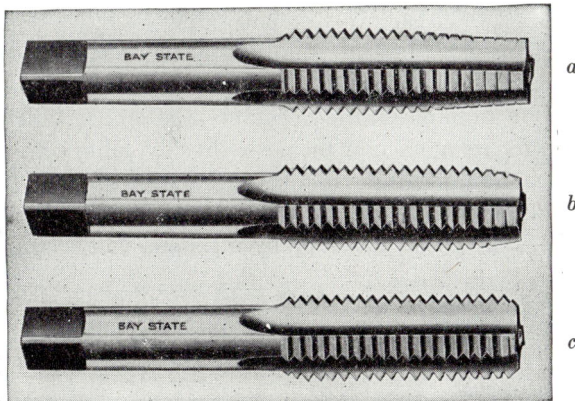

Fig. 9-19. Set of hand taps: (*a*) taper, (*b*) plug, and (*c*) bottoming. (*Bay State Tap & Die Company*)

Fig. 9-20. Adjustable tap wrench. (*Morse Twist Drill & Machine Company*)

Types of Taps. Several forms of taps are used in machine work, brief descriptions of which follow:

Hand Taps. Most internal threads are cut with taps, which are usually held in a tapping machine or with a tapping attachment in the drill press. Many threads, however, must be tapped by hand. Figure 9-19 shows a set of machinist's hand taps squared on the shank end to receive the wrench (Fig. 9-20). Hand taps are made in sets of three taps, called taper, plug, and bottoming. The first tap or taper tap is tapered or "chamfered" back from the end at least six threads, the plug tap is chamfered about three or four threads, while the bottoming tap is merely backed off on the end teeth. Taps furnished in sets are of the same diameter unless otherwise specified, so that to tap a *through hole* it is only necessary to use the taper tap. Where the hole does not go through the piece (blind hole) it is customary to start with the taper, follow with the plug, and, occasionally, if the hole is fairly shallow, finish with the bottoming.

Machine-screw Taps. Hand taps under $\frac{1}{4}$ in. diameter, such as 8–32, 10–24, etc., are catalogued as machine-screw taps and are used mostly in the form of plug taps. If necessary they may be quickly ground to either taper or bottoming form.

Tapered Taps. This tap has a uniformly tapering body or portion thereof and is used for tapping a full thread in a tapered hole. The most common example is the ordinary *pipe tap*. A tapered tap is best named for its particular purpose, thus avoiding confusion with the first tap or "taper tap" in a set of hand taps.

Tapper Tap (Fig. 9-21). This is the name given to the tap whose chief use is in a special nut-tapping machine. The shank is longer

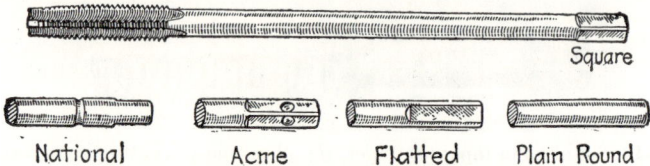

Square

National   Acme   Flatted   Plain Round

Fig. 9-21. Tapper tap and forms of shank ends.

than a hand tap of the same diameter and invariably is smaller than the root diameter of the thread. This is for the purpose of holding a number of nuts after tapping. When no more nuts can be held on the shank, the tap is removed and the tapped nuts slide off the shank. Usually the tapper tap is given a longer taper (chamfer) than the taper tap of a hand set, to lighten the work of each tooth. If considerable taper is given, care must be taken not to ream the hole instead of tapping it.

Some manufacturers turn the first six or eight threads taper, not merely turn the outside taper, but cut the threads on a taper. This eliminates to a certain extent the tendency otherwise to ream the hole and also improves the cutting qualities of the tap and produces a "cleaner cut" thread. Also several of the straight threads are chamfered to reduce the amount of work for the successive cutting edges. Tapper taps are provided with various forms of shank ends to fit the holders of nut-tapping machines in common use.

Pulley Taps. These taps are especially long hand taps for tapping the setscrew and oil-cup holes in the hubs of pulleys. The shank is long enough to reach through a hole drilled in the pulley rim which is made substantially the size of the shank and thus affords a means of aligning and steadying the tap. The extension drill for the hole in the hub may be made by soldering a straight-shank drill in a hole drilled in the end of a suitable piece of drill rod.

Machine Taps. These are made for general use in special tap holders in drilling machines. One of the best known and most efficient holders is the Beaman and Smith holder (see Fig. 9-22). A

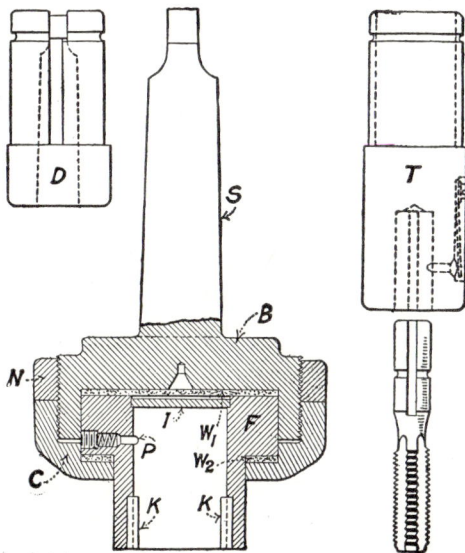

Fig. 9-22. Beaman and Smith safety drill and tap holder. S is the shank and B the body recessed to receive the friction socket F. The cap C screws on the body and holds the friction tap holder F as tight between the fiber disk W_1 and washer W_2 as is necessary to drive the drill or tap. N is a check nut for securing the cap C in place after the friction adjustment is made. Special sockets, T and D as shown, are required to hold the tap and drill. Taps with special shanks may be obtained from almost any tap manufacturer. Drill sockets are furnished with Morse taper holes for any desired size of drill. The sockets are inserted in the holder F and are kept from turning by the keys K and from falling out by the small spring plunger P. It will be observed that the tap is held in its socket in a similar way. The thrust of the socket T or D is against the disk I, which serves to protect the fiber disk W_1.

plug hand tap may be used as a machine tap in a drilling machine provided with spindle-reverse gears, or in certain tapping attachments if a suitable holder for the squared shank end is provided. Do not use a chuck to hold a tap over $\frac{3}{8}$ in. diameter because it **is** likely to injure the chuck.

Gun Taps (Fig. 9-23). This type is very efficient when used either as a hand tap or in a machine for power tapping. Because of the

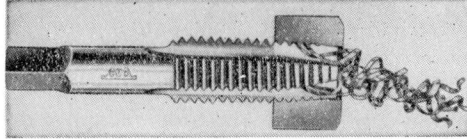

Fig. 9-23. Gun tap. (*Greenfield Tap & Die Company*)

shape of the initial cutting edges, which have both rake and shear, it is unnecessary to chamfer more than three or four threads, thus avoiding the tendency to ream. Further, it does not clog because the chip "shoots" out ahead of the tap.

Tap-size Drills.[1] The diameter of the hole to be drilled for the threads in a nut or other inside threaded piece is *theoretically* the minor diameter of the corresponding screw size. This will give a *full depth* of thread; however, it is not practical to tap a full thread; therefore the *tap-drill sizes* are larger than the minor diameter. Three-quarters of the full thread is enough to leave for tapping

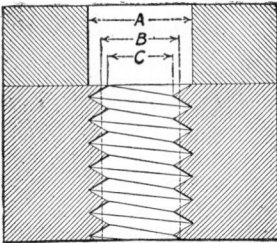

Fig. 9-24. *A* is a body size; *C* is minor diameter; *B* is tap-drill size that will leave enough stock for about three-quarters of a full thread as shown.

(Fig. 9-24). An ordinary nut so drilled and tapped will break the bolt before the thread will strip. Use the following:

RULE: The size of the tap drill for American National threads equals major diameter minus 1 divided by the number of threads per inch.

FORMULA: $T.D.S. = D - 1/N$

where $T.D.S.$ = tap drill size

D = diameter of tap

N = number of threads per inch

[1] For tap-drill sizes see Table 8, page 532.

EXAMPLE: $\frac{1}{2}$-in. tap − 13 threads.

SOLUTION: $T.D.S.$ = 0.500 − $\frac{1}{13}$ = 0.500 − 0.077 = 0.423.

The nearest drill under 0.423 in. is 0.421 in. ($\frac{27}{64}$ in.).

Advantages of Tapping by Power. Tapping by power reduces the expense and inaccuracy of tapping by hand. In addition to being much easier and quicker, it is steady and even, and effects a saving in the breakage of taps and also pro-longs the life of the cutting edges. Because of the firm manner of hold-ing and turning the tap, the thread produced is clean and true.

Figure 9-25 shows a tapping attach-ment used in power tapping. This piece of equipment is called the *Tap King* and is widely used in manu-facturing plants. Using this piece of equipment or any other similar piece, tapping becomes a routine operation. The tap may be withdrawn from the hole without stopping the machine.

Fig. 9-25. A tapping attach-ment. (*Procunier Safety Chuck Company*)

Tapping in a Drill Press

1. Make the setup carefully, having the holder or attachment tight in the spindle and properly adjusted, the work so held that it cannot twist or cramp, and the tap sharp and running true or arranged to float in the holder.

2. Use a slow spindle speed, especially until practice has given confidence.

3. The spindle must be perfectly free to slide in the sleeve, no feed being necessary in the tapping operation except in certain cases (a follow-up hand feed).

4. Have at hand plenty of cutting lubricant and apply it freely when tapping; provide a means of catching the surplus, however, in order to avoid wasting the lubricant and messing the machine. (Lard oil is best for steel, and soap or tallow works well for tap-ping cast iron.)

5. Have the work located against one or more stops so that it may be able to center itself.

6. A certain pressure is needed to start the taper tap and care must be taken to make the tap "bite" or "catch the thread" and not ream the top of the hole taper. After the tap is well started, it feeds itself and requires only to be turned. It is a good plan occasionally to turn the tap backward half a turn to break the chip. In tapping soft materials such as copper, babbitt, etc., it is necessary to remove the tap several times and clean away the chips.

7. When the hole is tapped to the required depth, reverse the direction of rotation of the tap and with a slight upward pressure on the feeding lever, back the tap out. It may be necessary in a fairly long hole to reverse part of a turn once or twice during the tapping operation to break the chip.

Tapping Troubles. There are many causes that make for poor tapped holes. The chart shown here is helpful in spotting the cause for trouble in tapping.

Tapping Trouble

Trouble	Probable Cause	Remedy
	Hole too small	Use larger drill
	Tap hitting bottom	Correct adjustment Exercise more care Use more positive reverse Drill hole deeper
Breakage	Misalignment	Make correction
	Tapping too deep	Use spiral pointed or serial taps
	Dull tap	Sharpen tap
	Cramped condition	Check holder and alignment
Chipping	Inadequate lubrication	Consult lubrication engineer
	Hitting bottom or chips packed in bottom	Check reversing stop Drill hole deeper

Tapping Trouble (Continued)

Trouble	Probable Cause	Remedy
Chipping	Hard spots in work	Check to see that hard spots are not caused by work hardening when drilled or bored
	Loading	Check lubrication
Torn or rough threads	Incorrect hook, relief or chamfer	Grind correctly
	Inadequate lubrication	Consult lubrication engineer
	Dull tap	Sharpen tap
	Loading	Check lubrication
Wavy threads	Misalignment of spindle	Correct condition
	Incorrect chamfer or thread relief	Grind proper chamfer Use tap with concentric thread
Tapping oversize or bell mouth holes	Loose spindle or worn holder	Correct condition
	Too much float in spindle or fixture	Correct condition
	Misalignment	Correct condition
	Excessive thrust pressure	Adjust pressure Use more care if manual
	Loading	Check lubrication
Undersize threads	Tap spreads hole which shrinks after tap is removed	Redesign part Use oversize tap Be sure tap cuts freely
	Dull tap	Sharpen tap
Excessive wear	Inadequate lubrication	Consult lubrication engineer
	Sand in cored hole	Clean hole before tapping
	Abrasive material	If bakelite, use oversize tap

Using a Piece Already Drilled as a Template. Very often in machine construction, when one part is fastened to another part by screws, it is advisable to "spot" through the body-size holes in one to locate the positions of the tap-size holes in the other. This operation is illustrated in Fig. 9-26. If several holes are to be spotted and drilled, it will be best to tap the first hole as soon as it is drilled—possibly the first two holes—and hold the pieces together while the other holes are spotted and drilled.

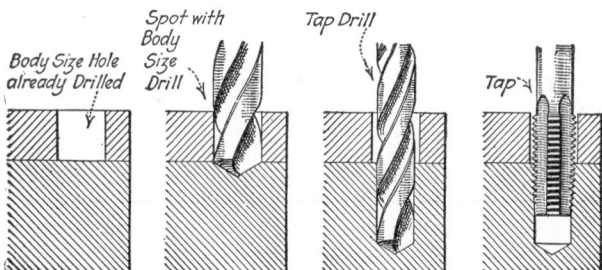

Fig. 9-26. Spotting and drilling for tap. In order to tighten the top piece to the other, the screw will go through the top piece (*body-size drill*) and screw into the bottom piece after this piece has been *spotted* with the body-size drill, drilled with the *tap drill* (a given amount smaller than the body size) and then tapped.

Checking a Tapped Hole (Fig. 9-27). This illustration shows an operator or an inspector checking a tapped hole just completed.

Fig. 9-27. Checking a tapped hole with a plug thread gage. (*The Sheffield Corporation*)

He is using a plug-type thread gage and has inserted the "go" end of the gage. This end should enter and fit accurately. If it does, then he will try the "no-go" end of the gage. This part of the gage should not fit.

This procedure is usually followed in all machine shops where tapped holes must be accurate for mass production. This ensures that the tapped hole is properly threaded and will fit with the mating part.

Threading Dies. When external threads are cut, especially on small diameter stock, a *die* is used. Figure 9-28 shows a few dies; when one is mounted in a die holder (Fig. 9-29), it will cut external threads by hand.

Fig. 9-28. Threading dies. (*Standard Tool Company*)

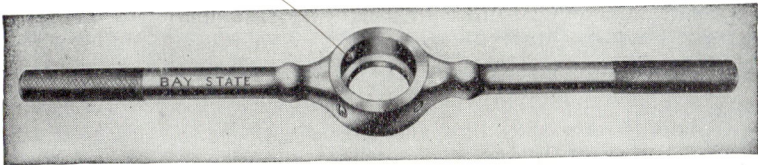

Fig. 9-29. A die holder. (*Bay State Tap & Die Company*)

The threading dies are manufactured in many sizes. The forms of threads cut with these dies are usually the National and pipe. Machinists, as a rule, use the die mounted in a die holder usually called a stock.

QUESTIONS ON TAPS, TAPPING, AND DIES

1. Name the three taps in a tap set. What is the purpose of each one?
2. When threads are tapped in tough metals, what should be done to keep them from tearing?
3. What lubricant is best when tapping cast iron? Steel? Brass? Aluminum? Copper?

4. How far should a screw enter a tapped hole in order to give sufficient strength?

5. What is a blind hole?

6. If the effort to turn the tap is continued after it bottoms, what will be the result?

7. How do you use a scale when counting the number of threads per inch? What is a pitch gage?

8. How may the pitch of the thread in a nut be determined with a whittled stick, if there is no tap or bolt to fit it?

9. What size is the largest drill that will pass through the nut?

10. What is a tap drill? What is meant by a body-size drill?

11. Why is a tap drill smaller than the outside diameter of the bolt?

12. Why are the screws used in automobile work of finer pitch than those used in machine-tool manufacture?

13. In common practice, is the tap-drill size equal to the root diameter of the thread? Is it larger or smaller?

14. State three objections to the use of a tap drill that will give a full thread.

15. When two pieces are to be held tightly together, why not tap both pieces?

16. If it is desired to tap a slightly larger hole in a nut so it will be a free fit on a thread, how can this be done with a standard size tap?

17. Before attempting to re-tap an old nut, what precaution should be taken? Why?

18. It occasionally happens that a ½-in. screw will not fit a tapped hole which appears all right. What caution must be observed when using ½-in. setscrews, ½-in. taps, and ½-in. dies?

19. How is a tap sharpened? How is it backed off?

20. Explain the principle of the operation of the bevel gears and the clutch in the reversing mechanism or tapping attachment.

21. State four advantages of tapping by power.

22. Explain by sketch and description the action of any auxiliary tapping attachment by means of which duplicate holes may be tapped the same depth using the spindle stop.

23. What is the meaning of the word *template?*

24. What is a die? When is it used?

25. What holds the die?

26. Who uses a pipe-thread die and why?

The Lathe

CHAPTER 10

Lathe Construction and Manipulation

The history of modern machinery started in the last years of the eighteenth century when Henry Maudslay, an Englishman, built the first practical screw-cutting lathe. When compared with a modern precision lathe, this machine was slow and clumsy, but from the basic principles of Maudslay's lathe have come nearly all modern machine tools.

Today, nearly 150 years after Maudslay, the screw-cutting lathe is still the heart of industrial manufacturing. It seems odd to consider the lathe so vitally important when large batteries of automatic machines are used in every modern factory. But pay a visit to the factory toolroom where the machining is done that makes possible the construction of these huge automatic machines. There you will find a lathe—easily the most important tool—busy at the hands of an expert machinist, turning the plans of designers and engineers into new tools and machines for modern industry.

More jobs of a mechanized nature can be done on a lathe than with a dozen of any other tools. In the machine shop, experimental shop, or home shop, the metal lathe is called upon for many operations. Turning, milling, grinding, drilling, and boring must be performed on iron and steel; wood, plastics, alloys, and soft metals must be shaped into form; springs and coils wound; threads of all sizes and shapes have to be cut; and machine parts need to be repaired or replaced. Manufacturers, tool and die makers, experimenters, automotive men, model builders, inventors—thousands of businesses, hobbies, and professions depend on a precision screw-cutting lathe with its many attachments.

The Engine Lathe. The lathe, as all engine lathes are usually called in machine shops, while being the most important machine-shop tool is also one of the simplest in its construction. Its simplicity, together with the wide range of operations of which it is capable, makes it especially interesting to the young machinist. This, in addition to the fact that so many basic elements of machine construction and machine-shop practice are involved in the construction and operation of the lathe, makes lathe work, without question, the proper elementary machine-shop work.

Function of the Lathe. The function of a lathe is the *removal of metal, by means of a suitably formed cutting tool of hardened and tempered steel, from a piece of work which is securely supported and made to revolve.*

You will notice as you progress in your apprenticeship that at times other machine tools have the work moving or the tool moving, or both the work and the tool moving. However, in the lathe, the work revolves and the tool usually moves along a straight line. Notice the planer, the shaper, the milling machine, etc., and note the difference.

Determining the Size of a Lathe. Lathes are classified as to their size by the maximum diameter of work which may be revolved over the ways, such as 10, 14, and 16 in. and for particular classifications, the total length between centers is also noted. Lathes used in the manufacturing of heavy ordnance pieces are long and may range from 10 to 100 ft. Swings of 36 in. and larger are also found in industrial machine shops, but they are not so common as the smaller ones.

General Lathe Operations. The general lathe operations are *straight (cylindrical) turning, taper turning, boring* (straight or tapered), *facing* (which is a cut at right angles to the axis of the piece), and *thread cutting.* Drilling, reaming, and tapping may also be done on the lathe.

Attachments of particular value are available for special operations such as relieving or backing-off, grinding, and taper turning.

Types of Lathes. Special lathes of a large variety and sizes are made for different kinds of work. The three common types of lathes usually found in a machine shop are the *bench* lathe, the *engine* lathe, and the *turret* lathe.

The *bench* lathe is a small lathe usually mounted on a bench and is used for small work. They are accurate and do an excellent job on most lathe operations. They usually have all the attachments that the larger lathes have.

The *engine* lathe, or just *plain* lathe, is larger than the bench lathe and is the machine tool on which many lathe operations are done. This lathe is the most valuable machine tool in the shop.

The *turret lathe* (Fig. 1-12) is a manufacturing machine. Considerable mechanical skill is required to make and adjust the several cutting tools in the turret head and cross slide, but when the tools are once made and adjusted and the stops set, it requires little mechanical skill to operate the machine. It is a semiautomatic machine. Several different operations can be done on a workpiece without resetting of work or tools.

Fig. 10-1. A standard change gear bench lathe. (*South Bend Lathe Works*)

Bench Lathes. Figure 10-1 illustrates a standard change gear bench lathe with power longitudinal feeds and power cross feeds. This lathe has a set of independent change gears which are used to connect the headstock spindle with the lead screw for cutting various pitches of screw threads and for obtaining a series of power longitudinal feeds for turning. The cross feed may also be operated automatically through a friction clutch and a series of gears in the apron.

Notice that there is no feed rod on this lathe. The feed is controlled by the hand knob at the bottom of the carriage. This operates the friction clutch that engages the lead screw, which in turn acts as a feed rod. By changing the ratio of the change gears in the left end of the lathe, the amount of feed may be controlled.

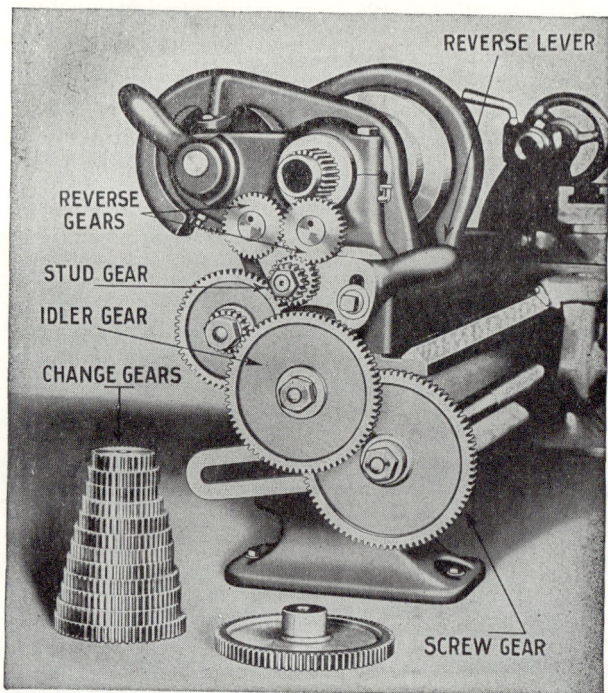

Fig. 10-2. End view of a standard change gear bench lathe with a set of change gears. (*South Bend Lathe Works*)

The end view of a standard change gear bench lathe and the gearing for connecting the headstock spindle with the lead screw of the lathe are shown in Fig. 10-2. The gears may be used and arranged so that practically any pitch of thread may be cut.

The standard change gear type of lathe is popular in the small shop because it is less expensive than the quick change gear lathe (Fig. 10-3). It is also used widely in industrial plants for production operations where few changes of threads and feeds are necessary. For this class of work, the standard change gear lathe has an advantage in that, when set up for an operation, the adjustments are not easily tampered with and changed as they may be on the quick change gear lathe.

Quick Change Gear Lathe (Fig. 10-3). A quick change gear lathe is one in which the gearing between the spindle and lead screw

Fig. 10-3. A quick change gear lathe. (*South Bend Lathe Works*)

is so arranged that changes for obtaining various pitches of screw threads may be made through a quick change gearbox without having to actually change any gears. The gears in this gearbox are shifted by levers operated from the front of the lathe and are quick and easy to operate.

The quick change gear lathe is very popular in busy shops where frequent changes of threads and feeds must be made, such as in tool and die work, general repair and maintenance, and for some production work.

Figure 10-4 shows a quick change gear mechanism with the parts identified. To obtain any desired feed, it is only necessary to arrange the levers on the gearbox according to the direct-reading index chart shown in Fig. 10-5. The threads per inch are shown in *large*

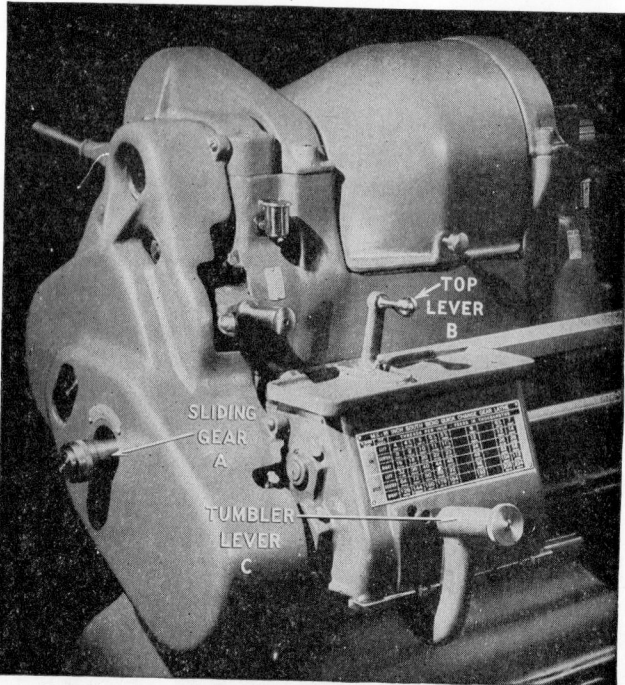

Fig. 10-4. Quick change gearbox with levers identified. (*South Bend Lathe Works*)

16-INCH SOUTH BEND QUICK CHANGE GEAR LATHE										
SLIDING GEAR	TOP LEVER	THREADS PER INCH—FEEDS IN THOUSANDTHS								
IN	LEFT	4 .0841	4½ .0748	5 .0673	5½ .0612	5¾ .0585	6 .0561		6½ .0518	7 .0481
	CENTER	8 .0421	9 .0374	10 .0337	11 .0306	11½ .0293	12 .0280		13 .0259	14 .0240
	RIGHT	16 .0210	18 .0187	20 .0168	22 .0153	23 .0146	24 .0140		26 .0129	28 .0120
OUT	LEFT	32 .0105	36 .0093	40 .0084	44 .0076	46 .0073	48 .0070		52 .0065	56 .0060
	CENTER	64 .0053	72 .0047	80 .0042	88 .0038	92 .0037	96 .0035		104 .0032	112 .0030
	RIGHT	128 .0026	144 .0023	160 .0021	176 .0019	184 .0018	192 .0017		208 .0016	224 .0015

AUTOMATIC CROSS-FEED EQUALS 375 TIMES LONGITUDINAL FEED

Fig. 10-5. Chart for a 16-in. South Bend quick change gear lathe. (*South Bend Lathe Works*) figures on the index chart. The *smaller* figures indicate the power longitudinal turning feeds in thousandths of an inch.

The pitch of the thread to be cut is determined by shifting the sliding gear A, top lever B, and the tumbler lever C so that they conform with the thread-cutting chart. For example, to cut six threads per inch, the sliding gear A is pushed "In," the top lever B is pushed to the extreme left position, and the tumbler lever C is placed just below the column in which the number 6 appears on the index chart.

The Engine Lathe. This type of lathe is described in detail in the later sections of this chapter.

Running a Lathe. Almost every young man in the shop—errand boy, apprentice boy, machinist's helper—wants to "run a lathe." It is a worthy ambition, but before he can hope to do much more than start or stop the machine, he must learn about the cutting tools—their shape, how they are sharpened, and how they are held to peel off the metal. He ought to know how to read the thirty-seconds and sixty-fourths of an inch on a rule or "scale" quickly and accurately, how to "feel" with a caliper to obtain a measurement within 0.002 in. He should learn as soon as possible the names and functions of the parts of the machine. He should appreciate, to a reasonable extent, the value of the proper cutting speeds and feeds. He should know how to oil the lathe carefully and thoroughly. After he has studied these things, "running the lathe" will be more interesting.

It is not to be expected that the beginner will learn all about the construction of a lathe in one or two lessons. This chapter covers information that should be acquired as rapidly as possible but may be acquired in connection with the doing of jobs in the lathe. The right kind of boy will not be satisfied with merely operating the lathe any more than he will be satisfied with sitting down to study names and functions of parts, and theory of why and how. *Experience* and *knowledge* go together and make for keener interest and faster progress.

The real mechanic understands the construction of his machine; he knows the names and uses of the parts and the principles underlying the operation of the mechanisms. The more one learns of these things the more interesting the work becomes.

Cleaning and Oiling (Fig. 10-6). One of the best ways for the beginner to start his acquaintance with a machine is to clean it thoroughly and oil it. Cleaning should be done while the machine is idle; *never when it is running.* A small piece of cloth moistened with kerosene will serve to cut the dirt and grease, after which wipe with dry waste. The ways and other exposed bearings should be especially clean before oiling. Use a stick to get in the corners, make a good job of it.

Fig. 10-6. Oiling chart for the lathe. (*South Bend Lathe Works*)

Oil the ways and other flat bearings (the dovetail bearing of the cross slide and over back of the bed where the carriage gib slides) by rubbing on the oil with the fingers.

Every piece that revolves has one or more bearings and every bearing has to have oil. Find every revolving part by turning the lathe by hand. Find the particular oil holes, be sure they are not stopped up with dirt, and put in sufficient oil to lubricate the bearings thoroughly. Common sense will help one to judge how often a bearing should be oiled and how much oil to use. It is perhaps sufficient to say that it is a crowning disgrace to let a machine get "stuck," and also that a bearing flooded until the oil drips on the floor is an indication of ignorance or carelessness.

Some of the later models of machine tools have pressure lubrication. A pump forces the oil from a reservoir through a filter and then through pipe lines to the bearings and gears. A gear splash, a cascade, or a pipe direct to the bearing may be used. Oil grooves are scientifically laid out in round and flat bearing surfaces. A strainer or settling basin is used to separate foreign matter, and a filter further to clean the oil is provided. *Having all these improvements in no wise lessens the responsibility of the machinist in being sure that his machine is properly oiled.*

While the student is cleaning and oiling is an excellent time to learn more concerning the features of the machine. Short descriptions of the parts of the lathe are given immediately after the following safety suggestions.

A FEW SAFETY SUGGESTIONS

1. Roll up your sleeves; remove your necktie.
2. Do not wear a ring or wrist watch.
3. Keep the wrenches, measuring tools, etc., arranged, not thrown, on the lathe board. Never put work, files, tools, etc., on the ways of the lathe, but do put a little oil on them occasionally.
4. Then put the oil can where you can't jab your face against the spout.
5. Keep your hands away from the revolving gears.
6. Ask questions after a reasonable amount of thought and study.
7. Do not move a handle to see what will happen, especially if the machine is running; reason out what the handle is for, or learn in some way, and then move it. Make sure you are right before starting the machine. If you are not sure, ask the instructor; it is better to be safe than sorry.
8. If you make a mistake, do not make the second one of trying to cover it up. The first may sometimes be excusable, the second never. Remember everyone respects an honest straightforward chap.
9. Do not make the same mistake twice.

Some Very Important Precautions. A habit one should cultivate when learning to run a lathe is make sure that the carriage
moves freely on the ways before starting the machine.

The first thing an experienced machinist always does when going
to work on a lathe is to move the carriage on the ways by hand to
make sure that

1. The half nut is not tightened.
2. The feed control is not tightened.
3. The carriage clamp screw is not tightened.
4. The ways are oiled.
5. The job clears the carriage when revolving.

DESCRIPTIONS AND FUNCTIONS OF LATHE PARTS

Figure 10-7 shows a quick change gear type lathe with all of the
important parts identified. Study this illustration very carefully
so that you may learn the names and the locations of these parts.

Fig. 10-7. Important parts of the lathe. (*South Bend Lathe Works*)

Although Fig. 10-7 shows a South Bend lathe, other lathes of the same type have about the same construction and location of parts. So by learning the parts on this lathe, it will make it so much easier when you have to operate any other make of lathe.

The Bed. The lathe bed (Fig. 10-8) is the foundation on which the lathe is built. It must be substantially constructed and scientifically designed.

Fig. 10-8. The ways of a lathe. (*South Bend Lathe Works*)

Prismatic V ways have been found to be the most accurate and serviceable type of ways for lathe beds and have been adopted by most of the leading machine-tool builders. There are two sets of ways on the lathe, the *outer* ways guide the carriage, and the *inner* ways keep the headstock and tailstock in line.

The V ways of the lathe bed are very carefully hand scraped so that the headstock, carriage, and tailstock are perfectly fitted and aligned parallel to the axis of the spindle through the entire length of the bed. These ways are usually about 90 deg. included angle and have the tops flat (in the new lathes) or rounded (in the old lathes) to prevent bruising.

The Headstock. The complete headstock comprises the headstock casting, the main spindle, the necessary mechanism for obtaining the various spindle speeds, and also certain gears which are used to operate the quick change gear mechanism.

Fig. 10-9. Headstock with cone-pulley cover opened. (*South Bend Lathe Works*)

Notice that in Fig. 10-7, this lathe does *not* have a feed rod. It has only a *lead screw* used for cutting threads. In this particular type of lathe, the feed rod is unnecessary because of the specially designed mechanisms in the gearbox and apron that control the feed.

The *main spindle* revolves on two bearings, one at each end of the headstock. A hole extends through the entire length of the main spindle and this hole is tapered at the front end to receive the live center. The main spindle controls the speed of the work when the work revolves. It must be mechanically true and perfectly aligned because the spindle "out of true" in any way, or in imperfect alignment, or with improperly adjusted bearings, will

Fig. 10-10. Phantom view of driving mechanism of lathe. (*South Bend Lathe Works*)

cause trouble. The main spindle is threaded to receive a chuck or faceplate.

Figure 10-9 shows the cone-pulley cover raised to illustrate how the belt fits over the pulley and the various steps on the cone pulley for speed adjustment.

The *live* center, which fits into the main spindle, is so called because it acts as a bearing surface on which the work rests. It revolves with the work. When compared with the hardness of the dead center in the tailstock, it is usually "soft" and is so made since it does no work.

Figure 10-10 shows a phantom view of the underneath belt motor drive. This drive is an efficient and practical direct equipment for a back-geared screw-cutting lathe. This drive is silent, powerful, and economical in operation.

The motor and driving mechanism are fully enclosed in the cabinet leg underneath the lathe headstock. There are no exposed pulleys, belts, or gears.

Power is transmitted from the motor to the countershaft by a V belt and from the countershaft up through the lathe bed to the headstock cone pulley by a flat leather belt.

Adjustments B and C are provided for taking up belt stretch and for obtaining any desired tension on the motor belt and cone-pulley belt. A belt tension release lever A, conveniently located on the front of the cabinet leg, permits easy shifting of the cone-pulley belt. A hinged cover encloses the headstock cone pulley when the lathe is in use.

DEFINITIONS: HEADSTOCK PARTS AND THEIR FUNCTIONS

Figure 10-11 identifies the parts of the headstock. The parts and functions are:

Cone Pulley. A four-step pulley and spindle; speeds are changed by shifting the belt from one step of the cone pulley to another.

Back-gear Lever. To engage the back gears for slow spindle speeds, pull the bull-gear lock pin out and push it down to disconnect the cone pulley from the spindle; then pull the back-gear lever forward. Revolve the cone pulley by hand to make sure the back gears are properly engaged. Do not engage the back gears while the lathe spindle is revolving.

Bull-gear Lock (plunger type). On some lathe headstocks the plunger-type bull-gear lock is used. For direct belt drive on these lathes, the bull-gear lock pin is pushed in, and for back-geared drive, it is pulled out.

Feed Reverse Lever. The feed reverse lever on the left end of the headstock has three positions; "Up," "Central," and "Down." The central position is neutral and when in this position all power carriage feeds are disconnected. When the lever is either in the up or down position, the carriage feeds by power will be in operation. The lathe should always be stopped before changing the position of the feed reverse lever.

Fig. 10-11. Parts of the headstock. (*South Bend Lathe Works*)

The Tailstock. The tailstock is for the purpose primarily of giving an outer bearing and support for work being turned on centers. To accommodate different lengths of work, it may be moved along the ways and clamped in any position, and in addition, the tailstock spindle, *A* in Fig. 10-12, which holds the dead center *B*, is adjustable longitudinally by means of the handwheel *C*, which operates the screw within the housing of the tailstock. The tailstock spindle is carefully fitted in its housing and is normally in exact alignment with the headstock spindle. There is *no vertical* adjustment whatever, but the tailstock may be adjusted *transversely*, that is, towards or away from the operator by means of the adjusting screws *D*, one on each side of the tailstock. The spindle may be locked in place by tightening the handle *E*, and the tailstock may be tightened in place by turning the nut *F*.

CAUTION. If the spindle is turned out so far as to run off the screw, be very careful to see that the keyway lines up with the

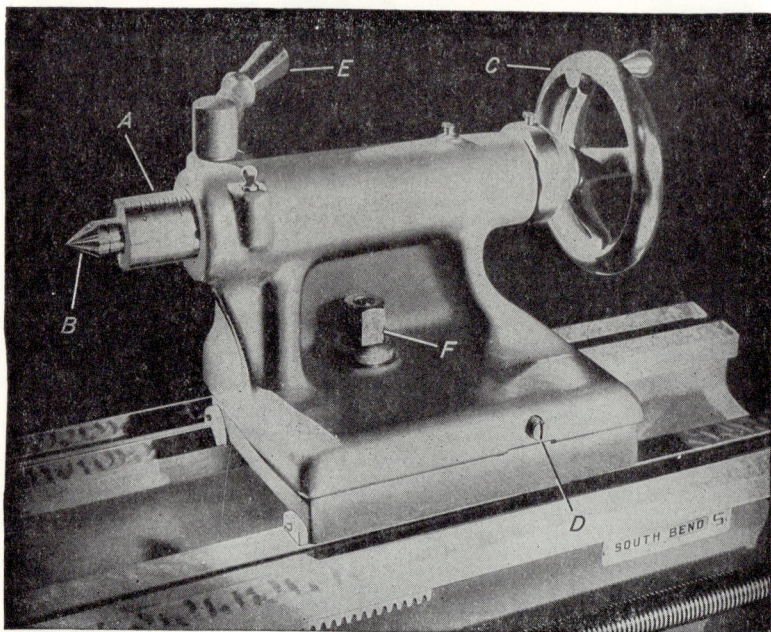

Fig. 10-12. Parts of the tailstock: *A*, tailstock spindle; *B*, dead center; *C*, hand wheel; *D*, adjusting screw; *E*, handle; *F*, nut. (*South Bend Lathe Works*)

key before turning it back. Be careful not to turn back too far or the spindle will jam against the shoulder of the screw. Notice that the spindle of the tailstock is graduated in eights of an inch so that the movement of the spindle may be measured.

The Dead Center. This center is called the *dead* center because it does not move with the work as the *live* center does. This center acts as a bearing for the work and supports it. It should be oiled before using.

To eliminate the rapid wear or burning of the steel tailstock center when high-rotating speeds are used (especially when using carbide-tipped cutting tools), current practice is to tip the point of the center with stellite or cemented carbide, or to replace the solid center with the so-called *live* or antifriction bearing center which revolves with the work just like the live center in the headstock. The bearings in these centers are made in a variety of designs in which roller or ball bearings are used. Figure 10-13 shows the South Bend ball-bearing center.

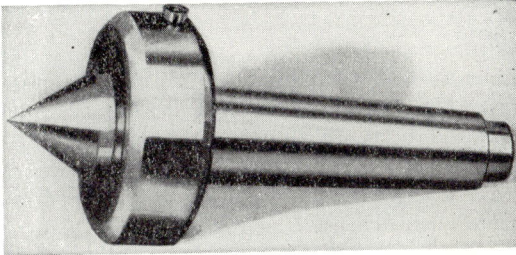

Fig. 10-13. Ball-bearing tailstock center. (*South Bend Lathe Works*)

To remove the dead center, turn the handwheel "back," or counterclockwise, until the end of the screw hits the end of the dead center and forces it out.

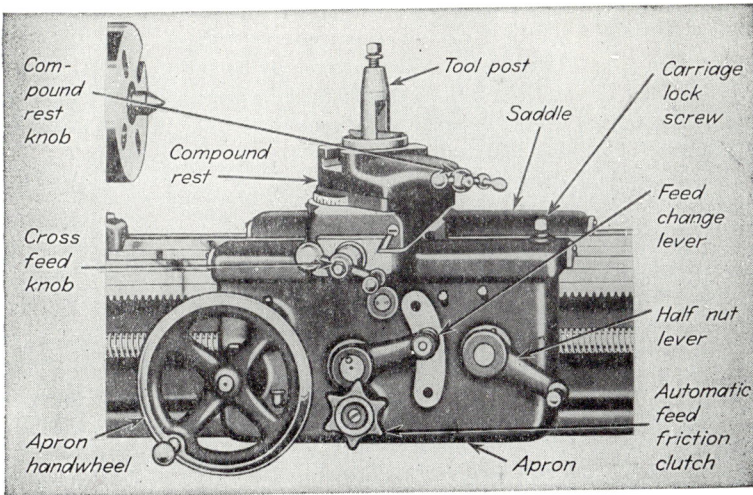

Fig. 10-14. Parts of the carriage. (*South Bend Lathe Works*)

The Carriage

PARTS OF THE CARRIAGE AND THEIR FUNCTIONS

Apron. This is the lower part in which there are gears which mesh with the rack (a straight gear mounted behind the apron and next to the outer ways) and other gears which adjusts the direction of the feed; the clutch mechanism and the split half nut.

Saddle. The saddle is fitted to the outer ways and is gibbed to the bed. It is in the form of the letter H, being bridged across the lathe bed to carry the cross slide and tool rest. It is gibbed in order to compensate the wear on these parts.

Tool Post. This part holds the tool holder in place. It consists of the tool post screw which tightens the tool holder in place; the ring at the bottom and the rocker which adjusts the position of the tool itself.

Compound Rest. This is a tool rest that may be swiveled on the cross slide to any desired angle. The swivel plate is graduated in degrees, and the zero mark (which is usually on the side of the plate) is in line with a mark on the cross slide when the compound rest is at right angles to the center line of the lathe.

DEFINITION: CARRIAGE ADJUSTMENTS

Compound-rest Knob. Used to move the tool held in the tool post.

Cross-feed Knob. Used to move the cross feed.

Apron Handwheel. Used to move the carriage by hand. (see APRON)

Carriage Lock Screw. Used to lock the carriage in place.

Feed-change Lever. Used to change the direction of feed. It has three positions: "Up" for longitudinal feeds, "Down" for cross feeds, and "Center" for the neutral position.

Half-nut Lever. Used to engage the lead screw when cutting threads. Although there is no thread chaser or thread dial indicator shown in the illustration (Fig. 10-14) many lathes are equipped with such a device. It is of great help in cutting threads. It is explained later in this section.

Automatic-feed Friction Clutch. Used to engage the power feed. The power-feed friction clutch controls the operation of both the power longitudinal feed and the power cross feed. To engage the clutch, turn the knob to the *right;* to disengage, turn to the *left.* The direction of the feed is controlled by the position of the reverse lever on the headstock.

How to Operate the Thread Dial (Fig. 10-15). This device is used primarily in the cutting of threads. By its use, the apprentice is able to "catch" the groove of a previous cut. The tool moves directly into the groove previously cut just by pushing the half-nut lever down.

Fig. 10-15. Threading dial or chasing dial. (*South Bend Lathe Works*)

On the South Bend lathe, when cutting all *even* threads per inch, close the half nut at *any line* on the dial.

For all *odd* threads per inch, close the half nut at *any numbered* line on the dial.

For all one-half threads, such as 4½, 5½, and 10½, close the half nut at *any odd-numbered* line.

Micrometer Collars (Fig. 10-16). Each graduation of the micrometer collars on the cross-feed knob and the compound-rest knob represent a movement of one-thousandth of an inch. The graduated collars may be set at zero by releasing the setscrews *A* which lock them in position.

Power Carriage Feeds on Quick Change Gear Lathes. A wide range of power longitudinal feeds and power cross feeds is available on all quick change gear lathes. To obtain any desired feed it is only necessary to arrange the levers shown in Fig. 10-17 on the gearbox according to the direct reading chart shown in Fig. 10-18. The threads per inch are shown in *large* figures and the

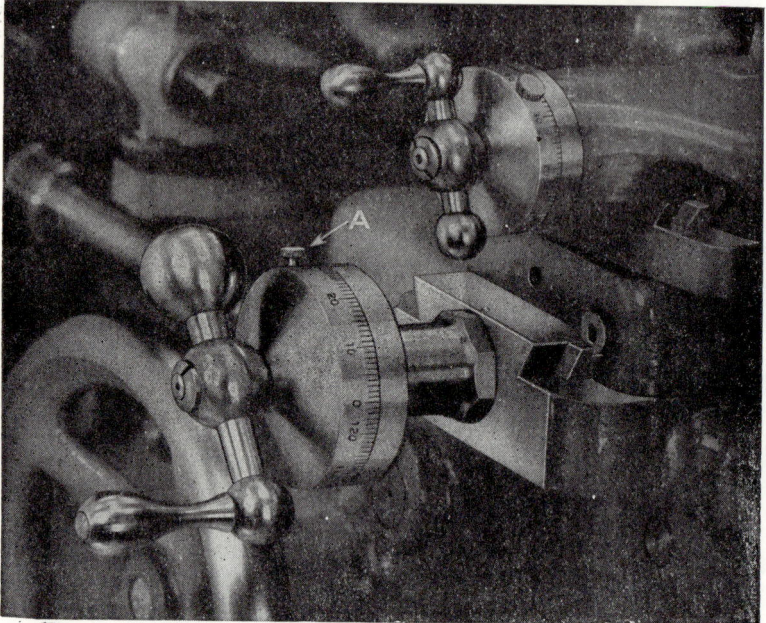

Fig. 10-16. Micrometer collar. *A*, setscrews. (*South Bend Lathe Works*)

smaller figures indicate the power longitudinal turning feeds in thousandths of an inch.

Power Carriage Feeds on Standard Change Gear Lathes. Standard change gear lathes are equipped with a set of independent gears for cutting screw threads and obtaining various power longitudinal feeds and power cross feeds.

In Fig. 10-19, a large screw gear *C* should be placed on the lead screw and a small stud gear *A* on the reverse stud. These two gears should be connected with idler gears *B*. To obtain finer or coarser feeds, use a smaller or larger stud gear.

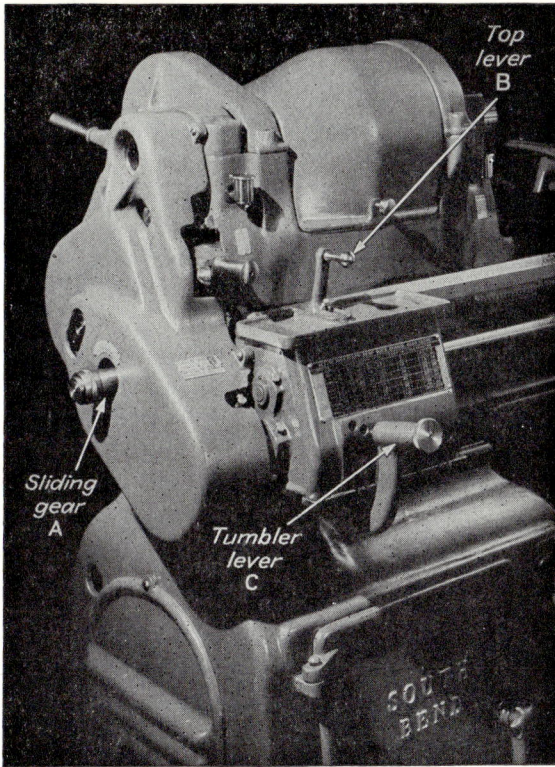

Fig. 10-17. Levers of the gearbox of a quick change gear lathe. (*South Bend Lathe Works*)

14½ - 16 INCH SOUTH BEND QUICK CHANGE GEAR LATHE										
SLIDING GEAR	TOP LEVER	THREADS PER INCH - FEEDS IN THOUSANDTHS								
IN	LEFT	4 .0841	4½ .0748	5 .0673	5½ .0612	5¾ .0585	6 .0561		6½ .0518	7 .0481	AUTOMATIC CROSS FEED EQUALS .375 TIMES LONGITUDINAL FEED
	CENTER	8 .0421	9 .0374	10 .0337	11 .0306	11½ .0293	12 .0280		13 .0259	14 .0240	
	RIGHT	16 .0210	18 .0187	20 .0168	22 .0153	23 .0146	24 .0140		26 .0129	28 .0120	
OUT	LEFT	32 .0105	36 .0093	40 .0084	44 .0076	46 .0073	48 .0070		52 .0065	56 .0060	
	CENTER	64 .0053	72 .0047	80 .0042	88 .0038	92 .0037	96 .0035		104 .0032	112 .0030	
	RIGHT	128 .0026	144 .0023	160 .0021	176 .0019	184 .0018	192 .0017		208 .0016	224 .0015	

Fig. 10-18. Chart showing positions of levers for threads per inch and feed in thousandths of an inch when using a quick change gear lathe. (*South Bend Lathe Works*)

Fig. 10-19. Position of gears in a standard change gear lathe. *A*, small stud gear; *B*, idler gear; *C*, large screw gear. (*South Bend Lathe Works*)

QUESTIONS ON LATHE CONSTRUCTION

1. What are the ways used for? How are they shaped? How are they finished? Why?

2. Explain how the carriage is moved along the ways by hand. What is the feed rack?

3. How are the ways cleaned and oiled properly? What will occur if they are allowed to become dry?

4. Where is the live center located? Where is the dead center located?

5. Why are the centers called dead and live? Which is hard? Which is soft? Why?

6. If through carelessness the tail spindle is run off the screw, what precaution must be taken regarding the keyway?

7. How is the tailstock adjusted sideways? Why is it necessary to first loosen the clamping bolts?

8. How is the tailstock spindle tightened?

9. Where is the main spindle of the lathe? Why must it be substantially made and accurate?

10. What establishes the center line of the lathe? What is it parallel to? When is the dead center in line?
11. How is the live center removed?
12. What part of the carriage is called the saddle? The apron?
13. Can you move the carriage by hand when the split nut is closed? When the feed-control knob is tightened? When the clamping screw is tightened? Give reasons.
14. Why does a machinist, before starting to work on a lathe, always try the carriage to make sure that it runs freely?

SPEEDS OF PULLEYS AND GEARS

The beginner should consider carefully the construction of the driving mechanism of the lathe, and understand thoroughly the method of obtaining the different speeds, because similar mechanical principles are involved in nearly every sort of machine tool. The first thing to understand when beginning a study of machine speeds is the driving and driven action of pulleys and gears.

Driving and Driven Pulleys. When two pulleys are connected by a belt, motion is transmitted from the driving pulley to the driven pulley.

If the driven pulley and the driving pulley are the same diameter, the driven pulley will make as many revolutions as the driving pulley, because the distance that the belt is carried along by frictional contact with the driving pulley during one revolution is equal to the circumference of the driving pulley, which is equal to the circumference of the driven pulley. If the *driven* pulley is *twice* the diameter of the driving pulley (Fig. 10-20), the driven pulley goes

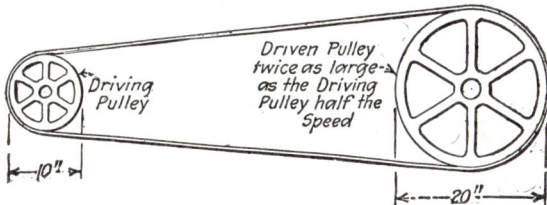

Fig. 10-20. Driving and driven pulleys.

half as fast as the driving pulley, because the distance that a point on the belt is carried along by frictional contact with the driving pulley during one revolution is equal to *half* the circumference of the driven pulley. If the *driven* pulley is *one-third as large* in diameter as the driving pulley, it will revolve three times as fast as the driving pulley because the circumference of the driving pulley is three times the circumference of the driven pulley. That is, the speeds of driving and driven pulleys are to each other *inversely* as their diameter.[1]

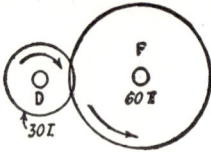

Fig. 10-21. Driver and follower gears.

Driving and Driven (Follower) Gears. The same reasoning is true with gears with different numbers of teeth as with pulleys of different diameters. If a driving gear having 30 teeth (Fig. 10-21) is in mesh with a gear having 60 teeth, when the driving gear has made one full revolution it has engaged only 30 of the 60 teeth of the follower gear and turned it only half around. If a driving gear *D* has 40 teeth (Fig. 10-22a), and the follower gear *F* has 20 teeth one revolution of the driving gear will revolve the follower gear two

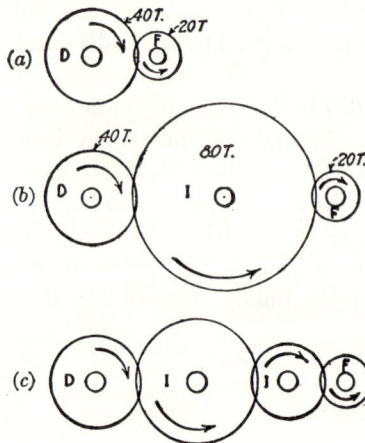

Fig. 10-22. Simple gear trains. (*a*) No intermediate, (*b*) one intermediate, (*c*) two intermediates.

revolutions. That is, the velocities of the driving and follower gears are to each other *inversely* as the numbers of their teeth.[2]

---

[1] For formulas on speeds of pulleys see Appendix (p. 515–516).
[2] For formulas on velocities of gears see Appendix (p. 516–518).

Simple Gear Train. Two gears in mesh are called a pair of gears. Three or more gears, the first meshing with the second, the second with the third, and so on, constitute a simple train of gears. The gear between the driving and follower gears in a simple train is known as an *idler* or *intermediate*. A small gear in a pair or a train or gears is often called a *pinion*.

Placing an intermediate gear (of any number of teeth) between two gears changes the direction of rotation of the follower gear but does not change the velocity ratio. This is illustrated in Fig. 10-22*b*. One revolution of D will engage 40 teeth in I (no matter how many teeth I has), and I will engage 40 teeth in F turning it around twice, the same as in *a* without the intermediate. Note, however, that in Fig. 10-22*b* the direction of rotation of the follower gear F is changed.

Any number of intermediates will not affect the *velocity ratio* between the driving and the follower gears, but the *direction of rotation of the follower gear depends on the number of intermediates;* thus with one intermediate the follower gear will revolve in the same direction as the driving gear (*b*, Fig. 10-22) and with two intermediates the direction will be reversed (Fig. 10-22*c*).

Compound Gear Train. If, however, there are two gears fastened to the same shaft, or to a quill, or fastened together in any way so that when one revolves the other must revolve at the same speed, one engaged by the driving gear and the other engaging the follower, these two gears *mounted on the same shaft* are not intermediates. They are respectively the follower gear of the first pair and the driving gear of the second pair of four gears which form a *compound gear train*. In a compound gear train the sizes of the gears between the first driver and the final follower cannot be disregarded as in a simple train. This is illustrated in Fig. 10-23. Suppose D_1

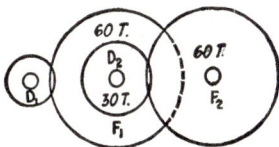

Fig. 10-23. Compound gear trains. Gears F_1 and D_2 are mounted on the same shaft and serve as the compound between D_1 and F_2.

revolves twelve times, F_1 will revolve four times being three times as large; D_2 will revolve four times because it is fastened to the same shaft as F_1, and the final driven gear F_2 will make *two* revolutions.

QUESTIONS ON PULLEY SPEEDS AND GEAR VELOCITIES

1. What is meant by the velocity of a gear?

2. The velocities of two gears in mesh (with teeth engaging) varies inversely as the numbers of teeth. What do you mean by "inversely"?

3. A driving gear *D* has 60 teeth and meshes with a gear *F* of 40 teeth. How many times will *F* (the follower gear) revolve when *D* makes 10 revolutions? Why?

4. Introduce an intermediate gear *I* of 120 teeth between *D* and *F*. How will this affect the result as to the relative speed of *F*? As to direction of *F*?

5. Introduce one more intermediate of any number of teeth in this train of gears. What will be the result as to relative speed of *F*? As to direction of *F*?

6. What is meant by a simple train of gears?

7. What does the introduction of one or more intermediates serve to do as regards the speed of the follower gear? As regards direction of follower gear? Is this always true in any simple train of gears?

8. When installing a lathe it is desired to have the slowest speed of the cone pulley 100 r.p.m. The largest step of the cone pulley on the lathe is 10 in. in diameter, the smallest step on the countershaft cone pulley is 6 in. in diameter, and the loose pulley is 12 in. in diameter. What diameter pulley will be required on the line shaft which runs at 250 r.p.m.?

9. A pulley 12 in. in diameter is running at 220 r.p.m. and is connected by a belt to a pulley 8 in. in diameter. How fast does the smaller pulley revolve?

10. What is meant by an inverse ratio?

Direct Spindle Speeds. There are usually two or more series of speeds in all except the smallest sizes of machine tools. They are commonly known as the *direct* speeds or "*back gears out*" and *indirect* speeds or "*back gears in.*"

Different *direct* speeds in a belt-driven (cone pulley) lathe are obtained by changing the driving belt to the various steps on the cone pulley. The cone pulley of the lathe is the *driven* pulley and changing the belt from a larger to a smaller step on this pulley (and a corresponding larger step on the counter-shaft cone pulley, which is the driving pulley) increases the speed.

The cone pulley (Fig. 10-25) is not fastened to the spindle but may revolve freely upon it. The spindle-driving gear D called the *face gear* is keyed to the spindle, and to cause the spindle to revolve, it is necessary to transmit the motion from the belt-driven cone pulley to the face gear D. The *direct* speeds are obtained by locking together the cone pulley and the face gear D by the *lockpin L*. As many different direct speeds may be thus obtained as there are steps on the cone pulley.

Lockpin (Fig. 10-24). The plunger P is really the locking pin; when it enters the cone pulley it locks the face gear to the pulley.

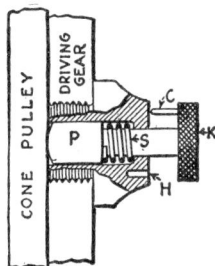

Fig. 10-24. Lockpin. When the lock-pin is arranged as shown, the cone pulley is free to revolve past the face gear (spindle-driving gear). There are three or more equidistant holes in the pulley which make it un-necessary to turn the pulley more than one-third of a revolution to bring a hole in front of the plunger.

The spring S tends to push the plunger into the hole in the cone pulley but in the position shown in Fig. 10-24 is kept from doing so by the pin C. To "put in" the lockpin, turn the knurled knob K until the pin enters the hole H and pull the belt *by hand* until one of the holes in the pulley comes in front of P and P enters the hole. *Never* start the machine by power until the plunger is in the hole of the pulley. When "taking out" the lockpin pull the knob K until the pin is out of the hole and turn the knob part way around.

Back Gears. In order to get a large number of different speeds, many engine lathes and other machine tools are equipped with back gears. The function of the back gears is to give a speed to the spindle which is slower than the speed of the cone pulley. This reduction in speed also gives a corresponding *increase* in power. Some lathes have two or more sets of back gears.

Referring to Fig. 10-25 the back gears B and C are both fastened to the quill[1] which revolves on the shaft E which is supported by brackets back of the spindle. It will be noted that the ends of this

---

[1] **Quill:** Hollow sleeve which revolves on a shaft and carries pulleys, gears, clutches, etc.

shaft, the bearings, are eccentric (out of center) with the part of the shaft on which the quill revolves.

This construction is for the purpose of changing the position of the back gears, putting them in to engage with the gears A and D or taking them out of mesh by partly rotating the shaft by means of the back-gear handle H.

Indirect Spindle Speeds, Back Gears (An Application of Compound Gearing). It will be observed (Fig. 10-25) that the back

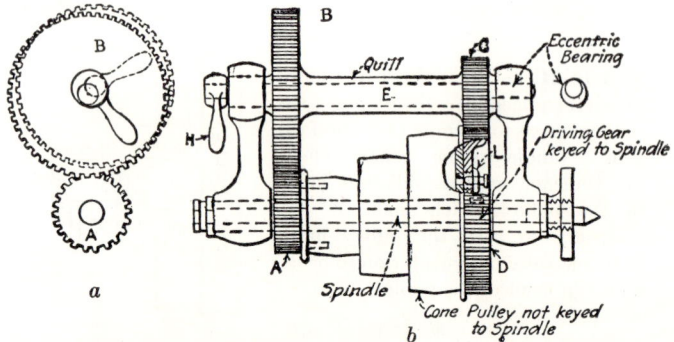

Fig. 10-25. Lathe headstock: (*b*) is a view looking down on the headstock with the back gears supported back of the cone pulley; (*a*) is an end view showing the two positions of the back gears and back-gear handle; heavy line "in," light line "out."

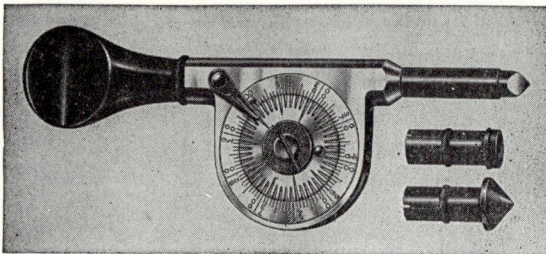

Fig. 10-26. Speed indicator. One hundred turns of the spindle cause one revolution of dial which is graduated in one hundred divisions, with every ten divisions numbered. Rubber tips may be applied to the indicator spindle.

gears are in and the *lockpin* is out. Gear A is fastened securely to the cone pulley and power is transmitted from the cone and gear A to back gears B and C, and from C to face gear D which is keyed to the spindle. If gear B is three times as large as A it will revolve one-third as fast. *B* and *C* are both fastened to the same quill and revolve at equal speeds. If *D* is three time as large as *C* it will revolve one-third as fast, with the result that *D* will revolve one-third of one-third or one-ninth as fast as *A*. There are, of course, as many back-gear speeds as there are steps on the cone pulley. A lathe with three steps on the cone pulley and with back gears would thus have six spindle speeds, three direct and three indirect.

Revolutions per Minute (R.P.M.). In order that the beginner may realize the different revolutions per minute (r.p.m.) of the lathe spindle at each of the positions of the speed-change levers (or of the belt on the different steps of the cone pulley if belt driven), he may ascertain the different speeds by counting the lower number of revolutions, and by using a speed indicator (Fig. 10-26) for the faster speeds (get the number of revolutions for $\frac{1}{2}$ min. and multiply by 2 to get the r.p.m.).

Sliding Gears. To obtain a number of speeds of a driven shaft, or of a spindle of a modern machine tool, a construction known as *sliding gears* is much used. These sliding gears consist of a cluster of gears, the parts of which are listed here.

Suitable levers are arranged

Fig. 10-27. (*a*) Multiple-spline gear and fork for moving gear, (*b*) multiple-spline shaft sometimes used as an integral key shaft, (*c*) yoke for moving gear.

to operate a fork as in Fig. 10-27*a*, or a yoke as in Fig. 10-27*c*, to slide the cluster of gears to the position desired.

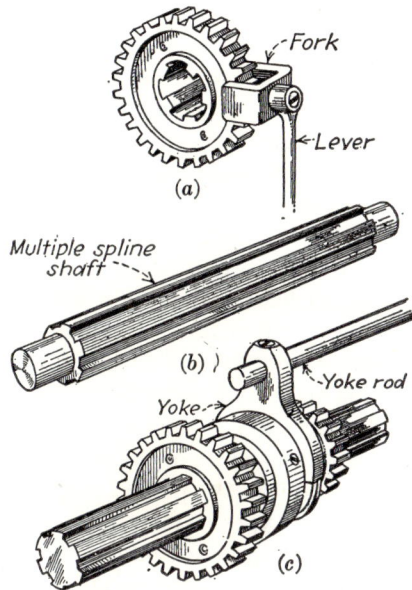

DEFINITIONS: CLUSTER OF GEARS

Gear Cluster. A number of gears mounted together to slide as a unit.

Key. A piece, usually rectangular section, used to fasten to a rod or shaft

a pulley or gear or similar part having a hole fitting the shaft, to keep
this part in place and to keep it from turning.

Keyway (or key seat): The groove in the rod or shaft, or in the hole in the
pulley or gear, to fit the key.

Spline. A comparatively long keyway in the shaft or rod to permit sliding
of the gear if desired.

Feather. A sliding key, fitting tight in the sliding part and easy in the spline.

Integral. Made in one piece.

Multiple. More than one, usually several.

Until quite recently one sliding key, or "feather," was all that
was needed to drive almost any gear, or bank or cluster of gears,
but since so much more power must be delivered by the heavier,
faster machines, the heat-treated alloy-steel gears that are now
used must have more than one key, and the shaft with the *multiple
spline*, sometimes called *integral key*, is commonly used (Fig. 10-27b).

An idea of the importance of this design may be gathered from
the fact that standards for broached-hole dimensions from $\frac{3}{4}$ to 3 in.
diameters have been established: for permanent fit, to slide when
not under load, and to slide when under load. Broaches for making
the holes and cutters for hobbing the shafts are manufactured.

Other Features of High-duty Lathes. The use of high-speed
cutting tools and the resulting increased power requirements have
made necessary in machine design a much stronger construction
of the various parts of the machine and a more efficient drive. Keen
competition on the part of the manufacturers has developed many
interesting types of direct-gear-driven and clutch-controlled mechanisms which give a greater number of spindle speeds than is possible
in the cone-pulley type, and also a considerable increase in the power
delivered. These machines are differentiated from the cone-pulley
type by the terms *geared head*, or sometimes *selective gear drive*,
and *constant speed drive*.

Among the advantages of the geared head are the ease and flexibility of the speed changes (by means of levers instead of changing
belts) and its adaptability to individual-motor drive, or for driving
direct to the single pulley from the line shaft.

With the increase in driving power of the geared-head lathe a
corresponding increase in strength and rigidity in the machine as a
whole is necessary, particularly in the apron and other parts of the

feeding mechanism. For this reason the high-duty lathe apron is provided with a back plate which affords a back support for the studs, the pinions and gears are made of specially selected steel, and the studs are heat treated and ground.

As has been stated, modern lathes up to 24 in. are provided with quick change gear mechanism for feeds and thread leads. This mechanism usually provides 36 or more (depending on the make) feeds and as many thread changes, any one of which is instantly available by operating one or possibly two levers. These levers, together with an index plate for showing the position of the levers for the given amount of feed or the pitch of the thread, are conveniently arranged on the gearbox.

A recent development in lathe design is the *flanged* spindle nose to replace the threaded nose for continuous chucking work or for mounting special fixtures in manufacturing. A centralizing taper is provided on the flange to accurately and quickly locate the chuck plate or fixture, which is then firmly fastened to the flange by bolts and driven by a substantial key. However, for the general run of shop jobs and toolroom work, requiring more frequent changes of faceplates, chucks, etc., the threaded nose is preferred. (It will be observed that the lathe illustrated in Fig. 10-28 has a flanged spindle nose.)

The original geared heads were noisy and many of them were far from smooth running. These faults have been corrected in many ways:

1. The gears themselves have been greatly improved in shape and finish and durability, hence in quiet and smooth running.

2. The use of too many friction and positive jaw clutches within the head has been avoided by the use of sliding gears. A simple movement of a conveniently arranged lever serves to engage the mating gears that give the gear run for the speed desired.

3. Increased strength, longer life, and much greater smoothness in operation result from having the gears on multiple-spline (integral-key) shafts.

4. Antifriction bearings, roller and ball types, have taken the place of most of the plain bearings.

5. Most machines may be instantly started or stopped by means of a friction clutch and a brake operated by a close-at-hand lever.

In some of the modern lathes a forward and reverse control of the *apron gearing* is provided in addition to the friction clutch and brake for the machine spindle. Electromagnetic brakes are also used on many modern lathes.

6. The entire head unit, including the clutch and brake, all bearings, the spindle, the shafts or the sleeves for the gears, are automatically oiled.

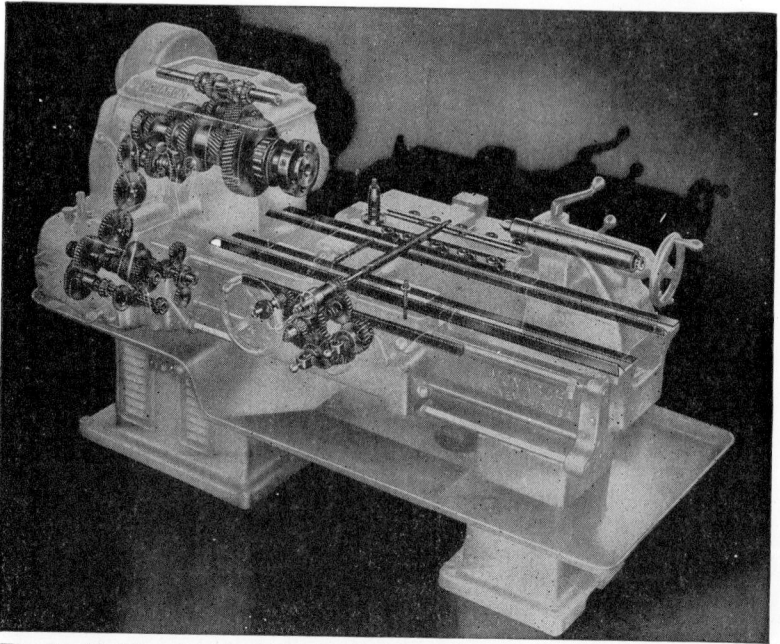

Fig. 10-28. Phantom view of a modern lathe. The parts shown in black are of special alloy steels, heat-treated. These parts include the main spindle, the tailstock spindle, all gears, studs, and shafts in the headstock, quick-change gearbox and apron, the feed rack and the feed-rack pinion. (*Monarch Machine Tool Company*)

The aim has been to improve the appearance of machines, make the speed and feed changes easier, lessen the need of repairs, and, by building the machines in units, make easier any necessary repairs or replacements; also to provide increased speed and greater strength in order to use up-to-date high-speed cutting tools. And all the while the purpose has been to give the machine *a smoother action* because the good work of any machine depends upon this. To the great credit of the machine-tool designers and builders the increased flexibility and speed of modern machines are combined with a smooth action that gives a high degree of accuracy and an excellent finish in the work produced.

It must not be lost sight of, however, that the lathe-operation essentials are practically unchanged. Certainly the lathe is faster, and many improvements make for the convenience of the operator,

Fig. 10-29. Cam-lock spindle nose. (*Pratt & Whitney*)

but setting the tool, turning a cylinder, turning a taper, cutting a thread, or boring a hole, and the knowledge, the knack, the skill, the judgment, remain about the same as always.

The Cam-lock Spindle Nose (Fig. 10-29). Adopted by the American Standards Association as the spindle nose that provides the most rigid and accurate means of holding chucks, faceplates, and fixtures to the spindle, this new holding device is fast replacing other means of holding faceplates and chucks. The pilot taper and flange face ensure permanent accuracy in holding the chuck or

faceplate central and square. There are no threads to be damaged or
to catch dirt or chips, the holding means being a series of cam-
locking studs on the back of the chuck or plate which fit into radial
holes in the spindle flange. There is no possibility of a chuck being
thrown off during high-speed operation or when the spindle is
stopped suddenly.

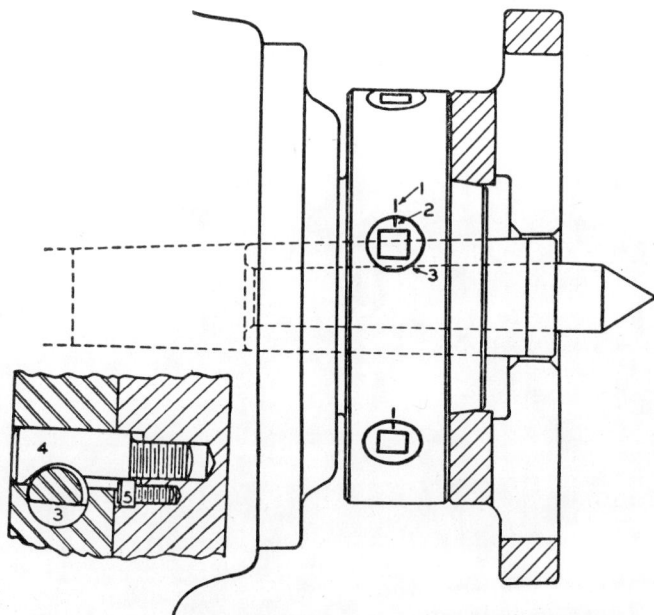

Fig. 10-30. Parts of a cam-lock spindle nose: (1) registration lines on spindle
nose, (2) registration lines on cam locks, (3) cam locks, (4) cam-lock mating
stud on chuck or faceplate, (5) hollow-head retaining screw. (*Pratt & Whitney*)

The cam-lock nose also provides the most convenience and safety
in mounting and removing chucks and faceplates. There is no need
to lock gears and pound a chuck loose, because it cannot "freeze"
on.

Still one more great advantage of the cam-lock nose is the fact
that it is the American Standard for toolroom lathes, engine lathes,
turret lathes, and automatic lathes. This ensures accurate inter-
changeability of chucks and fixtures on all lathes equipped with
this new nose without requiring an adapter plate.

The spindle is hardened, tempered, and accurately ground, leaving the front end very hard to prevent the embedding of chips and to assure permanent accuracy. It is mounted on preloaded super-precision ball bearings and requires no further adjustment.

To mount faceplates or chucks on the cam-lock spindle nose, proceed as follows (Fig. 10-30):

1. Wipe off all chips and dirt from the pilot and flange of the spindle nose and off the corresponding recess and shoulder on the face-plate or chuck so that no chips that would otherwise prevent their running true remain.

2. Place the registration lines No. 2 on the heads of the six cam locks so as to match the corresponding lines No. 1 on the outer rim of the spindle nose. Detents will hold them in these positions.

3. Lift the faceplate or chuck up in line with the spindle either by hand (resting it on a wooden block) or by using the sling of a crane, and push it onto the spindle nose.

4. Tighten the cam locks No. 3 by a clockwise turn of the wrench, pulling them up tight by hand. It is not necessary to use a hammer on the wrench. When the cam locks are tightened, the registration lines No. 2 on their heads should be between the "three o'clock" and "six o'clock" positions. If any one of these does not register within this range, the mating stud No. 4 in the faceplate or chuck should be adjusted.

To remove the faceplate or chuck reverse the operations, that is,

1. Unlock the cam-lock studs No. 3 by turning the wrench counter-clockwise until the registration lines No. 2 on the heads of the six cam locks match the corresponding lines No. 1 on the flange of the spindle nose.

2. Gently tap the faceplate or chuck with a lead hammer so as to loosen the pinch at the pilot, and then pull it away from the spindle nose.

Attachments. A great expense in manufacturing is the obsolescence of special machines. By building special units or attachments it is possible often to increase the production capacity of a standard machine, without destroying its flexibility, to practically the output of a special machine. If the machine is to be used in making a special part only a portion of the time, being a flexible machine tool, it may be used for other work the rest of the time. If the part produced becomes obsolete, then only the special unit is obsolete, not necessarily the whole machine.

The demand for special attachments to increase production, speed, and accuracy presents real problems for competent designers and for skilled machinists and toolmakers. It only means, however, the application of the old principles of machine-shop practice—the application of screws, gears, cams, levers, clutches, and properly sharpened cutting tools. It calls for real mechanical ability to design and build special mechanisms, and the machine shop is where the training is obtained.

The Electric Motor. It would be practically impossible to use many of the attachments, or even the improved units, of the modern machine tool, without the individual electric-motor drive, not only for the machine itself but for the attachment or unit. The speed obtained and the ease of operation are especially noticeable in the traverse of heavy units, as planer heads for example, and in the use of hand tools, as hand drills. Every young machinist should learn the principles of the construction, operation, and repair of electric motors and switches.

THE TURRET LATHE

There is one branch of the lathe family that is used only when and where parts are to be machined on a production basis. That is to say, many parts produced in the fastest time that are identical in size and shape and to a close tolerance. One setup can be made which will enable the operator to perform several operations on the same workpiece using several different cutting tools with exact results that can be duplicated on piece after piece. This branch of the lathe family includes both the horizontal and vertical turret lathes, automatic screw machines, automatic multistation lathes and automatic multispindle lathes. There are others.

The horizontal turret lathe (Fig. 10-31) is the most widely used of this branch of the lathe family. It is the "work horse" of the group, always operating at top speed, roughing out the excess metal with maximum depth of cut and feed, and revolving at the maximum speed possible. Coolants are usually used causing smoke and fumes to rise above the machine as though it were on fire.

Although the operator of a turret lathe does not need to have all of the skills of the first-class engine-lathe hand, he is, by no means, without skill. He must be able to set up tools and gages and tool stops for a smooth running sequence of operations without excessive tool travel or movement.

The turret lathe gets its name from the device that can hold many tools. It may be indexed so that each tool can be brought to the position where it is to be used on the job. This multiple tool-holding turret was first used as an accessory to the engine lathe. Originally it was a block that could hold more than a single tool. Then it became an indexed turret mounted in the tailstock of the

Fig. 10-31. A ram-type turret lathe. (*The Warner-Swasey Company*)

lathe. Later these features were refined and incorporated into an entirely new machine, similar in many respects to the engine lathe but different in several important ways.

The headstock of the turret lathe carries the spindle and the gear combinations that drive it. It is usually capable of six to twelve spindle speeds that can be reversed when it is needed. The handles that control the selection of the gears necessary for a required speed are located outside the headstock casting, just as they are found on an engine lathe. The spindle speeds differ in the various sized lathes, those for light work are capable of high speeds, close to

4,000 r.p.m. while the heavier turret lathes have a slower but more powerful drive.

The cross slide of the turret lathe differs in many respects from that of the engine lathe. It has its own turret, a square one, in which four cutting tools can be held. The square turret can be indexed so that the required tool can be brought into an operating position. It is then locked in place to prevent any possibility of a chatter caused by tool vibration. The crosswise movement of the tools as well as the longitudinal movement can be controlled by the setting of positive stops or by the automatic throwing out of the feed

Fig. 10-32. A saddle-type turret lathe. (*Jones and Lamson Machine Company*)

control (feed trip). Tools can also be fastened to the cross slide both at the front and back of the rest. This is usually the position of the tools used for shouldering, for cutting slots, or for parting off the piece after the last operation has been performed.

In place of the tailstock, the turret lathe uses a hexagonal shaped turret that carries the tools used for a variety of operations. The tools are mounted in the proper sequence required by the job being machined and are indexed at the completion of each operation.

Turret lathes are made with either a horizontal or vertical spindle. The vertical turret resembles a vertical boring mill, the difference being mainly in the turret arrangement of holding and indexing the tools. The work is fastened on a rotating table or chuck while the tools are held in the turret supported above the cross slide. Tools can also be held in a head in a square turret at the side of the table. It is possible for this machine to have more than one side head in use should the job require it.

Horizontal turret lathes are made in two types, namely, the ram (Fig. 10-31) and the saddle types (Fig. 10-32). They are designed for different kinds of work and get their names from the way the turret is mounted on the lathe. The ram type has the turret mounted on a slide that moves back and forth on a saddle that is clamped to the lathe bed. This machine is used mostly for bar work as well as light machining.

The saddle-type machine has its turret mounted on the saddle which moves back and forth while the turret-held tools are in operation. This type of lathe is more suitable for heavy chucking work. It is designed to give more rigid support to the tools. The stroke or tool movement can be much longer, making it suitable for long turning or boring operations.

There are many ways of supporting the job for turret-lathe operations. The standard six, four, three, and two jaw chucks are often used as well as special types of chucks such as the two jaw box chuck and the revolving jaw chucks. Chucks may be controlled by air, hydraulics, or electricity.

Bar work is usually held in collets when the stock is smaller than $2\frac{1}{2}$ in. in diameter or width size. Collets are of the spring type and of various sizes. They are shaped to hold round, hexagonal, or square stock.

Turret lathes may be equipped with steady rests to support long slender work. They are available in several sizes and types.

The methods and equipment used to support the cutting tools of a turret lathe are many and varied. They are usually selected on the basis of job requirements.

Many types of work are possible with a turret lathe. Among these are turning, boring, reaming, threading, taper turning, and internal and external threading. An experienced engine-lathe hand should have no difficulty in operating a turret lathe after receiving some explanation regarding the machine's controls. Study is required for the efficient placement of the tooling equipment.

CHAPTER 11

Cutting Tools and Cutting Speeds

In the beginning of a discussion of lathe tools, it is necessary to call attention to the work done by a committee under the sponsorship of the American Standards Association. The committee consisted of members of the National Machine Tool Builders' Association, the Society of Automotive Engineers, the Metal Cutting Tool Institute, and the American Society of Mechanical Engineers.

This committee set up standard terms and definitions for tools used in machine-shop practice. All such terms and definitions are used in this chapter with the permission of the American Standards Association. These terms and definitions are discussed and illustrated and it will be to the benefit of the apprentice to learn them just as soon as possible. Get to use the correct terminology at the very beginning of your trade apprenticeship.

KINDS AND CARE OF CUTTING TOOLS

Cutting-tool Efficiency.[1] A machine tool is no more efficient than its cutting tool. Plants that machine widely different types of material on a production basis find it economical to use tools especially designed for each material, rather than to use one design of tools for all jobs. Magnesium alloys call for tools of somewhat different design from those used on iron or copper alloys, while cast iron calls for tools of different design from those used on alloy steel.

Cutting tools must combine sufficient strength to maintain a sharp cutting edge, sufficient wear resistance to prevent wearing of the cutting edge, sufficient toughness to prevent chipping of the

[1] N. E. Woldman and R. C. Gibbons, *Machinability and Machining of Metals*, New York, McGraw-Hill Book Company, Inc., 1951.

cutting edge, and sufficient hardness to prevent picking up of the chips.

However, if a cutting tool is to give maximum production with the least amount of trouble and maintenance, it is necessary that the following five points be observed:

1. The right kind of tool material for the purpose of the tool must be selected.

2. The tool must be given the correct hardening heat-treatment.

3. The tool must be correctly designed.

4. The tool must be accurately made by the toolmaker.

5. The tool must be properly applied in the machining operation with the proper coolant and lubricant.

It is very necessary for the student in machine-shop practice to realize in the *beginning* that the cutting tool is a most important factor. There is nothing in shop work that should be given more thoughtful consideration than cutting tools. If one understands the principles underlying the successful action of the cutting tool, he has gone a long way in becoming expert in its use.

Time is always wasted if an improperly shaped tool is used. A dull tool is dangerous to use. It is fairly difficult for the beginner to hold a lathe tool against the grinding wheel and grind it just how and where it should be ground. He must first learn how it should be ground, and he must acquire by practice the knack of grinding it.

The action of a cutting tool depends primarily on three things: (1) the rigidity of the work, that is, of the piece itself, and the manner in which it is held in the machine; (2) the rigidity of the tool— its size and the way in which it is held; and (3) the shape of the cutting tool as it is ground, and as it is presented to the work.

The machine-tool builder takes care of the design of the machine to give the necessary strength and stability. The cutting action of the tool, however, depends on its shape and its adjustment in the holding device. This is especially interesting to the machinist because most of the cutting tools he uses in the shop must be shaped— or at least sharpened— and adjusted (set) by himself. The experienced workman will never use a dull tool, a poorly shaped tool, or a tool improperly set or insecurely held if he can help it.

Simple Fundamental Factors Governing Lathe Cutting-tool Design. If you look up the meaning of the word *cut* in a standard dictionary, you will find that it may mean any of the following: cleave, gash, incise, divide, carve, hew, trim, pare, remove, etc. Because one of the simplest words in the English language can be correctly used to convey so many different thoughts, each of a dozen different people might have his own particular impression of the meaning of the word *cut*. Little wonder then that so many people, including trained mechanics, find it difficult to describe clearly their own ideas of just how a cutting tool behaves, and why it behaves in a certain manner under certain conditions.

Perhaps our childhood experiences and our fear of being cut cause us to think of cutting as being primarily a "slicing" action, which can be brought about with little effort other than the effort of moving the cutting tool. Because of this, we seldom stop to think that when an instrument or tool cuts, *pressure*, as well as motion, is necessary. Broadly speaking, the thinner and the sharper the edge of the cutting tool, the less pressure is required to cut a piece of material.

In cutting metal with a machine-driven cutting tool, pressure is perhaps the most important factor in the cutting action. It is true that motion is also necessary, but the effect of motion is more noticeable and, therefore, more easily understood. Pressure, on the other hand—what causes it, how is it exerted on the tool, and how it affects both the tool and material—is not so easily understood without considerable study. However, it is largely because of the effect of pressure on the cutting action, that a machine tool is designed in a specific manner.

To begin with, it should be recognized that a metal-cutting tool actually "pushes" the metal apart. As a result, the pressures exerted on the cutting edge of a machine-driven cutting tool are very high, particularly as the rate of feed and depth of cut increases. This pressure force occurs in three different directions in the ordinary metal-turning operation: (1) the force exerted against the top or face of the tool in a downward direction, due to the rotation of the workpiece; (2) the force exerted against the flank or side of the tool due to the lateral motion or feed of the tool; and (3) the force exerted against the end or nose of the tool, due to the fact that the tool is forced into the material. These three forces, exerted on the tool from three different directions, are necessary because they make the cutting action possible. At the same time, as they increase, they increase the friction between the tool and the workpiece with its attendant heat and tool wear.

Primarily, the location of the cutting edge is determined largely by the direction in which cutting pressure is to be applied. That is, the tool blank is ground so as to create a cutting edge so located that the cutting pressure will force it into the material being cut. The objective is to produce a cutting edge that will require a minimum of pressure to force it through the metal, yet will withstand the application of cutting pressure without breaking, and will resist wear.

Simple Fundamentals Governing the Form and Application of Lathe Tools. Fundamentally, all cutting tools are provided with a cutting edge or edges which are adaptations of three basic forms, namely, the *point*, the *straight edge*, and the *shaped edge* (Fig. 11-1). A *pointed* cutting edge (Fig. 11-1*a*) is the part of

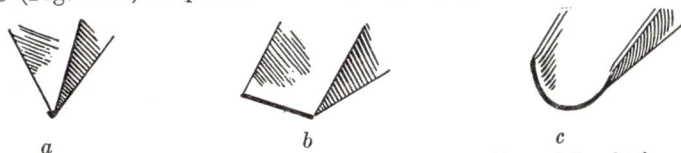

Fig. 11-1. Cutting edges: (*a*) Pointed cutting edge, (*b*) straight cutting edge, (*c*) shaped cutting edge. (*The Shell Oil Company*)

a tool where three or more surfaces come to form a point. A *straight* cutting edge (Fig. 11-1*b*) is the part of a tool where two flat surfaces intersect to form a straight line. A *shaped* cutting edge (Fig. 11-1*c*) is the part of a tool where two surfaces, one of which must be curved, intersect to form a curved line.

Examples of these basic forms as applied to cutting tools follow:

Tools with pointed *edges:* Scriber, handsaw, circular saw, rasp, grinding wheel, emery cloth.

Tools with straight *edges:* Cold chisels, wood chisels, mill file, keyway cutter, drill, countersink, tapered reamer with straight flutes.

Tools with shaped *edges:* Cape chisel, milling cutters (concave and convex), milling cutters with spiral cutting edges.

The cutting edge of a lathe tool is important for several reasons. In the first place, it is, strictly speaking, the only portion of the tool that actually cuts. The rest of the tool bit serves as a support for the cutting edge, carries away the heat generated by the cutting action, and aids in the removal of the chip. Thus, the cutting efficiency of any tool depends, to a great extent, upon the proper design and location of the cutting edge or edges. In addition, the location and shape of the cutting edges determine how the tool must be applied and what shape and surface finish it will produce.

Because the cutting edge of a lathe tool must always be advanced *into* the work, it is relatively easy to determine which lathe tool is intended for a certain type of operation by studying the shape and location of the cutting edge in relation to the tool's shank.

For instance, if you were seeking a tool suitable for use in a simple outside turning operation, wherein the cut is advanced by moving the tool either to the right or left, any tool having a cutting edge shaped like those in the two top rows in Fig. 11-2 (except second and third tool from the left, second row), would normally be satisfactory. This is because the primary cutting edges of these tools are located on the side of the tool's shank and, therefore, the tools must be fed from left to right, or right to left, in order to function correctly. The second and third tools from the left end of the second row, having their primary cutting edges located on the end of the tool's shank, would obviously be effective only when used for operations where they would be advanced into the work by feeding them "nose" first.

The shape and contour of the cutting edge also tell a story, if you study them very carefully. For instance, it is sometimes much simpler to grind the cutting edge of a tool convex or concave than it is to control the motion of a tool to make it produce concave or convex contours on the workpiece. Thus, lathe tools having cutting edges of such special shapes are designed primarily for special forming operations and are called *forming tools*.

If you examine the typical lathe tools illustrated in Fig. 11-2, you will notice that they have two characteristics in common. They are relatively sturdy tools, that is, they contain a considerable amount of metal in proportion to the size of the cutting edge; and they are fairly simple in design. This is especially true of all the

TYPICAL OUTSIDE TURNING TOOLS

TYPICAL BORING AND FACING TOOLS

TYPICAL THREAD CUTTING TOOLS

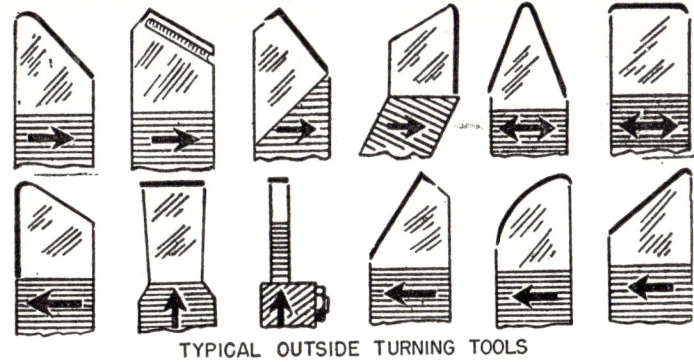

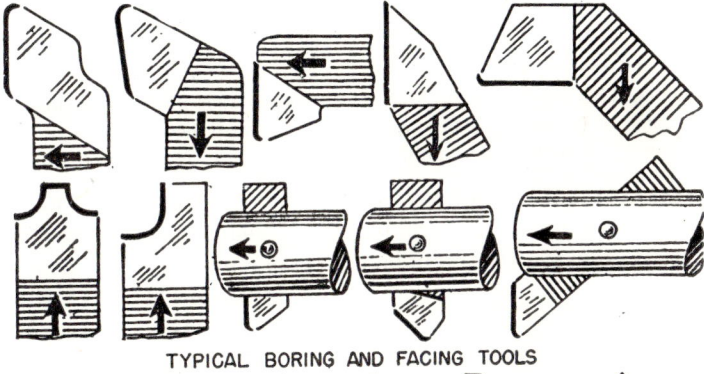

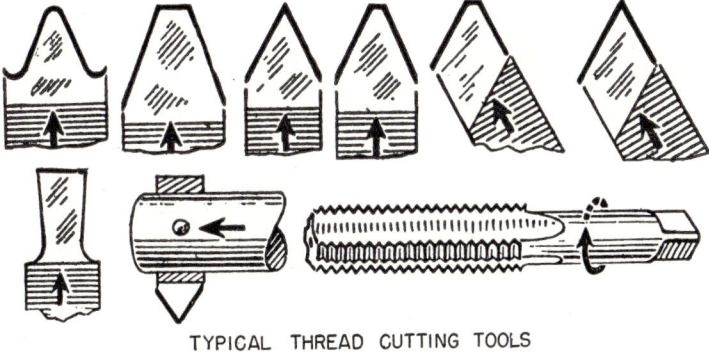

Fig. 11-2. Typical lathe tools. Arrows indicate the direction in which the tools are fed. (*The Shell Oil Company*)

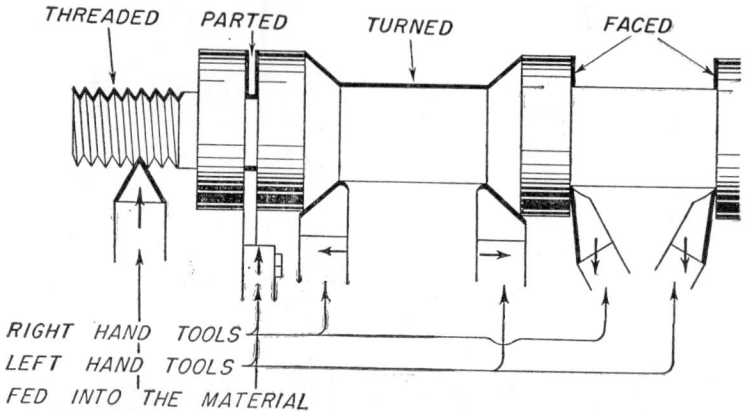

Fig. 11-3. This illustration establishes the terms that apply to various lathe operations performed on different surfaces of a workpiece. It also shows the character of tools used and the direction of tool movement. Note that right-

tools shown in the illustration which are designed to do standard lathe operations such as turning, boring, facing, and thread cutting.

The reason for these fundamental characteristics of lathe tool design are: the lathe is normally a fast-cutting machine tool. It takes a fairly heavy cut at a relatively high speed. This exerts a heavy pressure on the cutting edge and generates a great deal of heat. Unless plenty of metal is provided to support the cutting edge rigidly, and carry off the heat rapidly, its cutting efficiency will be quickly destroyed. However, as the lathe tool usually cuts "in the open," no great provisions for removing the chip as it is cut off are needed.

Cutting Tools Used in Lathe Work. Figure 11-2 illustrates many of the common cutting tools used in lathe work. Before going further, it will be well to explain the origin and reasons for the terms used in the naming of specific lathe tools and their various parts.

The system of names used in the machine shop to identify the various kinds of cutting tools is not too hard for the apprentice to grasp, providing the reasons why these names have been selected is clearly understood. Most lathe tool names are derived from the *operations each type of tool is designed to do;* for example, *roughing*

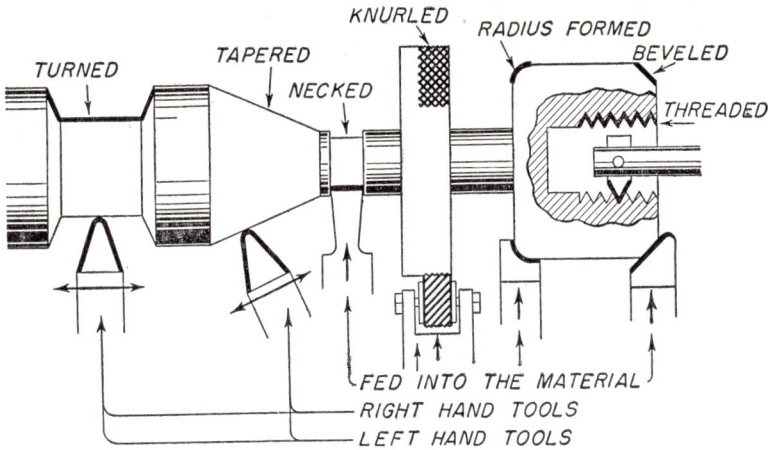

hand tools cut from right to left, while left-hand tools cut from left to right. (*The Shell Oil Company*)

tools take rough cuts, *turning* tools do simple cylindrical turning, *facing* tools turn the faces or ends of stock, etc.

Figure 11-3 shows a workpiece upon which a great many of the common operations have been done. In addition, the illustration shows the type of tool most commonly used for each type of operation. A study of this illustration will give some indication as to why different tools are used for threading, parting, turning, facing, etc. For example, a parting tool obviously could not be used efficiently to do a turning operation, chiefly because it has a cutting edge only on the end or nose of the tool.

Tool names are more specifically designated by prefixing those names with the terms *right-* or *left-hand*. For instance, right- (or left-) hand roughing tool, right (or left) turning tool, etc. The designation of a tool as a right-hand or left-hand is determined basically by the location of the tool side-cutting edges, but not in the manner that you would expect. A left-hand tool is one which has its side cutting edges on the *right* and *moves to the right*. The right-hand tool is one which has its cutting edges on the *left* and *moves to the left*. Thus a tool that began cutting on the operator's left was called a left-hand tool even though it moved to the right and had its side cutting edges on the right, and vice versa. Study Fig. 11-4 very carefully.

Steels of Which Cutting Tools Are Made. Cutting tools used in machine shops are made of high-carbon steel (tool steel), high-speed steel, and alloys such as stellite and the cemented carbides. The stellite and carbide tools are used only in special rapid-production work. Carbon steel for cutting tools, excepting hand tools, has almost entirely given way to high-speed steel.

Cutting tools, of whatever kind of steel, are hardened and tempered. Too much heat, when using the tool, will destroy the temper

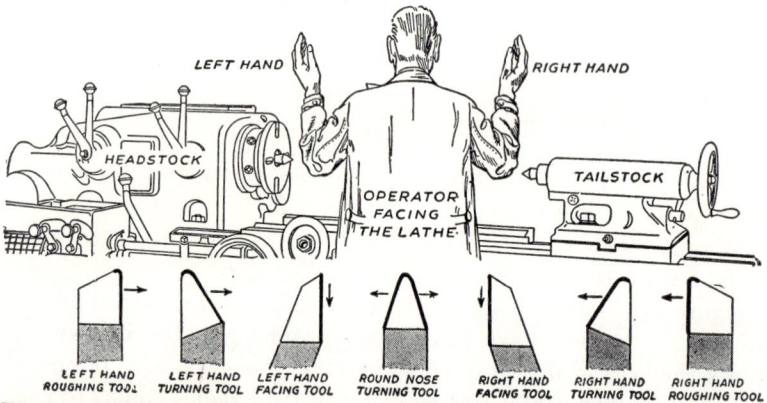

Fig. 11-4. How to distinguish between right- and left-hand tools. When the tool is held face up with the nose pointing away from the operator and the *cutting edge* is on the *right* side, it is considered a left-hand tool because it is used to make a cut that begins on the operator's left, even though it moves to his right; and vice versa, if the cutting edge of the tool is on the left side, it is called a right-hand tool. (*The Shell Oil Company*)

and make the cutting edge soft. In lathe work, or drilling, or milling—any machine operation where metal is cut—heat is generated. The chip is heated instantaneously, the work itself soon warms noticeably, and the tool point becomes very hot. In many machines a liquid coolant is used to carry away part of the heat, but in any case, if a *carbon-steel* tool is used and the speed of the cut is so high that enough heat is generated to blue the cutting edge, the temper is lost. The great value of *high-speed steel* lies in the fact that it will stand about three times as much heat as carbon steel and still retain its temper. A limit speed for carbon steel may be at least doubled when using high-speed steel; that is why *high-speed* steel is so named, and the reason for its success.

Terms Generally Used to Designate Different Lathe Tools. A *tool blank* when properly ground is a *tool bit* (Fig. 11-5). The tool

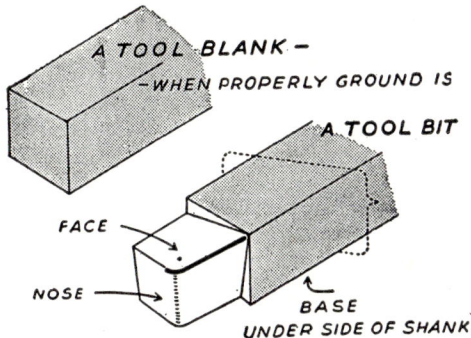

Fig. 11-5. Tool blank and ground tool. (*The Shell Oil Company*)

bit consists of a *face*, a *nose*, and a *shank*. The under side of the shank forms the *base*. The *cutting edge* is formed by the meeting of two surfaces, or *faces*, two planes, or one plane and one curved face, or two curved faces. In Fig. 11-5, the *heavy black line* indicates the cutting edge. The same holds true for all heavy black lines in the illustrations for tool bits.

Fig. 11-6. A round-nose tool. (*The Shell Oil Company*)

Fig. 11-7. A V-*threading tool*. (*The Shell Oil Company*)

Fig. 11-8. An American National form-threading tool. (*The Shell Oil Company*)

The cutting edge or edges of a tool may be visualized as being in the form of a straight line, or a curved line, or a combination of both. When this is done, a round-nosed turning tool may be viewed as being made up of two straight cutting edges, set at angles to the center line of the shank, and one curved cutting edge (Fig. 11-6).

A *V-threading tool*, on the other hand, may be visualized as being made up of two straight cutting edges that meet at a point, the angle with the center line of the shank being 30 deg. or 60 deg. between the two cutting edges (Fig. 11-7).

An American National threading tool (Fig. 11-8) may be visualized as being made up of three straight lines or cutting edges, two of which are set at angles to the one at the end.

A *necking tool* (Fig. 11-9) has only one straight cutting edge, set at right angles to the tool shank.

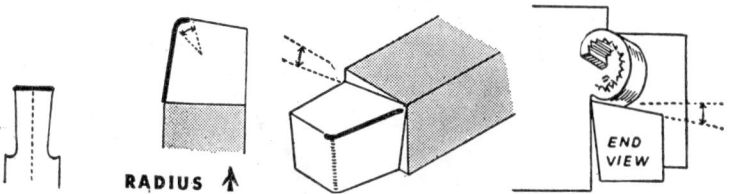

RADIUS ⋏

Fig. 11-9. A necking tool. (*The Shell Oil Company*)

Fig. 11-10. A radius. (*The Shell Oil Company*)

Fig. 11-11. Side rake angle. (*The Shell Oil Company*)

The term *radius* (Fig. 11-10) applies to the radius of a circle that would be formed if the part of the cutting edge of a tool that is rounded were completed. This arc of a circle is generally on the nose of a tool and may be ground to any radius required to do the given job.

A tool is ground to a given form for two reasons: (1) to produce a cutting edge of a given shape in a given position in relation to the shank of the tool; and (2) to produce a form that will permit the cutting edge to be fed into the workpiece so it can cut efficiently. The difference in form among tools is brought about by variations in the size of the angle to which the various planes involved are ground and in the radius to which portions of the cutting edge may be rounded.

DEFINITIONS: CUTTING-EDGE TERMS:

Side Rake. This term indicates that the plane that forms the face or top of a tool has been ground back at an angle sloping from the side cutting edge (Fig. 11-11). The extent of side rake influences the angle at which the chip leaves the workpiece as it is directed away from the side cutting edge.

Back Rake. This term indicates that the plane which forms the face or top of a tool has been ground back at an angle sloping from the nose. However, when a tool bit is held by a toolholder, the holder establishes the back-rake angle which normally is 16½ deg. The extent of back rake influences the angle at which the chip leaves the workpiece as it is directed away from the nose of the tool (Fig. 11-12).

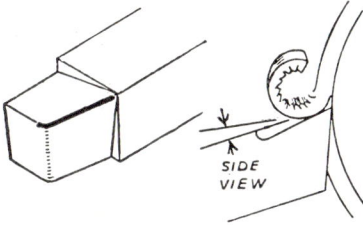

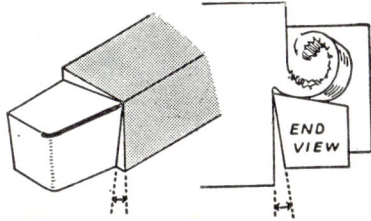

Fig. 11-12. Back rake angle. (*The Shell Oil Company*)

Fig. 11-13. Side clearance angle. (*The Shell Oil Company*)

Side Clearance. This term (or *side relief*) indicates that the plane that forms the flank or side of a tool has been ground back at an angle sloping down from the side cutting edge. Side clearance concentrates the thrust force exerted on the flank of a tool in a small area adjacent to the side cutting edge (Fig. 11-13).

End Clearance. This term (or *end relief*) indicates that the nose or end of a tool has been ground back at an angle sloping down from the end cutting edge (Fig. 11-14). End clearance concentrates the thrust force exerted on the nose of the tool in a small area adjacent to the end cutting edge.

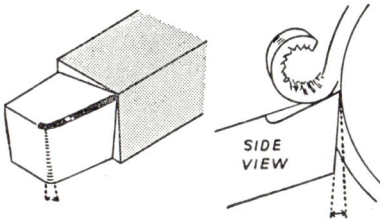

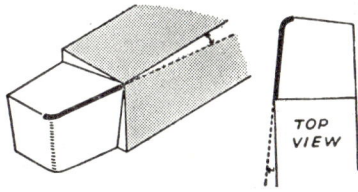

Fig. 11-14. End clearance angle. (*The Shell Oil Company*)

Fig. 11-15. Side cutting-edge angle. (*The Shell Oil Company*)

Side Cutting-edge Angle. This term indicates that the plane which forms the flank or side of a tool has been ground back at an angle to the side of the shank (Fig. 11-15), thereby establishing the angle of the side cutting edge in relation to the shank.

End Cutting-edge Angle. This term indicates that the plane which forms the end of a tool has been ground back at an angle sloping from the nose to the side of the shank, establishing the angle of the end of the tool in relation to the shank (Fig. 11-16).

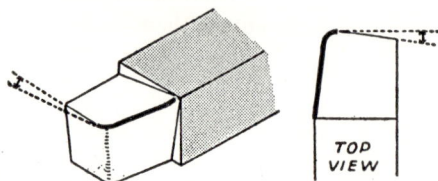

Fig. 11-16. End cutting-edge angle. (*The Shell Oil Company*)

Detailed explanations on these terms follow.

The Cutting Edge and the Faces That Form It. A cutting tool may have a single cutting edge, as a chisel or a lathe tool; two cutting edges as a twist drill; or several, as a reamer or a milling cutter. Any cutting edge is formed by the meeting of two surfaces, or *faces:* two plane surfaces, as for example, a flat chisel; or one plane and one curved; or both curved. Sometimes these faces are called merely the *front,* or *side,* or *top,* as in tools for lathe, shaper, and planer. Occasionally, a face is called the *lip* when referring to a lathe tool or a drill. The front of a tooth of a reamer or a milling cutter is called the *face* of the tooth, while the other cutting-edge surface is called the *land.*

In any tool, both surfaces that form the edge must be smooth to produce a keenness of edge. If either face is not smooth, the edge is not keen and it cannot produce a smooth cut. For example, if the groove of a milling cutter or a reamer is carelessly made, and the face of the tooth is torn and rough, no matter how smooth the land may be, the edge will be as rough as the rough face. Also, a smooth edge will stay sharp longer than a ragged edge; therefore, when sharpening any tool, the finishing cut of the grinding wheel should be light. The intelligent use of an oilstone is recommended.

When the cutting edge is broken or rounded it is dull and, to sharpen it, one of the faces (in some tools, both faces) must be ground. The grinding of a lathe tool is done, usually, by hand, moving the tool skillfully against the revolving abrasive wheel. To sharpen it skillfully means, first, to know the positions in which it must be held against the wheel to meet the requirements, and second, to gain the knack of holding it in these positions.

Contour of Turning Tool. For generations past the *roughing tool* was forged and ground to have a top face substantially as shown in Fig. 11-17a. That is, the top face was "egg shaped" with

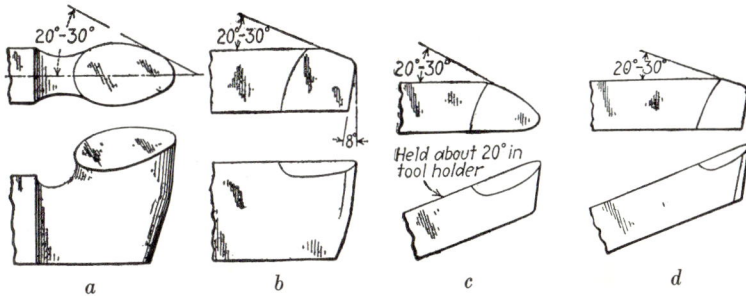

Fig. 11-17. Contours of turning tools.

the cutting edge presented to the work at an angle of 20 to 30 deg. and the nose rounded in proportion to the size of the tool. Taylor proved that such a shape, with the round nose modified to meet conditions, will answer in most cases for roughing and finishing cuts in either steel or cast iron in the run of shop jobs in a 14- or 16-in. lathe, and for roughing cuts in the shaper, planer, and larger lathes.

In Fig. 11-17b, is shown a shape of tool ground on a bar, which, as far as the cutting edge is concerned, is the same as the tool *A*. In 11-17c is shown a tool bit ground to resemble tool *a*, and in 11-17d the tool bit resembles the tool *b*. Practically, the four tools are alike in the shape of the cutting edges and in the cutting action.

If the round nose of a certain tool leaves feed marks too pronounced, a tool with a larger radius may be used. If in a different kind of job, the nose has too large a radius, and taking the wider chip seems to cause a chatter, it will be easy to substitute a tool with a narrower nose. Various other shapes of tools will be described from time to time.

Tool Angles. To grind the tool properly the edge must keep its shape—flat or curved as the case may be. Also, to cut well, the surfaces that form the edge must be "ground to certain angles." These tool angles are measured in degrees and are often described as so many degrees "with the horizontal" or "with the vertical." (In this case, *horizontal* means in a plane parallel to the base surface of the tool, and *vertical* means at right angles to the base surface. Lathe tools are held in the tool post practically in a horizontal position and no doubt this is the reason for these terms.)

When reading about the tool angles and when practicing grinding, the beginner should try to have "in his mind's eye" the value (size) of the given angle. A good way is to compare the angle to a right angle (90 deg.) in the same way one compares an eighth or a quarter of an inch with an inch. The hands of a clock set 15 min. (time) apart will measure an angle of 90 deg.; 10 min. apart will indicate 60 deg.; 1 min. apart, 6 deg. Just to make a test, draw angles of, say, 60, 45, and 20 deg. and then gage them with a protractor.

The angles of the tool are named thus: *cutting angle*, the angle of the wedge that cuts or peels; *clearance angle*, ground away so the tool will not rub; *rake angle*, the slope of the tool so it will peel instead of push off the chip. Discussions of these angles follow.

Cutting Angle. The action of any cutting tool in any material is that of a wedge prying apart or separating the substance of the material. The angle of the wedge is the *cutting angle of the tool* (see Fig. 11-18).

The harder the material to be cut, the more the cutting edge must be supported, that is, the cutting angle must be greater. The cutting angle that is correct for wood is not substantial enough to stand up under the strain of cutting iron or steel; the cutting edge, not being sufficiently supported against such a severe crushing force, would soon crumble and the value of the tool would be lost. The proper cutting angle for a metal-cutting cutting tool is 60 to 80 deg. depending largely upon the hardness of the metal to be cut.

A cutting tool must be correctly shaped and sharpened, and properly set in the machine, in order to have its cutting angle effective. Many tools, such as drills, milling cutters, and some lathe tools, are already shaped when the machinist gets them, but he must know how to sharpen them. The tool bits, so much used for turning, boring, and planing, must be shaped, as well as sharpened and set, by the man on the machine.

Metal is ground away from the forged lathe tool—and from the tool bit—to sharpen it, and to give it after it has been sharpened the shape it ought to have and (when set in the machine) the correct cutting angle. It is not enough to know that the cutting angle for a certain tool must be 70 deg.; the machinist must know how to grind and how to set the tool to get that angle. That is, when the tool is held against the grinding wheel to get the shape of a turning tool, for example, and a cutting angle of, say, about 70 deg., it i'

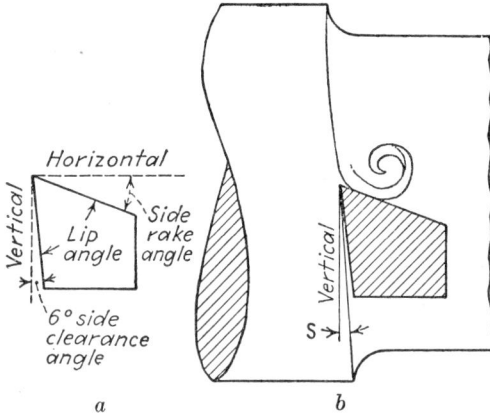

Fig. 11-18. In (a) are illustrated the side clearance angle of 6 deg. from the vertical, the cutting angle or lip angle of 60 to 80 deg. (depending on the material mainly, sometimes on the nature of the cut) and the side rake angle of average 12 deg. from the horizontal. In (b) is the *action* of the tool. Note the chip being peeled off because the tool has rake. Note also the separation of the material just ahead of the cutting edge. Attention is called to the slant of the cut as indicated by the angle S, which shows that since the tool feeds (to the left in this case) it must have clearance or it will rub. The coarser the feed and the smaller the diameter for a given feed, the greater the slant, but 6-deg. side clearance is usually enough.

ground on the side and on the front so that it will not rub on the work. This is grinding the *clearance*, side clearance and front clearance. It is also ground (or held in the toolholder) so that the top of the tool slopes, toward the back or toward the side, or both, and this angle of slope is called *rake*. Slope from the front to the back is called *front* rake (or, in some shops, back rake) and the slope to the side is called *side* rake.

Clearance Angles. When whittling with a jackknife, the back of the blade is raised a trifle, otherwise it will merely rub instead of cut. If it is raised 10 deg. the *clearance angle* is 10 deg. In most machine-shop cutting operations the action is similar; the cutting edge digs in, splitting or parting the metal ahead of itself, *one face* of the tool pries or peels off the chip, the *edge* tends to smooth the torn surface, and *the other face clears the work altogether.*

Three examples will illustrate the action:

1. The work in a lathe as it revolves is forced down against the cutting tool (Fig. 11-19*a*), the chip is pried off against the top of the tool, and the front and side clear the work.

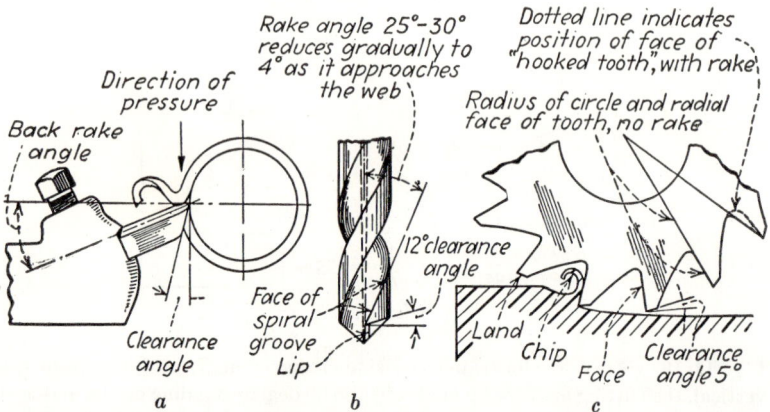

Fig. 11-19. Shows clearance and rake on three much-used machine-shop cutting tools: (*a*) lathe tool, (*b*) twist drill, and (*c*) milling cutter.

2. A twist drill, pressed (fed) into the work, cuts as it revolves. The cutting edges dig into the metal, the faces (of the spiral grooves) pry or peel off the chips, and the *lips* clear the work because they have been backed off, that is, given clearance (Fig. 11-19*b*).

3. In the case of a milling cutter the face of the tooth peels off the chip while the land just clears (Fig. 11-19*c*).

In all three of the above examples one face pries or peels off the chip and the other is ground at an angle, or as the machinist says, "backed off" or "given clearance" or "relieved," so it will not rub.

In general, the angle of *side clearance* on a lathe tool should not be more than 6 deg. (Fig. 11-20*a*), because the greater the amount of metal a cutting edge has under it, or the more it is backed up, the longer it will stay sharp.

The direction of the force which is exerted against the turning tool is along a line tangent to the circumference of the work at the cutting point (see Fig. 11-20). As the usual practice is to set the turning tool on center or a little above, it is necessary to have clearance at the front of the tool, so that it will not rub. This *front clear-*

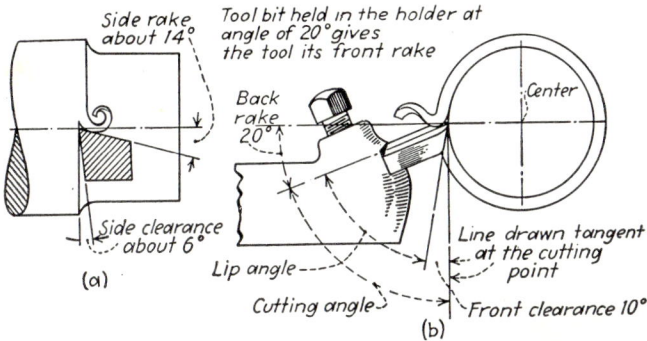

Fig. 11-20. (*a*) Side rake and side clearance; (*b*) back rake and front clearance. The line drawn tangent at the cutting point shows the direction of the force against the tool. Set "on center," this tool has 10-deg. front clearance. If it were set a little above center, it would have less effective front clearance, less cutting angle, and more rake.

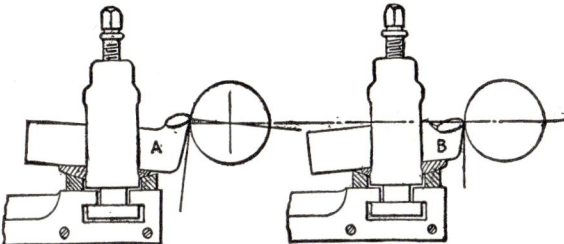

Fig. 11-21. Setting a lathe tool to get the proper clearance angle. A front clearance of 10 or 12 deg. is usually ground on a forged tool. Note the position above the center of the new tool *A* so as not to give excessive front clearance. Note *B*, which represents the position of the same tool after being sharpened several times, set on center to give correct clearance.

ance is usually about 10 deg. The design of the tool post (ring and rocker) permits of using tools of various heights. Since 10 deg. is practically a standard clearance, the height of the tool will determine the amount to set the tool above center to resist the tangential force of the cut and still have sufficient clearance. This is illustrated in Fig. 11-21. That is, a tool may be *ground* with 10 deg. front clear-

ance, yet when set above center have, in effect, much less than 10
deg. The amount it really has when in action in the lathe is known
as *effective* clearance.

From the above it will be understood that the *effective* front clearance of a lathe tool depends upon the tool setting; the more the
cutting edge is above center the less clearance it has. If set a little
too high the tool will rub, and if too low the edge will be more
quickly dulled.

The *effective* side clearance depends upon the amount of feed as
shown by the *slant* in Fig. 11-18.

NOTE: For many years machinists have spoken of the angle of the
wedge as the cutting angle, but there has been a difference of opinion as to whether or not the cutting angle included the clearance
angle. As a matter of fact the true cutting angle is the angle as
ground on the tool (the *lip angle*) plus the *effective* clearance. Also it
should be noted that on a tool having a curved cutting edge such as
the usual turning tool, the true cutting angle is the composite of
the side and end angles and is measured on the line of the chip flow.

It may help in understanding the effective clearance to imagine
two other conditions than are shown in Fig. 11-20, possibly making
a couple of sketches. In the figure the tool is ground with 60-*deg.*
lip angle, is held in the holder at an angle of 20 deg., and, being set
on center of the work, has, as shown, an angle of front clearance of
10 deg. and a cutting angle of 70 deg. Now imagine, first, that the
tool is ground to have only 1 deg. front clearance and set exactly
on center as shown in the figure; the lip angle would be 69 deg. and
the cutting angle would remain unchanged. Second, imagine the
front of the tool (as in the figure with 60-deg. lip angle) tipped up
until the cutting point is just high enough to bring the tangent line
to indicate 1 deg. front clearance instead of 10 deg. (Fig. 11-21*b*).
In this case the lip angle would remain 60 deg., but the cutting
angle would be 61 deg. instead of 70 deg. as before.

Rake Angles. A definition of rake is *an inclination from the vertical
or horizontal.* If a turning tool is set in a lathe so the top is flat and
horizontal, it will have no rake, or if a drill has straight grooves
it has no rake. Note in Fig. 11-19 that both the lathe tool and the
twist drill have rake, while the milling cutter, having a radial tooth,

has no rake. A milling cutter with a "hooked tooth" has rake (shown in one tooth in Fig. 11-19). When a tool has no rake it pushes off the metal, while if it has rake it tends to peel off the chip. Most tools have rake.

Sometimes a tool is given *negative* rake. For example, in planer work the roughing tool is often ground with regular side rake but with negative back rake, in order to ease the blow as the tool hits the work at the start of the cut. This is shown in Fig. 11-26*b*.

In lathe tools it usually is necessary to have the top of the tool on a double slope, from the front and from the side, otherwise the cutting angle will not be acute enough. Also, having the double slope causes the chip to "flow" in the desired direction. The slope from the front is called *back rake* (in some shops, front rake) and the slope from the side is called *side rake* (see Fig. 11-20). The number of degrees of these rake angles depends, of course, on the cutting angle required; the more rake a tool has, the less cutting angle it has, that is, the sharper the wedge is. A cutting angle of 70 deg. is average for cast iron and tool steel, and 60 deg. is average for machine steel. In a toolholder the back rake is taken care of, usually, by the position of the bit at an angle in the holder (Fig. 11-23). The side rake may be nicked in the bit or it may be ground as illustrated in Fig. 11-22.

Brass is a softer material and therefore would not seem to require so heavy a cutting angle as steel. However, no rake is given a cutting tool for brass because of the tendency of the tool to "hook in" or "dig in" the soft material.

Keep Cutting Tools Sharp. A cutting tool carefully ground will stay sharp under correct working conditions for a considerable time, but as soon as it is noticeably dull it should be reground or the tool and possibly the work will be ruined. A dull tool tears rather than cuts the material; it springs the work and does not make a smooth cut. To *keep cutting tools sharp* is a most important factor in efficient machine work.

It is an acknowledged fact that lack of judgment in the grinding of tools costs thousands of dollars every year in the wastage of materials alone. To sharpen a dull tool shall it be ground on the top, on the front, or on the side, or a little here and there? No rule can be given. Each tool grinding calls for judgment. Examine the particular tool; how many times may it be ground on the top before it is worn out? How much may it be ground on the side before it is too thin? How much of the life of the tool is lost by grinding it on the front? Keep these things in mind when sharpening a tool.

In this connection refer again to Fig. 11-22; regular tool bits for the lathe, shaper, and planer are sharpened by grinding on the end only, when previously beveled as shown. The tool bit is ground in a surface grinder for a side rake of 12 to 14 deg. its whole length. It is an improvement for the usual facing, shouldering, and turning tool

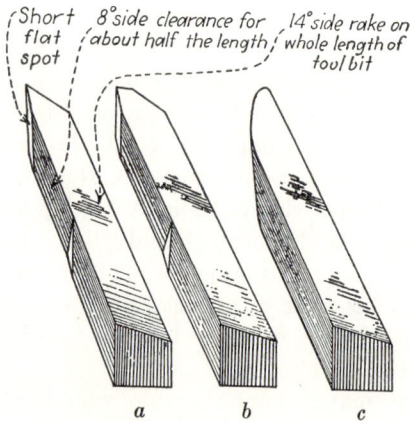

Fig. 11-22. Tool bits beveled on the top for side-rake angle. Sharpened by grinding on the end only. (*a*) Facing, (*b*) shoulder, and (*c*) turning.

and for standard thread tools. (For shaper and planer bits the bevel is from the opposite edge.) Side rake is thus provided once and for all. All sharpening is done on the end and the bits do not have the usual ugly nicked points. The economy in grinding time and the saving of the tools are notable.

Grinding Cutting Tools. The beginner should grind a practice piece of machine steel (preferably a little larger than the tool bit so as not to get them mixed) and acquire the knack before attempting to grind an expensive tool bit. It may be fairly difficult at the start to grind the proper front clearance because the bit when in use is held at an angle in the holder. Until the eye is trained, use a gage. The 60-deg. center gage is suitable, if 10-deg. front clearance is wanted, because in most of the holders the tool bit is set at an angle of 16½ deg. with the horizontal (Fig. 11-23). For any other than 60-deg. cutting angle it is easy to cut out a small sheet-metal gage of the angle desired.

When grinding carbon steel, care must be taken not to bear on too hard or the edge will become blue and the temper lost. A wet

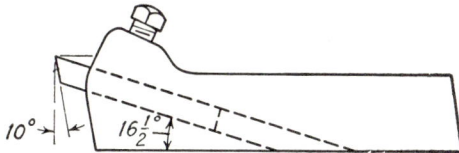

Fig. 11-23. Tool bit is held in the holder at an angle of 16½ deg. to give the back rake.

grinder should be used if one is available. It is not so easy to burn the temper out of a high-speed cutter but it is easy to cause surface cracks by not having water enough. Have plenty of water and do not bear on too hard; give the wheel a chance.

A tool bit should *not* be ground in a holder, first, because the method is clumsy and inefficient, and second, because one is liable to grind the holder. If occasionally the holder is ground a little, soon

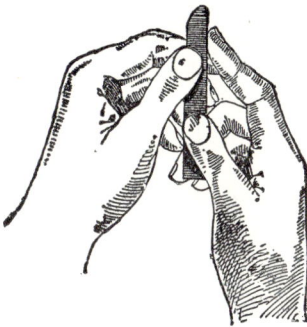

Fig. 11-24.

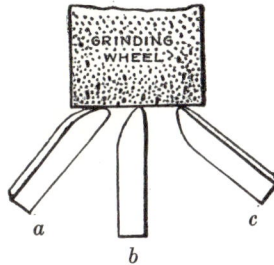

Fig. 11-25.

it is ruined. Figure 11-24 shows the correct way to hold the turning-tool bit. Hold it securely but not rigidly. As it is swung from *a* through *b* around to *c* (Fig. 11-25), it pivots slowly between the left thumb and forefinger, with the pressure mostly with the right fore-finger. Grind one continuous cut, keeping in mind the front and side clearance. Tip it a little to the right, as at *a*, to grind the side clearance, and to the left as it reaches *c* in order to finish the round nose.

Oilstoning the edge serves to produce a better finish on the work, and prolongs the life of the tool.

DONT'S IN TOOL GRINDING

Don't grind stupidly; know where and why and how to take off the metal.

Don't hold the tool as if your fingers were paralyzed; hold it securely enough to control it.

Don't whittle the tool; grind it.

Don't hold the tool left-handed or otherwise awkwardly; hold it properly—it's the easiest way.

Don't be afraid to use plenty of water.

Don't hold the tool in one place or you will cut a groove in the wheel.

Don't use a wheel that is grooved or out of round if you can help it.

Don't grind on the side of a wheel except when necessary. When it is necessary you will want a flat surface and it won't be flat if you or anyone else has cut grooves in it.

Don't hold the smaller tools on the tool rest; support them in the left hand and rest this hand.

Don't use the tool rest with more than $\frac{1}{16}$-in. space between it and the wheel.

Don't make a round nose of a thread tool or a thread tool of a round nose; it is wasteful of material and in the end wasteful of time.

Don't use the grinder without some sort of eye protection— goggles or guard.

Cemented Carbide Tools. A word should be said here about the cemented carbides, the wonderful superspeed cutting materials. First, what they are: Pure tungsten, carburized to form tungsten carbide, was produced about the end of the last century by Henri Moissan. It is one of the hardest known substances, but is brittle and porous. It was not commercially valuable until a method of *cementing* it (holding tiny particles together with a suitable binder) was developed (about 1927). Since then it has been found that carbides of tantalum, titanium, molybdenum, and several others are valuable, and mixtures of different carbides that will give various *grades* of product, each superior for its particular class of work, have been developed.

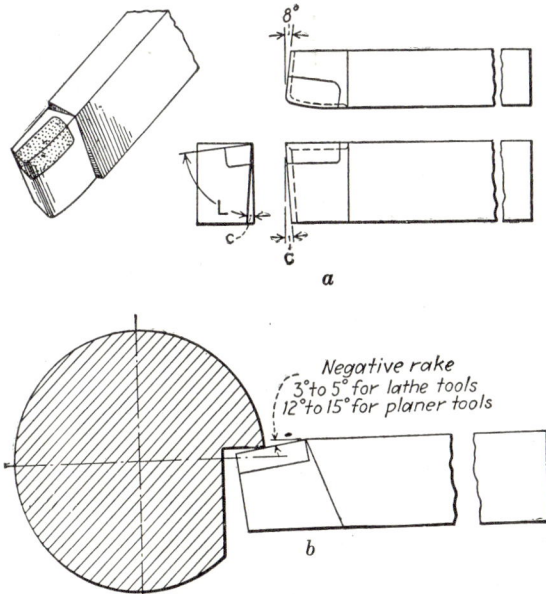

Fig. 11-26. Cemented carbide-tipped tools. (*a*) Turning tool, angles marked *c* are clearance angles and *L* is the lip angle; (*b*) shows how an interrupted cut in lathe work (or the beginning of a cut in a shaper or planer) strikes the tool having negative rake; the impact is some distance behind the nose and is less likely to break the tip.

The carbide, or a mixture of two or more carbides, and the binder (cobalt is much used) are powdered and mixed in the most thorough way, and then molded under hydraulic pressure into the shapes desired. These ingots or rough shapes are next pre-sintered at about 1500°F. and have then the consistency of the graphite in a pencil. In this condition they may be further shaped by turning, drilling, filing, etc., somewhat oversize to allow for later shrinkage. The pieces are final-sintered in special furnaces at temperatures ranging from 2500° to 2900°F., depending upon the grade. During this process the binder coalesces and cements the carbide particles together, forming a structure of extremely hard carbide crystals in a tough binder.

The cemented carbide thus produced has extraordinary hardness, high compression strength, low heat conductivity, but is quite brittle. Due to its brittleness, it cannot be used as a tool bit in a holder, like a high-speed-steel bit for example, but is fitted into and

Table of Angles for Carbide-tipped Tools

Material to be machined	Clearance angle, C	Lip angle, L
Soft gray cast iron	5°	74°–80°
Hard gray cast iron	4°	74°–80°
Chilled cast iron (65–90 scleroscope)	3°	82°–86°
Soft steel	6°	60°–65°
Hard steel	5°	65°–74°
12% manganese steel	4°	80°–84°
Stainless steel	5°	65°–74°
Soft steel castings	5°	68°–73°
Hard steel castings	5°	73°–78°
Bronze, brass, etc.	6°	65°–75°
Aluminum alloys	8°	50°–55°
Planer tools	As above but with negative back rake 12 to 15°	

brazed in place to be used as the cutting point in the end of a bar of steel (Fig. 11-26) or a reamer, drill, or other cutting tool. Because of its low conductivity of heat it never becomes hot enough to melt the brazing material.

Cemented carbides have qualities that make possible cutting speeds several times as fast as high-speed steel. Also they will freely cut hard substances that steel will not cut at all. Their first cost is high, but there is no doubt of their value in production work, not only as cutting tools, but also for parts that must be wear-resisting such as guides, gages, and wire dies. It should be emphasized, however, that particular *grades* are made for given purposes, and *cemented-carbide tools cannot be used indiscriminately on various materials.* Nor can cemented-carbide cutting tools give satisfactory results unless the greatest care is taken to eliminate all vibration in work holder and toolholder. Further, safety demands protection against the tendency of the red-hot chips to fly. Note the substantial toolholder illustrated in Fig. 11-27.

Catalogues furnished by the manufacturers give details of selection, grinding, and use, and are interesting and instructive, but expert advice in the selection of the suitable grade is always recommended. When necessary to sharpen the tool, knowledge, care, and

Fig. 11-27. Carbide-tipped tool ready for use. (*The South Bend Lathe Works*)

skill are needed. Carbides cannot be ground on ordinary wheels. Diamond wheels are needed for grinding.

QUESTIONS ON CUTTING TOOLS

1. What is the general shape of the cutting edge of a turning tool for lathe work? What are the disadvantages of a sharp point on a turning tool?

2. What is meant by cutting angle? How many degrees are included in the cutting angle of an average turning tool? Why not 90 deg.? Why not 30 deg.?

3. What is meant by clearance angle? How much side clearance has a lathe turning tool? How much front clearance? What is the disadvantage of too great a clearance angle?

4. What is meant by front rake? Side rake? What is the object in giving rake to a tool?

5. Other things being equal, will a tool with side rake cut equally well if fed in either direction?

6. What is meant by negative rake?

7. What is a right-hand turning tool?

8. What is a bent tool?

9. It may be stated that a cutting-off tool has five clearance angles; where are they?

10. It may be stated that a side tool has four clearance angles; where are they?

11. When it is necessary to sharpen a side tool, is it ground on the top, on the side, or on the front? Why must judgment be exercised?

12. What are the advantages of a tool that has been oilstoned?

13. If a tool rubs on the work, what faults may be found?

14. What is the chief advantage of a tool holder and bit?

15. Should the bit be ground in the holder or should it be removed before grinding? Give reasons.

16. Name three things on which the action of a cutting tool depends.

17. What is meant by the contour of a tool face?

18. What is meant by effective clearance?

19. What is the difference between the corner-rounding tool and the crowning tool?

20. What is the purpose of beveling the top surface of a tool bit?

21. What is meant by the term cemented in referring to carbide tools?

22. What is the difference between a tool bit and a tipped-tool?

23. What is the meaning of the word sintered?

24. What do you understand by the words tungsten, tantalum, and molybdenum?

25. How is the carbide tip fastened in place?

SPEED, FEED, AND DEPTH OF CUT

Roughing and Finishing Cuts. There are two kinds of cuts in machine-shop work called, respectively, the *roughing cut* and the *finishing cut*. When a piece is *roughed out*, it is fairly near the shape and size required, but enough metal has been left on the surface to finish smooth and to exact size.

Bars of steel, forgings, castings, etc., are obtained, if possible, of the shape and size that will machine to the greatest advantage, that is, usually with one roughing and one finishing cut. Sometimes, however, certain portions of a piece may require more than one roughing cut. Also, in some jobs, for example, when great accuracy is not needed, or when a comparatively small amount of metal must be removed, a finishing cut may be all that is required.

The *roughing cut*, to remove the greater part of the excess material, should be reasonably heavy, that is, all the machine, or cutting tool, or work, or all three, will stand. One need not worry much about the machine being overworked, and it will soon be quite easy to judge the capabilities of the given tool. The machinist's purpose is to remove the excess stock as fast as he can without leaving a surface too torn and rough, without bending the piece if it is slender, and without spoiling the centers.

The *finishing cut*, to make the work smooth and accurate, is a finer cut. The emphasis here is refinement—very sharp tool, comparatively little metal removed, and a higher degree of accuracy in measurement.

Whether roughing or finishing, the machinist must set the lathe for the given job. He must consider the size and shape of the work and the kind of material, also the kind of tool used and the nature of the cut to be made; then he proceeds to set the lathe for the correct speed and feed and to set the tool to take the depth of cut desired.

Definitions. *Cutting speed* in any machine-shop operation is expressed in *feet per minute*. In lathe work it is the number of feet measured on the circumference of the work that passes the cutting edge of the tool in 1 min. If it were possible to measure the exact length of the chip removed in 1 min., it would measure the cutting speed in feet per minute.

The *feed* in lathe work is the amount the tool advances for each revolution of the work. For example, in turning a cylinder with $\frac{1}{32}$-in. feed it will require 32 revolutions of the work to move the carriage 1 in. The machinist speaks of "coarse feed" and "fine feed." These terms mean nothing except when applied to lathes of practically the same size. What might be regarded as fine feed on a large lathe would be a coarse feed on a small lathe.

By the term *cut* in lathe work is meant the *depth of cut.* Suppose a cylinder of machine steel 2 in. in diameter is put in a lathe and a cut made reducing the diameter to 1⅞ in. Regardless of the speed or feed, the depth of the cut is ¹⁄₁₆ in. It should now be clear what the foreman means when he says "Give it a higher speed," "Try a coarser feed," or "Take a deeper cut."

The Time Element. One of the most important problems entering into machine-shop work is the time element. The time it takes to produce a finished piece of work depends largely on the rate at which the metal is removed from the original stock. The rate at which the metal is cut off depends on three things, namely, the depth of cut, the feed, and the cutting speed. Take for example the turning operation.

1. It is obvious that the cutting edge of the tool takes a deeper cut if it reduces the diameter ¼ in. than if it reduces it only ⅛ in. It will be folly to take two cuts if ¼-in. reduction in roughing size is necessary. One factor then is the depth of cut.

2. If every time the work revolves the tool is fed ¹⁄₆₄ in., it will remove a chip only half as thick as if it were fed ¹⁄₃₂ in. If practicable to set the feed for ¹⁄₃₂ in., why not get the piece turned in half the time? Another factor then is the amount of feed.

3. If this work is 2 in. in diameter and revolves 70 times in 1 min. a point on the circumference will travel about 30 ft. in 1 min. If the cutting tool will stand 60 ft. per minute cutting speed it will not be efficient to turn at half this speed. The third factor then is the cutting speed.

There is a new problem of cutting speed, feed, and depth of cut for every job on every machine in the shop. After awhile the workman becomes expert enough to attend to these things automatically. At the start, however, these problems require close attention and certain calculations.

Cutting Feeds and Speeds. There are so many conditions that determine the proper depth of cut and feed that it is impossible to give any set rule for either. The shape of the tool, the way in which it is held, the kind of steel from which it is made are factors; also the kind of material being cut, whether machine steel or tool steel, brass or cast iron; the shape of the piece being cut, whether it is rigid or inclined to spring; the nature of the cut, whether it is rough-ing or finishing, are all factors which must be taken into considera-tion when obtaining an efficient depth of cut or amount of feed.

Conditions also govern the rate at which the tool will cut, and no table can be given that will apply in all cases. Fortunately how-ever, there are certain well-established *average* cutting speeds for various metals.

Average Cutting Speeds with Tools of High-speed Steel*

Stainless steel and Monel metal	50 ft. per min.
Annealed tool steel	60 ft. per min.
Machine steel, wrought iron, and cast iron	80 ft. per min.
Brass	200 ft. per min.
Aluminum	300 ft. per min.

* Average cutting speed with tools of carbon steel is about half the above.

Cutting speeds must not be confused with revolutions per minute (r.p.m.). A piece 2 in. in diameter will have to make five times as many r.p.m. as a piece 10 in. in diameter to give the same cutting speed. In other words, each different diameter must have a different number of r.p.m. to give the same cutting speed. If the beginner will calculate for the first few jobs the r.p.m. necessary to give the required cutting speeds, after awhile he will become so accustomed to seeing the machine work properly that he will be able to set up without calculations and almost without thought.

Cutting-speed Calculations. Cutting speed (excepting the shaper and planer) is the rate at which a point on the *circumference* travels. In the case of a lathe it is the circumference of the work; in the case of a milling machine or drill press it is the circumference of the milling cutter or of the drill. And remember, in machine-shop practice, when speaking of sizes, the *diameter* is expressed, not the circumference. Also these diameters are given in *inches*, while cut-ting speed is expressed in feet. To find the circumference of a piece of work (or of a drill or milling cutter) multiply the diameter by 3.14 and, to reduce to feet, divide by 12. However, instead of mul-tiplying the diameter by 3.14 and dividing by 12 in every problem it is much quicker to multiply the diameter by 0.26. The diameter multiplied by 3.14 and this divided by 12 is equal to 0.26 times the diameter.

$$\frac{\text{diameter} \times 3.14}{12} = 0.26 \times \text{diameter}$$

That is, the circumference in feet is always equal to 0.26 times the diameter in inches.

Further, if one had a job that figured 2 ft. in circumference it would take 20 r.p.m. to give a cutting speed of 40 ft. per min.; if the job figured ½ ft. in circumference it would take 80 r.p.m. to give a cutting speed of 40 ft. In both cases the number of r.p.m. is equal to the cutting speed divided by the circumference in feet. From these examples the following may be deduced: To obtain the r.p.m. necessary to give any required cutting speed, multiply the diameter (in inches) by 0.26 and divide the cutting speed by this product.

Since 0.26 is so nearly ¼, it may be stated that for all practical purposes the number of r.p.m. may be calculated by the following:

RULE: To obtain the number of r.p.m. necessary to give any required cutting speed, divide ¼ of the diameter into the cutting speed; OR multiply the cutting speed by 4 and divide by the diameter.

EXAMPLE: A piece of steel 2½ in. in diameter is to be turned in a lathe. What number of r.p.m. is necessary to give a cutting speed of 80 ft. per min.?

SOLUTION: $$\text{R.p.m.} = \frac{CS}{\frac{1}{4}D} = \frac{80}{\frac{1}{4} \times 2\frac{1}{2}} = \frac{80}{\frac{5}{8}} = 128 \ Ans.$$

or $$= \frac{4CS}{D} = \frac{4 \times 80}{2.5} = 128 \ Ans.$$

Value of High Speed. In a previous paragraph it was stated that the edge of the tool parted the metal "ahead of itself," and it might have been said further that the metal has a tendency to "pile up" on the nose of the tool, tearing the turned surface similarly as with a dull tool.

Every machinist knows that this tendency is less at the faster speeds, but the cemented-carbide cutting tools have made it possible to prove that above a "critical speed" (over 250 ft. per min. for most steels) this piled-up edge does not form, nor is there a parting ahead of the metal, and the chip and turned surface are not torn.

It is under the same principle that a bullet from a rifle will pierce a pane of glass, and thrown by hand will shatter the glass.

During a recent test, using a multiproduction lathe (The American Tool Works Company, Cincinnati, Ohio) with a cemented-carbide cutting tool, bars of steel were successfully turned at 350 ft. per min. The chip breaker curled and disposed of a ⅜-in.-wide chip which was "as smooth as glass," and the turned surface was clean cut. The same kind of steel was being turned with a high-speed steel tool in a nearby lathe at 80 ft. per min., with much inferior results.

Of course cemented-carbide tools are expensive. The modern lathe is fast, accurate, and rigid in construction and therefore is able to use these cutting tools. The machinists now employed have been trained in the use of these cutting tools, and it can be clearly seen that, with all the above factors, the trend today is toward almost universal use of cemented-carbide cutting tools. They definitely save time in production and thereby save money for the manufacturer and the consumer.

QUESTIONS ON CUTTING FEEDS AND SPEEDS

1. What do you understand by time element in machining a piece of work?
2. Name four things that may determine the proper feed for turning.
3. What is the difference between cutting speed and revolutions per minute?
4. How many r.p.m. are necessary to turn a piece of work 1½ in. in diameter at a speed of 30 ft. per min?
5. What number of r.p.m. is necessary to give a cutting speed of 40 ft. per minute on work 2¼ in. in diameter?
6. What rule is used to find the r.p.m. of a drill to give a required cutting speed?
7. Is this same rule used to obtain the r.p.m. of work in a lathe to give the required cutting speed?
8. In turning a cast-iron pulley 12 in. in diameter, how many r.p.m. will be necessary to give a cutting speed of 40 ft. per minute?
9. Why is it that machine steel can be turned at a higher speed than tool steel?
10. If the r.p.m. and the diameter of the work are known, how may the cutting speed be found?
11. What is the property that gives high-speed steel its value?
12. Name three things to emphasize in considering the finishing cut.

What Happens When Metals Are Cut. Maybe, when you were a kid, one spring afternoon when the gang switched from marbles to baseball, you made the mistake of sliding into second base on a hip pocket full of marbles. If you had been a winner that day, there might have been several layers of marbles between you and the ground, but those next to you were pressed into you as firmly as though they were in contact with the ground. The explanation, of course, was merely that the pressure of the ground on the outer layer of marbles was transmitted from marble to marble until it finally got to you. If you keep the behavior of those marbles in mind throughout the next few pages, it will help you to understand what "goes on" in a piece of metal while it is being cut.

Another point that should be understood clearly is that metals, for all their density and apparent solidity, are not as solid or uniform in their physical structure as you might think. They are much like a piece of concrete—a mixture of grains held together by cement. As a result, when pressure is applied to the grains in a limited area, as happens when a cutting tool bites into the metal, the pressure is passed along from one grain to another in areas next to the point where the cutting pressure is applied, just as was the case with the marbles.

There is another characteristic feature of the structure of metals that is even more important in its influence on the behavior of metals under the effect of the cutting action. Without getting too deep into the science of metallurgy, we can explain briefly that the grains which make up all metals have a characteristic structure that science describes as crystalline. This merely means that the atoms which make up the grains are all arranged in a definite order and orderly pattern. In metals, this pattern takes the form of a series of interlocked cubes. So, in a given metal, all the grains have the same characteristic cubical internal structure, although the lines of the cubical pattern in no two adjacent grains line up or are parallel. The material that binds the grains together, however, does not have this orderly arrangement of the atoms which compose it. Its atoms are thrown together in a random pattern giving it a structure that is called *amorphous*, meaning having no regular form or structure.

As a result of the grains of metal having this crystalline structure, every grain has certain cross-sectional planes which the atoms do not hold together as strongly as in other parts of the grain. These planes are described generally as *planes of weakness*. When pressure is applied to a grain, sections of it begin to "slip" along these planes. Up to a certain point, this slipping merely causes the grain to be deformed. Beyond that point the grain will be sheared apart. The extent to which a grain can slip without breaking varies in different types of metals. If it can slip considerably, the metal is said to be *ductile*. If it fractures without slipping far, the metal is called *brittle*. So long as grain sections merely slip along these planes of weakness, it is usual to refer to the planes along which they slip as *slip planes*. However, if the movement is sufficient to fracture the grain, they are usually called *cleavage planes*. This is apt to be confusing, for the same planes of weakness are involved in either case. What these planes are called is simply a matter of whether the grains are only deformed or actually broken by the pressure. Since we are interested in this discussion on the actual breaking apart of the grains of metal, we will consider the planes in question to be *cleavage* planes.

The importance of the presence of these cleavage planes in metals will become more apparent after the fundamentals of cutting have been made clear. Cutting requires pressure and motion of the cutting edge or the material being cut. The value or intensity of the cutting action depends upon the keenness of the cutting edge, the velocity of motion, and the degree of pressure involved. For instance, you can squeeze a knife blade quite hard without cutting your hand, yet if you attempt to withdraw it without loosening your grasp, your hand will be instantly cut. But you can move your hand fairly rapidly over the same cutting edge without being cut, if you touch it lightly enough.

As you will see in Fig. 11-28, there are three basic methods by which material can be cut, and they are distinguished primarily by the amount of pressure, that is, the force per unit area, and speed of motion applied. In Fig. 11-28a, the motion of the cutting edge is along the line of cut. The cutting edge travels at a relatively high speed, and under relatively light pressure. In Fig. 11-28b, the cutting edge moves towards the line of cut. It may travel at a relatively low rate of speed but necessitates a relatively high pressure to cut. In Fig. 11-28c, the cutting edge travels toward the line of cut, but it moves at a high rate of speed and also under high pressure.

The first type of cutting motion produces what we can call a *slicing action*, the familiar cutting motion used in carving a roast or slicing bread. The cutting is accomplished almost entirely by the relatively rapid movement of the cutting edge. Just enough pressure is required to cause the sides of the tool to "spread" the material slightly so that the edge can reach the area to be cut as the cut progresses. Because the pressure is low, the edge requires little support, so the tool is "thin," and the sides forming the cutting edge are very nearly parallel.

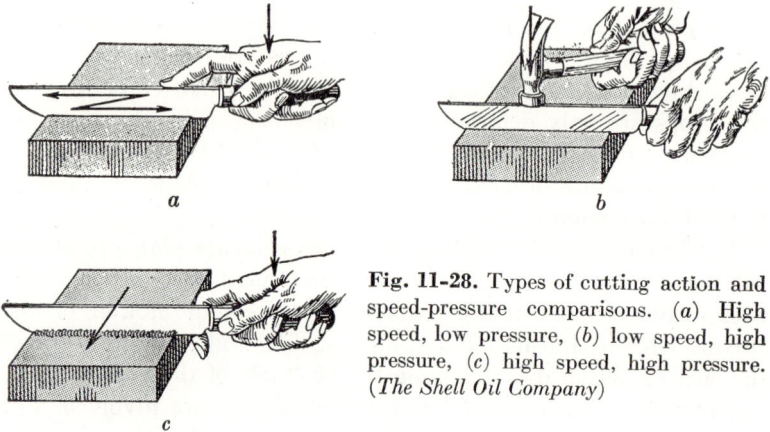

a

b

c

Fig. 11-28. Types of cutting action and speed-pressure comparisons. (*a*) High speed, low pressure, (*b*) low speed, high pressure, (*c*) high speed, high pressure. (*The Shell Oil Company*)

The second cutting motion might be described as a *wedging action*. The action of a cold chisel and that of an ax used to cut a log are typical examples. Great pressure, usually applied suddenly, accounts for most of the cutting action. Thus the cutting edge must be supported by a much greater amount of material. As a result, a wedging tool is fairly thick, that is, the sides forming the cutting edge meet at a wider angle than those of a slicing tool.

The final cutting motion, and the one that concerns us most in lathe operations can be described as a *scraping action*. The pressure applied to the cutting edge and the speed of the cutting motion are both relatively high. For this reason, the cutting edge of a scraping tool requires maximum support to "hold up," so it is designed with the sides forming the cutting edge meeting at a wider angle than either the slicing or wedging tool. See Fig. 11-29 for the comparisons.

of these angles. It should also be noted that the tool is designed to enter the material at such an angle that most of the pressure is concentrated on one side of the cutting edge.

While it is commonly considered that to cut, the cutting tool must be much harder than the material being cut, you may recall such phenomena as a straw being driven into solid wood by a tornado, your foot punching a clean hole in a sheet of hard but thin ice, and a baseball neatly penetrating a pane of glass. In other words, a softer material can cut, providing the energy it exerts on the material cut (as determined by the velocity and the weight of, or

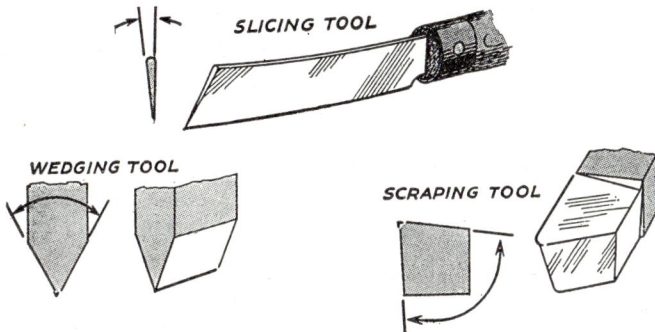

SLICING TOOL

WEDGING TOOL

SCRAPING TOOL

Fig. 11-29. Difference in amount of metal that supports the cutting edge. (*The Shell Oil Company*)

the pressure behind, the cutting object) is great enough. In the case of the straw, though its weight was light, its velocity was high. In the case of your foot, its velocity was low but the weight great. In the case of the baseball, its weight and velocity, while only moderate, combined to produce relatively great energy.

Thus we find that the slicing action, which involves a relatively high velocity but little pressure, only permits the cutting of material considerably softer than the tool. The wedging action, with relatively high pressure applied—often with considerable speed for a brief period, as when the cold chisel is struck with a hammer—permits cutting of a material much more nearly equal the hardness of the cutting tool; while the scraping action, which combines relatively high pressure and high speed of cutting movement, makes possible, under proper conditions, the cutting of materials almost as hard as the cutting tool.

The fact still remains, however, that for practical purposes, to cut a piece of material we use a cutting tool considerably harder than the material being cut, because it is ordinarily impractical to achieve sufficient velocity and pressure simultaneously. However, as we shall see, the cutting of the harder metals would be an almost impossible job were it not for the crystalline structure of metal and the cleavage planes which this structure introduces.

If you will study Figs. 11-28 to 11-32, you will notice that even the thinnest cutting edge applies some wedging action to the material after the edge has entered. In the case of a slicing motion, this wedging action is very slight, due to the fact that a slicing tool must be quite thin. In the so-called *wedging type of cutting motion*, material

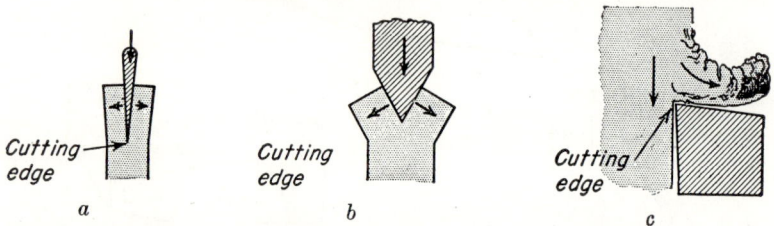

Fig. 11-30. Effects of (*a*) slicing, (*b*) wedging, and (*c*) scraping actions. (*The Shell Oil Company*)

on both sides of the tool is subjected to a still greater degree of wedging pressure. Yet, the actual displacement of the material is only moderate, because the wedging action takes place equally on both sides of the cutting edge of the tool that is only moderately "thick." Under the influence of scraping action, however, as shown in Fig. 11-30*c*, the extreme wedging pressure, resulting from the wide angle between the sides of the tool forming the cutting edge, is concentrated on one side of the cutting edge. The deformation, or displacement, of the material in such cases is relatively great.

As we will recall, metal is made up of many grains. Pressure applied to one grain or layer of grains passes on to other individual grains or layers of grains. Pressure of the wedging action of the cutting tool, therefore, passes from grain to grain of the metal. Since it is not applied uniformily to all surfaces of the grains, it subjects them to a sort of shearing action. This shearing action causes the grains to slip and finally break along their cleavage planes. When enough grains are thus fractured, a piece of metal is separated from the workpiece. What happens when a piece of metal is being cut on a lathe, therefore, is simply that by applying a wedging action behind a cutting edge, the metal is "split" along the lines of cleavage

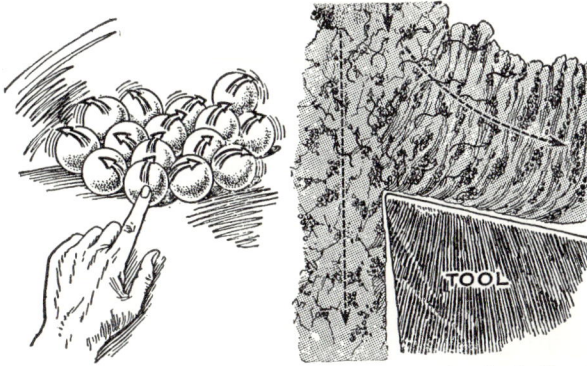

Fig. 11-31. The pressure effect of tools on metal grains is similar to that of pressure applied to one marble in a group—it is transmitted from marble to marble. (*The Shell Oil Company*)

of the grains subjected to the greatest pressure, and a chip is released and passes up over the face of the tool. From this, it may be seen that it is the wedging action of the face of the tool that does most of the work; the cutting edge itself does little actual cutting.

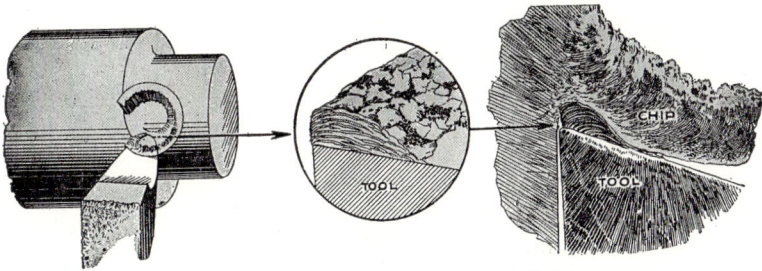

Fig. 11-32. The false cutting edge. (*The Shell Oil Company*)

It serves merely to start the wedging action and perhaps smooth off small parts left behind as the chip separates from the workpiece. However, the sharper the cutting edge, the more the wedging action tends to be concentrated on a relatively few grains of the workpiece material. As a result, a cleaner separation of chip and workpiece occurs, and hence a smoother finish.

Since the tool meets the workpiece at an angle that concentrates the wedging action on the face of the tool, the greatest pressure and the resultant cleavage is not in a line parallel with the direction of cutting motion, but approximately perpendicular to the face of the tool. As a result, the chip removed is not a continuous one, like that removed by a carpenter's plane when planing with the grain, but a number of chip parts or segments which may or may not cling together, depending upon the type of metal and other conditions.

While all metals behave basically in the manner just described when being cut, variations in the characteristics of different metals necessitate certain variations in the cutting methods required for most efficient results. It is impossible here to take up these factors in detail. However, as an illustration of the problems involved we might recall that some metals, which are called *ductile*, are composed of grains which are able to slip considerably along their lines of cleavage before breaking. Such grains tend to be deformed, rather than fractured, when subjected to the cutting pressure. This causes part of them, in effect, to "flow" up over the face of the tool, before the actual separation takes place. This produces a continuous chip and a smoother cutting action. In such cases, a high speed of workpiece motion at a moderate feed and depth of cut, which results in moderate pressure, is desirable. That is why such metals are cut best at high speeds.

On the other hand, the metals that have been described as brittle, being composed of grains which tend to fracture rather than deform under pressure, are inclined to "split," in effect, ahead of the cutting edge. This produces a rough, jerky cutting action and if performed at high speeds would cause excessive vibration, tool wear, and uneven finish. Therefore, brittle metals are best cut at moderate speeds with fairly high rate of feed and depth of cut, which result in a fairly heavy pressure on the tool.

As a final word, study the figures in this section very carefully. Follow the text and you should be able to understand just what happens when metals are cut.

CHAPTER 12

Centering

Holding Work in the Lathe. Work to be turned in the lathe may be held between centers, fastened in a chuck, clamped to the faceplate, or clamped to the saddle. Work that is to be faced or turned true with a finished hole is held either on a mandrel be-

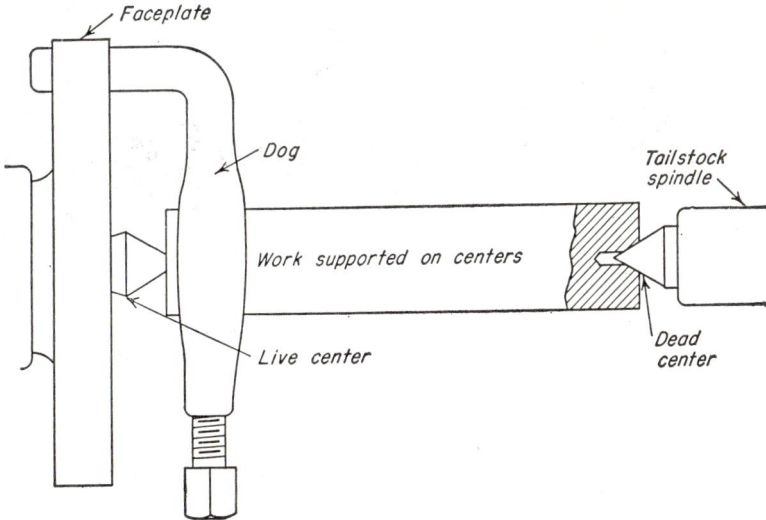

Fig. 12-1.

tween centers, or on a special mandrel the shank of which fits the spindle, or on a plug which is fastened in the chuck and turned to fit the hole.

A large proportion of lathe work is mounted on centers. Sixty-degree countersunk holes, called *centers*, are drilled and reamed in both ends of the piece to be turned. These holes fit the 60-deg. lathe centers and the work is thus supported (Fig. 12-1).

The work thus centered is usually driven from the faceplate by means of a *dog* which is securely clamped to it on the live-center end. The work turns *with* the live center, which acts as a support only, and *on* the dead center, which acts as a support and also as a bearing (see Fig. 12-1).

Lathe Dogs for Driving Work on Centers. The common lathe dog shown in Fig. 12-2*a* is the most popular type. Figure 12-2*b*

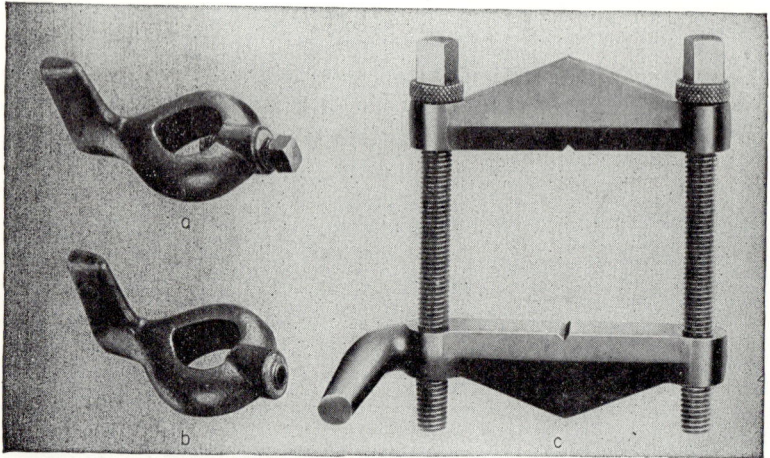

Fig. 12-2. Lathe dogs: (*a*) common lathe dog, (*b*) safety lathe dog, and (*c*) clamp lathe dog. (*The South Bend Lathe Works*)

shows a safety lathe dog which has a headless setscrew and is not likely to catch in the operator's sleeve. Figure 12-2*c* shows a clamp lathe dog, used principally for rectangular work in the lathe. When attaching a lathe dog to the work, make sure that the setscrew is securely fastened.

If ever a finished end is put in a dog, it should be protected by a piece of copper or soft brass between the work and the hardened end of the setscrew.

Importance of Carefully Locating the Center. It is very important to carefully center a piece of work to be turned. A piece carelessly centered may not have sufficient stock to clean up, that is, finish all over, and therefore be spoiled. Even if it has sufficient stock to clean up, the fact that the centers are out of true will necessitate a big chip on one side of the diameter and a small chip on the other. This unevenness of cut takes more time and may cause inaccuracy.

It is especially important to center tool steel accurately and carefully. In its manufacture, the heating necessary for rolling the steel into bars of various shapes and sizes causes a decarburized[1] surface to the depth of perhaps $\frac{1}{32}$ in. If this is not altogether removed in machining a piece of tool steel, when the piece is heat-treated that part of the piece from which the decarburized portion has not been removed will not harden.

The rolling process also causes a difference of density of the metal toward the center of the bar, and turning off more from one side of the bar than the other will cause the piece to warp in hardening.

Care must be taken in centering cast iron. In making an iron casting, the molten metal is poured into a sand mold. The hot metal coming in contact with the cold sand causes the surface of the casting, called the *scale*, to become considerably harder than the interior. Also a considerable amount of sand is fused with the iron in the surface of the casting. These conditions serve to render the surface of a casting very hard and brittle, and when machining, it is important that the point of the cutting tool be well under this scale in order not to rub off the cutting edge and ruin the tool.

Methods of Locating Centers. First, measure the stock to see if it will finish to the length required, and then rub chalk on the ends to make the center-locating lines more distinct.

There are several good methods for accurately locating the center holes which must be drilled in each end of the work before it can be mounted on the lathe centers for machining. Some of these methods are explained here.

Divider Method. Chalk the ends of the work, set the dividers to approximately one-half the diameter of the piece, and scribe four lines across each end, as shown in Fig. 12-3. The center of the square in the piece will be the center of the work.

Hermaphrodite-caliper Method. Set the caliper (Fig. 6-5) to about the radius of the piece. Place the caliper leg on the circumference

---

[1] Tool steel has a definite content of carbon, usually about 1 per cent. When the steel is heated and exposed to the air, as in rolling, the carbon on the surface is lost and this surface layer is said to be *decarburized*.

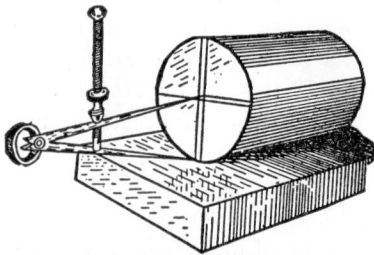

Fig. 12-3. Locating centers with dividers. (*The South Bend Lathe Works*)

Fig. 12-4. Centering with hermaphrodite caliper. (*The South Bend Lathe Works*)

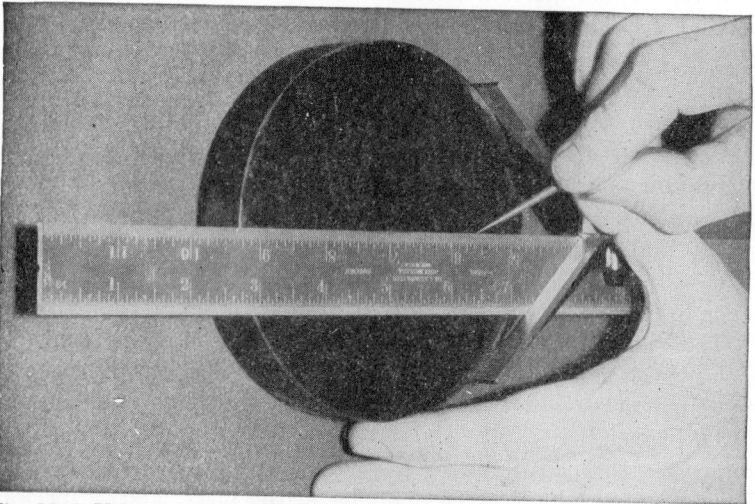

Fig. 12-5. Using a centerhead to locate the center. (*The L. S. Starrett Company*)

at the extreme end of the piece and with the point draw an arc near the center of that end. Move the caliper leg about one-quarter of the circumference of the end each time and draw three more arcs. The four arcs will form an approximate square, the center of which is the center required (Fig. 12-4).

Center-head Method (Fig. 12-5). Hold both limbs of the center-

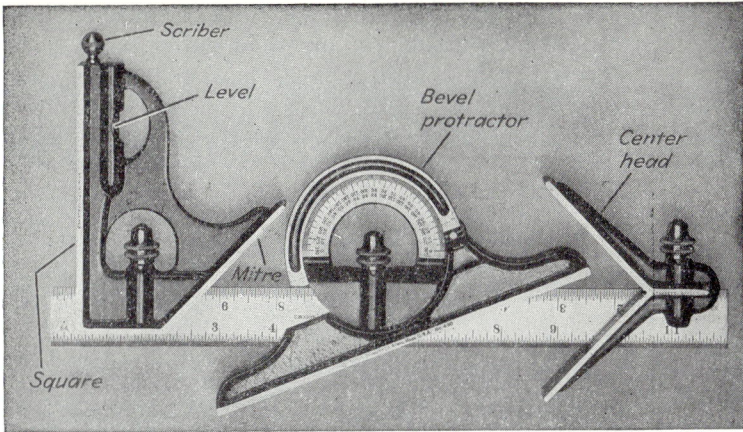

Fig. 12-6. Combination set: a rule, a square, a mitre, a center square, a bevel protractor, a level, and a scriber. (*The L. S. Starrett Company*)

head of a combination square (Fig. 12-6) against the surface of the work and, with a scriber, rule lines at about right angles to each other. The intersection of these lines is the required center.

Surface-gage Method (Fig. 12-7). When the center in an irregular-shaped casting or forging is required, a surface gage may be used (see Chapter 6, pages 155–156). For example, a bolt blank may

be forged with the head offset. If the head is centered true, the body of the bolt will run out of true and may not clean up. To properly center such a

Fig. 12-7. Using a surface gage to locate the center. (*The South Bend Lathe Works*)

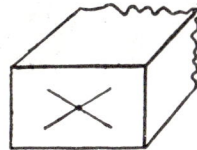

Fig. 12-8.

piece, place the bolt on parallels or on V blocks, adjust the sur-face-gage scriber to the approximate center of the body, and draw lines on both ends forming squares. The centers of these squares are the desired centers.

Diagonal-line Method (Fig. 12-8). Rectangular pieces are easily centered by drawing diagonal lines.

Centering-machine Method (Fig. 12-9). Modern machine-shop equipment includes a centering machine which automatically holds round pieces central with the drill spindle, thus making it unnecessary to locate the centers otherwise. There are several kinds of these machines on the market, some of which are provided with three-

Fig. 12-9. A centering machine. (*Pines Engineering Company*)

jaw chucks and cannot be used for holding and centering square stock.

In many shops, a centering machine may not be available, and further, many of the larger and irregular-shaped pieces cannot be held in such a machine even if one is at hand; therefore, other methods of locating the centers must be used. Some of these methods have just been explained.

Use of Center Punch. After the center is located, tighten the piece in a vise and select a center punch (see Chapter 6, page

148) with a point ground to about 90-deg. Place the center punch vertically at the center point and tap with a hammer (Fig. 12-10), making a mark sufficiently deep so that the work will revolve on the center points when placed in the lathe. It is important to test

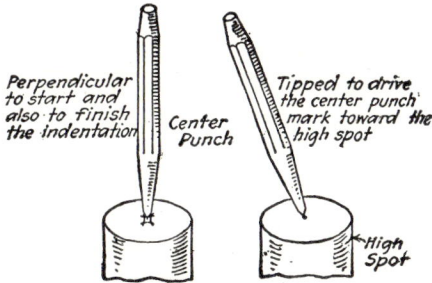

Perpendicular
to start and
also to finish
the indentation

Center
Punch

Tipped to drive
the center punch
mark toward the
high spot

High
Spot

Fig. 12-10.

the accuracy of the center-punch marks, especially until experience has trained the eye. Do not put on a dog, or do not start the lathe, but revolve the work by hand on dead centers, marking the high spot on each end with chalk (Fig. 12-11).

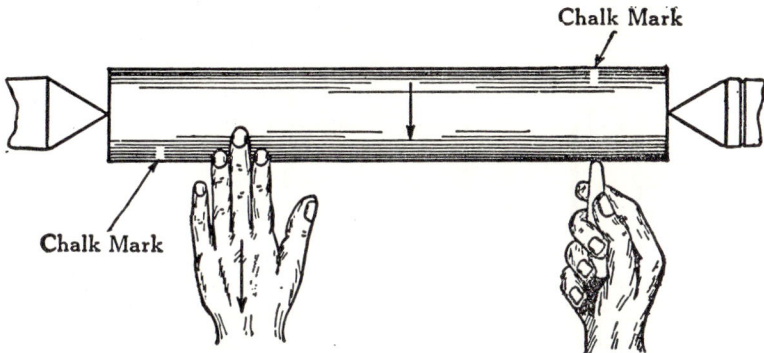

Chalk Mark

Chalk Mark

Fig. 12-11. Testing the accuracy of center-punch marks. (*The South Bend Lathe Works*)

1. Do not tighten the dead center too much, but allow the work to spin freely.
2. Spin the work slowly at first to see if it runs out of true; if you spin it too fast, the blur makes it appear to run true.

3. If it does run out too much, then spin it fast and, with a piece of chalk, just touch the spinning work about one-half inch from each end. The chalk will not mark all around the piece but will mark the high spot.

4. Clamp the work in the vise again, and by tipping the center punch, drive the center toward the high spot to bring it right. Then hold the punch perpendicular and make the indentation symmetrical. Where the chalk marks the piece (the high spot) indicates the greatest radius. To shorten this radius serves to bring the center-punch mark toward the center. Sometimes the beginner may need to change the center-punch mark and test the location two or three times before the work runs true enough.

5. Before placing the piece to be tested for centers on these centers, test to see whether these centers are in "line" or alignment. The dead center and live center should be in line for all operations except taper turning. Form the habit, when going to work on the lathe, of making sure that the centers are in approximate alignment.

6. To ascertain if a lathe is in approximate alignment: (1) Note that the live center runs true and carefully bring the dead center to within $\frac{1}{16}$ in. of the live center (Fig. 12-12). A very little

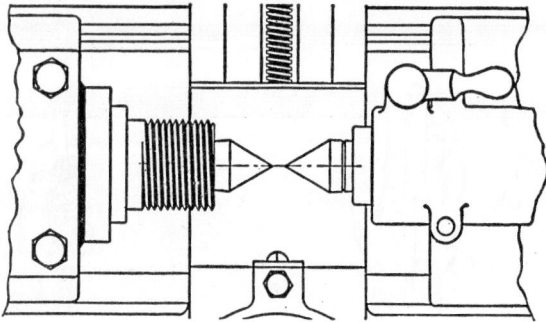

Fig. 12-12. Checking the alignment of the lathe centers. (*The South Bend Lathe Works*)

offset will be easily seen. (2) Note *witness marks* on slide and base of the tailstock. These usually indicate whether or not alignment is close. Setting a lathe in *accurate* alignment is explained in Chapter 14.

Drilling and Reaming the Center. The combination drill and countersink (Fig. 12-13) is the correct tool to use for making the center hole. The hole may be made as follows (Fig. 12-14):

Fig. 12-13. Combination center drill and countersink. (*South Bend Lathe Works*)

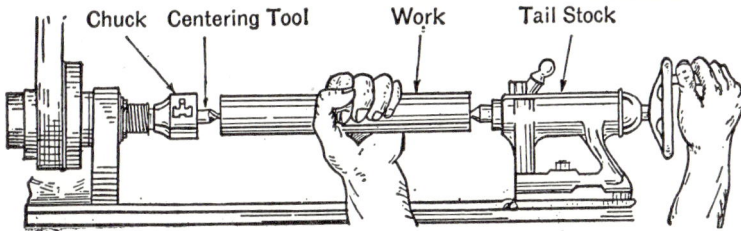

Fig. 12-14. Drilling the center hole in the end of a shaft. (*The South Bend Lathe Works*)

1. Obtain a combination drill and countersink of the right size and be sure it is sharp. Get also a small drill chuck with a taper shank that will fit the taper hole in the main spindle of an engine lathe.
2. See that the centers are in approximate alignment.
3. With a suitable steel rod through the spindle hole, knock out the live center, holding it so it will not fall.
4. Be sure the taper shank of the chuck is clean and fits the taper hole; then thrust it tightly into place.
5. Fasten the combination drill and countersink firmly in the chuck.
6. Let the tail spindle project about an inch, move the tailstock to such a position that the work may be held between the point of the drill and the dead center, and then clamp the tailstock to the ways.
7. Put one of the center-punch marks on the drill point and, steadying the work, bring the dead center carefully into the other punch mark.
8. Hold the work fairly tight with the left hand, allowing the tool rest to support the wrist.
9. Apply lard oil or cutting compound for steel. Drill cast iron dry.
10. Start the lathe (fastest speed), and feed by turning the tail-

spindle handwheel slowly until the center hole is reamed to the correct size.

11. Be careful not to break the drill when drawing the work back from the center reamer. It is best to keep the work against the tail center as it is backed away from the drill, thus avoiding any tendency to pry off the drill.

If the drill should be broken in the center hole, it may often be removed by a sharp blow on the side or end of the piece of work; if not, it must be softened by annealing. Then it may be drilled out.

Size of Centers. Combination drills and countersinks are furnished in various sizes. There is no rule for the sizes of centers. The proportion of the size of the center to the diameter of the work is largely a matter of judgment and depends on the material, the amount of stock to be removed, the cut to be taken, the number and kinds of operations to be performed, and the shape of the piece.

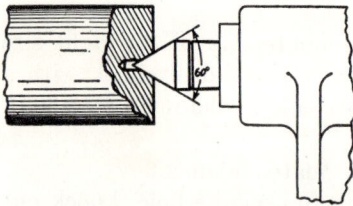

Do not make the centers too big; they should be just large enough to withstand the resistance of the cut. If, after facing, the center is too small, it is easy to make it larger.

Correct Center Hole (Fig. 12-15).

Fig. 12-15. A correctly drilled and countersunk hole. (*The South Bend Lathe Works*)

To be correct, the center hole must be the size required for the diameter of the piece, as listed below:

Finished diameter of work (inches)	Diameter of center (inches)	Diameter of center drill (inches)
$\frac{1}{2}$	$\frac{1}{8}$	$\frac{1}{16}$
1	$\frac{3}{16}$	$\frac{3}{32}$
$1\frac{1}{2}$	$\frac{1}{4}$	$\frac{3}{32}$
2	$\frac{5}{16}$	$\frac{1}{8}$

There must also be sufficient clearance at the bottom of the countersink.

When drilling center holes, allow for the thickness of the metal that will be faced off the end; otherwise, the center holes will be too small to support the piece after the ends are faced.

Poorly Drilled Center Holes. One of the most common causes of unsatisfactory lathe work is poorly drilled center holes. Figure 12-16 shows a shallow center hole with incorrect angle and no clear-

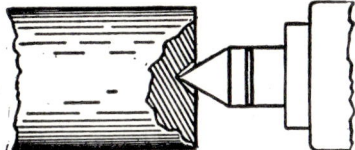

Fig. 12-16. A poorly drilled center hole, too shallow and at incorrect angle. (*The South Bend Lathe Works*)

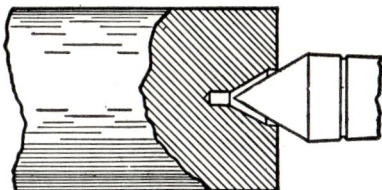

Fig. 12-17. An incorrect center hole, drilled too deep to fit the lathe center. (*The South Bend Lathe Works*)

ance for the tip of the center point. Figure 12-17 shows a center hole that has been drilled too deep. Accuracy cannot be expected when center holes are poorly made. Furthermore, the lathe centers may be damaged.

QUESTIONS ON CENTERING

1. Does it make any difference whether the "morphy" is set a little more or a little less than the radius?
2. Why do you rub chalk on the ends of the stock?
3. How large an indentation do you make with the center punch before testing? Why? What is the angle of the point of the center punch?
4. After both centers are located and center-punched, how are they tested for accuracy? What does the high spot indicate?
5. If the center-punch marks need changing slightly, how is this done?
6. Why should care be taken to have the centers in the work fairly true?
7. Why is the combination drill and countersink an efficient tool?
8. How many r.p.m. should the combination drill and countersink be run?
9. Name at least two things that determine the proper size of the centers to be reamed.
10. Why does the drill break so easily? What is a good way to pry it out?
11. How tightly do you grasp the work when you are drilling it? Where do you rest your hand? Give reasons.
12. On what materials is a cutting lubricant used when drilling or reaming? What is the use of the lubricant?

13. How is the center square used for finding the center?

14. If the nature of the work is such that the use of a "morphy" of a center square is not practicable (for example, a bolt head that is forged off center from the body), how may the centers be located so that the body will run true?

15. What is a centering machine? What are its advantages?

16. Give two reasons for the drilled hole being deeper than the point of the lathe center.

17. If a drill has been broken off in the center hole, why must it be annealed before it can be drilled out?

CHAPTER 13

Facing

General Information. The lathe operation of finishing the ends of the work, to make the ends flat and smooth and to make the piece the required length, is called *facing;* in some shops *squaring.*

The work may be held on centers or in a chuck.[1] An advantage of holding the work in a chuck lies in the fact that the work does not have to be centered before facing, consequently one end may usually be faced clean and then all the overlength taken off the other end without worrying about the relative size of the centers. Also, a shoulder tool or a regular turning tool may be used, and this is often an advantage especially when removing the scale from cast iron. A disadvantage is the time it takes to put on the chuck and afterward to remove it. Further, many pieces cannot be held in a chuck and faced because they would project too far; 3 or 4 in. is the limit.

The term *radial facing* is applied to work of a comparatively large diameter and may be discussed more properly under the subject of chuck work (see page 370).

The ends of a properly faced piece will be square (flat). The surface may be tested with the edge of a rule. To produce a flat surface when facing on centers, the lathe centers must be in line; a surface like Fig. 13-1a, indicates

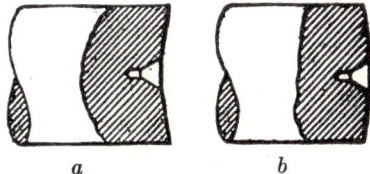

a *b*

Fig. 13-1.

that the dead center is offset towards the operator, a surface like Fig. 13-1b shows the center is offset away from the operator.

If considerable material is to be removed later in the turning

[1] For information concerning chucks, see p. 370.

operation, it is better not to face to exact length until all the rough turning cuts are taken. This will provide a larger center for the roughing cuts than would look well in the finished piece. Also, finishing the ends after roughing out the work will remove the burr around the center caused by the great pressure of the heavy roughing cut that tends to enlarge the hole as the work revolves.

A piece of steel is usually cut off somewhat over the finished length because the hacksaw or cutting-off machine of any kind is not meant for accuracy. The machinist before starting to work on any special piece measures the stock to be sure it is long enough. If there is any doubt about the stock being long enough, a *telltale* (an unfinished portion of the end) is left *on each end* of the piece to prove, if necessary, that it was short.

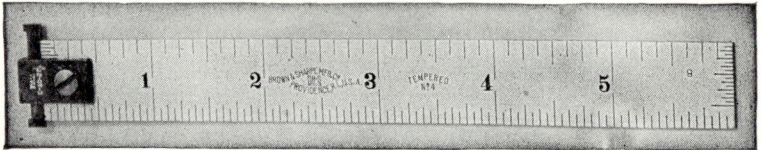

Fig. 13-2. Hook rule. This rule is useful for taking measurements and for setting or reading the measure of an inside caliper. (*The Brown & Sharpe Manufacturing Company*)

Suppose the work is to be faced on centers. Face off about half the overlength from one end; remove the dog; lay off the length (with the hermaphrodite caliper if the piece is short, otherwise with rule and scriber); place the dog on the end that has been faced and finish the other end practically to the line. If a chuck is used instead of centers, just as much care must be used in laying off and measuring.

An accurate way of measuring the length of the shorter pieces is with an outside caliper. Sometimes on the longer pieces it is necessary to use a rule to measure direct or possibly two rules end to end. When using this method one must be particularly careful to have the end of the rule flush (even) with the end of the work. A hook rule (Fig. 13-2) is very useful.

Remember always that the function of the tool is to cut the metal, not scrape it. Do not take a great number of chips. Learn as quickly as possible to judge the facing chip that will remove a given amount of stock.

Facing accurately and quickly is a job that requires attention to business and good judgment. The beginner who with reasonable speed can face a piece on centers to length and have the ends square and smooth, with no ridges, no undercut near the center, and no fin, has a right to be proud of his work.

Facing on Centers: Adjusting the Work. After the work is carefully centered, tighten a dog firmly on one end (a protecting piece of copper under the dog screw is unnecessary unless that end of the work is finished). Put a drop of oil in the center hole in the other end. Place the work between centers and *adjust* the tail center. The experienced machinist always puts the work on the live center first, being sure the tail of the dog does not bind in the slot of the faceplate (Fig. 13-3). Then he runs the tail center into the center

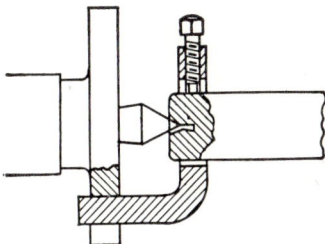

Fig. 13-3. When using a dog larger than necessary, it is likely to bind on the sides of the faceplate slot and may also bind on the bottom. In either case, the work will not fit on the lathe center and will not run true.

hole and is careful that it enters without hitting around the hole two or three times. To avoid chatter, he brings the center up until there is no shake of the work between centers, but *not too tight* because the work must be free to turn or the center will be scored and possibly spoiled. That is, he *adjusts* the work between the centers carefully. Unless the work is too large, the machinist always tries this adjustment by wiggling the tail of the dog in the faceplate slot.

When placing the work between centers do not hold it at arm's length or try and reach over the tool post. Hold the piece steady by resting the hand against the tool rest or the tail spindle or in any convenient way.

The Facing Operation. A side tool is used for facing. There are several patented holders with bits or blades for facing, but perhaps the regular turning-tool holder with a bit ground as shown in Fig. 13-4 is as satisfactory as any of these.

The whole cutting edge of the side tool should not be set at right angles to the center line of the work, but the point of the tool should be slightly in, that is, toward the work.

To obtain a smooth finish the point of the side tool should be slightly rounded with an oilstone, or so ground as to present a short flat surface to the work (see Fig. 13-4). The length of this flat surface should be greater than the amount of the cross feed.

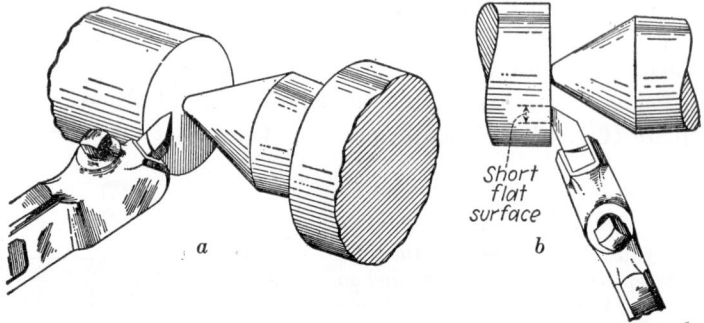

Fig. 13-4. Facing, or squaring.

To make sure that the flat spot is set square, take a light facing cut with the tool set fairly near right "by eye." Then run the tool in toward the center and also a trifle away from the end of the work. Now, watching the cut, carefully feed the tool (hand longitudinal feed) to just touch the work and note if the heel and toe of the flat spot both touch on the squared surface. If they do, the flat spot is set square; if they do not, it will be easy to reset the tool.

The work may be roughed by feeding from the center hole outward or from the circumference toward the center. *The finishing cut is made from the center hole outward.* (If considerable overlength is to be removed by facing, it may be advisable to rough by feeding the tool *sideways*, that is, "stepping off" the excess material by several hand-fed side cuts instead of radial cuts, and perhaps a turning-tool bit properly ground for this purpose may be more efficient.)

If there are several pieces to face, it will be advisable to get a half center (Fig. 13-5) from the toolroom, but having only one or two pieces, or in the event of a half center not being available, the following method is used.

Adjust the work between the centers (no slack and not too tight), start the lathe, and, with the right hand on the cross-feed handle and the left hand on the long-feed handwheel, bring the tool as close to the center as convenient and then into the work until a light chip is taken around the center hole. Stop feeding with the left hand (long feed) and with the right hand feed slowly outward, that is, toward the circumference, thus squaring or facing the end. The amount of chip and feed must be determined by conditions. The machinist usually prefers to face the smaller pieces (under 1 in. diameter) by hand feed. The beginner will go slowly on the first piece.

The above method of facing will leave a slight *fin* around the center hole. Sometimes the machinist purposely leaves a fairly heavy fin, say, ¼ in. or more in diameter, around the center hole until he is ready to take the finishing cut. He judges by the looks (length) of the fin how much he has removed from the end of the stock. To remove this fin bring the side tool to the surface just faced and to the fin. Ease the tail center about ¹⁄₃₂ in. and clamp

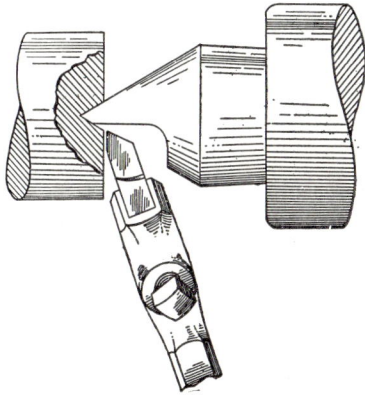

Fig. 13-5. The use of a half-center for facing.

the tail spindle; when the lathe is started the work will have a tendency to ride on the tool and make a clean cut around the center hole. Do not feed toward the circumference again but stop the lathe and remove the work.

A Typical Facing Job. If there are a dozen pieces to be faced, they may be held either on centers or in a chuck. If the work may be held conveniently either way, there is not much choice between the methods except that if the centers are used, care must be taken not to face too much off one end and thus leave the center holes unequal in size. In either case, on centers or in a chuck, a facing tool or a shoulder tool may be used. Proceed as follows:

1. Lay the pieces side by side, ends flush (even); pick out the shortest one and measure the length in order to judge how much to face off one end of this and succeeding pieces.
2. Set the tool with the facing *flat spot* square.
3. Face one end of each piece. If a shoulder tool is used, the roughing cut may be made by feeding from the circumference toward the center. Then face "in" a trifle with the same tool and feed from the center out to give a smooth finishing cut.
4. When all the pieces are faced on one end, lay off the lengths and face the other ends; the roughing cuts very close to the line, the finishing cuts splitting the line.

QUESTIONS ON FACING

1. Why should the piece be measured before proceeding to face?
2. It may be stated that a side tool has four clearance angles; where are they? What three are ground on the tool?
3. If a patent holder is used, why should the blade be removed from the holder before grinding?
4. If it is necessary to sharpen a side tool, should it be ground on the top, on the front, or on the side? Why?
5. Should a side tool be oilstoned? Give reason.
6. Why must the centers be in line? What is the effect if the tailstock slide is offset toward the operator? Away from the operator?
7. How do you adjust the work between centers?
8. Do you always finish one end before rough facing the other end? Give reasons.
9. What is a telltale?
10. If you have several pieces to face, is it advisable to rough face them all before finishing any? Give reason.
11. When is hand feed used in facing? When is power feed used? Give reasons for both.
12. Is the tool fed in a direction toward or away from the center? Why?
13. Why is it advisable to slightly round the point of the side tool?
14. What do you mean by setting the side tool on center and pointing slightly in toward the work?
15. For a facing cut, how do you lay off the length? How do you measure the length?
16. When should a piece not be faced to exact length before the turning operation?

17. When facing an end, one roughing cut and one finishing cut are usually sufficient. Why take more?

18. If considerable metal is to be removed what tool other than a side tool may be used? Why is it more efficient? How may it be fed?

19. What causes a wavy or chattered appearance of the surface being squared?

20. What is a half-center? Why is it more than half?

21. What is a fin? What is the best way of removing a fin? Another way?

22. When is a lubricant used in facing?

23. Name at least two reasons why a piece is faced.

CHAPTER 14

Turning in a Lathe

Turning in a lathe is accomplished by causing the work to revolve while the tool, being fed longitudinally, peels off a chip. The same definition may be applied to turning in a turret lathe or to turning outside or inside (boring) in a boring mill. The principles and methods involved in turning and boring are the same for the larger machines as for the smaller machines. The cutting action of the tool is the same whether the work is held between centers or in a chuck, on the faceplate of a lathe, on the table of a boring mill, or in a special fixture in either machine. The principles of feeds and speeds, of alignment, of measurement, etc., are fundamental machine-shop principles.

In rapid-production work where hundreds or thousands of duplicate pieces are made within narrow limits of exactitude, the turret lathe with its special holding fixtures, its facing, turning boring, and other tools, each arranged in the turret head or on the cross slide for its particular operation, is most advantageously used. For the larger castings and forgings the boring mill is most adaptable for many turning, facing, or boring operations. It must be remembered that these machines are, after all, modifications of the lathe. The lathe is the most important machine; it is the most widely used and the most adaptable of machine-shop tools, and turning in a lathe is one of the most important operations in a machine shop.

In order to be able intelligently to set up a lathe for an accurate turning job it is necessary to understand certain of the *principles* and *methods* involved.

PRINCIPLES OF TURNING

Position of the Dead Center. The center line of the lathe is determined by the center of rotation, or the axis, of the main spindle and is parallel to the ways. It is therefore parallel to the line of travel of the carriage which moves on the ways, and it is also parallel to the line of travel of the turning tool.

The live center and the dead center are equidistant from the horizontal plane of the ways. The live center, having no adjustment, is fixed in its position.

The design of the tailstock, however, permits of transverse adjustment of the dead center, that is, the dead center may be moved *off center* toward or away from the operator, or it may be adjusted from off center to an exact central position.

When turning work in a lathe, if the dead center is exactly *in line* with the live center, the distance from both centers to the line of travel of the tool is the same. In this case the radii and consequently the diameters of the turned work are everywhere equal, and the turned piece is a perfect cylinder. It is said to be *turned straight* (Fig. 14-1a).

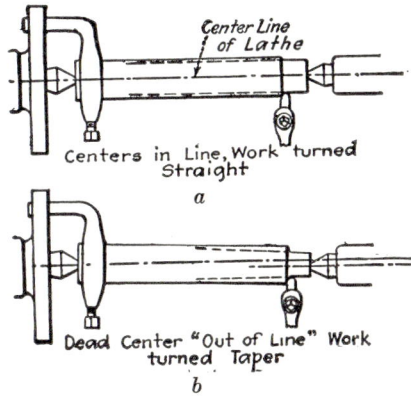

Fig. 14-1.

If, when turning, the dead center is *offset* or *out of line*, the distance from the line of travel of the turning tool to one center is greater than it is to the other, and the diameter of the work which is being turned changes constantly from one end to the other so that the work is not straight. It is said to be *turned taper* (Fig. 14-1b). Methods of obtaining accurate alignment of centers are explained beginning page 345.

Accuracy of the Live Center. The method of procedure in turning a cylinder in a lathe is to turn half its length or more from one end, then reverse the piece on centers (changing the dog to the opposite end of the work) and turn the rest of the cylinder. The circumference of any properly turned piece is concentric with its center line. If the live center runs true and a piece is turned as above, it will be found that the part of the cylinder first turned will run absolutely true when reversed, and when the remainder is turned the two cuts will meet exactly. This work is right and is possible only when the live center runs perfectly true.

Suppose that the live center runs out and the above operations are made. When the piece is reversed it will be noticed that the middle of the work runs out one-half the amount the live center is out of true. It is impossible to have the cut that is made after the piece is reversed meet flush with the cut already made, and the piece cannot be turned straight to size (Fig. 14-2). Further, suppose the

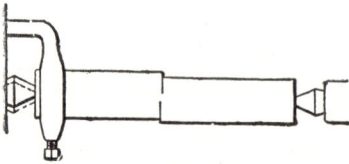

Fig. 14-2. Result of attempting to turn a cylinder with the live center "out of true."

live center runs out of true and a portion only of the length of the work is turned. If the center does not run out too much and the stock is large enough to clean, the turned portion will be round and straight *but it will not run true* on dead centers and it will not run true in a lathe or other machine in which the centers are true. Many times it has been discovered after several later operations (in which the centers were not used) that the work has been spoiled in turning; this means delay and waste. The live center *must* run true.

How to Determine if the Live Center Runs True. One method of determining if the live center runs true is as follows: Tighten a toolholder (reversed) in the tool post and bring the end fairly close to the center; hold a piece of paper under the revolving center and look down between the toolholder and the center. Any eccentricity of the center may readily be observed.

Cleaning and Truing the Lathe Centers. The shanks of the lathe centers are tapered and fit taper holes in their respective spindles. Any dirt, chips, or burrs, either on the shank or in the taper hole, will cause the center to run out of true. Clean the center with the palm of the hand, and if any nick or burr is felt, oilstone it off. Clean the tail-spindle hole with clean waste on a stick, or with your finger. To clean the main-spindle hole, push a piece of waste through the whole length and wipe the taper hole with your finger *but never while the lathe is running. Never clean any moving part of any machine.* If the live center runs out after cleaning, it may be trued up with a square-nose tool (Fig. 14-3) or with a turning tool if the compound rest is used. A center should be filed very little, if at all, after turning. Test the angle of the center with a center gage as shown in Fig. 14-4. Some lathes have been abused to

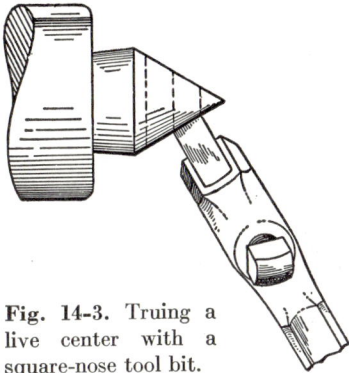

Fig. 14-3. Truing a live center with a square-nose tool bit.

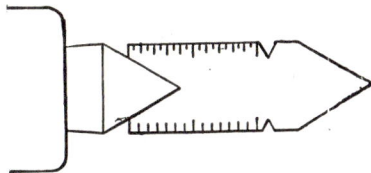

Fig. 14-4. Center gage. A tool used for testing the accuracy of 60-deg. centers. Used also when grinding and setting 60-deg. threading tools

such an extent that the taper hole in the main spindle runs out of true. In such a case it is necessary to have a witness mark (perhaps a center-punch mark) on both the spindle and center and bring these two in line when putting in the live center.

The dead center is hardened and if damaged must be ground. It should be smooth. The dead center is a bearing on which the work revolves; therefore *it must be kept well oiled* or it will run dry in the center of the work and become roughened and probably twisted off.

Some machinists advocate a hardened live center. It is no doubt stronger than a soft center. To have the live center, either soft or hard, run *true*, it is usually best to true it when it is in position in the lathe spindle, and therefore in the case of a hard center, it is necessary to use the special grinding attachment. For most operations the soft live center is satisfactory.

There are several styles of grinding attachments that are designed especially for truing centers. If one of these attachments is not available, the dead center may be cold-water annealed and trued up and then rehardened. Such a center is good enough for the dead center but is not likely to be true enough, after hardening, for the live center.

Setting the Tool[1]

1. *Catch the tool short* (Fig. 14-5). The farther the cutting edge of any tool projects from the tool post, the greater the leverage and

a   *b*

Fig. 14-5. (*a*) *Correct:* Tool caught short with only sufficient room to use wrench for removing tool point. (*b*) *Incorrect:* Too much leverage permits spring and vibration, causes chatter and inaccurate work.

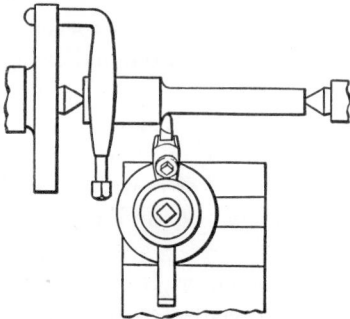

Fig. 14-6. Shows tool post on left-hand side of tool rest. In this position, there is less tendency to feed so far that the dog will strike the tool rest.

the more the spring of the tool. This causes chattering and often worse evils and should be avoided wherever possible.

2. The tool post should be located at the *left-hand end* of the T slot in the tool rest (Fig. 14-6). If it is clamped in the middle or

[1] It is assumed that the beginner in lathe work will be provided with properly sharpened cutting tools until such a time as it is convenient to have him learn to grind them for himself. Information concerning cutting tools for lathe work is given in the text, Chapter 11.

right-hand end of the slot the danger of the dog hitting the tool rest is greatly increased. If the dog hits the tool rest when the lathe is running, the point of the live center will be broken off and the center hole in the work spoiled.

3. The position of the cutting edge as presented to the work has a considerable influence on the finished appearance of the work and

Fig. 14-7. The cutting edge as presented to the work. (a) Most efficient turning tool, (b) does not remain sharp as long or produce as good work as (a), (c) very inefficient except for certain finishing cuts.

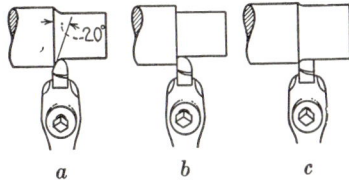

also on the life of the tool. It may be easily proved that a cutting edge at right angles to the center line of the work will not cut so efficiently as when arranged at an angle of about 20 deg. with this perpendicular (Fig. 14-7).

4. The usual practice with modern lathe turning tools (tool-holders with high-speed tool bits) is to set the tool point toward the dog (Fig. 14-8a), thus obtaining approximately the proper side rake with less grinding on the top of the tool bit. This is all right for light cuts if care is taken to tighten the tool securely in the tool post. For heavy cuts, however, it is best, if possible, to have the tool point a little away from the dog for if it slips it will move away from the work and not into it (Fig. 14-8b).

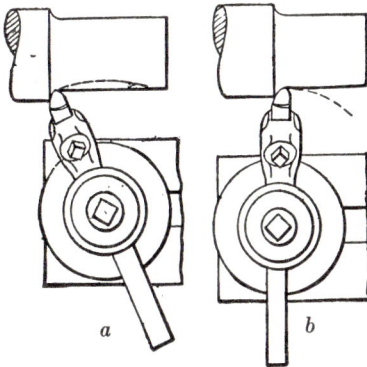

Fig. 14-8.

5. Have the point of the tool on center or a trifle above in order to have the correct amount of front clearance (this is illustrated in Chapter 11).

Direction of the Feed. In machining a piece of work on centers the feed should be toward the headstock because then the pressure is on the live center, which revolves with the work. The dead center is a bearing on which the work revolves. If a heavy feed is directed against it, undue friction will result which will tend to score the center hole in the work and may possibly twist off the end of the lathe center.

The Use of a Protecting Piece. A finished surface that has been scored or dented by the sides of the dog or by the dog screw is an indication of extreme carelessness or ignorance. To avoid that sort of thing, the machinist uses a protecting piece of copper or soft brass of reasonable thickness. He does not use sheet steel because steel is too hard and the dent the dog makes in it is carried through into the work. He does not use paper or cardboard because these are too soft and the dog screw crushes through.

Adjusting Work on Centers. It is quite necessary in the beginning of one's machine-shop experience to acquire the habit of making a proper *machine setup* and *work adjustment*. It is one of the habits that distinguishes an expert on any machine in any shop.

Have the tail spindle projecting about 3 in. (usually) and move the tailstock to about the distance from the headstock necessary to hold the work between the centers; then clamp the tailstock to the bed.

Tighten the dog securely, using a protecting piece of copper or brass if necessary, and put a drop of oil in the center hole. Put the other center hole on the live center and, holding the work against the live center with the left hand supported on the tool rest, run the dead center into its center hole. Then adjust the work carefully, wiggling the tail of the dog to make sure the adjustment is tight enough but *not too tight.*

Oiling and Readjusting the Centers. It is very important to keep sufficient oil (or white lead) on the dead center. The heat generated in turning, especially during a heavy roughing cut, will quickly burn up the oil on the bearing surface, and a dry bearing always cuts. Also the heat of a heavy cut may expand the work enough to unduly tighten it between the centers. It is not enough to squirt some oil at the center—stop the lathe, draw back the center, put the oil where it will do the most good, and *readjust* the dead center. A dry bearing will sometimes give warning by a faint squeak. *Always investigate a squeak.*

A *live* tailstock center with antifriction bearings has been developed for high-production lathes. It must be remembered, however, that even though this center turns with the work and oil in the center hole is not required, the heated work expands just the same, and if the expansion is such that the work lengthens appreciably, this, as well as any other tailstock center, must be kept in mind and readjusted if necessary.

Lubricating the Tool. There is no doubt that a good flow of oil or cutting compound on a turning tool will make for longer life of the tool, more work, and a better finish, when machining steel or wrought iron. Most engine lathes, however, are not equipped to obtain a flow of oil, and the small amount that can be applied with a brush is not usually considered worth while except when cutting threads.

Graduations on Cross-feed Screw. Most lathes are equipped with a graduated bushing on the cross-feed screw which will show in thousandths of an inch the movement of the cross slide. For example, the cross-feed screw in Fig. 14-9 has 8 threads per inch; one complete turn of the handle advances the cross slide $\frac{1}{8}$ in. The

Fig. 14-9. The micrometer collar on cross-feed screw. (*The South Bend Lathe Works*)

bushing is graduated into 100 equal divisions; therefore a movement of one of these divisions past the line on the nut (shown in line with the 0 graduation on the bushing) will indicate a movement of the cross slide of $\frac{1}{100}$ of $\frac{1}{10}$ in. or $\frac{1}{1000}$ in. Remember that this movement affects the *radius* of the work and is *doubled* on the diameter.

CAUTION: All lathes are not *graduated* to read thousandths, but the *numbers* stamped on the graduations read thousandths. For example: if there are 10 graduated spaces between the numbers 0 and 10 the graduations read thousandths, but if there are only 5 graduations between 0 and 10 then each graduation will indicate 0.002 in. When going to work on a strange machine note the graduations, whether they indicate 2 thousandths, 1 thousandth, or $\frac{1}{2}$ thousandth.

Lost Motion in the Cross Feed. There is always back lash or lost motion between any freely revolving screw and the nut. The amount of lost motion depends on the looseness of the thread in the nut and is, of course, increased by wear. The amount of lost motion in the cross-feed screw in a new lathe may be 0.005 in. and in an old lathe 0.020 in. or more. Suppose the lathe operator runs the cross slide in 0.005 in. too far and then merely moves the handle back 0.005 in.; the cross slide has not moved and will not move until the lost motion is taken up. The best way to correct an error of this kind is to move the handle back more than is really necessary, then take up the lost motion in the other direction and feed in again to the proper mark.

Cutting Speed and Feed. One of the most important principles in lathe work, or any machine work, is involved in cutting the metal at the proper speed and feed. The reader is referred to Chapter 11.

AN EXAMPLE OF TURNING

As an example let it be supposed that a machine steel cylinder is to be finished $6\frac{1}{2}$ in. long and $1\frac{3}{8}$ in. in diameter. The stock furnished is $1\frac{1}{2}$ in. in diameter and $6\frac{9}{16}$ in. long. Be sure the live center runs true and note that the lathe centers are approximately in line. Center the work carefully (centers about $\frac{3}{16}$ in. in diameter) and, in this case, face to length. The next operation is rough turning. In order to turn *straight* it is necessary to have the lathe centers exactly in line.

Alignment of Centers. With the turning tool take a cut (No. 1, Fig. 14-10) quite near the dog just deep enough to get under the scale and about ¼ in. wide. *Without changing the position of the cross feed*, move the dead center away from the work, swing the piece clear from the turning tool, and run[2] the carriage back to take cut No. 2. Put the work back on the centers and take cut No. 2. Caliper both cuts. If they are of the same diameter the lathe is turn-

ing straight because the two cuts indicate exactly the same effect as if one cut had been made the whole length to the dog. If the two cuts do not measure alike and cut No. 2 is the larger diameter, the tailstock slide should be moved

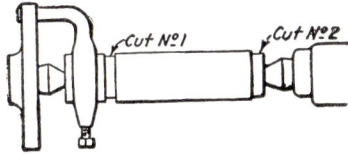

Fig. 14-10.

toward the operator. If cut No. 2 is the smaller the tailstock should be moved away from the operator.

Quicker Methods of Aligning Centers. If a test piece (a piece 8 or 10 in. long, turned round and straight) and an indicator are available, the lathe centers may be quickly aligned. Place the test piece on centers without a dog and the indicator in the tool post.

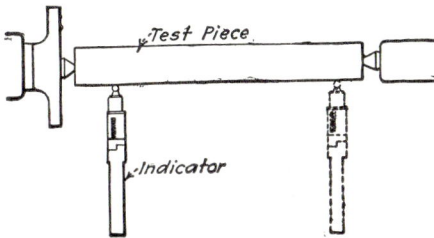

Fig. 14-11. Best method for aligning centers.

Run the indicator along the length of the test piece (Fig. 14-11), and when no movement of the indicator needle is observed, the centers are in line. If no indicator is available, lightly pinch a piece of paper between the butt end of a toolholder and the test piece near one end, and then near the other end, and note the graduations on the cross-feed screw for each position. The reading of the graduations will indicate whether or not the centers are in line.

Setting the Speed. The next step is to get the proper number of revolutions of the spindle to give a correct cutting speed (in

---

[2] "Run" means to cause to perform a characteristic motion, hence the shop terms *run the tail center back, run the carriage back, run the tool in*, etc.

this case, with a high-speed tool, say about 70 ft. per min.). The formula is

$$\text{r.p.m.} = \frac{4 \times \text{cutting speed}}{\text{diameter of work}}$$

Substituting values and solving,

$$\text{r.p.m.} = \frac{4 \times 70}{1.5} = 186$$

Then fix the spindle speed as near 186 r.p.m. as possible.

The Roughing Cut. Tighten the dog securely on one end of the work, put a drop of oil in the opposite center, and adjust between the lathe centers (no slack and not too tight).

With the tool post at the left-hand side of the tool rest, set the tool well back in the tool post. For roughing, it usually is set square or pointing a little to the right. In this case, work $1\frac{1}{2}$ in. in diameter, set the tool about $\frac{1}{32}$ in. above center.[3]

An accurate job is required, so it will be necessary to take two cuts, a roughing cut and a finishing cut. The diameter is to be reduced $\frac{1}{8}$ in. (stock $1\frac{1}{2}$ in. to finish $1\frac{3}{8}$ in.), that is, the depth of cut is less than $\frac{1}{16}$ in., so a coarse *feed* (say up to $\frac{1}{32}$ in.) may be used without strain and without tearing the surface.

Leave about $\frac{1}{32}$ in. for the finishing cut. Being careful not to turn undersize, feed by hand for $\frac{1}{8}$ or $\frac{3}{16}$ in., stop the lathe, and measure the cut. When the diameter measures about $\frac{1}{32}$ in. oversize, throw in the feed and turn about half the length. Throw out the feed first, then stop the lathe, but do not touch the cross-feed handle. Now take out the work and without moving the cross feed run the carriage back to the beginning of the cut. Change the dog end-for-end on the work, and now use a protecting piece under the screw. Adjust the work on centers again and turn to meet the cut already made.

The Finishing Cut. Approximately $\frac{1}{32}$ in. is left on the diameter for finishing. The amount to leave for the finishing cut depends largely on the character of the roughing cut (a very coarse roughing

[3] Until the beginner's eye has been trained, it may be better to set the tool before putting the work in the lathe, and to use the point of the center to gage the height of the tool. The trained machinist sets the tool after adjusting the work.

feed has a tendency to tear the surface even if a fairly sharp tool is used). At least $\frac{1}{64}$ in. should be left for the finishing cut ($\frac{1}{32}$ in. on the diameter) because less than $\frac{1}{64}$ in. does not give the cutting point a chance to get under the chip and the result is a rubbing or burnishing effect which rapidly dulls the edge and produces a poor finish. The feed for finishing is finer than for roughing, say $\frac{1}{64}$ in. or less for this job.

A keen cutting edge is essential for a good finish. If several pieces have been roughed with the tool it may be necessary to regrind it, but if only one or two, probably a few rubs with the oilstone is sufficient. Adjust the cross feed until the tool just touches the rough-turned surface of the work; then run the tool off the work toward the dead center. Using the graduations on the cross feed run the tool in, but not quite the full amount. Take a cut wide enough to caliper and measure the work again. (*NOTE:* This precaution takes only a moment and is always advisable.) Having noted the extra amount to be removed, start the lathe, throw out the feed, run the tool off the work again, move the cross slide in the required amount, and turn half the length of the work. Throw out the feed, then stop the lathe, and, being careful not to touch the cross-feed handle, remove the work and run the tool back to the starting point. Change the dog to the finished end and keep the protecting piece of brass or copper under the screw. Oil the dead center, adjust the work between centers, and turn to meet the finished cut already made. *If the position of the cross slide has not been changed, the ends of the piece will measure the same; if the live center runs true, the two cuts will meet exactly; if the centers are in line, the piece will be straight.*

Turning Duplicate Pieces. When turning a number of duplicate pieces, set the tool for the first piece, cut the required length, throw out the feed, then stop the lathe, remove the piece, run the carriage back to the starting point, and put in the next piece. Measure each piece when it is taken from the lathe to make sure the setting is unchanged.

If the cut is of sufficient length to give the necessary time, put a dog on the next piece and oil the center so that it will be ready to put in the lathe when the other is taken out. "Time is money."

When the first cut is made on all the pieces, take the next operation or cut in the same way—piece by piece, and so on till all are roughed, then take the finishing cuts by the same method of procedure.

These directions apply in general to any lathe operation, and as a matter of fact to most machine-shop work involving more than one piece. Machining several pieces without changing the setting of the tool or the adjustment of the machine makes for speed and accuracy.

Filing in a Lathe. No matter how much care is used in turning, it is usually impossible to secure a finish that is smooth and polished enough to be used directly in service. It is unquestionably better to grind the finished surface whenever possible, but many times a grinding machine is not available. Under such circumstances, work is usually filed to size and polished.

Very little work requires any filing, although it often happens that a few strokes with the file will save considerable time in turning. For example, if a special taper is turned nearly correct, a few strokes of the file will make it right much more quickly than it could be turned, or if a shaft is nearly exact, a very little filing will make it correct. Sometimes it may be necessary to file and polish such work as a filleted corner, rounded edge or end, or some special part of a machine such as a bushing or a handle or a pulley.

The following steps are suggested for good results when filing in the lathe:

1. Clean centers and see that there are no burrs around the center holes.
2. Put center lubricant on tailstock center.
3. Put dog on work, protecting surface under clamp screw with a small piece of copper or brass.
4. Place work on headstock center and run up tailstock center with right hand until tight. Loosen tailstock center slightly and start lathe, adjusting center to be just loose enough to allow the dog to click in faceplate but not loose enough to rattle or for work to have end shake.
5. Shift gears in headstock to give about twice the finish-turning speed on surface to be filed.
6. Select a 12-in. mill file[4] and be sure the handle is secure. If the file is clean, it is ready for use on brass, cast iron, etc., but for

---

[4] For a description of files, see Chapter 5, pp. 128–141.

use on steel, it should be rubbed with chalk until evenly covered (chalk prevents the steel filings from clogging the file teeth).

7. Be sure your shirt sleeves are rolled up above the elbow.

8. Start the lathe and file the work holding the file as shown in Fig. 14-12. *Hold the left arm well above the top of the faceplate.*

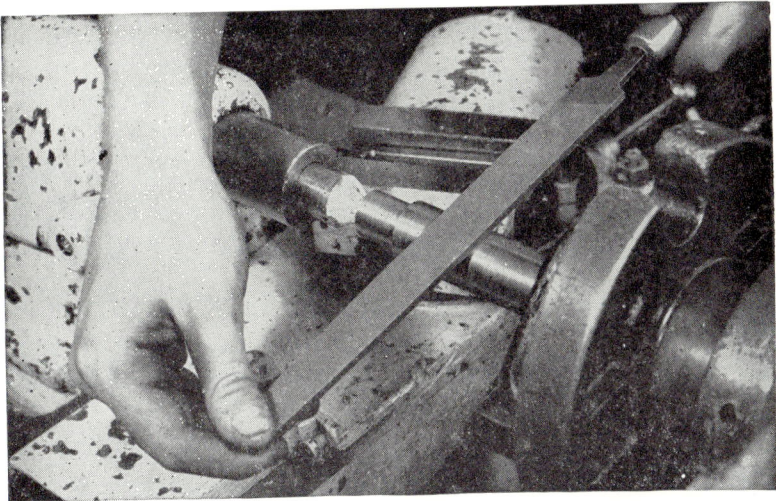

Fig. 14-12. Filing in the lathe.

9. When filing, use a long, slow, forward stroke and press firmly and evenly on the revolving piece.

10. Relieve the pressure on the return stroke.

NOTE: Filing left handed is very much safer than filing right handed. There is no danger to either hand in left-hand filing. The great number of accidents in the past resulting from right-hand filing has caused today's instructors to teach left-hand filing.

Suggestions When Filing

1. Do not revolve the workpiece too fast.

2. Do not move the file too rapidly across the work. If you do, the work will be out-of-round.

3. Do not lift the file off the work on the return stroke.

4. Do not bear down too hard on the work on the forward or cutting stroke.

5. Keep the file pointed practically straight ahead, but the stroke

should be from right to left or left to right, to avoid the tendency to file more from one portion than another. Crossing the strokes in this way will also help to keep the file clean.

6. Many machinists leave too much for filing. With a fairly smooth cut, two-thousandths is enough for filing and polishing.

Polishing in the Lathe. Most polishing in the lathe is done with emery cloth. Emery cloth may be obtained in various sizes of grain from fine to coarse. Usually polishing is done with a fairly fine grain of emery cloth and the best finishes are obtained with a piece of emery cloth practically worn out. A better finish and a more lasting polish may be obtained by applying a reasonable amount of lard oil.

Suggestions for Polishing

1. After filing is completed, the finished surface should be polished.

2. On work that is well balanced, set change levers to give the highest possible speed. On unbalanced work, run at highest possible speed without causing undue vibration.

3. On straight shafts, 1 in. or under in diameter, work should be polished in speed lathes if possible.

4. Use strip of emery cloth of fine grade and press against work, moving the abrasive cloth from side to side to cross lines and bring work to a rough polish and to avoid cutting rings in work.

5. Use very fine emery cloth or a worn-out piece of fine grade cloth and use oil on work to bring to final polish. Use crocus cloth for very fine finish polishing.

6. When polishing, check size and straightness frequently with mike to be sure dimensions are correct on finished piece.

7. The best polishing requirements are (*a*) high speed of work, (*b*) fine grade of emery cloth, (*c*) use of oil on abrasive cloth (lard oil), and (*d*) greatest possible pressure on work.

NOTE: Polishing and filing heat the work. When measuring diameter with micrometer, either cool work by dipping in water or make allowance of one or two ten-thousandths for cooling of work. This may not be true in all cases since the coefficient of expansion varies with the material and size.

Polishing in the lathe may also be done by placing a piece of emery cloth on a file as shown in Fig. 14-13. The emery cloth is usually dipped in oil before using.

Fig. 14-13. Using emery cloth with a file.

Do not try to file or polish work with grooves or slots or holes in the surface. If it is necessary to polish such a piece in a lathe, plug these holes or grooves with hard wood.

QUESTIONS ON TURNING — I

1. What do you mean by adjusting the work between centers?
2. How do you make sure the dog does not bind in the slot of the faceplate?
3. Why is it necessary to have the live center running true? Name two methods of truing a live center.
4. Why must both centers be in line? How are the centers aligned approximately? How are they aligned accurately?
5. Why is it necessary to put oil in the dead-center hole? Why is the dead center hardened?
6. What occurs if the tool is not caught short?
7. What occurs if the tool is set below the center? If set too far above the center? What is the best way of determining when the tool is set right as regards the center?

8. What occurs if, when turning, the dog hits the tool rest? How does laxity in setting the tool often account for an accident of this kind?

9. How may the proper cutting speed be calculated?

10. What determines the roughing chip? The roughing feed?

11. What determines whether the finishing chip shall be $\frac{1}{64}$ in. or more than that?

12. Why does a finishing chip of $\frac{1}{64}$ in. give better results than a finishing chip of $\frac{3}{1000}$ in.?

13. How is the roughed diameter measured? When is the measurement made? Why?

14. Explain the method of using, and the value of the graduations on the cross-feed screw.

15. If it is advisable to oil the center during the cut, how is it done? Why not simply put oil on the outside?

16. If machine oil is not heavy enough what may be used instead?

17. What determines the proper feed for the finishing cut?

18. How is the finished diameter measured? When is the measurement made? Why?

19. When is a protecting piece under the dog screw necessary? Why is a piece of copper or brass better than sheet iron?

20. Describe in detail the method of turning duplicate pieces, and explain the advantages of this method of procedure.

21. Why is a mill file best for filing work in a lathe?

22. What causes pinning in a file?

23. What two mistakes are often made when learning to file in a lathe?

24. When it is practical to finish round work by filing in a lathe?

SHOULDER TURNING

When turning to a shoulder it is assumed that the work on which the shoulder or shoulders must be made has been faced. It may or may not have been turned.

Figure 14-14 illustrates four types of shoulders. The *rounded*

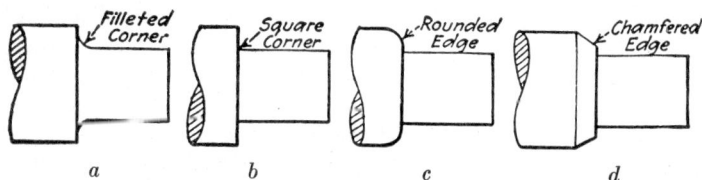

Fig. 14-14. Shoulders: (*a*) filleted corner, (*b*) square corner, (*c*) rounded edge, (*d*) chamfered edge.

edge and the *chamfered* edge apply to the ends of a piece as well as to the edges of a shoulder. To *break* an edge is to touch it lightly with a file or emery cloth and take away the extreme sharpness.

Roughing to the Shoulder. When it is required to turn to a shoulder, first lay off the distance from the end. Use a hermaphrodite caliper, or a scale and scriber, and make a clean sharp line. Chalking the spot in which the line is to be scribed will serve to make it more distinct.

If more than one shoulder is to be cut on the end of a piece, it is a matter of *judgment* whether the shoulder nearest the end or farthest from the end should be turned first. The usual practice is to lay off the longest distance and rough turn to that shoulder, then lay off the shoulder nearer the end and rough turn to that, etc. This might involve unnecessary roughing cuts, however, if the shoulders were not very deep.

If there are several pieces, lay off the shoulder distance on several of them before shouldering any. Put the pieces between centers *without the dog* and revolve once or twice by hand and mark the line. Rough turn in the usual way, with the regular turning tool, until within $\frac{1}{8}$ or $\frac{1}{16}$ in. of the line; then throw out the power feed and feed *to the line* by hand.

It is well to grind the turning tool with a small round nose and to set it in such a way as to leave as little stock at the shoulder as possible for the finishing tool. When there are a number of pieces, rough-turn all of them with the same setting of the tool.

Finishing the Diameter and the Square Shoulder. On the longer shoulder cuts the regular turning tool used for roughing may be used also for finishing the diameter nearly to the fillet. Do not, however, turn quite to the fillet because then the last chip will be as heavy as the roughing chip and is likely to dig in and spoil the work.

The *shoulder tool* (Fig. 14-15) is used to rough out the fillet and also, at the same setting, to finish the diameter where the fillet was, and the square shoulder (on the shorter shoulder cuts it is used to finish the diameter its whole length). It is ground to have two cut-

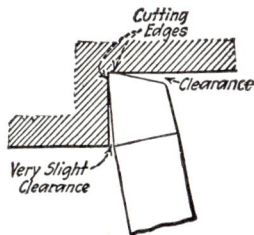

Fig. 14-15.

ting edges at right angles to each other and ⅟₁₆ in. or more wide; one edge to turn the diameter and the other edge to face the shoulder. Have the two cutting edges wide enough to give a good finish but not so wide as to tend to dig in. Extreme care must be taken when grinding and setting a square-shoulder tool. Then proceed as follows:

1. Using the square-shoulder tool, *with hand feed*, carefully cut out the fillet left in the corner by the roughing tool to leave the corner fairly square (taking two or more cuts to remove this material is called *stepping out* the fillet).
2. Take a cut on the diameter, leaving it only 0.015 to 0.020 in. oversize, and note the setting (graduations) for this cut.
3. Face the shoulder to the line.
4. When the shoulder is faced to the line and the diameter is the small amount oversize, feed in to the graduation noted and take a light cut on the shoulder, *splitting* the line.
5. Feed in again to the graduation noted, and, in addition, *half* the number of thousandths the diameter is oversize, and turn the diameter to finish size.

NOTE: The reason for noting the cross-feed setting is this: It may be necessary to take a second facing cut to get the right dimension and it will be easy to run the tool in exactly far enough and not risk under-cutting the diameter. Also, if several pieces have been roughed, the finish cuts can be made quickly after the first setting because it has been determined how far in to run the tool. The smaller filleted corners are turned in the same way as explained above. The finishing tool is substantially the same except that it is rounded to give the required radius.

The reason for hand feed *always* when turning near a shoulder is the impossibility of throwing out the power feed at exactly the right instant. One-eighth inch is close enough to the shoulder to feed (long feed) by power.

The reason for leaving 0.015 to 0.020 in. on the diameter and splitting the shoulder line before turning the diameter to exact size is the less likelihood of digging in and undercutting the diameter near the shoulder.

Have the two cutting edges of the shoulder tool a trifle less than 90 deg., rather than more.

Many machinists prefer to face a shoulder by feeding in from the circumference. In this case the tool is set to split the line and is fed towards the corner. In either case rough practically to the line; do not leave too much for the finishing cut or the corner of the finishing tool will become dull sooner than need be.

If possible a piece should usually be roughed all over before any finish cut is taken. Where the end is turned smaller to a shoulder it should be roughed first, thereby possibly saving a second roughing cut over this portion of the piece; that is, a piece need not necessarily be roughed to a straight cylinder before roughing the shoulder cuts. After roughing, face to length. The next operation is to finish-turn the larger diameters. Then lay off the exact shoulder dimensions on these finished diameters, finish the small diameters, and face the shoulders to the lines, checking the diameters with a micrometer and the lengths by scale measurement.

The Forming Tool. The larger filleted corners are best roughed out with a large round-nose tool, using both hand feeds simultaneously. An approximately correct gage cut from sheet metal may be advisable. The best tool to use for finishing a large fillet or a rounded corner of almost any size over ⅛-in. radius is termed a *forming tool*. Forming tools are often forged and then filed to the desired shape. Figure 14-16 illustrates a selection of typical forming tools that are used with a tool

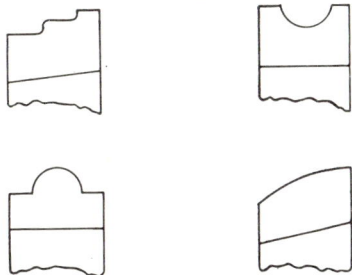

Fig. 14-16. Forming tools.

holder made suitable to accept them. In principle it resembles the old-fashioned "gooseneck" or "spring tool" in that any tendency of the tool spring is *away* from the work and not into it. Usually a better finish is produced on steel if oil is used to lubricate the forming tool. The cutting speed is fairly slow to avoid chattering.

Necking (Fig. 14-17). Occasionally it is desirable when turning

shouldered work, especially when roughing, to cut a groove, or
neck, of nearly the correct depth and turn either to the groove or
from the groove depending on which end of the piece it is most convenient to place the dog.

When a piece is afterward to be ground to a shoulder it is often
advisable to neck it just under the size to be ground (Fig. 14-17*b*)
so that the grinding wheel will not have to be fed close to the
shoulder. If a thread is to be cut to a shoulder, it usually is considered better to cut a neck for the thread tool to run into (Fig.
14-17*c*). The necking tool may be round-nosed or square-nosed, as
desired.

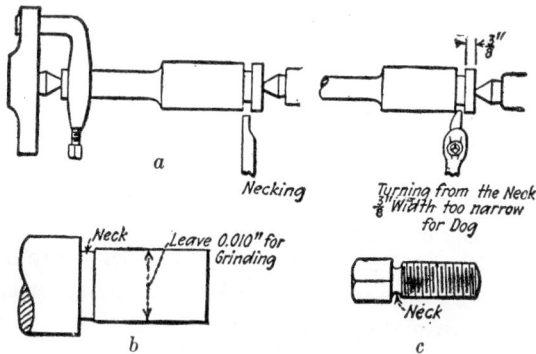

Fig. 14-17.

The Center Rest. The center rest, or steady rest (Fig. 14-18),
is a very valuable accessory to the lathe when slender pieces of any
considerable length are to be turned. The base is planed to fit the
inside ways of the lathe, and by means of a clamp the center rest
may be held in the required position. The three jaws are adjustable.

A spot, slightly wider than the jaws of the steady rest, is very
carefully turned near the center of the work (Fig. 14-19). If the
piece is to be turned the whole length and other operations afterward made on one or both ends, the machinist usually prefers the
center rest to the follower rest for steadying the work during the
first operation of turning the cylinder as well as for the later operations. In such a case the spot should be turned somewhat nearer the
live center than the middle of the piece, in order that the first cut
may be turned at least half the length of the work. When one-half

Fig. 14-18. A center rest. (*The South Bend Lathe Works*)

Fig. 14-19. Center rest, or steady rest, in use. (*The South Bend Lathe Works*)

the length of the piece is turned, reverse the piece and readjust the jaws to the diameter of the turned part of the work. To protect this part from being roughened a thin piece of brass or copper should be placed around the piece under the jaws; use oil to lubricate, and do not adjust the jaws too tight.

The spot should be turned smooth and preferably of some standard mandrel size. The reason for the particular diameter of the spot is to enable the operator to adjust the jaws on a short mandrel

Fig. 14-20. Center rest being used with a chuck. (*The South Bend Lathe Works*)

rather than on the piece itself, because a long slender piece springs so easily that it makes a true adjustment on such a piece very difficult.

Do not adjust the jaws without first securely clamping the center rest to the ways, for unless this is done, the adjusting of the jaws is apt to lift it from the ways, and when it is finally clamped down the work is sprung.

A long piece of work placed in a chuck for the purpose of boring or turning may not be held rigidly enough, in which case the center rest may be used as a support for the outer end (Fig. 14-20). A spot for the jaws is first carefully turned concentric with the axis of the work.

If one end of the work is supported by the live center, drilling and boring may be done on the other end when the center rest is used as a support (see Fig. 14-21). In this case it is necessary to tie the work to the faceplate (usually with a belt lacing) in order to keep it tight against the live center. To tie the work to the faceplate, unscrew the faceplate three or four revolutions and tie the lacing as tight as possible. After thus tying, screw the faceplate home; this draws the work securely against the live center.

Fig. 14-21. A center rest being used. (*The South Bend Lathe Works*)

The *cathead* (Fig. 14-22) may be used where it is impracticable to turn a spot for the center rest. Great care must be taken to adjust the cathead before putting it in the center rest so that it will run perfectly true when the work is revolving on centers.

Fig. 14-22. By adjusting the set screws the bushing (cathead) may be made to run true on bar of casting.

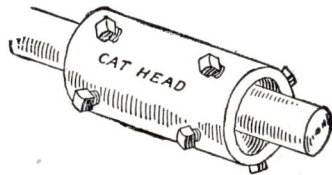

The Follower Rest. The follower rest (Fig. 14-23) is used to prevent slender work from springing away from the tool during the cut. The diameter is turned for a short distance to the desired size and the two jaws are adjusted to this diameter. As the follower rest is bolted to the carriage and moves with it, the two jaws constantly

Fig. 14-23. Using the follower rest.

Fig. 14-24. Both the steady rest and follower rest being used. (*The South Bend Lathe Works*)

offer resistance to the spring of the work away from the tool. Figure 14-24 shows both steady rest and follower rest being used.

Knurling. Knurling may be defined as *the process of checking the surface of a piece by rolling depressions into the surface.* The knurled portion of a nut, a screw, or of a handle that is to be adjusted by

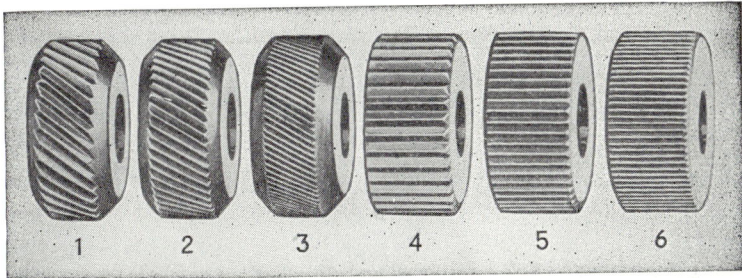

Fig. 14-25. Various knurls: (1) and (4) coarse pattern, (2) and (5) medium, (3) and (6) fine, (1), (2), and (3) diamond, (4), (5), and (6) straight.

hand (for example, a tap wrench) gives an excellent gripping surface.

Most knurled jobs in machine-shop work are of the pattern as fine, medium, coarse, straight, and diamond (Fig. 14-25). The knurls are small wheels with the marking cut in their faces and all are hardened.

Figure 14-26 shows a typical knurling tool, and Fig. 14-27 shows a typical knurling job.

Fig. 14-26. Typical knurling tool. (*Armstrong Bros. Tool Company*)

The advantage of the particular kind of knurling tool shown in Fig. 14-26 lies in the fact that the tool is self centering and the knuckle or joint has ample bearing to resist the severe strains of both end and side thrust. It also has a disadvantage in that both knurls tend to push the work away from the tool thus distorting the center holes in the work.

Knurling will tend to increase slightly the diameter of the part knurled due to the fact that the outer surface of the metal will be raised above the normal size of the piece.

Care must be taken in starting the knurl to see that one wheel does not split the diamond. The knurls should be pressed hard into

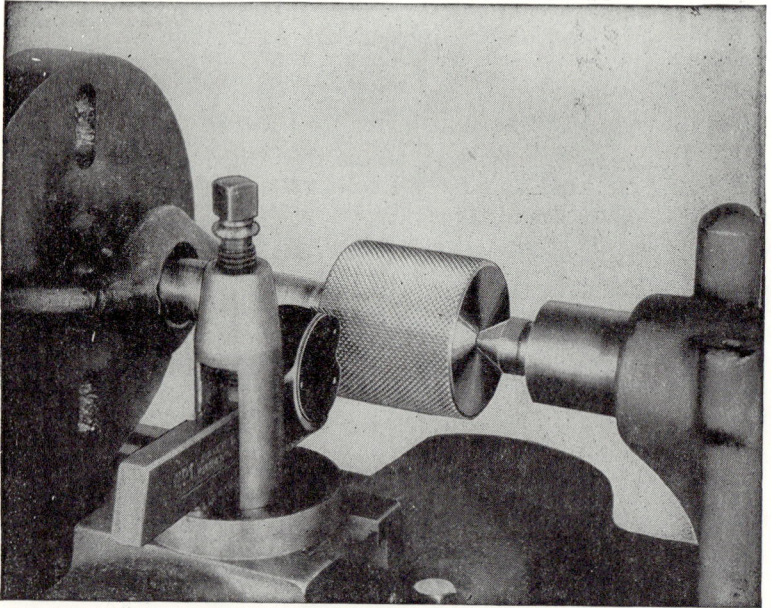

Fig. 14.27. A typical knurling job. (*The South Bend Lathe Works*)

the work at the start and the pressure relieved somewhat after making sure they track. The finished job should show as in the illustration with the diamond shape clean and sharp.

After a knurl is started right it will usually track right along at a medium or fairly coarse feed. If in the beginning the wheels do not track but one of them splits the diamond, try another place on the work and then, when the tool does make the proper knurl, going over the split part will probably correct it.

Power feed may be used and usually one or possibly two "cuts" will be enough. Oil is used to lubricate when knurling any kind of material.

HOLDING WORK ON A MANDREL

The Standard Mandrel. A mandrel—a very helpful lathe accessory—is a tool which, when pressed into a finished hole in a piece of work, provides centers on which the piece may be turned or otherwise machined.

A mandrel is a master tool and should be treated as such. Too frequently one sees a mandrel with the surface scored and cut, and the centers ruined. Such a tool is worse than useless; it had better be discarded altogether and not spoil more work. Furthermore, hundreds of jobs have been utterly ruined by reason of the operator

Fig. 14-28. A mandrel. (*The South Bend Lathe Works*)

not starting the mandrel straight, or trying to force it, large end first, into the hole, or forgetting to put a little oil on the mandrel or in the hole. Cultivate habits of carefulness, keep the tools in good shape, and make your work right.

Standard hardened and ground lathe mandrels (Fig. 14-28) are manufactured in various sizes. The mandrel tapers about 0.008 in. per foot, and the nominal size is near the middle. It is driven or pressed into the hole in the work and holds by friction. *To prevent damage to the work, the mandrel should always be oiled before being forced into the hole.*

The ends are turned somewhat smaller than the body, so that any nicks or burrs, caused by the clamping of the dog, will not injure the accuracy of the mandrel.

It is very important that the centers are large enough to withstand the severe strain that may be caused by turning a heavy piece; that they are exactly 60 deg. to fit the lathe center; and that they are very smooth to ensure a good bearing. The centers are recessed, that is, cut out a trifle around the center, for protection, but even so, a mandrel should never be driven with a steel hammer without protecting the end. It is better to use a babbitt hammer, or a press (Fig. 14-29) made especially for forcing a mandrel in or out. *Be sure the mandrel is started straight* or it will score one side of the hole. If the hole is properly sized, the mandrel should enter a considerable distance before it begins to bind, thus serving to start itself square. It is important to remember that *the size of a mandrel is always marked on the large end.* The other end is, of course, the entering end. To avoid pressure against the arms or the web of a pulley when forcing a mandrel in or out, put a collar under the hub; if a collar is not available a pair of short parallel pieces will answer.

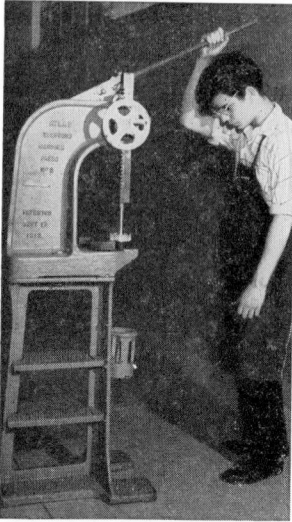

Fig. 14-29. Pressing a mandrel into a gear blank using an arbor press.

Using a Mandrel. It is especially important when using a mandrel that the live center *runs exactly true.* Otherwise the mandrel will run out of true and the work will not be faced or turned true with the hole. Great care must be taken when adjusting a mandrel between centers and also in attention to the dead center during the turning operation. If the mandrel gets hot, burns the oil out, and twists the center off, not only is the center damaged but the mandrel also is ruined.

Turning and facing operations on work held on a mandrel are not different from other turning and facing operations and require the same conditions of tool grinding and setting.

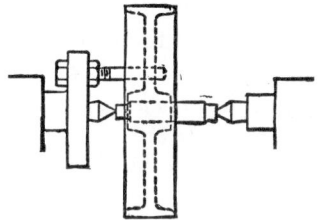

Fig. 14-30.

When turning work on a mandrel feed toward the large end of the mandrel, if convenient. This tends to tighten the work on the mandrel. When turning comparatively large work on a small mandrel care must be taken that the mandrel does not spring or bend and also that the work does not turn on the mandrel. It is often advisable in such a case to drive the work directly from the faceplate instead of by means of a dog (Fig. 14-30).

Always remember that, even if the mandrel is hard, the cutting tool is harder and it is easy, through carelessness, to injure the mandrel. Set the facing tool with a thickness of paper between it and the mandrel and thus avoid cutting into the mandrel.

Other Forms of Mandrels

Homemade Mandrels. A machine-steel mandrel with case-hardened ends is often found efficient; or, if it is a rush job, a piece of machine steel carefully turned (on good-sized centers) to fit the hole will answer. On large sizes a satisfactory mandrel may be made of cast iron by inserting in the ends hardened tool-steel plugs with centers.

Expansion Mandrels. Expansion mandrels of various types are manufactured. These mandrels are expensive and are not so accurate as the solid ground mandrel. *Taper mandrels* with cast-iron expansion bushings (Fig. 14-31a) are extensively used, especially in the

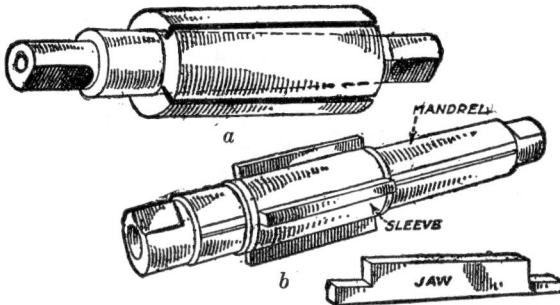

Fig. 14-31. Two types of expansion mandrels: (a) taper mandrel with cast-iron expansion bushings, (b) mandrel with tapered adjustable jaws.

larger sizes. Do not try to force the bushing to bind in a hole that is oversize or it is likely to ruin the bushing.

Another form of expansion mandrel is shown in Fig. 14-31b. It consists of the mandrel proper which has four or more grooves cut lengthwise, uniformly deeper toward one end; a sleeve with slots opposite the grooves in the mandrel and of the same width; and the jaws which fit into the grooves of the mandrel and through the slots in the sleeve. The jaws taper in length to correspond to the incline of the slots and therefore bear evenly in a straight hole. The take-up or release is made by sliding the mandrel in the sleeve. The particular value of this mandrel lies in the fact that it may be adjusted to bind in a hole somewhat larger or smaller than its nominal size.

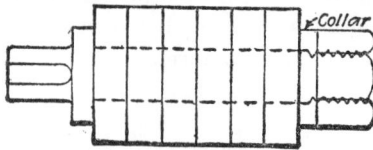

Fig. 14-32. A gang mandrel.

Gang Mandrel. A gang mandrel (Fig. 14-32) is useful for turning or milling several pieces such as gear blanks or cutter blanks at the same time. It is especially useful when turning thin pieces.

Threaded Mandrel. The threaded mandrel, or nut arbor, (Fig. 14-33) is used for facing nuts or otherwise machining inside threaded pieces. Unless one face of the work is square with the axis of the

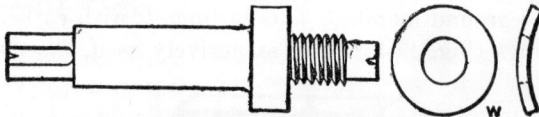

Fig. 14-33. A thread mandrel. *W* an equalizing washer.

thread an equalizing washer *W* is necessary to make sure that the nut takes up true on the thread of the mandrel and is not canted. Such a washer is quickly made from an ordinary iron washer by bending it slightly.

Fig. 14-34. A taper-shank mandrel.

Taper-shank Mandrel. The taper-shank mandrel (Fig. 14-34) may be fitted to the taper hole in the spindle of the machine. The projecting portion may be of the form desired. A nut mandrel made in this way is used for machining blind nuts, that is, a nut in which the hole does not go through.

To Turn a Crankshaft or an Eccentric. When a cylindrically turned surface of a piece has an axis parallel to, but not coincident with, the normal axis of the piece, this surface is said to be *turned eccentric.* The work itself may be called an eccentric or a cranksnaft as shown in Fig. 14-35. Both are much used in machine construction

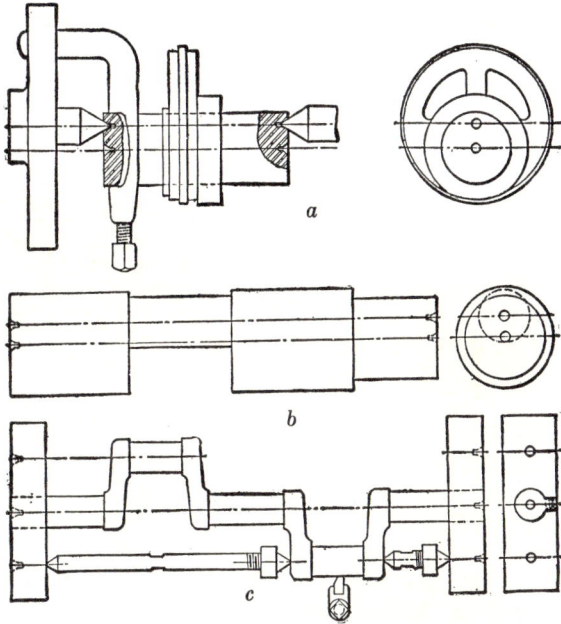

Fig. 14-35. Types of turning work: (*a*) eccentric, (*b*) and (*c*) crankshaft.

to convert rotary into reciprocal motion or the contrary. To turn the eccentric surface it is necessary to provide centers offset from the centers of the normal axis an amount equal to one-half the throw desired, that is, one-half the amount of the reciprocating motion to be imparted or converted as the case may be. Three methods of providing the offset centers for turning eccentric cylindrical surfaces are illustrated in Fig. 14-35. An eccentric (Fig. 14-35*a*) is usually keyed to a shaft when in use and consequently is located on a mandrel, by a key or by a witness mark, and then turned. A mandrel with offset centers is shown in Fig. 14-35*a*. The crankshaft, Fig. 14-35*b*, is itself provided with an extra pair of centers. When the amount of eccentricity is too great to allow the extra pair of centers within the diameter of the normal bearing, special pieces with centers properly arranged may be fitted on the ends of the shaft as shown in (Fig. 14-35c). A suitable counterweight should be provided, and also braces to eliminate spring.

QUESTIONS ON TURNING—II

1. If considerable metal is to be removed, is it advisable to face to exact length? Give reason.
2. Why is it usually advisable to lay off the shoulder distance from one end of the work?
3. What tools may be used to lay off these distances? When is chalk used? When is blue vitriol used?
4. Is care used in laying off shoulder distances when roughing? Why?
5. If you are going to rough a square shoulder, how does the shape of the tool differ from a regular turning tool? How is the tool set? Why?
6. If one or more diameters are to be turned on a piece, is it necessary to rough to straight cylindrical shape before roughing the smaller diameters?
7. When roughing out, how much stock do you try to leave for finish facing the shoulder? Why?
8. Why is it good practice to throw out the power feed when $\frac{1}{16}$ in. or more from the shoulder, and feed the rest by hand?
9. When turning, how much do you leave for a finishing cut?
10. How do you grind a combination turning and facing tool for finish-turning the diameter and finish-facing the shoulder? Is such a tool efficient? Why? Explain its action in detail.
11. Explain how the graduations on the cross-feed screw may be of great help in turning shouldered pieces.
12. Sometimes when turning shoulders it is convenient to neck the work. How is this done?
13. If the work, when faced, is left somewhat overlength because of the amount of stock to be turned off, when should it be faced to length? Why at this time?
14. What is meant by a square corner when turning a shoulder? A filleted corner?
15. What is a square edge? A rounded edge? A chamfered edge?
16. Why must care be taken when starting the knurling tool?
17. How do you tell when a piece is sufficiently knurled?
18. Why are two wheels used to produce the diamond-pattern knurl?

19. What is meant by turning a spot for the steady rest?
20. Why is it advisable to make the spot a nominal size if convenient?
21. Why not turn the spot in the middle of the piece?
22. When is it necessary to tie the dog to the faceplate? How is it done?
23. What is the difference between a steady rest and a follower rest?
24. Why is a mandrel tapered slightly?
25. Why is a mandrel not marked on both ends?
26. How is a mandrel started and how is it pressed in the hole?
27. What precaution must always be taken before forcing a mandrel in a hole? Why?
28. Name three kinds of mandrels and explain the particular value of each.
29. What is a nut arbor? What do you understand to be the value of the bent washer on the nut arbor?
30. What do you mean by a blind nut? Can you find a blind nut holding any part of the lathe?
31. How may a blind nut be held while being faced or turned?
32. A special bushing 3 in. long has a hole 0.990 in. in diameter. What kind of mandrel, if available, could be used?
33. If no mandrel for a hole 0.990 in. in diameter were available what would you do?
34. Why should the center holes in a mandrel be clean cut, smooth, and fairly large?
35. Why are the ends of a mandrel recessed around the centers?
36. Explain how work of fairly large diameter, mounted on a mandrel, may often be driven direct from the faceplate. What is the advantage of this method of driving?
37. What is an eccentric?
38. What do you understand as the difference between an eccentric and a crankshaft?
39. What do you mean by turning eccentrically?
40. Using one or more V blocks and a surface gage how would you proceed to lay out the positions of the two pairs of centers in Fig. 14-34b.

CHAPTER 15

Chucking Work

Work that cannot be readily mounted between the lathe centers is usually held in a *chuck*, shown in Fig. 15-1. Many machining operations are performed on work held in a chuck, such as threading, boring (straight and taper), and turning.

Fig. 15-1. Work being done on work held in a chuck. (*South Bend Lathe Works*)

Kinds of Chucks. There are several types of chucks used in machine-shop work, the most popular being the 4-jaw *independent* chuck and the 3-jaw *universal* chuck. The other types are the *com-*

bination, headstock spindle, and the *draw-in-collet* chuck. Each will be described.

The Independent Chuck (Fig. 15-2). A 4-jaw independent chuck has four reversible jaws, each of which may be independently adjusted. This means simply that each jaw may be moved separately; they do *not* move simultaneously. This type of chuck is used more than any other type because it will hold practically any shape of work and can be adjusted to any degree of accuracy desired.

Concentric rings, scribed on the surface or face of the chuck, permit centering round work approximately, as it is placed in the chuck. To center more accurately, see Figs. 15-9 to 15-12 in this chapter.

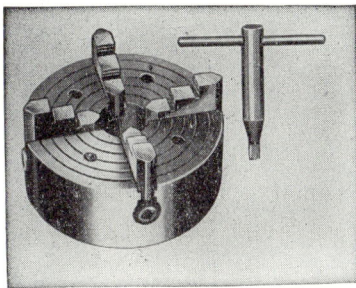

Fig. 15-2. A 4-jaw independent chuck and key. (*South Bend Lathe Works*)

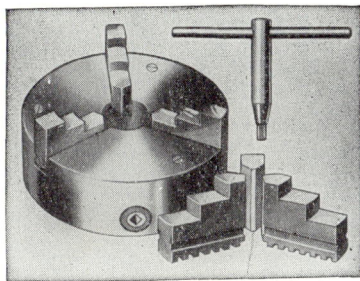

Fig. 15-3. A 3-jaw universal chuck and key. (*South Bend Lathe Works*)

The Universal Chuck (Fig. 15-3). Round and hexagonal work may be chucked quickly in this type of chuck since all three jaws move simultaneously (all together) and automatically center the work within a few thousandths of an inch. This type of chuck will usually center work within 0.003 in. when new, but when the scroll becomes worn, this degree of accuracy cannot be expected.

Since there is no way to adjust the jaws independently, this chuck is not used where extreme accuracy is required. The 4-jaw independent type should always be used when work must be centered to run dead true. However, if no independent chuck is available, shims may be placed between the chuck jaws and the work, to compensate for the inaccuracy of the universal type.

Two sets of jaws are usually provided with universal chucks, one set used for outside chucking, and the other for inside chucking. These jaws cannot be reversed.

The Combination Chuck. A chuck that may be used as either an independent or universal chuck is called a *combination* chuck. Practically all larger chucks are independent or a combination, while the small lathe and drill chucks are universal.

Headstock Spindle Chuck (Fig. 15-4). This chuck is similar to a drill chuck except that it is hollow and is threaded so that it may be screwed on to the spindle nose of the lathe.

Fig. 15-4. Work being machined while being held in a headstock spindle chuck. (*South Bend Lathe Works*)

The Drill Chuck. This type is explained in Chapter 8, page 176.

The Draw-in-collet Chuck (Fig. 15-5). This type of chuck is the most accurate of all types and is used for high precision work, such as making small tools and manufacturing small parts for watches, typewriters, etc. The collets (Fig. 15-6) are made for round, square, and other shapes of work.

Figure 15-7 shows a handwheel draw-in-collet chuck with its parts. The adapter fits the taper hole in the main spindle and the chuck fits into the adapter. The hollow draw-in spindle goes through

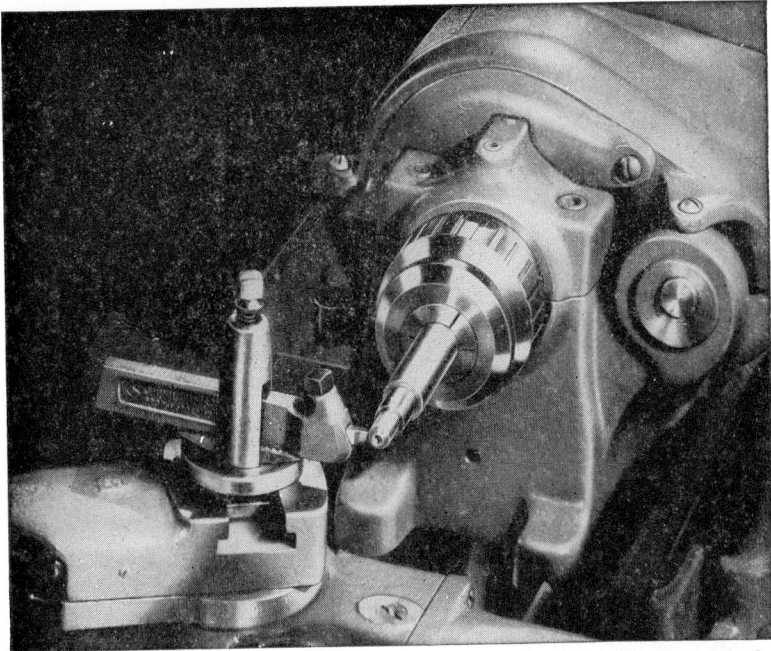

Fig. 15-5. Machining a part held in a draw-in-collet chuck. (*South Bend Lathe Works*)

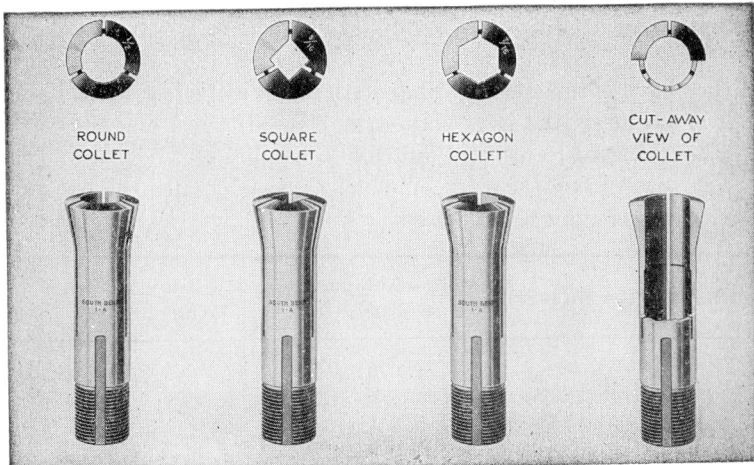

ROUND COLLET   SQUARE COLLET   HEXAGON COLLET   CUT-AWAY VIEW OF COLLET

Fig. 15-6. Various types of collets: (*South Bend Lathe Works*)

the hole in the lathe spindle, and the end, being threaded inside, screws over the threaded portion of the chuck and draws it back into the adapter until it grips the work. This form of chuck is often called a *spring collet chuck*.

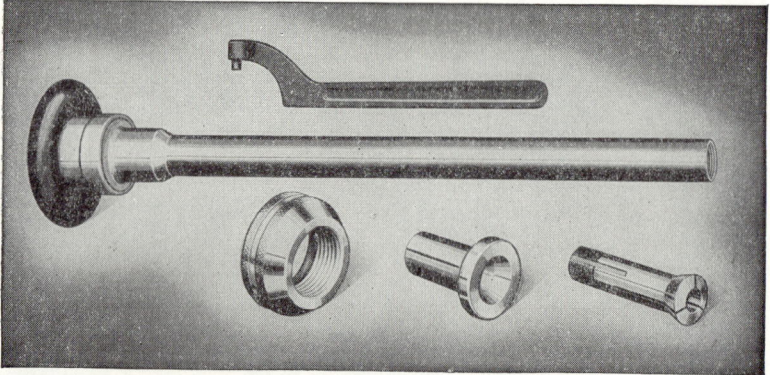

Fig. 15-7. A handwheel draw-in-collet chuck with parts. (*South Bend Lathe Works*)

The work held in the collet should not be more than 0.001 in. smaller or larger than the collet size. Collets are usually made of heat-treated steel, but for some classes of work, brass collets are often used.

Selecting a Chuck. Lathe chucks should be carefully selected for the size of the lathe and the work for which they are to be used. If the chuck is too small, the capacity of the lathe is restricted, but if it is too large, the jaws may strike the lathe bed and the chuck will be awkward to use and difficult to handle.

The most practical sizes of chucks, as recommended by some manufacturers, are listed below:

Size of lathe (inches)	4-jaw independent lathe chuck (inches)	3-jaw universal lathe chuck (inches)
9	6	5
10	6	5
13	7½	6
14½	9	7½
16 and 16 to 24	10	7½

Removing Chuck from Lathe Spindle. To start a chuck so that it can be removed from the lathe spindle, engage the back gears, place a wood block between the chuck jaw and back ways of the bed (Fig. 15-8), and turn the cone pulley by *hand*. After start-

Fig. 15-8. Using a wooden block to remove a chuck from the spindle nose of a lathe.

ing the chuck, place a board across the bed ways to protect them from damage in case the chuck is dropped off the spindle. This procedure also applies to *faceplates*.

CAUTION: A chuck or faceplate should never be run off or on a spindle by machine power. Either may sometimes be *started off* for one or two threads. but *never started on.*

Mounting the Chuck on the Spindle. Remove the live center and if short work is to be machined, put waste in the center hole to keep out chips and dirt. Remove the lathe faceplate and place it where chips and dirt will not get into the threaded hole. Be sure the thread on the spindle and also the shoulder of the spindle and the chuck plate are perfectly clean and free from any burr. Oil the thread thoroughly. A chuck 10 in. in diameter or over should be brought in line with the spindle by placing it on a suitable block laid across the ways of the lathe; start it square on the thread, turning the spindle by hand (the same care should be taken when removing the chuck). The chuck should screw on the spindle easily. It should be screwed tight against the shoulder by hand but must *not* be brought up with a bang.

Methods of Adjusting the Work in a Chuck

Chalk Method. Relatively long workpieces that are chucked in 3- or 4-jaw chucks should be checked to see if they are chucked true,

Fig. 15-9. Chalk method for testing work for on-center position. (*The Shell Oil Company*)

that is, to determine whether the center line of the workpiece corresponds with a line running from the chuck center to the dead center.

The so-called *chalk method* of checking a workpiece for on-center accuracy is simple, although less accurate than mechanical methods. The workpiece is rotated slowly and, as shown in Fig. 15-9, a piece of chalk held in a fixed position is brought in contact with the rotating surface. If not mounted true, only the high side will be marked. The workpiece should then be adjusted to bring it to an on-center position. When this is accomplished, a chalk line will be drawn around the entire circumference.

The length of the line drawn on the surface of the workpiece that is out of true indicates the extent and direction of adjustment that should be made. The shorter the line, the more the workpiece is off center and the greater the adjustment. To center it, the point midway of the chalk line on its circumference should be moved toward center, a greater distance if the chalk mark is short, a lesser distance if the mark is long. If the workpiece is relatively short, and it is chucked in a 4-jaw chuck, it is moved by adjustment of the individual jaws. If a 3-jaw chuck is used, shims will have to be inserted between the jaws and the workpiece on the high side. If the workpiece is long and its extended end is to be adjusted, the chuck jaws should be slightly loosened before making an adjustment; so as not to subject them to strain.

The Scriber Method (Fig. 15-10). The scriber method of determining whether a workpiece is chucked accurately is efficient when

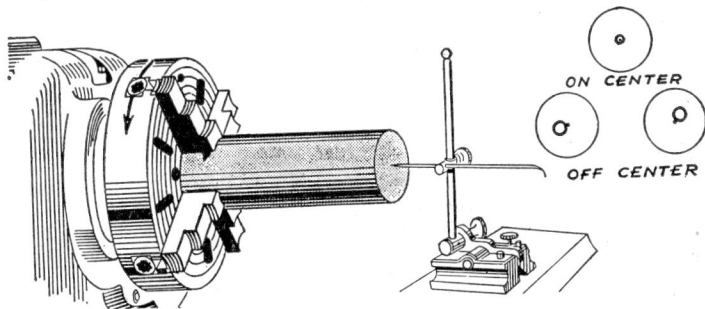

Fig. 15-10. Scriber method for testing work for on-center position. (*The Shell Oil Company*)

a moderate degree of mounting accuracy is required. This method employs a surface gage. The end of the workpiece should first be faced to assure a smooth surface, which is then coated with layout fluid or chalk so that the scriber marks will be plainly seen. The exact center must also be located and marked. The scriber point is located on this center mark, and the workpiece is rotated slowly. If it is mounted true, the point of the scriber will remain on the center mark; if not, a circle will be scribed to one side. The location of this circle in relation to the center mark will indicate the direction it is out of true, while its size will indicate the extent. The workpiece should be moved toward the center.

The scriber of a surface gage may also be used in a different manner, wherein no center mark is used. By this method, adjustments are made to bring the point of the scriber to the same height as the lathe centers. It is then swung around to point toward the workpiece and is brought in contact with the end surface, close to the actual center. In this position, the workpiece is rotated. This action will cause the scriber to scratch a circle on the workpiece surface. The dead center is then brought in contact with the workpiece end surface, and the location of its point in relation to the circle will indicate whether or not the workpiece is mounted true. If mounted true, the dead center of the lathe will point to the center of the scribed circle. If not, it will point to one side of this circle, indicating the extent and direction in which the workpiece should be adjusted. Either of these procedures described should be repeated until a true setting is made.

The Wiggler Method (Fig. 15-11). The wiggler method is comparatively simple and accurate. The entire assembly is made up of a

Fig. 15-11. Wiggler method for testing work for on-center position. (*The Shell Oil Company*)

holder supporting a universal joint which acts as a fulcrum for a long, pointed bar called a *wiggler*. This fulcrum is located close to one end of the wiggler; thus, any movement of the end projecting a short distance from the fulcrum will be greatly exaggerated at the other end. The holder is mounted in the tool post, and the short arm of the wiggler is inserted in the hole punched in the exact center of the workpiece and surface. Then the workpiece is rotated. If it is not chucked true, the long arm of the wiggler will describe a circle, and the setting must be adjusted until the wiggler point remains in a stationary position opposite the dead center.

In order to determine the direction in which the workpiece should be moved, the tool post should be adjusted so that the circle described by the wiggler will be uniformly around the point of the dead center, as shown in Fig. 15-11. The lathe is then stopped, and the workpiece is moved to bring the end of the wiggler opposite the point of the dead center. It should be remembered, however, that because the wiggler is pivoted on a universal joint the workpiece must be moved in a direction *opposite* to that in which the point of the wiggler is off the dead center. Each adjustment should be checked and this procedure should be repeated until the long end of the wiggler remains in a fixed position opposite the point of the dead center. For absolute accuracy, both the wiggler and the dead center should be ground to a fine point so that even minute variations in alignment may be found.

Dial Indicator Method (Fig. 15-12). A dial indicator makes possible the greatest accuracy in checking the on-center position of a workpiece. This is the case because any variation from center is

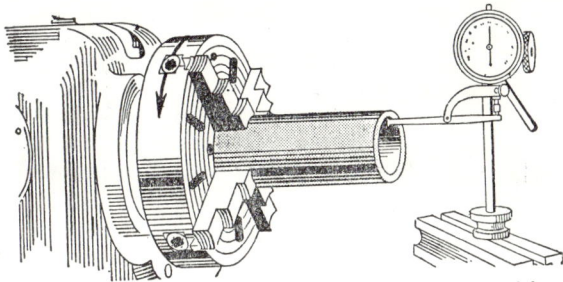

Fig. 15-12. Indicator method for testing work for on-center position. (*The Shell Oil Company*)

visibly recorded in graduations on the dial of the indicator. These graduations may be as fine as thousandths or ten-thousandths of an inch. Briefly, the procedure followed is this: First, adjust the center point of the indicator on the workpiece so it is subjected to sufficient pressure to cause the hand on the dial to make one complete revolution. Second, adjust the face of the dial so the zero mark is opposite the hand. Third, rotate the workpiece by hand and determine the extent to which it is out of true. Fourth, stop the workpiece at the point of highest dial reading; then move it in a direction from this point toward its center. The extent of workpiece adjustment is *one-half* the maximum distance the hand moves from zero.

Different methods are used to bring a dial indicator to the correct position on the workpiece surface to get a reading. In Fig. 15-13, a

Fig. 15-13. A dial indicator being used to determine the on-center position of work held in a chuck. (*South Bend Lathe Works*)

reading is being taken on an interior surface, which is something that cannot be done by any of the methods so far described. In the type of holder shown, any variation in off-center setting is transmitted to the dial indicator mechanism through a lever. It will be seen that this construction permits the checking of either an interior or exterior surface with equal ease.

Other holding devices use an arm, leading from a securely clamped base. This holds the dial in a position that will allow the contact point to be brought to position on the workpiece surface. Sometimes, this base is clamped to a fixed part of the lathe, and in other instances, it is securely held by the toolholder (Fig. 15-13).

It should always be remembered that a dial indicator is a very delicate instrument and, if its accuracy is to be kept, must be handled with great care.

Radial Facing. The term *radial facing* may be applied to the truing of the faces of work of a comparatively large diameter when held in a chuck or on a faceplate (Fig. 15-14). The shovel-nose tool may be used for the roughing cut. When using this sort of a tool or a similar tool, face from the circumference of the work toward the center. When finishing, an ordinary turning tool or side tool, whichever is preferred, may be used. In radial facing, care must be taken that there is little or no end motion in the main spindle bearings. Also, to prevent the tool working away from the cut, and thus producing a surface which is not flat and true, it is necessary to tighten the carriage clamping screw. A much better finished appearance may be obtained on cast iron if the chip is very light and the feed is very coarse. A square-nosed tool makes an excellent cast-iron finishing tool. It is good practice when facing steel in a lathe to apply a suitable amount of lard oil or other cutting compound with a brush. Cast iron and brass are machined dry.

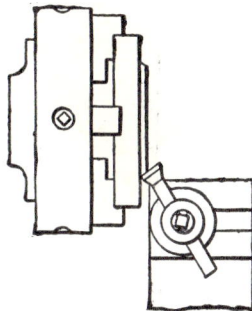

Fig. 15-14. Radial facing.

CUTTING OFF BAR STOCK IN A LATHE

The Cutting-off Tool. Select an offset cutting-off tool (sometimes called a *parting* tool) with the blade protruding only a trifle longer than half the diameter of the stock.

The cutting edge of a cutting-off tool (Fig. 15-15) is the widest part of the blade. The front clearance is the same as for any turning tool, about 10 deg. Besides the front clearance it has clearance on both sides, toward the bottom, and also toward the body. The width of the cutting edge depends on various conditions, but it should always be wide enough to make the blade strong and not so wide as to waste the stock unnecessarily. A cutting-off tool never has side rake and seldom if ever any back rake. The reason for no back rake is the decided tendency for the tool to hook into the work due to the slack in the cross-feed screw. To sharpen a cutting-off tool, grind it on the front. Cut-off tools are sometimes ground diagonally to avoid a teat on the work.

The Cutting-off Operation. Set the tool on center; if too high it will "ride" as it approaches the small diameter; if too low it will "dig." If the work is steel or wrought metal, use plenty of lard oil or

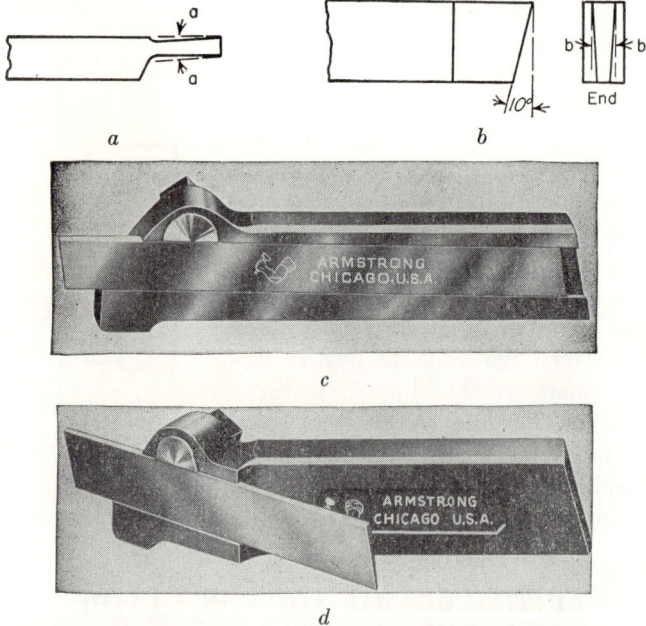

Fig. 15-15. The cutting-off tool: (*a*) top, (*b*) side. The amount of clearance at *a* and also at *b* is very small, just enough to clear the sides of the groove being cut. Excessive clearance weakens the tool. One particular advantage of the patent cutting-off toolholder and blade is that the blade may be adjusted to project only the distance necessary. Another advantage is that the tool requires grinding in front and top *only*, *never* on the sides. (*c*) Shows a straight holder with blade and (*d*) shows a right-hand offset holder and blade. (*Armstrong Bros. Tool Company*)

some good cutting compound and provide means of catching the surplus, thus keeping the lathe clean. Feed by hand and be sensitive to the cutting conditions. The lathe, especially if motor driven, may be speeded faster as the diameter is decreased. It requires strict attention to business to do a good job in grinding, setting, and using a cutting-off tool. When cutting off stock held in a chuck it is best to use an offset tool to permit working close to the chuck (Fig. 15-16).

It should be emphasized here that spring of the work or of the tool is always a decided disadvantage. When using the cutting-off tool particular care should be taken that the work and the tool both be as rigid as the nature of the job will permit.

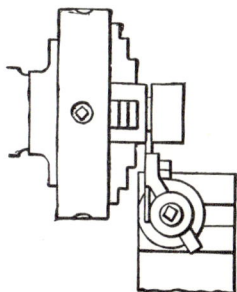

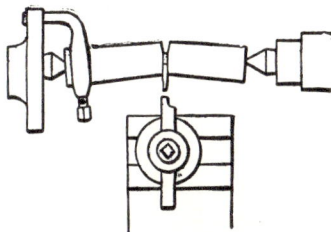

Fig. 15-16. Correct use of cutting-off tool.

Fig. 15-17. A sure way of spoiling the work and breaking the tool.

Do not attempt to cut in two a piece of work held between centers; do not attempt to even neck the piece if it is slender, because it will almost certainly be bent and ruined and the tool will be broken (Fig. 15-17).

Chattering. The rapid vibration of the tool and the work, which is called *chattering*, frequently takes place when using a cutting-off tool and may be due to one or more of several reasons: to a tendency of the tool or work to spring; to the fact that the tool is set too high; to the looseness of the cross slide; or to the looseness of the lathe spindle in its bearings.

QUESTIONS ON THE USE OF LATHE CHUCKS

1. How is the chuck started on the thread? If it is a heavy chuck how is it best held when starting?

2. What is the danger of having the spindle revolve by power when starting the chuck on the thread? When screwing it home?

3. Why should the chuck not be screwed against the shoulder with a bang? Why should it be screwed up tight?

4. To make the work run more nearly true, should you adjust two opposite jaws to push the high spot *toward* the center or *away* from the center? Why?

5. If the high spot should come between two jaws, how would these jaws be adjusted?

6. What is the purpose of the rings in the face of the chuck?

7. If you had several pieces of the same size to machine in the chuck, explain how you could save time by marking two jaws of the chuck.

8. Find as many of the following chucks as are available: 6-in. three-jaw universal; 8-in. four-jaw independent; and a combination chuck.

9. What is the advantage of the universal chuck?

10. What advantages has the independent chuck?

11. How is the combination chuck changed from independent to universal? How are the jaws adjusted to make them true before the change is made?

12. There is a proper method of removing a chuck from the lathe spindle. How is it started? How is it held when being unscrewed? What is the danger of starting the lathe by power?

13. What type of chuck jaw is used to hold bar stock or pieces of small diameter?

14. How would you hold in a 6-in. chuck a piece 6 in. in diameter to bore it? How would you hold it to turn off the circumference?

15. What is meant by reversible jaws?

16. What is meant by jaws with reversible tops?

17. How do you size up the workman who hammers the chuck wrench or who uses a pipe extension to the wrench?

18. What is the danger of stopping the chuck by clapping the hand on it?

19. What is the small chuck with a taper arbor which fits into the tail spindle usually called?

20. What are two advantages of the split chuck (spring collet)?

21. Explain in detail the action of the draw-in sleeve in closing the split chuck?

22. What is the advantage of an offset cutting-off tool in chuck work?

23. How many clearance angles has a cutting-off tool?

24. When is a cutting-off tool set properly?

25. What is the objection to holding work between centers to cut in two?

26. What is meant by chattering? How may it be prevented?

27. When radial facing, what tool may be used for roughing?

28. What is the object of clamping the carriage when radial facing?

DRILLING AND REAMING IN A LATHE

Introduction. *Drilling* a hole may be defined as *one process of making a hole where none existed previously.*

Boring may be differentiated from drilling in that it is the process of enlarging, by turning inside with some form of boring tool, a hole already existing; for example, a hole already drilled, or a cored hole in a casting.

Reaming is the process of finishing a hole to the required size by means of either a machine reamer or a hand reamer.

Many holes do not have to be especially accurate, and merely drilling the hole may be enough. For example, a hole may be sufficiently accurate and smooth enough if drilled $\frac{1}{64}$ or $\frac{1}{32}$ in. undersize and then finished with a machine reamer; or possibly a hole drilled $\frac{1}{32}$ in. undersize and machine-reamed with a machine reamer $\frac{3}{1000}$ to $\frac{5}{1000}$ in. undersize and finished with a hand reamer will be satisfactory. However, none of these holes has to be bored.

While the drill press is essentially the machine for drilling and reaming, it often happens that it is more profitable to finish the holes in a lathe.

The twist drills and reamers used in lathe work are the same as those used in drill-press work. For a complete explanation and description of drills and reamers, see Chapters 7 and 8.

Drilling in a Lathe: Spotting the Center. Suppose it is required to finish a hole, say 1 in. in diameter, in a piece of solid metal. Usually the first operation, after truing the work in the chuck, is to face the piece, especially if it is cast iron. The next operation is spotting a center for the drill, using the bent spotting tool (Fig. 15-18).

Fig. 15-18. Spotting tool.

Fig. 15-19. Tool bit.

This tool is ground to an angle of about 120 deg. to correspond with the angle formed by the lips of the drill. Note that each lip is given clearance but in opposite directions, because the cutting force is up on one lip and down on the other. Set the spotting tool on center and square, that is, in such a position that both lips will cut evenly. Start the lathe and run the tool up to the work. If the point of the tool is not exactly in the center, a small ring will be turned in the face of the work. It is very easy to adjust the point to the center of this ring. Make the spot nearly as large as the diameter of the drill to be used.

A tool bit may be ground and used for a spotting tool if it is given sufficient side clearance (Fig. 15-19). Care must be taken or the point, being very delicate, will break.

Operation of Drilling the Hole. Select a drill somewhat under-size ($\frac{1}{64}$ or $\frac{1}{32}$ in.), to allow for reaming, and a drill holder (Fig. 15-20) to fit the taper shank of the drill. Be sure that both the taper

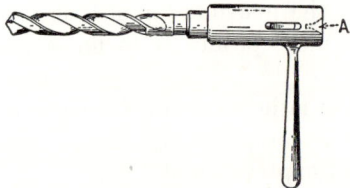

Fig. 15-20. Drill holder fits the taper shanks of drills and machine reamers. Has a large center hole at A and is provided with a suitable handle.

shank of the drill and the taper hole in the holder are clean and *free from oil*. Tapers will not hold if oily, and if the taper does not help hold the drill from turning, the tang of the drill may be twisted off under the pressure of the cut.

NOTE: If the drill has a straight shank a dog may be used to keep it from turning, provided the drill has a good center hole. Place a protecting piece of brass or copper under the dog screw.

It is important before starting the drill to note that the tail center is not offset.

Place the point of the drill in the spot and the center of the drill holder on the tail center of the lathe (Fig. 15-21). Have the spindle well back in the tailstock and the tailstock tightly clamped to the bed. Upon revolving the work the drill may be fed into the work by turning the tailstock handwheel.

As the drill breaks through the inside end of the piece, it has a tendency to pull away from the dead center, due to the spiral and to the lack of resistance. *CAUTION:* Do not try to hold the drill back against the center by hand because it is dangerous. Many drills have been broken and many hands have been severely injured by ignorance or carelessness in this respect. There will be no trouble if a tool clamped in the tool post is arranged against the handle of the drill holder so that the drill cannot pull away from the tailstock unless it pulls the carriage along. This setup is shown in Fig. 15-21.

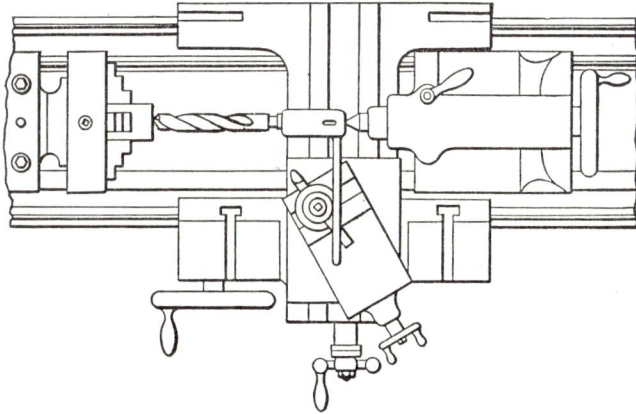

Fig. 15-21. Drilling in a lathe. It is very important to have the tool post tight and the handle of the drill holder against it. Turning the tailstock handwheel will feed the drill and at the same time push the carriage along the ways.

Do not wait until the drill starts to break through, but arrange as above when making the setup. While the carriage moves easily enough by the screw pressure against the drill holder and does not make the feeding of the drill noticeably harder, it still offers resistance enough to keep the drill holder against the center when the drill has a tendency to dig. *CAUTION:* Never loosen the tailstock or withdraw the dead center from the drill while the lathe is running. After the hole has been drilled, *stop the lathe* and, keeping the drill holder against the dead center, either run the tail spindle back or loosen the tailstock and pull it back until the drill can be removed.

In lathe drilling the speed is nearly always too slow, probably due to the fact that the chuck, being so much larger than the drill, seems to be going fast enough. Calculate the required r.p.m. and set the speed accordingly, especially until experienced.

Machine Reaming. Reaming is the next operation. The machine reamer is held in a drill holder or by a dog. It should be held against any tendency to pull away from the center as explained in "Operation of Drilling the Hole," page 386, not only when the reamer breaks through but *during the whole length of the cut.* This precaution is absolutely necessary or the reamer will catch and bend or break, and the hole will be spoiled.

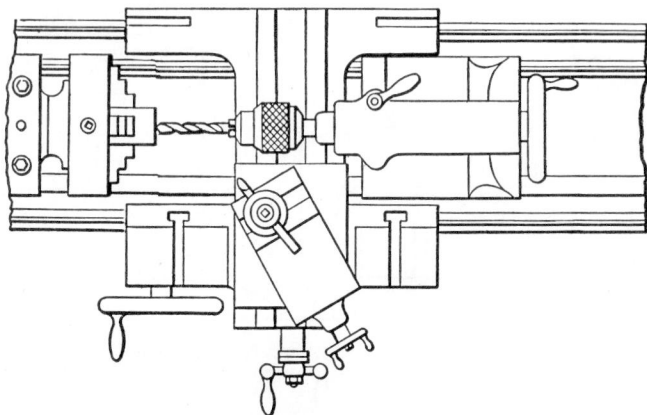

Fig. 15-22. For holes under ½ in., use the drill chuck with a shank that fits the taper hole in the tailstock spindle.

The speed for reaming is usually somewhat slower than for drilling (especially in cast iron) to avoid any tendency to overheat and ruin the reamer. The feed should not be crowded or the reamer is likely to tear the surface of the hole.

Place the reamer in position with the end in the hole, get everything ready, then start the lathe and start to feed immediately by turning the handwheel. Ream cast iron dry, except sometimes when a little oil may be rubbed on the lands of a rose reamer to keep it from scoring. Always use a lubricant when reaming steel or other alloys.

Use of Drill Chuck. Straight-shank drills and reamers up to ½ or ⅝ in. diameter may be held in a drill chuck, the taper shank of which fits the tailstock spindle hole. If a reamer is held in this way one must be careful to have it true in the chuck or it will ream the hole slightly taper. In any case have the shank of the chuck *tight* in the spindle or it may loosen and score both shank and spindle. This setup is shown in Fig. 15-22.

Hand Reaming. If for any reason it is necessary to finish the hole with a hand reamer, it is usually better to start the reamer while the work is in the lathe. Keep the dead center against the reamer and turn the reamer by hand with a wrench. After the reamer is well started the work may be removed and the hole finished in a vise.

It is especially important to *know* that the dead center is in line when starting a reamer in a lathe as above. If the dead center is even slightly offset the reamer will not start true.

Sometimes when the work is held in the vise and the reamer turned with the wrench, a chatter will occur at the start. This may often be avoided by holding the reamer in the vise and, with a suitable wrench or clamp, turning the work on the reamer.

A burr on the edge of a reamer may spoil the hole. When the reamer is obtained from the toolroom, feel along the edge of each tooth and if any burr is felt, oilstone it off.

REMINDER: Do not leave over 0.005 in. for a hand reamer to remove. Never turn a reamer backwards. Use a cutting lubricant when drilling or reaming steel, but cast iron is drilled and reamed dry.

QUESTIONS ON DRILLING AND REAMING

1. If the point of the centering tool is not exactly on center, what kind of cut will be made in the face of the work?
2. How may the center then be easily found?
3. What shape is the end of the spotting tool? Why?
4. How is clearance on the cutting edge of the spotting tool nearer the operator ground? How is it ground on the other edge? Why?
5. How large a spot should be made?
6. If the work is a rough casting or any piece that is not fairly square, why should it be faced before drilling?
7. Can the spotting tool be used to clean a portion of the face around the spot?
8. How may a tool bit be ground to produce a satisfactory spot?

9. What is the effect in drilling if the tail center is offset?
10. How do you feed the drill?
11. Should the cutting speed be the same as if the drill revolved? Why?
12. What is the number of r.p.m. necessary to give 30 ft. per min. cutting speed for a 1-in. diameter drill? For $\frac{1}{2}$-in. diameter drill? For $1\frac{1}{4}$-in. diameter drill?
13. How do you judge the proper feed?
14. As the drill breaks through at the end of the hole the tendency is for it to draw in, or dig in. This will pull the drill holder off the center and probably break the drill. How is this prevented?
15. If it is a fairly deep hole in steel, how is cutting compound applied?
16. What does a squeak indicate?
17. If a straight-shank drill is used, how may it be held with a dog? What about the center in the drill?
18. How is the dog arranged on the drill? How is it arranged to keep the drill from drawing in?

BORING IN A LATHE

Reasons for Boring. It is sometimes necessary after drilling to enlarge a hole with a boring tool because the drill used for drilling does not leave sufficient metal for reaming or because a reamer of proper size is not available. However, the most common reason for boring a hole is to obtain a hole that is correct in size and true.

If it is important to have a hole run true and central with the piece, as set up in the chuck or on the faceplate, the hole should be bored. It is not safe to assume that a drill will run perfectly true through solid metal, even though it starts true; it might strike a blowhole, or a hard spot in the work, or it may become dull. These conditions will cause the drill to wobble. A reamer will follow the general direction of the hole as drilled, and the result, if the hole is not straight, will be most unsatisfactory.

A cored hole, if it is to be finished true, must invariably be bored. A three-lipped drill is steadier and stronger and is therefore better than a two-lipped drill for drilling a cored hole, but the hole must be bored round and true after any drilling operation if accuracy is required.

Occasionally a core is not properly set in a mold and the hole in the casting is consequently out of center. In many such cases the casting may be adjusted in the chuck so that the eccentricity is divided, half in the hole, half on the outside, and both surfaces may be finished to size (Fig. 15-23). In this event the hole should be trued up by boring at least deep enough to give a fair start for the drill and possibly its full length.

Fig. 15-23. (*a*) Shows the casting trued up by the outside and the dotted line; the hole (as bored) does not clean up. (*b*) Shows the eccentricity divided, so that both the hole and the outside will clean.

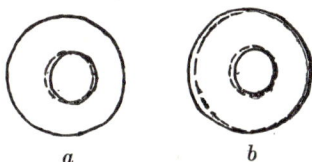

a   *b*

The Boring Tool. The boring tool (the part that cuts) is a turning tool held in a bar or holder or forged on the end of the bar (Fig. 15-24). It is ground like a turning tool that cuts from left to right. It has side rake (Fig. 15-25*a*); a cutting angle of about 60 to 70 deg. (being a metal turning tool), and a rounded cutting point to

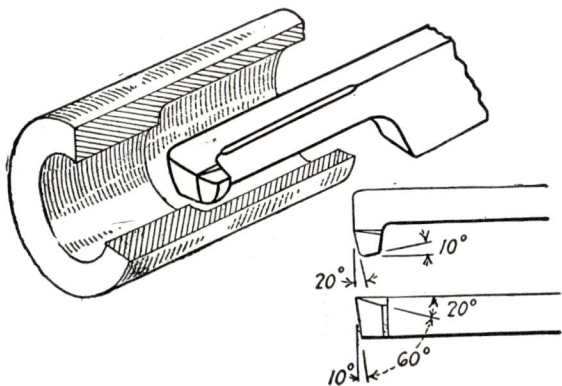

Fig. 15-24. The forged boring tool.

give the tool a longer life and the work a smoother finish. The cutting edge is not at right angles to the axis of the work but should be about 20 deg. from this perpendicular as shown in the figure. This causes the chip to curl away from the finished cut and also reduces the tendency for the tool to spring into the work. The boring tool must have *side clearance* (Fig. 15-25*b*) to permit its feeding into the

work and thus peel off the chip; and also *front clearance* (Fig. 15-25c)
so as not to rub on the finished work.

The clearance must be sufficient to preclude any chance of rubbing but should not be excessive or the cutting edge, not being
backed up, will break away and dull quickly.

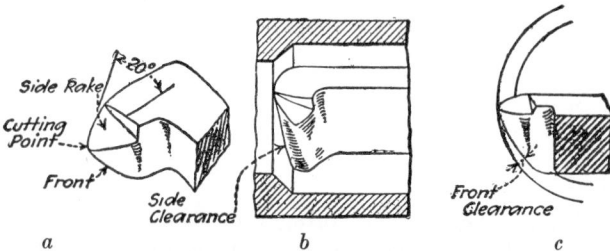

Fig. 15-25. Turning tool part of a boring tool. Note side rake (*a*) and side (*b*)
and front (*c*) clearance.

Have the boring-tool bar as short as the length of the hole will
permit and *be very sure that the bar will clear* as the tool works into the
hole.

The Boring-tool Holder. A boring-tool holder in which the
length of the bar and the position of the cutting edge of the tool
may be adjusted will usually give better satisfaction than the forged

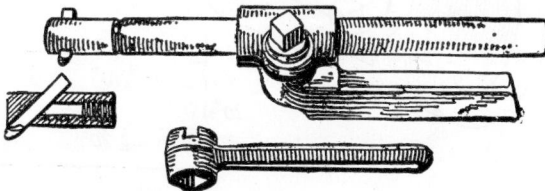

Fig. 15-26. Armstrong boring-tool holder and wrench for adjusting or tightening either the cap or the bar. (*Armstrong Bros. Tool Company*)

tool. Figure 15-26 represents a boring-tool holder having these
advantages. The tool bit may be sharpened and reset without disturbing the toolholder, which advantage is especially desirable when
cutting an inside thread. The extra hole, which holds the tool point
at an angle, is useful when boring to a shoulder or when squaring the
bottom of a hole.

OPERATION SHEET

Grinding and Setting a Boring Tool

SAFETY RULES

1. *Wear goggles* when turning brittle metals.
2. *Do not hold* tool bit in the toolholder when grinding.

Operations

1. Determine the side clearance angle, top and back rake angles, and the front clearance angle required for such a tool. *Keep in mind the material to be bored.*
2. Grind the required side clearance angle. Keep tool bit cool. Dip in water if necessary.
3. Grind the required top and back rake angles. Keep tool bit cool. Dip in water if necessary.
4. If the tool bit is to be used for a finishing cut, *hone* the cutting edge.
5. Secure boring bar long enough for the job.
6. Insert the tool bit in boring bar with only the ground portion sticking out of the toolholder (boring bar).
7. Tighten securely by tightening cap on boring bar. Be sure that the tool bit is tight.
8. Adjust the boring bar in holder with just sufficient length projecting from the holder so that you can bore to the required length without hitting the work.
9. Adjust point of tool *exactly* on the center of the job.
10. Adjust tool so that the boring bar is level and parallel to the ways of the lathe.
11. Tighten holder.
12. Tighten tool-post screw on toolholder. Make sure that the tool setting has not been changed. Check before using.
13. Boring tool is now ready to go to work.

OPERATION SHEET

Boring in the Lathe

Operations

1. Mount work in chuck and center.
2. Set boring tool.
3. Revolve lathe spindle by hand to be sure work will clear carriage at all points throughout the travel of the carriage as hole is bored.
4. Select proper spindle speed for size of drill being used. Set lathe for this speed.
5. For rough boring, set lathe for medium feed. If tool chatters and vibrates when boring is started, reduce spindle speed and cut down the feed.
6. Start the lathe.
7. Move tool to start of cut with hand-feed controls. (Remember, the tool is moved toward you by the cross feed to increase depth of chip when boring.)
8. Take trial cut using hand feed. Note how tool cuts. Make any necessary adjustments of speed and feed.
9. Stop the lathe.
10. Measure the start of bore. Leave about 0.010 or 0.020 in. for finishing cut.
11. Start the lathe. Engage power longitudinal feed for carriage.
12. If work vibrates or tool chatters, adjust speed and feed until this stops.
13. As tool nears the end of cut, disengage power feed and finish by hand feed.
14. When the end of cut is reached, turn cross-feed crank to right so that the tool clears the bore.
15. Stop the lathe. Run boring bar out of bore by hand.
16. For a finishing cut, hone the cutting edge of the tool.
17. Set lathe for a slow longitudinal feed.
18. Move boring bar into position by hand. Start the lathe.
19. Take trial cut and measure bore.
20. Check size of finished bore. Reset tool and turn start of bore until finished using power longitudinal feed.
21. Stop the lathe *first*. Check size of finished hole.

Hints on Boring in the Lathe

1. Always select a boring tool with a shank *small* enough to clear the hole and not too long.

2. Be sure that the boring tool is *always* sharp and ground with the proper clearance angles.

3. Be sure that the rake angles on the cutter are correct for the metal being bored.

4. Extreme care *must* be taken to avoid springing or breaking the work when clamping in a chuck. This is especially true with thin rim or thin wall pieces.

5. Take *light* cuts at the start of the boring operation.

6. It is advised to use cutting lubricants when boring steel. Put it on *before* job is started. During the boring operation, in order to put some more lubricant on the piece, a squirt gun may be used. This is especially true for long bores assuming that the lubricant is put on by hand.

7. Before taking the final finishing cut, make *sure* that the size of the bore is correct.

QUESTIONS ON BORING AND REAMING

1. What is the difference between drilling and boring?
2. Is the boring tool a turning tool? Explain your answer.
3. Where on a job does the boring tool cut?
4. State two reasons for rounding the cutting point of a boring tool.
5. Should the tool for boring cast iron and steel be given front rake and side rake? State reasons.
6. In what respects should a tool for boring brass differ from a tool for boring steel? State reasons.
7. In which two directions does a boring tool have a tendency to spring?
8. How may this spring be largely overcome?
9. What particular care must be taken regarding the shank, or bar, of a boring tool when setting up?
10. How is the proper feed for boring determined?
11. How is the proper chip size for boring determined?
12. What is the reason for boring a hole?
13. When is it advisable to bore a hole that is to be reamed later?
14. When is a machine reamer that is up to size used in lathe work?
15. When is a machine reamer slightly undersized used?
16. How much undersized should it be?

17. How is a taper-shank reamer held?

18. How is a straight-shank reamer held?

19. Why must the reamer be held against the center during the entire cut?

20. How does the cutting speed of a reamer compare with that of a drill?

21. How does the feed of a reamer compare with that of a drill?

22. When is the hand reamer used in the lathe?

23. How much undersized should a hole be left for hand reaming?

24. How is the hand reamer turned when used in a lathe?

25. How is the hand reamer kept square when used in a lathe?

CHAPTER 16

Tapers and Angles

Tapers. One of the most important principles in machine-shop practice is that involved in taper work, particularly the round-taper shank and the round-taper hole (Fig. 16-1).

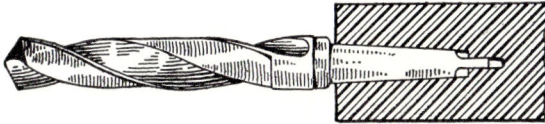

Fig. 16-1. Round-taper shank and round-taper hole.

There is hardly a revolving spindle in any machine that is not provided with a taper hole. This taper hole will receive and securely and rigidly hold the taper shanks of various tools such as centers, drills, and reamers. The correct position of the tool thus used is immediately obtained and indefinitely maintained, yet a slight blow serves to remove the shank from the hole.

Taper in round work may be defined as *the difference in diameters, for any length, measured along the axis of the work.* It is usually stated in tables, on drawings, etc., as the amount of taper *per inch* or taper *per foot.*

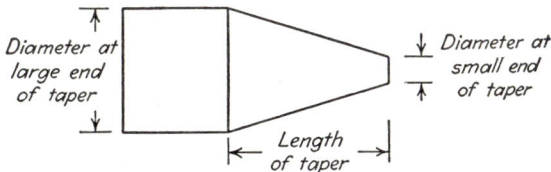

Fig. 16-2.

There are four parts to every taper: (1) the taper per inch or taper per foot; (2) the length of the tapered part; (3) the large diameter; and (4) the small diameter (Fig. 16-2).

Standard Tapers. There are various systems of standard tapers in common commercial use, the most important being the *Morse standard*, the *Brown & Sharpe standard*, the *Jarno standard*, and the *taper-pin standard* (see list of tables, page xvii).

Twist drills are made with Morse standard taper shanks, up to, and including, $\frac{9}{16}$ in. with No. 1 taper; from $\frac{9}{16}$ in. up to, and including, $\frac{29}{32}$ in. with No. 2 taper, etc.

The Brown & Sharpe standard taper is used in milling machines; the arbors, collets, end mills, etc., have shanks with Brown & Sharpe tapers, with one exception—the new standard milling-machine spindles have the hole for the arbor, etc., with a taper of $3\frac{1}{2}$ in. per foot for quick release.

There is no standard taper for the shanks of lathe centers. Each manufacturer seems to have established sizes of his own. Do not attempt to use a center made for one lathe in another kind of lathe, and do not use in a lathe a chuck with a shank fitted to a drill press. The chances are the taper will not fit.

A disturbing fact in machine work, which often results in considerable confusion, is the number of mongrel sizes in the various systems. For example, there are seven different amounts of taper per foot in the seven Morse standard tapers. No one tries to remember the lengths, diameters, etc.; a table of sizes is necessary.

The Jarno system of tapers is the most sensible system. In this series the number of the taper is the key by which all the dimensions are immediately known. Thus, the number of the taper is the number of *eighths* of an inch in diameter at the large end, the number of *tenths* of an inch in diameter at the small end, and the number of *halves* of an inch in length. The taper is 0.600 in. per ft. in each size. It is too late to incorporate the Jarno system in drilling machines and milling machines; there are too many million drills, reamers, end mills, etc., in the shops to make a change feasible, but there seems to be no real reason why the Jarno system cannot be used in the new lathes.

To preserve the accuracy and efficiency of tapers (shanks and holes) they must be free from dirt, chips, nicks, or burrs. A most distressing sight is a taper, either a shank or a hole, practically spoiled by being nicked or dented. The most important single direction in regard to tapers is to *keep them clean*. The next important thing is to wipe them dry, because an oily taper will not hold.

TAPER TURNING

There are three methods of turning tapers in the lathe: (1) by offsetting the tailstock; (2) by using the compound; and (3) by using the taper attachment of the lathe. The method used depends on the (1) length of the taper; (2) the angle of taper; and (3) the number of pieces to be machined.

Each method will be thoroughly discussed in the following paragraphs.

Setover Tailstock Method. The oldest and probably most used method of taper turning is the setover tailstock method. The tailstock is made in two pieces, the lower fitted to the bed, while the upper part is fitted to a cross keyway machined on the lower section. To turn straight diameters, the tailstock spindle is set exactly in line with the headstock center. To turn taper diameters, the upper half of the tailstock is set over the amount necessary to produce the taper required. Figure 16-3 shows a taper being cut with the setover of the tailstock.

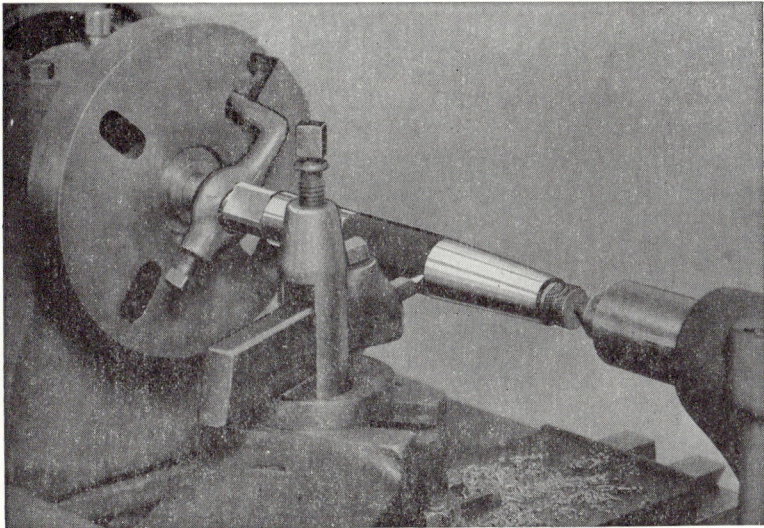

Fig. 16-3. Taper cut by offsetting the tailstock. (*South Bend Lathe Works*)

To find the proper amount to offset the tailstock for a given taper on a piece of work requires a simple calculation, but there are a few things about offsetting the tailstock for turning tapers that must be thoroughly understood before calculations can be made intelligently.

1. The more the given piece is offset the greater will be the amount of taper.

2. The longer the piece of work the more the offset required to obtain a given taper. For example: An offset of $\frac{1}{16}$ in. for a piece 2 in. long would give a fairly steep taper, but the same offset for a piece 24 in. long would give a taper hardly noticeable, in fact, only one-twelfth as much as the first piece.

3. The length of the taper itself, that is, the distance a taper is cut on a piece of work, has nothing to do with the offset. When making calculations do not get length of the taper confused with the length of the work.

4. Since the work revolves in the lathe, only one-half as much offset is required to give the same amount of taper as if the work did not revolve.

5. The taper is proportional to the length—so much taper per foot. The offset is proportional, but in the ratio of one-half the length because the work revolves.

Measurements in machine-shop work, including lengths up to 2 ft. or more, are expressed in the denomination of *inches*. Therefore, when calculating the offset, where the length is given in inches, the taper per foot is always reduced to taper per *inch* (divide taper per foot by 12). Then the proportion will be

$$\text{Offset: taper per inch} = \frac{\text{length of work in inches}}{2} : 1 \text{ inch.}$$

that is,
$$\text{Offset: } T = \frac{L}{2} : 1$$

or
$$\text{Offset} = \frac{TL}{2}$$

where T = taper per inch
L = entire length of work in inches

Rule for Offset When Turning Taper. From the preceding formula the rule for offset is derived. Multiply the length of the work *in inches* by the taper *per inch* and divide by two. The result will be the amount to offset the tailstock.

NOTE: When measuring work and calculating offset, disregard eighths and take the nearest quarter inch under. For example: If the work measures $9\frac{7}{16}$ or $9\frac{3}{8}$, call the length $9\frac{1}{4}$ in your calculation. As a matter of fact, the centers of the lathe enter the work a little way and no doubt the offset as calculated, using $9\frac{1}{4}$, will be nearer right.

Methods of Gaging Offset. Assume that the lathe is set for straight turning and that a certain amount of offset is required to turn the taper. Hold the tool post rigid by clamping a tool as in Fig. 16-4.

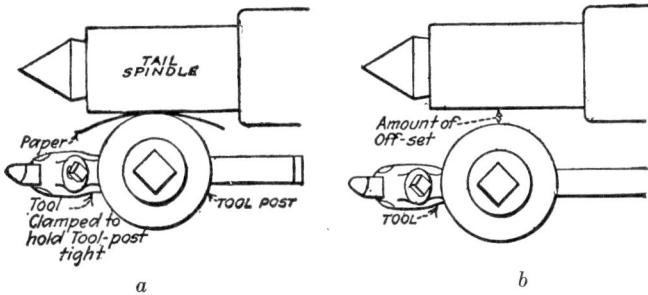

Fig. 16-4. Offsetting tailstock for taper turning.

Run the cross slide in until a piece of paper is lightly pinched between the tool post and the tailstock spindle (Fig. 16-4a). *Take up the lost motion in the cross-feed screw*, and using the graduations on the collar, run the cross slide away from the spindle until the distance between the tool post and the spindle is equal to the amount of the required offset (Fig. 16-4b). Then adjust the *tailstock slide* until paper is pinched between the spindle and the tool post, thus obtaining the required offset.

If necessary to offset in a direction away from the operator, use a similar method. Arrange as in Fig. 16-4a, offset the tail spindle a little farther than necessary, run the cross slide in the proper amount, and adjust the tailstock back toward the operator until the piece of paper is pinched between the spindle and the tool post.

Setting of Turning Tool. When calculating the required offset, it may be readily proved that the three lines of the problem (the center line of the lathe, the center line of the work, and the offset line) are in the same plane. Therefore in turning or boring taper it is absolutely necessary to have the cutting point of the tool on center.

Methods of Measuring Tapers. For the reason that the centers enter the work a short distance, which fact is usually ignored in calculations, and also that there is a possibility of other errors, it is necessary always to *test the amount of taper before turning the work to size.*

The taper per inch of any turned piece may be easily obtained by dividing the difference in diameters by the length in inches measured along the axis of the work between these diameters. For example: To find the taper of a sample piece, or to ascertain if a taper being turned is correct, the following method may be used to obtain an approximately accurate result. With pencil or scriber draw two lines on the surface of the taper parallel with the end and, if convenient, a whole number of inches apart. Measure the diameters at these lines and divide their difference by the number of inches between them. The result will be the taper per inch.

When obtaining the taper per inch it is the usual practice to consider the length as measured on the surface as near enough for practical purposes, because the difference between the length of an ordinary taper measured along the axis of the work and the length measured on the surface of the work is so small that it is, in most cases, not worth considering.

Fitting a Taper to a Gage. It is difficult to accurately measure the diameters of a taper with a spring caliper or a micrometer. A taper should be finally fitted to a gage (Fig. 16-5), or to the spindle

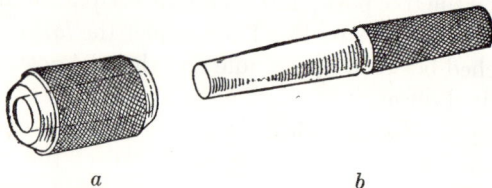

a   *b*

Fig. 16-5. Standard taper gages: (*a*) external, or taper-ring gage and (*b*) internal, or taper-plug gage.

or sleeve for which it is intended. To try a taper draw three light chalk lines about equidistant along the length of the work and then wring the taper (to the left and it will not stick) a part of a turn in the gage. If the chalk marks do not rub off evenly, the taper is incorrect. When extreme accuracy is required, a very thin application of prussian-blue oil paint may be used instead of the chalk marks.

Standard taper gages, external and internal (Fig. 16-5), are practically indispensable where accurate taper work is done.

Gaging the Size of a Taper. A very quick, accurate method of gaging the *size* of a taper is to note the distance it goes into the gage. If too large, it will not go in far enough; if too small it will go in too far. For example: say a shank 0.600 in. per foot taper (0.050 per inch) does not enter the gage within ½ in. of correct *depth* because it is 0.025 in. too large in *diameter;* if it goes into the gage 0.200 in. too far it is 0.010 in. too small in diameter. Be sure to understand this. For instance, how much too large in diameter is a tapered piece that sticks out of the gage 1 in. too far?

Duplicating a Taper Piece. When a taper on a piece of work is to be duplicated, it may be put, if it has centers, in the lathe. Then the offset of tail spindle, or the adjustment of the taper attachment or of the compound rest, may be quickly obtained by means of an indicator placed in the tool post. When the setting is correct, the reading of the indicator will not change when moved along the length of the taper.

Turning a Taper with a Square-nose Tool. It often happens that the easiest and quickest way to get an abrupt taper or angular cut on a piece is by means of a square-nose tool. For example: The live center may be trued up with a square-nose tool very efficiently (this is illustrated in Fig. 14-3). It is necessary only to have a fairly broad square-nose tool properly sharpened, set on center, and to the desired angle.

Filing a Taper. Most round work is either turned or ground to size. There are times, however, when a few strokes with a file will serve to fit a taper that is nearly right and wanted in a hurry much more quickly than it could be turned or ground.

THE TAPER ATTACHMENT

Introduction. The taper attachment (Fig. 16-6) has many features of especial value among which are the following: (1) The lathe centers are in line and the center holes in the work are not distorted. (2) The length of the work need not be considered, for once the taper is set, that particular taper will be turned on any length of piece. (3) The alignment of the lathe need not be disturbed, thus saving considerable time and trouble. (4) Taper boring is accomplished as easily as turning. (5) A much wider range is possible than by the offset method; for example, to turn a taper $3/4$ in. per ft. on the end of a bar 4 ft. long would require a setover of $1\frac{1}{2}$ in. which is outside the limit of a regular 14- or 16-in. lathe.

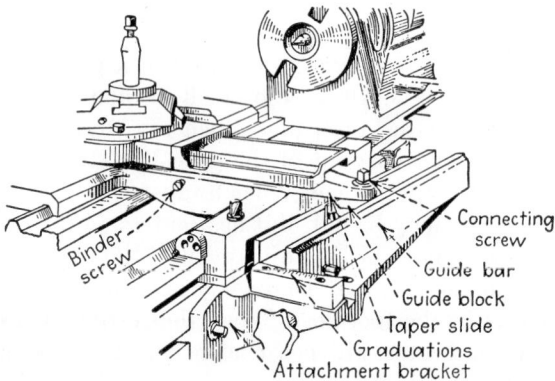

Fig. 16-6. Taper attachment. The taper slide acts also as the connection. See Fig. 16-9.

Further, it is often convenient to use a combination of the offset of the tailstock and taper attachment when turning tapers too steep for either method alone.

Ordinarily, when the lathe centers are in line, the work is turned straight, because as the carriage feeds along, the tool is always the same distance from the center line. The purpose of the taper attachment is to make it possible to keep the lathe centers in line, but by freeing the cross slide and then guiding it (and the tool) gradually away from the center line to cause a taper to be turned, as in Fig. 16-7a, or by guiding it gradually nearer the center line, as in Fig. 16-7b, to cause a taper hole to be bored.

By *freeing* the cross slide is meant the loosening of binder screws, the *position* of which, and the *number* (in some lathes one, in others half a dozen), depend upon the design of the attachment. The purpose of the binder screws is (1) to *bind* the cross slide so it may be moved only by turning the crossfeed handle, or (2) when loosened, to *free* the cross slide for use with the taper attachment. When the cross slide is free it may be moved an inch or more by pushing against the tool post.

Parts of the Taper Attachment. There must be a guide to control the movement of the cross slide. and there must be a connection

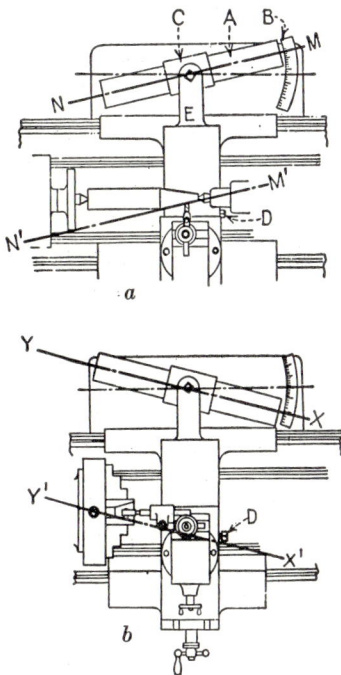

Fig. 16-7. Using the taper attachment: (*a*) turning a taper; *A*, guidebar unit; *B*, graduations on circular part of scale; *C*, guide block, or sliding shoe; *D*, binding screw; *E*, connection; *MN*, center line of guide bar; *M'N'*, path of tool cutting taper set by guide bar. These apply only when cutting a taper. (*b*) Boring a taper; *XY*, center line of guide bar; *X'Y'*, path of tool boring the taper set by guide bar. These apply only when boring a taper.

of some kind between the guide and the cross slide. It is the combination of the free cross slide, the guiding arrangement, and the connection that makes the taper attachment. There are a number of designs of these attachments, but the principle of operation is the same for all. The main features are shown in Fig. 16-7.

Guide-bar Unit. The guide bar is pivoted at its center; it may be swiveled to the desired position and rigidly secured. In some lathes the bracket upon which the guide bar rests is bolted to a planed surface on the back of the bed, and in others is carried on the back of the carriage. In the latter arrangement the guide bar, when in use, is anchored through a rod and locking arm to the rear V on the lathe bed.

Graduations. Graduations at one or both ends of the guide bar indicate the setting in taper per *foot* (not per inch). Usually graduations in degrees are also provided.

Guide Block (or sliding shoe). The guide block, or sliding shoe, is fitted to slide along the bar. (The guide *block* fits in a groove in the guide bar and a *shoe* fits over the sides and top of the bar.)

Cross-slide Unit. The cross-slide unit is the regular cross slide with a few additional parts and so designed for the taper attachment that it may be loosened and is then quite free to slide (without turning the cross-feed screw). A sectional view is shown in Fig. 16-9.

Binder Screw (or screws). A binder screw loosens, or tightens, the cross-slide unit.

Connection. A connection is provided between the cross-slide unit and the guide block.

Types of Connections. If the student understands that the cross slide must be free and then is connected to the block or shoe on the guide bar, he can read the following and note which of the three types of connection is used in his lathe:

Yoke. A yoke connection is between the regular cross slide and the guide. The disadvantage is that the cross feed cannot be used for additional depths of cuts. In most cases, however, the compound-rest feed may be used.

Telescopic Feed Screw. By the use of the telescopic feed screw, in which the cross-feed screw is connected to the guide (see Fig. 16-8), it is possible to use the regular cross feed for additional cuts, but for heavy work the pull of the connection puts a considerable strain on the screw.

Taper Slide. The use of an extra sliding member, called the *taper slide*, between the cross slide and the saddle (see Fig. 16-9) is the oldest and simplest type. It is perhaps the most costly but has neither of the drawbacks of the others.

Using the Taper Attachment. Do not cut the taper to size until the *fit* has been checked by gage or otherwise. The graduations at the end of the bar are for convenience, not for a high degree of accuracy.

Just as much judgment and care must be exercised in fitting a taper when using the taper attachment as when cutting a taper by any other method.

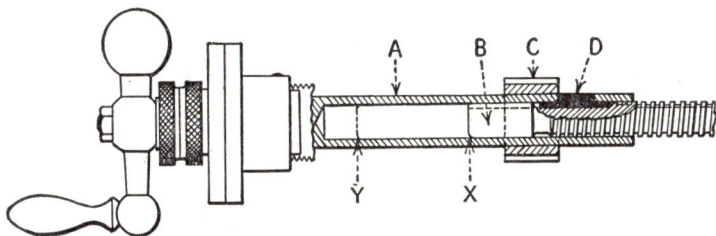

Fig. 16-8. Telescopic feed screw, the screw *B* telescoping into the sleeve *A*. The feed screw is extended to the connection with the guide block and thus governs the movement of the cross slide *C* for a given taper. The lines *X* and *Y* indicate different positions of the screw for the larger and smaller diameters of the taper. In any position, the cross slide may be fed in or out as usual because the key *D*, feathered in the screw, turns the screw and moves the cross slide.

Fig. 16-9. The taper slide *D* is provided between the cross slide *B* and the saddle *F*. When the taper attachment is not being used, *D* is tightened by the binder screw *E*, and the cross slide *B*, when fed either in or out, moves on *D* as a base. When the binder screw is loosened, the unit, comprising *A*, *B*, *C*, and *D*, is free to move on the saddle *F* as a base. In this design, the taper slide *D* serves also as a *connection* (see Fig. 16-6), and when fastened to the guide block, it is no longer free, but is controlled by the movement of the guide. The cross-feed screw *C* serves equally well whether or not the taper attachment is being used.

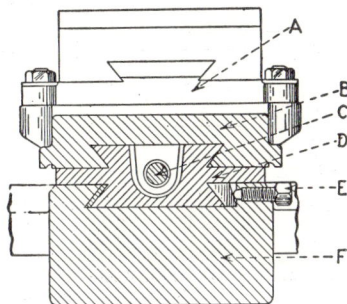

To set up and use the taper attachment, proceed as follows:

1. The guide block should not project over the end of the guide bar either at the beginning or at the end of the cut, so make sure its position is right.
2. Clean and oil the guide bar and block.
3. Set the bar for a trial cut, using the graduations.

4. Loosen the binder screws (and remember when loosening a screw that one turn is as good as half a dozen turns).

5. Oil the flat bearing surfaces of the cross-slide unit.

6. Fasten the connection to the guide block.

7. Adjust the work between centers, and set the tool.

3. Take up the lost motion and proceed to take the first cut.

Figure 16-10 shows the taper attachment in use.

Fig. 16-10. Taper attachment in use. (*South Bend Lathe Works*)

Taking Up Lost Motion. When using certain kinds of taper attachments, the machinist's enemy, "lost motion" (backlash), must be taken care of or serious trouble will result. In every slide and every freely revolving screw there is a certain amount of lost motion. This is very noticeable if the parts are worn. In a taper attachment so designed that lost motion may occur anywhere between the tool and the guide, care must be taken that the lost motion is taken up in the right direction before proceeding to cut. *Otherwise the piece will be turned or bored straight for a short distance before the* *taper attachment begins to work.* To take up lost motion when turning taper, run the carriage back toward the dead center at least ¾ in. (use a half-center if the diameter of the work is small), then feed forward by hand until the beginning of the cut, when the power feed may be thrown in. This operation must be repeated for every cut.

Boring Tapers with Taper Attachment. The best way to bore a taper in a lathe is by the use of the taper attachment (Fig. 16-7b). Extreme care must be exercised that the backlash, or lost motion, is taken care of when tapers are being bored with the taper attachment. Otherwise the hole will be bored straight for a certain distance, before the taper starts. Be sure that the boring tool is small enough to operate without rubbing at the small end of the hole.

Boring Tapers with Compound Rest. Another method of boring a taper and one often used for very abrupt tapers (or angles) is by means of the compound rest. The compound rest is set around a certain amount to cut the desired taper or angle, and the boring tool is fed by hand.

Fitting Taper Holes. Taper holes are fitted to *taper-plug gages* similarly as taper shanks are fitted to taper-ring gages.

Taper holes are usually finished by reaming.

QUESTIONS ON TAPERS

1. Having found the taper per inch, how do you know the taper per foot?

2. How many parts, that is, dimensions, must be measured to determine the amount of taper?

3. When measuring a tapered piece with a caliper or micrometer, what care must be taken?

4. In measuring the taper why do you lay off a whole number of inches and not such a distance as $3\frac{9}{16}$ in., or $4\frac{3}{32}$ in.?

5. What is the taper per inch of 0.6 in. taper per foot? Of ½ in. taper per foot? Of ¾ in. taper per foot?

6. What is the taper per foot of 0.050 in. taper per inch? Of 0.042 in. taper per inch? Of 0.062 in. taper per inch?

7. How do you try a taper in a gage? Why do you make three chalk marks? Why not one chalk mark? Why not cover the taper with chalk?

8. If the taper fits, but is too large and does not go in the gage far enough, how do you determine from the amount it sticks out how much more to turn off?

9. Suppose the shank of a reamer is 0.600 in. taper per foot, and that it is required to leave 0.010 in. for grinding. How much farther into the gage will the shank go after it is ground?

10. Is there a taper hole in the spindle of the milling machine? Drilling machine? Grinding machine? Is there any revolving spindle in the shop which does not have a taper hole?

11. What are some of the cutting tools held by means of tapers? Are they held securely? Is the friction of the taper alone sufficient to hold them?

12. What are some of the advantages of the taper in machine-shop work?

13. What is one of the most important considerations regarding tapers? What does a mechanic think of an ill-fitting or a damaged taper? What does he think of a taper that is nicked or burred?

14. Why are tangs milled on the ends of twist drills, machine reamers, and end mills? Why not on lathe centers?

15. What do you understand by the term standard taper? Name two systems of standard tapers in commercial use for holding cutting tools and state their chief difference.

16. Why will the Brown & Sharpe taper not fit in a drill press? Why will the taper shank of a chuck fitted to a lathe spindle not fit in a milling-machine collet or in a drill socket?

17. What common cutting tools are provided with Morse standard tapers?

18. In what machines are Brown & Sharpe tapers mostly used?

19. Do lathe centers have any standard taper?

QUESTIONS ON TAPER TURNING

1. If the dead center is in line with the live center, a cylinder is turned. Why?

2. If the dead center is offset, what shape is turned? Why? What does the position of the dead center determine?

3. If the center is offset toward the operator, which end of the taper is smaller? If the offset is in a direction away from the operator, which end is smaller?

4. When offsetting the tailstock, how do you take care of the lost motion in the cross-feed screw?

5. If a piece of work is 1 ft. long and the dead center is offset $\frac{1}{4}$ in., the taper turned on this piece will be $\frac{1}{2}$ in. per ft. Why?

6. If a piece of work is 2 ft. long and the offset of the tailstock is $\frac{1}{4}$ in. what will be the taper per foot? Why?

7. In the two preceding questions with the same offset we have two different tapers. Give reason.

8. Suppose the machinist has two pieces of steel, one 12 in. long and the

other 24 in. long, and it is required to turn the same taper on each piece, What will be the difference in the offset? Which piece will require the more offset? Why?

9. If the dead center is offset ¼ in. and a piece of work is turned taper a distance of 4 in., and another piece, of the same size and the same offset, is turned taper a distance of 6 in., will the taper per foot be the same in both cases? Give reason.

10. It may be stated that two factors, one of them being the offset, determine the amount of taper that will be turned. What is the other factor?

11. Does the length of the taper have anything to do with the offset? Give reason.

12. What is the rule for offsetting the tailstock when turning taper?

13. In the above rule, why divide by two?

14. How is the amount of taper given on drawings? How is it expressed in charts of standard tapers?

15. A piece of work 7½ in. long is to have a taper 4 in. long ½ in. per ft. What offset is required?

16. Calculate the amount of offset for the following:
   a. Length of work 8½ in.; taper 0.600 in. per ft.
   b. Length of work 6½ in.; taper ½ in. per ft.
   c. Length of work 9 in.; taper ¾ in. per ft.
   d. Length of work 6¾ in.; taper 0.500 in. per ft.

17. Two pieces of the same length are to be turned taper; one has large centers, the other has small centers. Which will require the more offset? Why?

18. If calculations are exactly right and setover of tailstock is made accordingly, and to a thousandth of an inch, is it safe to assume that the taper will be correct and therefore turn to size before trying it? Give reason.

19. To make sure the correct taper is being turned, how may the piece be measured with a caliper or a micrometer?

20. If a micrometer is used, why is the measurement made with the edges of the spindle and anvil?

21. Why should the cutting tool be set on center when turning taper?

22. If a tapered piece is to be duplicated, how may the tailstock be adjusted without calculating the offset? Can this be done if the new piece is longer or shorter than the sample? Give reason.

23. Under what circumstances is it proper to fit a taper by filing?

24. If the centers of the lathe were in line, but as the tool was fed along, it worked back gradually and uniformly, what shape piece would be turned?

25. In the taper attachment, how is the block guided? How is the guide bar pivoted? How adjusted? How is it tightened? Why is it tightened?
26. Explain in detail the principle and construction of the taper attachment.
27. State at least four advantages of the taper attachment.
28. On what sort of a taper would the use of both the offset and the taper attachment be advisable?

TURNING ANGLES

Angles. An angle is the amount of the divergence between two straight lines that either meet in a common point, or would meet if sufficiently prolonged. The straight lines are called the sides of the angle and the meeting point is called the vertex of the angle. An

Fig. 16-11.

angle is *measured* on the circumference of a circle drawn with the vertex as a center. The sides of the angle lay off a certain portion of the circumference. The circumference is divided into 360 parts or degrees and the number of degrees between the sides of the angle is the measure of the angle. For example, if one-fourth of the circumference is intercepted between the sides, the angle is measured by 90 deg. (one-fourth of 360 deg.), and is commonly spoken of as an angle of 90 deg., or a right angle (Fig. 16-11). Also if one-sixth of the circumference is intercepted by the sides of the angle, the angle is measured by 60 degrees, or, in other words, it is an angle of 60 deg. (Fig. 16-11). For fine angular measurements, the degree is subdivided into 60 parts called *minutes* and the minutes are subdivided into 60 parts, called *seconds*. The notations used are degrees (°), minutes ('), seconds ("). The subdivisions of seconds are not used in ordinary machine work.

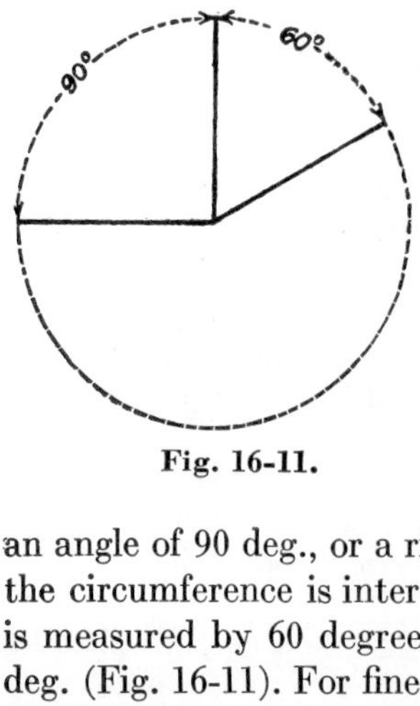

Classification of Angles

A *right angle* is equal to an angle of 90 deg.
An *acute angle* is less than 90 deg.
An *obtuse angle* is greater than 90 deg.
Two angles are called *complementary angles* when their sum is

equal to a right angle and each is called the *complement* of the other. For example, 55 deg. is the complement of 35 deg.; 35 deg. is the complement of 55 deg.; 40 deg. is the complement of 50 deg., etc.

Two angles are called *supplementary angles* when their sum is equal to two right angles (180 deg.). For example, 55 deg. is the supplement of 125 deg.

On drawings and blueprints, the angle is usually dimensioned as shown in Fig. 16-12a. In formulas and calculations, it may be named by a small italic letter as shown in Fig. 16-12b.

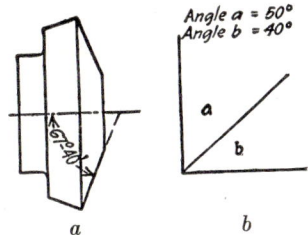

Angle a = 50°
Angle b = 40°

Fig. 16-12.

Tapers and Angles.[1] Tapering pieces up to an included angle of 8 deg.,[2] which is about 1¾ in. taper per foot, are known as tapers and are measured as having "taper per foot." Pieces which are turned or bored to an included angle of greater than 8 deg. are usually spoken of and are measured as having *included angle* or as having an *angle with the center line* (the angle with the center line is half the included angle).

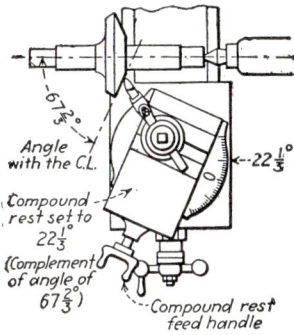

Fig. 16-13. Using compound rest for turning angles.

To illustrate: On almost all lathe centers, the shank is turned *taper* 0.600 in. per ft., and the center is turned to an *angle* of 60 deg. (60 deg. is the included angle; the angle with the center line is 30 deg.).

The Use of the Compound Rest for Turning Angles. The best method of turning an angle on a piece of work is to use a tool rest that may be swiveled on the cross slide to any desired angle. This tool rest is known as the *compound rest* (Fig. 16-13). The swivel plate of the rest is graduated in degrees, and the zero mark, which is usually on the side of the plate, is in line with a mark on the

---

[1] For table of tapers and corresponding angles see p. 530.

[2] A tapered piece over 8 deg. included angle approximately will not hold in a taper hole.

cross slide when the compound rest is at right angles to the center line of the lathe. There are a number of methods, used by various lathe manufacturers, for graduating the compound rest, but it does not make much difference whether the zero is on the front or on either side so long as the zero on the degree graduations coincides with the zero on the slide when the slide is set at right angles to the center line of the lathe. However, it is necessary to remember, when setting for a given angle, that there may be any one of several *numbers*, due to the several methods of graduating, that may represent the correct setting. Graduating the compound rest is a feature of the lathe that needs standardization.

Setting the Compound Rest. Setting the compound rest is comparatively easy if the operator realizes, first, that the compound rest is normally set at 90 deg. from the center line of the lathe; and, second, that the travel of the tool is to be at a certain angle other than 90 deg. with the center line of the lathe. In order to cut at a certain angle with the center line of the lathe, the compound rest must be swiveled either (1) the number of degrees which is the *complement* of the angle with the center line, or (2) 90 deg. plus *the angle* with the center line.

To illustrate (1): Suppose a bevel gear blank is to be turned to an angle of 67 degrees 40 minutes with its axis, that is, 67 degrees 40 minutes ($67\frac{2}{3}$ deg.) with the center line. The complement of $67\frac{2}{3}$ deg. is $22\frac{1}{3}$ deg. Set the compound rest around $22\frac{1}{3}$ deg. from its normal position (Fig. 16-13).

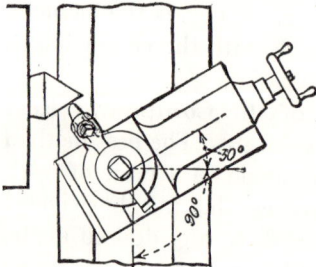

Fig. 16-14. Setting compound rest.

To illustrate (2): Suppose it is required to turn a lathe center 60 deg. included angle, the angle with the center line is then 30 deg. Swivel the rest to the right, 90 deg. from its original position; then swivel it 30 deg. more as shown (Fig. 16-14). If the compound rest were swiveled 60 deg., the complement of 30 deg., to the right it would be necessary to run the lathe backward and turn on the back side of the center. This is sometimes done. If the compound rest were set 60 deg. to the left, the handle would probably interfere with the faceplate.

There are different methods of dimensioning the degrees of the angles on a drawing. The dimension may be given as an included angle, Fig. 16-15a; as the angle with the axis, Fig. 16-15b; or as the angle with a line perpendicular to the axis, Fig. 16-15c. It is always best to find *the angle with the center line* and then set the compound rest in one of the ways suggested in the preceding illustrations. A sketch will help in determining the correct position at which to set the compound rest.

Turning the Angle. The compound rest is provided with a hand feed which is independent of the cross feed. Turning an angle is accomplished by turning the compound-rest handle. This is hand feed; there is no power feed for the compound rest. The tool will feed at the angle for which the compound rest is set, but remember, *not always according to the figures on the graduations.*

If fairly heavy cuts are to be taken, it will be a good idea to tighten the carriage-clamp screw. After the first cut is made, run the tool back to the starting point by turning the compound-rest handle; then feed in to take the next cut by moving the cross-feed handle. Be careful not to take too deep a cut, especially near the finish.

The Bevel Protractor. The instrument used in machine shops for measuring angles is called the bevel protractor (Fig. 16-16).

The principle of construction of a bevel protractor is as follows: Two members, the beam and the blade, are so arranged as to swivel on a pivot at the center of the dial, which is graduated in degrees. When the edges of the beam and blade are parallel, a small line on

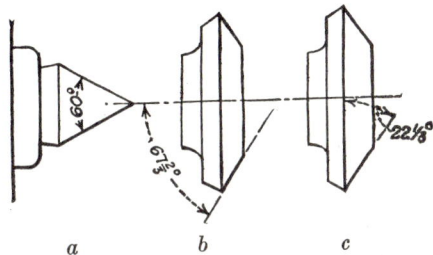

Fig. 16-15. Different methods of dimensioning the degrees of angles: (*a*) included angle, (*b*) angle with the axis, and (*c*) angle with line perpendicular to axis.

the swivel plate coincides with the zero line on the dial, and when any measurement of an angle between the beam and the blade *of 90 deg. or under* is desired, the reading may be obtained direct from the position of the line on the swivel plate with regard to the graduation numbers on the dial. *But remember this:* To obtain the measure-

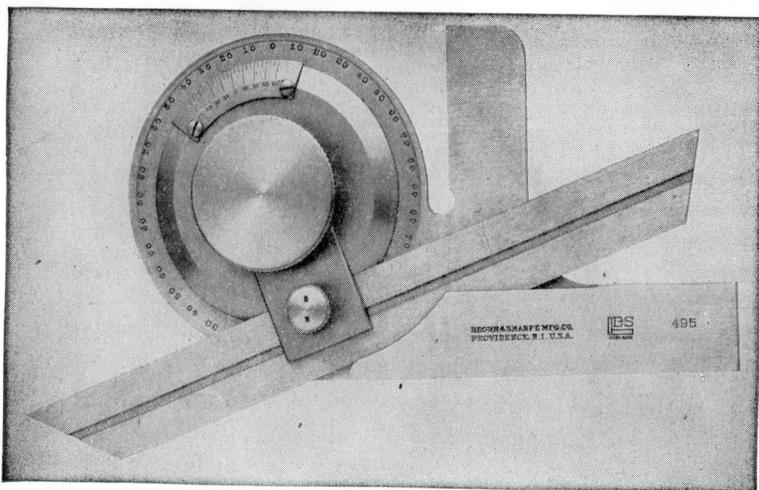

Fig. 16-16. Brown & Sharpe bevel protractor. (*Brown & Sharpe Manufacturing Company*)

ment of the angle between the beam and the blade of *over* 90 deg. subtract the number of degrees as indicated on the dial from 180 deg. As will be noted, this is because the dial is graduated from opposite zero marks to 90 deg. each way.

QUESTIONS ON ANGLES

1. What is an angle and how is it measured?

2. What is an acute angle? An obtuse angle?

3. In what way is an angle usually dimensioned on a drawing?

4. What is meant by the term included angle? Angle with the center line?

5. What is meant by the complement of an angle? Complementary angles? Give an example of each.

6. How is the compound rest of a lathe graduated?

7. If the compound rest is set around 30 deg. from normal position, what will be the included angle of the piece turned?

8. Why must extreme care be taken when setting a compound rest to turn a given angle?

9. Why is it best before setting the compound rest to determine at what angle with the center line the given cut is to be?

10. Explain the principle of the construction of the bevel protractor.

11. What caution must be taken when reading the measurement of an angle over 90 deg. on the bevel protractor?

CHAPTER 17

Threads and Thread Cutting

Screw threads are applied to many devices for various purposes. They may be used to *transmit power* and to *increase its effect*, as in an auto jack; to *control movement*, as in a micrometer; to *convey material*, as in the feed screw of a kitchen food grinder; and, of course, to *hold* parts together. Except for threads used in conveying materials, which are generally cast, the threads for all of these various uses are cut on a lathe or a thread-cutting machine belonging to the lathe family.

Thread work is a very important part of machine-shop practice. This chapter includes (1) terminology, the definitions and symbols of the parts of a thread, and the terms used in connection with making threaded parts; (2) a discussion of shapes and sizes; (3) dimensions and calculations for the parts of a thread; (4) taps and dies for cutting threads; (5) gearing a lathe for cutting threads; (6) cutting a thread in a lathe; (7) measuring a thread; and (8) brief discussion of various threading operations.

All of these are related thread subjects which an intelligent machinist must understand. It is not one lesson but at least a dozen lessons. It is not difficult to learn about threads and thread cutting, but it does call for real understanding. It cannot be learned by reading the chapter through once or twice—it must be *studied*.

THREADS, TAPS, AND DIES

Thread Standards. Until a few generations ago, each manufacturer producing threaded parts cut the threads to fit his particular ideas of the most suitable forms and dimensions. As a result, few threaded parts were interchangeable, and replacement of a simple bolt or nut usually involved making one to fit. Today, thread forms and dimensions are largely standardized in a relatively few widely accepted thread systems. The following thread systems are a few of those you will be most likely to meet.

Amercian National Thread System. By far, the most of the threads used in this country are cut according to this system. This was formerly known as the *National Standard* system, hence the old designations of NC, NF, N-8, N-12, and N-16 are still used to indicate the five series: coarse, fine, 8-pitch, 12-pitch, and 16-pitch, which make up the system. (NC stands for National Coarse threads; NF means National Fine threads; 8-pitch means that there are 8 threads per inch of length, measured along the axis of the bolt or workpiece; 12-pitch means that there are 12 threads per inch of length, measured along the axis of the bolt or workpiece; and 16-pitch means that there are 16 threads per inch of length, measured along the axis of the bolt or workpiece.)

S.A.E. Standard Thread System. This system, set up by the Society of Automotive Engineers (S.A.E.), is widely used throughout the automotive, aircraft, and related industries. It uses the same thread form as the American National system and has coarse, fine, 8-pitch, 12-pitch, and 16-pitch series identical with that system. In addition, the SAE system includes an extra-fine and a special-pitch series, and frequently only these two series are specifically designated as SAE threads.

American National Acme Thread System. This system uses the Acme thread form, the sides of which are much steeper than those of the American National and S.A.E. threads. It is standardized in a series which is fairly coarse, and the Acme thread form is frequently cut in nonstandard pitch and diameter combinations, for special purposes.

The Unified Thread System. This *new* thread is a combination of the American National form and the Whitworth thread form (a British thread), specifically designed so that parts manufactured in this country, Canada, and Great Britain may be interchangeable.

American National Pipe Thread. This thread system uses a thread form similar to the American National, except that the crest and root (these terms will be explained later in this chapter) are much narrower. In addition, it is tapered to ensure a progressively tighter fit as the matching parts are screwed together.

In addition to the standardized thread systems mentioned, there are three commonly used thread forms which are not generally standardized as to relationship of diameter and pitch. These are the *square* thread, the 29-deg. *worm* thread, and the *sharp* V thread.

Each of the above thread systems are explained and described later in this chapter. Formulas are given and sample problems are solved.

There are many thread systems used in foreign countries, but not commonly used here. These include the *British Standard Whitworth* and the *British Association Standard* systems, and the German, French, and International Metric systems. In addition, there are numerous specialized standard threads in use in this country, such as *gas fixture, American Standard hose coupling*, and *National Standard fire hose coupling*.

A working knowledge of the more common thread systems and forms will be helpful not only to those engaged in producing threads, but also to those merely interested in the maintenance of machinery as well.

DEFINITIONS: THREAD TERMS

The following terms are generally used in designating different parts of screw threads:

Screw Thread. A screw thread may be visualized as a flexible form, like a piece of string that has been wrapped around a cylinder, or the sides of a cylindrical hole, at a uniform rate of advance, producing a form known as a *helix*. It may also be considered as a raised form produced on the outside of a cylinder, or on the inside walls of a cylindrical hole, after a thread-cutting operation has been completed.

External Thread. A thread on the outside of a member.

Internal Thread. A thread on the inside of a member.

Major Diameter. The largest diameter of a screw thread. The term *major diameter* applies to both internal and external threads, and replaces the term outside diameter as applied to the thread of a screw and also the term full diameter as applied to the thread of a nut.

Minor Diameter. The smallest diameter of a screw thread. The term *minor diameter* applies to both internal and external threads, and replaces the terms core diameter and root diameter as applied to the thread of a screw and also the term inside diameter as applied to the thread of a nut.

Pitch Diameter. The diameter of an imaginary cylinder the surface of which would pass through the threads at such points as to make equal the widths of the threads and the widths of the grooves cut by the surface of the cylinder. It is equal to the major diameter less an amount equal to the single depth of thread. The allowance and tolerance in the sizing of threads are given as on the pitch diameter. Also the pitch

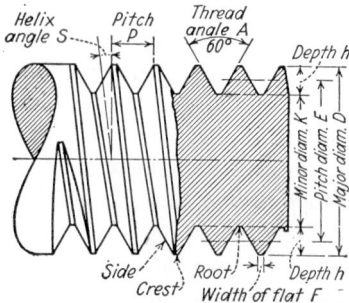

Fig. 17-1. American National screw thread.

diameter is used in determining the outside diameter of the *blanks* for rolled threads. As that part of the groove of the thread below the pitch line is rolled (depressed) into the blank the metal is squeezed up to form the part of the thread above the pitch line. Hence the diameter of the blank for rolled threads is equal to the pitch diameter of the screw to be rolled. A great proportion of commercial threads are rolled.

Axis of a Screw. The longitudinal central line through the screw.

Pitch. The distance from a point on a screw thread to the corresponding point on the next thread measured parallel to the axis.

$$\text{Pitch (in inches)} = \frac{1}{\text{number of threads per inch}}$$

Lead. The distance a screw thread advances axially in one turn. On a single-thread screw, the lead and the pitch are identical; on a double-thread screw, the lead is twice the pitch; on a triple-thread screw the lead is three times the pitch, etc.

Angle of Thread. The angle included between the sides of the thread measured in an axial plane.

Half Angle. The angle included between a side of the thread and the normal to the axis, measured in an axial plane.

Helix Angle. The angle made by the helix of the thread at the pitch diameter with a plane perpendicular to the axis.

Crest. The top surface joining the two sides of a thread.

Root. The bottom surface joining the sides of two adjacent threads.

Side. The surface of the thread which connects the crest with the root.

Depth of Thread. The distance between the crest and the root of a thread measured normal to the axis.

Length of Engagement. The length of contact between two mating parts, measured axially.

Depth of Engagement. The depth of thread contact of two mating parts, measured radially.

Thickness of Thread. The distance between the adjacent sides of the thread measured along or parallel to the pitch line.

Terms Relating to Fits

Fit. The relation between two mating parts with reference to ease of assembly. The quality of fit is dependent upon both the relative size and the quality of finish of the mating surfaces. When any classes of fits are established in machine-shop practice it means that certain allowances and tolerances are specified.

Allowance. An intentional difference in the dimensions of mating parts. It is the minimum clearance or the maximum interference which is intended between mating parts.

EXAMPLES: The following examples are of allowances for three classes, 1, 2, and 4 respectively, of screw and nut ¾ in. diameter, 10 threads per inch, American National Coarse-thread Series.

1. ¾″—10NC—1 (class 1 is the least exacting fit).

Minimum pitch diameter of nut	0.6914
Maximum pitch diameter of screw	0.6850
Allowance (positive)	0.0064

This means that the closest fitting screw and nut, class 1, will have 0.0064 in. clearance (space) (play) between sides of threads.

2. ¾″—10NC—2 (class 2 is recommended for general use).

Minimum pitch diameter of nut	0.6850
Maximum pitch diameter of screw	0.6850
Allowance (none)	0.0000

This means that the closest fitting screw and nut, class 2, will have no clearance.

3. ¾″—10NC—4 (class 4 is the most exacting fit).

Minimum pitch diameter of nut	0.6850
Maximum pitch diameter of screw	0.6854
Allowance (negative)	−0.0004

This means that the closest fitting screw and nut, class 4, will be a *tight* fit, with the screw-pitch diameter 0.0004 in. larger (maximum interference) than the pitch diameter of the nut.

Tolerance. The amount of variation permitted in the size of a part.

EXAMPLE: Screw ¾ in. diameter, 10 threads per inch, American National Coarse-thread Series, class 2 (¾″—10NC—2).

1. Maximum pitch diameter	0.6850
Minimum pitch diameter	0.6786
Tolerance	0.0064
2. Maximum major diameter	0.7500
Minimum major diameter	0.7372
Tolerance	0.0128

NOTE: In American National screw threads, all series and all classes, tolerances are applied *plus* to the threaded hole or nut, *minus* to the screw. Thus the variations from basic will always favor the free fit rather than the tight fit.

Basic. The theoretical or nominal standard size from which all variations are made.

Limits. The extreme permissible dimensions of a part. In the example given above, the sizes 0.6850 and 0.6786 in. are the limits.

    a. Clearance in nut at minor diameter is such that the basic depth of thread shall be reduced by one-sixth (or more in some cases).

    b. Tolerance in nut at minor diameter is such that the basic depth of thread may be further reduced by one-twelfth (or more for some sizes of threads).

NOTE: What (*a*) and (*b*) mean practically is this: For any class of American National form of internal thread (nuts, etc.) the tap-size drill selected may be large enough to leave only three-quarters of a full thread (one-sixth reduced for clearance, plus one-twelfth tolerance, equals one-fourth of thread and leaves three-fourths of full thread) (see Fig. 17-2) and Table 8, page 532).

Tolerance on major diameter of nut is such as to result in a flat one-third of the basic flat.

Crest Clearance. Defined on a screw form as the space between the crest of the thread and the root of the mating part.

NOTE: What the two preceding definitions mean practically is this: The crest of the tap thread forms (cuts) the major diameter of the nut, and to be sure to have crest clearance between the crest of the screw and its mating surface in the nut, the crest of the *tap* is extended. That is, the tap is made oversize on the major diameter, and instead of having the crest equal one-eighth of the pitch it may be only one twenty-fourth of the pitch. Taps are usually made with about 40 per cent truncation (Fig. 17-2*b*).

h = Basic depth
  = 0.6495 × p
  = $\frac{0.6495}{n}$

c = Clearance = ⅛ of basic depth

t = Tolerance = 1/12 of basic depth

¾h = ¾ of basic depth (or ¾ full thread in the nut)

b = Extended major diam. on tap to give say 40% truncation instead of 100% truncation as at f

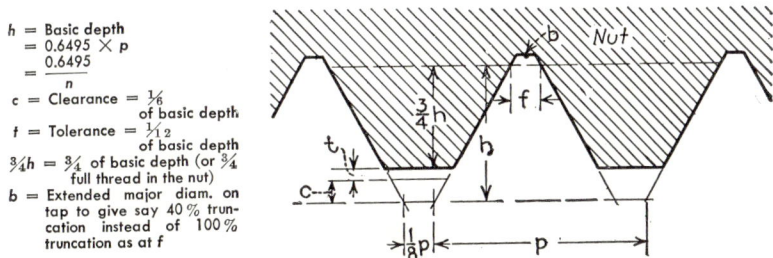

Fig. 17-2. Shows portions of a standard nut.

For other crest clearance on the screw, see "tolerance on major diameter," the second example and the note under "tolerance." For crest clearance on nut thread, see definitions under "limits."

Right-hand and Left-hand Threads. A right-hand thread advances clockwise, a left-hand thread counterclockwise. Looking at the side of a screw, the slant of the right-hand thread is down towards the right, left-hand thread down towards the left.

Wire Measurement Symbols. For method of measuring American National threads by three-wire method see page 452.

Measurement over wires	*M*
Diameter of wire	*G*
Corresponding radius (½*G*)	*g*

Dimensional Symbols. For use in formulas, on drawings, etc., the following dimensional symbols should be used:

Major diameter	D
Corresponding radius	d
Minor diameter	K
Corresponding radius	k
Pitch diameter	E
Corresponding radius	e
Angle of thread	A
One-half angle of thread	α
Number of turns per inch	N
Number of threads per inch	n
Lead	$L = \dfrac{1}{N}$
Pitch	$p = \dfrac{1}{n}$
Helix angle	s
Tangent of helix angle	$S = \dfrac{L}{3.14159 \times E}$
Width of basic flat at top, crest, or root	F
Depth of basic truncation	f
Depth of sharp V thread	H
Depth of basic American National thread	h

Identification Symbols. These are for use in correspondence, on drawings, shop and storeroom cards, specifications for parts, taps, dies, tools, and gages.

The basis of the system is the initial letters of the series, preceded by the diameter in inches (or the screw number if under $\frac{1}{4}$ in. in diameter) and the number of threads per inch. The initial letters are followed by the classification of fits, all in arabic characters. If the thread is left-hand the symbol "LH" shall follow the class of fit. No symbol is used to distinguish right-hand threads.

Examples   Mark

American National Coarse-thread Series: To specify a threaded part 1 in. in diameter, 8 threads per inch, right-hand, and class 2 fit   1″—8NC—2

American National Fine-thread Series: To specify a threaded part 1 in. in diameter, 14 threads per inch, left-hand thread, and class 3 fit   1″—14NF—3LH

American National 8-*Pitch*-, 12-*Pitch*-, *and* 16-*Pitch-thread*   2″—8N—2
Series: To specify a threaded part 2 in. in diameter   2″—12N—2
in each of these special series, class 2 fit   2″—16N—2

NOTE: The number of threads must be indicated in all cases, irrespective of whether it is the standard number of threads for that particular size of threaded part or a special number.

General Dimensions and Characteristics of Screw-thread Forms. The diagrams in this section establish the dimensional formulas used in the production of each commonly used screw-thread form. These dimensional relations must be adhered to, regardless of the size of the thread form produced. The size varies with the number of threads per inch.

The Sharp V Thread (Fig. 17-3). The sharp V-thread form is one of what is known as the *locking* threads. As a matter of fact, match-

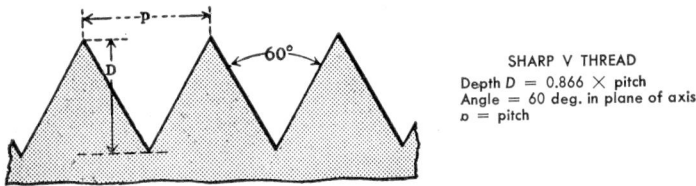

SHARP V THREAD
Depth D = 0.866 $\times$ pitch
Angle = 60 deg. in plane of axis
p = pitch

Fig. 17-3. Sharp V thread. Although the crest and root theoretically are sharp, actually they are rounded or flat. (*The Shell Oil Company*)

ing threaded parts cut to this form fit closer and will seal better than any other thread form produced, because of the wedging action of the sharp top and bottom. However, this characteristic also tends to cause the thread to jam when subjected to strain, which may result in the top of one thread galling in the bottom of the matching part, and a stripped thread is a possibility when an attempt is made to unscrew them. For these and other reasons, this thread form is seldom used except on steam fittings requiring a seal.

Another disadvantage of this thread is the fact that the sharp top of the thread can withstand very little abuse without serious damage. Its sides are at an included angle of 60 deg., as illustrated, and theoretically come to a point at both the top and bottom. However, it is practically impossible to produce this form exactly to formula, especially at the bottom, because the sharp point of the tool, having very little support, is likely to round off or break down in a short time. As a result, the bottom of the thread produced is rounded off accordingly. The sharp V-thread form may be cut on a lathe by a V-threading tool, or any of numerous types of taps and dies. There is this important difference, however: The same lathe cutting tool can be used in the production of different numbers of threads per inch, but a given tap or die is capable of producing only a given number of threads per inch.

The American National Thread (Fig. 17-4). The American National thread form is now recognized as the standard locking thread form in the United States, principally because it is similar to the sharp V thread in every respect except one—the top and bottom of the threads are *flat*. This means that the strength and locking characteristics of the sharp V thread are largely retained, yet the thread will withstand more abuse without injury. At the same time,

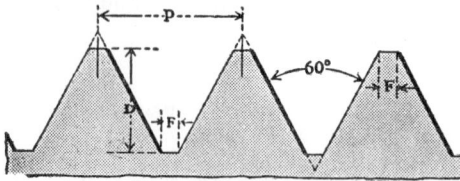

AMERICAN NATIONAL THREAD
Depth D = 0.6495 x pitch
Width of flat F = 0.125 x pitch
Angle = 60 degrees in plane of axis

Fig. 17-4. American National thread. (*The Shell Oil Company*)

the tools, taps, or dies used to produce this thread will hold their original shape much longer.

Still another advantage of this thread form is that its cross section can be held to more accurate dimensions than practically any other thread form. This is because it has an included angle of 60 deg., which is a wide angle, and because the flat crest and root are one-eighth the pitch. Thus, the tool can be fed at an angle when

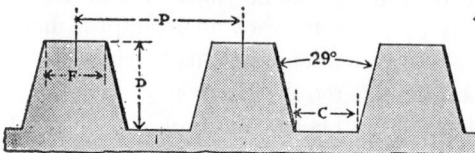

AMERICAN NATIONAL ACME THREAD
Min. depth D = 0.5 x pitch
Max. depth D = 0.5 x pitch
   + 0.010 inch
Width F = 0.3707 x pitch
Width C = width F for min. depth
Width C = width F — 0.0052 inch
   for max. depth
Angle = 29 degrees in plane of axis

Fig. 17-5. American National Acme thread. (*The Shell Oil Company*)

the thread is being cut, yet the flat end area is broad enough to withstand the forces of cutting without breaking down. This is important.

The American National Acme Thread (Fig. 17-5). The American Acme thread is classified as a power-transmission type of thread. This is because the 29-deg. included angle at which its sides slope reduces the amount of friction when matching parts are under load. Further, because of the wide root and crest, this thread form is strong and capable of carrying heavy loads.

This thread, when used on lead screws or similar parts, has a distinct advantage in that the split nut can easily be engaged and disengaged, due to the slope of the sides of the matching parts. And because the sides slope, an adjustable split nut may be compensated for wear, allowing it to seat a little closer, and thus eliminating possible backlash or lost motion. When cutting the thread, the tool

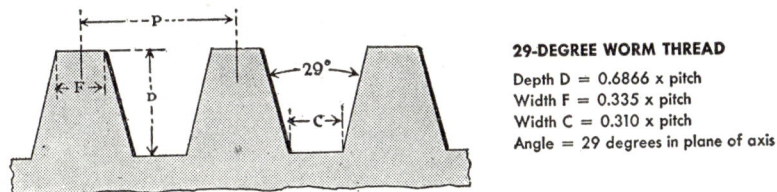

29-DEGREE WORM THREAD

Depth D = 0.6866 x pitch
Width F = 0.335 x pitch
Width C = 0.310 x pitch
Angle = 29 degrees in plane of axis

Fig. 17-6. The 29-deg. worm thread. (*The Shell Oil Company*)

is set at 90 deg. to the center line of the part to be threaded while the compound is offset 14½ deg. to the right.

The 29-deg. Worm Thread (Fig. 17-6). The 29-deg. worm thread is practically the same as the Acme. The only difference is that the depth is a little greater, while the width of the crest and root are proportionally less. This thread form is generally used where a fast or quick-action thread is required.

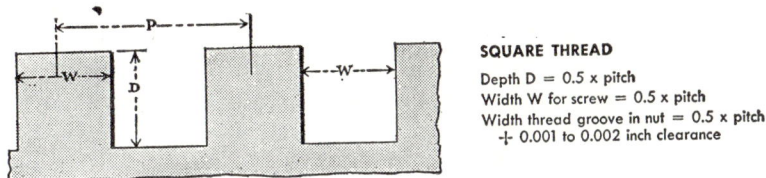

SQUARE THREAD

Depth D = 0.5 x pitch
Width W for screw = 0.5 x pitch
Width thread groove in nut = 0.5 x pitch
+ 0.001 to 0.002 inch clearance

Fig. 17-7. The square thread. (*The Shell Oil Company*)

The Square Thread (Fig. 17-7). All surfaces of the square thread form are square with each other, and the sides are perpendicular to the center of the axis of the work. The depth, as well as the width, of the crest and root are equal. Because of the relatively small contact areas and lack of wedging characteristics, friction between matching threads is reduced to a minimum. Thus, this thread form is used for maximum transmission power.

The cutting of this thread form presents some difficulty because it is square, and a thread progresses in the form of a helix. This gives the thread a slight twist. The thread groove on a nut is generally cut a little deeper to allow clearance between the crest and root of the matching parts. Some operators prefer to produce this thread in two cuts—the first taken with a narrow tool to the full depth, and the second with a tool ground to size. This procedure relieves cutting pressure on the tool nose.

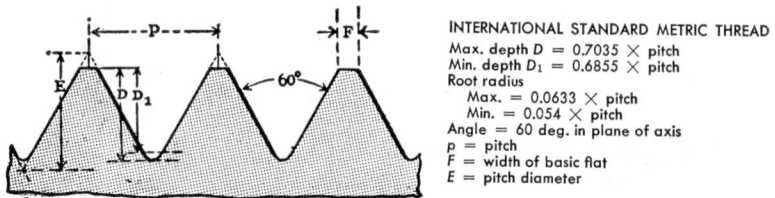

INTERNATIONAL STANDARD METRIC THREAD
Max. depth D = 0.7035 × pitch
Min. depth D_1 = 0.6855 × pitch
Root radius
    Max. = 0.0633 × pitch
    Min. = 0.054 × pitch
Angle = 60 deg. in plane of axis
p = pitch
F = width of basic flat
E = pitch diameter

Fig. 17-8. The International Standard Metric thread. (*The Shell Oil Company*)

The International Standard Metric Thread (Fig. 17-8). The International Standard Metric thread form has sides set at a 60-deg. included angle, the same as for the sharp V thread and the American National. It differs from the American National, however, in that the depth is a little greater and that the bottom is rounded to a radius of approximately $\frac{1}{16}$ of the pitch. But the top flat is the same as the American National, or $\frac{1}{8}$ of the pitch. The advantages of this thread form is the added strength provided by the greater depth, and the clearance between the flat top of one thread and the round root of a matching thread which eliminates the possibility of binding.

The method of producing this thread form is similar to that used in the cutting of the sharp V thread and American National in that the tool is generally fed at an angle of 29 deg. or 30 deg. This is an advantage in that most of the cutting is done by a side-cutting edge of the tool, and as a result the point is not subjected to so severe pressure as when fed straight in. The tool, however, should be machine-ground to assure the correct radius of the point, which is difficult to accomplish when grinding by hand. This thread form is considered one of the locking types and is not widely used in this country. In the majority of the European countries, however, it has been adopted as the standard thread.

The British Standard Whitworth Thread (Fig. 17-9). The British Standard Whitworth thread form is another of the locking threads but its sides are set at an included angle of 55 deg. instead of 60 deg. Because of this steeper slope of thread form, it has greater strength. Also, because of the long radius of the root and crest, it has exceptional locking characteristics.

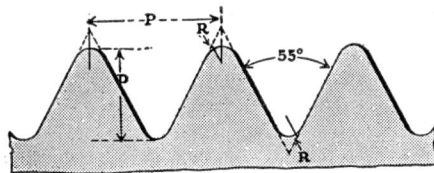

BRITISH STANDARD WHITWORTH THREAD
Depth D = 0.6403 x pitch
Radius R at crest and root = 0.137329 x pitch
Angle = 55 degrees in plane of axis

Fig. 17-9. The British Standard Whitworth thread. (*The Shell Oil Company*)

However, because the crest and root of this thread form are rounded to a specific radius, the tool must be machine-ground so that the radii and angles may be accurately cut. This means that the tool is, in effect, a forming tool and that the thread produced is a formed thread. Therefore, when cutting this thread, the tool cannot be advanced into the piece at an angle, as is possible for some of the other threads. A British Whitworth tool must be advanced directly into the piece, as is necessary when cutting a square thread.

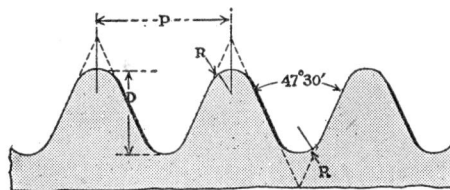

BRITISH ASSOCIATION THREAD
Depth D = 0.6 x pitch
Radius R at crest and root = 2 x pitch ÷ 11
Angle = 47½ degrees in plane of axis

Fig. 17-10. The British Association thread. (*The Shell Oil Company*)

The British Association Thread (Fig. 17-10). This thread is similar to the British Whitworth, but its use is confined to the fine-thread series or threads of $\frac{1}{4}$ in. diameter and less. Because of the small dimensions of the thread, extra strength is desirable. This is accomplished by setting the sides of the thread at an angle of 47½ deg. instead of 55 deg., which makes them slightly steeper.

The Unified Screw Thread (Figs. 17-11 and 17-12). Effort toward reaching agreement on a common system of screw threads for use in English speaking countries was started as a result of experience in the First World War. Little was accomplished, however, until the Second World War had again demonstrated the overwhelming

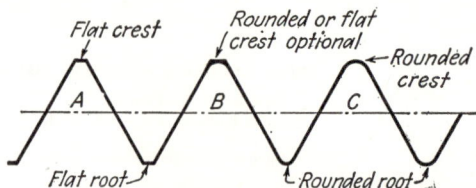

Fig. 17-11. A comparison between the American National form and the new unified form of thread. *A*, Original American National form of thread; *B* and *C*, new standard forms. (*The American Society of Mechanical Engineers*)

need for a unified thread system. Meetings of the Combined Production and Resources Board were held during the years 1943–1945. Final work was accomplished through a meeting of representatives of the A.S.M.E. (American Society of Mechanical Engineers), the S.A.E. (Society of Automotive Engineers) and the

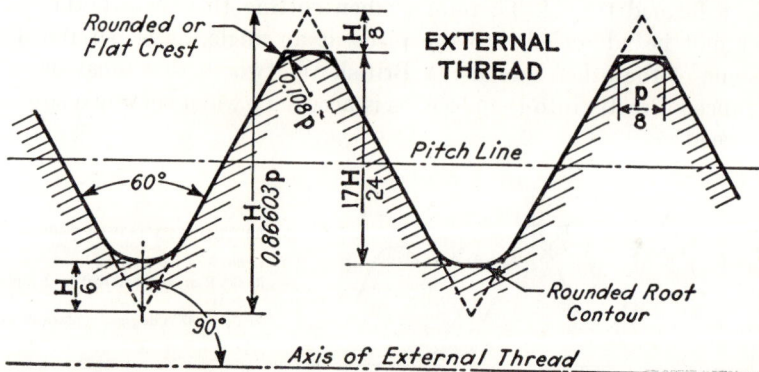

Fig. 17-12. The unified thread. $H = 0.86603p$; $p =$ pitch $= \dfrac{1}{N}$ (*The American Society of Mechanical Engineers*)

A.S.A. (American Standards Association), which worked closely with members of the standard associations, industries, and armed forces of all three nations (United States, Canada, and England).

No longer will American manufacturers who export to English-speaking countries have to maintain vast inventories of gages, taps, dies, and other tools for screw, bolt, and nut production. No longer will it be necessary to manufacture a product of one mechanical design for the American market and another for export. All in all, manufactured articles in one country will be used in the other two countries without any trouble at all. For example, United States nuts would not fit onto British bolts, and vice versa, while Canada necessarily was on a double standard, having to produce both British and American threads. The new Unified Screw Thread System will be common in all English-speaking, inch-using countries.

Figure 17-11 shows a comparison between the American National thread and the new unified thread. Notice that the crest of the new thread may either be flat or rounded while the root *must* be rounded.

Figure 17-12 shows the actual dimensions of the new unified thread.

QUESTIONS ON THREADS

1. Name four uses of threads. Give an example of each.

2. What is the function of thread standardization?

3. Name the various standard thread systems in use today.

4. What do the following stand for: NC, NF, N-12, N-16, S.A.E.?

5. What is the difference between pitch and lead of a thread?

6. Define major diameter, minor diameter, pitch diameter, pitch, angle of thread, crest, root, fit.

7. What is meant by a locking thread? Name some.

8. What are the advantages and disadvantages of the sharp V thread?

9. What is the accepted and standardized locking thread in this country?

10. What are the decided advantages of the American National over the sharp V thread?

11. How is the American National Acme thread classified?

12. What are the advantages in using an Acme thread? Where are they used and when?

13. What difference is there between the Acme and the 29 deg. worm thread?

14. Why is the square thread so seldom used today? What thread has taken its place? Why?

15. Of what importance to us in the United States are the British threads?

16. Why was the unified thread designed?

17. Of what use will the unified thread be to the peoples of the United States, Canada, and Great Britain?

18. What do the following mean?
  a. ⅞″—9 NC—2
  b. ¼″—20NF—1

Tapping in the Lathe. Tapping is the process of cutting a thread on the inside surface of a hole by means of a tool called a *tap.* For a complete description of taps, see Chapter 9, pages 226. Holes of small diameter are usually threaded by means of a tap. Work to be tapped in a lathe must be held and supported in a chuck or in the steady rest while being tapped.

The hole, whether drilled or bored, should be free of chips, before starting the tapping operation.

It is not necessary to thread a tapped hole very deep for the purpose of holding metal parts together. A good rule to follow is to make the length of the threads in the tapped hole not more than one and one-half times the diameter of the screw. This leaves a large margin of safety against stripping the thread. The shorter the length of the thread to be cut, the easier it is to cut the thread.

Tapping in the lathe may be done in two ways, namely, hand tapping and machine tapping. Hand taps are used on *blind* holes (holes that do not go all the way through). Jobs which are to be tapped for their full length should be threaded by the use of a *taper* tap or a *machine* tap (see Chapter 9). It is very difficult to use a hand tap with a power feed; the tap is likely to break under the stress induced by the power feed.

Hand tapping in a lathe takes considerable time. It is thus an expensive process and should be done only where it is absolutely necessary. The hole should not be tapped any deeper than is consistent with the strength of the threads in the tapped hole. If possible, a hole that is to be tapped should be drilled deeper than the length of the threads to be cut. This allows the taper tap to cut most of the thread, which makes for an easier tapping operation.

Taps are not easily broken if the proper lubricant is used. Lard oil, sperm oil, graphite and tallow mixtures are good lubricants to use on steel and iron. Lard oil or soap compounds are good lubricants to use when tapping cast iron which is usually cut dry. Mineral oils are poor cutting lubricants.

Pressure must be exerted to start the tap in the hole until it *bites* into the work. When the tap has been properly started, no further pressure is required because the tap will follow in the path started by the first cutting edges.

If the tap starts to cut in the right direction, it will continue to cut properly. Use plenty of cutting lubricants. An ordinary tap is a poor cutting tool because it seldom has clearance and it has no rake; the so-called *gun tap* is an example of this type of tap (Fig. 9-23).

Tap-drill Sizes. Before a hole is tapped, the proper size hole must be drilled. For a complete explanation of tap-drill sizes, see Chapter 9. However, this phase of tapping is so important for the correct size drill and tap to be used, that it is worth while to repeat some parts of it here.

The diameter of the drill that should be used on a tapped hole (American National thread) may be found by using the formula

$$T.D.S. = D - \frac{1}{N}$$

where $T.D.S.$ = tap drill size, D = diameter of the screw, and N = the number of threads per inch.

EXAMPLE: What size tap drill should be used to cut a full thread to fit a ⅞-in. American National screw?

SOLUTION: A ⅞-in. American National form thread has 9 threads per inch.

Therefore, using the preceding formula for the tap-drill size, we get

$$T.D.S. = 0.875 - \frac{1}{9} = 0.875 - 0.111 = 0.764 \text{ in.}$$

From a table of decimal equivalents, it will be found that 0.764 in. is almost equal to ⁴⁹⁄₆₄ in. Therefore, a ⁴⁹⁄₆₄-in. drill should be used.

In Table 8, page 532, you can readily determine the size of tap drill to be used for a 75-per cent thread, which is the size usually used in commercial threads. For a ⁷⁄₈-in. diameter American National thread, it will be found, if the table is consulted, that a ⁴⁹⁄₆₄-in. drill is recommended. The size of drill to be used, therefore, depends upon the type of thread to be cut; that is, a full 100-per cent thread or a 75-per cent of the full thread. In the above example, for the 75-per cent thread, a ⁴⁹⁄₆₄-in. drill is used.

OPERATION SHEET

Hand Tapping in a Lathe (Fig. 17-13)

1. Mount the work in the chuck and true-up, making sure that it is centrally located.
2. If a hole has to be drilled, center-drill the hole.
3. Secure proper size tap drill and drill hole.
4. Secure a set of three taps of the required size.
5. Place the square head of the No. 1 tap (starting tap) in the jaws of the tap wrench.
6. Tighten the jaws of the tap wrench.
7. Place the threaded end of the tap in the hole; adjust the tail-stock center in the hole in the square end of the tap (Fig. 17-13).

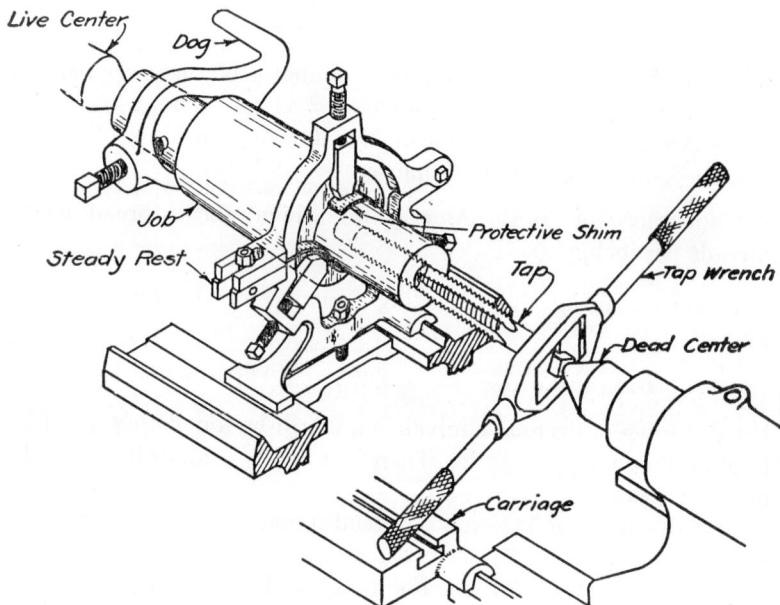

Fig. 17-13. Tapping in the lathe.

Use enough pressure so that the tap will enter the hole in the piece. Be sure that the length of the tailstock center sticking out of the tailstock is not too long but long enough to be able to force the tap through the entire length of the hole to be tapped without moving the tailstock.

8. Clamp the tailstock to the lathe bed.
9. Use oil on the tap and in the hole.
10. Move the tailstock center forward by means of the hand wheel until the tap *bites* into the job. *Do not use more pressure than is necessary.*
11 Revolve the wrench as far around the center as possible, keeping the tailstock center in contact with the job.

NOTE: If the lathe is belt driven, it is safer to have a helper pull down on the belt to revolve the job. The tap feeds in as the spindle revolves, therefore the operator must keep the tailstock center in contact with the tap so that the tapped hole will be concentric with the job.

12. Revolve the job by power if the lathe is motor driven, for about one-third of a revolution. Then stop the lathe and turn the tap by means of the wrench as far as possible.

NOTE: It is not necessary to tap the job completely in the lathe. If the threads are started right, the finishing taps (Nos. 2 and 3) will follow in the path of the starting tap. The tapping operation may then be finished on a bench where it is more easily done.

13. Continue the hand operation until the tap has cut several threads.
14. Reverse the motion of the lathe after the tap has cut three or four threads.
15. Release the tailstock center from the job as the reversing process proceeds. Proceed very carefully because the tap may easily be broken.
16. Clean the chips from the hole.
17. Continue the tapping operation by hand, as indicated, until the full depth has been reached.
18. Use plenty of cutting lubricant.
19. Test the job by means of a thread gage.

Machine Tapping. Machine tapping is generally done on a turret lathe or other form of automatic machine. A taper tap or machine tap is used. The tapping operation is usually done on a *through* hole (all the way through the hole). The taps have a long tapered section and thus each thread has very little cutting to do. Collapsible taps are used to a large extent in turret lathe work of large diameter.

When a *blind* hole is to be tapped with a power feed, some form of a friction clutch must be used. This friction clutch slips after a certain safe load has been exceeded. This prevents the tap from breaking.

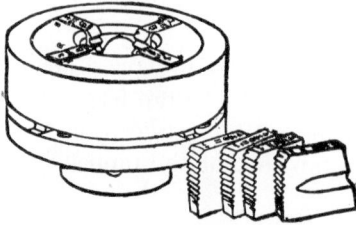

Fig. 17-14. Adjustable die. (*Pratt & Whitney*)

The Threading Die. A *die* is a tool for cutting external threads. In general the threading die is so arranged as to permit the cutting edges of four cutters or chasers to do an equal share toward cutting their shape (the form of the thread desired) into a cylindrical rod, when turned or screwed on the end of the rod for a distance of the required length of the thread.

Some dies are made solid, some in two halves within a body or head, and still others with the four separate chasers properly and securely held in the head. The last named (Fig. 17-14) is perhaps the best type since the chasers can be easily removed and sharpened. It also permits considerable adjustment which is a decided advantage when a screw slightly oversize or undersize is required, or when

Fig. 17-15. Die holder or diestock. (*Standard Tool Company*)

a roughing and a finishing cut are desirable. The complete die when locked together seems to have all the advantages of a solid die.

Most threads used in manufacturing are cut with dies in screw machines and bolt machines. Very often, however, it is practicable to size a fairly long thread or even to cut the whole thread by hand, in which case the die is held in the *diestock* or *screwplate* (see Fig. 17-15).

When threading a piece by hand the end of the rod should be

chamfered about 45 deg. for at least the depth of the thread and care must be exercised in starting the die true. As in starting a tap, pressure must be exerted when starting the die, but after it is well started it will feed itself. Use lard oil when cutting a thread on steel and wrought metals, and turn backward part of a turn occasionally to break the chip.

QUESTIONS ON TAPS AND DIES

1. Name the three taps in a tap set. What is the purpose of each?
2. What is an adjustable tap wrench?
3. What is meant by clearance on a tap? Why is it put there?
4. What lubricant is best for cast iron? Steel? Brass? Aluminum? Copper?
5. How far should a screw enter a tapped hole in order to give sufficient strength?
6. What is a blind hole?
7. Why must the lathe be run at its slowest speed when tapping?
8. Why should a tap be backed out slowly?
9. How can you chamfer the stock with a file? By what other means may it be chamfered?
10. Give two reasons for chamfering.
11. What care must be taken in starting a die? Why is it necessary?
12. Is it better to cut the entire thread in one cut or in two cuts? Why? How do you adjust the die for this?
13. What lubricant is best to use when cutting a thread on steel or wrought iron?
14. How do you protect the thread already cut on one end of a stud when threading the other end?
15. What is a die? Die holder? Diestock?
16. What is meant by an adjustable die? Solid die?
17. What advantage has an adjustable die?

GEARING A LATHE FOR CUTTING THREADS

Two types of lathes are generally used in machine shops for cutting threads. These lathes are the quick change gear lathe and the standard change gear lathe. For a detailed explanation of these types, see Chapter 10, Lathe Construction.

To cut a thread in a lathe involves the use of gears. It is therefore essential that the beginner understand the first principles of spur gearing in order to set up his machine intelligently.

DEFINITIONS: GEAR TERMS

Spur Gear. A spur gear is a toothed wheel or cylinder with the teeth parallel to the axis. The smaller of the two gears in mesh is often called the *pinion*.

Train of Gears. A train of gears is a series of two or more gears with their teeth meshed together. The motion of the first gear causes each gear in the train to move.

Bank of Gears. A bank of gears is a number of gears arranged together and revolving on, or keyed to, the same shaft or sleeve. When there is a bank of gears of different sizes arranged successively, the collection is often called a *cone of gears*.

Cluster of Gears. A cluster of gears is a unit of several gears arranged as sliding gears to give a series of speeds.

Driving Gear. In a simple gear train, the gear to which motion is first imparted is the driving gear.

Driven Gear. The gear of the simple gear train to which motion is *finally* transmitted is the driven gear, or *follower*.

Intermediate Gear. A gear in mesh between the driving and follower gears is called the *intermediate*. The purpose of an intermediate gear is to connect two gears that are too far apart to mesh with each other.

In a gear train the speeds of the gears are *inversely proportional* to the number of their teeth. For example, a driving gear has 20 teeth and a follower gear has 40 teeth; one revolution of the driving gear will engage 20 teeth of the follower gear and cause it to make one-half of a revolution, that is, the follower gear, which is *twice as large* as the driving gear will revolve *half as fast*. In the same way the follower gear *half as large* as the driving gear will revolve *twice as fast*. The speeds are not directly proportional to the number of the teeth of the gears, but are indirectly or *inversely* proportional.

In a gear train each gear revolves in the opposite direction to that of the gear with which it meshes; therefore, adding an intermediate gear serves to change the direction of the follower gear. An intermediate of any number of teeth or any number of intermediates may be used, and not change the relative velocities of the driving and follower gears.

EXAMPLE: Driving gear, 28 teeth; driven gear, 28 teeth; one revolution of the driving gear will cause one revolution of the driven gear. Introduce one intermediate of any number of teeth, say, 60 teeth, one revolution of the driving gear will engage 28 teeth of the intermediate and it in turn will engage 28 teeth of the follower gear causing it to make one revolution or the same as was obtained without the intermediate. The direction of rotation of the follower gear, however, is changed.

In simple gearing then, the size of the intermediate may be disregarded. The velocity of the driving gear is to the velocity of the follower gear inversely as the numbers of their teeth.

Gearing the Lathe for Cutting Threads. As has been previously stated, the more modern lathes are provided with *quick change gears* for feeds and thread leads. It is not enough, however, for a machinist to be able merely to move a handle or two to set the gears to cut a given thread, he must know the *reason why*. Perhaps the best way to learn about the lathe gears for thread cutting is to get an understanding of the older method of change gears, a description of which is given here. On pages 440 to 441 a brief discussion of quick change gears will be found.

Thread cutting in an engine lathe is accomplished by causing the lathe carriage to move, *positively*, a certain distance for each revolution of the main spindle.

The positive movement of the carriage is obtained by, first, connecting the main spindle to the lead screw by gears, thus transmitting any movement of the spindle, positively, to the lead screw; and, second, closing tightly the split nut upon the lead screw, thereby ensuring a positive movement of the carriage for each revolution of the lead screw.

When cutting threads in a lathe the motion of the spindle is transmitted to the *stud shaft* by the *tumbler-gear train* and from the *stud shaft* to the *lead screw* by the *change gear train* (see Fig. 17-16).

The tumbler-gear train consists of a gear keyed to the spindle, two *tumbler gears* (or *reverse gears*), and the fixed stud gear which is keyed to the inside end of the *stud shaft* (Fig. 17-16).

The two tumbler gears are intermediate gears between the spindle gear and the fixed stud gear and are so mounted on a bracket as to make it possible for the operator to have one intermediate or two intermediates in mesh between the driving and driven gears or to throw them both out of mesh with the driving gear as shown by the three positions of the handle in (Fig. 17-17).

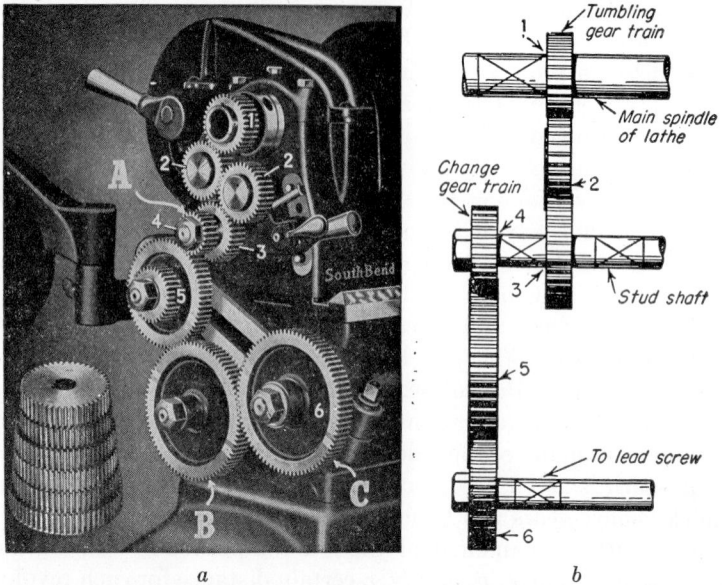

Fig. 17-16. Gearing in lathe. (*a*) *A*, Stud gear; *B*, intermediate gear; *C*, gear on screw. (*b*) Tumbling gear train: (1) spindle gear, (2) tumbling gear, (3) inside stud gear. Change gear train: (4) gear on stud, (5) intermediate, (6) gear on screw. (*South Bend Lathe Works*)

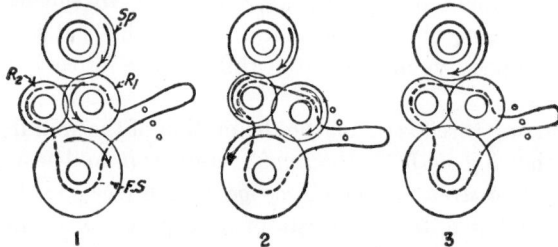

Fig. 17-17. Illustrates operation of reverse gears or tumble gears. (1) Forward, (2) reverse, (3) neutral. R_1 and R_2, Reversing gears; *Sp*, spindle gear; *FS*, fixed-stud gear.

The function of the tumbler gears is to reverse the direction of rotation of the feed rod, if for any reason it is desired to feed toward the tailstock, or of the lead screw when cutting left-hand threads. With a forward motion of the spindle and of the lead screw, the carriage advances toward the headstock and a right-hand thread is cut.

To cut a left-hand thread, the work turns forward just the same but the direction of the lead screw is reversed, thus moving the carriage toward the tailstock.

The *change gear train* (so called because the driving and follower gears may be changed at the will of the operator) consists of the *gear on stud*, the *intermediate*, and the *gear on screw* (Fig. 17-16). A series of different gears called *change gears* are furnished with the lathe and by changing the sizes of the gears on stud and screw various velocity ratios between the two may be obtained.

Operation of the Gears. When the spindle gear and the inside stud gear of the tumbler-gear train (Fig. 17-16) are of the same size, and the gears on stud and screw are equal, one revolution of the stud shaft will cause one revolution of the lead screw. If the lead screw is $\frac{1}{6}$-in. pitch the carriage will advance $\frac{1}{6}$ in. The number of threads per inch which will be cut on the work will be the same as the number of threads per inch on the lead screw.

However, *a great many lathes are made with the inside stud gear larger than the spindle gear.* Suppose the spindle gear has 30 teeth and the inside stud gear has 40 teeth; one revolution of the spindle will cause three-fourths of a revolution of the stud shaft and with equal gears on stud and screw cause three-fourths of a revolution of the lead screw.

If the lead screw is $\frac{1}{6}$-in. pitch, the carriage will advance three-fourths of $\frac{1}{6}$ in., or $\frac{1}{8}$ in., and 8 threads per inch will be cut on the work.

If the inside stud gear is twice as large as the spindle gear and the lead screw has 6 threads per inch, 12 threads per inch will be cut on the work with equal gears on stud and screw.

Lead Number. The number of threads per inch that are cut with equal gears on stud and screw is the basis of all calculations for change gears for thread cutting and is called the *lead number*. The lead number for any lathe may be found as follows: Find the ratio of the number of turns of the *spindle* to the number of turns of the *stud shaft* (whole numbers) and multiply the number of threads per inch on the lead screw by this ratio. *For example:* 4 turns of *spindle* to 3 turns of *stud shaft*, 6 threads per inch of lead screw, $6 \times \frac{4}{3} = 8 = lead$ *number.*

Any lathe with a lead number of 8 will cut 8 threads per inch with equal gears on stud and screw, and will cut 16 threads per inch if the gear on screw is twice as large as the gear on stud, or it will cut 4 threads per inch if the gear on screw is half as large as the gear on stud.

Calculating the Sizes of Gears to Cut a Given Thread. The *rule for change gears* may best be stated in the form of an equation:

$$\frac{\text{Lead number}}{\text{Number of threads per inch}} = \frac{\text{gear on stud (driving gear)}}{\text{gear on screw (follower gear)}}$$

or

$$\frac{L}{N} = \frac{D}{F}$$

By this equation the correct gears to cut any thread, whole or fractional, may be quickly ascertained.

EXAMPLE: Lead number 6; threads per inch 10; available gears 20 to 80, progression[1] 4; six-tenths is the ratio of the driving gear to the follower gear (gear on stud to gear on screw).

SOLUTION: A 6-tooth gear on stud and a 10-tooth gear on screw would cut the thread, but no such gears are available. To multiply both numerator and denominator of a fraction by the same number does not alter the ratio, therefore, multiply by 4 and the result equals

$$\frac{6 \times 4}{10 \times 4} = \frac{24}{40}$$

Use a 24-tooth gear on stud and 40-tooth gear on screw

EXAMPLE: To cut 11½ threads per inch.

SULUTION:

$$\frac{6}{11\frac{1}{2}} \times \frac{6}{6} = \frac{36}{69}$$

Use a 36-tooth gear on stud and 69-tooth gear on screw.

NOTE: A 69-tooth gear is usually furnished with a lathe.

An index plate is fastened to the side of the lathe to show which change gears to use when cutting threads. However, a specified gear

---

[1] *Change Gear Progression.* By *progression* in change gears is meant the regular increase in the number of teeth in each succeeding gear in a set of gears. The sizes of the gears increase by a certain number of teeth from the smallest to the largest gear—in the above case by 4 teeth from 20 teeth to 80 teeth.

may be mislaid or broken, or a thread not given on the plate may be required. The *thinking* mechanic is *resourceful.*

Compound Gearing. Suppose the smallest gear available is a 24-tooth gear and it is necessary to have the follower gear revolve one-sixth as fast as the driving gear; for example, to cut 36 threads with a lead number of 6. In a simple train this would require a 144-tooth follower gear $\left(\dfrac{6}{36} = \dfrac{24}{144} \right)$. If such a gear is not available, or if the center distance between the shafts does not permit of its use, an arrangement known as compound gearing may be used to obtain the required result.

Either arrangement in Fig. 17-18 (*a* or *b*) illustrates a compound of two simple gear trains. While the compounding gears *B* and *C*

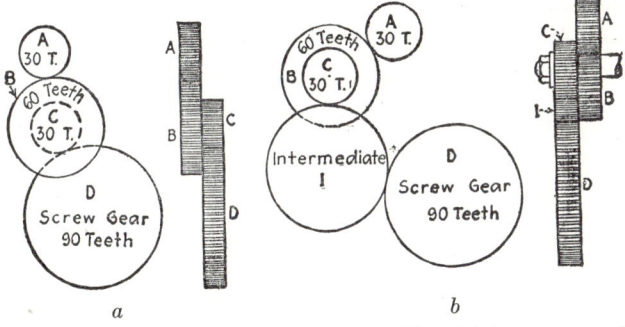

Fig. 17-18. Illustrates compound gearing. *A*, The driving gear, and *B*, the follower gear of the first train; *C*, the driving gear, and *D*, the follower gear of the second train.

are arranged between the original driving gear *A* and the final follower gear *D*, it is evident that their sizes are not disregarded as is an intermediate in a simple train of gears. Suppose gear *A* to revolve 6 r.p.m., *B* would revolve three times, *C* keyed to the same shaft as *B*, would revolve three times and would cause *D* to revolve once because *D* has three times as many teeth as *C*. The gears *B* and *C* are together known as the compound. In many lathes a compound is furnished with the machine. It consists of two gears, one having twice as many teeth as the other, fastened together and arranged on a special bracket between the stud gear and the intermediate. This is illustrated in Fig. 17-18*b*, the gears *B* and *C* forming the compound. In other lathes provision is made to substitute compounding gears for the intermediate as shown in Fig. 17-18a.

In compound gearing the velocity of the original driving gear is to the velocity of the final follower gear, inversely as the product of the driving gears is to the product of the follower gears. The formula used for a compound train is the same as for a simple train if D equals the *product* of the driving gears and F equals the *product* of the follower gears. Therefore to ascertain the proper gears to use for compound gearing the same rule is used to find the four gears as for finding the two gears in a simple train, namely:

$$\frac{\text{Lead number}}{\text{Number of threads required}} = \frac{\text{driving gears}}{\text{follower gears}}$$

EXAMPLE: Required to cut 28 threads per inch, lead number 6, progression 4.

SOLUTION: Arrange the ratio of the lead number to the number of threads to be cut (6:28) as a fraction $\frac{6}{28}$ and factor. Then,

$$\frac{6}{28} = \frac{2 \times 3}{4 \times 7}$$

Now multiplying the numerator 2 and the denominator 4 by the same number does not change the value of the fraction and multiplying 3 and 7 by the same number does not change the value of this fraction. Multiplying 2 and 4 by 16 equals $\frac{32}{64}$, and multiplying 3 and 7 by 8 equals $\frac{24}{56}$; that is,

$$\frac{6}{28} = \frac{2 \times 3}{4 \times 7} = \frac{32 \times 24}{64 \times 56}$$

Gears 32 and 24 are the driving gears and 64 and 56 are the follower gears. If a compound gear in a 1:2 ratio is furnished with the machine it may be used instead of the 32 and 64 gears. If either the 24 or the 56 gear is not available multiply 3 and 7 by any number which will give two gears that are available; for example, multiplying by 12 gives 36 driver and 84 follower, and these gears may be at hand.

NOTE: One of the best examples of compound gearing in the machine shop is to be found in the back gears.

THREAD CUTTING

Preliminary Hints on Thread Cutting

1. Grind the thread tool accurately to gage (center gage, Fig. 17-19).

2. Do not grind the point flat for pitches under $\frac{1}{20}$ in.; round it slightly with an oilstone.

3. Set the compound rest 30 deg. to the right. This gets the compound-rest handle away from the cross-feed handle and also makes it easy to adjust the tool to catch the thread if necessary.

4. The cutting point of a thread tool should be exactly on center, and the cutting edges set exactly to gage (Fig. 17-20). Do not jam the thread tool into the V of the gage, but leave a little space between. With the gage against the work, move one side of the little V against one cutting edge of the tool and, by holding a piece of paper underneath, see if the light is shut out. If one side is all right try the other side, and thus check the grinding of the tool.

5. The friction feed is never used when cutting a thread. Be sure the feed-control knob is not

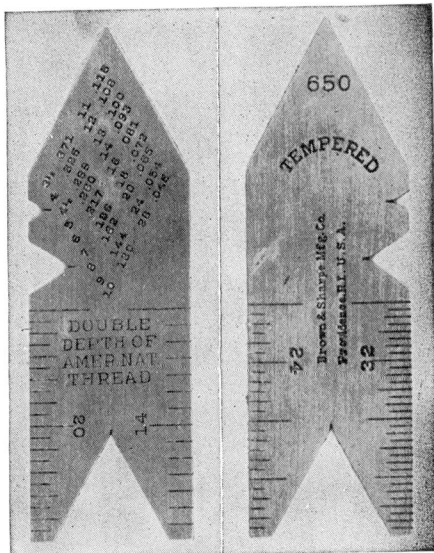

Fig. 17-19. A center gage. (*Brown & Sharpe Manufacturing Company*)

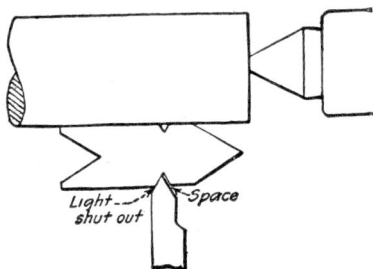

Fig. 17-20. Setting the thread tool.

tightened. Having the split nut and the feed both in will break the apron when the lathe is started.

6. *Be sure* the gears are right for the pitch required. Many jobs are spoiled by carelessness in this respect. Measure the pitch after the first light cut. This may be done by counting the number for 1

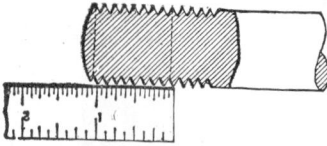

Fig. 17-21. Eight threads per inch.

in. or for ½ in. (Fig. 17-21), but a screw-pitch gage (Fig. 17-22), is quicker and there is less chance of error.

7. Be sure that the split nut is closed *tight* on the lead screw. If the threads on the nut do not go into the grooves of the screw, move the carriage a trifle by hand.

8. See if there is plenty of clearance for the dog when the thread tool is at the end of the cut.

9. If the thread being cut is of steel or wrought iron, apply good lard oil or cutting compound with a brush. Do not cut dry, and do not slush the lathe.

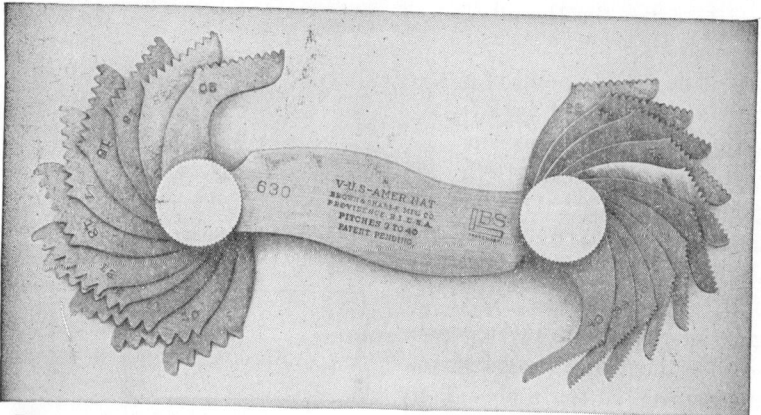

Fig. 17-22. Thread-pitch gage. (*Brown & Sharpe Manufacturing Company*)

10. If there is more than one slot in the faceplate, mark the one used with chalk. If necessary to remove the work from the lathe be sure to put the dog in the marked slot otherwise the thread will be "split" and ruined.

11. Even with a sharp thread tool, a burr will form on top of the

thread. This burr should be rubbed off with a file before the finish cut is taken.

12. If the outside diameter is the correct size, the depth of the thread may be gaged fairly close by the amount of the flat left. When approaching the finish, work carefully. It is often advisable, especially when cutting several screws, to first rough the threads. Finish with a keen tool correctly ground to 60 deg. and take light cuts.

13. To correct a ragged appearance of the first thread, the end of the work should be chamfered. This is done, usually after the thread is finished, by opening the split nut and hand feeding the thread tool carefully against the corner and chamfering it to the depth of the thread.

The Thread Stop. It is usually advisable for the beginner to use the thread stop (Fig. 17-23). The thread stop A is arranged on

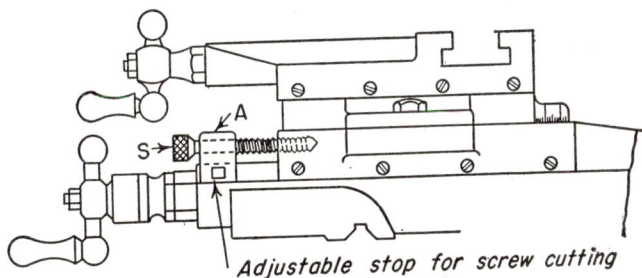

Fig. 17-23. Thread stop, A, for screw cutting. S is the adjustable screw.

the carriage in front of the cross slide and the screw S slides freely in a hole in the stop and screws into a hole in the cross slide. Turn the screw S until it enters the hole in the cross slide $\frac{1}{4}$ in. or more. Set the thread tool by the gage, and on center, and run the cross slide in until the point of the tool nearly touches the work to be threaded. Then by clamping the stop, the cross slide (and tool) cannot be fed in except as the screw S is loosened.

In order to feed the thread tool in a certain definite amount for each cut, the screw S is loosened sufficiently to allow the tool to move this amount. The feed, of course, should be less as it approaches the full width of the cut, that is, as it approaches the finish of the thread. Many machinists prefer to use only the graduations of the cross-feed screw for gaging the depth of cut. It will probably save time and trouble, especially for the beginner, to use both the thread stop and the graduations.

Four Ways of "Catching the Thread" after Resetting the Tool. If it is necessary for any reason to remove the tool before the thread is finished, *the tool must be reset accurately to gage*, and then, using one of the following methods, make sure the tool exactly enters the partly cut groove. Be careful to have both the work and the carriage as if going forward rather than reverse, that is, be sure all backlash is taken up.

1. If the lathe is provided with a compound rest, adjust the tool to the desired position in the groove by manipulating the cross-feed handle and the compound-rest handle.
2. If the lathe is not provided with a compound rest loosen the dog and turn the work until the tool enters the groove centrally.
3. If this is impractical, put the reverse-gear handle in neutral position and revolve the work *forward* by hand, until the tool is exactly opposite the groove; then connect the reverse gears as before.
4. Another way is to disengage the intermediate gear from the screw gear and revolve the spindle forward by hand until the tool will enter the groove of the thread centrally, then reengage the intermediate.

Using the Apron-control Handle. Some lathes are provided with an apron-control lever to start, stop, or reverse the apron without stopping the spindle. This lever, at the right of the apron, serves to move a single-tooth clutch between the forward and reverse gears within the headstock.

The fact that the clutch is single tooth keeps the revolutions of the stud gear exactly timed with the revolutions of the spindle, and therefore the thread tool will exactly enter the groove to take succeeding cuts. If there were two teeth instead of one on the clutch member, the thread tool would, just as likely as not, exactly split the thread rather than enter the groove.

Operation of Cutting a Thread in a Lathe. The following operations are performed when cutting a screw thread in a lathe equipped with a threading or chasing dial and a quick change gearbox. This is a common job, done especially by apprentices and by most machinists. The apprentice should learn how to cut a thread with the greatest possible speed and accurateness.

The step-by-step procedure in cutting an American National form thread is as follows:

OPERATION SHEET

1. Select stock to be threaded.
2. Face both ends using a facing tool.
3. Center stock, first making sure that the live and dead centers are in line.
4. Mount stock between centers in the lathe.
5. Turn the piece to the proper outside diameter. Use a round nose tool. "Mike" the piece to make sure that the diameter is correct.
6. Chamfer the right end of the piece.
7. Set the gearbox for the correct number of threads per inch.
8. Set the lathe for the proper cutting speed which is four times slower than for ordinary turning.
9. Set the compound rest at 29 deg. for thread cutting.
10. Place a right-hand threading tool, ground to the American National form, in a toolholder and tighten. Leave about ½ in. of the tool protruding from the toolholder.
11. Place the toolholder in the tool post and adjust tool so that the point is exactly at the same height as the point of the dead center.
12. Hold the tool in this position and tighten the tool-post setscrew.
13. Set the tool with the aid of a center gage to the center line of the lathe.
14. Adjust threading stop.
15. Adjust lead screw so that the carriage runs from right to left or toward the headstock for a right-hand screw.
16. Move the carriage so that the tool clears the end of the job.
17. Adjust the cross slide into the stop with the cross-feed screw.
18. Set the compound-rest micrometer collar to 0.
19. Calculate the proper depth of the cut.
20. Start the lathe.
21. Adjust the tool to take a cut about 0.002 in. deep with the compound-rest screw.

22. Engage the half nuts (see Chap. 10, page 257).
23. Take a trial cut.
24. After cut has been taken, move the tool away from the work, toward you.
25. Disengage the half nuts. Stop the lathe.
26. Check threads, that is, make sure that you are cutting the required number of threads per inch. Use a thread-pitch gage if necessary.
27. Move the carriage back so that the tool clears the end of the work.
28. Move the cross slide in to the stop.
29. Adjust the compound-rest screw to take about a 0.005-in. cut.
30. Start the machine and engage the half nuts. Use cutting oil now.
31. Take a cut across the entire length to be threaded.
32. At end of cut, disengage the half nuts and repeat the operations until the thread has been cut to the proper depth.
33. Finish the end of the thread by cutting a 30-deg. chamfer on the end, or round the end with a forming tool.
34. Check threads once more, using the proper thread gage.

How to Cut a Screw Thread in a Lathe without a Threading Dial. The thread is cut in the same manner as using the threading dial. The only difference is that the half nut is not disengaged when the carriage is reversed. The half nuts are engaged when the thread is started and left in that position until the cutting of the thread is completed.

When the tool gets to the end of the part to be threaded, the tool is backed away from the work and the machine is reversed. This runs the carriage backward. When the carriage is run far enough back to clear the work, the cross slide is screwed against the thread stop. The machine is again run in the forward motion, taking the second cut in the material. These operations are repeated until the thread is completed.

The apprentice should take special care when the machine is reversed so that the point of the tool does not strike the lathe center, breaking the point of the tool. Although this method is much slower than by using the dial, the thread produced is much better because the half nuts are never disengaged from the lead screw. This seems to be the better procedure because the half is always in the same relative position.

Measuring Threads

The Three-wire Method. The three-wire method of measuring pitch diameters of screw threads is recommended by the Bureau of Standards at Washington, D.C., and by the National Screw Thread Commission as the best means of securing uniformity. This method is accurate and satisfactory when properly carried out.

Today industry no longer uses odd sizes of soft drill rod for measuring purposes but demands highly accurate, hardened, and lapped cylinders, or wires, of the correct size for the part to be measured.

The three-wire method consists in measuring the pitch diameter of a thread over the diameters of three small wires. Two of these wires are inserted between the threads and measuring anvil of the micrometer on one side and the third wire is placed on the opposite side midway between the two wires (see Fig. 17-24). The size of wire that touches exactly at the mid-slope of a perfect thread of a given pitch is termed as the *best sized wire* or *best wire* for that pitch.

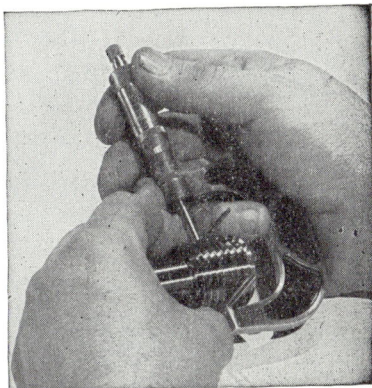

Fig. 17-24. Measuring threads by the three-wire method.

Larger and smaller wires may be used to measure external threads if the wires are not so large as to contact the corners of the thread, or so small as to give a measurement over the wires less than the outside or major diameter of the screw being measured. However, wires close to the "best size" give the most accurate results. In any case, the use of wires of extra size is to be avoided.

Great care must be taken not to apply too much pressure in making the measurement over the wires.

The three wires are of the same size and this size may be determined by the formula for G shown below. After calculating G and placing the wires on the screw as shown in Fig. 17-24, make the measurement with the micrometer.

Measuring the American National Form of Thread

FORMULAS:

$$M = D + 3G - \frac{1.5155}{N} \qquad G = \frac{0.57735}{N}$$

where M = measurement of the wires, D = major diameter of the screw, and N = the number of threads per inch.

EXAMPLE 1: Find the pitch diameter of an 1″—8 NC thread.

SOLUTION: 1. Calculate the value for G.

$$G = \frac{0.57735}{N} = \frac{0.57735}{8} = 0.0722$$

2. Calculate the value for M.

$$M = D + 3G - \frac{1.5155}{N}$$
$$= 1.000 + 3 \times 0.0722 - \frac{1.5155}{8}$$
$$= 1.000 + 0.2166 - 0.1894$$
$$= 1.2166 - 0.1894 = 1.0272″$$

If the threads are perfect, the micrometer will read 1.0272 in. If the reading is above this figure, then the threads must be brought to that dimension by further cutting. If below, then the threads are cut too deep and the piece is scrapped.

The Van Keuren Company, manufacturers of thread-measuring instruments, has simplified the mathematical procedure shown in Example 1 by calculating a wire constant or the amount to be *subtracted* from the measurement over the wires to get the pitch diameter of the screw. This constant is plainly printed on the label of the glass or plastic container holding the wires. To further help the machinist and reduce the amount of time necessary for mathematical calculations when making measurements over wires, this company has calculated the best-sized wires for many pitches of threads.

EXAMPLE 2: Find the pitch diameter of an 1″—8 NC thread.

SOLUTION: 1. Calculate or look up the best-sized wire to use.
2. Secure these wires and arrange on screw as shown in Fig. 17-24.

3. Make the measurement over wires with a micrometer. It should read 1.0272 in.

4. *Subtract* the wire constant 0.10826 that is printed on the label of the container.

$$1.0272 - 0.10826 = 0.91894 \text{ in.}$$

5. By checking the basic pitch diameter of an 1″—8 NC thread, you will find that it should be 0.9188 in. This thread is slightly oversized but accurate enough for practical purposes.

Notice that in both examples, the measurement over the wires are exactly the same. You may use either method if necessary but be sure to have the wire constants if you use the second method.

Measuring the V Thread. In the V thread, instead of using the constant $1.5155/N$, the constant $1.732/N$ is used.

Measuring the Whitworth Thread. In the Whitworth form of thread the constant $1.6008/N$ is used, and for "three times the diameter of the wire" in the rule, substitute "3.1657 times the diameter of the wire."

The Use of the Compound Rest for Cutting Threads. The great disadvantage of the thread tool cutting on both sides of the 60-deg. angle is the fact that it cannot have rake and cut correctly. If a thread tool that is supposed to cut an equal amount on each side of the angle is given rake from one side, the other side will automatically be given a *negative* rake and will not cut. The objection to back rake is shown in Fig. 17-25. It will be observed that any

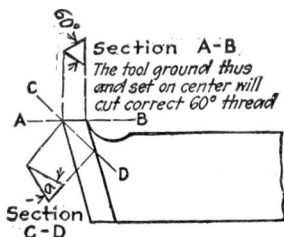

Fig. 17-25. If top rake is ground on tool as on line *C-D*, the angle *a* is much less than 60°.

angle of back rake decreases the angle between the cutting faces, and this angle grows smaller as the rake is increased.

If, however, the lathe is provided with a compound rest, a tool having side rake as shown in Fig. 17-26a may be used.

Set the compound rest so that the tool may be fed in at an angle of 30 deg. to form one side of the thread. Some machinists prefer to use 29 deg. instead of the 30 deg., claiming that the difference in setting permits a scraping action of the following edge of the tool. Grind the tool to 60 deg. and set it with the center gage as usual, Fig. 17-26b. The setup is shown at Fig. 17-26d.

The thread stop is used as a stop only and not to gage the depth of cut because the tool is fed into the work by the compound-rest handle. One side of the tool does all of the cutting (Fig. 17-26c) and may be given the desired rake. The adjacent side, if the tool is properly ground, will just clear the other side of the thread. That

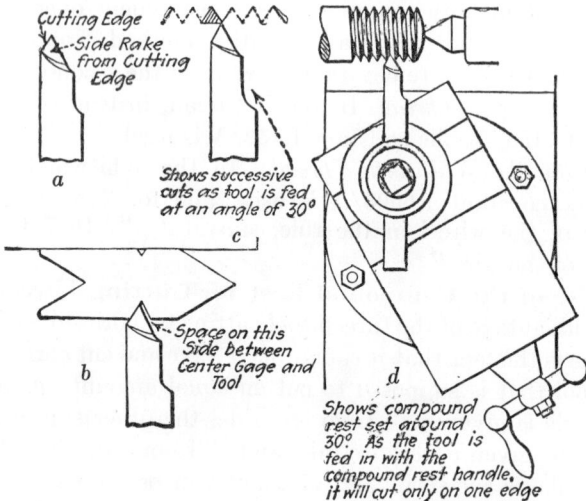

Fig. 17-26. Use of the compound rest for cutting threads.

is, the tool is pulled out of the groove at the end of the cut and fed back to the stop just before the start of the next cut, but the successive cuts, to make the groove deeper and deeper, are fed in by moving the compound-rest handle.

This method of cutting threads is recommended as being two or three times as fast as with a tool having no rake.

Cutting a Thread without the Reverse Belt. Sometimes when cutting a long thread the time wasted in the return of the tool from the end of the thread is a serious consideration, so serious that some shop foremen forbid the use of the reverse belt[2] when thread cutting.

[2] *Reverse Belt.* Sometimes called the *back belt* and often the *cross belt.* It reverses the direction of rotation of the countershaft and consequently of the machine spindle.

To cut a thread without the reverse belt, the tool is withdrawn at the end of the thread, as is the usual practice, but, instead of reversing the lathe, the split nut is opened and the carriage run back by hand a certain *definite distance*, at which point the split nut may be closed and the operator be assured that the tool will track in the original groove. This definite distance depends of course on the length of the thread but it also depends on the pitch of the thread being cut, and on the pitch of the lead screw.

Many lathes are now equipped with a chasing dial (see Fig. 17-27). A brass plate giving directions for using the chasing dial on

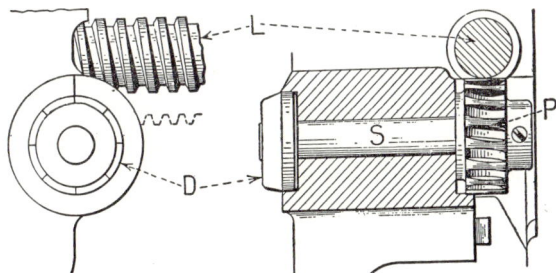

Fig. 17-27. Thread chasing dial: *D*, dial; *L*, lead screw; *P*, pinion engaging lead screw. In some lathes, the position of the shaft *S* is horizontal as above; in others, it is vertical. The operation is the same.

the particular lathe is screwed to the lathe. The dial (being connected with a small gear which meshes into the threads of the lead screw) is caused to revolve once for every 4 in. travel of the carriage. The dial is graduated into eight divisions; consequently each division will indicate travel of the carriage of ½ in. and show at a glance the time when the lead screw and carriage bear exactly the same relative positions as before, at which time the split nut is closed and the thread tool will track.

If the lathe has no chasing dial, the place to close the split nut may be determined as follows:

1. If the number of threads required is the same as the number of threads on the lead screw, close the split nut at any point.

2. If the number of threads on the lead screw is a factor of the number of threads required, close the split nut at any point.

3. For all other even threads, close the split nut at any ½-in. distance from the stopping point, if the number of threads on the

screw is even; if lead screw is odd, close the split nut on any inch distance from the stopping point.

4. For all odd threads close the split nut on any inch distance from the stopping point.

5. For half-threads (for example 11½ threads per inch), close the split nut any 2-in. distance from the stopping point.

It is advisable to mark the definite distance from the stopping point of the carriage, perhaps with a lead pencil on the ways of the lathe. Then when the carriage is run back by hand to this mark the split nut will properly engage the lead screw and the thread tool will track. This operation is often spoken of as *catching the thread.*

To Cut a Left-hand Thread. To cut a left-hand thread it is necessary to reverse the direction of rotation of the lead screw. This causes the carriage to move toward the tailstock with a forward motion of the spindle. When cutting a left-hand thread start the cut on the end of the thread nearest the dog (usually in a groove already turned) and cut toward the tailstock. Set compound rest 30 deg. to the left.

To Cut a Thread on a Taper. When cutting a thread on a tapering piece (for example, on a pipe) the thread tool should be set square with the *center line* of the piece to be threaded. The taper attachment is best and, if available, should be used; if one is not available, and the piece is provided with centers, the tailstock may be offset to give the desired amount of taper. If the work must be held in a chuck and the lathe is not provided with a taper attachment, a fairly good job can be done by slowly feeding the tool towards the operator as the work turns.

The Square Thread. For transmitting motion an Acme thread or a square thread is nearly always used, as for example on a lead screw or on a feed screw. These threads are much used for obtaining and maintaining pressure as on vise screws and jackscrews.

If one has learned to cut an American National thread intelligently, he should have no great difficulty in learning quickly to cut a square thread. That is, if it is understood that the centers must be true and in line; that the tool must be the right shape with sharp cutting edges, set accurately to gage and on center; that there must be room for the carriage to travel without interference from the beginning to the end of the thread; that the gears must be right for the given pitch of thread; that the depth of the cut is important; and that smoothness of the finished thread is very necessary, then nine-tenths of the art of cutting any kind of thread has been learned.

The chief difference in cutting a 60-deg. thread and a square thread is in the tool, although it should be added that to cut a square thread probably calls for patience, carefulness, and strict attention to a somewhat greater degree.

The Square-thread Tool. Although the square-thread tool (Fig. 17-28a) looks something like a short cutting-off tool, it differs in

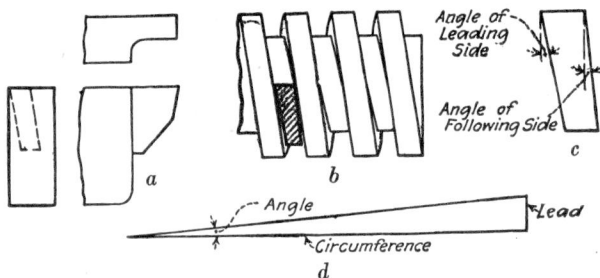

Fig. 17-28. The square-thread tool.

one very important respect: The blade is not square with the bottom as in a cutting-off tool but is canted to conform to the "slant"[3] of the thread. This is illustrated in Fig. 17-28b. Before attempting to make a tool for cutting a square thread one should know how to determine the correct amount of slant of the tool for the given thread.

The amount the tool slants depends upon two things: (1) The slant angle changes for each different *lead* of thread on a given diameter. The greater the lead the greater the angle. (2) It changes for each different diameter of thread of any given lead. The larger the diameter the less the slant.

In addition to the slant which the tool blade must have, it must be made thinner toward the bottom, otherwise it could not enter

[3] The reason that the thread slants is because it is a helix, and the amount the thread slants depends on the helix angle, "the angle made by the helix of the thread at the pitch diameter with a plane perpendicular to the axis."

the thread at all, let alone have clearance, because a piece with parallel sides cannot fit in a curved slot, and the groove of a square thread is a curved slot. The slant of the leading side of the tool therefore must be greater than the slant of the following side of the tool. But notice that both slant in the same general direction (Fig. 17-28c).

The amount of the slant of either side for any thread may be represented by a right triangle (Fig. 17-28d). One of the right-angle sides equals the *lead* of the thread and the other the *circumference* (1) of the minor diameter of the thread for the leading side, and (2) of the major diameter of the thread for the following side. The number of degrees of slant is measured between the hypotenuse and the side representing the circumference (Fig. 17-28d). (The triangle may be drawn to larger scale if desired.)

EXAMPLE: Find the slant of the following side and of the leading side of the blade of a tool for cutting 1¼ in.–4 square threads.

SOLUTION:

Lead equals 0.250 in.
Major diameter = 1.250 in.
Minor diameter = 1.000 in.
   1.250 in. × 3.14 = 3.92 in. = circumference (major diameter of thread).
   1.000 in. × 3.14 = 3.14 in. = circumference (minor diameter of thread).

Draw a right triangle, one right-angle side equal to 0.250 in. (lead) and the other equal to 3.92 in. (circumference of major diameter); draw the hypotenuse and measure the angle between the circumference line and the hypotenuse. It will equal 3⅔ deg. as nearly as can be measured with a bevel protractor. This is the angle of the following side. Draw another right triangle with L (lead) equal to 0.250 in. and C (circumference) equal to 3.14 in. (circumference at the minor diameter of thread); draw the hypotenuse and measure the angle. It will equal 4½ deg. as nearly as can be measured with the protractor. This is the angle of the leading side.

Another way of finding the slant angles of a square-thread tool is by means of a simple calculation if a table of tangents is at hand.

On the next page the above example is solved by this method. The portion of the table of tangents given is sufficient for any square thread.

Clearance. Theoretically a cutting-off tool need have no side clearance, but for practical purposes it must be given clearance, say, 1 deg. on each side, or it will rub. In the same way a square-thread tool must have clearance; *in addition to its theoretical shape* it must be made still thinner at the bottom, say, about 1 deg. on each side (Fig. 17-28b). Suppose the square-thread tool in the example just solved is given 1-deg. clearance on each side; then the angle to grind on the leading side will be the calculated angle *plus* 1 deg. (4½ deg. plus 1 deg equals 5½ deg.), and on the following side the angle will be 1 deg. *less* than the calculated theoretical angle (3⅔ deg. *minus* 1 deg. equals 2⅔ deg.). This is illustrated in Fig. 17-29. It is difficult at first to reason why the clearance on a square-thread tool is plus on one side and minus on the other, but it is very necessary to understand it. It is a typical machine-shop problem.

Suggestions. Have the tool a trifle wider than half the pitch, say, 0.003 in. on a quarter-inch pitch thread (tool, 0.125 plus 0.003 in.).

Fig. 17-29. Showing the *theoretical* and the *clearance* angles for a 1¼-in., four square threads.

Most machinists prefer to grind the tool in a surface grinder or in some other exact way rather than by hand.

If impracticable to grind it, then file the annealed tool to shape and harden and temper it.

If many threads are to be cut, it will be advisable to set a blade of the right thickness in a toolholder having a slot milled to fit the blade and at an angle to conform to the slant of the thread. The part of the blade that projects from the holder may be given clearance by grinding a little on each side, making it a little thinner at the bottom. Do not, however, change the thickness of the top of the tool, that is, the width of the cutting edge.

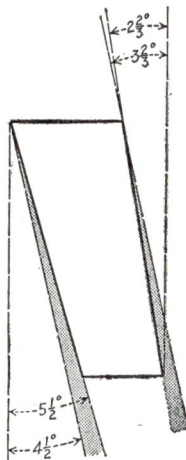

Cutting a Square Thread. The operation of cutting a square thread differs in no particular respect from cutting an American National thread. If the thread is half-inch pitch or greater it is usually advisable to cut it somewhat narrower with a stocking tool before finishing. Some mechanics prefer to finish the sides of the thread with a side tool; others prefer the regular square-thread tool ground to full size. In any event the object is to secure a thread with smooth sides. Proceed as follows:

OPERATION SHEET

1. Set the work in the lathe. Be sure the centers are in line. Tighten the dog on the work securely, using a protecting piece of soft brass or copper, and adjust the work fairly tight between centers with plenty of oil (check up on this adjustment occasionally because the strain of the cut tends to enlarge the dead-center hole).
2. Set the compound rest at an angle 30 deg. to the right. This is to get it out of the way of the cross-feed handle, and to be able to use it later if necessary to catch the thread.
3. Set the lathe for lead of thread desired; oil lead screw and ways.
4. Set the tool to the left of the tool rest, on center and square.
5. Put in the split nut and "cut air" to the end of the thread. This is to make sure that there is room for the travel of the carriage to the end of the thread, and also that the thread will end exactly in the center of the hole, if a hole has been drilled for this purpose. If necessary move both the compound-rest feed and the cross feed until the thread ends exactly in the hole.
6. Run the tool in to touch the work, note the graduation, and calculate what the graduation should read when the thread is cut the full depth (depth equals one-half pitch plus three or four thousandths for clearance).

   Square- and Acme-threaded screws are frequently designed to permit the end to be turned for a distance of $\frac{1}{16}$ in. or more to the minor diameter size. This helps in determining when the thread has been cut full depth. The tool as set for the thread may be used to turn this short shoulder distance.
7. If the length of the thread warrants it, use the chasing dial.
8. Proceed to cut the thread full depth and fit to a nut or gage. Feed-in for each cut will depend upon size of thread, say, 0.005 to 0.010 in. for a $\frac{1}{4}$-in. pitch. Use lard oil or cutting compound.

The Square-thread Tap. A tap may be used to finish the inside thread; or several taps, each succeeding tap being larger, should be used to cut the smaller threads, especially when fairly long in proportion to diameter.

When making a square-thread tap the thread is somewhat wider than the groove in order that the screw that goes into the tapped hole will have a trifle clearance on the side. Also the diameter of the tap should be a few thousandths oversize to prevent the outside of the screw thread from rubbing in the tapped hole. Further, the groove should be cut a trifle deeper than the root diameter because this part of the tap does not cut since the hole for the thread is bored at least full root-diameter size. Great care must be taken to back off the sides and top of a square-thread tap clear to the cutting edge, but only a very little. If too much clearance is given a tap, chips will wedge between the tap and the thread when turning the tap backward thus scoring and perhaps spoiling the thread.

The Acme Thread.[4] The Acme thread (Fig. 17-30) is intended to take the place of the square thread because (1) it is easier to cut

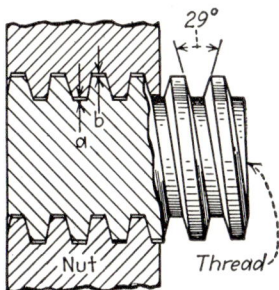

Fig. 17-30. Acme screw in nut: *a*, clearance of 0.010 in. is obtained by cutting the thread 0.020 in. larger than the major diameter of the screw; *b*, clearance of 0.010 in. is obtained by making the major diameter of the tap 0.020 in. larger than the major diameter of the screw.

Acme threads with taps and dies, and (2) the Acme thread is stronger.

It is important to know about the standard clearance in Acme threads. The bearing between any screw and nut is on the *sides* of the threads, and clearance is provided between crest and root, in American National form, square, Acme, and other shapes. The *tap-drill size*, that is, the hole in the nut, is made large enough and the major diameter of the tap is made enough oversize to take care of the clearance.

[4] Table of Acme threads, page 534.

The square thread, external and internal, has sides parallel and the depth is equal to one-half the pitch, plus a small amount for clearance (no standard amount).

The Acme thread has sides forming an angle of 29 deg., and the normal or working depth is equal to one-half the pitch. The clearance, for both crest and root, is 0.010 in. *for all sizes of Acme threads.* To get this, the major diameter of taps, for all pitches of Acme threads, are made 0.020 in. oversize to give 0.010 in. major-diameter clearance in nuts and other internal threads, and Acme thread tools are properly shaped[5] (to gage) and the screws are cut 0.010 in. deeper (than normal) to give minor-diameter clearance in the threads.

Having these clearances provided in the tap and in the screw, the minor diameter of the Acme nut or other internal Acme thread is the normal minor diameter

$$D - \frac{1}{n}$$

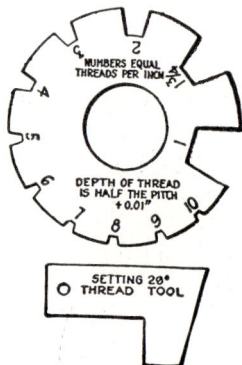

Fig. 17-31. Gages for grinding and setting Acme-thread tools.

Cutting an Acme Thread

1. The Acme-thread tool, external and internal, is ground to gage for the pitch required (see Fig. 17-31).

2. The screw thread is cut 0.010 in. deeper than half the pitch on all sizes of threads. That is, minor diameter always equals

$$D - \frac{1}{n} + 0.020 \text{ in.}$$

3. The tap is turned 0.020 in. over major diameter of screw. It is cut with the same width of tool as the screw thread, and the minor diameter is the same for tap and screw.

4. The hole for the nut or other internal Acme thread is made a size equal to the major diameter minus an amount equal to the pitch $\left(D - \frac{1}{n}\right)$. This minor diameter will have clearance since the screw thread is cut 0.010 in. deeper than half the pitch.

[5] The end of the tap thread and the end of the thread tool are extended 0.010 in. and are consequently narrower than the normal shape of the thread.

5. The side of an Acme thread is 14½ deg.; therefore move the compound rest 14½ deg. to the right when cutting a screw, to the left when boring an internal thread. Set the thread stop and feed for successive cuts by moving the compound-rest handle.

6. The procedure for cutting a square thread may be followed when cutting an Acme thread (see page 460).

Boring an Internal Thread. Cutting an internal thread of whatever shape is to cutting an external thread as boring is to turning—a little more care for the spring of the tool, a little more difficulty in measuring. The compound rest is moved around to the *left* instead of the right, and the tool (cross slide) is moved towards the operator for the cut, away from the operator before reversing. Make the setup carefully, follow directions when cutting the first thread and the second will be easy.

1. Internal threads are best finished with a tap, but if no tap is available the thread must be bored to size. If the piece to be fitted is heavy or awkward to handle it will save time and trouble if a cheap gage is made before the thread is started. To make such a gage, take careful measurement of the thread to be fitted and cut a short screw of the same diameter and pitch.

2. It will be wise for the beginner to make a sketch of the internal thread to be cut. Give the sizes of the major diameter, depth of thread, and minor diameter, in thousandths of an inch. Except in special cases, the hole for *American National form of thread* may be larger than the exact minor diameter by an amount equal to one-half the single depth of thread (one-half of 0.6495 in. $\times p$). For a *square thread* the hole should be bored a trifle (0.005 in.) over the minor diameter (square-thread minor diameter equals major diameter of screw minus an amount equal to the pitch). *For example:* Minor diameter for 1⅛ in.—4 square thread equals 1.125 minus 0.250 equals 0.875. The hole will be bored about 0.005 larger or 0.880. For the *Acme* thread the hole is bored 0.020 in. over the minor diameter. To obtain the size to bore the hole for an Acme thread, subtract an amount equal to the pitch from the major diameter of the thread.

3. Nearly always, it is necessary to bore the hole to a certain size before cutting the thread, first to have the hole run true; second, to give it the correct size. It may be advisable to have two tool bits

and possibly two complete boring-tool holders, one for boring, the other for threading. An excellent boring-tool holder (with the bit set at right angles to the bar, as required for cutting threads) is shown top view, in Fig. 15-26, page 392.

4. If the thread is not to go all the way through, an inside recess should be bored. This recess (Fig. 17-32) is a groove at least as

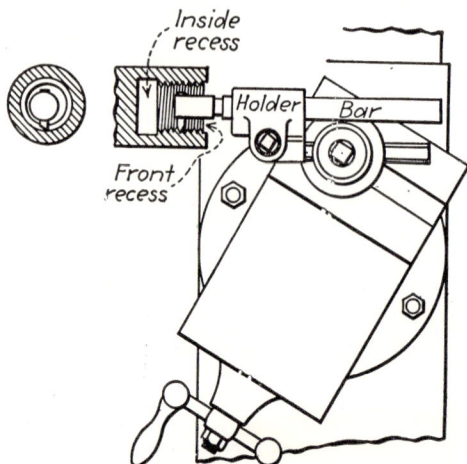

Fig. 17-32. Showing setup for boring a thread. The compound rest is set around to the left 30 deg. for the American National thread, 14½ deg. for an Acme thread. Set the thread stop as explained in the text and use the compound-rest handle for feeding successive cuts.

deep as, and somewhat wider than, the thread, for the thread to run into.

5. It will be easier to bore the thread if the tool has rake, as explained on page 453; therefore set the compound rest around 30 deg. as shown in Fig. 17-32. It is better to set the compound rest around (1) to get the handle away from the cross-feed handle, and (2) to make it easier to reset the tool if necessary. (For a square thread, set the compound rest around, but *feed* with the cross-feed handle. For an Acme thread, set the compound rest around 14½ deg. and feed with the compound-rest handle.)

6. The thread tool is carefully ground with special attention to clearance and sharpness.

7. To prevent unnecessary spring, the bar of the tool should be reasonably large in diameter and caught as short in its holder as the length of the thread will permit. Set the thread tool on center.

8. In most cases it will be permissible, before proceeding to cut the thread, to bore a slight front recess, equal to the major diam-

eter, to act as a gage for the depth of the thread. This small shoulder may be bored with the thread tool after it is set for threading.

9. Set the thread stop to act in a double capacity, in one direction to limit the size of the cut, in the opposite direction to prevent the tool from being run too far back, in which event it will rub off the top of the thread.

10. It will be advisable to have some mark, on the bar perhaps, that will indicate the point of reversal.

11. Have the setup right, proceed carefully, use cutting oil for steel. The depth of successive cuts will depend upon conditions. The cut with 60-deg. thread tool is merely a deep line at first—wider and wider as the finish is approached, but less depth of cut on account of the increasing width.

Cutting Metric Screw Threads. A meter, the standard of length in the metric system of measurement, is equal to 39.37 inches.

For purposes of finer measurement the meter is divided into 100 equal parts called centimeters and the centimeter into 10 equal parts called millimeters.

Therefore a millimeter is equal to 0.03937 inch ($\frac{1}{1000}$ of a meter or $\frac{1}{1000}$ of 39.37 inches). Also if 39.37 inches (one meter) equals 1000 millimeters *one inch equals* 25.4 *millimeters* (1000 millimeters divided by 39.37).

In all threads except the metric it is customary to speak of the number of threads per inch, that is, the thread of $\frac{1}{13}$-in. pitch, for example, is thought of and spoken of not as a "$\frac{1}{13}$ pitch" thread but as "13 threads per inch." In the metric thread, however, it is the usual practice to think and speak in terms of pitch and the pitch of the thread is given in millimeters. [See Appendix for list of tables: French (Metric), Standard, and International Standard Threads.]

For example the 26-mm. thread (1.024 in. diameter) has a pitch of 3 mm. (0.118 in.).

In order to determine the number of threads per inch of a metric thread it is necessary to divide 25.4 by the pitch in millimeters. That is,

$$\frac{25.4}{\text{pitch (in mm.)}}$$

is the number of threads per inch.

The formula for gearing a lathe to cut any desired number of threads per inch is:

$$\frac{\text{Lead number}}{\text{Number of threads per inch required}} = \frac{\text{driving gears}}{\text{follower gears}}$$

Substituting "pitch (mm.)" for the "number of threads per inch required" in the above formula and

$$\frac{\text{Lead number}}{\dfrac{25.4}{\text{Pitch (in mm.)}}} = \frac{\text{driving gears}}{\text{follower gears}}$$

Suppose the lead number is 8 and the pitch is 3 mm., then:

$$\frac{8}{\dfrac{25.4}{3}} = 8 \div \frac{25.4}{3} = 8 \times \frac{3}{25.4} = \frac{24}{25.4}$$

The denominator being fractional, both terms of the fraction are multiplied by 5 (in this case) to get a whole number.

$$\frac{24 \times 5}{25.4 \times 5} = \frac{120}{127} = \frac{\text{driving gear (stud)}}{\text{follower gear (screw)}}$$

Now 127 is a prime number (it cannot be factored) so it is impossible to cut a metric thread on a lathe with an English-measure lead screw without a 127-tooth gear, and, further, this gear is always a *driven* or *follower* gear. It is called a *translating* gear.

In the above example 120 stud gear and 127 screw gear will serve, but few lathes are equipped with a gear of 120 teeth.

It will be necessary to compound.

$$\frac{120}{127} = \frac{60 \times 2}{127 \times 1} = \frac{60 \times 40}{127 \times 20} = \frac{60 \text{ and } 40 \text{ (driving gears)}}{127 \text{ and } 20 \text{ (follower gears)}}$$

Some lathes are provided with compounding gears in the ratio of $\frac{50}{127}$, especially for cutting metric threads. In such lathes the gears on stud and screw may be figured to conform to this compounding ratio. Thus in the above example:

Factoring $\frac{120}{127}$ to obtain 50 in the numerator will give

$$\frac{120}{127} = \frac{50 \times 2.4}{127 \times 1} = \frac{50 \times 96 \text{ (driving gear)}}{127 \times 40 \text{ (follower gear)}}$$

or

$$\frac{50 \times 48 \text{ (driving gear)}}{127 \times 20 \text{ (follower gear)}}$$

or

$$\frac{50 \times 72 \text{ (driving gear)}}{127 \times 30 \text{ (follower gear)}}$$

Multiple Threads. In a single thread the lead is equal to the pitch.

A double thread is one having two thread pitches to one lead; a triple thread has three pitches to one lead; a quadruple thread has four pitches to one lead, etc. These threads are known as multiple threads and are much used in machine construction and may be of any recognized form of thread (Fig. 17-33a, which represents a square thread).

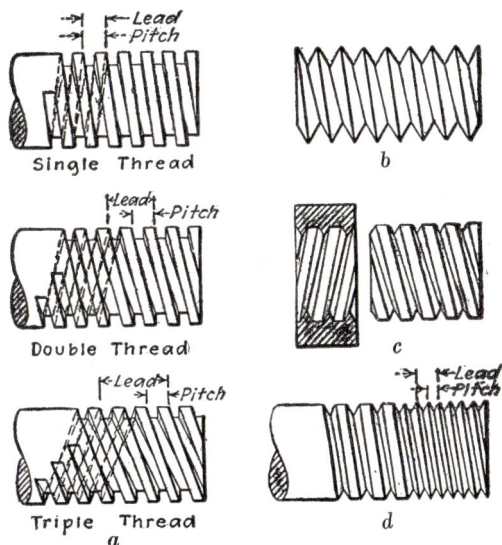

Fig. 17-33. Multiple threads: (a) square thread, (b) single-cut screw, (c) thread cut half the depth as that in (b), (d) double thread.

Suppose it is required to operate a part of a machine by screw action; that the movement must be ¼ in. per revolution of the screw; and that the diameter of the screw cannot be over 1 in. A single-cut screw of 1 in. diam. ¼-in. pitch will look like Fig. 17-33*b*, which is not a good-looking screw and moreover the cross section at the root of its thread is proportionally weak. If a thread of the same *lead* but half the depth were cut, it would look like Fig. 17-33*c*, still faulty in appearance and the nut would be very weak, in fact only half as strong as it should be.

If a thread of the same depth as in Fig. 17-33*c* is cut halfway between the grooves of the first thread as shown in Fig. 17-33*d*, the *double thread* will be pleasing in appearance and of the required strength. It is, of course, understood that the nut also must have the double thread.

Cutting a Multiple Thread. To cut a double thread (American National, for example), proceed as if cutting a single thread of the *required lead* until the thread is half the depth, and the groove is half the width of a single thread *of the same lead*. It is then necessary to give the work exactly half a turn without turning the lead screw. This may be accomplished by having a special faceplate with the slot for the tail of the dog exactly opposite the one used for the thread groove already cut.

In the absence of an accurately slotted faceplate, the method used is to disengage the intermediate gear from the screw gear and move the lathe spindle (and the work) one half turn. Before disconnecting these gears bring a tooth of the stud gear exactly between two teeth of the intermediate and mark this tooth with chalk. The distance this tooth moves shows how much the spindle has moved and here is where a serious mistake is liable to occur.

If the gear on spindle and the inside stud gear are of the same number of teeth, the marked stud gear will move one-half revolution when the work is turned half around, but most lathes are now constructed with the spindle gear smaller than the inside stud gear in a ratio of 3:4 or 2:3. This means that the stud gear will not go half around; it will go three-fourths or two-thirds of half around as the case may be.

Suppose the spindle gear has 30 teeth and the inside stud gear has 40 teeth; the ratio is 3:4. Instead of the marked stud gear revolving half around it will revolve three-fourths of one-half revolution, or three-eighths revolution. For this reason it will be necessary to select a stud gear with a number of teeth divisible by 8.

Beginning with the tooth *next* to the marked tooth count (in the proper direction) the number of teeth necessary to show the half revolution of the spindle and mark the last one. Turn the spindle to bring that tooth into exactly the proper position with respect to the intermediate gear and engage the screw gear.

The principle of cutting triple threads and quadruple threads is the same as for cutting double threads.

QUESTIONS ON CUTTING A THREAD IN A LATHE

1. How is thread cutting accomplished in an engine lathe?
2. What is the purpose of the tumbler gears?
3. Why are there a number of change gears furnished with the lathe?
4. With equal gears on stud and screw, the lathe will cut a certain number of threads per inch. This is called the lead number. The lead number may or may not be the same as the number of threads per inch on the lead screw; give the reason for this.
5. State a rule or formula in the form of a proportion that will serve for calculating change gears.
6. If the lead number of a lathe is 8, what gears are suitable to cut 12 threads per inch? 10 threads? 6 threads? 11½ threads?
7. In any lathe, does it make any particular difference how many teeth the intermediate gear has? Give reason.
8. Why is the intermediate gear adjustable on the bracket? Why is the bracket adjustable?
9. What is meant by compound gearing?
10. When is compound gearing used in thread cutting?
11. With a lead number of 6, gear progression 4, what gears may be used to cut 36 threads per inch?
12. What is the object of having a flat on the top of the thread? On the bottom?
13. What is the angle of a thread tool (American National)?
14. What gage is used when grinding the thread tool?
15. How much clearance has a thread tool? Which side? Why?
16. Why is the point rounded slightly instead of being flattened an exact amount? How is it rounded?
17. If a thread tool is to cut on both sides of the angle, can it be given rake? Give reason.
18. Why is it wrong to pinch the gage between the tool and the work? How should the gage be used?

19. What is the purpose of the thread stop? How is it arranged?

20. Why is it necessary to withdraw the thread tool at the end of the thread before reversing?

21. Why do you use a lubricant? How is it applied?

22. How much of a chip is advisable when cutting a thread? Why not more?

23. How do you judge when the thread is nearly cut?

24. How do you remove the burr from the thread?

25. Which is the better method of gaging a thread, with a nut or by the three-wire method?

26. When gaging with a nut, can you tell exactly how much more you have to cut? Can you tell with the three-wire method?

27. Why do you use three wires instead of two?

28. Why is a $\frac{1}{32}$-in. wire too small for $\frac{1}{10}$-in. pitch thread? Why is $\frac{1}{4}$-in wire too large? How do you judge the size?

29. State the rule for measuring American National threads by the three-wire method.

30. Why is the three-wire method particularly valuable if a special tap is to be made?

31. If for any reason the tool is removed before the thread is finished, what care must be taken when resetting it?

32. State two ways of resetting the tool central with the part of the thread already cut.

33. When resetting the tool why must the lost motion of the lead screw be taken into consideration?

34. What is meant by change-gear progression in a lathe?

35. Is it advisable to use the compound rest when cutting a thread? Give reasons.

36. Explain the setup for using the compound rest for thread cutting.

37. Explain the way in which a left-hand thread is cut in a lathe.

38. What is the advantage of the chasing dial on the apron of the lathe?

39. Is the chasing dial necessary when cutting threads without the reverse belt? Explain.

40. What gear is necessary when it is desired to cut a metric thread with a lead screw of $\frac{1}{8}$-in. pitch? Why?

41. When is a double thread used?

42. How is a double thread cut in a lathe?

CHECKING THREADS

Mass production demands that all pieces manufactured be thoroughly checked for size, finish, and many other factors. These pieces must be correct for the dimensions specified if they are to fit the mating parts.

There are many threaded parts that must fit their mating parts. If the threads are too shallow or too deep, they will not fit and thereby time, money, and materials are wasted. Nuts have to fit bolts and studs have to fit mating parts. In order that such parts be correct, they are checked very carefully by *thread gages*, which may be considered as standard equipment for all machine shops doing threading.

Thread Gages. In dealing with thread gages, we must remember that a screw thread must be formed in accordance with certain

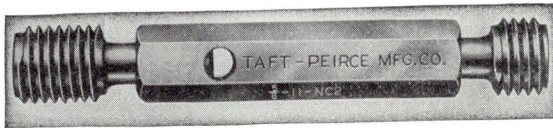

Fig. 17-34. A plug-type thread gage. (*The Taft-Peirce Manufacturing Company*)

established dimensions for each type of thread. For this reason, a thread gage is designed to check at one time the major diameter, the minor diameter, the pitch, and also whether the threads have been properly formed to ensure a correct fit. Figure 17-34 shows a thread gage designed to check an internal thread having a major diameter of ⅝ in., 11 threads per inch, National Coarse type of thread, and for a No. 2 fit. The longer end is the "go" gage and the shorter end, the "no go" gage. The "go" gage checks all the features just mentioned, but the "no go" gage checks only one thing, that is, whether the threads are so cut to make a proper contact or fit with the mating part when assembled. Figure 17-34 is usually called a *plug*-type gage.

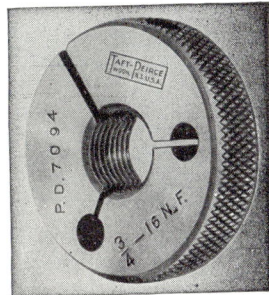

Fig. 17-35. A ring-type thread gage. (*The Taft-Peirce Manufacturing Company*)

Figure 17-35 illustrates a *ring* gage used for checking external threads. This type also has the "go" and "no go" sizes. The gage is designed to check a ¾-in. major diameter having 16 National Fine threads per inch. The pitch diameter is also shown for this size.

Until recently, no more than one and one-half turns of the "no go" gage were permissible for acceptance of the part; but, under new provisions of the National Bureau of Standards, a "no go" thread plug gage may enter a threaded hole for the full length of the gage and still be acceptable, provided the gage fits snugly after three full turns. Likewise, a thread ring gage may engage an ex-

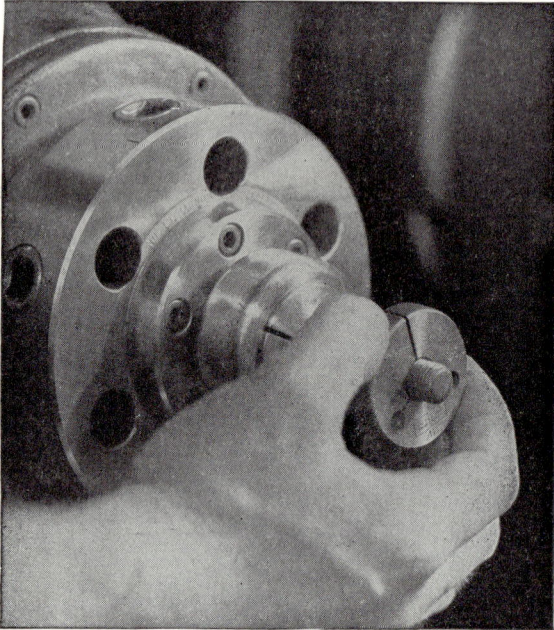

Fig. 17-36. A ring-type thread gage being used. (*The Taft-Peirce Manufacturing Company*)

ternal thread for its full width, provided there is no shake after four full turns.

This applies to a No. 3 fit. For No. 1 and No. 2, $3\frac{1}{2}$ turns are permitted for internal threads and $4\frac{1}{2}$ turns for external threads. For a No. 4 fit, 2 turns are allowed, and for a stud fit, $1\frac{1}{2}$-turns.

Thread plug gages, used for checking internal screw threads, usually have a chip groove cut the full length of the gage to pick up any loose chips of metal or bits of dirt in the threads. However, if the hole appears not to be clean, it should be cleaned out before using the gage. The gage should enter the hole easily and be run down to the bottom of the hole. The gage should not rock or show a loose fit.

When the gage is in the hole, see if the handle of the gage is square with the work. If not, the hole has been improperly drilled or tapped at an angle. When a hole does not go completely through a piece (a blind hole), check to see if it has been cut deep enough as the specifications on the blueprint.

Thread ring gages are the counterpart of the thread plug gage and are used to check external threads. Figure 17-36 shows a ring thread gage being used.

Fig. 17-37. Using a roller-type thread gage. (*The Taft-Peirce Manufacturing Company*)

A convenient tool widely used for gaging external threads is the *roll thread snap gage* (Fig. 17-37). This is capable of much more rapid work and use than the other types. The work should pass the "go" rolls freely and of course should be stopped by the "no go" rolls. Figure 17-38 shows such a thread gage being used on work mounted in the machine.

Figure 17-39 shows a plug thread gage being used in checking a number of pieces having the same size thread. This procedure is usually carried on by an inspector in the machine shop.

Fig. 17-38. Using a roller-type thread gage on a piece mounted on the machine. (*The Taft-Peirce Manufacturing Company*)

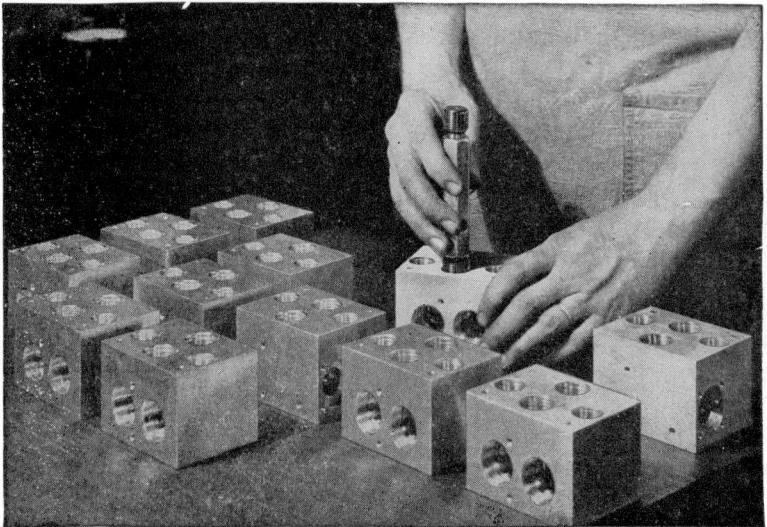

Fig. 17-39. An inspector using a plug-type thread gage. (*The Taft-Peirce Manufacturing Company*)

How to Select the Proper Thread Gage. When selecting the proper thread gage for a specific size thread, read the blueprint *first* to make sure of the size of the thread. Then, secure that size from the toolroom or the rack on which the gages are kept. Before using the gage, read the size on the gage (they are marked) and check once more with the print.

Pipe Threads. Pipe threads may also be checked using thread plug and ring gages. The procedure is similar to that used for regular threads.

Checking Threads with a Thread Micrometer. The thread micrometer may be used to check the pitch diameters of threads. These micrometers have a pointed spindle and a double-V anvil. Both are correctly shaped to contact the screw thread. The micrometer reading gives the true pitch diameter in thousandths of an inch. This equals the outside diameter less the depth of one thread. Figure 17-40 shows a thread micrometer being used.

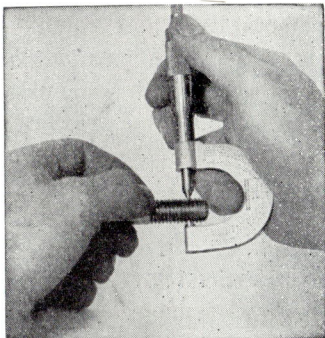

Fig. 17-40. Thread micrometer being used. (*Brown & Sharpe Manufacturing Company*)

QUESTIONS ON CHECKING THREADS

1. Is the thread on a bolt external or internal?
2. What is the standard term used to denote the outside diameter of a screw thread? The inside diameter?
3. What types of thread gages may be used in checking threads?
4. What does the "no go" end of a plug gage check? The "go" end?
5. How many classes of fits are there? Which is the best? The poorest?
6. Why are gages used at all in checking threads?
7. What does a thread micrometer actually measure?
8. Getting the outside diameter of a thread and knowing the depth, how can you check the reading on the thread micrometer?

CHAPTER 18

Faceplate Work

Workpieces that cannot be chucked, or turned between centers because of their unusual shapes, may be clamped to a faceplate, or mounted on an angle plate bolted to a faceplate, so that the surfaces to be worked are concentric with the lathe centers.

A faceplate is machined so that it will be square with the lathe centers when mounted on the spindle. It generally has four T slots as well as four elongated holes to accommodate clamp bolts. Thus, regardless of the shape of the workpiece, the section upon which an operation is to be performed can be held in an on-center position. Workpieces mounted in this manner should be checked for mounting accuracy by some method explained in Chapter 15, Chuck Work, before a cutting operation is started.

It is of course essential that the work is accurately fastened or clamped in position on the faceplate, and for this purpose certain accessories are necessary. Sketches and descriptions of some of these are here given (Fig. 18-1), and examples showing their use follow.

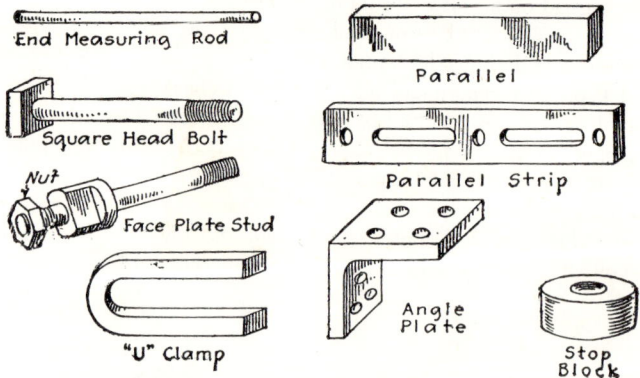

End Measuring Rod

Square Head Bolt

Nut

Face Plate Stud

"U" Clamp

Parallel

Parallel Strip

Angle Plate

Stop Block

Fig. 18-1. Accessories for faceplate work.

DEFINITIONS: FACEPLATE ACCESSORIES (Fig. 18-1)

Square Head Bolt. This bolt may be used in any of the faceplate slots for clamping pieces to the faceplate.

Shouldered Stud. Threaded each end and so designed that it may be fastened in any desired position on the faceplate.

U Clamp. Used with either a bolt or a stud in clamping the work; is easily adjustable and is light and strong.

Parallel Strip. Made with at least two adjacent sides straight and square; is provided with slots and either straight or tapped holes as shown in the figure, so that it may be easily clamped by bolts or screws in any position on the faceplate.

Angle Plate. Made in various sizes usually with an angle of 90 deg. between the finished faces, but may have any desired angle; provided with the necessary holes for clamping purposes; is used for a large variety of jobs in faceplate work.

Stop Block. A small piece of iron or steel, with a hole through it, so that it may be bolted securely to the faceplate forming a positive step in relocating a piece, or locating several duplicate pieces in the same position on the faceplate.

End Measuring Rod. Sometimes called *pin gage*, made from a piece of drill rod or similar material in any desired length; rounded sufficiently on the ends to offer a point contact and used for relocating work at certain definite distances from the stop block.

Parallel. A standard shop tool, opposite sides parallel, adjacent sides square; very useful in faceplate work when used in connection with the parallel strip.

Indicator. There are several different forms of universal indicators by means of which work may be accurately located either from a cylindrical projection on the work, or a hole in the work, or a prick-punch mark in the work (Figs. 18-2 and 18-3). For a complete and detailed explanation of indicators, see Chapter 3, Measuring Tools of the Machine Shop.

Weights for Counterbalance. Very necessary in faceplate work. Any piece of iron or steel that may be picked up in the shop that is of sufficient weight to counterbalance the work when fastened to the faceplate may be used.

Typical Faceplate Setups. Figure 18-4 shows a flat piece of cast iron clamped to the faceplate located by means of a parallel strip and stop block. This piece has been indicated to drill and bore

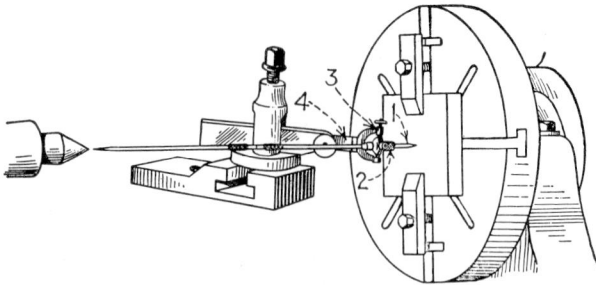

Fig. 18-2. Center tester, or *wiggler*. The needle (1) is adjustable lengthwise in ball chuck (2). The ball chuck is pivoted to form a universal joint (3) when indicating a prick-punch mark. It may be converted to a single pivot and a $\frac{3}{16}$-in. steel ball slipped over the point of the needle for indicating holes or buttons. The flexible steel ribbon (4) keeps the even pressure of the needle or ball against the work. (*The L. S. Starrett Company*)

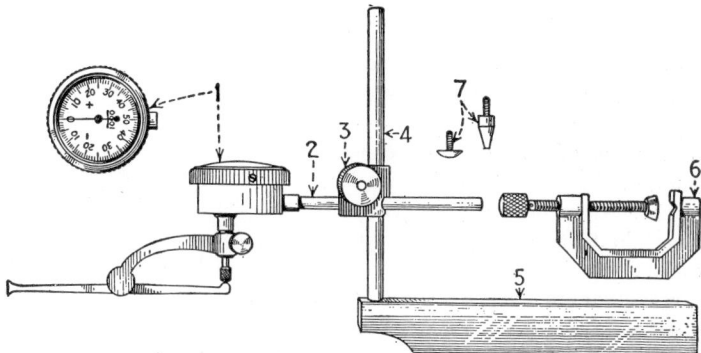

Fig. 18-3. Universal dial indicator. The advantage of a dial indicator is that the error can be read in thousandths of an inch. (1) Dial gage; (2) rod, fits hole in dial gage; (3) sliding swivel, adjustable on rod (2), or on upright (4), which is fastened in the bar (5); (6) clamp, hole in end fits rod (2). With either the bar (5) or the clamp (6) it is possible to use this tool in any machine for almost any indicating testing purpose. (7) Types of indicator points. (*Brown & Sharpe Manufacturing Company*)

a hole at one end. With the work in the position shown it would be out of balance were it not for the weight used as a counterbalance.

Figure 18-5 shows this same piece of iron moved along on the parallel strip and relocated by means of this strip and the gage between it and the stop block. With the proper number of lengths of gages a series of holes at any distance apart may be bored in such a piece, and by using a parallel strip for locating the edge, these holes will be in line.

Figure 18-6 shows the use of a parallel by means of which two rows of holes may be drilled in parallel lines; the weights, clamps, etc., are not shown. These operations are used in toolmaking, that is, in making jigs, fixtures, gages, etc.[1]

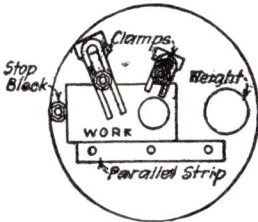

Fig. 18-4. Faceplate with a flat piece of cast iron clamped to it.

Fig. 18-5. Same piece of iron shown in Fig. 18-4 relocated.

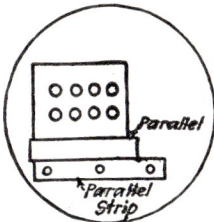

Fig. 18-6. Use of a parallel to drill two rows of holes.

Fig. 18-7. Faceplate set up as a temporary fixture.

Sometimes when it is required to hold on the faceplate and machine a number of duplicate pieces, the faceplate may be set up as a temporary fixture by using parallel strips, or angle irons, or stop blocks, or possibly all three, together of course with the necessary clamps. Figure 18-7 shows a typical faceplate job of this kind. The hole in the work must be bored at an angle of 65 deg. with the

[1] Instead of using the parallel as shown, *gage blocks* may be used. Gage blocks are rectangular pieces of hardened steel with two opposite sides ground and lapped to an exact dimension. Gage blocks may be used also instead of the pin gage for spacing the holes. The most accurate of these gages are the Johansson gage blocks, or *Jo-blocks*, which measure accurately in millionths of an inch. They are made by the Brown & Sharpe Manufacturing Company. It will be understood that these gages are used only where extreme accuracy is necessary.

finished flat surface. The special block *A* is planed at an angle of 25 deg. (complement of 65 deg.) to give the required seat for the work. After the block is once set it is not disturbed and duplicate pieces may be quickly and accurately located and machined.

Figure 18-8 will give an idea of how, in a number of duplicate pieces, the hole may be bored accurately, a certain distance from a finished surface, by locating each piece with the finished surface against a parallel strip, and then clamping to the faceplate as shown.

Figure 18-9 shows the value of the angle plate in faceplate work. The angle plate must be square and true. It is usually held against

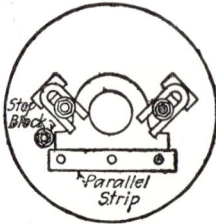

Fig. 18-8. Use of faceplate to bore duplicate pieces.

Fig. 18-9. Using an angle plate in faceplate work.

the faceplate by screws coming through from the back of the faceplate and screwing into tapped holes in the angle plate, though often straight holes are drilled through the angle plate and it may then be bolted fast to the faceplate. It is often necessary in order to get the angle plate in the position desired on the faceplate, to drill new holes. In such a case a certain amount of common sense should be exercised in regard to the position of these new holes.

Hints on Faceplate Work

1. Be sure that both the shoulder on the spindle and the face of the hub of the plate are free from burrs or nicks, and that both threads are clean.

2. The faceplate should screw freely on the spindle and tight against the shoulder. It should not be forced too hard against the shoulder or it will jam. If a chuck or a faceplate is run against the shoulder with a bang, removal is difficult.

3. The faceplate should run perfectly true and if advisable may be tested with an indicator.

4. After the piece is clamped, try every screw, and every nut, to make sure that each is sufficiently tight.

5. See that the faceplate is free to turn, that no bolts or clamps project in any way that will come in contact with either the carriage, the ways, or the headstock. Turn once around by hand to make sure.

6. A piece of paper between two flat surfaces will reduce the tendency to slip. This is true in planer work, or shaper work, or boring-mill work, and especially true in faceplate work, where facilities for clamping are not always of the best.

7. Remember in clamping, that it is the work that is to be clamped, not the blocking under the other end of the clamp.

8. Use the dead center to hold the work against the faceplate while clamping. If the work has a large hole in it a piece of flat stock slightly larger than the hole may be used between the work and the dead center.

9. The work and necessary counterweights, etc., may often be more easily clamped to the plate when it is lying in a horizontal position on the bench. The clamps may be tightened sufficiently to hold the work, after which the faceplate is mounted in its place, and then the work carefully adjusted to the desired position and made fast.

10. Use bolts long enough to obtain the full strength of the nut, or the thread of both will be strained and may be spoiled.

11. Avoid using bolts that are much too long; it is dangerous. If other bolts are not available put all excess of length possible back of the faceplate.

The Button Method of Locating Holes. Toolmaker's buttons, Fig. 18-10a, are steel bushings which may be tightened in exact positions on the work for locating purposes. The hole in the button is larger than the screw to permit of a certain amount of sidewise adjustment of the button after preliminary fastening. The buttons are hardened. They are ground to a given diameter in even tenths, 0.300, or 0.400, or 0.500 in., and the ends ground square at the same time. The hole is usually $\frac{3}{16}$ in. and the screw 5—40NC—2, that is, $\frac{1}{8}$ in. in diameter.

The method of using the buttons is: (1) Set all the buttons on the work in the exact positions the holes are to be bored; (2) set the work on the faceplate with the No. 1 button trued with the indicator; (3) remove this button, drill and bore the hole, ream if advisable; (4) readjust the work and true up each button in turn and proceed as in (3). The whole procedure in detail follows.

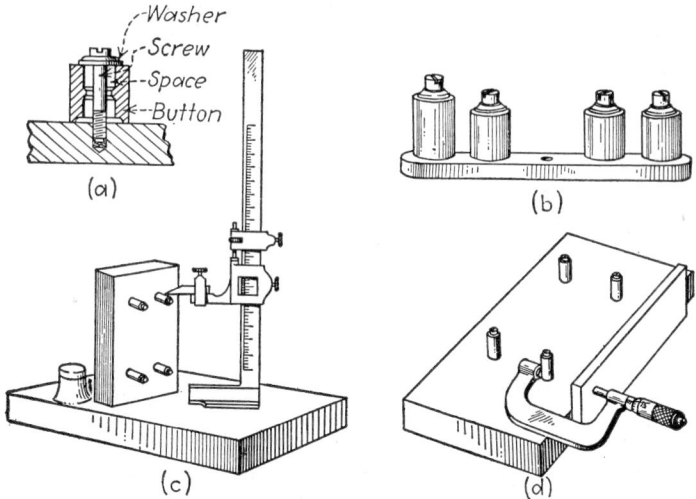

Fig. 18-10. Toolmakers' buttons. (*a*) Button in place; (*b*) the set of four, one longer than the rest to permit adjustment when close to another; (*c*) setting with height gage; and (*d*) setting with parallel and micrometer.

Setting the Buttons

1. The work must be surfaced flat and true.
2. Make a careful layout of intersecting lines to indicate the centers of the holes.
3. Make prick-punch marks at intersections, and *check*.
4. Make larger indentations with center punch, and drill for tap (for 5—40 tap, No. 38 drill is used, $\frac{1}{4}$ to $\frac{5}{16}$ in. deep).
5. Tap the holes and file off the burrs.
6. Fasten the No. 1 button (only fairly tight so that later it may be adjusted, that is, rapped this way or that with comparative ease).
7. Adjust the No. 1 button in right relation to the base and edge of work. Use micrometer and parallel, or height gage.
8. *Tighten* the No. 1 button, and *check*.

9. Proceed in the same way to adjust and tighten the No. 2 button, then No. 3, and so on; each in its proper relation to the base and to the side or to other buttons as the case may be.

Setting the Work

1. Being careful not to disturb the buttons, clamp the work on the faceplate approximately in position.
2. Mount the faceplate on the lathe spindle.
3. Adjust the *work* until the No. 1 button runs true as shown by the indicator.
4. Remove the button, drill, bore, and ream the hole (if the previous work has been done carefully the small tap-drill hole should not run out enough to hurt).
5. Move the work and adjust it until No. 2 hole runs true, and proceed as with No. 1. The same with remaining holes.

QUESTIONS ON FACEPLATE WORK

1. Jobs are sometimes clamped to the faceplate. Why?
2. Why is the faceplate machined square?
3. What precautions are taken when the large faceplate is put on the spindle?
4. What operations may be done on work fastened to the faceplate?
5. What tools are used to fasten work to the faceplate?
6. What is a test indicator?
7. When is a test indicator used?
8. Weights are at times bolted to the faceplate with the job. Why?
9. Show by sketch how duplicate pieces may be set up on a faceplate for boring.
10. Why should a piece of paper placed between the work and faceplate serve as an aid to hold the job?
11. How is a clamp arranged so that the work is held securely?
12. What is an angle plate?
13. How is the angle plate used in faceplate work?
14. What is a parallel?
15. How would you use a parallel? Show by a sketch.
16. How is a pin gage made?
17. Why is the pin gage rounded on the ends?
18. For what type of work is the faceplate valuable?

19. For what are toolmakers' buttons used?
20. Why is the hole in the toolmakers' button larger than the diameter of the screw?
21. Why are buttons ground on the ends?
22. What instruments would you use in setting buttons?
23. Why must the surface of the job on which buttons are to be used be flat and true?
24. What must be done before drilling holes in the job for receiving the buttons?
25. After the holes are drilled, what must be done to them?
26. After the buttons are in place, what must be done?
27. What precautions must be taken in setting toolmakers' buttons accurately?

Forge Work

CHAPTER 19

Soldering, Brazing, and Babbitting

The Principle of Soldering. Soldering is the process of joining pieces of metal by fusing their surfaces together with solder, an alloy of tin and lead. (An alloy is a mixture of metals, brought about generally by melting or fusion.) The solder commonly used is composed of lead and tin and has a melting temperature of 401°F., which is lower than that of either lead or tin.

If molten solder is placed on a piece of metal that has been cleaned, fluxed (that is, treated with certain chemicals or materials), and heated somewhat above the melting point of solder, then the solder will spread over the metal and stick to it. In fact, the solder and the surface of the piece fuse and mix together, forming an alloy of solder and the metal. When two pieces of metal are joined by soldering, the molten solder runs between them, fills up any spaces, and fuses with and penetrates into the surfaces of the pieces. Upon cooling, the solder solidifies and binds the pieces together.

Soldering is, therefore, an alloying process, and it is important that conditions be kept favorable for alloys to form while soldering. The two most important conditions are:

1. The metals to be joined must be thoroughly cleaned of all grease, dirt, and rust or tarnish, and kept clean (usually with the aid of fluxes).

2. The pieces themselves must be heated and kept somewhat above the melting point of solder for a short time.

If insufficient heat is applied to the pieces, the solder will not intermix well with the surfaces being joined, and poor work will result.

Cleaning the Work: Action of Fluxes. Solder will not stick

485

to metal that is dirty or coated with rust or tarnish. One of the first steps in soldering, therefore, is to remove thoroughly all dirt and oxide. This is commonly done by mechanical means, such as scraping with a dull knife, filing, or rubbing with steel wool or very fine emery cloth (Fig. 19-1). All metals oxidize (rust or tarnish) to some extent when exposed to the air even for short periods of time. When

Fig. 19-1. One of the first steps in soldering is to clean the work thoroughly. This may be done by scraping with a dull knife.

metal is heated, as it must be in soldering, the oxidation takes place more rapidly. Therefore, after a piece is cleaned, a flux, usually in the form of a liquid or paste, is applied to exclude the air and thus prevent oxidation until the part can be soldered (Fig. 19-2).

Most fluxes also have a certain solvent action to remove any oxide not removed by mechanical means. Some fluxes have a very strong solvent action and can be used to remove oxides without first scraping the work. Such fluxes are usually hard on the hands and their use is advised only when absolutely necessary.

Flux fills the space between the soldering iron and the piece being soldered and thus better enables the heat to flow from the iron to the work.

A flux, therefore, may be considered as helping the soldering process in the following ways: (1) removing the oxides, (2) preventing oxidation while the work is being heated, and (3) aiding the flow of heat from the soldering iron to the work.

Kinds of Fluxes. Various materials in the form of pastes, liquids, or powders are used as soldering fluxes on different materials.

Soldering pastes under different trade names are available at hardware stores. They are compounded from various materials, and most of them make excellent fluxes for most common metals. They

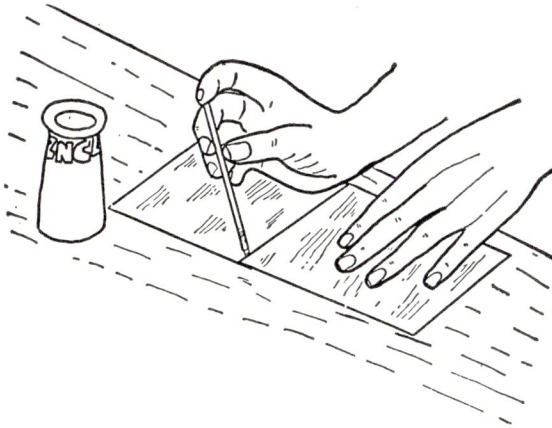

Fig. 19-2. After the work is cleaned, flux is applied. Liquid fluxes can be applied easily with a medicine dropper or a hollow glass tube.

are easily applied and are generally less messy and less corrosive than liquid fluxes.

Muriatic acid (commercial hydrochloric acid) is a very effective flux for soldering galvanized iron and zinc. It may be bought at drugstores. Because of its corrosive nature, muriatic acid must be used sparingly and with care.

Zinc chloride, or *cut acid,* as it is frequently called, is a common flux that can be used on most metals. It may be prepared as follows:

1. Drop small pieces of zinc into a bottle about one-half full of muriatic acid, adding more pieces of zinc from time to time until no more zinc will dissolve and there is a slight excess of zinc left in the bottle. The resulting liquid is zinc chloride. Zinc may be obtained from an old fruit-jar lid or the shell of an old dry-cell

battery. Zinc from such sources should be carefully cleaned before using.

2. After all chemical action has stopped, strain the zinc chloride through a cloth, or allow the dirt to settle and pour off the clear liquid.

3. Dilute the zinc chloride with one-fourth to one-half its volume of water.

Care should be taken not to get the acid on the hands or clothing. *Neither the acid nor zinc chloride should be kept around tools;* nor should zinc chloride be made around tools, as the vapors or fumes will cause severe corrosion. If acid or other flux should be spilled on tools, it should be wiped off at once and a liberal coating of grease or oil applied.

Rosin is sometimes used for soldering bright tin. A small quantity of powdered rosin is sprinkled on the part to be soldered, and when the hot soldering iron is applied, it melts and spreads over the surface. Rosin is a very mild flux. It is used where extreme caution must be taken against corrosion.

Tallow is a good flux for soldering lead. After the lead is thoroughly scraped, it should be heated slightly, after which the tallow is applied to the warm surface.

Sal ammoniac is a good flux for cleaning and tinning soldering irons. It may be obtained in cakes or in lumps or powdered form. A teaspoon of powdered sal ammoniac, or the equivalent in lump form, dissolved in water makes a good cleaning solution into which soldering irons may be dipped quickly while hot and thus cleaned.

Small cakes of sal ammoniac, especially prepared for cleaning and tinning irons, are available at hardware stores. These are quite satisfactory, and their use is generally recommended.

Kinds of Solder. There are many special kinds of solder, but the two most generally used are (1) lead-and-tin solders, or soft solders; and (2) silver solders, or hard solders.

Lead-tin solders are available in the form of bars, solid wire filled with a flux core, or ribbon. For large jobs requiring considerable solder, it is usually bought in bars. For the occasional job, acid-core solder or paste-core solder is very convenient and very satisfactory. Flux-core wire solders are more expensive than plain bar, wire, or ribbon solder, but where only a small amount of soldering is to be done, the added convenience of having the flux in the solder is well worth the small extra cost.

Silver solders are composed principally of silver, copper, and zinc in varying amounts. They are used for high-strength joints or where high temperatures are encountered. They have higher melting points than lead-tin solders, which are far more commonly used in the shop.

Soldering Irons. Soldering irons are really made of copper. In fact, they are sometimes called soldering *coppers*. Copper is used because of its resistance to oxidation and corrosion and because of its ability readily to absorb and give up heat. Soldering coppers (Fig. 19-3) are made in different shapes and of varying weights.

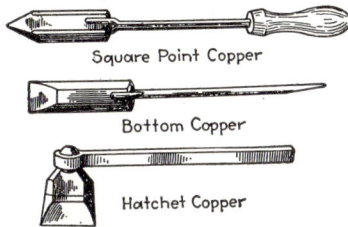

Square Point Copper

Bottom Copper

Hatchet Copper

Fig. 19-3. Soldering irons, or coppers.

The square-pointed copper is used more for general work than such shapes as the blunt roofing copper or the chisel-shaped bottom copper. A small copper should not be used on heavy work because it will not keep its heat long enough. On the other hand a copper that is too heavy is unnecessarily clumsy for light work. It is very necessary that the copper be properly "tinned" and that in heating care be exercised not to overheat. If it is overheated a scale of copper oxide is formed on the point and this scale, being practically a nonconductor of heat, renders the copper almost useless until it is retinned.

Tinning a Copper. To tin a soldering copper it is necessary to file or otherwise smooth and clean the end for about ¾ in. back. The copper is then heated enough to melt solder, after which the flux and the solder are applied. There are several ways of applying the flux and solder when tinning the copper, the method employed depending almost altogether on the material at hand.

1. The soldering iron may be dipped in the acid and then the solder applied.

2. The point of the copper may be rubbed with a piece of sal ammoniac and then the solder applied. This is the quickest and best way.

3. A piece of solder and some powdered rosin may be placed on a brick and the heated copper rubbed thereon until it is tinned.

Dipping Solution. If the copper while being heated becomes discolored by reason of the kind of fuel used (charcoal, gas, or gasoline) it may be cleaned by dipping it quickly in a solution made by dissolving a teaspoonful of powdered sal-ammoniac in a quart of water.

Soldering Operation. When soldering it is often convenient to *tack* one piece to the other, that is, a few drops of solder are put here and there to hold the piece in position. When finishing the operation care must be taken to let one portion cool before proceeding to the next. The copper should be so applied that as much of the available heat as possible may be utilized and further it must be placed in such a position on the work over the joint that the solder will flow into the seam and not merely along the outer edge.

Oftentimes it is good practice to solder two or more thin pieces together and machine them as one, afterwards melting them apart. It is usually best when soldering steel to steel to be sure both are tinned, because steel does not alloy with solder as readily as does copper or brass. If the steel pieces are properly cleaned and heated, flux applied generously, and solder rubbed on with the heated copper and the excess rubbed off with a piece of waste, the surfaces will show bright with a thin coating of solder. Like the soldering copper they are tinned. If a little flux is applied and the tinned surfaces are held together and heated they will be perfectly soldered or, as sometimes called, *sweated* together.

BRAZING

A much stronger joint can be made by brazing than by soldering. Brazing is a process of joining metal parts which is similar to soldering except that *spelter* is used instead of solder. Spelter is a compound of copper and zinc and is often called hard solder. It is usually about half and half copper and zinc; adding more copper up to two-thirds copper and one-third zinc serves to produce a stronger joint, but makes it more difficult to work. A spelter made of half copper, three-eighths zinc, and one-eighth tin makes an excellent spelter. Spelter is used in either granular or wire form. Brass rod is a combination of substantially two-thirds copper and one-third zinc (with a small amount of lead added to make it machine easier) and if prepared spelter is not available brass filings will make an excellent substitute.

The flux used for brazing is powdered borax. A small amount is mixed with water to form a paste and applied to the surfaces to be brazed before they are heated. During the process of brazing the dry borax is sprinkled on the joint where it melts and flows between the surfaces to be joined. The use of too much flux should be avoided because it hardens the surfaces of the joint and makes the filing and finishing difficult. When the flux begins to flow the spelter is placed on the joint and the heat continued until the spelter flows into the joint and no longer. A spatula for placing the flux and also the spelter on the joint may be made by flattening the end of a steel rod of suitable diameter and length.

To produce a strong joint it is necessary to have the surfaces fitted and held together tightly. Copper, brass, wrought iron, malleable iron, or steel may be brazed. Care must be taken when brazing copper or brass not to overheat and melt the work.

QUESTIONS ON SOLDERING AND BRAZING

1. Of what materials is soft solder composed?
2. Steel is an alloy. Brass is an alloy. What is an alloy? Is solder an alloy?
3. When a piece of solder is melted on a piece of copper is a new alloy formed?
4. What is meant by the term fuse?
5. When a piece of solder is melted on a piece of copper, why does the solder cling to the copper?
6. What is rust? What is meant by oxidation?
7. If a piece of steel is polished, it will retain its brightness in ordinary temperature for several days or maybe weeks, but if heated sufficiently it will quickly become almost black. Why is this?
8. Why will not solder cling to an oxidized surface?

9. What is the action of a flux?
10. Why is a flux used in soldering?
11. What flux is commonly used in machine shops? How is it made?
12. How is the soldering copper tinned?
13. What care must be taken when heating a copper? Why?
14. How are pieces of metal sweated together?
15. What is the difference between soldering and brazing?
16. Of what materials is spelter composed?
17. What flux is used for brazing?
18. How is the flux applied to the surfaces to be joined?

BABBITTING

Babbitt. Babbitt metal is an alloy of copper (4 parts), tin (88 parts), and antimony (8 parts). It is widely used as a lining for bearings for the following reasons: The bearings (boxes and caps) do not have to be bored; the shaft or spindle of the machine may be aligned and the babbitt melted and poured around it. It is practically an antifriction metal. It is strong, tough, and durable. It may be readily machined if necessary, and scrapes much easier than cast iron or bronze. When the bearing becomes worn the babbitt is easily broken out with a chisel, remelted, and poured to form a new bearing surface.

Lead is added in the cheaper grades of babbitt. This is all right for shafts having light duties to perform, but to produce good babbitt bearings requires a high grade of babbitt metal, of which there are several brands in the market.

Babbitting a Bearing. There are several methods of pouring babbitt bearings:

1. The bearing box or housing is cylindrical in shape and the metal is poured around the shaft, or around a rod or "babbitting mandrel" the exact size of the shaft to be used.

2. The metal to form the bearing is poured around a mandrel somewhat smaller than the exact size of the shaft. The bearing is afterward bored to the size required.

3. The bearing is split on a center line horizontally, separating the upper and lower halves. Both the lower and upper parts of this bearing are poured at the same time. Pieces of cardboard called liners are placed between the two, and against the shaft, holes being

made in the liners near the shaft for the passage of the metal from the upper to the lower part. (The narrow portions of metal may be easily broken when the cap is removed.)

4. The bearing metal is poured in the upper and lower parts separately, the lower part being poured first, after which the upper part or cap is adjusted and the babbitt metal poured in to form the lining for the cap.

It should be understood that in either of the above methods (3) or (4), the metal may be poured around a shaft or mandrel to the exact size and merely scraped to form a suitable bearing surface, or it may be poured around a shaft or mandrel or a suitable rod somewhat smaller than the exact size of the bearing required and afterward machined to size. If before machining, light blows are struck with a ball-peen hammer over the entire surface, it will serve to harden the surface and make the grain of the alloy closer when machined and a more durable bearing is produced. This method is considered the best.

The bearing boxes are usually cored to the required size. On the smaller sizes the cored holes are straight and cylindrical. To prevent the babbitt lining from working loose, small holes may be drilled at right angles to the axis of the bearing and the metal running into these holes, when poured, serves to tie the lining securely to the box or cap. To serve the same purpose in the larger bearings the box or cap may have two or more dovetail recesses cored parallel to the axis. Where a thrust load is taken on the bearings, the casting is either cored or counterbored somewhat larger in the end taking the thrust in order to provide against any tendency for the load to loosen the lining.

If the shaft or babbitting mandrel is painted with a mixture of graphite and gasoline it will make removal easier. This is especially true in a solid bearing, that is, one in which the metal forms a solid sleeve around the shaft. A coating of lampblack, applied by holding a candle flame against the shaft, will serve the same purpose.

It is advisable to preheat the mandrel and also the casting of the bearing. Otherwise the cold casting may chill the babbitt enough to prevent its filling the space, and in any event the bearing surface will not be as smooth as if the box and shaft were heated. The heating may be done with a blowtorch or by any convenient means.

If the bearing is to be poured "to size" considerable care should be taken to align the shaft. If many boxes are to be babbitted it will save time to make a suitable fixture for holding the shaft in position.

Fire clay mixed with water to the consistency of putty may be used to close the openings between the shaft and the box and thus keep the metal from running out. It may be well to cut cardboard washers and back them up with the clay.

The babbitt metal should be slowly heated until it will quickly burn a pine stick to a dark brown. Too much heat will injure the metal and when insufficiently heated it does not pour well. If a small amount of crushed rosin is put in the babbitt just before pouring a smoother bearing surface will result.

Care must be taken that no water comes in contact with the melted babbitt. Even a few drops of water will cause the metal to spatter.

The pouring must be continuous. If it is interrupted the additional metal will not fuse with that already poured and the lining will be cracked. It is sometimes necessary when pouring large bearings to use two ladles, pouring from both at the same time.

QUESTIONS ON BABBITTING

1. Of what materials is babbitt made?

2. What causes the difference in the grades of babbitt?

3. What is babbitt used for?

4. Name three advantages of babbitt for the purpose for which it is used.

5. Explain how the cheapest type of babbitted bearing is produced.

6. Explain the principal features of the best type of babbitted bearing.

7. Would a bearing such as suggested in question 5 be suitable for shafts having heavy duty to perform? Why?

8. Would a bearing such as suggested in question 6 be practicable for a 1-in. diameter shaft? Why?

9. How is a small babbitt bearing kept from working loose?

10. How is a large babbitt bearing kept from working loose?

11. When a thrust load is to be taken on the bearing, what provision is made to keep the babbitt in place?

12. When proceeding to babbitt a bearing, how do you get the boxes ready?

13. How do you get the shaft or mandrel ready?

14. How do you separate the cap from the box? Why?

15. Why do you heat the box and the shaft?
16. How do you prevent the babbitt from sticking to the journal?
17. How do you prevent it from running out at the ends of the box?
18. How much babbitt do you melt? Why?
19. Why is a bearing spoiled if the pouring is interrupted?
20. How slowly should the babbitt be melted? Why?
21. How may you tell when the babbitt is hot enough to pour?
22. What does it matter if the babbitt is too hot?
23. How does a little rosin affect the babbitt?
24. When do you put it in?
25. What will cause the melted babbitt to spatter?

Hand Forging in a Machine Shop

It is probably true that a machinist or toolmaker does more hardening and tempering of steel than he does forging; nevertheless, to understand the fundamentals of hand forging, of heating, holding, and hammering a piece of wrought iron or steel saves time. Such knowledge often makes unnecessary a sketch or drawing or an explanation to the smith in another shop.

On succeeding pages are definitions of the common hand-forging operations, introductory descriptions and illustrations of the forge tools, together with a few notes concerning common processes.

The following are definitions of the forging operations for shaping properly heated wrought iron or steel by means of hammer blows.

DEFINITIONS: FORGING OPERATIONS

Drawing or Drawing-out. The process of lengthening a piece of stock while the cross-sectional area is being reduced.

Spreading. The process of making a part wider and correspondingly thinner. (Spreading is mostly drawing out crosswise instead of lengthwise.)

Upsetting. The process of increasing the cross-sectional area of a given portion or possibly of the whole piece. (And, of course, this decreases the length.)

Welding. The process of joining two surfaces by fusion when they are properly heated and (in hand-forging practice) hammered together.

Forging. Consists of all the operations needed to form the required shape and size. It may include one or more of the foregoing operations and also *bending, twisting, heading,* etc.

Most general-purpose machine shops are equipped with a forge (gas forge usually) for heating the metal and also with tools used in the forging operations. The forge may be used also for heating steel for hardening and tempering, and near by are two quenching tanks, containing water and oil, respectively. Ash cans make suitable quenching tanks for most small jobs.

The Gas Forge. The proper mixture of gas and low-pressure compressed air under combustion in a gas forge (or gas furnace) gives an intense heat. The *mixture* of gas and air that will give the best combustion, as well as the amount of this mixture that will give the degree of heat desired, is easily regulated and controlled. A type of gas forge commonly used in toolmaking departments and in general-purpose machine shops is shown in Fig. 20-1. The air,

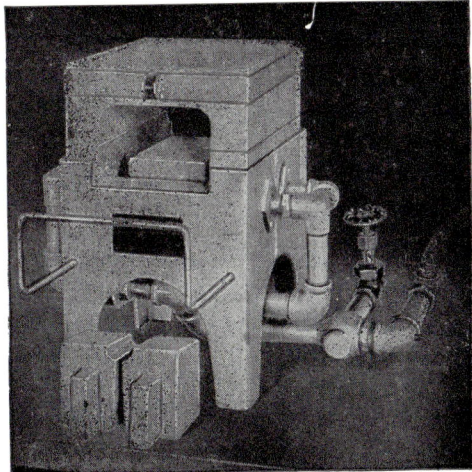

Fig. 20-1. Convertible bench forge. Has removable cover brick, and front and back bricks easily handled by tongs. Has adjustable rack for work support. May be used as oven furnace for heat-treating carbon or high-speed steel. (*American Gas Furnace Company*)

under pressure of approximately 1 lb. per sq. in., comes to the air cock (lever handle). The gas from the main comes to the gas valve (wheel handle). The mixture required, regulated by means of the two handles, goes through the mixture pipes and the four burners (two on each side) to the combustion chamber. The burners are arranged to give an intense heat with very little air impinging on the work. Too much air oxidizes the surface of the steel and causes a heavy coating of iron oxide (scale). The combustion chamber is of specially molded refractory material (hard-burned firebrick) and will last for years.

To light the forge:

1. Light a suitable piece of paper, and with a pair of tongs place it in the combustion chamber.
2. Turn on the air (lever handle) about halfway—air cock handle about 45 deg.
3. Keep your face away from the opening in the forge (*safety first*), and turn on the gas slowly until the "combustion roar" is heard.
4. Adjust the air cock and gas valve to give the proper flame of the force desired. A soft bluish flame at the burners is considered good combustion. With very little practice the right mixture is regulated for low heat or high heat, as desired.

An improved type of gas forge or furnace, with a special feature called *Single Valve Ratio Control*, as manufactured by the American Gas Furnace Company[1] or *Single Valve Control Proportional Mixer*, as manufactured by the Chicago Flexible Shaft Company,[2] *automatically* mixes and sends to the burners the correct proportions of gas and air for any degree of heat desired.

The first cost of this furnace is somewhat higher than that of the two-valve-control type illustrated in Fig. 20-1, but guesswork concerning the mixture is eliminated. It is necessary only to open the gas shutoff valve and then regulate the control valve in the air line to give the degree of heat required. The lighting is similar to that explained above.

Tongs and Their Use. Except in working on the end of a fairly long bar, the piece being forged must be held and handled with tongs. Many forms and sizes of tongs are used; some are standard; others have jaws especially shaped. The types commonly used are illustrated in Fig. 20-2a.

Flat tongs (Fig. 20-2a) are used ordinarily for holding flat stock. When they have a small groove running lengthwise in each jaw, they may be used for holding the smaller sizes of rods.

Hollow-bit tongs (Fig. 20-2b) are used for holding round or square or flat stock. The wide space behind the jaws provides room for the

---

[1] American Gas Furnace Company, Elizabeth, New Jersey.

[2] Stewart Industrial Furnace Division, Chicago Flexible Shaft Company, Chicago, Illinois.

head of a bolt or a similar enlarged part of a given job. It is comparatively easy to fit these tongs.

Pickup tongs (Fig. 20-2c) are used more often for handling hot pieces than for holding them during the forging process. When properly shaped, they are not at all clumsy.

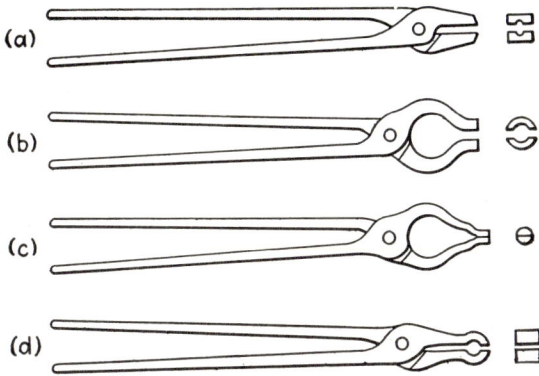

Fig. 20-2. Types of tongs commonly used: (a) flat, (b) hollow-bit, (c) pick-up, and (d) link or ring.

Link or *ring tongs* (Fig. 20-2d) are used primarily for holding curved pieces. Being fairly narrow, the jaws grip closely on a short part of the curve as the piece is being forged. When it is necessary to hold a rod at right angles with the tongs, this type may be used.

Fitting Tongs. This is a matter of *safety first*. With faulty tongs (Fig. 20-3b and c) the work is likely to fly out, with consequent serious injury to the smith or someone near by. Use tongs of approximately the right size, and *be sure they are properly fitted*. To fit the tongs, heat the jaws red hot, and hammer them tight on the work, as in Fig. 20-3a. To keep the handles the right distance apart in fitting the jaws, pinch a suitable piece of steel between them close to the joint. If the handles are too far apart, bend them by hammering close to the joint.

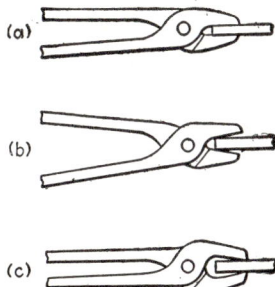

Fig. 20-3. Holding work in tongs: (a) right, (b) and (c) wrong.

The Anvil. The usual anvil weighs around 150 lb. and stands about 26 in. high. To bring it to this height, it is fastened on a cast-iron base or a heavy wooden block. Many prefer the wood on account of its greater resiliency.

The body (Fig. 20-4) and the horn are of wrought iron or a special grade of steel. The face is a tool steel plate, $\frac{1}{2}$-in. or more thick, welded to the body. The face is heat-treated (hardened and tempered) to resist the sledge-hammer blows on the work being forged. It is smooth and practically flat, being slightly convex crosswise. The horn is primarily for the purpose of bending curved parts. The base of the horn has a flat top on which the work is laid when it is being cut with a chisel. The corners of the face next to the horn are slightly rounded for about 4 in. The round hole through the tail of the anvil, or the *pritchel hole*, is useful

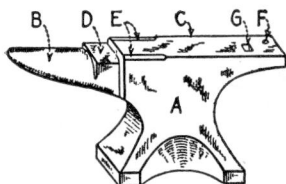

Fig. 20-4. Anvil: *A*, body; *B*, horn; *C*, face; *D*, base; *E*, face corners; *F*, pritchel hole; *G*, hardie hole.

for punching holes and for heading and also for bending the smaller sizes of rods. The square hole, or *hardie hole*, receives various tools with square shanks (Fig. 20-7*c*, also Fig. 20-8*a* and *b*). The position of the smith is in front of the anvil with the horn at his left.

The Swage Block. This forge-shop tool (Fig. 20-5*a*) is used for many squaring, sizing, heading, bending, and forming operations. It is 1 ft. or more wide and may be used either flat or edgewise in its stand.

The Forge-shop Cone. The forge-shop mandrel or cone (Fig. 20-5*b*) is used for truing and sizing rings. It is made in various sizes, the average being about 3 ft. high and tapering from 2 in. at the top to 12 in. at the base.

The Vise. A vise is a necessity in forge-shop practice. When using a vise and hammer, hammer the work, not the vise! Do not hold a heavy piece of hot metal in the vise, for to do so will destroy the temper of the vise jaws.

Hammers. The face of a hammer is used for ordinary hammering; the peen for drawing out, riveting, scarfing, etc. The familiar ball-peen hammer (Fig. 20-6*a*) is much used by the smith. The weight depends upon his choice for the job at hand and may vary

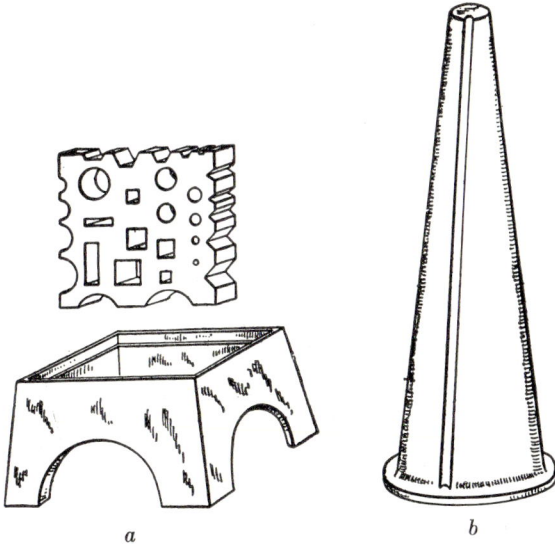

Fig. 20-5. (*a*) Swage block and stand and (*b*) forge-shop cone.

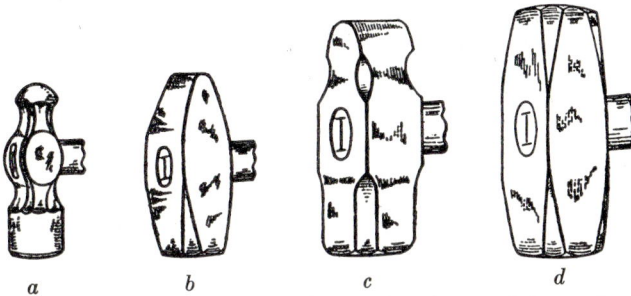

Fig. 20-6. Hammers and sledges: (*a*) ball-peen hammer, (*b*) heavy hammer or hand sledge with cross peen, (*c*) sledge with straight peen, and (*d*) swing sledge with two faces.

from 1 to 2½ lb. The heavy cross-peen hammer (Fig. 20-6*b*) is really a one-hand sledge and weighs from 2½ to 4 lb.

The sledges (Fig. 20-6*c* and *d*) are handled by the smith's helper. The lighter type, (*c*), weighs 10 or 12 lb. and usually has a straight peen. In use it is raised head high for a snappy blow. The double-faced sledge, (*d*), which weighs up to 20 lb., is for heavier striking with a full overarm swing.

Handles, of course, vary in size and length. On sledges they are about 26 in. long. It is imperative that handles for hammers and sledges are fitted tight and wedged. *Never use a hammer or sledge with a loose head or a split handle.*

Anvil Tools and Their Use. For a considerable part of anvil work the piece itself is struck, either by the smith with his hammer or by the helper with his sledge. In the latter case the smith directs

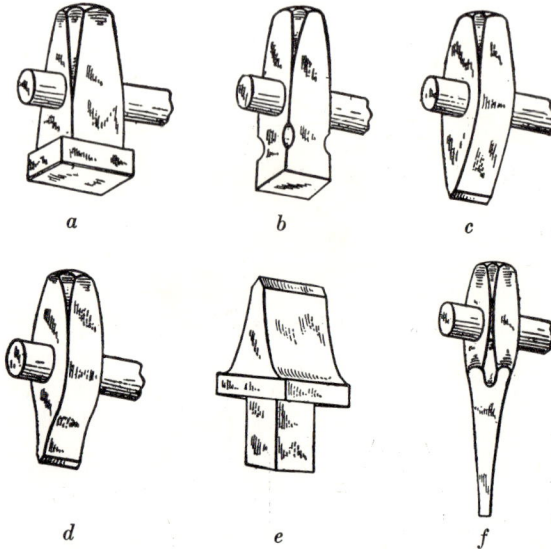

Fig. 20-7. Anvil tools: (*a*) flatter, (*b*) set hammer or square set, (*c*) cold chisel, (*d*) hot chisel, (*e*) hardie, and (*f*) punch.

the helper's stroke by himself striking a light blow where he wants the sledge to land and a light blow on the anvil as a signal to stop striking. Frequently, however, special anvil tools (Figs. 20-7 and 20-8) are held by the smith and struck by the helper. Some anvil tools are made in pairs (Fig. 20-8), the upper one fitted with a handle, the lower one provided with a square shank that fits the hardie hole.

The old-time blacksmith used discarded buggy spokes for anvil-tool handles. A similar type of handle is still used. It should never be wedged in the eye like a hammer handle but should project an inch or more through the eye, as shown in Figs. 20-7 and 20-8. This is for safety; the loosening of the tool on the handle will be noticed at once.

The flatter (Fig. 20-7a) is used for flattening and smoothing surfaces, removing hammer marks, etc. The face is smooth, about 2½ in. to 3 in. square, with rounded edges.

The set hammer (Fig. 20-7b) is used for finishing corners in shouldered work where the flatter would be inconvenient. It is also used for drawing out. It is about 1¼ in. square and is made in both square- and rounded-corner types.

The cold chisel (Fig. 20-7c) is used for nicking cold stock preparatory to breaking off. The bar is nicked all around. To break off the pieces, the bar is held down on the anvil with the sledge, with the nick on the far edge of the anvil, while the smith strikes a sharp blow on the projecting part. By another method the bar is tightened in the vise with the nick at the edge, and, with the projecting part covered by the end of a pipe sufficiently long to give a good leverage, the pipe is given a sudden snappy jerk.

The hot chisel (Fig. 20-7d) is thinner than the cold chisel. Hot metal cuts quite easily. Do not use a hot chisel over the face of the anvil; cut either at the edge of the anvil or on a fairly heavy copper strip placed on the base of the horn of the anvil. To cut off square, tip the chisel a trifle, enough to have one face perpendicular.

The hardie (Fig. 20-7e) also is used for cutting hot metal. Place the work in position on the cutting edge, and strike with hammer or sledge. Use judgment in the force of the blow.

The punch (Fig. 20-7f) is used for making a hole in hot metal by driving the punch halfway through from each side. First, make adequate center punch marks on opposite sides of the work to indicate clearly, when the metal is red hot, where the hole is to be. Second, drive the punch halfway through from one side. Third, turn the work over, locate the second center punch mark over the center of the pritchel hole or the hardie hole, and drive the punch to meet the first half of the hole. Fourth, make the hole the required size.

If is often convenient to use the blacksmith's punch to enlarge a given hole or to make a square, oval, or other shape of hole.

Fullers and swages (Fig. 20-8) are made in many sizes, the top part fitted with a handle and the bottom part held in the hardie hole. Most swages are shaped for finishing cylindrical parts, but other shapes, such as square, and hexagonal are used. Top swages may be used with the swage block (Fig. 20-6).

Fullers are used for finishing round corners, for making grooves, and frequently for drawing out and for spreading. It is often convenient to use a bottom swage and a top fuller to bend small plates or similar parts.

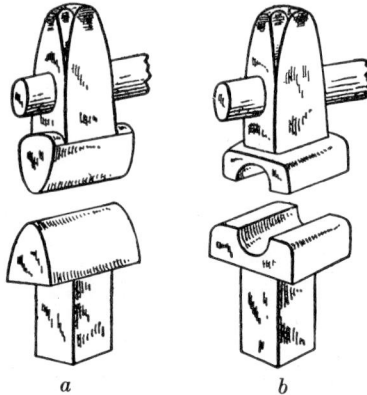

a   *b*

Fig. 20-8. Anvil tools: (*a*) top and bottom fullers and (*b*) top and bottom swages for round work.

QUESTIONS ON FORGE-SHOP TOOLS

1. Name five forging operations.

2. What is the combustion mixture in a gas forge?

3. What kind of handle has the gas valve?

4. What are the successive steps in lighting the gas forge?

5. Name three kinds of tongs.

6. What is likely to happen when faulty tongs are used?

7. Which hole in the anvil is square?

8. Which side is the front of the anvil?

9. How is the lighter type of sledge used? The heavier type?

10. What is the smith's signal to his helper to stop striking?

11. Are the handles of anvil tools such as flatters and chisels wedged? Give reason.

12. State the procedure of punching a hole through hot metal.

13. Which type of the smith's chisels is used to cut the metal entirely off?

14. For what purpose may the bottom swage and the top fuller be used together?

FORGING PRACTICE

Heating. Wrought iron and steel are the metals commonly forged. They are soft (plastic) when properly heated and will flow easily under the hammer blows. The forging heat for steel is a light yellow, considerably above the red-hot color; for wrought iron it may be even hotter, almost the so-called *white hot.*

NOTE: It is impossible to describe exactly the proper colors of heats for forging, welding, or hardening. "Cherry red" does not help much; neither does "white hot." Some experience is necessary to learn the right heats. It may be stated, however, that "when the shadows disappear" describes the correct color for hardening. Also, "bright yellow" or "light yellow" describes forging color about as nearly as possible, and the steel must be practically scintillating or sparking for the welding operation.

The American Gas Furnace Company gives the following table of colors and equivalent degrees of temperature:

Color	°F.	Color	°F.
Faint red	930	Salmon	1550
Blood red	1075	Dark orange	1634
Dark cherry	1175	Orange	1725
Medium cherry	1275	Lemon	1830
Cherry	1375	Light yellow	1975
Bright cherry	1450	White	2200

Proper forging will improve rather than injure the grain of the steel. Do not hammer the work when it is dull red, for to do so will probably cause cracks to develop. Reheat as often as necessary, but remember that each reheating causes extra scale on the surface of the work. Too high a degree of heat will burn and spoil the steel. *Heat the work slowly, thoroughly, and carefully; hammer it quickly.*

Drawing Out. The smaller sections may be drawn out by laying the heated bar across the face of the anvil and striking with a suitable hammer. Use the face of the hammer or either type of peen, whichever will best serve the purpose. The larger sections are drawn out when the work is laid on the horn of the anvil. This will lessen the tendency to spread. Further to reduce this tendency, the top fuller may be used with the sledge.

To draw out a piece to a *square* or *rectangular* cross section, keep

it fairly square or rectangular as it is worked smaller. Give it frequent quarter and half turns, thus: side *A* (Fig. 20-9), then a
quarter-turn to side *B*, half-turn to side *C* (opposite *B*), quarter-
turn to side *D*, then back to side *A*, and repeat.

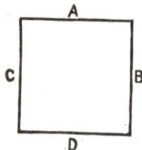

Fig. 20-9.

To draw out a *round* cross section, from round,
square, or other shape, *first draw the piece out square*,
as explained above, to about the thickness of the
shape (cylindrical or pointed) desired. Then hammer
the corners to make it approximately octagonal, and
finally round it. If this procedure is not followed,
cracks will probably develop.

Shoulders. When a piece is to be drawn out to a shoulder on one
side only and the stock is not too large, it may be forged with a hammer as shown in Fig. 20-10*a*. The shoulder location point of the
heated metal is placed directly over the inside edge of the anvil. If
it spreads too much as it is being drawn out, hammer the edges
occasionally to keep working toward the general shape required in
the finished forging. For the larger bars, as in Fig. 20-10*b*, the set

a   b   c

Fig. 20-10. Shouldering: (*a*) shoulder on one side, smaller stock; (*b*) shoulder on
one side, heavier stock; and (*c*) double shoulder.

hammer and sledge may be used for both drawing out and shouldering. Hold the work well forward on the anvil, thus avoiding a tendency to form a shoulder on the underside.

To forge shoulders on both sides, place the heated bar on the
anvil with the shoulder location point directly over the inside edge
of the anvil, and hold the set hammer with its edge directly above,
as shown in Fig. 20-10*c*. Give the work a half-turn occasionally to
keep both sides even.

To draw out a bar uniformly to a shoulder (for example, a cylindrical or a square reduction along the center line of a given bar)
the reduced portion is first forged square to about the size required.
This is done in a manner similar to that for the shoulder on both

sides, (Fig. 20-10c). That is, it is forged with the shoulder at the edge of the anvil and the edge of the set hammer directly above. If the reduced portion is to be cylindrical, remember that it is first forged square, then octagonal, and finally rounded.

Upsetting. To enlarge the cross-sectional area of a given portion of a piece of steel or wrought iron, heat slowly and thoroughly until almost white hot that part of the bar (usually one end) at which the enlargement is wanted. If the bar is fairly long, the cold part may be grasped in the hands and the heated end struck against the face or side of the anvil. Shorter pieces are held vertically on the anvil with link tongs (Fig. 20-2d) and the colder end struck with hammer or sledge. In either case heavy blows and perhaps occasional straightening are necessary.

Bending. Be sure that the bend is started in the right place. It is especially true that the sharper bends must be started right, and one or more center-punch marks may be used to show where the inside corner is to be.

The longer bends—rounded corners—are made over the horn; the sharper bends, over the slightly rounded corners of the anvil face (*E*, Fig. 20-4). In either case, except in rods smaller than $\frac{3}{8}$ or $\frac{1}{2}$ in., the helper usually presses the piece down hard on the face or horn of the anvil with his sledge while the smith hammers down the projecting end. The smaller rods may be bent while they are held in the vise without overheating or otherwise injuring the vise.

Length of Stock for Bending. Sometimes for an angle bend, and almost always for a curve bend (as for an eye, a ring, or a link), it is necessary to know the length of the stock needed. This is always calculated as the *length of the center line.* For example, in the right-angle bend shown in Fig. 20-11a, the outside measurement is 11 in., the inside measurement is 10 in., and the length of the center line is $10\frac{1}{2}$ in. ($6\frac{1}{4}$ plus $4\frac{1}{4}$ in.). The smith usually allows a little extra length to cut off one end or the other, perhaps both.

The length of stock to cut off for the ring (Fig. 20-11b) is the length at the center line. The diameter at the center line, the *mean diameter*, is 6 in.; the mean circumference (6 in. multiplied by 3.14) is 18.84 in., or practically $18\frac{7}{8}$ in. for the length to cut off.

Bending Rings and Links. To bend a rod in a circular direction, as for a ring or a link, it may be forged on the horn of the anvil or over a suitable cylindrical piece held in the vise. To avoid deep hammer marks, strike the projecting portion—not directly over the anvil.

In forging rings or links, the stock is cut off the proper length. This is the length of the mean circumference (Fig. 20-11b) plus the little the smith may allow for squaring the ends just before closing. If the piece is to be welded, an amount equal to about one-half the diameter of the stock is allowed to make up for the waste due to scaling.

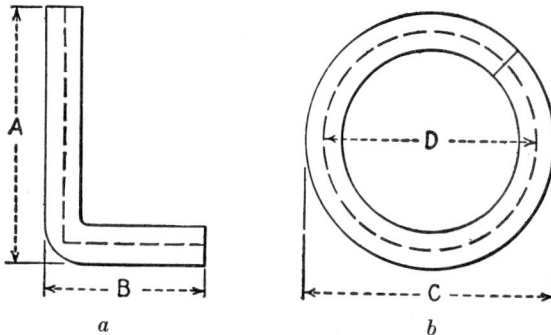

a   *b*

Fig. 20-11. (*a*) Stock ½ in. Outside measurements: A equals 6½ in., B equals 4½ in. Length of center line equals 10½ in. (*b*) Stock ½ in. Outside diameter C equals 6½ in., mean diameter D equals 6 in., mean circumference equals 18.84 in.

Rings and links are usually welded. Cut off the stock, upset the ends, forge the scarves, and bend the piece. Curve the ring by bending approximately halfway from each end, finally overlapping the scarfed ends. Curve the link by bending first in a U shape with ends even; then bend the scarfed ends to overlap. Make the weld, and finish to shape and size.

Bending Eyes. When it is required to forge an eye on the end of a rod or bar, enough of the piece to form the eye is bent at a right angle having nearly a square corner, as shown in Fig. 20-12a. This amount is equal to the mean circumference of the eye.

When a center-punch mark to lay off the distance would injure the finished job, the smith makes a chalk mark on the anvil a distance from the end of the anvil equal to the length required for the eye. When the work is heated, ready to bend, it is laid along the anvil with the end of the work flush with the end of the anvil, as in Fig. 20-12b, or flush with the chalk mark, as in Fig. 20-12c, whichever is preferred. Then the edge of the hammer is placed on the piece at the point where the bend is to be made, and, with the hammer in this position, both work and hammer are moved to the slightly

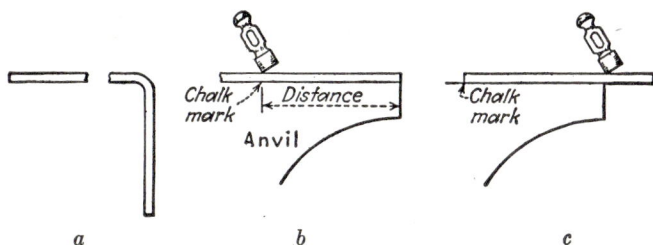

Fig. 20-12. Laying off the length for a bend.

rounded edge of the anvil; the overhang will be the amount to bend down.

After the right-angle bend is made, the ring is reheated and forged as illustrated in Fig. 20-13, starting at the end and gradually completing the curve.

Welding. The ends to be joined must first be upset, as in Fig. 20-14a. This is to provide for the reduction in the cross-sectional

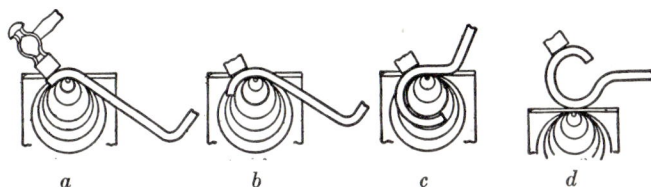

Fig. 20-13. Bending an eye: (a) starting, (b) continuing, (c) nearly ready to close, and (d) closing.

area due to hammering the joint in welding. Heat white-hot for upsetting, and upset plenty rather than not enough.

After the ends are upset they will have to be *scarfed*, which means forming the ends preparatory to welding. In hand forging, the lap weld[3] is used mostly for round, square, and rectangular bars. In

---

[3] Other welds, such as butt weld, V weld, and split weld are not discussed in this book.

Fig. 20-14b, the scarfed ends for a lap weld are shown. The upset ends are beveled with the ball peen, and the surfaces to be welded are finished with the face of the hammer. In length, these surfaces are about one and one-half times the thickness of the upset. They are slightly convex, because the first hammer blow should start the weld in the center, and succeeding blows will tend to squeeze out the melted scale and slag. A flux[4] should be used, particularly in welding steel, to promote the fusion of the metal and make a strong weld.

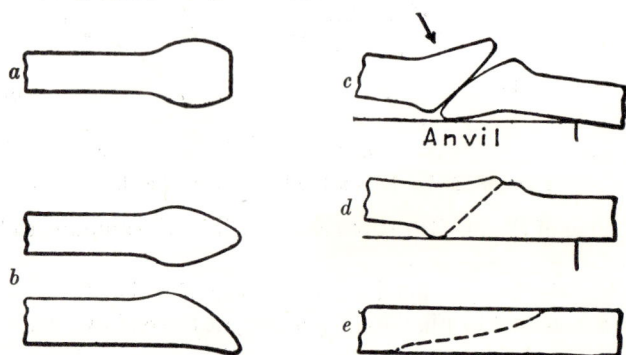

Fig. 20-14. Steps in welding: (a) the upset end, (b) face and side of scarf, (c) on anvil ready for first welding blow, (d) ready for cleaning and finishing, and (e) finished weld.

The scarfed ends and the area for a short distance back should be thoroughly heated to a white scintillating heat—both ends the same. As quickly as possible after heating, sprinkle with flux, and hit the bar with a hammer, or tap it on the anvil horn to shake the scale from the welding surfaces. Place the job on the anvil carefully and quickly, with the point of the top scarf overlapping a trifle the heel of the lower scarf, as shown in Fig. 20-14c. Strike a hard blow in the center, as indicated by the arrow, and work rapidly from the

[4] A flux (borax, or fine, sharp, clean sand) is used in welding iron or steel to lower the melting point of the scale (oxide of iron) so that it will flow off the surface. An oxidized surface will not weld properly. A flux is a necessity in welding steel because the steel would be injured if heated high enough to melt the scale. It also helps to make a good weld in wrought iron. Sprinkle the flux on the welding surfaces just before or immediately after removing the work from the furnace.

center with hard, snappy blows. Weld the thinner ends as quickly as possible, because they cool very rapidly. Reheat if, in the operation, the joint falls below the welding heat. Finally, clean off the scale with a file and smooth to size (Fig. 20-14e).

QUESTIONS ON FORGING PRACTICE

1. What do you understand by steel flowing under the hammer?
2. Which is hotter, cherry or yellow? About how many degrees?
3. Explain how work is drawn to a square cross section.
4. Explain how work is drawn to a round cross section.
5. Explain the method of drawing equal opposite shoulders on the end of a bar.
6. What type of tongs are used to hold a short piece in upsetting?
7. What is meant by the mean circumference of a forged ring?
8. Why does the smith need to know the approximate mean circumference in forging an eye?
9. Explain how the smith uses a chalk mark on the anvil to lay off on the work the length to be bent.
10. After the work is bent at a right angle, how do you proceed to forge the eye?
11. What is the operation of scarfing?
12. What is the purpose of a flux in welding?
13. Why must the work be very hot in order to weld?
14. Why does the smith work so fast in making a weld?

EXAMPLE OF FORGING, HARDENING, AND TEMPERING

Making a Cold Chisel. Every machinist should know how to forge, harden, and temper a cold chisel or a screw driver. Frequently a special chisel or screw driver is needed, or one that is much used needs to be redressed. Directions given here concerning a cold chisel apply as well to a screw driver.

Examine, if possible, a flat chisel, a cape chisel, and a gouge chisel. Make a flat chisel first; it is easier. Refer to Fig. 20-15.

Chisel steel is octagon shape. Steel suitable for cold chisels and screw drivers is around 80-point carbon, which is high enough to hold an edge and low enough to withstand a forging heat. Get a piece, say, ⅝-in. octagon, 6 in. long.

Heat the steel a bright red for forging. Allow a sufficient time for the steel to heat thoroughly, making sure the heat has penetrated

to the center. This is called *a soaking heat.* Heat it slowly in order
that the outside will not become overheated before the soaking heat
is given. A bright red is not a white heat, a white heat is too hot.
No carbon steel can be heated above a bright red without injuring it.

When forging *make the flats of the chisel parallel with opposite flats
of the octagon stock.* This is important for the appearance of the completed chisel. Strike only fairly hard blows. It is better to hammer

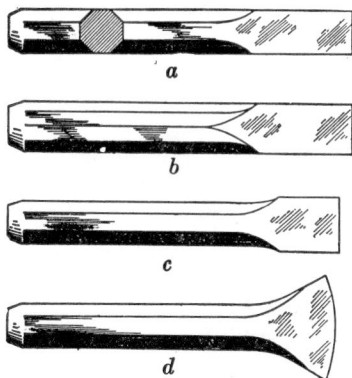

rather lightly at first, until one
has a little practice, than to give
too heavy blows and get the
chisel out of shape. A blacksmith
holds his thumb on top of the
hammer handle with an easy
grasp but with full control. He
strikes solid, snappy blows with
the face of the hammer—not the
edge.

*Do not forge the end fish-tail
shape as shown in* Fig. 20-15d.

Fig. 20-15. Forging a flat cold
chisel: (*a*) right; (*b*) wrong, not
forged parallel with flat of stock; (*c*)
right, edges kept parallel and about
the right width; and (*d*) wrong,
forged fan-shaped.

After flattening the end somewhat, turn the chisel a quarter-
turn and, holding the shank horizontally, hammer the narrow sides
to make them parallel. Alternate
the blows, four or five on the wider
surface, then four or five on the narrow surface, and so on until the
chisel is the shape desired. When forging do not allow the heat to get
below a dull red, because hammering the steel after it has cooled
too much will set up strains that may crack the steel when the chisel
is hardened. Reheat the piece two or three times if necessary—not
too hot and not too quickly. As the chisel gets thinner on the forged
end, be careful when reheating it not to overheat the thin section.

After the chisel is forged the next operation is *annealing.* Reheat
to a cherry red (a little hotter than a dull red) and lay aside to cool.
The slower it cools the better. Sometimes it may be left in the furnace to cool with the furnace, or it may be buried in ashes or in
powdered charcoal. Ordinarily it is sufficient, however, merely to
cool in the air. Annealing serves to relieve the strains set up by

forging and to give the steel an even, close grain or texture. (Annealing also serves to soften hardened steel, or hard spots that may be in the steel. Manufacturers of steel anneal most of the carbon steel after rolling because rolling acts to a certain extent as does hammering.) Annealing any piece, after forging and *before hardening*, is a very important step and is frequently overlooked.

The next step is *hardening*. Heat the chisel about 2 in. back from the cutting edge to a cherry red (hotter than a dull red but not a bright red—the heat for hardening is not so high as for forging). Give it a soaking heat until the shadows disappear. Be very careful that the fire is not hot enough to overheat and ruin the thin section of the chisel.

The sequence of the following directions, (1), (2), and (3), for *quenching* the chisel is important. Understand each of the directions and the reason therefor thoroughly so that each step may be made carefully and deliberately without further reference to these instructions.

1. When it is exactly the right heat, remove the chisel from the fire and quickly but deliberately dip it in water about ½ in. and keep it moving up and down for another ¼ or ½ in. This movement is to avoid having too sharp a line between the hardened and unhardened portions. If this is not done the piece is liable to crack at the water line. Keep the ½ in. of chisel *in the water* all of the time until it is finally removed.
2. When the ½ in. of the chisel end is black (hardened) plunge the whole chisel under water and quickly back, nearly out, that is, out to the ½-in. portion that must be left in the water. Repeat this two or three times until the red is gone from the sides of the chisel and a dull-red streak only remains along the center.
3. Now quickly remove the chisel from the water and plunge it into the tempering oil. Move it around in the oil and allow to cool. This treatment will give a hardened portion ½ in. or more back from the cutting edge; also the sides are hard and the quenching in oil of the center part while red gives a maximum toughness.

If no oil bath is available, cool the chisel slowly by occasionally dipping it in the water.

Tempering is the next operation. When the chisel is cool remove it from the oil bath and with a piece of emery cloth or broken grinding wheel polish the flat back far enough from the cutting edge to see the temper color run. Draw the temper by holding the chisel over a flame, heating the shank and the heavier section of the forged end and allowing the color to run, that is, draw the temper from the shank towards the cutting edge. The color on the cutting end should be purple flecked with blue (530° to 540°F.), and this color should extend at least ½ in. back. The chisel is now hardened and properly tempered ½ in. back of the cutting edge and may be sharpened several times before the hardened section is ground away.

Screw drivers should be drawn a trifle more than cold chisels. Draw them to blue (540° to 550°F.).

Tempering heat should penetrate all through the steel and the longer the piece is held at the tempering heat the tougher it will be. Toolmakers have learned that in punch and die work it is wise to leave the die in the tempering oil for several hours. It is much less liable to break when in use and the cutting edge lasts longer.

Reasoning as above, it will be found that if, after the color has been drawn on a screw driver or a chisel, it is polished and drawn again and possibly once again, it will greatly improve the toughness and in no way affect the hardness.

Finally grind the chamfer on the head of the chisel and sharpen the cutting edge by grinding two even parallel facets or bevels.

QUESTIONS ON MAKING A COLD CHISEL

1. What content of carbon has the average cold chisel?
2. In what careful manner is the chisel steel heated for forging?
3. What surfaces of the chisel stock are considered when the flats of the chisel are forged?
4. What is the next step after forging a screw driver or a chisel?
5. Which has the temper drawn more, the chisel or the twist drill? Why?
6. Besides relieving forging stresses and giving steel an even texture, what does annealing do?
7. What is the remedy if a chisel edge breaks when in use?
8. What is the remedy if a chisel edge bends or flattens when in use?
9. What is likely to happen if the piece being hardened is not kept in motion in the quenching bath?
10. State how properly to harden and temper a cold chisel.
11. How many degrees has the cutting angle of a cold chisel?

Appendix

RULES FOR FINDING THE DIAMETERS AND SPEEDS OF PULLEYS

The speed (r.p.m.) of driving and driven pulleys are to each other *inversely* as their diameters. That is, the *speed* of the driving pulley is to the *speed* of the driven pulley as the *diameter* of the driven pulley is to the *diameter* of the driving pulley, or

$$S:s = d:D$$

This is usually written $DS = ds$ and is the fundamental formula for the *fundamental rule for speeds of pulleys*. The diameter of the driving pulley multiplied by its speed is equal to the diameter of the driven pulley multiplied by its speed.

Knowing any three of the quantities, the fourth can be calculated by substituting values in the proper one of the following equations:

$$D = \frac{ds}{S} \tag{1}$$

$$S = \frac{ds}{D} \tag{2}$$

$$d = \frac{DS}{s} \tag{3}$$

$$s = \frac{DS}{d} \tag{4}$$

EXAMPLE: A pulley 12 in. in diameter is running 220 r.p.m. and is connected by a belt to a pulley 7 in. in diameter. How many r.p.m. will the smaller pulley make?

SOLUTION: Use equation (4) and substitute the known values

$$\text{r.p.m.} = \frac{DS}{d} = \frac{12 \times 220}{7} = 377+ \quad Ans.$$

Pulley Train. The principal driving shafts in a shop are called *main lines* and the smaller shafts that carry the pulleys over the machines are called *countershafts*. Often the speed must be reduced between the engine and the main line in which case a *jackshaft* carries the speed-reducing pulleys. When motion of one shaft is transmitted to another and from that to a third and so on to any number of shafts, the pulleys that carry the belts, which transmit the motion, make up what is called a pulley train.

Suppose power is transmitted from a pulley on the motor to a pulley on the line shaft. The motor pulley is the *driving* pulley and the line shaft pulley is the *driven*. The power is further transmitted from another pulley (a driving pulley) on the line to a driven pulley on the countershaft and from another *driving*) pulley on the countershaft to the (*driven*) pulley on the machine.

The problem of calculating the speeds, etc., in a pulley train is the same in principle as for two pulleys. Instead of calculating for each pair of pulleys in the train separately, a combination of the different proportions will give the same result.

Rule for Pulley Speeds. The continued product of the diameters of the driving pulleys and the speed of the first driver is equal to the continued product of the diameter of the driven pulleys and the speed of the last driven pulley.

EXAMPLE: A certain line shaft runs at 250 r.p.m. A 15-in. pulley on this shaft is connected by a belt to a 10-in. pulley on the countershaft. From a 12-in. pulley on the countershaft, motion is transmitted to the machine. What diameter must the pulley on the machine be to give a spindle speed of 600 r.p.m.?

SOLUTION: Let x = diameter of pulley on machine.

$$\underset{5}{\cancel{250}} \times 15 \times \cancel{12} = 10 \times x \times \underset{12}{\cancel{600}}$$
$$15 = 2x \quad \text{or} \quad x = 7\frac{1}{2} \text{ in. } Ans.$$

RULES FOR FINDING THE NUMBER OF TEETH AND VELOCITY OF GEARS

The velocity (r.p.m.) of the driving gear and the follower gear are to each other *inversely* as the numbers of their teeth. That is, the velocity of the driving gear is to the velocity of the follower gear as the number of teeth in the follower gear is to the number of teeth of the driving gear, or

$$V:v = n:N$$

This is usually written $NV = nv$ and is the formula used for determining velocity.

The Fundamental Rule for Velocities of Gears. The number of teeth in the driving gear multiplied by its velocity is equal to the number of teeth of the driven gear multiplied by its velocity.

Knowing any three of the quantities, the fourth can be found by substituting values in the proper one of the following equations.

$$NV = nv$$

Then
$$N = \frac{nv}{V} \tag{1}$$

$$V = \frac{nv}{N} \tag{2}$$

$$n = \frac{NV}{v} \tag{3}$$

$$v = \frac{NV}{n} \tag{4}$$

EXAMPLE: A gear with 40 teeth meshes with a gear having 96 teeth. If the small gear makes 120 r.p.m., what will be the velocity of the larger gear?

SOLUTION: Use equation (4),

$$v = \frac{NV}{n} = \frac{\overset{5}{\cancel{40}} \times \overset{10}{\cancel{120}}}{\underset{8}{\cancel{96}}} = 50 \text{ r.p.m. } Ans.$$

A compound gear train is a train of gears composed of two or more pairs, or simple trains, of gears. The problem of calculating velocities, etc., in compound gearing is the same in principle as for two gears. Instead of calculating for each pair of gears in the train separately a combination of the different proportions will give the same result.

Rule for Compound Gear Velocities. The continued product of the *numbers* of teeth in the driving gears and the velocity of the first driving gear is equal to the continued product of the *numbers* of teeth in the follower gears and the velocity of the final follower gear.

MACHINE FITS

There are four different kinds of cylindrical fits used in machine work, namely, the running (and sliding) fit, the drive fit, the force fit, and the shrink fit.

In most cases, excepting the shrink fit, the hole should be finished to a standard size, the shaft or stem or other part then fitted to it. Babbitted bearings are an exception.

Sliding and Running Fit. For a sliding or running fit the diameter of the shaft should be enough smaller to allow for a film of oil for lubrication. This allowance, as it is called, depends on (1) the purpose of the bearing, (2) the diameter of the shaft, (3) the length of the bearing, (4) the kind of metal used for each.

For an average length of bearing an allowance of 0.001 in. per inch of diameter of bearing is sufficient. A longer bearing requires usually a trifle more allowance.

The speed of the shaft is a factor in running fits and the necessity of high speeds and close running fits has developed bearing metals such as babbitt, bronze, and hardened steel, which are much used in machine construction. Hardened and ground spindles in hardened and ground bearings require very little allowance; likewise hardened and ground shafts in bronze bearings. Unlike metals work best in running fits, with the exception of hardened steel. Like metals may be used for sliding fits. The bar of a sliding fit is usually finished lengthwise by drawfiling to give it a longer life and a better appearance.

Drive Fit. When two pieces are to retain indefinitely a fixed relative position, they may be so held by driving the one in the other as a key in a shaft, or a straight dowel pin in a hole. The allowance depends on the length and cross section or diameter of the bearing surfaces, and the smoothness of the surface and the form of the surrounding part. The longer bearing surfaces and the larger diameter require less allowance; a carefully ground surface will hold better than a turned or filed surface and therefore does not require so much allowance; and a thin or weak pulley hub for example will not stand the driving allowance for a key that might be used in a heavy solid hub.

Force Fit. When two pieces are to retain permanently a fixed relation a greater allowance than a drive fit may be used and the one part is forced into the other in a screw press or in a hydraulic press. For example, in forcing the axles into locomotive driving wheels, a pressure of 150 tons is not uncommon.

Shrink Fit. When two pieces are to remain permanently together but the shape of one or both would make it impracticable or impossible to force one within the other, the enveloping piece is heated and thereby expanded sufficiently to slide over the other and then cooled slowly with water. Care must be taken when a piece is to be shrunk on another against a shoulder to prevent the piece shrinking away from the shoulder, leaving a space between. Cool the part against the shoulder first and then gradually away from the shoulder.

FASTENING A BELT

There are many kinds of patented metal belt fasteners in the market. Some of them are quickly applied and very serviceable but none, except perhaps the wire lacing, or the clipper lacing, is as flexible and smooth running as the old-fashioned rawhide belt lacing, which is still very generally used. It is desirable that every boy in the shop should know how to lace a belt.

The tools used comprise a belt punch, a belt awl, a pair of pliers, a try square, and a sharp knife.

General Directions

1. Cut the ends of the belt *square.*
2. The "grain" side or hair side of the belt should run against the pulleys (the grain side is the smooth side).
3. The lacing should be crossed on the flesh side (outside) of the belt and *not* on the grain side (side toward pulley).
4. The holes in both ends should be exactly opposite.
5. The belt should not be too tight or it will injure both the belt and the bearings.
6. A belt is made of sections of leather lapped and cemented together. The belt should be put on so that the points of the laps will run against the pulley.

The following directions apply particularly to belts from 2 to 5 in. wide.

1. Put the belt around the pulleys and pull tight letting one end lap over the other and note the amount. A good strong pull will indicate the amount the belt must be shortened to give it the proper tension.
2. Lay off the amount to be trimmed with the point of the knife, using the try square as a guide, and then cut straight on the line.
3. Punch holes approximately $\frac{3}{16}$ in. diameter about $\frac{3}{4}$ in. from center to center and not nearer than $\frac{1}{2}$ in. from the end or from the sides.
4. Select a lace, a trifle longer than is required, that will pull fairly easy through the holes. Butt the ends of the belt together with edges flush. Put lace up through holes 3 and 6 from the *flesh* side (see Fig. A-1) pulling ends of lace even. Put lace *a* down through 7, up through 4 (and pull tight, using the pliers if necessary), down through 8, up through 4 once more, down through 8 again, up through 3, down through 7, up through 2. Punch a hole $\frac{1}{2}$ in. back of hole 2 and pull the lace through this hole. Cut off lace, leaving tab end of about $\frac{3}{8}$ in. Cut lace nearly half through at the surface of the belt and twist tab end one-half turn, thereby fastening it.

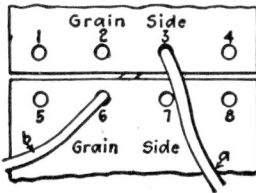

Fig. A-1.

Put lace *b* down through 2, up through 5, down through 1, up through 5, down through 1, up through 6, down through 2, and up through 7. Fasten lace directly back of 7.

Cementing Belts. Cementing together the lapped ends of a belt, Fig. A-2, is considered the best method of fastening. The ends are

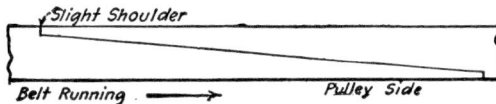

Fig. A-2.

shaved down as shown so that the lapped portion is not noticeably thicker than the rest of the belt, and the shaved parts should be flat and fit snugly together.

Get two pieces of board about 6 and 12 in. long, respectively, (for a belt under 4 in. wide) and a little wider than the belt, and arranging the lap about the middle (lengthwise) of the longer board lightly clamp at each end. Then fix the lap exactly right, with the edges of the belt flush and straight, and set the clamps tight.

Put a piece of paper between the belt and the board and lifting the upper lap apply the cement to both shaved surfaces, rubbing it in well and being careful not to put on too much. Make the joint tight by rubbing out the air pockets, perhaps with the face of a hammer, paying particular attention to the ends and edges. Put a piece of paper over the joint, then the short piece of board, and clamp tightly the two boards with the belt between them. Allow to set for several hours at least, and overnight if convenient. The object of the paper is to keep the boards from sticking to the belt; what little paper cannot be torn off will soon wear off.

GEOMETRICAL PROGRESSION

A series of numbers is said to be in geometrical progression when any number of the series equals the preceding number multiplied

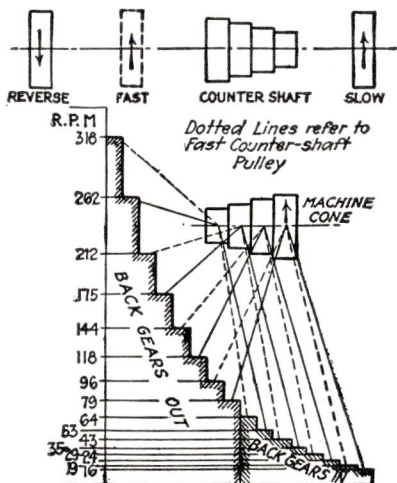

Fig. A-3.

by a given constant. For example 2, 4, 8, 16, 32 is such a series and the constant is equal to 2. Any one of these numbers is equal to the preceding number multiplied by 2. Also, in other words, this constant equals the *ratio* of any number of the series to the next lower number. For example in the series given 16 divided by 8 is equal to 2.

The speed changes and usually the feed changes of most machine tools advance from the slowest to the fastest in geometrical progression. The reason for this is that, in this arrangement, speeds for the larger diameters of work or cutters (milling cutters, drills, etc.) increase slowly, giving a greater number of available speeds, and the speeds for the smaller diameters increase more rapidly, which is as it should be because a comparatively small difference in diameter requires a considerable change in speeds. The *ratio* used is usually around 1:2. For example, in Fig. A-3, if each speed is multiplied by the ratio 1:2, the quotient will be approximately the next higher speed.

SCREW-THREAD MICROMETER

The distinctive feature in the construction of this micrometer is that the end of the movable spindle is pointed and the fixed end or

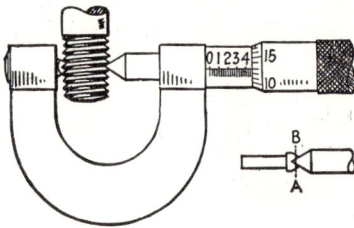

Fig. A-4.

"anvil" is V shaped. Enough is taken from the end of the point, and the bottom of the V is carried down low enough, so that they will not rest on the bottom or top of the thread to be measured but on the cut surface. As the thread itself is measured, it will be seen that the actual outside diameter of the piece does not enter into consideration.

As one-half of the depth of the thread from the top is measured on each side, the diameter as indicated by the caliper is the pitch diameter,[1] that is, the full size of the screw less the depth of one thread. When the spindle point and the anvil points are in contact the 0 represents a line drawn through the plane *AB* and if the caliper is opened, for example, to 0.463 in., it represents the distance of the two planes, 0.463 in. apart.

[1] *Pitch diameter* of a thread is equal to the nominal outside diameter less the depth of one thread and may be found as follows:

Depth of V thread equals 0.866 ÷ number of threads per inch.

Depth of Am. Std. thread equals 0.6495 ÷ number of threads per inch.

Depth of Whitworth thread equals 0.640 ÷ number of threads per inch.

The pitch diameters for the various sizes of machine screws and standard screws are given in Tables 7, 14, and 15.

The screw-thread micrometer has certain limitations. The given V on the anvil may be used for only a few pitches, for example, one size is used for 8 to 14 threads, the next for 14 or 20 threads, etc. Also the reading is somewhat distorted owing to the slant angle of the thread; consequently, for accuracy, the micrometer should be set to a standard thread plug of the given size. This tool is more useful as a gage than as a measuring tool. The three-wire method has proved more satisfactory as a means of measuring threads.

WIRE GAGES AND SHEET-METAL GAGES

Considerable confusion exists in regard to the gage numbers or the decimal equivalent of the gage numbers when ordering wires and sheets of the various metals, owing to the fact that there are so many gages listed in the tables given in handbooks, catalogues, text books, etc. Fortunately most of these older standards are obsolete or practically obsolete and only a few are now generally accepted and used in the trade. These are listed in Table 7.

Steel Wire Gage, formerly called the *Washburn & Moen Gage* and also the *American Steel & Wire Company* steel wire gage, is the standard gage for steel and iron wire excepting music wire (see Music Wire Gage), and drill rods.

The American Wire Gage, also known as the *Brown & Sharpe* gage, is the generally accepted standard for copper wire (other than telephone and telegraph wire, see British Imperial Standard Wire Gage), brass wire, german silver wire, and also for the thickness of *sheets* of these materials.

The A. S. & W. Co. New Music Wire Gage is regarded as standard in the United States, the older Washburn & Moen music wire gage being obsolete. Foreign music wires are sized according to the respective makers gages.

Music steel spring wire or "music wire," or "piano wire," is the best quality of steel wire and has, as noted, its own particular gage. Numbers 13 to 27 inclusive are used in pianos, some of the smaller sizes in other musical instruments. It is a tough wire of great tensile strength and resilience without extreme hardness. It is particularly useful for making springs since it does not have to be hardened and tempered. Do not confuse music wire with spring wire. *Spring wire* **is** made to the steel wire gage. It may be obtained with any desired carbon content for the purpose desired, but it is not so high grade as music steel spring wire.

The Stubs' Steel Wire Gage is commonly used in this country as well as in England for measuring drill rods. Do not get the Birmingham or Stubs' iron wire gage confused with Stubs' steel wire gage.

The Birmingham or *Stubs' Iron Wire Gage* (B.W. gage) was formerly used in the United States and in Great Britain to designate soft steel and iron wire. It is the gage used for iron telephone and telegraph wire, but for gaging other iron and steel wire, has been superseded to a great extent in Great Britain by the British Imperial gage and in the United States by the steel wire gage.

British Imperial Standard Wire Gage is now the standard gage of Great Britain. It is used by the American Telephone and Telegraph Co. as a gage for copper telephone and telegraph wire and is referred to as the New British Standard (N.B. Std.).

RÉSUMÉ

Wires

For steel wire, use steel wire gage.

For copper telephone or telegraph wire, use British Imperial Standard gage. For iron telephone or telegraph wire, use Birmingham gage.

For copper, brass, and german silver wire, use American (Brown & Sharpe) gage.

For music wire use A. S. & W. *new* music wire gage, and for imported music wire use gage of maker.

For drill rod use Stubs' steel wire gage.

Sheets

For iron and steel sheets and plates use United States Standard gage.

For sheet copper, brass and german silver, use American (Brown & Sharpe) gage.

NOTE: When ordering, it is always well to give the decimal equivalent of the gage size and also the limits, plus or minus, that will be acceptable.

Table 1. Decimal and Millimeter Equivalents of Fractional Parts of an Inch

Inches		Inches	Millimeter	Inches		Inches	Millimeter
	$\frac{1}{64}$	0.01563	0.397		$\frac{33}{64}$	0.51563	13.097
$\frac{1}{32}$		0.03125	0.794	$\frac{17}{32}$		0.53125	13.494
	$\frac{3}{64}$	0.04688	1.191		$\frac{35}{64}$	0.54688	13.890
$\frac{1}{16}$		0.0625	1.587	$\frac{9}{16}$		0.5625	14.287
	$\frac{5}{64}$	0.07813	1.984		$\frac{37}{64}$	0.57813	14.684
$\frac{3}{32}$		0.09375	2.381	$\frac{19}{32}$		0.59375	15.081
	$\frac{7}{64}$	0.10938	2.778		$\frac{39}{64}$	0.60938	15.478
$\frac{1}{8}$		0.125	3.175	$\frac{5}{8}$		0.625	15.875
	$\frac{9}{64}$	0.14063	3.572		$\frac{41}{64}$	0.64063	16.272
$\frac{5}{32}$		0.15625	3.969	$\frac{21}{32}$		0.65625	16.669
	$\frac{11}{64}$	0.17188	4.366		$\frac{43}{64}$	0.67188	17.065
$\frac{3}{16}$		0.1875	4.762	$\frac{11}{16}$		0.6875	17.462
	$\frac{13}{64}$	0.20313	5.159		$\frac{45}{64}$	0.70313	17.859
$\frac{7}{32}$		0.21875	5.556	$\frac{23}{32}$		0.71875	18.256
	$\frac{15}{64}$	0.23438	5.953		$\frac{47}{64}$	0.73438	18.653
$\frac{1}{4}$		0.25	6.350	$\frac{3}{4}$		0.75	19.050
	$\frac{17}{64}$	0.26563	6.747		$\frac{49}{64}$	0.76563	19.447
$\frac{9}{32}$		0.28125	7.144	$\frac{25}{32}$		0.78125	19.844
	$\frac{19}{64}$	0.29688	7.541		$\frac{51}{64}$	0.79688	20.240
$\frac{5}{16}$		0.3125	7.937	$\frac{13}{16}$		0.8125	20.637
	$\frac{21}{64}$	0.32813	8.334		$\frac{53}{64}$	0.82813	21.034
$\frac{11}{32}$		0.34375	8.731	$\frac{27}{32}$		0.84375	21.431
	$\frac{23}{64}$	0.35938	9.128		$\frac{55}{64}$	0.85938	21.828
$\frac{3}{8}$		0.375	9.525	$\frac{7}{8}$		0.875	22.225
	$\frac{25}{64}$	0.39063	9.922		$\frac{57}{64}$	0.89063	22.622
$\frac{13}{32}$		0.40625	10.319	$\frac{29}{32}$		0.90625	23.019
	$\frac{27}{64}$	0.42188	10.716		$\frac{59}{64}$	0.92188	23.415
$\frac{7}{16}$		0.4375	11.113	$\frac{15}{16}$		0.9375	23.812
	$\frac{29}{64}$	0.45313	11.509		$\frac{61}{64}$	0.95313	24.209
$\frac{15}{32}$		0.46875	11.906	$\frac{31}{32}$		0.96875	24.606
	$\frac{31}{64}$	0.48438	12.303		$\frac{63}{64}$	0.98438	25.003
$\frac{1}{2}$		0.5	12.700	1		1.00000	25.400

Table 2. Cutting Speeds Lathe Work, Drills, Milling Cutters

Formulas: $C.S. = \dfrac{D \times \text{r.p.m.}}{4}$, and r.p.m. $= \dfrac{4\,C.S.}{D}$

Dia.	20	30	40	50	60	70	80	90	100	110	120	130	140	150	160	170	180
¼	306	458	611	764	916	1070	1222	1376	1528	1681	1833	1986	2139	2292	2462	2615	2780
⅜	204	306	407	509	612	712	814	916	1019	1120	1222	1324	1426	1528	1632	1735	1836
½	153	229	306	382	458	534	612	688	764	840	917	993	1070	1146	1221	1298	1374
⅝	122	183	244	306	366	428	488	550	611	672	733	794	856	917	976	1036	1098
¾	102	153	204	255	306	356	408	458	509	560	611	662	713	764	816	867	918
⅞	87	131	175	218	262	306	350	392	437	480	524	568	611	655	699	742	786
1	76	115	153	191	230	268	306	344	382	420	458	497	535	573	611	649	687
1⅛	68	102	136	170	204	238	272	306	340	373	407	441	475	509	542	576	610
1¼	61	92	122	153	184	214	244	274	306	336	367	397	428	458	489	520	551
1⅜	56	83	111	139	167	194	222	250	278	306	333	361	389	417	444	472	500
1½	51	76	102	127	152	178	204	228	255	280	306	331	357	382	407	433	458
1⅝	47	71	94	118	141	165	188	212	235	259	282	306	329	353	377	400	423
1¾	44	65	87	109	130	152	174	196	218	240	262	284	306	327	349	371	393
1⅞	41	61	82	102	122	143	163	183	204	224	244	265	285	306	326	346	366
2	38	57	76	95	114	134	152	172	191	210	229	248	267	287	306	324	344
2⅛	36	54	72	90	108	126	144	162	180	198	216	234	252	270	288	306	323
2¼	34	51	68	85	102	119	136	153	170	187	204	221	238	255	272	289	306
2⅜	32	48	64	80	97	112	129	145	161	177	193	210	225	241	257	273	290
2½	31	46	61	76	92	106	122	134	153	168	183	199	214	229	244	260	275
2⅝	29	44	58	73	88	102	117	130	146	160	175	189	204	218	233	248	262
2¾	28	42	56	70	83	97	111	125	139	153	167	181	194	208	222	236	250
2⅞	27	40	53	67	80	93	106	119	133	146	159	173	186	199	213	226	239
3	25	38	51	64	76	90	102	114	127	140	153	166	178	191	204	216	229

Cutting speeds in feet per minute — Revolutions per minute

Table 3. Morse Tapers

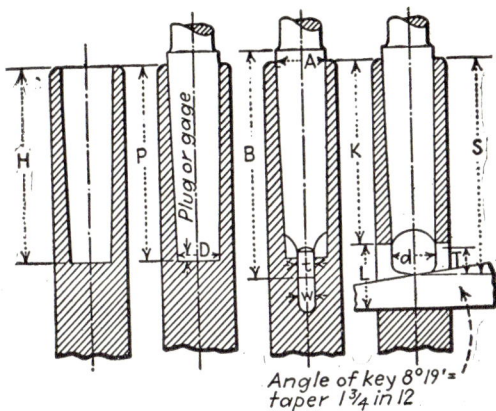

Angle of key 8°19' =
taper 1¾ in 12

Number of taper	Diameter of plug at small end	Diameter at end of socket	Whole length of shank	Shank depth	Depth of hole	Standard plug depth	Thickness of tongue	Length of tongue	Diameter of tongue	Width of keyway	Length of keyway	End of socket to keyway	Taper per foot
	D	A	B	S	H	P	t	T	d	w	L	K	
0	0.252	0.356	2 11/32	2 7/32	2 1/32	2	5/32	1/4	0.235	0.160	9/16	1 15/16	0.6246
1	0.369	0.475	2 9/16	2 7/16	2 3/16	2 1/8	13/64	3/8	0.343	0.213	3/4	2 1/16	0.5986
2	0.572	0.700	3 1/8	2 15/16	2 5/8	2 9/16	1/4	7/16	17/32	0.260	7/8	2 1/2	0.5994
3	0.778	0.938	3 7/8	3 11/16	3 1/4	3 3/16	5/16	9/16	23/32	0.322	1 3/16	3 1/16	0.6023
4	1.020	1.231	4 7/8	4 5/8	4 1/8	4 1/16	15/32	5/8	1 13/32	0.478	1 1/4	3 7/8	0.6232
5	1.475	1.748	6 1/8	5 7/8	5 1/4	5 3/16	5/8	3/4	1 13/32	0.635	1 1/2	4 15/16	0.6315
6	2.116	2.494	8 9/16	8 1/4	7 3/8	7 1/4	3/4	1 1/8	2	0.760	1 3/4	7	0.6256
7	2.750	3.270	11 1/4	11 5/8	10 1/2	10	1 1/8	1 3/8	2 5/8	1.135	2 5/8	9 1/2	0.6240

NOTE: The figures in the "Taper per foot" column have been revised to conform with the standard end diameters and lengths.

Table 4. Brown & Sharpe Tapers

Taper 0.500 in. per ft. except No. 10, which is 0.5161 in. per ft.

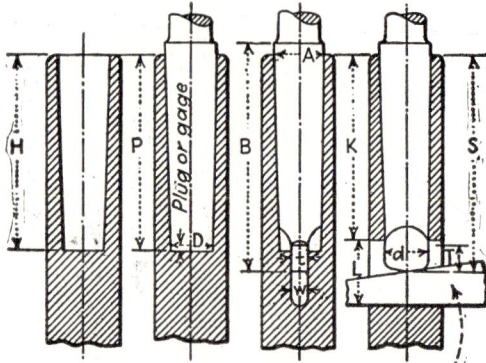

Angle of key 8°19' = taper 1¾ in 12

Number of taper	Diameter of plug at small end	Plug depth	Diameter at end of socket	Whole length of shank	Shank depth	Depth of hole	Thickness of tongue	Diameter of tongue	Length of tongue	Width of keyway	Length of keyway	End of socket to keyway
	D	P	A	B	S	H	t	d	T	w	L	K
4	0.350	$1\frac{11}{16}$	0.420	$2\frac{3}{16}$	$2\frac{3}{32}$	$1\frac{13}{16}$	$\frac{7}{32}$	0.320	$1\frac{1}{32}$	0.228	$1\frac{1}{16}$	$1\frac{41}{64}$
5	0.450	$2\frac{1}{8}$	0.539	$2\frac{21}{32}$	$2\frac{9}{16}$	$2\frac{1}{4}$	$\frac{1}{4}$	0.420	$\frac{3}{8}$	0.260	$\frac{3}{4}$	$2\frac{1}{16}$
6	0.500	$2\frac{3}{8}$	0.599	$2\frac{31}{32}$	$2\frac{7}{8}$	$2\frac{1}{2}$	$\frac{9}{32}$	0.460	$\frac{7}{16}$	0.291	$\frac{7}{8}$	$2\frac{19}{64}$
7	0.600	$2\frac{7}{8}$	0.720	$3\frac{1}{2}$	$3\frac{13}{32}$	3	$\frac{5}{16}$	0.560	$\frac{15}{32}$	0.322	$\frac{15}{16}$	$2\frac{25}{32}$
8	0.750	$3\frac{9}{16}$	0.898	$4\frac{1}{4}$	$4\frac{1}{8}$	$3\frac{11}{16}$	$\frac{11}{32}$	0.710	$\frac{1}{2}$	0.353	1	$3\frac{29}{64}$
9	0.900	$4\frac{1}{4}$	1.077	5	$4\frac{7}{8}$	$4\frac{3}{8}$	$\frac{3}{8}$	0.860	$\frac{9}{16}$	0.385	$1\frac{1}{8}$	$4\frac{1}{8}$
10	1.0446	5	1.260	$5\frac{27}{32}$	$5\frac{23}{32}$	$5\frac{1}{8}$	$\frac{7}{16}$	1.010	$\frac{21}{32}$	0.447	$1\frac{5}{16}$	$4\frac{27}{32}$
11	1.250	$5\frac{15}{16}$	1.498	$6\frac{25}{32}$	$6\frac{21}{32}$	$6\frac{1}{16}$	$\frac{7}{16}$	1.210	$\frac{21}{32}$	0.447	$1\frac{5}{16}$	$5\frac{25}{32}$
12	1.500	$7\frac{1}{8}$	1.797	$8\frac{1}{16}$	$7\frac{15}{16}$	$7\frac{1}{4}$	$\frac{1}{2}$	1.460	$\frac{3}{4}$	0.510	$1\frac{1}{2}$	$6\frac{15}{16}$

Table 5. Taper Pins and Reamers
(Pratt & Whitney Company)
Taper = $\frac{1}{4}$ in. per ft., or 0.0208 in. per in.

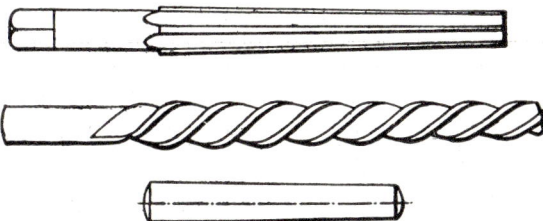

Size (No.)	Diameter of small end of reamer	Diameter of large end of reamer	Length of flute	Total length of reamer	Size drill for reamer	Longest limit length of pin	Diameter of large end of pin	Approx. fractional size at large end of pin
0	0.135	0.162	$1\frac{5}{16}$	2	28	1	0.156	$\frac{5}{32}$
1	0.146	0.179	$1\frac{9}{16}$	$2\frac{3}{8}$	25	$1\frac{1}{4}$	0.172	$\frac{11}{64}$
2	0.162	0.200	$1\frac{13}{16}$	$2\frac{11}{16}$	19	$1\frac{1}{2}$	0.193	$\frac{3}{16}$
3	0.183	0.226	$2\frac{1}{16}$	3	12	$1\frac{3}{4}$	0.219	$\frac{7}{32}$
4	0.208	0.257	$2\frac{3}{8}$	$3\frac{7}{16}$	3	2	0.250	$\frac{1}{4}$
5	0.240	0.300	$2\frac{7}{8}$	$4\frac{1}{8}$	$\frac{1}{4}$	$2\frac{1}{4}$	0.289	$\frac{19}{64}$
6	0.279	0.354	$3\frac{5}{8}$	5	$\frac{9}{32}$	$3\frac{1}{4}$	0.341	$\frac{11}{32}$
7	0.331	0.423	$4\frac{7}{16}$	$6\frac{1}{16}$	$\frac{11}{32}$	$3\frac{3}{4}$	0.409	$\frac{13}{32}$
8	0.398	0.407	$5\frac{1}{4}$	$7\frac{1}{16}$	$\frac{13}{32}$	$4\frac{1}{2}$	0.492	$\frac{1}{2}$
9	0.482	0.609	$6\frac{1}{8}$	$8\frac{1}{8}$	$\frac{31}{64}$	$5\frac{1}{4}$	0.591	$\frac{19}{32}$
10	0.581	0.727	7	$9\frac{1}{2}$	$\frac{19}{32}$	6	0.706	$\frac{23}{32}$
11	0.706	0.878	$8\frac{1}{4}$	$11\frac{1}{4}$	$\frac{23}{32}$	$7\frac{1}{4}$	0.857	$\frac{55}{64}$
12	0.842	0.050	10	$13\frac{3}{8}$	$\frac{55}{64}$	$8\frac{3}{4}$	0.013	$1\frac{1}{64}$
13	1.009	1.259	12	16	$1\frac{1}{64}$	$10\frac{3}{4}$	1.233	$1\frac{15}{64}$

NOTE: These reamer sizes are so proportioned that each overlaps the size smaller about $\frac{1}{2}$ in. The helical reamers are designed especially for machine reaming on a production basis. They are very free cutting, the chips do not pack in the flutes, and there is a minimum of breakage.

Table 6. Tapers per Foot and Corresponding Angles

Taper per foot	Included angle	Angle with center line	Taper per foot	Included angle	Angle with center line
1/16	0°18′	0°9′	1⅛	5°22′	2°41′
⅛	0°36′	0°18′	1¼	5°57½″	2°58¾′
3/16	0°53½′	0°26¾′	1⅜	6°33½′	3°16¾′
¼	1°11½′	0°35¾′	1½	7°9′	3°34½′
5/16	1°29½′	0°44¾′	1⅝	7°45′	3°52½′
⅜	1°47½′	0°53¾′	1¾	8°20½′	4°10¼′
7/16	2°5½′	1°2¾′	1⅞	8°56′	4°28′
½	2°23′	1°11½′	2	9°31½′	4°45¾′
9/16	2°41′	1°20½′	2¼	10°43½′	5°21¾′
⅝	2°59′	1°29½′	2½	11°53½′	5°56¾′
11/16	3°10½′	1°38¼′	2¾	13°9½′	6°34¾′
¾	3°35′	1°47½′	3	14°15′	7°7½′
13/16	3°53′	1°56½′	3½	16°35½′	8°17¾′
⅞	4°10½′	2°5¼′	4	18°55½′	9°27¾′
15/16	4°28½′	2°14¼′	4½	21°37′	10°48½′
1	4°46½′	2°23¼′	5	23°32′	11°46′

Table 7. Different Standards for Wire Gages and Sheet-metal Gages in Use in the United States

Dimensions of sizes in decimal parts of an inch

Gage numbers	Steel wire gage	American or Brown & Sharpe gage	American S. & W. Co. *new* music wire gage	Stubs' *steel* wire gage	Birmingham or Stubs' *iron* wire gage	British Imperial Standard wire gage	U.S. Standard gage for sheet and plate iron and steel	Gage numbers
6/0	.4615	.5800	.004	....	....	.464	.4687	6/0
5/0	.4305	.5165	.005	....	.500	.432	.4375	5/0
4/0	.3938	.4600	.006	....	.454	.400	.4062	4/0
3/0	.3625	.4096	.007	....	.425	.372	.375	3/0
2/0	.3310	.3648	.008	....	.380	.348	.3437	2/0
1/0	.3065	.3249	.009	....	.340	.324	.3125	1/0
1	.2830	.2893	.010	.227	.300	.300	.2812	1
2	.2625	.2576	.011	.219	.284	.276	.2656	2
3	.2437	.2294	.012	.212	.259	.252	.25	3
4	.2253	.2043	.013	.207	.238	.232 —	.2344	4
5	.2070	.1819	.014	.204	.220	.212	.2187	5
6	.1920	.1620	.016	.201	.203	.192	.2031	6
7	.1770	.1442	.018	.199	.180	.176	.1875	7
8	.1620	.1285	.020	.197	.165	.160	.1719	8
9	.1483	.1144	.022	.194	.148	.144	.1562	9
10	.1350	.1019	.024	.191	.134	.128	.1406	10
11	.1205	.0907	.026	.188	.120	.116	.125	11
12	.1055	.0808	.029	.185	.109	.104	.1094	12
13	.0915	.0720	.031	.182	.095	.092	.0937	13
14	.0800	.0641	.033	.180	.083	.080	.0781	14
15	.0720	.0571	.035	.178	.072	.072	.0703	15
16	.0625	.0508	.037	.175	.065	.064	.0625	16
17	.0540	.0452	.039	.172	.058	.056	.05625	17
18	.0475	.0403	.041	.168	.049	.048	.05	18
19	.0410	.0359	.043	.164	.042	.040	.04375	19
20	.0348	.032	.045	.161	.035	.036	.0375	20
21	.0317	.0285	.047	.157	.032	.032	.03437	21
22	.0286	.0253	.049	.155	.028	.028	.03125	22
23	.0258	.0226	.051	.153	.025	.024	.02812	23
24	.0230	.0201	.055	.151	.022	.022	.025	24
25	.0204	.0179	.059	.148	.020	.020	.02187	25
26	.0181	.0159	.063	.146	.018	.018	.01875	26
27	.0173	.0142	.067	.143	.016	.0164	.01718	27
28	.0162	.0126	.071	.139	.014	.0149	.01562	28
29	.0150	.0113	.075	.134	.013	.0136	.01406	29
30	.0140	.01	.080	.127	.012	.0124	.0125	30
31	.0132	.0089	.085	.120	.010	.0116	.01093	31
32	.0128	.00795	.090	.115	.009	.0108	.01015	32
33	.0118	.00708	.095	.112	.008	.0100	.00937	33
34	.0104	.0063	.100	.110	.007	.0092	.00859	34
35	.0095	.0056	.106	.108	.005	.0084	.00781	35
36	.0090	.005	.112	.106	.004	.0076	.00703	36
37	.0085	.00445	.118	.103	....	.0068	.00664	37
38	.0080	.00396	.124	.101	....	.0060	.00625	38
39	.0075	.00353	.130	.099	....	.0052	......	39
40	.0070	.00314	.138	.097	....	.0048	......	40
41	.0066	.00280	....	.095	....	.0044	......	41
42	.0062	.00249	....	.092	....	.0040	......	42
43	.0060	.00222	....	.088	....	.0036	......	43
44	.0058	.00198	....	.085	....	.0032	......	44
45	.0055	.00176	....	.081	....	.0028	......	45
46	.0052	.00157	....	.079	....	.0024	......	46
47	.0050	.00140	....	.077	....	.0020	......	47
48	.0048	.00124	....	.075	....	.0016	......	48
49	.0046	.000986	....	.072	....	.0012	......	49
50	.0044	.000878	....	.069	....	.001	......	50

Table 8. American National Screw Threads: National Coarse (NC) and National Fine (NF)

Thread Dimensions and Tap-drill Sizes

n = number of threads per inch

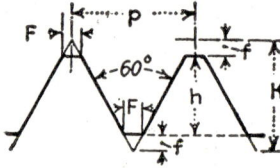

$$p \text{ (pitch)} = \frac{1}{\text{number of threads per inch}} = \frac{1}{n}$$

$$h \text{ (depth)} = 0.649519p = \frac{0.649519}{n}$$

$$H \text{ (depth, sharp V thread)} = 0.866025p$$

$$f = \frac{H}{8} = \text{depth of basic truncation}$$

$$F = 0.125p = \frac{p}{8} = \text{width of basic flat at}$$
top, crest or root

National Coarse is the former U.S. Standard for sizes ¼ in. and larger, while for sizes under ¼ in. it is the coarse threads of the former A.S.M.E. machine-screw sizes.

National Fine is the former S.A.E. Standard for sizes ¼ in. and larger, while for sizes under ¼ in. it is the fine threads of the former A.S.M.E. machine-screw sizes.

Nominal size and number threads per inch	Major diameter	Pitch diameter	Minor diameter	Commercial tap drill to produce approx. 75% full thread	Decimal equivalent of tap drill
*0—80	0.0600	0.0519	0.0438	3-64	0.0469
*1—64	0.0730	0.0629	0.0527	53	0.0595
72	0.0730	0.0640	0.0550	53	0.0595
*2—56	0.0860	0.0744	0.0628	50	0.0700
64	0.0860	0.0759	0.0657	50	0.0700
*3—48	0.0990	0.0855	0.0719	47	0.0785
56	0.0990	0.0874	0.0758	45	0.0820
*4—40	0.1120	0.0958	0.0795	43	0.0890
48	0.1120	0.0985	0.0849	42	0.0935
*5—40	0.1250	0.1088	0.0925	38	0.1015
44	0.1250	0.1102	0.0955	37	0.1040
*6—32	0.1380	0.1177	0.0974	36	0.1065
40	0.1380	0.1218	0.1055	33	0.1130
*8—32	0.1640	0.1437	0.1234	29	0.1360
36	0.1640	0.1460	0.1279	29	0.1360
*10—24	0.1900	0.1629	0.1359	25	0.1495
32	0.1900	0.1697	0.1494	21	0.1590
*12—24	0.2160	0.1889	0.1619	16	0.1770
28	0.2160	0.1928	0.1696	14	0.1820
¼—20	0.2500	0.2175	0.1850	7	0.2010
28	0.2500	0.2268	0.2036	3	0.2130
⁵⁄₁₆—18	0.3125	0.2764	0.2403	F	0.2570
24	0.3125	0.2854	0.2584	I	0.2720

* American National Standard wood screws are made in same numbers and corresponding body diameters as starred sizes.

Table 8. American National Screw Threads: National Coarse (NC) and National Fine (NF) (Continued)

Nominal size and number threads per inch	Major diameter	Pitch diameter	Minor diameter	Commercial tap drill to produce approx. 75% full thread	Decimal equivalent of tap drill
⅜—16	0.3750	0.3344	0.2938	5-16	0.3125
24	0.3750	0.3479	0.3209	Q	0.3320
⁷⁄₁₆—14	0.4375	0.3911	0.3447	U	0.3680
20	0.4375	0.4050	0.3726	25-64	0.3906
½—13	0.5000	0.4501	0.4001	27-64	0.4219
20	0.5000	0.4675	0.4351	29-64	0.4531
⁹⁄₁₆—12	0.5625	0.5084	0.4542	31-64	0.4844
18	0.5625	0.5264	0.4903	33-64	0.5156
⅝—11	0.6250	0.5660	0.5069	17-32	0.5312
18	0.6250	0.5889	0.5528	37-64	0.5781
¾—10	0.7500	0.6850	0.6201	21-32	0.6562
16	0.7500	0.7094	0.6688	11-16	0.6875
⅞— 9	0.8750	0.8029	0.7307	49-64	0.7656
14	0.8750	0.8286	0.7822	13-16	0.8125
1— 8	1.0000	0.9188	0.8376	7-8	0.8750
14	1.0000	0.9536	0.9072	15-16	0.9375
1⅛— 7	1.1250	1.0322	0.9394	63-64	0.9844
12	1.1250	1.0709	1.0168	1 3-64	1.0469
1¼— 7	1.2500	1.1572	1.0644	1 7-64	1.1094
12	1.2500	1.1959	1.1418	1 11-64	1.1719
1⅜— 6	1.3750	1.2667	1.1585	1 7-32	1.2187
12	1.3750	1.3209	1.2668	1 19-64	1.2969
1½— 6	1.5000	1.3917	1.2835	1 11-32	1.3437
12	1.5000	1.4459	1.3918	1 27-64	1.4219
1¾— 5	1.7500	1.6201	1.4902	1 9-16	1.5625
2 — 4½	2.0000	1.8557	1.7113	1 25-32	1.7812
2¼— 4½	2.2500	2.1057	1.9613	2 1-32	2.0312
2½— 4	2.5000	2.3376	2.1752	2 1-4	2.2500
2¾— 4	2.7500	2.5876	2.4252	2 1-2	2.5000
3 — 4	3.0000	2.8376	2.6752	2 3-4	2.7500
3¼— 4	3.2500	3.0876	2.9252	3	3.0000
3½— 4	3.5000	3.3376	3.1752	3 1-4	3.2500
3¾— 4	3.7500	3.5876	3.4252	3 1-2	3.5000
4 — 4	4.0000	3.8376	3.6752	3 3-4	3.7500

REASONS FOR FINER PITCHES (NATIONAL FINE)

Threads in automobile work are cut in hard, tough materials and do not require to be so coarse as threads cut in cast iron. A screw or bolt of a given size and of finer pitch has greater minor diameter and consequently greater strength than a coarse-pitch screw of same size. A fine-pitch screw or nut may be set up tighter and does not shake loose so readily as one of coarse pitch.

Table 9. Acme 29-deg. Screw Threads

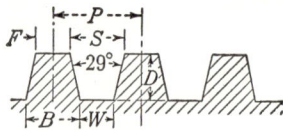

N = number of threads per inch

$P = \dfrac{1}{N}$ = linear pitch $W = 0.3707P - 0.0052$

$D = 0.5P + 0.010$ $S = 0.6293P$

$F = 0.3707P$ $B = 0.6293P + 0.0052$

The Acme standard thread is an adaptation of the most commonly used style of worm thread and is intended to take the place of the square thread.

It is a little shallower than the worm thread, but the same depth as the square thread and much stronger than the latter.

The various parts of the Acme standard thread are obtained as follows:

Width of tool point for screw thread $= \dfrac{0.3707}{\text{number of threads per inch}} - 0.0052$

Width of screw or nut thread $= \dfrac{0.3707}{\text{number of threads per inch}}$

Minor diameter $=$ major diameter $- \left(\dfrac{1}{\text{number of threads per inch}} + 0.020 \right)$

Depth of thread $= \dfrac{1}{2 \times \text{number of threads per inch}} + 0.010$

Table of Acme 29-deg. Screw-thread Parts

Number of threads per inch	Pitch of single thread	Depth of thread	Width of top of thread	Width of space at bottom of thread	Width of space at top of thread	Thickness at root of thread
N	P	D	F	W	S	B
1	1.0	0.5100	0.3707	0.3655	0.6293	0.6345
1⅓	0.750	0.3850	0.2780	0.2728	0.4720	0.4772
2	0.500	0.2600	0.1853	0.1801	0.3147	0.3199
3	0.3333	0.1767	0.1235	0.1183	0.2098	.02150
4	0.250	0.1350	0.0927	0.0875	0.1573	0.1625
5	0.200	0.1100	0.0741	0.0689	0.1259	0.1311
6	0.1666	0.0933	0.0618	0.0566	0.1049	0.1101
7	0.1428	0.0814	0.0529	0.0478	0.0899	0.0951
8	0.125	0.0725	0.0463	0.0411	0.0787	0.0839
9	0.1111	0.0655	0.0413	0.0361	0.0699	0.0751
10	0.10	0.0600	0.0371	0.0319	0.0629	0.0681

Table 10. American (N.P.T.) Standard Taper Pipe Taps
(Drill sizes for tapping without reaming)

Size of pipe	Threads per inch	Actual inside diameter	Actual outside diameter	Minor diameter small end of tap	Minor diameter small end of pipe and gage	Tap drill Size	Tap drill Decimal equivalent
1/8	27	0.270	0.405	0.3145	0.3339	R	0.339
1/4	18	0.364	0.540	0.4043	0.4329	7/16	0.437
3/8	18	0.494	0.675	0.5393	0.5676	37/64	0.578
1/2	14	0.623	0.840	0.6651	0.7013	23/32	0.719
3/4	14	0.824	1.050	0.8751	0.9105	59/64	0.921
1	11 1/2	1.048	1.315	1.1017	1.1441	1 5/32	1.156
1 1/4	11 1/2	1.380	1.660	1.4447	1.4876	1 1/2	1.500
1 1/2	11 1/2	1.610	1.900	1.6828	1.7265	1 47/64	1.734
2	11 1/2	2.067	2.375	2.1578	2.1995	2 7/32	2.218
2 1/2	8	2.468	2.875	2.5617	2.6195	2 5/8	2.625
3	8	3.067	3.500	3.1828	3.2406	3 1/4	3.250
3 1/2	8	3.548	4.000	3.6789	3.7375	3 3/4	3.750
4	8	4.026	4.500	4.1750	4.2344	4 1/4	4.250

NOTE: Standard pipes and pipe fittings go to 12 in. diameter.

It is frequently necessary to drill holes which are to be tapped for pipes and fittings. The American Standard is used throughout the United States. The "nominal" inside diameter of the pipe is used to designate the size of the pipe. The fact that there is considerable difference in the "nominal" diameter and actual diameter, especially in the smaller sizes, is often confusing.

For five or six threads the outside diameter of the pipe tapers and the diameter at the root of the thread follow the same taper. In this part the threads have full depth. For the next two threads the taper at the root continues, but the outside not being tapered these threads have imperfect tops. The remaining threads are increasingly imperfect on the top and also on the bottom because of the chamfer or bell mouth of the threading die.

In extra strong, or double extra strong, or hydraulic pipe the additional thickness is on the inside of the pipe and does not affect the thread dimensions. When cutting threads on pipe or pipe fittings set the tool at right angles to the axis of the piece.

Table 11. British Standard Whitworth Threads

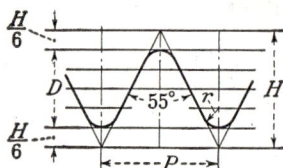

P (pitch) $= \dfrac{1}{\text{number of threads per inch}}$

D (depth) $= 0.6403P = \dfrac{0.6403}{n}$

$H = 0.9605P$

$\dfrac{H}{6} = 0.1600P$

$r = 0.1373P$

n = number of threads per inch

Nominal diameter of screw, inches	No. of threads per inch	Std. single depth of thread	Effective diameter (pitch diameter)	Commercial tap drill to produce 75% full thread	Nominal diameter of screw, inches	No. of threads per inch	Std. single depth of thread	Effective diameter (pitch diameter)	Commercial tap drill to produce 75% full thread
1/4	20	0.0320	0.2180	13/64	1	8	0.0800	0.9200	7/8
5/16	18	0.0356	0.2769	F	1 1/8	7	0.0915	1.0335	1
3/8	16	0.0400	0.3350	O	1 1/4	7	0.0915	1.1585	1 7/64
7/16	14	0.0457	0.3918	U	1 1/2	6	0.1067	1.3933	1 11/32
1/2	12	0.0534	0.4466	27/64	1 3/4	5	0.1281	1.6219	1 9/16
9/16	12	0.0534	0.5091	31/64	2	4 1/2	0.1423	1.8577	1 25/32
5/8	11	0.0582	0.5668	35/64	2 1/4	4	0.1601	2.0899	2
3/4	10	0.0640	0.6860	21/32	2 1/2	4	0.1601	2.3399	2 1/4
7/8	9	0.0711	0.8039	49/64					

Table 12. British Standard Fine Threads

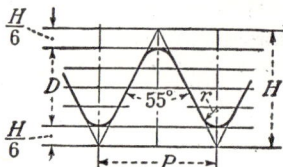

P (pitch) $= \dfrac{1}{\text{number of threads per inch}}$

D (depth) $= 0.6403P = \dfrac{0.6403}{n}$

$H = 0.9605P$

$\dfrac{H}{6} = 0.1600P$

$r = 0.1373P$

n = number of threads per inch

Nominal diameter of screw, inches	No. of threads per inch	Std. single depth of thread	Effective diameter (pitch diameter)	Commercial tap drill to produce 75% full thread	Nominal diameter of screw, inches	No. of threads per inch	Std. single depth of thread	Effective diameter (pitch diameter)	Commercial tap drill to produce 75% full thread
1/4	26	0.0246	0.2254	No. 3	13/16	12	0.0534	0.7591	47/64
9/32	26	0.0246	0.2566	D	7/8	11	0.0582	0.8168	25/32
5/16	22	0.0291	0.2834	M	1	10	0.0640	0.9360	29/32
3/8	20	0.0320	0.3430	21/64	1 1/8	9	0.0711	1.0539	1 1/64
7/16	18	0.0356	0.4019	W	1 1/4	9	0.0711	1.1789	1 9/64
1/2	16	0.0400	0.4600	7/16	1 3/8	8	0.0800	1.2950	1 17/64
9/16	16	0.0400	0.5225	1/2	1 1/2	8	0.0800	1.4200	1 25/64
5/8	14	0.0457	0.5793	9/16	1 3/4	7	0.0915	1.6585	1 39/64
11/16	14	0.0457	0.6418	5/8	2	7	0.0915	1.9085	1 55/64
3/4	12	0.0534	0.6966	43/64					

Table 13. British Association Screw Threads

Angle of thread $47\frac{1}{2}$ deg.

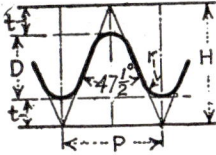

$P \text{ (pitch)} = \dfrac{1}{\text{number of threads per inch}}$

$D \text{ (depth)} = 0.6P$

$H = 1.136P$

$t = 0.268P$

$r = 0.182P$

$n = \text{number of threads per inch}$

Seventy-five per cent of the full depth of thread is amply strong for all ordinary work.

Number	Diameter (major diameter), mm.	Approximate diameter, inches	Pitch, mm.	Depth of thread, mm.	Effective diameter (pitch diameter), mm.	Core diameter (minor diameter), mm.	Drill sizes nearest commercial drill to produce 75% depth of thread
0	6.0	0.236	1.00	0.600	5.400	4.80	No. 7
1	5.3	0.209	0.90	0.540	4.760	4.22	16
2	4.7	0.185	0.81	0.485	4.215	3.73	22
3	4.1	0.161	0.73	0.440	3.660	3.22	29
4	3.6	0.142	0.66	0.395	3.205	2.81	31
5	3.2	0.126	0.59	0.355	2.845	2.49	37
6	2.8	0.110	0.53	0.320	2.480	2.16	43
7	2.5	0.098	0.48	0.290	2.210	1.92	46
8	2.2	0.087	0.43	0.260	1.940	1.68	48
9	1.9	0.075	0.39	0.235	1.665	1.43	$\frac{1}{16}$ in.
10	1.7	0.067	0.35	0.210	1.490	1.28	54
11	1.5	0.059	0.31	0.185	1.315	1.13	56
12	1.3	0.051	0.28	0.170	1.130	0.96	59

Table 14. French (Metric) Standard Screw Threads

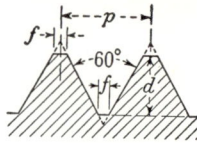

p = pitch
d = depth = $p \times 0.64952$
f = flat = $\dfrac{p}{8}$

Diameter of screw, mm.	Pitch, mm.	Diameter at root of thread, mm.	Width of flat, mm.	Diameter of screw, mm.	Pitch, mm.	Diameter at root of thread, mm.	Width of flat, mm.
3	0.5	2.35	0.06	30	3.5	25.45	0.44
4	0.75	3.03	0.09	32	3.5	27.45	0.44
5	0.75	4.03	0.09	33	3.5	28.45	0.44
6	1.0	4.70	0.13	34	3.5	29.45	0.44
7	1.0	5.70	0.13	36	4.0	30.80	0.5
8	1.0	6.70	0.13	38	4.0	32.80	0.5
8	1.25	6.38	0.16	39	4.0	33.80	0.5
9	1.0	7.70	0.13	40	4.0	34.80	0.5
9	1.25	7.38	0.16	42	4.5	36.15	0.56
10	1.5	8.05	0.19	44	4.5	38.15	0.56
11	1.5	9.05	0.19	45	4.5	39.15	0.56
12	1.5	10.05	0.19	46	4.5	40.15	0.56
12	1.75	9.73	0.22	48	5.0	41.51	0.63
14	2.0	11.40	0.25	50	5.0	43.51	0.63
16	2.0	13.40	0.25	52	5.0	45.51	0.63
18	2.5	14.75	0.31	56	5.5	48.86	0.69
20	2.5	16.75	0.31	60	5.5	52.86	0.69
22	2.5	18.75	0.31	64	6.0	56.21	0.75
22	3.0	18.10	0.38	68	6.0	60.21	0.75
24	3.0	20.10	0.38	72	6.5	63.56	0.81
26	3.0	22.10	0.38	76	6.5	67.56	0.81
27	3.0	23.10	0.38	80	7.0	70.91	0.88
28	3.0	24.10	0.38				

Table 15. International Standard Screw Threads*
(Dimensions in millimeters)

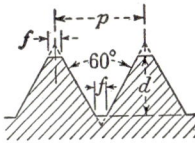

$p = \text{pitch}$
$d = \text{depth} = p \times 0.6495$
$f = \text{flat} = \dfrac{p}{8}$

Diam. of screw	Pitch	Diam. of screw	Pitch	Diam. of screw	Pitch	Diam. of screw	Pitch
6	1.00	18	2.50	42	4.50	76	6.50
7	1.00	20	2.50	45	4.50	80	7.00
8	1.25	22	2.50	48	5.00	88	7.50
9	1.25	24	3.00	52	5.00	96	8.00
10	1.50	27	3.00	56	5.50	116	9.00
11	1.50	30	3.50	60	5.50	136	10.00
12	1.75	33	3.50	64	6.00		
14	2.00	36	4.00	68	6.00		
16	2.00	39	4.00	72	6.50		

* The International Standard is the same, with modifications noted, as that now in general use in France.

INTERNATIONAL STANDARD THREADS

At the "Congrés International pour l'Unification des Filetages," held in Zurich, October 24, 1898, the following resolutions were adopted:

"The Congress has undertaken the task of unifying the threads of machine screws. It recommends to all those who wish to adopt the metric system of threads to make use of the proposed system. This system is the one which has been established by the 'Society for the Encouragement of National Industries,' with the following modification adopted by this Congress.

"1. The clearance at the bottom of thread shall not exceed 1⁄16 part of the height of the original triangle. The shape of the bottom of the thread resulting from said clearance is left to the judgment of the manufacturers. However, the Congress recommends rounded profile for said bottom.

"3. The table for Standard Diameters accepted is the one which has been proposed by the Swiss Committee of Action. [This table is given above.] It is to be noticed especially that 1.25 mm. pitch is adopted for 8 mm. diameter, and 1.75 mm. pitch for 12 mm. diameter. The pitches of sizes between standard diameters indicated in the table are to be the same as for the next smaller standard diameter."

Table 16. The Metric System of Measurement

MEASURES OF LENGTH

1 millimeter (mm.) = 0.03937079 in., or about $\frac{1}{25}$ in.
10 millimeters = 1 centimeter (cm.) = 0.3937079 in.
10 centimeters = 1 decimeter (dm.) = 3.937079 in.
10 decimeters = 1 meter (m.) = 39.37079 in., 3.2808992 ft., or 1.09361 yd.
10 meters = 1 decameter (Dm.) = 32.808992 ft.
10 decameters = 1 hectometer (Hm.) = 19.927817 rods
10 hectometers = 1 kilometer (Km.) = 1093.61 yd., or 0.621377 mi.
10 kilometers = 1 myriameter (Mn.) = 6.21377 mi.
  1 inch = 2.54 cm., 1 foot = 0.3048 m., 1 yard = 0.9144 m.
  1 rod = 0.5029 Dm., 1 mile = 1.6093 Km.

MEASURES OF WEIGHT

1 gramme (g.) = 15.4324874 gr. Troy, or 0.03215 oz. Troy, or 0.03527398 oz. avoir.
10 grammes = 1 decagramme (Dg.) = 0.3527398 oz. avoir.
10 decagrammes = 1 hectogramme₂ (Hg.) = 3.527398 oz. avoir.
10 hectogrammes = 1 kilogramme (Kg.) = 2.20462125 lb.
1000 kilogrammes = 1 tonne (T.) = 2204.62125 lb. or 1.1023 tons of 2000 lb. or 0.9842 ton of 2240 lb. or 19.68 cwt.
1 grain = 0.0648 g., 1 oz. avoir. = 28.35 g., 1 pound = 0.4536 Kg., 1 ton 2000 lb. = 0.9072 T., 1 ton 2240 lb. = 1.016 T., or 1016 Kg.

MEASURES OF CAPACITY

1 liter (l.) = 1 cubic decimeter = 61.0270515 cu. in., or 0.03531 cu. ft. or 1.0567 liquid qt. or 0.908 dry qt. or 0.26417 Amer. gal.
10 liters = 1 decaliter (Dl.) = 2.6417 gal., or 1.135 pk.
10 decaliters = 1 hectoliter (Hl.) = 2.8375 bu.
10 hectoliters = 1 kiloliter (Kl.) = 61027.0515 cu. in., or 28.375 bu.
  1 cubic foot = 28.317 l., 1 gallon, Amer. = 3.785 l., 1 gallon, Brit. = 4.543 l.

Table 17. Metric Conversion Table*

Millimeters	×	0.03937	= inches
Millimeters	=	25.400	× inches
Meters	×	3.2809	= feet
Meters	=	0.3048	× feet
Kilometers	×	0.621377	= miles
Kilometers	=	1.6093	× miles
Square centimeters	×	0.15500	= square inches
Square centimeters	=	6.4515	× square inches
Square meters	×	10.76410	= square feet
Square meters	=	0.09290	× square feet
Square kilometers	×	247.1098	= acres
Square kilometers	=	0.00405	× acres
Hectares	×	2.471	= acres
Hectares	=	0.4047	× acres
Cubic centimeters	×	0.061025	= cubic inches
Cubic centimeters	=	16.3866	× cubic inches
Cubic meters	×	35.3156	= cubic feet
Cubic meters	=	0.02832	× cubic feet
Cubic meters	×	1.308	= cubic yards
Cubic meters	=	0.765	× cubic yards
Liters	×	61.023	= cubic inches
Liters	=	0.01639	× cubic inches
Liters	×	0.26418	= U. S. gallons
Liters	=	3.7854	× U. S. gallons
Grams	×	15.4324	= grains
Grams	=	0.0648	× grains
Grams	×	0.03527	= ounces, avoirdupois
Grams	=	28.3495	× ounces, avoirdupois
Kilograms	×	2.2046	= pounds
Kilograms	=	0.4536	× pounds
Kilograms per sq. cm.	×	14.2231	= lb. per sq. in.
Kilograms per sq. cm.	=	0.0703	× lb. per sq. in.
Kilogram per cubic meter	×	0.06243	= lb. per cu. ft.
Kilogram per cubic meter	=	16.01890	× lb. per cu. ft.
Metric tons (1000 kilograms)	×	1.1023	= tons (2000 lb.)
Metric tons (1000 kilograms)	=	0.9072	× tons (2000 lb.)
Kilowatts	×	1.3405	= horsepower
Kilowatts	=	0.746	× horsepower
Calories	×	3.9683	= B.t.u.
Calories	=	0.2520	× B.t.u.
Francs	×	0.193	= dollars
Francs	=	5.18	× dollars

* *The American Machinist*, New York.

Table 18. Decimal Equivalents of the Number and Letter Sizes of Twist Drills

No.	Size in decimals	No.	Size in decimals	No.	Size in decimals	No.	Size in decimals
1	0.2280	21	0.1590	41	0.0960	61	0.0390
2	0.2210	22	0.1570	42	0.0935	62	0.0380
3	0.2130	23	0.1540	43	0.0890	63	0.0370
4	0.2090	24	0.1520	44	0.0860	64	0.0360
5	0.2055	25	0.1495	45	0.0820	65	0.0350
6	0.2040	26	0.1470	46	0.0810	66	0.0330
7	0.2010	27	0.1440	47	0.0785	67	0.0320
8	0.1990	28	0.1405	48	0.0760	68	0.0310
9	0.1960	29	0.1360	49	0.0730	69	0.02925
10	0.1935	30	0.1285	50	0.0700	70	0.0280
11	0.1910	31	0.1200	51	0.0670	71	0.0260
12	0.1890	32	0.1160	52	0.0635	72	0.0250
13	0.1850	33	0.1130	53	0.0595	73	0.0240
14	0.1820	34	0.1110	54	0.0550	74	0.0225
15	0.1800	35	0.1100	55	0.0520	75	0.0210
16	0.1770	36	0.1065	56	0.0465	76	0.0200
17	0.1730	37	0.1040	57	0.0430	77	0.0180
18	0.1695	38	0.1015	58	0.0420	78	0.0160
19	0.1660	39	0.0995	59	0.0410	79	0.0145
20	0.1610	40	0.0980	60	0.0400	80	0.0135

LETTER SIZES OF DRILLS

Letter	Size in decimals	Letter	Size in decimals
A $15/64$	0.234	N	0.302
B	0.238	O $5/16$	0.316
C	0.242	P $21/64$	0.323
D	0.246	Q	0.332
E $1/4$	0.250	R $11/32$	0.339
F	0.257	S	0.348
G	0.261	T $23/64$	0.358
H $17/64$	0.266	U	0.368
I	0.272	V $3/8$	0.377
J	0.277	W $25/64$	0.386
K $9/32$	0.281	X	0.397
L	0.290	Y $13/32$	0.404
M $19/64$	0.295	Z	0.413

Table 19. Mensuration
AREA

Parallelogram	= base × perpendicular height.
Trapezoid	= half the sum of the parallel sides × perpendicular height.
Triangle	= base × ½ perpendicular height.
Circle	= diameter squared × 0.7854, or circumference squared × 0.07958.
Sector of a circle	= length of arc × half radius.
Segment of a circle	= { area of sector of equal radius—triangle when segment is less, and + area of triangle when segment is greater than the semicircle.
Side of square of equal area as circle	= diameter × 0.8862, or circumference × 0.2821.
Diameter of a circle of equal area as square	= side × 1.1284.
Parabola	= base × ⅔ height.
Ellipse	= long diameter × short diameter × 0.7854.
Regular polygon	= sum of sides × half perpendicular distance from center to sides.
Cylinder	= circumference × height + area of both ends.
Sphere	= diameter squared × 3.1416, or diameter × circumference.
Segment of sphere	= height of segment × circumference of sphere of which it is a part + area of base.
Pyramid or cone	= circumference of base × ½ slant height + area of base.
Frustrum of pyramid	= sum of circumference at both ends × ½ slant height + area of both ends.

LENGTH

Circumference of circle = diameter × 3.1416.
Diameter of circle = circumference × 0.3183.
Side of square of equal periphery as circle = diameter × 0.7854.
Diameter of circle of equal periphery as square = side × 1.2732.
Side of an inscribed square = diameter of circle × 0.7071.
Length of arc = number of degrees × diameter × 0.008727.
Circumference of circle whose diameter is 1 = 3.14159265.
English statute miles = linear feet × 0.00019.
English statute miles = linear yards × 0.000568.

SOLID CONTENTS

Prism or cylinder = area of end × length.
Sphere = cube of diameter × 0.5236.
Segment of sphere = (height squared + three times the square of radius of base) × (height × 0.5236).
Side of an equal cube = diameter of sphere × 0.806.
Length of an equal cylinder = diameter of sphere × 0.6667.
Pyramid or cone = area of base × 13 altitude.
Frustrum of cone = { add to the product of the two diameters the square of the large diameter and the square of the small diameter; multiply the sum by 0.7854 and the product by ⅓ the altitude.

Table 20. Diagonals of Hexagons and Squares

Across flats	Across corners		Across flats	Across corners		Across flats	Across corners	
	Hexagon	Squares		Hexagon	Squares		Hexagon	Squares
1⁄16	0.072	0.088	1⅜	1.587	1.944	2¹¹⁄₁₆	3.103	3.800
⅛	0.144	0.177	1⁷⁄₁₆	1.659	2.032	2¾	3.175	3.889
3⁄16	0.216	0.265	1½	1.732	2.121	2¹³⁄₁₆	3.247	3.979
¼	0.288	0.353	1⁹⁄₁₆	1.804	2.209	2⅞	3.319	4.065
5⁄16	0.360	0.441	1⅝	1.876	2.298	2¹⁵⁄₁₆	3.391	4.154
⅜	0.432	0.530	1¹¹⁄₁₆	1.948	2.386	3	3.464	4.242
7⁄16	0.505	0.618	1¾	2.020	2.470	3¹⁄₁₆	3.536	4.331
½	0.577	0.707	1¹³⁄₁₆	2.092	2.563	3⅛	3.608	4.419
9⁄16	0.649	0.795	1⅞	2.165	2.651	3³⁄₁₆	3.680	4.507
⅝	0.721	0.883	1¹⁵⁄₁₆	2.237	2.740	3¼	3.752	4.596
11⁄16	0.793	0.972	2	2.309	2.828	3⁵⁄₁₆	3.824	4.684
¾	0.865	1.060	2¹⁄₁₆	2.381	2.916	3⅜	3.897	4.772
13⁄16	0.938	1.149	2⅛	2.453	3.005	3½	4.041	4.949
⅞	1.010	1.237	2³⁄₁₆	2.525	3.093	3⅝	4.185	5.126
15⁄16	1.082	1.325	2¼	2.598	3.182	3¾	4.330	5.303
1	1.155	1.414	2⁵⁄₁₆	2.670	3.270	3⅞	4.474	5.480
1¹⁄₁₆	1.226	1.502	2⅜	2.742	3.358	4	4.618	5.656
1⅛	1.299	1.591	2⁷⁄₁₆	2.814	3.447	4⅛	4.763	5.833
1³⁄₁₆	1.371	1.679	2½	2.886	3.535	4¼	4.904	6.010
1¼	1.443	1.767	2⁹⁄₁₆	2.958	3.623	4⅜	5.051	6.187
1⁵⁄₁₆	1.515	1.856	2⅝	3.031	3.712	4½	5.196	6.363

Diagonal of hexagon equals 1.155 times distance across flats.
Diagonal of square equals 1.414 times distance across flats.
Largest square that can be inscribed in circle equals 0.707 times the diameter.
Largest hexagon that can be inscribed in circle equals 0.866 times the diameter.
Largest square that can be cut on cylinder equals diameter times 0.707.
Largest hexagon that can be cut on cylinder equals diameter times 0.866.

Table 21. Weights of Flat Bar Steel per Linear Foot

Thickness	1/2	5/8	3/4	7/8	1	1 1/8	1 1/4	1 3/8	1 1/2	1 3/4	2	2 1/4	2 1/2	2 3/4	3	3 1/2	4	5	6
1/8	0.213	0.266	0.320	0.372	0.426	0.479	0.530	0.585	0.640	0.745	0.850	0.955	1.07	1.18	1.28	1.49	1.70	2.13	2.56
3/16	0.319	0.399	0.480	0.558	0.639	0.718	0.790	0.878	0.960	1.12	1.28	1.43	1.60	1.76	1.92	2.24	2.55	3.20	3.83
1/4	0.425	0.533	0.640	0.743	0.852	0.958	1.06	1.17	1.28	1.49	1.70	1.91	2.13	2.34	2.56	2.98	3.40	4.26	5.11
5/16	0.531	0.665	0.800	0.929	1.06	1.20	1.33	1.46	1.60	1.86	2.13	2.39	2.66	2.92	3.19	3.72	4.25	5.32	6.38
3/8	0.638	0.798	0.960	1.12	1.28	1.43	1.59	1.75	1.91	2.23	2.55	2.87	3.20	3.51	3.83	4.46	5.10	6.40	7.66
7/16	0.744	0.931	1.12	1.30	1.49	1.67	1.86	2.05	2.23	2.60	2.98	3.35	3.72	4.09	4.46	5.21	5.95	7.44	8.92
1/2		1.07	1.28	1.49	1.70	1.91	2.13	2.34	2.55	2.98	3.40	3.83	4.26	4.68	5.10	5.96	6.80	8.52	10.20
9/16		1.20	1.44	1.67	1.91	2.15	2.39	2.63	2.87	3.35	3.83	4.30	4.78	5.26	5.74	6.69	7.65	9.56	11.50
5/8			1.60	1.86	2.12	2.39	2.66	2.92	3.19	3.72	4.26	4.79	5.32	5.86	6.39	7.44	8.52	10.64	12.78
11/16			1.76	2.04	2.34	2.63	2.92	3.22	3.51	4.09	4.68	5.26	5.84	6.43	7.01	8.18	9.35	11.70	14.00
3/4				2.23	2.55	2.86	3.19	3.50	3.83	4.46	5.10	5.74	6.40	7.02	7.65	8.92	10.20	12.80	15.30
13/16				2.41	2.76	3.11	3.45	3.80	4.14	4.83	5.53	6.22	6.91	7.60	8.29	9.67	11.10	13.80	16.60
7/8					2.98	3.34	3.72	4.09	4.46	5.21	5.96	6.70	7.46	8.19	8.94	10.42	11.92	14.92	17.88
15/16					3.19	3.59	3.98	4.38	4.78	5.58	6.38	7.17	7.97	8.77	9.56	11.20	12.80	15.90	19.10
1						3.82	4.25	4.68	5.10	5.96	6.80	7.66	8.52	9.36	10.20	11.92	13.60	17.04	20.40
1 1/8							4.78	5.27	5.74	6.71	7.65	8.61	9.59	10.54	11.48	13.41	15.30	19.17	22.95
1 1/4								5.85	6.38	7.45	8.50	9.57	10.65	11.71	12.76	14.90	17.00	21.30	25.61
1 1/2								7.02	7.67	8.94	10.20	11.49	12.78	14.04	15.30	17.88	20.40	25.56	30.00

Table 22. Weights of Steel and Wrought Iron

Diameter across flats	Steel				Iron	
	Weight per foot				Weight per foot	
	Round	Square	Hexagon	Octagon	Round	Square
1/16	0.010	0.013	0.012	0.011	0.010	0.013
1/8	0.042	0.053	0.046	0.044	0.041	0.052
3/16	0.094	0.119	0.103	0.099	0.092	0.117
1/4	0.167	0.212	0.185	0.177	0.164	0.208
5/16	0.261	0.333	0.288	0.277	0.256	0.326
3/8	0.375	0.478	0.414	0.398	0.368	0.469
7/16	0.511	0.651	0.564	0.542	0.501	0.638
1/2	0.667	0.850	0.737	0.708	0.654	0.833
9/16	0.845	1.076	0.932	0.896	0.828	1.055
5/8	1.043	1.328	1.151	1.107	1.023	1.302
11/16	1.262	1.608	1.393	1.331	1.237	1.576
3/4	1.502	1.913	1.658	1.584	1.473	1.875
13/16	1.763	2.245	1.944	1.860	1.728	2.201
7/8	2.044	2.603	2.256	2.156	2.004	2.552
15/16	2.347	2.989	2.591	2.482	2.301	2.930
1	2.670	3.400	2.947	2.817	2.618	3.333
1 1/16	3.014	3.838	3.327	3.182	2.955	3.763
1 1/8	3.379	4.303	3.730	3.568	3.313	4.219
1 3/16	3.766	4.795	4.156	3.977	3.692	4.701
1 1/4	4.173	5.312	4.605	4.407	4.091	5.208
1 5/16	4.600	5.857	5.077	4.858	4.510	5.742
1 3/8	5.049	6.428	5.571	5.331	4.950	6.302
1 7/16	5.518	7.026	6.091	5.827	5.410	6.888
1 1/2	6.008	7.650	6.631	6.344	5.890	7.500
1 9/16	6.520	8.301	7.195	6.905	6.392	8.138
1 5/8	7.051	8.978	7.776	7.446	6.913	8.802
1 11/16	7.604	9.682	8.392	8.027	7.455	9.492
1 3/4	8.178	10.41	9.025	8.635	8.018	10.21
1 13/16	8.773	11.17	9.682	9.264	8.601	10.95
1 7/8	9.388	11.95	10.36	9.918	9.204	11.72
1 15/16	10.02	12.76	11.06	10.58	9.828	12.51
2	10.68	13.60	11.79	11.28	10.47	13.33
2 1/8	12.06	15.35	13.31	12.71	11.82	15.05
2 1/4	13.52	17.22	14.92	14.24	13.25	16.88
2 3/8	15.07	19.18	16.62	15.88	14.77	18.80
2 1/2	16.69	21.25	18.42	17.65	16.36	20.83
2 5/8	18.40	23.43	20.31	19.45	18.04	22.97
2 3/4	20.20	25.71	22.29	21.28	19.80	25.21
2 7/8	22.07	28.10	24.36	23.28	21.64	27.55
3	24.03	30.60	26.53	25.36	23.56	30.00
3 1/8	26.08	33.20	28.78	27.50	25.57	32.55
3 1/4	28.20	35.92	31.10	29.28	27.65	35.21
3 3/8	30.42	38.78	33.57	32.10	29.82	37.97
3 1/2	32.17	41.65	36.10	34.56	32.07	40.83
3 5/8	35.09	44.68	38.73	37.05	34.40	43.80
3 3/4	37.56	47.82	41.45	39.68	36.82	46.88
3 7/8	40.10	51.05	44.26	42.35	39.31	50.05
4	42.73	54.40	47.16	45.12	41.89	53.33

Table 23. Trigonometric Functions

Angle	Sine	Cosine	Tan.	Cotan.	Secant	Cosec.	
0°00′	.00000	1.0000	.00000	Infinite	1.0000	Infinite	90°00′
5	.00145	1.0000	.00145	687.55	1.0000	687.55	55
10	.00291	.99999	.00291	343.77	1.0000	343.77	50
15	.00436	.99999	.00436	229.18	1.0000	229.18	45
20	.00582	.99998	.00582	171.88	1.0000	171.89	40
25	.00727	.99997	.00727	137.51	1.0000	137.51	35
30	.00873	.99996	.00873	114.59	1.0000	114.59	30
35	.01018	.99995	.01018	98.218	1.0000	98.223	25
40	.01163	.99993	.01164	85.940	1.0001	85.946	20
45	.01309	.99991	.01309	76.390	1.0001	76.396	15
50	.01454	.99989	.01454	68.750	1.0001	68.757	10
55	.01600	.99987	.01600	62.499	1.0001	62.507	5
1°00′	.01745	.99985	.01745	57.290	1.0001	57.299	89°00′
5	.01891	.99982	.01891	52.882	1.0002	52.891	55
10	.02036	.99979	.02036	49.104	1.0002	49.114	50
15	.02181	.99976	.02182	45.829	1.0002	45.840	45
20	.02326	.99973	.02327	42.964	1.0003	42.976	40
25	.02472	.99969	.02473	40.436	1.0003	40.448	35
30	.02618	.99966	.02618	38.188	1.0003	38.201	30
35	.02763	.99962	.02764	36.177	1.0004	36.191	25
40	.02908	.99958	.02910	34.368	1.0004	34.382	20
45	.03054	.99953	.03055	32.730	1.0005	32.745	15
50	.03199	.99949	.03201	31.241	1.0005	31.257	10
55	.03344	.99944	.03346	29.882	1.0005	29.899	5
2°00′	.03490	.99939	.03492	28.636	1.0006	28.654	88°00′
5	.03635	.99934	.03638	27.490	1.0007	27.508	55
10	.03781	.99928	.03783	26.432	1.0007	26.450	50
15	.03926	.99923	.03929	25.452	1.0008	25.471	45
20	.04071	.99917	.04075	24.542	1.0008	24.562	40
25	.04217	.99911	.04220	23.694	1.0009	23.716	35
30	0.4362	.99905	.04366	22.904	1.0009	22.925	30
35	.04507	.99898	.04512	22.164	1.0010	22.186	25
40	.04652	.99892	.04657	21.470	1.0011	21.494	20
45	.04798	.99885	.04803	20.819	1.0011	20.843	15
50	.04943	.99878	.04949	20.205	1.0012	20.230	10
55	.05088	.99870	.05095	19.627	1.0013	19.653	5
	Cosine	Sine	Cotan.	Tan.	Cosec.	Secant	Angle

Table 23. Trigonometric Functions (Continued)

Angle	Sine	Cosine	Tan.	Cotan.	Secant	Cosec.	
3°00′	.05234	.99863	.05241	19.081	1.0014	19.107	87°00′
5	.05379	.99855	.05387	18.564	1.0014	18.591	55
10	.05524	.99847	.05532	18.075	1.0015	18.103	50
15	.05669	.99839	.05678	17.610	1.0016	17.639	45
20	.05814	.99831	.05824	17.169	1.0017	17.198	40
25	.05960	.99822	.05970	16.750	1.0018	16.779	35
30	.06105	.99813	.06116	16.350	1.0019	16.380	30
35	.06250	.99804	.06262	15.969	1.0019	16.000	25
40	.06395	.99795	.06408	15.605	1.0020	15.637	20
45	.06540	.99786	.06554	15.257	1.0021	15.290	15
50	.06685	.99776	.06700	14.924	1.0022	14.958	10
55	.06830	.99766	.06846	14.606	1.0023	14.640	5
4°00′	.06976	.99756	.06993	14.301	1.0024	14.335	86°00′
5	.07121	.99746	.07139	14.008	1.0025	14.043	55
10	.07266	.99736	.07285	13.727	1.0026	13.763	50
15	.07411	.99725	.07431	13.457	1.0027	13.494	45
20	.07556	.99714	.07577	13.197	1.0029	13.235	40
25	.07701	.99703	.07724	12.947	1.0030	12.985	35
30	.07846	.99692	.07870	12.706	1.0031	12.745	30
35	.07991	.99680	.08016	12.474	1.0032	12.514	25
40	.08136	.99668	.08163	12.250	1.0033	12.291	20
45	.08281	.99656	.08309	12.035	1.0034	12.076	15
50	.08426	.99644	.08456	11.826	1.0036	11.868	10
55	.08571	.99632	.08602	11.625	1.0037	11.668	5
5°00′	.08715	.99619	.08749	11.430	1.0038	11.474	85°00′
5	.08860	.99607	.08895	11.242	1.0039	11.286	55
10	.09005	.99594	.09042	11.059	1.0041	11.104	50
15	.09150	.99580	.09189	10.883	1.0042	19.929	45
20	.09295	.99567	.99335	10.712	1.0043	10.758	40
25	.09440	.99553	.09482	10.546	1.0045	10.593	35
30	.09584	.99540	.09629	10.385	1.0046	10.433	30
35	.09729	.99525	.09776	10.229	1.0048	10.278	25
40	.09874	.99511	.09922	10.078	1.0049	10.127	20
45	.10019	.99497	.11069	9.9310	1.0050	9.9812	15
50	.10163	.99482	.10216	9.7882	1.0052	9.8391	10
55	.10308	.99467	.10363	9.6493	1.0053	9.7010	5
	Cosine	Sine	Cotan.	Tan.	Cosec.	Secant	Angle

Table 23. Trigonometric Functions (Continued)

Angle	Sine	Cosine	Tan.	Cotan.	Secant	Cosec.	
6°00′	.10453	.99452	.10510	9.5144	1.0055	9.5668	84°00′
5	.10597	.99437	.10657	9.3831	1.0057	9.4362	55
10	.10742	.99421	.10805	9.2553	1.0058	9.3092	50
15	.10887	.99406	.10952	9.1309	1.0060	9.1855	45
20	.11031	.99390	.11099	9.0098	1.0061	9.0651	40
25	.11176	.99373	.11246	8.8918	1.0063	8.9479	35
30	.11320	.99357	.11393	8.7769	1.0065	8.8337	30
35	.11465	.99341	.11541	8.6648	1.0066	8.7223	25
40	.11609	.99324	.11688	8.5555	1.0068	8.6138	20
45	.11754	.99307	.11836	8.4489	1.0070	8.5079	15
50	.11898	.99290	.11983	8.3449	1.0071	8.4046	10
55	.12042	.99272	.12131	8.2434	1.0073	8.3039	5
7°00′	.12187	.99255	.12278	8.1443	1.0075	8.2055	83°00′
5	.12331	.99237	.12426	8.0476	1.0077	8.1094	55
10	.12476	.99219	.12574	7.9530	1.0079	8.0156	50
15	.12620	.99200	.12772	7.8606	1.0080	7.9240	45
20	.12764	.99182	.12869	7.7703	1.0082	7.8344	40
25	.12908	.99163	.13017	7.6821	1.0084	7.7469	35
30	.13053	.99144	.13165	7.5957	1.0086	7.6613	30
35	.13197	.99125	.13313	7.5113	1.0088	7.5776	25
40	.13341	.99106	.13461	7.4287	1.0090	7.4957	20
45	.13485	.99086	.13609	7.3479	1.0092	7.4156	15
50	.13629	.99067	.13757	7.2687	1.0094	7.3372	10
55	.13773	.99047	.13906	7.1912	1.0096	7.2604	5
8°00′	.13917	.99027	.14054	7.1154	1.0098	7.1853	82°00′
5	.14061	.99006	.14202	7.0410	1.0100	7.1117	55
10	.14205	.98986	.14351	6.9682	1.0102	7.0396	50
15	.14349	.98965	.14499	6.8969	1.0104	6.9690	45
20	.14493	.99844	.15648	6.8269	1.0107	6.8998	40
25	.14637	.98923	.14796	6.7584	1.0109	6.8320	35
30	.14781	.98901	.14945	6.6911	1.0111	6.7655	30
35	.14925	.98880	.15094	6.6252	1.0113	6.7003	25
40	.15068	.98858	.15243	6.5605	1.0115	6.6363	20
45	.15212	.98836	.15391	6.4971	1.0118	6.5736	15
50	.15356	.98814	.15540	6.4348	1.0120	6.5121	10
55	.15500	.98791	.15689	6.3737	1.0122	6.4517	5
	Cosine	Sine	Cotan.	Tan.	Cosec.	Secant	Angle

Table 23. Trigonometric Functions (Continued)

Angle	Sine	Cosine	Tan.	Cotan.	Secant	Cosec.	
9°00′	.15643	.98769	.15838	6.3137	1.0125	6.3924	81°00′
5	.15787	.98746	.15987	6.2548	1.0127	6.3343	55
10	.15931	.98723	.16137	6.1970	1.0129	6.2772	50
15	.16074	.98700	.16286	6.1402	1.0132	6.2211	45
20	.16218	.98676	.16435	6.0844	1.0134	6.1661	40
25	.16361	.98652	.16585	6.0296	1.0136	6.1120	35
30	.16505	.98628	.16734	5.9758	1.0139	6.0588	30
35	.16648	.98604	.16884	5.9928	1.0141	6.0066	25
40	.16791	.98580	.17033	5.8708	1.0144	5.9554	20
45	.16935	.98556	.17183	5.8196	1.0146	5.9049	15
50	.17078	.98531	.17333	5.7694	1.0149	5.8554	10
55	.17221	.98506	.17483	5.7199	1.0152	5.8067	5
10°00′	.17365	.98481	.17663	5.6713	1.0154	5.7588	80°00′
5	.17508	.98455	.17783	5.6234	1.0157	5.7117	55
10	.17651	.98430	.17933	5.5764	1.0159	5.6643	50
15	.17794	.98404	.18083	5.5301	1.0162	5.6197	45
20	.17937	.98378	.18233	5.4845	1.0165	5.5749	40
25	.18080	.98352	.18383	5.4396	1.0167	5.5308	35
30	.18223	.98325	.18534	5.3955	1.0170	5.4874	30
35	.18366	.98299	.18684	5.3521	1.0173	5.4447	25
40	.18509	.98272	.18835	5.3093	1.0176	5.4026	20
45	.18652	.98245	.18985	5.2671	1.0179	5.3612	15
50	.18795	.98218	.19136	5.2257	1.0181	5.3205	10
55	.18938	.98190	.19287	5.1848	1.0184	5.2803	5
11°00′	.19081	.98163	.19438	5.1445	1.0187	5.2408	79°00′
5	.19224	.98135	.19589	5.1049	1.0190	5.2019	55
10	.19366	.98107	.19740	5.0658	1.0193	5.1636	50
15	.19509	.98078	.19891	5.0273	1.0196	5.1258	45
20	.19652	.98050	.20042	4.9894	1.0199	5.0886	40
25	.19794	.98021	.20194	4.9520	1.0202	5.0520	35
30	.19937	.97992	.20345	4.9151	1.0205	5.0158	30
35	.20079	.97963	.20497	4.8788	1.0208	4.9802	25
40	.20222	.97934	.20648	4.8430	1.0211	4.9452	20
45	.20364	.97904	.20800	4.8077	1.0214	4.9106	15
50	.20506	.97875	.20952	4.7728	1.0217	4.8765	10
55	.20649	.97845	.21104	4.7385	1.0220	4.8429	5
	Cosine	Sine	Cotan.	Tan.	Cosec.	Secant	Angle

Table 23. Trigonometric Functions (Continued)

Angle	Sine	Cosine	Tan.	Cotan.	Secant	Cosec.	
12°00′	.20791	.97815	.21256	4.7046	1.0223	4.8097	78°00′
5	.20933	.97784	.21408	4.6712	1.0226	4.7770	55
10	.21076	.97754	.21560	4.6382	1.0230	4.7448	50
15	.21218	.97723	.21712	4.6057	1.0233	4.7130	45
20	.21360	.97692	.21864	4.5736	1.0236	4.6817	40
25	.21502	.97661	.22017	4.5420	1.0239	4.6507	35
30	.21644	.97630	.22169	4.5107	1.0243	4.6201	30
35	.21786	.97598	.22322	4.4799	1.0246	4.5901	25
40	.21928	.97566	.22475	4.4494	1.0249	4.5604	20
45	.22070	.97534	.22628	4.4194	1.0253	4.5311	15
50	.22211	.97502	.22781	4.3897	1.0256	4.5021	10
55	.22353	.97470	.22934	4.3604	1.0260	4.4736	5
13°00′	.22495	.97437	.23087	4.3315	1.0263	4.4454	77°00′
5	.22637	.97404	.23240	4.3029	1.0266	4.4176	55
10	.22778	.97371	.23393	4.2747	1.0270	4.3901	50
15	.22920	.97338	.23547	4.2468	1.0273	4.3630	45
20	.23061	.97304	.23700	4.2193	1.0277	4.3362	40
25	.23203	.97271	.23854	4.1921	1.0280	4.3098	35
30	.23344	.97237	.24008	4.1653	1.0284	4.2836	30
35	.23486	.97203	.24162	4.1388	1.0288	4.2579	25
40	.23627	.97169	.24316	4.1126	1.0291	4.2324	20
45	.23768	.97134	.24470	4.0867	1.0295	4.2072	15
50	.23910	.97099	.24624	4.0611	1.0299	4.1824	10
55	.24051	.97065	.24778	4.0358	1.0302	4.1578	5
14°00′	.24192	.97029	.24933	4.0108	1.0306	4.1336	76°00′
5	.24333	.96994	.25087	3.9861	1.0310	4.1096	55
10	.24474	.96959	.25242	3.9616	1.0314	4.0859	50
15	.24615	.96923	.25397	3.9375	1.0137	4.0625	45
20	.24756	.96887	.25552	3.9136	1.0321	4.0394	40
25	.24897	.96851	.25707	3.8900	1.0325	4.0165	35
30	.25038	.96815	.25862	3.8667	1.0329	3.9939	30
35	.25179	.96778	.26017	3.8436	1.0333	3.9716	25
40	.25319	.96741	.26172	3.8208	1.0337	3.9495	20
45	.25460	.96704	.26328	3.7983	1.0341	3.9277	15
50	.25601	.96667	.26483	3.7759	1.0345	3.9061	10
55	.25741	.96630	.26639	3.7539	1.0349	3.8848	5
	Cosine	Sine	Cotan.	Tan.	Cosec.	Secant	Angle

Table 23. Trigonometric Functions (Continued)

Angle	Sine	Cosine	Tan.	Cotan.	Secant	Cosec.	
15°00′	.25882	.96592	.26795	3.7320	1.0353	3.8637	76°00′
5	.26022	.96555	.26951	3.7104	1.0357	3.8428	55
10	.26163	.96517	.27107	3.6891	1.0361	3.8222	50
15	.26303	.96479	.27263	3.6679	1.0365	3.7018	45
20	.26443	.96440	.27419	3.6470	1.0369	3.7816	40
25	.26584	.96402	.27576	3.6263	1.0373	3.7617	35
30	.26724	.96363	.27732	3.6059	1.0377	3.7420	30
35	.26864	.96325	.27889	3.5856	1.0382	3.7224	25
40	.27004	.96285	.28046	3.5656	1.0386	3.7301	20
45	.27144	.96245	.28203	3.5457	1.0930	3.6840	15
50	.27284	.96206	.28360	3.5261	1.0394	3.6651	10
55	.27424	.96166	.28517	3.5066	1.0399	3.6464	5
16°00′	.27564	.96126	.28674	3.4874	1.0403	3.6279	74°00′
5	.27703	.96086	.28832	3.4684	1.0407	3.6096	55
10	.27843	.96045	.28990	3.4495	1.0142	3.5915	50
15	.27983	.96055	.29147	3.4308	1.0146	3.5736	45
20	.28122	.95964	.29305	3.4124	1.0420	3.5559	40
25	.28262	.95923	.29463	3.3941	1.0425	3.5383	35
30	.28401	.95882	.29621	3.3759	1.0429	3.5209	30
35	.28541	.95840	.29780	3.3580	1.0434	3.5037	25
40	.28680	.95799	.29938	3.3402	1.0438	3.4867	20
45	.28820	.95757	.30096	3.3226	1.0443	3.4698	15
50	.28959	.95715	.30255	3.3052	1.0448	3.4532	10
55	.29098	.95673	.30414	3.2879	1.0452	3.4366	5
17°00′	.29237	.95630	.30573	3.2708	1.0457	3.4203	73°00′
5	.29376	.95588	.30732	3.2539	1.0461	3.4041	55
10	.29515	.95545	.30891	3.2371	1.0466	3.3881	50
15	.29654	.95502	.31051	3.2205	1.0471	3.3722	45
20	.29793	.95459	.31210	3.2041	1.0476	3.3565	40
25	.29932	.95415	.31370	3.1877	1.0480	3.3409	35
30	.30070	.95372	.31530	3.1716	1.0485	3.3255	30
35	.30209	.95328	.31690	3.1556	1.0490	3.3102	25
40	.30348	.95284	.31850	3.1397	1.0495	3.2951	20
45	.30486	.95239	.32010	3.1240	1.0500	3.2801	15
50	.30625	.95195	.31271	3.1084	1.0505	3.2653	10
55	.30763	.95150	.32331	3.0930	1.0510	3.2506	5
	Cosine	Sine	Cotan.	Tan.	Cosec.	Secant	Angle

Table 23. Trigonometric Functions (Continued)

Angle	Sine	Cosine	Tan.	Cotan.	Secant	Cosec.	
18°00′	.30902	.95106	.32492	3.0777	1.0515	3.2361	72°00′
5	.31040	.95061	.32653	3.0625	1.0520	3.2216	55
10	.31178	.95015	.32814	3.0475	1.0525	3.2074	50
15	.31316	.94970	.32975	3.0326	1.0530	3.1932	45
20	.31454	.94924	.33136	3.0178	1.0535	3.1792	40
25	.31592	.94878	.33298	3.0032	1.0540	3.1653	35
30	.31730	.94832	.33459	2.9887	1.0545	3.1515	30
35	.31868	.94786	.33621	2.9743	1.0550	3.1379	25
40	.32006	.94740	.33783	2.9600	1.0555	3.1244	20
45	.32144	.94693	.33945	2.9459	1.0560	3.1110	15
50	.32282	.94646	.34108	2.9319	1.0566	3.0977	10
55	.32419	.94599	.34270	2.9180	1.0571	3.0845	5
19°00′	.32557	.94552	.34433	2.9042	1.0576	3.0715	71°00′
5	.32694	.94504	.34595	2.8905	1.0581	3.0586	55
10	.32832	.94457	.34758	2.8770	1.0587	3.0458	50
15	.32969	.94409	.34921	2.8636	1.0592	3.0331	45
20	.33106	.94361	.35085	2.8502	1.0598	3.0206	40
25	.33243	.94313	.35248	2.8370	1.0603	3.0081	35
30	.33381	.94264	.35412	2.8239	1.0608	2.9957	30
35	.33518	.94215	.35576	2.8109	1.0614	2.9835	25
40	.33655	.94167	.35739	2.7980	1.0619	2.9713	20
45	.33792	.94118	.35904	2.7852	1.0625	2.9593	15
50	.33928	.94068	.36068	2.7725	1.0630	2.9474	10
55	.34065	.94019	.36232	2.7600	1.0636	2.9355	5
20°00′	.34202	.93969	.36397	2.7475	1.0642	2.9238	70°00′
5	.34339	.93919	.36562	2.7351	1.0647	2.9122	55
10	.34475	.93869	.36727	2.7288	1.0653	2.9006	50
15	.34612	.93819	.36892	2.7106	1.0659	2.8892	45
20	.34748	.93769	.37057	2.6985	1.0664	2.8788	40
25	.34884	.93718	.37223	2.6865	1.0670	2.8666	35
30	.35021	.93667	.37388	2.6746	1.0676	2.8554	30
35	.35157	.93616	.37554	2.6628	1.0682	2.8444	25
40	.35293	.93565	.37720	2.6511	1.0688	2.8334	20
45	.35429	.93513	.37887	2.6394	1.0694	2.8225	15
50	.35565	.93462	.38053	2.6279	1.0699	2.8177	10
55	.35701	.93410	.38220	2.6164	1.0705	2.7010	5
	Cosine	Sine	Cotan.	Tan.	Cosec.	Secant	Angle

Table 23. Trigonometric Functions (Continued)

Angle	Sine	Cosine	Tan.	Cotan.	Secant	Cosec.	
21°00′	.35837	.93358	.38386	2.6051	1.0711	2.7904	69°00′
5	.35972	.93306	.38553	2.5938	1.0717	2.7799	55
10	.36108	.93253	.38720	2.5826	1.0723	2.7694	50
15	.36244	.93201	.38888	2.5715	1.0729	2.7591	45
20	.36379	.93148	.39055	2.5605	1.0736	2.7488	40
25	.36515	.93095	.39223	2.5495	1.0742	2.7386	35
30	.36650	.93042	.39391	2.5386	1.0748	2.7825	30
35	.36785	.92988	.09559	2.5278	1.0754	2.7184	25
40	.36921	.92935	.39727	2.5171	1.0760	2.7085	20
45	.37056	.92881	.39896	2.5065	1.0766	2.6986	15
50	.37191	.92827	.40065	2.4960	1.0773	2.6888	10
55	.37326	.92773	.40233	2.4855	1.0779	2.6791	5
22°00′	.37461	.92718	.40403	2.4751	1.0785	2.6695	68°00′
5	.37595	.92664	.40752	2.4647	1.0792	2.6599	55
10	.37730	.92609	.40741	2.4545	1.0798	2.6504	50
15	.37865	.92554	.40911	2.4443	1.0804	2.6410	45
20	.37999	.92499	.41081	2.4342	1.0811	2.6316	40
25	.38134	.92443	.41251	2.4242	1.0817	2.6223	35
30	.38268	.92388	.41421	2.4142	1.0824	2.6131	30
35	.38403	.92332	.41592	2.4043	1.0830	2.6040	25
40	.38537	.92276	.41762	2.3945	1.0837	2.5949	20
45	.38671	.92220	.41933	2.3847	1.0844	2.5859	15
50	.38805	.92164	.42105	2.3750	1.0850	2.5770	10
55	.38939	.92107	.42276	2.3654	1.0857	2.5681	5
23°00′	.39073	.92050	.42447	2.3558	1.0864	2.5593	67°00′
5	.39207	.91993	.42619	2.3463	1.0870	2.5506	55
10	.39341	.91936	.42791	2.3369	1.0877	2.5419	50
15	.39474	.91879	.42963	2.3276	1.0884	2.5333	45
20	.39608	.91822	.43136	2.3183	1.0891	2.5247	40
25	.39741	.91764	.43308	2.3090	1.0897	2.5163	35
30	.39875	.91706	.43481	2.2998	1.0904	2.5078	30
35	.40008	.91648	.43654	2.2907	1.0911	2.4995	25
40	.40141	.91590	.43827	2.2817	1.0918	2.4912	20
45	.40275	.91531	.44001	2.2727	1.0925	2.4849	15
50	.40408	.91472	.44175	2.2637	1.0932	2.4748	10
55	.40541	.91414	.44349	2.2548	1.0939	2.4666	5
	Cosine	Sine	Cotan.	Tan.	Cosec.	Secant	Angle

Table 23. Trigonometric Functions (Continued)

Angle	Sine	Cosine	Tan.	Cotan.	Secant	Cosec.	
24°00′	.40674	.91354	.44523	2.2460	1.0946	2.4586	66°00′
5	.40806	.91295	.44697	2.2373	1.0953	2.4506	55
10	.40939	.91236	.44872	2.2286	1.0961	2.4426	50
15	.41072	.91176	.45047	2.2199	1.0968	2.4347	45
20	.41204	.91116	.45222	2.2113	1.0975	2.4269	40
25	.41337	.91056	.45397	2.2028	1.0982	2.4191	35
30	.41469	.90996	.45573	2.1943	1.0989	2.4114	30
35	.41602	.90936	.45748	2.1859	1.0997	2.4037	25
40	.41734	.90875	.45924	2.1775	1.1004	2.3961	20
45	.41866	.90814	.46101	2.1692	1.1011	2.3886	15
50	.41998	.90753	.46277	2.1609	1.1019	2.3811	10
55	.42130	.90692	.46454	2.1527	1.1026	2.3735	5
25°00′	.42262	.90631	.46631	2.1445	1.1034	2.3662	65°00′
5	.42394	.90569	.46808	2.1364	1.1041	2.3588	55
10	.42525	.90507	.46985	2.1283	1.1049	2.3515	50
15	.42657	.90445	.47163	2.1203	1.1056	2.3443	45
20	.42788	.90383	.47341	2.1123	1.1064	2.3371	40
25	.42920	.90321	.47519	2.1044	1.1072	2.3299	35
30	.43051	.90258	.47697	2.0965	1.1079	2.3228	30
35	.43182	.90196	.47876	2.0887	1.1087	2.3158	25
40	.43313	.90133	.48055	2.0809	1.1095	2.3087	20
45	.43444	.90070	.48234	2.0732	1.1102	2.3018	15
50	.43575	.90006	.48414	2.0655	1.1100	2.2949	10
55	.43706	.89943	.48593	2.0579	1.1118	2.2880	5
26°00′	.43837	.89879	.48773	2.0503	1.1126	2.2812	64°00′
5	.43968	.89815	.48953	2.0427	1.1134	2.2744	55
10	.44098	.89751	.49134	2.0352	1.1142	2.2676	50
15	.44229	.89687	.49314	2.0278	1.1150	2.2610	45
20	.44349	.89623	.49495	2.0204	1.1158	2.2543	40
25	.44489	.89558	.49677	2.0130	1.1166	2.2477	35
30	.44620	.89493	.49858	2.0057	1.1174	2.2411	30
35	.44750	.89428	.50040	1.9984	1.1182	2.2348	25
40	.44880	.89363	.50222	1.9912	1.1190	2.2282	20
45	.45010	.89298	.50404	1.9840	1.1198	2.2217	15
50	.45140	.89232	.50587	1.9768	1.1207	2.2153	10
55	.45269	.89166	.50769	1.9697	1.1215	2.2090	5
	Cosine	Sine	Cotan.	Tan.	Cosec.	Secant	Angle

Table 23. Trigonometric Functions (Continued)

Angle	Sine	Cosine	Tan.	Cotan.	Secant	Cosec.	
27°00′	.45399	.89101	.50952	1.9626	1.1223	2.2027	36°00′
5	.45528	.89034	.51136	1.9556	1.1231	2.1964	55
10	.45658	.88968	.51319	1.9486	1.1240	2.1902	50
15	.45787	.88902	.51503	1.9416	1.1248	2.1840	45
20	.45917	.88835	.51687	1.9347	1.1257	2.1178	40
25	.46046	.88768	.51872	1.9278	1.1265	2.1717	35
30	.46175	.88701	.52057	1.9210	1.1274	2.1657	30
35	.46304	.88634	.52242	1.9142	1.1282	2.1596	25
40	.46433	.88566	.52447	1.9074	1.1291	2.1536	20
45	.45561	.88499	.52612	1.9007	1.1299	2.1477	25
50	.46690	.88431	.52798	1.8940	1.1308	2.1418	10
55	.46819	.88363	.52984	1.8873	1.1317	2.1359	5
28°00′	.46947	.88295	.53171	1.8807	1.1326	2.1300	62°00′
5	.47075	.88226	.53358	1.8741	1.1334	2.1242	55
10	.47204	.88158	.53545	1.8676	1.1343	1.1185	50
15	.47332	.88089	.53732	1.8611	1.1352	2.1127	45
20	.47460	.88020	.53919	1.8546	1.1361	2.1070	40
25	.47588	.87951	.54107	1.8482	1.1370	2.1014	35
30	.47716	.87882	.54295	1.8418	1.1379	2.0957	30
35	.47844	.87812	.54484	1.8354	1.1388	2.0901	25
40	.47971	.87742	.54673	1.8291	1.1397	2.0846	20
45	.48099	.87673	.54862	1.8227	1.1406	2.0790	15
50	.48226	.87603	.55051	1.8165	1.1415	2.0735	10
55	.48354	.87532	.55241	1.8102	1.1424	2.0681	5
29°00′	.48481	.87462	.55431	1.8040	1.1433	2.0627	61°00′
5	.48608	.87391	.55621	1.7979	1.1443	2.0573	55
10	.48735	.87320	.55812	1.7917	1.1452	2.0519	50
15	.48862	.87250	.56003	1.7856	1.1461	2.0466	45
20	.48989	.87178	.56194	1.7795	1.1471	2.0413	40
25	.49116	.87107	.56385	1.7735	1.1480	2.0360	35
30	.49242	.87035	.56577	1.7675	1.1489	2.0308	30
35	.49369	.86964	.46769	1.7615	1.1499	2.0256	25
40	.49495	.86892	.56962	1.7555	1.1508	2.0204	20
45	.49622	.86820	.57155	1.7496	1.1518	2.0152	15
50	.49748	.86748	.57348	1.7437	1.1528	2.0101	10
55	.49874	.86675	.57541	1.7379	1.1537	2.0050	5
	Cosine	Sine	Cotan.	Tan.	Cosec.	Secant	Angle

Table 23. Trigonometric Functions (Continued)

Angle	Sine	Cosine	Tan.	Cotan.	Secant	Cosec.	
30°00′	.50000	.86603	.57735	1.7320	1.1547	2.0000	60°00′
5	.50126	.86530	.57929	1.7262	1.1557	1.9950	55
10	.50252	.86457	.58123	1.7205	1.1566	1.9900	50
15	.50377	.86383	.58318	1.7147	1.1576	1.9850	45
20	.50503	.86310	.58513	1.7090	1.1586	1.9801	40
25	.50628	.86237	.58709	1.7033	1.1596	1.9752	35
30	.50754	.86163	.58904	1.6977	1.1606	1.9703	30
35	.50879	.86089	.59100	1.6920	1.1616	1.9654	25
40	.51004	.86015	.59297	.16864	1.1626	1.9606	20
45	.51129	.85941	.59494	1.6808	1.1636	1.9558	15
50	.51254	.85866	.59691	1.6753	1.1646	1.9510	10
55	.51379	.85791	.59888	1.6698	1.1656	1.9463	5
31°00′	.51504	.85717	.60086	1.6643	1.1666	1.9416	59°00′
5	.51628	.85642	.60284	1.6588	1.1676	1.9369	55
10	.51753	.85566	.60483	1.6534	1.1687	1.9322	50
15	.51877	.85491	.60681	1.6479	1.1697	1.9276	45
20	.52002	.85416	.60881	1.6425	1.1707	1.9230	40
25	.52126	.85340	.61080	1.6372	1.1718	1.9184	35
30	.52250	.85264	.61280	1.6318	1.1728	1.9139	30
35	.52374	.85188	.61480	1.6265	1.1739	1.9093	25
40	.52498	.85112	.61681	1.6212	1.1749	1.9048	20
45	.52621	.85035	.61882	1.6160	1.1760	1.9004	15
50	.52745	.84959	.62083	1.6107	1.1770	1.8959	10
55	.52868	.84882	.62285	1.6055	1.1781	1.8915	5
32°00′	.52992	.84805	.62487	1.6003	1.1792	1.8871	58°00′
5	.53115	.84728	.62689	1.5952	1.1802	1.8827	55
10	.53238	.84650	.62892	1.5900	1.1813	1.8783	50
15	.53361	.84573	.63095	1.5849	1.1824	1.8740	45
20	.53484	.84495	.63299	1.5798	1.1835	1.8697	40
25	.53607	.84417	.63503	1.5747	1.1846	1.8654	35
30	.53730	.84339	.63707	1.5697	1.1857	1.8611	30
35	.53852	.84261	.63912	1.5646	1.1868	1.8569	25
40	.53975	.84182	.64117	1.5596	1.1879	1.8527	20
45	.54097	.84104	.64322	1.5547	1.1890	1.8485	15
50	.54220	.84025	.64528	1.5497	1.1901	1.8443	10
55	.54342	.83946	.64734	1.5448	1.1912	1.8402	5
	Cosine	Sine	Cotan.	Tan.	Cosec.	Secant	Angle

Table 23. Trigonometric Functions (Continued)

Angle	Sine	Cosine	Tan.	Cotan.	Secant	Cosec.	
33°00′	.54464	.83867	.64941	1.5399	1.1924	1.8361	57°00′
5	.54586	.83788	.65148	1.5350	1.1935	1.8320	55
10	.54708	.83708	.65355	1.5301	1.1946	1.8279	50
15	.54829	.83629	.65563	1.5252	1.1958	1.8238	45
20	.54951	.83549	.65771	1.5204	1.1969	1.8198	40
25	.55072	.83469	.65980	1.5156	1.1980	1.8158	35
30	.55193	.83388	.66188	1.5108	1.1992	1.8118	30
35	.55315	.83308	.66398	1.5061	1.2004	1.8078	25
40	.55436	.83228	.66608	1.5013	1.2015	1.8039	20
45	.55557	.83147	.66818	1.4966	1.2027	1.7999	15
50	.55678	.83066	.67028	1.4919	1.2039	1.7960	10
55	.55799	.82985	.67239	1.4872	1.2050	1.7921	5
34°00′	.55919	.82904	.67451	1.4826	1.2062	1.7883	56°00′
5	.56040	.82822	.67663	1.4779	1.2074	1.7844	55
10	.56160	.82741	.67875	1.4733	1.2086	1.7806	50
15	.56280	.82659	.68087	1.4687	1.2098	1.7768	45
20	.56401	.82577	.68301	1.4641	1.2110	1.7730	40
25	.56521	.82495	.68514	1.4595	1.2122	1.7693	35
30	.56641	.82413	.68728	1.4550	1.2134	1.7655	30
35	.56760	.82330	.68942	1.4505	1.2146	1.7618	25
40	.56880	.82247	.69157	1.4460	1.2158	1.7581	20
45	.57000	.82165	.69372	1.4415	1.2171	1.7544	15
50	.57119	.82082	.69588	1.4370	1.2183	1.7507	10
55	.57238	.81998	.69804	1.4326	1.2195	1.7471	5
35°00′	.57358	.81915	.70021	1.4281	1.2208	1.7434	55°00′
5	.57477	.81832	.70238	1.4237	1.2220	1.7398	55
10	.57596	.81748	.70455	1.4193	1.2233	1.7362	50
15	.57714	.81664	.70673	1.4150	1.2245	1.7327	45
20	.57833	.81580	.70891	1.4106	1.2258	1.7291	40
25	.57952	.81496	.71110	1.4063	1.2270	1.7256	35
30	.58070	.81411	.71329	1.4019	1.2283	1.7220	30
35	.58189	.81327	.71549	1.3976	1.2296	1.7185	25
40	.58307	.81242	.71769	1.3933	1.2309	1.7151	20
45	.58425	.81157	.71990	1.3891	1.2322	1.7116	15
50	.58543	.81072	.72211	1.3848	1.2335	1.7081	10
55	.58661	.80987	.72432	1.3806	1.2348	1.7047	5
	Cosine	Sine	Cotan.	Tan.	Cosec.	Secant	Angle

Table 23. Trigonometric Functions (Continued)

Angle	Sine	Cosine	Tan.	Cotan.	Secant	Cosec.	
36°00′	.58778	.80902	.72654	1.3764	1.2361	1.7013	54°00′
5	.58896	.80816	.72877	1.3722	1.2374	1.6979	55
10	.59014	.80730	.73100	1.3680	1.2387	1.6945	50
15	.59131	.80644	.73323	1.3638	1.2400	1.6912	45
20	.59248	.80558	.73547	1.3597	1.2413	1.6878	40
25	.59365	.80472	.73771	1.3555	1.2427	1.6845	35
30	.59482	.80386	.73996	1.3514	1.2440	1.6812	30
35	.59599	.80299	.74221	1.3473	1.2453	1.6779	25
40	.59716	.80212	.74447	1.3432	1.2467	1.6746	20
45	.59832	.80125	.74673	1.3392	1.2480	1.6713	15
50	.59949	.80038	.74900	1.3351	1.2494	1.6681	10
55	.60065	.79951	.75128	1.3311	1.2508	1.6648	5
37°00′	.60181	.79863	.75355	1.3270	1.2521	1.6616	53°00′
5	.60298	.79776	.75584	1.3230	1.2535	1.6584	55
10	.60413	.79688	.75812	1.3190	1.2549	1.6552	50
15	.60529	.79600	.76042	1.3151	1.2563	1.6521	45
20	.60645	.79512	.76271	1.3111	1.2577	1.6489	40
25	.60761	.79424	.76502	1.3071	1.2591	1.6458	35
30	.60876	.79335	.76733	1.3032	1.2605	1.6427	30
35	.60991	.79247	.76964	1.2993	1.2619	1.6396	25
40	.61107	.79158	.77196	1.2954	1.2633	1.6365	20
45	.61222	.79069	.77428	1.2915	1.2647	1.6334	15
50	.61337	.78980	.77661	1.2786	1.2661	1.6303	10
55	.61451	.78890	.77895	1.2838	1.2675	1.6273	5
38°00′	.61566	.78801	.78128	1.2799	1.2690	1.6243	52°00′
5	.61681	.78711	.78363	1.2761	1.2705	1.6212	55
10	.61795	.78622	.78598	1.2723	1.2719	1.6182	50
15	.61909	.78532	.78834	1.2685	1.2734	1.6153	45
20	.62023	.78441	.79070	1.2647	1.2748	1.6123	40
25	.62137	.78351	.79306	1.2609	1.2763	1.6093	35
30	.62251	.78261	.79543	1.2572	1.2778	1.6064	30
35	.62365	.78170	.79781	1.2534	1.2793	1.6034	25
40	.62479	.78079	.80020	1.2497	1.2807	1.6005	20
45	.62592	.77988	.80258	1.2460	1.2822	1.5976	15
50	.62706	.77897	.80498	1.2423	1.2837	1.5947	10
55	.62819	.77806	.80738	1.2386	1.2852	1.5919	5
	Cosine	Sine	Cotan.	Tan.	Cosec.	Secant	Angle

Table 23. Trigonometric Functions (Continued)

Angle	Sine	Cosine	Tan.	Cotan.	Secant	Cosec.	
39°00′	.62932	.77715	.80978	1.2349	1.2867	1.5890	51°00′
5	.63045	.77623	.81219	1.2312	1.2883	1.5862	55
10	.63158	.77531	.81461	1.2276	1.2898	1.5833	50
15	.63270	.77439	.81703	1.2239	1.2913	1.5805	45
20	.63383	.77347	.81946	1.2203	1.2929	1.5777	40
25	.63495	.77255	.82190	1.2167	1.2944	1.5749	35
30	.63606	.77162	.82434	1.2131	1.2960	1.5721	30
35	.63720	.77070	.82678	1.2095	1.2975	1.5694	25
40	.63832	.76977	.82923	1.2059	1.2991	1.5666	20
45	.63944	.76884	.83169	1.2024	1.3006	1.5639	15
50	.64056	.76791	.83415	1.1988	1.3022	1.5611	10
55	.64167	.76698	.83662	1.1953	1.3038	1.5584	5
40°00′	.64279	.76604	.83910	1.1917	1.3054	1.5557	50°00′
5	.64390	.76511	.84158	1.1882	1.3070	1.5530	55
10	.64501	.76417	.84407	1.1847	1.3086	1.5503	50
15	.64612	.76323	.84656	1.1812	1.3102	1.5477	45
20	.64723	.76229	.84906	1.1778	1.3118	1.5450	40
25	.64834	.76135	.85157	1.1743	1.3134	1.5424	35
30	.64945	.76041	.85408	1.1708	1.3151	1.5398	30
35	.65055	.75946	.85660	1.1674	1.3167	1.5371	25
40	.65166	.75851	.85912	1.1640	1.3184	1.5345	20
45	.65276	.75756	.86165	1.1605	1.3200	1.5319	15
50	.65386	.75661	.86419	1.1571	1.3217	1.5294	10
55	.65496	.75566	.86674	1.1537	1.3233	1.5268	5
41°00′	.65606	.75471	.86929	1.1504	1.3250	1.5242	49°00′
5	.65716	.75375	.87184	1.1470	1.3267	1.5217	55
10	.65825	.75280	.87441	1.1436	1.3284	1.5192	50
15	.65934	.75184	.87698	1.1403	1.3301	1.5166	45
20	.66044	.75088	.87955	1.1369	1.3318	1.5141	40
25	.66153	.74992	.88213	1.1336	1.3335	1.5116	35
30	.66262	.74895	.88472	1.1303	1.3352	1.5092	30
35	.66371	.74799	.88732	1.1270	1.3369	1.5067	25
40	.66479	.74702	.88992	1.1237	1.3386	1.5042	20
45	.66588	.74606	.89253	1.1204	1.3404	1.5018	15
50	.66697	.74509	.89515	1.1171	1.3421	1.4993	10
55	.66805	.74412	.89777	1.1139	1.3439	1.4969	5
	Cosine	Sine	Cotan.	Tan.	Cosec.	Secant	Angle

Table 23. Trigonometric Functions (Continued)

Angle	Sine	Cosine	Tan.	Cotan.	Secant	Cosec.	
42°00′	.66913	.74314	.90040	1.1106	1.3456	1.4945	48°00′
5	.67021	.74217	.90304	1.1074	1.3474	1.4921	55
10	.67129	.74119	.90568	1.1041	1.3492	1.4897	50
15	.67237	.74022	.90834	1.1009	1.3509	1.4873	45
20	.67344	.73924	.91099	1.0977	1.3527	1.4849	40
25	.67452	.73826	.91366	1.0945	1.3545	1.4825	35
30	.67559	.73728	.91633	1.0913	1.3563	1.4802	30
35	.67666	.73629	.91901	1.0881	1.3581	1.4778	25
40	.67773	.73531	.92170	1.0849	1.3600	1.4755	20
45	.67880	.73432	.92439	1.0818	1.3618	1.4732	15
50	.67987	.73333	.92709	1.0786	1.3636	1.4709	10
55	.68093	.73234	.92980	1.0755	1.3655	1.4686	5
43°00′	.68200	.73135	.93251	1.0724	1.3673	1.4663	47°00′
5	.68306	.73036	.93524	1.0692	1.3692	1.4640	55
10	.68412	.72937	.93797	1.0661	1.3710	1.4617	50
15	.68518	.72837	.94071	1.0630	1.3729	1.4595	45
20	.68624	.72737	.94345	1.0599	1.3748	1.4572	40
25	.68730	.72637	.94620	1.0568	1.3767	1.4550	35
30	.68835	.72537	.94896	1.0538	1.3786	1.4527	30
35	.68941	.72437	.95173	1.0507	1.3805	1.4505	25
40	.69046	.72337	.95451	1.0476	1.3824	1.4483	20
45	.69151	.72236	.95729	1.0446	1.3843	1.4461	15
50	.69256	.72136	.96008	1.0416	1.3863	1.4439	10
55	.69361	.72035	.96288	1.0385	1.3882	1.4417	5
44°00′	.69466	.71934	.96569	1.0355	1.3902	1.4395	46°00′
5	.69570	.71833	.96850	1.0325	1.3921	1.4374	55
10	.69675	.71732	.97133	1.0295	1.3941	1.4352	50
15	.69779	.71630	.97416	1.0265	1.3960	1.4331	45
20	.69883	.71529	.97700	1.0235	1.3980	1.4310	40
25	.69987	.71427	.97984	1.0206	1.4000	1.4288	35
30	.70091	.71325	.98270	1.0176	1.4020	1.4267	30
35	.70194	.71223	.98556	1.0146	1.4040	1.4246	25
40	.70298	.71121	.98843	1.0117	1.4060	1.4225	20
45	.70401	.71018	.99131	1.0088	1.4081	1.4204	15
50	.70555	.70916	.99420	1.0058	1.4101	1.4183	10
55	.70608	.70813	.99709	1.0029	1.4122	1.4163	5
45°00′	.70711	.70711	1.0000	1.0000	1.4142	1.4142	45°00′
	Cosine	Sine	Cotan.	Tan.	Cosec.	Secant	Angle

Table 24. Mathematical Method of Finding Slant Angles of Square-thread Tools

In any right-angle triangle, for example *d*, Fig. 17-29, the *side opposite* divided by *side adjacent* equals the *tangent of the angle*. Therefore dividing the lead (side opposite) by the circumference (side adjacent) will give the tangent of the angle to be found. In the example given (page 458), find the slant angle of the following side: lead is 0.250, circumference of major diameter is 3.92 in. Then 0.250 ÷ 3.92 = 0.0637. Looking in the table below, the nearest number to 0.0637 is 0.0641, which is the tangent of the angle 3 degrees 40 minutes, the same angle as was found by drawing the figure and measuring with a protractor. (For square threads the angle within one-third of a degree is near enough; the table shows every 10 minutes, or one-sixth degree.)

Find the slant angle of the leading side: lead is 0.250, circumference of minor diameter is 3.14 in. Then 0.250 ÷ 3.14 = 0.0796. Looking in the table below, the nearest number to 0.0796 is 0.0787, which is the tangent of 4 degrees 30 minutes.

Table of Tangents up to 14 Degrees 50 Minutes

Angles	Tan.	Angles	Tan.	Angles	Tan.	Angles	Tan.	Angles	Tan.
0°00′	0.0000	3°00′	0.0524	6°00′	0.1051	9°00′	0.1584	12°00′	0.2126
10	0.0029	10	0.0553	10	0.1080	10	0.1614	10	0.2156
20	0.0058	20	0.0582	20	0.1110	20	0.1644	20	0.2186
30	0.0087	30	0.0612	30	0.1139	30	0.1673	30	0.2217
40	0.0116	40	0.0641	40	0.1169	40	0.1703	40	0.2247
50	0.0145	50	0.0670	50	0.1198	50	0.1733	50	0.2278
1°00′	0.0175	4°00′	0.0699	7°00′	0.1228	10°00′	0.1763	13°00′	0.2309
10	0.0204	10	0.0729	10	0.1257	10	0.1793	10	0.2339
20	0.0233	20	0.0758	20	0.1287	20	0.1823	20	0.2370
30	0.0262	30	0.0787	30	0.1317	30	0.1853	30	0.2401
40	0.0291	40	0.0816	40	0.1346	40	0.1883	40	0.2432
50	0.0320	50	0.0846	50	0.1376	50	0.1914	50	0.2462
2°00′	0.0349	5°00′	0.0875	8°00′	0.1405	11°00′	0.1944	14°00′	0.2493
10	0.0378	10	0.0904	10	0.1435	10	0.1974	10	0.2524
20	0.0407	20	0.0934	20	0.1465	20	0.2004	20	0.2555
30	0.0437	30	0.0963	30	0.1495	30	0.2035	30	0.2586
40	0.0466	40	0.0992	40	0.1524	40	0.2065	40	0.2617
50	0.0495	50	0.1022	50	0.1554	50	0.2095	50	0.2648

Table 25. Constants for 5-in. Sine Bar
When using 10-in. sine bar multiply constant by two.

M	0°	1°	2°	3°	4°	5°
0	0.00000	0.08725	0.17450	0.26170	0.34880	0.43580
1	.00145	.08870	.17595	.26315	.35025	.43725
2	.00290	.09015	.17740	.26460	.35170	.43870
3	.00435	.09160	.17885	.26605	.35315	.44015
4	.00580	.09310	.18030	.26750	.35460	.44155
5	0.00725	0.09455	0.18175	0.26895	0.35605	0.44300
6	.00875	.09600	.18320	.27040	.35750	.44445
7	.01020	.09745	.18455	.27185	.35895	.44590
8	.01165	.09890	.18615	.27330	.36040	.44735
9	.01310	.10035	.18760	.27475	.36185	.44880
10	0.01455	0.10180	0.18905	0.27620	0.36330	0.45025
11	.01600	.10325	.19050	.27765	.36475	.45170
12	.01745	.10470	.19195	.27910	.36620	.45315
13	.01890	.10615	.19340	.28055	.36765	.45460
14	.02035	.10760	.19485	.28200	.36910	.45605
15	0.02180	0.10905	0.19630	0.28345	0.37055	0.45750
16	.02325	.11055	.19775	.28490	.37200	.45895
17	.02475	.11200	.19920	.28635	.37345	.46040
18	.02620	.11345	.20065	.28780	.37490	.46185
19	.02765	.11490	.20210	.28925	.37635	.46330
20	0.02910	0.11635	0.20355	0.29070	0.37780	0.46475
21	.03055	.11780	.20500	.29220	.37925	.46620
22	.03200	.11925	.20645	.29365	.38070	.46765
23	.03345	.12070	.20795	.29510	.38215	.46910
24	.03490	.12215	.20940	.29655	.38360	.47055
25	0.03635	0.12360	0.21085	0.29800	0.38505	0.47200
26	.03780	.12505	.21230	.29945	.38650	.47345
27	.03925	.12650	.21375	.30090	.38795	.47490
28	.04070	.12800	.21520	.30235	.38940	.47635
29	.04220	.12945	.21665	.30380	.39085	.47780
30	0.04365	0.13090	0.21810	0.30525	0.39230	0.47925
31	.04510	.13235	.21955	.30670	.39375	.48070
32	.04655	.13380	.22100	.30815	.39520	.48210
33	.04800	.13525	.22245	.30960	.39665	.48355
34	.04945	.13670	.22390	.31105	.39810	.48500
35	0.05090	0.13815	0.22535	0.31250	0.39955	0.48645
36	.05235	.13960	.22680	.31395	.40100	.48790
37	.05380	.14105	.22825	.31540	.40245	.48935
38	.05525	.14250	.22970	.31685	.40390	.49080
39	.05670	.14395	.23115	.31830	.40535	.49225
40	0.05820	0.14540	0.23265	0.31975	0.40680	0.49370
41	.05965	.14690	.23410	.32120	.40825	.49515
42	.06110	.14835	.23555	.32265	.40970	.49660
43	.06255	.14980	.23700	.32410	.41115	.49805
44	.06400	.15125	.23845	.32555	.41260	.49950
45	0.06545	0.15270	0.23990	0.32700	0.41405	0.50095
46	.06690	.15415	.24135	.32845	.41550	.50240
47	.06835	.15560	.24280	.32990	.41695	.50385
48	.06980	.15705	.24425	.33135	.41840	.50530
49	.07125	.15850	.24570	.33280	.41985	.50675
50	0.07270	0.15995	0.24715	0.33425	0.42130	0.50820
51	.07415	.16140	.24860	.33570	.42275	.50960
52	.07565	.16285	.25005	.33715	.42420	.51105
53	.07710	.16430	.25150	.33865	.42565	.51250
54	.07855	.16580	.25295	.34010	.42710	.51395
55	0.08000	0.16725	0.25440	0.34155	0.42855	0.51540
56	.08145	.16870	.25585	.34300	.43000	.51685
57	.08290	.17015	.25730	.34445	.43145	.51830
58	.08435	.17160	.25875	.34590	.43290	.51975
59	.08580	.17305	.26028	.34735	.43435	.52120
60	0.08725	0.17450	0.26170	0.34880	0.43580	0.52265

Table 25. Constants for 5-in. Sine Bar (Continued)

M	6°	7°	8°	9°	10°	11°
0	0.52265	0.60935	0.69585	0.78215	0.86825	0.95405
1	.52410	.61080	.69730	.78360	.85965	.95545
2	.52555	.61225	.69875	.78505	.87110	.95690
3	.52700	.61370	.70020	.78650	.87255	.95835
4	.52845	.61510	.70165	.78790	.87395	.95975
5	0.52985	0.61655	0.70305	0.78935	0.87540	0.96120
6	.53130	.61800	.70450	.79080	.87685	.96260
7	.53275	.61945	.70595	.79225	.87825	.96405
8	.53420	.62090	.70740	.79365	.87970	.96545
9	.53565	.62235	.70885	.79510	.88115	.96690
10	0.53710	0.62380	0.71025	0.79655	0.88255	0.96830
11	.53855	.62520	.71170	.79795	.88400	.96975
12	.54000	.62665	.71315	.79940	.88540	.97115
13	.54145	.62810	.71460	.80085	.88685	.97260
14	.54290	.62955	.71600	.80230	.88830	.97405
15	0.54435	0.63100	0.71745	0.80370	0.88970	0.97545
16	.54580	.63245	.71890	.80515	.89115	.97690
17	.54725	.63390	.72035	.80660	.89260	.97830
18	.54865	.63530	.72180	.80800	.89400	.97975
19	.55010	.63675	.72320	.80945	.89545	.98115
20	0.55155	0.63820	0.72465	0.81090	0.89685	0.98260
21	.55300	.63965	.72610	.81230	.89830	.98400
22	.55445	.64110	.72755	.81375	.89975	.98545
23	.55590	.64255	.72900	.81520	.90115	.98685
24	.55735	.64400	.73040	.81665	.90260	.98830
25	0.55880	0.64540	0.73185	0.81805	0.90405	0.98970
26	.56025	.64685	.73330	.81950	.90545	.99115
27	.56170	.64830	.73475	.82095	.90690	.99255
28	.56315	.64975	.73615	.82235	.90830	.99400
29	.56455	.65120	.73760	.82380	.90975	.99540
30	0.56600	0.65265	0.73905	0.82525	0.91120	0.99685
31	.56745	.65405	.74050	.82665	.91260	.99825
32	.56890	.65550	.74190	.82810	.91405	.99970
33	.57035	.65695	.74335	.82955	.91545	1.0011
34	.57180	.65840	.74480	.83100	.91690	.0016
35	0.57325	0.65985	0.74625	0.83240	0.91835	1.0039
36	.57470	.66130	.74770	.83385	.91975	.0054
37	.57615	.66270	.74910	.83530	.92120	.0068
38	.57760	.66415	.75055	.83670	.92260	.0082
39	.57900	.66560	.75200	.83815	.92405	.0096
40	0.58045	0.66705	0.75345	0.83960	0.92545	1.0110
41	.58190	.66850	.75485	.84100	.92690	.0125
42	.58335	.66995	.75630	.84245	.92835	.0139
43	.58480	.67135	.75775	.84390	.92975	.0153
44	.58625	.67280	.75920	.84530	.93120	.0168
45	0.58770	0.67425	0.76060	0.84675	0.93260	1.0182
46	.58915	.67570	.76205	.84820	.93405	.0196
47	.59060	.67715	.76350	.84960	.93550	.0210
48	.59200	.67860	.76495	.85105	.93690	.0225
49	.59345	.68000	.76635	.85250	.93835	.0239
50	0.59490	0.68145	0.76780	0.85390	0.93975	1.0253
51	.59635	.68290	.76925	.85535	.94120	.0267
52	.59780	.68435	.77070	.85680	.94260	.0281
53	.59925	.68580	.77210	.85820	.94405	.0296
54	.60070	.68720	.77355	.85965	.94550	.0310
55	0.60215	0.68865	0.77500	0.86110	0.94690	1.0324
56	.60355	.69010	.77645	.86250	.94835	.0338
57	.60500	.69155	.77785	.86395	.94975	.0353
58	.60645	.69300	.77930	.86540	.95120	.0367
59	.60790	.69445	.78075	.86680	.95260	.0381
60	0.60935	0.69585	0.78215	0.86825	0.95405	1.0395

Table 25. Constants for 5-in. Sine Bar (Continued)

M	12°	13°	14°	15°	16°	17°
0	1.0395	1.1247	1.2096	1.2941	1.3782	1.4618
1	.0410	.1261	.2110	.2955	.3796	.4632
2	.0424	.1276	.2124	.2969	.3810	.4646
3	..0438	.1290	.2138	.2983	.3824	.4660
4	.0452	.1304	.2152	.2997	.3838	.4674
5	1.0466	1.1318	1.2166	1.3011	1.3852	1.4688
6	.0481	.1332	.2181	.3025	.3865	.4702
7	.0495	.1346	.2195	.3039	.3879	.4716
8	.0509	.1361	.2209	.3053	.3893	.4730
9	.0523	.1375	.2223	.3067	.3907	.4743
10	1.0538	1.1389	1.2237	1.3081	1.3921	1.4757
11	.0552	.1403	.2251	.3095	.3935	.4771
12	.0566	.1417	.2265	.3109	.3949	.4785
13	.0580	.1431	.2279	.3123	.3963	.4799
14	.0594	.1446	.2293	.3137	.3977	.4813
15	1.0609	1.1460	1.2307	1.3151	1.3991	1.4827
16	.0623	.1474	.2322	.3165	.4005	.4841
17	.0637	.1488	.2336	.3179	.4019	.4855
18	.0651	.1502	.2350	.3193	.4033	.4868
19	.0665	.1516	.2364	.3207	.4047	.4882
20	1.0680	1.1531	1.2378	1.3221	1.4061	1.4896
21	.0694	.1545	.2392	.3235	.4075	.4910
22	.0708	.1559	.2406	.3250	.4089	.4924
23	.0722	.1573	.2420	.3264	.4103	.4938
24	.0737	.1587	.2434	.3278	.4117	.4952
25	1.0751	1.1601	1.2448	1.3292	1.4131	1.4966
26	.0765	.1615	.2462	.3306	.4145	.4980
27	.0779	.1630	.2477	.3320	.4159	.4993
28	.0793	.1644	.2491	.3334·	.4173	.5007
29	.0808	.1658	.2505	.3348	.4187	.5021
30	1.0822	1.1672	1.2519	1.3362	1.4201	1.5035
31	.0836	.1686	.2533	.3376	.4214	.5049
32	.0850	.1700	.2547	.3390	.4228	.5063
33	.0864	.1714	.2561	.3404	.4242	.5077
34	.0879	.1729	.2575	.3418	.4256	.5091
35	1.0893	1.1743	1.2589	1.3432	1.4270	1.5104
36	.0907	.1757	.2603	.3446	.4284	.5118
37	.0921	.1771	.2617	.3460	.4298	.5132
38	.0935	.1785	.2631	.3474	.4312	.5146
39	.0949	.1799	.2645	.3488	.4326	.5160
40	1.0964	1.1813	1.2660	1.3502	1.4340	1.5174
41	.0978	.1828	.2674	.3516	.4354	.5188
42	.0992	.1842	.2688	.3530	.4368	.5201
43	.1006	.1856	.2702	.3544	.4382	.5215
44	.1020	.1870	.2716	.3558	.4396	.5229
45	1.1035	1.1884	1.2730	1.3572	1.4410	1.5243
46	.1049	.1898	.2744	.3586	.4423	.5257
47	.1063	.1912	.2758	.3600	.4437	.5271
48	.1077	.1926	.2772	.3614	.4451	.5285
49	.1091	.1941	.2786	.3628	.4465	.5298
50	1.1106	1.1955	1.2800	1.3642	1.4479	1.5312
51	.1120	.1969	.2814	.3656	.4493	.5326
52	.1134	.1983	.2828	.3670	.4507	.5340
53	.1148	.1997	.2842	.3684	.4521	.5354
54	.1162	.2011	.2856	.3698	.4535	.5368
55	1.1176	1.2025	1.2870	1.3712	1.4549	1.5381
56	.1191	.2039	.2884	.3726	.4563	.5395
57	.1205	.2054	.2899	.3740	.4577	.5409
58	.1219	.2068	.2913	.3754	.4591	.5423
59	.1233	.2082	.2927	.3768	.4604	.5437
60	1.1247	1.2096	1.2941	1.3782	1.4618	1.5451

Table 25. Constants for 5-in. Sine Bar (Continued)

M	18°	19°	20°	21°	22°	23°
0	1.5451	1.6278	1.7101	1.7918	1.8730	1.9536
1	.5464	.6292	.7114	.7932	.8744	.9550
2	.5478	.6306	.7128	.7945	.8757	.9563
3	.5492	.6319	.7142	.7959	.8771	.9576
4	.5506	.6333	.7155	.7972	.8784	.9590
5	1.5520	1.6347	1.7169	1.7986	1.8797	1.9603
6	.5534	.6361	.7183	.8000	.8811	.9617
7	.5547	.6374	.7196	.8013	.8824	.9630
8	.5561	.6388	.7210	.8027	.8838	.9643
9	.5575	.6402	.7224	.8040	.8851	.9657
10	1.5589	1.6416	1.7237	1.8054	1.8865	1.9670
11	.5603	.6429	.7251	.8067	.8878	.9683
12	.5616	.6443	.7265	.8081	.8892	.9697
13	.5630	.6457	.7292	.8095	.8906	.9711
14	.5644	.6471	.7242	.8108	.8919	.9724
15	1.5658	1.6484	1.7306	1.8122	1.8932	1.9737
16	.5672	.6498	.7319	.8135	.8946	.9750
17	.5686	.6512	.7333	.8149	.8959	.9764
18	.5699	.6525	.7347	.8162	.8973	.9777
19	.5713	.6539	.7360	.8176	.8986	.9790
20	1.5727	1.6553	1.7374	1.8189	1.8999	1.9804
21	.5741	.6567	.7387	.8203	.9013	.9817
22	.5755	.6580	.7401	.8217	.9026	.9830
23	.5768	.6594	.7415	.8230	.9040	.9844
24	.5782	.6608	.7428	.8244	.9053	.9857
25	1.5796	1.6622	1.7442	1.8257	1.9067	1.9870
26	.5810	.6635	.7456	.8271	.9080	.9884
27	.5824	.6649	.7469	.8284	.9094	.9897
28	.5837	.6663	.7483	.8298	.9107	.9911
29	.5851	.6676	.7496	.8311	.9120	.9924
30	1.5865	1.6690	1.7510	1.8325	1.9134	1.9937
31	.5879	.6704	.7524	.8338	.9147	.9951
32	.5893	.6718	.7537	.8352	.9161	.9964
33	.5906	.6731	.7551	.8365	.9174	.9977
34	.5920	.6745	.7565	.8379	.9188	.9991
35	1.5934	1.6759	1.7578	1.8392	1.9201	2.0004
36	.5948	.6772	.7592	.8406	.9215	.0017
37	.5961	.6786	.7605	.8419	.9228	.0031
38	.5975	.6800	.7619	.8433	.9241	.0044
39	.5989	.6813	.7633	.8447	.9255	.0057
40	1.6003	1.6827	1.7646	1.8460	1.9268	2.0070
41	.6017	.6841	.7660	.8474	.9282	.0084
42	.6030	.6855	.7673	.8487	.9295	.0097
43	.6044	.6868	.7687	.8501	.9308	.0110
44	.6058	.6882	.7701	.8514	.9322	.0124
45	1.6072	1.6896	1.7714	1.8528	1.9335	2.0137
46	.6085	.6909	.7728	.8541	.9349	.0150
47	.6099	.6923	.7742	.8555	.9362	.0164
48	.6113	.6937	.7755	.8568	.9376	.0177
49	.6127	.6950	.7769	.8582	.9389	.0190
50	1.6141	1.6964	1.7782	1.8595	1.9402	2.0204
51	.6154	.6978	.7796	.8609	.9416	.0217
52	.6168	.6991	.7809	.8622	.9429	.0230
53	.6182	.7005	.7823	.8636	.9443	.0244
54	.6196	.7019	.7837	.8649	.9456	.0257
55	1.6209	1.7032	1.7850	1.8663	1.9469	2.0270
56	.6223	.7046	.7864	.8676	.9483	.0283
57	.6237	.7060	.7877	.8690	.9496	.0297
58	.6251	.7073	.7891	.8703	.9510	.0310
59	.6264	.7087	.7905	.8717	.9523	.0323
60	1.6278	1.7101	1.7918	1.8730	1.9536	2.0337

Table 25. Constants for 5-in. Sine Bar (Continued)

M	24°	25°	26°	27°	28°	29°
0	2.0337	2.1131	2.1918	2.2699	2.3473	2.4240
1	.0350	.1144	.1931	.2712	.3486	.4253
2	.0363	.1157	.1944	.2725	.3499	.4266
3	.0376	.1170	.1958	.2738	.3512	.4278
4	.0390	.1183	.1971	.2751	.3525	.4291
5	2.0403	2.1197	2.1984	2.2764	2.3538	2.4304
6	.0416	.1210	.1997	.2777	.3550	.4317
7	.0430	.1223	.2010	.2790	.3563	.4329
8	.0443	.1236	.2023	.2803	.3576	.4342
9	.0456	.1249	.2036	.2816	.3589	.4355
10	2.0469	2.1262	2.2049	2.2829	2.3602	2.4367
11	.0483	.1276	.2062	.2842	.3614	.4380
12	.0496	.1289	.2075	.2855	.3627	.4393
13	.0509	.1302	.2088	.2868	.3640	.4405
14	.0522	.1315	.2101	.2881	.3653	.4418
15	2.0536	2.1328	2.2114	2.2893	2.3666	2.4431
16	.0549	.1341	.2127	.2906	.3679	.4444
17	.0562	.1354	.2140	.2919	.3691	.4456
18	.0575	.1368	.2153	.2932	.3704	.4469
19	.0589	.1381	.2166	2945	.3717	.4482
20	2.0602	2.1394	2.2179	2.2958	2.3730	2.4494
21	.0615	.1407	.2192	.2971	.3743	.4507
22	.0628	.1420	.2205	.2984	.3755	.4520
23	.0642	.1433	.2218	.2997	.3768	.4532
24	.0655	.1447	.2232	.3010	.3781	.4545
25	2.0668	2.1460	2.2245	2.3023	2.3794	2.4558
26	.0681	.1473	.2258	.3036	.3807	.4570
27	.0695	.1486	.2271	.3048	.3819	.4583
28	.0708	.1499	.2284	.3061	.3832	.4596
29	.0721	1512	.2297	.3074	.3845	.4608
30	2.0734	2.1525	2.2310	2.3087	2.3858	2.4621
31	.0748	.1538	.2323	.3100	.3870	.4634
32	.0761	.1552	.2336	.3113	.3883	.4646
33	.0774	.1565	.2349	.3126	.3896	.4659
34	.0787	.1578	.2362	.3139	.3909	.4672
35	2.0801	2.1591	2.2375	2.3152	2.3922	2.4684
36	.0814	.1604	.2388	.3165	.3934	.4697
37	.0827	.1617	.2401	.3177	.3947	.4709
38	.0840	.1630	.2414	.3190	.3960	.4722
39	.0853	.1643	.2427	.3203	.3973	.4735
40	2.0867	2.1656	2.2440	2.3216	2.3985	2.4747
41	.0880	.1670	.2453	.3229	.3998	.4760
42	.0893	.1683	.2466	.3242	.4011	.4773
43	.0906	.1696	.2479	.3255	.4024	.4785
44	.0920	.1709	.2492	.3268	.4036	.4798
45	2.0933	2.1722	2.2505	2.3280	2.4049	2.4811
46	.0946	.1735	.2518	.3293	.4062	.4823
47	.0959	.1748	.2531	.3306	.4075	.4836
48	.0972	.1761	.2544	.3319	.4087	.4848
49	.0986	.1774	.2557	.3332	.4100	.4861
50	2.0999	2.1787	2.2570	2.3345	2.4113	2.4874
51	.1012	.1801	.2583	.3358	.4126	.4886
52	.1025	.1814	.2596	.3371	.4138	.4899
53	.1038	.1827	.2609	.3383	.4151	.4912
54	.1052	.1840	.2621	.3396	.4164	.4924
55	2.1065	2.1853	2.2634	2.3409	2.4177	2.4937
56	.1078	.1866	.2647	.3422	.4189	.4949
57	.1091	.1879	.2660	.3435	.4202	.4962
58	.1104	.1892	.2673	.3448	.4215	.4975
59	.1117	.1905	.2686	.3460	.4228	.4987
60	2.1131	2.1918	2.2699	2.3473	2.4240	2.5000

Table 25. Constants for 5-in. Sine Bar (Continued)

M	30°	31°	32°	33°	34°	35°
0	2.5000	2.5752	2.6496	2.7232	2.7959	2.8679
1	.5012	.5764	.6508	.7244	.7971	.8690
2	.5025	.5777	.6520	.7256	.7984	.8702
3	.5038	.5789	.6533	.7268	.7996	.8714
4	.5050	.5802	.6545	.7280	.8008	.8726
5	2.5063	2.5814	2.6557	2.7293	2.8020	2.8738
6	.5075	.5826	.6570	.7305	.8032	.8750
7	.5088	.5839	.6582	.7317	.8044	.8762
8	.5100	.5851	.6594	.7329	.8056	.8774
9	.5113	.5864	.6607	.7341	.8068	.8786
10	2.5126	2.5876	2.6619	2.7354	2.8080	2.8798
11	.5138	.5889	.6631	.7366	.8092	.8809
12	.5151	.5901	.6644	.7378	.8104	.8821
13	.5163	.5914	.6656	.7390	.8116	.8833
14	.5176	.5926	.6668	.7402	.8128	.8845
15	2.5188	2.5938	2.6680	2.7414	2.8140	2.8857
16	.5201	.5951	.6693	.7427	.8152	.8869
17	.5214	.5963	.6705	.7439	.8164	.8881
18	.5226	.5976	.6717	.7451	.8176	.8893
19	.5239	.5988	.6730	.7463	.8188	.8905
20	2.5251	2.6001	2.6742	2.7475	2.8200	2.8916
21	.5264	.6013	.6754	.7487	.8212	.8928
22	.5276	.6025	.6767	.7499	.8224	.8940
23	.5289	.6038	.6779	.7512	.8236	.8952
24	.5301	.6050	.6791	.7524	.8248	.8964
25	2.5314	2.6063	2.6803	2.7536	2.8260	2.8976
26	.5327	.6075	.6816	.7548	.8272	.8988
27	.5339	.6087	.6828	.7560	.8284	.8999
28	.5352	.6100	.6840	.7572	.8296	.9011
29	.5364	.6112	.6852	.7584	.8308	.9023
30	2.5377	2.6125	2.6865	2.7597	2.8320	2.9035
31	.5389	.6137	.6877	.7609	.8332	.9047
32	.5402	.6149	.6889	.7621	.8344	.9059
33	.5414	.6162	.6902	.7633	.8356	.9070
34	.5427	.6174	.6914	.7645	.8368	.9082
35	2.5439	2.6187	2.6926	2.7657	2.8380	2.9094
36	.5452	.6199	.6938	.7669	.8392	.9106
37	.5464	.6211	.6951	.7681	.8404	.9118
38	.5477	.6224	.6963	.7694	.8416	.9130
39	.5489	.6236	.6975	.7706	.8428	.9141
40	2.5502	2.6249	2.6987	2.7718	2.8440	2.9153
41	.5514	.6261	.7000	.7730	.8452	.9165
42	.5527	.6273	.7012	.7742	.8464	.9177
43	.5539	.6286	.7024	.7754	.8476	.9189
44	.5552	.6298	.7036	.7766	.8488	.9200
45	2.5564	2.6310	2.7048	2.7778	2.8500	2.9212
46	.5577	.6323	.7061	.7790	.8512	.9224
47	.5589	.6335	.7073	.7802	.8523	.9236
48	.5602	.6348	.7085	.7815	.8535	.9248
49	.5614	.6360	.7097	.7827	.8547	.9259
50	2.5627	2.6372	2.7110	2.7839	2.8559	2.9271
51	.5639	.6385	.7122	.7851	.8571	.9283
52	.5652	.6397	.7134	.7863	.8583	.9295
53	.5664	.6409	.7146	.7875	.8595	.9307
54	.5677	.6422	.7158	.7887	.8607	.9318
55	2.5689	2.6434	2.7171	2.7899	2.8619	2.9330
56	.5702	.6446	.7183	.7911	.8631	.9342
57	.5714	.6459	.7195	.7923	.8643	.9354
58	.5727	.6471	.7207	.7935	.8655	.9365
59	.5739	.6483	.7220	.7947	.8667	.9377
60	2.5752	2.6496	2.7232	2.7959	2.8679	2.9389

Table 25. Constants for 5-in. Sine Bar (Continued)

M	36°	37°	38°	39°	40°	41°
0	2.9389	3.0091	3.0783	3.1466	3.2139	3.2803
1	.9401	.0102	.0794	.1477	.2150	.2814
2	.9413	.0114	.0806	.1488	.2161	.2825
3	.9424	.0125	.0817	.1500	.2173	.2836
4	.9436	.0137	.0829	.1511	.2184	.2847
5	2.9448	3.0149	3.0840	3.1522	3.2195	3.2858
6	.9460	.0160	.0852	.1534	.2206	.2869
7	.9471	.0172	.0863	.1545	.2217	.2879
8	.9483	.0183	.0874	.1556	.2228	.2890
9	.9495	.0195	.0886	.1567	.2239	.2901
10	2.9507	3.0207	3.0897	3.1579	3.2250	3.2912
11	.9518	.0218	.0909	.1590	.2262	.2923
12	.9530	.0230	.0920	.1601	.2273	.2934
13	.9542	.0241	.0932	.1612	.2284	.2945
14	.9554	.0253	.0943	.1624	.2295	.2956
15	2.9565	3.0264	3.0954	3.1635	3.2306	3.2967
16	.9577	.0276	.0966	.1646	.2317	.2978
17	.9589	.0288	.0977	.1658	.2328	.2989
18	.9600	.0299	.0989	.1669	.2339	.3000
19	.9612	.0311	.1000	.1680	.2350	.3011
20	2.9624	3.0322	3.1012	3.1691	3.2361	3.3022
21	.9636	.0334	.1023	.1703	.2373	.3033
22	.9647	.0345	.1034	.1714	.2384	.3044
23	.9659	.0357	.1046	.1725	.2395	.3054
24	.9671	.0369	.1057	.1736	.2406	.3065
25	2.9682	3.0380	3.1069	3.1748	3.2417	3.3076
26	.9694	.0392	.1080	.1759	.2428	.3087
27	.9706	.0403	.1091	.1770	.2439	.3098
28	.9718	.0415	.1103	.1781	.2450	.3109
29	.9729	.0426	.1114	.1792	.2461	.3120
30	2.9741	3.0438	3.1125	3.1804	3.2472	3.3131
31	.9753	.0449	.1137	.1815	.2483	.3142
32	.9764	.0461	.1148	.1826	.2494	3153
33	.9776	.0472	.1160	.1837	.2505	.3163
34	.9788	.0484	.1171	.1849	.2516	.3174
35	2.9799	3.0495	3.1182	3.1860	3.2527	3.3185
36	.9811	.0507	.1194	.1871	.2538	.3196
37	.9823	.0519	.1205	.1882	.2550	.3207
38	.9834	.0530	.1216	.1893	.2561	.3218
39	.9846	.0542	.1228	.1905	.2572	.3229
40	2.9858	3.0553	3.1239	3.1916	3.2583	3.3240
41	.9869	.0565	.1251	.1927	.2594	.3250
42	.9881	.0576	.1262	.1938	.2605	.3261
43	.9893	.0588	.1273	.1949	.2616	.3272
44	.9904	.0599	.1285	.1961	.2627	.3283
45	2.9916	3.0611	3.1296	3.1972	3.2638	3.3294
46	.9928	.0622	.1307	.1983	.2649	.3305
47	.9939	.0634	.1319	.1994	.2660	.3316
48	.9951	.0645	.1330	.2005	.2671	.3326
49	.9963	.0657	.1341	.2016	.2682	.3337
50	2.9974	3.0668	3.1353	3.2028	3.2693	3.3348
51	.9986	.0680	.1364	.2039	.2704	.3359
52	.9997	.0691	.1375	.2050	.2715	.3370
53	3.0009	.0703	.1387	.2061	.2726	.3381
54	.0021	.0714	.1398	.2072	.2737	.3391
55	3.0032	3.0725	3.1409	3.2083	3.2748	3.3402
56	.0044	.0737	.1421	.2095	.2759	.3413
57	.0056	.0748	.1432	.2106	.2770	.3424
58	.0067	.0760	.1443	.2117	.2781	.3435
59	.0079	.0771	.1454	.2128	.2792	.3445
60	3.0091	3.0783	3.1466	3.2139	3.2803	3.3456

Table 25. Constants for 5-in. Sine Bar (Continued)

M	42°	43°	44°	45°	46°	47°
0	3.3456	3.4100	3.4733	3.5355	3.5967	3.6567
1	.3467	.4110	.4743	.5365	.5977	.6577
2	.3478	.4121	.4754	.5376	.5987	.6587
3	.3489	.4132	.4764	.5386	.5997	.6597
4	.3499	.4142	.4774	.5396	.6007	.6607
5	3.3510	3.4153	3.4785	3.5406	3.6017	3.6617
6	.3521	.4163	.4795	.5417	.6027	.6627
7	.3532	.4174	.4806	.5427	.6037	.6637
8	.3543	.4185	.4816	.5437	.6047	.6647
9	.3553	.4195	.4827	.5448	.6058	.6657
10	3.3564	3.4206	3.4837	3.5458	3.6068	3.6666
11	.3575	.4217	.4848	.5468	.6078	.6676
12	.3586	.4227	.4858	.5478	.6088	.6686
13	.3597	.4238	.4868	.5489	.6098	.6696
14	.3607	.4248	.4879	.5499	.6108	.6706
15	3.3618	3.4259	3.4889	3.5509	3.6118	3.6716
16	3629	.4269	.4900	.5519	.6128	.6726
17	.3640	.4280	.4910	.5529	.6138	.6736
18	.3651	.4291	.4921	.5540	.6148	.6745
19	.3661	.4301	.4931	.5550	.6158	.6755
20	3.3672	3.4312	3.4941	3.5560	3.6168	3.6765
21	.3683	.4322	.4952	5570	.6178	.6775
22	.3693	.4333	.4962	.5581	.6188	.6785
23	.3704	.4344	.4973	.5591	.6198	.6795
24	.3715	.4354	.4983	.5601	.6208	.6805
25	3.3726	3.4365	3.4993	3.5611	3.6218	3.6814
26	.3736	.4375	5004	.5621	.6228	.6824
27	.3747	.4386	.5014	.5632	.6238	.6834
28	.3758	.4396	5024	.5642	.6248	.6844
29	.3769	.4407	.5035	.5652	.6258	.6854
30	3.3779	3.4417	3.5045	3.5662	3.6268	3.6864
31	.3790	.4428	.5056	.5672	.6278	.6873
32	.3801	.4439	.5066	.5683	.6288	.6883
33	.3811	.4449	.5076	.5693	.6298	.6893
34	.3822	.4460	.5087	.5703	.6308	.6903
35	3.3833	3.4470	3.5097	3.5713	3.6318	3.6913
36	.3844	.4481	.5107	.5723	.6328	.6923
37	.3854	.4491	.5118	.5734	.6338	.6932
38	.3865	.4502	.5128	.5744	.6348	.6942
39	.3876	.4512	.5138	.5754	.6358	.6952
40	3.3886	3.4523	3.5149	3.5764	3.6368	3.6962
41	.3897	.4533	.5159	.5774	.6378	.6972
42	.3908	.4544	.5169	.5784	.6388	.6981
43	.3918	.4554	.5180	.5795	.6398	.6991
44	.3929	.4565	.5190	.5805	.6408	.7001
45	3.3940	3.4575	3.5200	3.5815	3.6418	3.7011
46	.3950	.4586	.5211	.5825	.6428	.7020
47	.3961	.4596	.5221	.5835	.6438	.7030
48	.3972	.4607	.5231	.5845	.6448	.7040
49	.3982	.4617	.5242	.5855	.6458	.7050
50	3.3993	3.4628	3.5252	3.5866	3.6468	3.7060
51	.4004	.4638	.5262	.5876	.6478	.7069
52	.4014	.4649	.5273	.5886	.6488	.7079
53	.4025	.4659	.5283	.5896	.6498	.7089
54	.4036	.4670	.5293	.5906	.6508	.7099
55	3.4046	3.4680	3.5304	3.5916	3.6518	3.7108
56	.4057	.4691	.5314	.5926	.6528	.7118
57	.4068	.4701	.5324	.5936	.6538	.7128
58	.4078	.4712	.5335	.5947	.6548	.7138
59	.4089	.4722	.5345	.5957	.6558	.7147
60	3.4100	3.4733	3.5355	3.5967	3.6567	3.7157

Table 25. Constants for 5-in. Sine Bar (Continued)

M	48°	49°	50°	51°	52°	53°
0	3.7157	3.7735	3.8302	3.8857	3.9400	3.9932
1	.7167	.7745	.8311	.8866	.9409	.9940
2	.7176	.7754	.8321	.8875	.9418	.9949
3	.7186	.7764	.8330	.8884	.9427	.9958
4	.7196	.7773	.8339	.8894	.9436	.9967
5	3.7206	3.7783	3.8349	3.8903	3.9445	3.9975
6	.7215	.7792	.8358	.8912	.9454	.9984
7	.7225	.7802	.8367	.8921	.9463	.9993
8	.7235	.7811	.8377	.8930	.9472	4.0001
9	.7244	.7821	.8386	.8939	.9481	.0010
10	3.7254	3.7830	3.8395	3.8948	3.9490	4.0019
11	.7264	.7840	.8405	.8958	.9499	.0028
12	.7274	.7850	.8414	.8967	.9508	.0036
13	.7283	.7859	.8423	.8976	.9516	.0045
14	.7293	.7869	.8433	.8985	.9525	.0054
15	3.7303	3.7878	3.8442	3.8994	3.9534	4.0062
16	.7312	.7887	.8451	.9003	.9543	.0071
17	.7322	.7897	.8460	.9012	.9552	.0080
18	.7332	.7906	.8470	.9021	.9561	.0089
19	.7341	.7916	.8479	.9030	.9570	.0097
20	3.7351	3.7925	3.8488	3.9039	3.9579	4.0106
21	.7361	.7935	.8498	.9049	.9588	.0115
22	.7370	.7944	.8507	.9058	.9596	.0123
23	.7380	.7954	.8516	.9067	.9605	.0132
24	.7390	.7963	.8525	.9076	.9614	.0141
25	3.7399	3.7973	3.8535	3.9085	3.9623	4.0149
26	.7409	.7982	.8544	.9094	.9632	.0158
27	.7419	.7992	.8553	.9103	.9641	.0167
28	.7428	.8001	.8562	.9112	.9650	.0175
29	.7438	.8011	.8572	.9121	.9659	.0184
30	3.7448	3.8020	3.8581	3.9130	3.9667	4.0193
31	.7457	.8029	.8590	.9139	.9676	.0201
32	.7467	.8039	.8599	.9148	.9685	.0210
33	.7476	.8048	.8609	.9157	.9694	.0219
34	.7486	.8058	.8618	.9166	.9703	.0227
35	3.7496	3.8067	3.8627	3.9175	3.9712	4.0236
36	.7505	.8077	.8636	.9184	.9720	.0244
37	.7515	.8086	.8646	.9193	.9729	.0253
38	.7525	.8096	.8655	.9202	.9738	.0262
39	.7534	.8105	.8664	.9212	.9747	.0270
40	3.7544	3.8114	3.8673	3.9221	3.9756	4.0279
41	.7553	.8124	.8683	.9230	.9765	.0288
42	.7563	.8133	.8692	.9239	.9773	.0296
43	.7573	.8143	.8701	.9248	.9782	.0305
44	.7582	.8152	.8710	.9257	.9791	.0313
45	3.7592	3.8161	3.8719	3.9266	3.9800	4.0322
46	.7601	.8171	.8729	.9275	.9809	.0331
47	.7611	.8180	.8738	.9284	.9817	.0339
48	.7620	.8190	.8747	.9293	.9826	.0348
49	.7630	.8199	.8756	.9302	.9835	.0356
50	3.7640	3.8208	3.8765	3.9311	3.9844	4.0365
51	.7649	.8218	.8775	.9320	.9853	.0374
52	.7659	.8227	.8784	.9329	.9861	.0382
53	.7668	.8236	.8793	.9338	.9870	.0391
54	.7678	.8246	.8802	.9347	.9879	.0399
55	3.7687	3.8255	3.8811	3.9355	3.9899	4.0408
56	.7697	.8265	.8820	.9364	.9896	.0416
57	.7707	.8274	.8830	.9373	.9905	.0425
58	.7716	.8283	.8839	.9382	.9914	.0433
59	.7726	.8293	.8848	.9391	.9923	.0442
60	3.7735	3.8302	3.8857	3.9400	3.9932	4.0451

Table 25. Constants for 5-in. Sine Bar (Continued)

M	54°	55°	56°	57°	58°	59°
0	4.0451	4.0957	4.1452	4.1933	4.2402	4.2858
1	.0459	.0966	.1460	.1941	.2410	.2866
2	.0468	.0974	.1468	.1949	.2418	.2873
3	.0476	.0982	.1476	.1957	.2425	.2881
4	.0485	.0991	.1484	.1965	.2433	.2888
5	4.0493	4.0999	4.1492	4.1973	4.2441	4.2896
6	.0502	.1007	.1500	.1981	.2448	.2903
7	.0510	.1016	.1508	.1989	.2456	.2910
8	.0519	.1024	.1517	.1997	.2464	.2913
9	.0527	.1032	.1525	.2004	.2471	.2925
10	4.0536	4.1041	4.1533	4.2012	4.2479	4.2933
11	.0544	.1049	.1541	.2020	.2487	.2940
12	.0553	.1057	.1549	.2028	.2494	.2948
13	.0561	.1066	.1557	.2036	.2502	.2955
14	.0570	.1074	.1565	.2044	.2510	.2963
15	4.0578	4.1082	4.1573	4.2052	4.2517	4.2970
16	.0587	.1090	.1581	.2060	.2525	.2978
17	.0595	.1099	.1589	.2067	.2533	.2985
18	.0604	.1107	.1597	.2075	.2540	.2992
19	.0612	.1115	.1606	.2083	.2548	.3000
20	4.0621	4.1124	4.1614	4.2091	4.2556	4.3007
21	.0629	.1132	.1622	.2099	.2563	.3015
22	.0638	.1140	.1630	.2107	.2571	.3022
23	.0646	.1148	.1638	.2115	.2578	.3029
24	.0655	.1157	.1646	.2122	.2586	.3037
25	4.0663	4.1165	4.1654	4.2130	4.2594	4.3044
26	.0672	.1173	.1662	.2138	.2601	.3052
27	.0680	.1181	.1670	.2146	.2609	.3059
28	.0689	.1190	.1678	.2154	.2617	.3066
29	.0697	.1198	.1686	.2162	.2624	.3074
30	4.0706	4.1206	4.1694	4.2169	4.2632	4.3081
31	.0714	.1214	.1702	.2177	.2639	.3089
32	.0722	.1223	.1710	.2185	.2647	.3096
33	.0731	.1231	.1718	.2193	.2655	.3103
34	.0739	.1239	.1726	.2201	.2662	.3111
35	4.0748	4.1247	4.1734	4.2208	4.2670	4.3118
36	.0756	.1255	.1742	.2216	.2677	.3125
37	.0765	.1264	.1750	.2224	.2685	.3133
38	.0773	.1272	.1758	.2232	.2692	.3140
39	.0781	.1280	.1766	.2240	.2700	.3147
40	4.0790	4.1288	4.1774	4.2247	4.2708	4.3155
41	.0798	.1296	.1782	.2255	.2715	.3162
42	.0807	.1305	.1790	.2263	.2723	.3170
43	.0815	.1313	.1798	.2271	.2730	.3177
44	.0823	.1321	.1806	.2278	.2738	.3184
45	4.0832	4.1329	4.1814	4.2286	4.2745	4.3192
46	.0840	.1337	.1822	.2294	.2753	.3199
47	.0849	.1346	.1830	.2302	.2760	.3206
48	.0857	.1354	.1838	.2309	.2768	.3213
49	.0865	.1362	.1846	.2317	.2775	.3221
50	4.0874	4.1370	4.1854	4.2325	4.2783	4.3228
51	.0882	.1378	.1862	.2333	.2791	.3235
52	.0891	.1386	.1870	.2340	.2798	.3243
53	.0899	.1395	.1878	.2348	.2806	.3250
54	.0907	.1403	.1886	.2356	.2813	.3257
55	4.0916	4.1411	4.1894	4.2364	4.2821	4.3265
56	.0924	.1419	.1902	.2371	.2828	.3272
57	.0932	.1427	.1909	.2379	.2836	.3279
58	.0941	.1435	.1917	.2387	.2843	.3286
59	.0949	.1443	.1925	.2394	.2851	.3294
60	4.0957	4.1452	4.1933	4.2402	4.2858	4.3301

SURFACE FINISHES AND THEIR MEASUREMENT

Introduction. Much emphasis has been given to the advances made in the science of measurement. The ability to maintain sizes to close tolerances in the manufacture of machine parts has made possible the mass production of such intricate mechanisms as self-winding watches, delicate weighing machines, and all types of electronically controlled computers and their components.

The importance of size measurement in our manufacturing processes cannot be overemphasized and yet there is another type of measurement that is of equal importance. This is called *the measurement of surface finish*. Measuring the smoothness, or roughness, of a machined surface is a comparatively recent development. For many years parts were machined to one of three requirements: Smooth, Medium, or Rough. The machine operator used these terms as a guide to the speed with which the cutting tool traveled across the work; in other words, the *feed*.

F.A.O. is an abbreviation that was used on blueprints to signify "Finish all over." A lower case *f* placed on a line that represented a surface signified that it required a machine finish. The kind of finish was specified by a note on the blueprint: "Lap," "Grind," "Ream," etc.

When the requirements of industry made necessary the need for further refinement in classifying the type of finish, a 60-deg. "V" was used to denote a finished surface. The sharp point of the V touched the surface to be machined and within the opening of the V a code number was added to denote the kind and grade of finish required. $\overset{68}{\bigvee}$ Grind to a No. 8 finish. $\overset{t9}{\bigvee}$ Lap to a No. 10 finish.

Surface Finish. Present-day standards for surface finish are very exacting. The requirements of modern industry permit little or no allowance for a "running-in" period; there is no allowable tolerance for wear.

Whenever a surface moves in contact with another, friction is created. Friction generates heat and causes wear. The amount of friction affects the speed of the machine and reduces its load-carrying capabilities.

Lubrication is used to prevent friction between metal surfaces that are in moving contact. If these surfaces are not smooth, the high points will interfere with the flow of the lubricant and break the film of oil that separates metal from metal.

By reducing the irregularity of the surface, in other words, by making surfaces smoother, less friction will result and greater efficiency will be obtained.

Surface Roughness. The condition of a surface has nothing to do with the size or shape of a piece or job. It can be the result of a machine defect, such as a worn slide or gib, a dull cutting tool, an imperfect bearing surface, or an excess of tooth clearance between meshing gears. The surface that results from this machining will be made up of tiny hills, valleys, waves, and bumps. There may also be flaws in the surface caused by the rupture of the metal by a dull tool or a faulty metal structure.

Surface Measurement. In order to measure the condition of a surface and to specify surface requirements in definite understandable terms, certain standards and measurements have been adopted and special instruments devised. The following will define the terms recommended and adopted by The American Standards Association.

Definitions

Surface. The surface of an object is the boundary that separates the object from another substance. Its shape and extent are usually defined by a drawing or descriptive specifications.

Profile. The contour of any specified section through a surface.

Roughness. Relatively finely spaced irregularities. On surfaces produced by machining and abrasive operations, the irregularities produced by the cutting action of tool edges and abrasive grains and by the feed of the machine tool are roughness. Roughness may be considered as being superposed on a wavy surface.

Waviness. The surface irregularities that are of greater spacing than the roughness. On machined surfaces such irregularities may result from machine or work deflections, vibrations, etc. Irregularity of similar geometry may occur as a result of warping, strains, or other causes.

Flaws. Irregularities that occur at one place or at relatively infrequent intervals in the surface, for example, a scratch, ridge, hole, peak, crack, or check.

Lay. The direction of the predominant surface pattern.
Microinch. One millionth of an inch. (0.000001 in.)

The symbol used to designate surface irregularities is a check mark with a horizontal extension $\sqrt{}$. The point of the symbol is shown touching the line representing the surface (Fig. A-5).

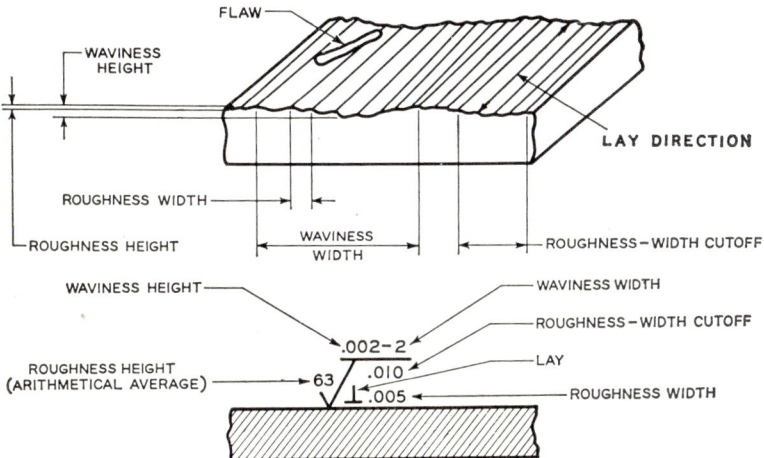

Fig. A-5. The relation of symbols to surface characteristics.

Methods of Measurement. The shopman judges the quality of a finish by first its visual appearance, how it looks; and then by running a thumbnail over the surface, how it feels. To provide him with a means of comparison a set of "Surface Roughness Scales and Specimens" is available. These scales have the number of the finish stamped on the surface it identifies. There are two types of scales and one set of specimens in general use. The specimens come in sets of ten and are packed in a wooden box. The scales are in sets of two: one set is for the comparing of flat surfaces, the other set is for internal and external cylindrical surfaces. The scales fit into a pocket case.

The Profilometer. While there are numerous methods of measuring the quality of surfaces, the one chosen for most shop applications is the type that makes use of a stylus, or tracer, to move across the surface profile. The irregularities of the surface are then magnified and shown on the meter of the instrument in microinches. The best known measuring instrument of this type is the Profilometer (Fig. A-6).

The Profilometer is a direct-reading shop instrument for measuring surface-roughness height in microinch units. It was first developed in 1936. It has proved to be a very important contribution

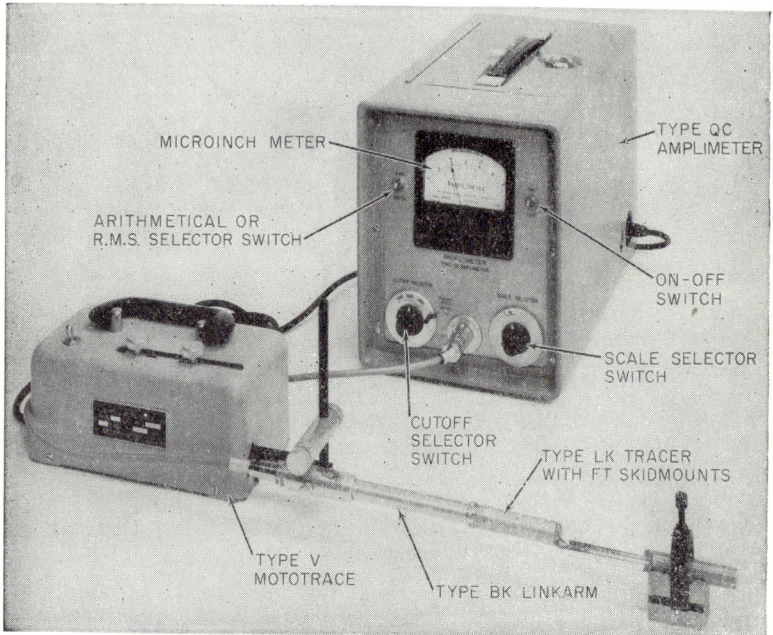

Fig. A-6. The Profilometer. (*Micrometrical Manufacturing Company*)

toward raising the standard of surface finishes. It measures both flat and cylindrical surfaces, either internal or external. It is comparatively simple to operate. There are models for toolroom use and portable models for shop use.

The important subject of surface finishes has been explained here in brief fashion. It is a subject that many books have been written about. It is hoped that this brief explanation will give some understanding of the subject and will encourage the reader to further his knowledge of the subject by reading and observation.

Index